LANGUAGE
DEVELOPMENT
AND
LANGUAGE
DISORDERS

Wiley Series on Communication Disorders
Thomas J. Hixon, Advisory Editor

This collection of books has been developed by John Wiley & Sons to meet some of the needs in the field of communication disorders. The collection includes books on both normal and disordered speech, hearing, and language function. The authors of the collection have been selected because they are scientific and clinical leaders in their field and, we believe, are eminently qualified to make significant and scholarly contributions to the professional literature.

Language Development and Language Disorders
Lois Bloom and Margaret Lahey

Readings in Language Development
Lois Bloom

Readings in Childhood Language Disorders
Margaret Lahey

Elements of Hearing Science: A Programmed Text
Arnold M. Small

Language
Development
and
Language
Disorders

LOIS BLOOM
Teachers College, Columbia University

MARGARET LAHEY
Hunter College of the City University of New York

JOHN WILEY & SONS   New York   Santa Barbara   London
Sydney   Toronto

Library of Congress Cataloging in Publication Data:

Bloom, Lois.
    Language development and language disorders.

    (Wiley series on communication disorders)
    Bibliography: P.
    Includes indexes.
    1. Children—Language.   2. Language arts—

Remedial teaching. I. Lahey, Margaret, Date—joint author. II. Title. Series.
LB1139.L3B578   371.9′14   77-21482
ISBN 0-471-08220-1

Printed in the United States of America

10 9 8 7 6 5

FOREWORD

Language Development and Language Disorders is the first book to be published in the John Wiley & Sons collection on communication disorders. A synthesis of the research findings in normal language development with a practical approach to the evaluation and management of children with language disorders has long been needed in the field of communication disorders. Too often, those who do the research are unfamiliar with the concerns of those who work with the children, and those who work with the children are unsure about how to evaluate and apply the research. Lois Bloom and Margaret Lahey are two of those all too few people who are competent both as researchers and as clinicians. Their book reflects their dual focus by the way in which it brings research and practical application together. *Language Development and Language Disorders* constitutes a significant change in the state of thought about normal and disordered language development. Researchers and clinicians will be better able to communicate with one another after reading this book. More important, many children will profit from the enlightened and scholarly work of these two authors.

Thomas J. Hixon
ADVISORY EDITOR IN
COMMUNICATION DISORDERS

PREFACE

If you watch and listen to young children talk you may be amused, impressed, puzzled, or curious, and you are bound to learn something. You will learn that they can say sounds, or words, or phrases; you will learn that they typically talk about what they are doing, or about to do, or want someone else to do; and you will learn that they use speech to influence and control the events around them. When a child does not do such things, or does only some of them, or does them later than you might expect, you would suspect that there is a problem. Individuals who are professionally concerned with children who have such problems have always been aware that information about normal language ought to guide planning for such children. However, just which aspects of normal language are most relevant and how to use information about normal language have not been agreed on.

For both of us, the beginning of our professional careers was taken up with the needs of children who, for whatever reason, had difficulty in learning to talk. Although we did not know one another in those days, the experience that we each had in learning about such children made us realize that we needed to learn considerably more than we knew about the nature of language and normal language development. This textbook represents the result of what followed from that realization.

We have since learned more about language development so that we now feel we can take some first steps toward closing the gap between knowing something about children with normal language and doing something about children with disordered language.

We are taking our metaphor from Miller, Galanter, and Pribram (1960) in proposing a plan for exploiting new knowledge to solve an old problem. This book is about language, language development, and language disorders in children. The first half of the book presents new knowledge; the second half of the book exploits this knowledge for a plan for language learning.

Two fundamental assumptions underlie our view of language learning. The first assumption is that language is a means for representing information in messages. It should follow that children with language disorders need to learn how the linguistic forms of sounds, words, and phrases encode elements of content that have to do with knowledge of objects and events in the world. Linguistic forms and elements of content come together so that one aspect of messages cannot be considered apart from the other; the form of language always relates to content.

The second assumption is that the use of language is a social act, and that children learn language as a means for obtaining, maintaining, and regulating contact with other persons. It should follow that children with language disorders need to learn how to use messages to inquire, converse, direct, and otherwise enjoy social interaction with others. The form of a message and the content that is represented in the message have to do with how individuals use their messages in communication contexts; the form and content of language always relate to language use.

The information in this textbook concerns the early period of language development in children's first three or four years of life, because everything that happens in these early years has to do with the nature of language in general and is fundamental to the later, subsequent development of language. This textbook was written in conjunction with two books of readings—one in language development, edited by Lois Bloom, and another in childhood language disorders, edited by Margaret Lahey—both published by John Wiley and Sons, 1978. Accordingly, we refer to cited works with the accompanying notation: "in *RLDev*" or "in *RLDis*," to alert the reader that more information than is reported here is available from the *Readings in Language Development* and the *Readings in Childhood Language Disorders*, respectively.

The material presented in the following pages is limited primarily to empirical descriptions of children's language behavior, from observational, longitudinal investigations of a relatively small group of children learning American English as a first language. Much of the research evidence has come from investigations of the language development of five children whose names appear frequently in the text: Allison, Eric, Gia, Kathryn, and Peter. These children were studied longitudinally from about 16 to 19 months through 36 months of age. The evidence of their language development has made it possible to form a number of tentative hypotheses for a plan for considering language disorders in children. It is assumed that extensive and intensive information, from well-documented evidence, of the language development of even a small group of normal children, will provide more reasonable hypotheses for assessment and intervention with children with language disorders than is possible with either (1) more superficial information from a large number of children, (2) a comparison of children's language with the forms of adult language, or (3) the intuitions that an adult might have about the relative simplicity or ease of one or another linguistic form.

The exploitation of knowledge about normal language development for children with language disorders is presented here as an hypothesis—we expect that it will evolve and change as we come to know more about language development and as we learn more about the use of such knowledge with children who have language problems.

Many persons have participated in the preparation of this book, and it is a pleasure for us to acknowledge their contributions here. Our greatest debt is to the students who have participated in our research activities in the study of children's language development; we thank, in particular, Lois Hood, Patsy Lightbown, Peggy Miller, Lorraine Rocissano, Bambi Schieffelin, and Karin Lifter. Each, in addition, has read and generously commented on numerous drafts of the manuscript. Karin Lifter and Kathleen Fiess bore the major responsibility for the heroic effort of compiling the bibliography and cross-checking references.

The research that is referred to here was supported by Fellowship F1-MH-30,001 from the National Institute of Mental Health, Research Grant HD03828 from the National Institute of Child Health and Development, and Research Grants SOC74-28126 and 76-15528 from the National Science Foundation, to Lois Bloom. Without such support, neither the research into normal language development that is reported on here nor our thinking about children with language disorders would have been possible in their present form.

An early draft of part of the manuscript was used as a preliminary text for courses that each of us taught from 1974 to 1976. Students in these courses applied the ideas and information in the manuscript to the assessment of hundreds of children with language disorders, in clinical and educational settings, for class projects. Their abundant, insightful comments on and criticisms of the text have influenced this book in an important way.

We have benefited greatly from sharing our ideas and hypotheses about the intersection of language development and language disorders in children with students and colleagues at Teachers College, Columbia University (where L. Bloom is a member of the faculty, and M. Lahey is a Research Associate), and at Montclair State College (where M. Lahey was a member of the faculty). Some of these ideas were also presented at numerous colloquia and workshops in the United States and Canada. A number of clinicians have attempted to use the information and suggestions that we have presented in these sessions and have been kind enough to share these experiences with us. In particular, we thank Marcia Bass, Lorraine Harris, Steve Lewis, Patsy Pearce, and Sandy Taenzer for their encouragement and enthusiasm for our continued efforts.

The early drafts of portions of the manuscript were circulated among a number of people who provided us with their comments and suggestions for improving the book on its way to publication. We thank, in particular, Elaine Barden, Lila Braine, Carol Lee De Filippo, Claudette Feier, Herbert Garber, Judith Johnston, Edward Mysak, Norma Rees, Naomi Schiff, Audrey Simmons-Martin, and Carol Wilder, as well as the publisher's reviewers who read and critiqued the manuscript, in particular, Philip Dale. As a result, we were able to sharpen our thinking, clarify the conceptual and empirical presentation of our information, and avoid at least a few serious blunders.

Because children learn language in contexts that include other persons and different objects and events, we have included a number of dialogues with children along with the descriptive and interpretive information that is presented. These dialogues have been with a handful of children—Allison, Eric, Gia, Kathryn, and Peter—whose language development until their third birthdays has been the subject of intensive study by our research group. This textbook is, in large part, about what we have learned from them through our thousands of dialogues with them. Our debt to them is enormous.

Finally, each of us has a family—a husband and children—who have each contributed something of themselves to this book. In particular, Robert H. Bloom and Henry Lahey provided important advice and many helpful questions and suggestions. The contribution of our families is measured in large part by the numbers of hours, days, and weeks that they did without us. Their tolerance and their support were considerable and so, with appreciation and with love, this book is dedicated to them.

                                             Lois Bloom
                                           Margaret Lahey

CONTENTS

To
Bob and Hank
Allison, Denise, and Diane

Part 1
LANGUAGE DESCRIPTION

The first two chapters are concerned with the basic tasks of defining language and presenting certain principles and procedures for describing language behavior. The rest of the book depends on how language is defined in the first place. Language can be defined in different ways for different purposes. This book describes normal language development in order to be able to understand language disorders in children. Accordingly, language is defined and described in terms of the forms of messages—words and the relations between words; the content of messages—meaning or semantics; and the use of messages—the functions for which individuals speak and the ways in which they vary message form according to the requirements of different linguistic and nonlinguistic contexts.

Chapter 1
A DEFINITION OF LANGUAGE

There is usually little need to reflect on the behaviors of speech and communication in the everyday course of events, and most people rarely think about language. If one should think about language at all, it would be immediately apparent that it is difficult to separate and define the behaviors that contribute to communication, and something is usually lost in the process. Ethologist C. G. Beer has commented on this point in connection with descriptions of observations of behavior in general:

> Description involves division and classification which exclude other possible divisions and classifications and hence other possible descriptions ... of necessity, all description is limited. (1973, pp. 53–54)

However, only by attempting to classify and describe the components of language can one hope to be able to understand and perhaps eventually to explain how language behaviors are learned and how they develop.

DEFINING LANGUAGE

A definition of language depends on the context in which one asks the question "What is language?" The answer to the question can vary according to whether one is interested in, for example, dialects and those who speak them, words and their histories, how languages differ in different cultures, the formal properties of language systems, language as an art medium, the ways that language is used, and the like (Halliday, 1975). The present context is one in which an attempt is made to understand what children learn about language and how children with language problems can be helped to learn language. To begin with, then, language will be defined for these purposes, and the answer to the question "What is language?" will specify the component parts that seem to be most relevant to the descriptions of language development and language disorders that will follow. A language is a code whereby ideas about the world are represented through a conventional system of arbitrary signals[1] for communication. The key words in the definition are *code, ideas, convention, system,* and *communication.* Perhaps the best way to understand language would be to consider what each term means and what each contributes to the definition of what languages are and how they work.

LANGUAGE IS A CODE

A code is a means of representing one thing with another, and language is a means of representation. Given an object, event, or relationship, one can represent it schematically—with a picture, a map, a graph, a word, a sentence, or other such device—so that it is possible to consider it, to preserve it, and to share it. In this way, the picture, map, graph, word, or sentence can be said to stand for or represent the object, event, or relationship.

As an example, a *cookie* is an object that can be baked, eaten, dropped, moved, and so forth. A picture of a cookie would have to represent its characteristic shape—usually roundness and flatness—and its texture— smoothness or lumpiness. A picture of the event *eating a cookie* would

---

[1] Throughout this book we have used three terms that are susceptible to interpretations that may be different from our intentions. The words "signal," "sign," and "symbol" are used in the following senses. Linguistic signals are units of sound (words, sentences, etc.) that are vocally produced, or units of movement that are manually produced. The word "sign" is used in its visual sense: the movement of the hands and the body that is made or that is seen as a linguistic signal. The word "symbol" is the use of a signal to represent or *stand for* some element of experience or meaning. Thus the linguistic signal /kæt/ is the event that symbolizes or represents a small, furry creature with four legs and whiskers; the linguistic signal /kæt/ is the symbol for the object cat.

represent the action relation between a person (the eater) and an object (the cookie). A picture of the event *taking a cookie* would represent the action relations between a person (the taker), an object (the cookie), and the place it is taken from (a surface or a container). A map of a cookie would represent relations between details of the cookie with precise accounting of sizes and distances (perhaps of bumps on the cookie and the distances between bumps). A graph of the cookie might represent information such as the size of the cookie in relation to the number of bumps on the cookie or the number of bites it takes to eat it.

Representations such as pictures, maps, and graphs are fairly direct schematic reproductions that preserve the proportions and relations of whatever is being represented. Words and sentences differ in that they represent an object, event, or relationship without reproducing it, either directly (as with a picture or map) or indirectly (as with a graph). The word "cookie" and the sentence "The girl eats the cookie" represent the object and the event by means of a *code*. The code is separate from actual cookies or eating cookies or any particular object or event. The code is the means or ways in which a finite number of elements (sounds and movements) correspond with all possible objects and events—including cookies and eating—so that more or less arbitrary sequences of sounds and movements can function as words, signs, or sentences to represent objects and events. In *en*coding, one recalls and combines the elements of the code to represent information in a message; in *de*coding, one recognizes and segments the elements of the code to extract information from a message. The code provides the form of language.

LANGUAGE REPRESENTS IDEAS ABOUT THE WORLD

The code or means of representing information can operate only in relation to what the speaker and hearer of the language *know* about objects and events in the world. Speakers of a language need to know about objects and actions in order to know the names for objects and actions. Knowing just the sounds in "cookie" is literally quite meaningless unless one also knows what cookies are. One cannot know about sentences and the relations between the parts of a sentence unless one also knows about relations between persons and objects in different kinds of events. For example, one cannot use and understand a syntactic structure for coding possession unless one understands that certain objects are within the domains of certain people because of their habitual use or association, and so on. It is the knowledge that individuals have about objects, events, and relations in the world that is coded by language—ideas about events are coded, not events themselves.

As in the figure in Box I-1, a speech event (A) does not represent events in the world (B) directly but, instead, represents an intervening cognitive representation (C) of events in the world.

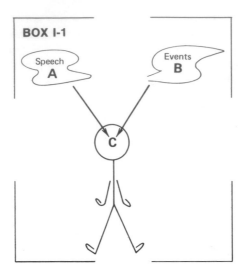

Even a concrete noun such as "cookie" or "house" represents an idea, a category, a concept. This point is basic in linguistic as well as psychological views of language. For example, Edward Sapir pointed out that

> the word "house" is not a linguistic fact if by it is meant merely the acoustic effect produced on the ear by its constituent consonants and vowels, pronounced in a certain order; nor the motor processes and tactile feelings which make up the articulation of the word; nor the visual perception on the part of the hearer of this articulation . . . nor the memory of any or all of these experiences. It is only when these, and possibly still other, associated experiences are automatically associated with the image of a house that they begin to take on the nature of a symbol, a word, an element of language . . . The elements of language [are] associated with whole groups, delimited classes, of experience rather than with the single experiences themselves . . . The single experience lodges in an individual consciousness and is, strictly speaking, incommunicable . . . Thus, the single impression which I have had of a particular house must be identified with all my other impressions of it. Further, my generalized memory or my "notion" of this house must be merged with the notions that all other individuals who have seen the house have formed of it . . . [and ultimately] this house and that house and thousands of other phenomena of like character are thought of as having enough in common, in spite of great and obvious differences of detail, to be classed under the same heading. In other words, the speech element "house" is the symbol, first and foremost, not of a single perception, nor even of the notion of a particular object, but of a "concept," in other words, of *a convenient capsule of thought that embraces thousands of distinct experiences and that is ready to take in thousands more.* (emphasis added, 1921, pp. 11–13)

An individual learns to use and understand a language in relation to (or as a representation of) the ideas or mental concepts that have been formed through experience. An individual's experience consists of many encounters with many different objects (e.g., houses, cups, apples, raisins, books, and cookies), some of which are more like one another than are others. Although there are cookies of different shapes, sizes and textures, these objects also share the constant features that differentiate them as cookies from other objects such as books, which also share certain constant features even though they differ in size, color, or content, and so on. The experience of different objects is an active process whereby persons perceive patterns of structure and invariance in the environment, such as similarities among different cookies and the movability of certain objects and not others (J. Gibson, 1966; see also Riegel, 1975). Based on encounters with objects, an individual perceives and remembers the constant features of an object class so that a similar object will be recognized in future encounters.

Individuals also have many encounters with persons and objects in relationships with one another: persons doing things to objects, objects being affected by certain actions, persons habitually associated with objects, and so forth. Children perceive the similarities in repeated encounters between persons and objects and form a mental record of the consistencies or constant features of a relationship in memory so that future encounters will be recognized. Words or signs take on significance or meaning by themselves, or grammatically in relation to one another, only in connection with such underlying cognitive representations of objects and object relations.

Thus, one can know that words ending in *-ment* or *-ness* are nouns and refer to things or concepts but, unless one also knows more about what those things are, the words will have no meaning. One can know that some nouns precede verbs and other nouns follow verbs in sentences. But, unless one also knows about the relationships between the objects and actions that such nouns and verbs represent, one cannot use or understand such words in sentences. For example, nouns before verbs can mean different things in relation to different verbs. A noun such as "boy" can be the agent of an action (as in "The *boy* ate the cookie"); a noun such as "key" can be the instrument of an action (as in "The *key* opened the door"); and a noun such as "girl" can be the object affected by some state (as in "The *girl* felt sad,"). The linguistic code cannot be used apart from such knowledge that individuals have about objects, events, and relations between objects; such knowledge provides the content of language.

LANGUAGE IS A SYSTEM

The ways in which sounds combine to form words and words combine to form sentences for representing knowledge are determined by a system of rules. In the construction of words, such rules specify which sounds can combine with one another and which sounds cannot be combined. For example, in English, a word cannot consist of only consonants but must also include a vowel; nasal consonants can precede other consonants at the ends of words ("dump" and "dunk"), but nasal consonants cannot precede other consonants at the beginning of a word (e.g., "nkup" and "mput" are not acceptable for words in English).

The rules for sentences in English specify how linguistic elements—words and morphemes (the elements of meaning such as -ing, -s, and -ness that cannot occur alone but must be attached to some other word or morpheme)—are combined to code meaning. For example, in simple active declarative sentences in English the word that represents the agent of an action, such as "girl," must occur before the word that represents the object affected by the action, such as "cookie." If attention is to be drawn to the cookie in an action, it is possible to reverse the order in which the words "cookie" and "girl" are mentioned in a sentence, but only if one also changes or adds other parts of the sentence, for example, "The cookie was eaten by the girl," or "It is the cookie the girl eats."

The ways in which rules of language operate are predictable. Given information about the rules for a particular sentence or a group of sentences, it is possible to make predictions about other possible sentences. Furthermore, given a group of sentences—"The boy baked the apple," "The girl climbed the tree," "The man carried the bag"—one could predict that the words "woman," "the," "tower," and "construct" would combine to form the sentence "The woman constructed the tower." Such a prediction would follow from the inductions about the given set of sentences that (1) names of persons that act precede the name of an action, (2) names of objects that are affected by an action follow the name of the action, (3) a word "the" precedes the names for persons and objects but not actions, and so on.

The number of elements and the number of rules in a language system are limited and finite. That is, one can count the number of words in a dictionary or lexicon; there are a fixed number of rules in a grammar for forming sentences. However, the number of possible combinations of elements (the number of sentences in a language) is unlimited and infinite. The use of finite means (elements and rules for relating elements) to produce indefinitely many expressions is *linguistic creativity*. Linguistic creativity in the behaviors of speakers and hearers is evidence that language users know rules that are related to one another and form a system.

Noam Chomsky made this relationship between linguistic behavior and linguistic knowledge explicit:

Having mastered a language, one is able to understand an indefinite number of expressions that are new to one's experience . . . and one is able, with greater or less facility, to produce such expressions on an appropriate occasion, despite their novelty and independently of detectable stimulus configurations, and to be understood by others who share this still mysterious ability. The normal use of language is, in this sense, a creative activity. ... A person who knows a language has mastered a system of rules that assigns sound and meaning in a definite way for an infinite class of possible sentences. ... Of course, the person who knows the language has no consciousness of having mastered these rules or of putting them to use, nor is there any reason to suppose that this knowledge of the rules of language can be brought to consciousness. (1972, pp. 100–104)

Thus, the number of all possible sentences that a speaker can produce and that a hearer can understand is indefinitely many. Moreover, a speaker can say and a hearer can understand new sentences that neither has ever said nor heard before because they know the system of rules for the language.

LANGUAGE IS A CONVENTION

"What lies behind the notion that facts about language are arbitrary is the view that . . . linguistic facts exist by virtue of a social rather than a logical or empirical constraint" (Fodor, Bever, and Garrett, 1974, p. 150). People speaking a language agree among themselves that certain forms correspond with certain content and can be used in specific ways. In this sense, the correspondences between form and meaning in language, and the ways in which languages are used are arbitrary or conventional facts about language. Just as new words can be introduced and accepted by members of a speech community, any of the facts about language can be changed— although it may be highly inconvenient and a nuisance to do so. For example, a 5-year-old child announced one day that from that moment on she intended to call apples "peaches" and to call peaches "apples." It was pointed out to her that she would have a hard time at the market, because when she asked for "apples" she would be given peaches. She immediately understood the dilemma and said that she would then have to tell the people at the market, who would then have to tell the truckers who transport the fruit, who would then have to tell the farmers who grow the fruit, who would then have to tell all the others farmers as well as the scientists who grow the seeds for planting the trees, and many others besides. Although it would hardly be worth the effort, the important fact is that it could be done, which is an essential fact about language. Words and sentences are used as they are only because the speakers in a language community agree on such matters; there is a set of community norms, operations, principles, strategies, and values that guide the production and interpretation of speech, the "community ground rules for speaking" (Bauman and Sherzer, 1974, p. 7).

It is certainly possible to make up a list of elements and rules for combining them but, if such knowledge about the dictionary of elements and the rules of grammar for their combination was not shared with anyone else, then one would not have a language. An important fact about a language is that it represents shared knowledge, that the elements of the system and the way in which the system works have been agreed on and accepted by the members of a particular community. It is not enough that an individual (1) perceive a particular instance of an object such as a cookie, (2) recognize other instances of the object, and (3) formulate a word or sign for the class of objects. Unless the class of objects conforms to a similar classification by other persons, and the word or sign is accepted by other persons as a means of representing the object class, then one cannot use the word or sign to formulate a message about the object. The form and content of language are coordinated with one another by such convention among speakers.

The fact that any group of speakers (a linguistic community of any size) recognizes and accepts a particular word or accepts a sentence as grammatical is evidence enough for including the word in the dictionary and the rules for the sentence in the language of that community. Of course, in this context, "agreement" and "acceptance" of an aspect of a language is always implicit and understood among the speakers of the language without their having to talk about it or, indeed, without their even being able to talk about it. Most adult speakers of a language would find the task of describing or explaining their language—or even explaining what language is—a very difficult task. Nonetheless, these same people know what they can and cannot say, and they know that unless they share the same information about words and combinations of words with other persons, they cannot use the language. This fact is attested to whenever a speaker enters a foreign community and finds that the language he or she speaks is strange and unacceptable.

LANGUAGE IS USED FOR COMMUNICATION

First, language is used for many and varied purposes, most of which involve interactions with other persons. As people interact in different circumstances in the course of a day, they need to use language in order to maintain contact with others, gain information, give information, and accomplish goals. Thus people do not just talk; instead, they do things with words and sentences. Knowing what can be done with language is an important part of knowing language. Halliday (1975) has made this point in his studies of child language that "relate the [linguistic] system to its social contexts [and] to the functions that language serves in the young child's life" (pp. 79-80).

Second, language use also consists of the ways in which speakers vary what they say according to the needs of different listeners in different circumstances. Speakers of a language have alternative means for saying the same thing or achieving the same purpose, and which alternative is used depends on the context. For example, it is possible to get a drink of water by asking a question ("Do you have any water?"), making a statement ("I'm thirsty"), or issuing a directive ("Give me a glass of water, please"). It is also possible to talk about objects by referring to them by name ("Here comes the *bus*") or by a pronoun ("Here *it* comes"). The ability to decide among the alternative forms of a message—whether, for example, to use a noun or a pronoun; to ask a question or make a statement—depends on the ability to make inferences about what the listener already knows and needs to know, as well as things such as how well the speaker knows the listener, and status relations between speaker and listener (Ervin-Tripp, 1970; Garvey, 1975a, in RLDev and others). Thus, in addition to (1) learning about the world for the content of language, and (2) learning the linguistic code for the form of representing language content, it is also necessary to (3) learn to recognize different kinds of circumstances that require different kinds of language use.

THE THREE DIMENSIONS OF CONTENT, FORM, AND USE IN LANGUAGE

Given the foregoing definition of what language is and how it works, it is possible to identify three major components of language: content, form, and use. Language consists of some aspect of *content* or meaning that is coded or represented by linguistic *form* for some purpose or *use* in a particular context. This three-dimensional view of language is basic to describing the development of language and for understanding language disorders. Selected aspects of each of these three components will be presented, and each will be described more fully in the chapters that follow.

THE CONTENT OF LANGUAGE

Words or signs and the relations between words or signs represent information or meaning in messages. One can conceive of language content in terms of the topics that are represented in particular messages, and categorizations of topics according to how they relate or are similar to one another in different messages. A topic is the particular idea encoded in a message—such as reference to a particular object, a chair; or to a particular action, sitting down; or to a particular relation, such as between a father and his chair or a mother and her coat (Box I-2). Thus, one can talk about Mommy or about the family dog or about cookies, or one can talk about eating cookies or riding a bike or a new pair of shoes. There are probably indefinitely many topics in the world or things that can be talked about in different settings.

Language content is the broader, more general categorization of the topics that are encoded in messages: objects in general (including Mommy, Daddy, cookies, plants, etc.); or actions in general (throwing, hitting, eating, etc.); or the possession relation in general (the relation between Mommy and her coat, Daddy and his chair, baby and her doll, etc.). Thus, Mommy's

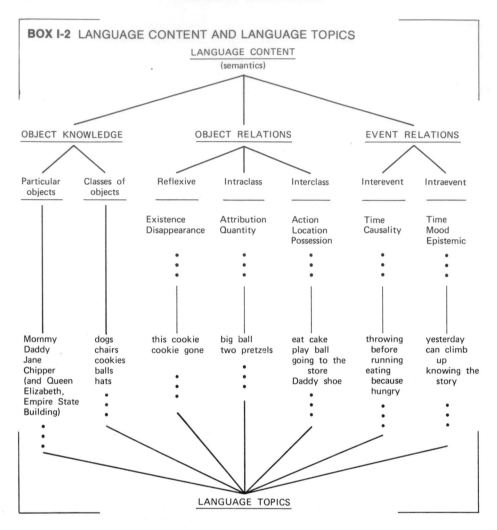

BOX I-2 LANGUAGE CONTENT AND LANGUAGE TOPICS

LANGUAGE CONTENT
(semantics)

OBJECT KNOWLEDGE   OBJECT RELATIONS   EVENT RELATIONS

Particular objects	Classes of objects	Reflexive	Intraclass	Interclass	Interevent	Intraevent
		Existence Disappearance	Attribution Quantity	Action Location Possession	Time Causality	Time Mood Epistemic
Mommy Daddy Jane Chipper (and Queen Elizabeth, Empire State Building)	dogs chairs cookies balls hats	this cookie cookie gone	big ball two pretzels	eat cake play ball going to the store Daddy shoe	throwing before running eating because hungry	yesterday can climb up knowing the story

LANGUAGE TOPICS

coat may be the *topic* of a message, but the *content* represented in the message has to do with the concept of the possession relation—a concept that also includes Daddy's chair and baby's doll.

Given the distinction between language topic and language content—the difference between a particular idea encoded in a message, such as with reference to a particular object (topic) and the broader, more general categorization of topics in many messages, such as reference to objects in general (content)—one can understand how virtually all children can be alike in the content of their messages. For example, all children learn to talk about objects and actions, and relations such as possession and location. At the same time, children can also be different in the topics that they can understand and talk about, with the result that there are differences in the vocabularies of children from a single culture, as well as differences in the vocabularies of children from different cultures.

There is also a continuity of language content from earliest language to progressively later and eventually mature language: 2-year-olds, 5-year-olds, and adults all talk about the same content (i.e., they talk about objects, actions, and relations). But whereas the content of language is cumulative and continuous as it evolves in the course of development, the topics of language are variable, with respect to age as well as culture. Two-year-olds talk about bouncing balls, 5-year-olds talk about baseballs, and adults talk about golf balls. Similarly, all children talk about moving, animate objects but, whereas children from middle-class urban homes talk about their pet fish, dogs, or cats, children from farm homes may talk about cows and chickens. The topics of language are varied and probably indefinitely many in number, but the content of language is constrained by the limits of categorization and classification.

The distinction between language content and language topic is analogous to the distinction in cognitive psychology between "semantic" and "episodic" memory, a distinction that was introduced by Tulving (1972) and elaborated on by Kintsch (1974).

> Semantic memory refers to a person's knowledge; episodic memory to his store of experiences. Obviously, most or all knowledge is derived in some way from personal experiences at one time or another, but these experiences have become depersonalized, at least in part, separated from their original context, and are thus much more broadly useful than specific, personal, context-bound experiences. (Kintsch, 1974, p. 4)

Similarly, whereas language topic is particular, personal, and contextual, language content is general, depersonalized, and independent of particular context. One could add that language topic can be more or less idiosyncratic with individual societies or cultures, whereas language content is shared by common human experience and may well be universal.

The content of children's language derives from individual topics through a process of generalization, and generalization involves the division and classification of events. As a result, language content can be presented as consisting of a taxonomy of categories, with rules for the assimilation of new topics as well as rules for relating categories to one another. The development of content in language consists of the acquisition of this taxonomy of categories and rule relations having to do with the nature of objects and the ways in which objects behave and relate to one another.

The development of language content depends on the interaction between children's knowledge (the information about objects and events in the world that is represented in memory) and context (the persons, objects, and events that are around the children). The interaction between knowledge and context is information processing, whereby like events are related and generalizations are formed to be represented in memory.

There are three primary categories of language content, then, as represented in Box I-2: object knowledge, relations between objects, and relations between events. In the first category, particular objects and classes of objects are straightforward classifications of language topics. Mommy, Daddy, Chipper (the family dog), and so forth, are topics in the category of *particular* objects; dogs, chairs, cookies, balls and boxes are topics in the category of *classes* of objects. The second category (relations among objects) is more complicated. Reflexive object relations have to do with the relation of an object to itself (or to another object from the same class). Thus, an object can simply exist ("this a cookie"), or disappear ("cookie gone"), or the same object or one just like it can reappear ("more cookie"). Intraclass relations are the attributions or properties that distinguish among objects in the same class of objects according to relative size ("the big ball" and "the little ball"), color ("the red shirt" and "the yellow shirt"), or some other differentiating dimension.

Interclass relations involve locative, action, and possession relations between objects—either a particular object such as Mommy and an instance of an object class such as hat, or between instances of different object classes such as a dog and a shoe, or a book and a shelf. A locative relation is the relation between objects according to their locations or places in space, for example, "in," "on," and "above," relative to one another; an action relation is the movement of an object or the way in which an object is affected by some movement. For example, one object can be "eaten," "thrown," or "pushed" by another object. A possession relation has to do with the domains of persons and with the objects that are associated within a person's domain.

The third category (relations between events) involves the ways in which different events, such as throwing a ball and running away, are related to each other in terms of, for example, time (before and after) or causality (one thing happening because of something else). Finally, there are certain relations within an event that are not object relations, such as the time that an event occurs, the mood of the speaker toward the event, or what the speaker knows or thinks about the event.

Thus, the content of language is its meaning or semantics—the linguistic representation of what persons know about the world of objects, events, and relations. The facts about objects and the ways in which objects relate to themselves and to one another can be represented by different kinds of words or signs and by relations between words or signs. Such linguistic representation depends on a code—a conventional system of arbitrary signals—that gives language its form.

THE FORM OF LANGUAGE

The form of utterances can be described in terms of their acoustic, phonetic shape, and the form of signed communication can be described in terms of its configurational properties. Both sound and sign utterances can be described in terms of the sounds or movements that are the parts or segments of an utterance, and the features of stress and intonation and emphasis that form the rhythm of sequences of segments, and are imposed on the segments or are suprasegmental. In describing only form, one is limited to describing the shape or contour of the surface features in an utterance or in a sample of utterances.

Form can be described in several ways, for example, in terms of the units of sound, or *phonology*, the units of meaning that are words or inflections, or *morphology*, and the ways in which units of meaning are combined with one another, or *syntax*. (See Box I-3.)

The sounds that occur in an utterance or a corpus of utterances can be described phonetically, as with the International Phonetic Alphabet, or in terms of articulatory features (the movements of the lips and tongue) and phonatory features, (pitch, resonance, voicing qualities, etc.). Words can be classified according to adult parts of speech as nouns, verbs, adjectives, and so forth, and reported with the frequency of occurrence of each part of speech. Sentences can be described according to sentence types, such as declaratives, negatives, and questions; clause types, such as relative clauses (The rat that ate the cheese is . . . .) and nominalized clauses (Hitting the policeman was a . . . .); and phrase structures, such as verb phrases (. . . is eating dinner) and attributive phrases (. . . the long blue bench). The sequences of phrases or clauses in a sentence can be described according to whether one clause is subordinate to another (complex sentences), or the clauses are otherwise coordinated with one another (compound sentences).

Regardless of how successful one can be in describing linguistic form alone, form in language is the means for connecting sounds or signs with meaning. The general categories of language content referred to earlier can be represented by different kinds of words as well as by syntactic relations between words. One can talk about (1) kinds of words or signs in terms of the kinds of meaning the words encode, such as substantive words and relational words; (2) combinations of words or signs in terms of the semantic-syntactic relations between them; (3) the use of morphological inflection to indicate time and number; and (4) the use of suprasegmental prosody

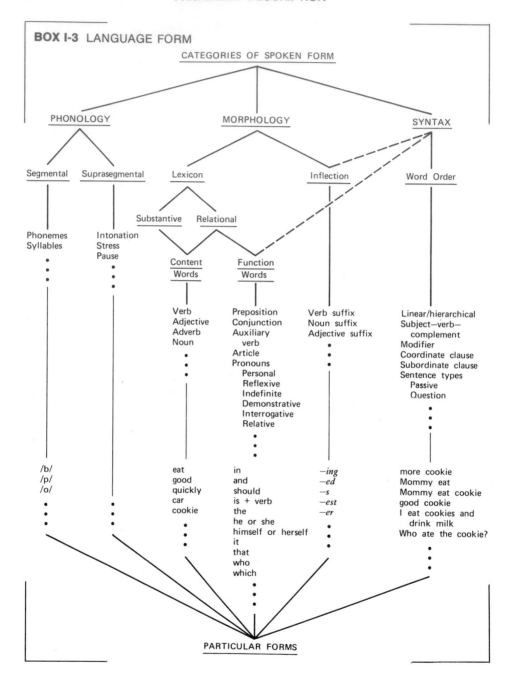

BOX I-3 LANGUAGE FORM

(different stress and intonation) to distinguish between different meanings of the same sentence.

Substantive Words and Relational Words

Specific objects and classes of objects can be named by substantive words: "Mommy," "Daddy," and "Kathryn," and "cookie," "car," and "ball." Such words refer to objects that have certain configurational properties (such as roundness), or functions (such as being rollable or eatable).

Relational words are not defined according to constant configurational and functional features but, instead, are defined by some relation that different objects can share—either with themselves (reflexive object relations) or with one another (intraobject and interobject relations involving attribution, action, location, possession, etc.). The meanings of relational words such as "good," "big," "tiny," "more," and "gone" are difficult to think about apart from an instance of an object or event. Even though one has some intuitive sense of what such words mean (i.e., "more" means recurrence, "big" means large size), the meaning cannot be truly represented except *in relation to* some particular object. One comes closer to a conceptualization for color words (we can think of redness or blueness) but, invariably, the concept of blue will include skies and the concept of red will include valentines.

Semantic-Syntactic Relations Between Words

Relational words are adjectives, adverbs, verbs, and prepositions, and they occur in syntactic relation to nouns and pronouns in sentences. The syntax of a sentence is the arrangement or order of words according to the meaning relation between them. Words such as "in," "on," "between," "above," and "below," are inherently relational in that they code or represent an array in which one object appears in a particular spatial relation to another object or objects. Thus, in the sentences, "The book is *on* the table" and "The shelf is *above* the table," the words "on" and "above" determine the order of words and how the objects book and shelf are located in relation to the object table. Such relations usually hold between objects from different classes (such as books and tables), and are interclass relations. If spatial relations between objects of the same class are specified (an intraclass relation), then it is necessary to distinguish them as different members of the same class, for example, "The *red* book is on the *blue* book."

Other relational words represent action relations that can take place among objects, for example, "eat," "read," and "throw." In the sentences, "the girl *threw* the ball" and "The boy *ate* the apple," the words "threw" and "ate" determine the meaning relation between the words "girl" and "ball" and between "boy" and "apple," respectively (the semantic relation between the words) and, in English, "threw" and "ate" determine the word order of the two nouns (the syntactic relation). Thus, the forms for representing the interclass locative and action relations include single relational words (prepositions and verbs) and semantic-syntactic relations between words in combination.

Morphological Inflections

The grammatical morphemes that are attached to nouns, verbs, and adjectives signal different kinds of meaning. The morpheme -s, when added to count nouns such as "dog," "cat," "bed," or "glass," indicates "more than one" or plurality; when added to an animate noun such as "Mommy," "baby," or "dog," -s can indicate possession; and when added to a verb such as "go" or "fit," -s indicates present or habitual action. Morphological inflections add what Brown (1973) has characterized as the "modulations of meaning," providing as they do, indicators of *time* (present -s or -ing, past -əd, etc.), *number* (with nouns to indicate plurality; with verbs to indicate one versus more than one actor, for example, "she sits" but "they sit."), and *aspect* to refer to the relative completeness of an action (the perfect, "He has (or had) eaten the cookie," and the progressive, "He is (or was) eating the cookie."). Meanings such as time, number, and aspect modulate the major meanings of sentences that come from the semantic-syntactic relations among nouns, verbs, and adjectives.

Suprasegmental Prosody

Words and morphological inflections are the segments of sentences. The form of a sentence can be varied by changing the *pitch* or *intonation* contour of the sentence; by changing the *stress* from one word to another in a sentence; or by changing the *pauses* between segments. Such changes in pitch, stress, or pause time provide the prosody or rhythm of an utterance and are *supra*segmental changes in form—extending as they do across the segments of an utterance. By changing the intonation contour of a sentence from falling, ⌐↓, to rising, ⌐↑, a sentence can be changed from a statement, "She's coming to the party↓," to a question "She's coming to the party↑?" By changing the pattern of stress, different information can be conveyed about the content of a sentence. For example, "Í rode the bay horse," with emphatic stress on "I," indicates that some other person rode some other horse, and "I rode the báy horse," with stress on "bay" indicates that there was a choice among horses to ride. By changing the pause pattern of a sentence (or, more accurately, by inserting a pause between segments), the several meanings of an ambiguous sentence can be made clear. For example, "Flying planes can be dangerous" is a famous ambiguous sentence. With a pause (#) inserted, "Flying planes # can be dangerous," one meaning (it is dangerous to fly planes) can be separated from another (it is dangerous to get too close to flying planes).

In summary, there are levels of formal description and the forms that are used by the language for representing information can be described in alternative ways. However, regardless of the ways in which linguistic form can be described, form in language is the means for connecting sound with meaning and consists of an inventory of linguistic units and the system of rules for their combination. Furthermore, information about the purpose of the utterance and the context of the utterance (use) will combine with content information to determine the form of the utterance.

THE USE OF LANGUAGE

There are two major aspects of the use of language. The first has to do with the goals or functions of language, the reasons why people speak; the second has to do with the influence of linguistic and nonlinguistic context that determines how individuals understand and choose among alternative forms of language for reaching the same or different goals (Box I-4).

The functions of language have traditionally been represented in linguistic terms as the structures for the declarative, interrogative, imperative, exclamative grammatical mood of the sentence (e.g., Lyons, 1968). More recently,

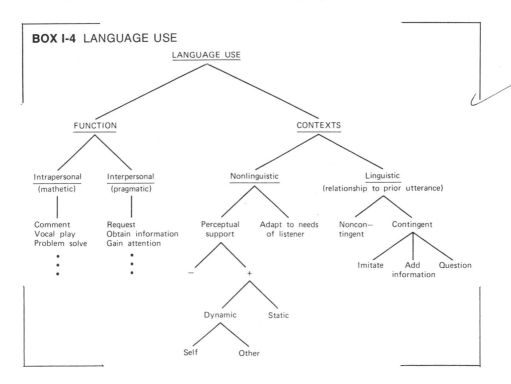

BOX I-4 LANGUAGE USE

Halliday (1975) has conceived of the functions of language in more social terms involving interaction, regulation, and personal control. Language use consists of the socially and cognitively determined selection of behaviors according to the goals of the speaker and the context of the situation. Such choices change the relationship between speaker and hearer in a particular context, or between the speaker and the context. Thus, one aspect of use has to do with the effect of the message on the relation between the speaker and the context—in terms of personal functions.

The second aspect of use has to do with rules for deciding which form of the message will serve the function of the message, considering who the other participants are in the context, and the rest of the situation. Speech does not occur in a vacuum—speech is behavior that occurs in relation to other persons. The speaker's ability to take information about the listener into account (to infer, for example, what the listener already knows and does not know) will determine how he or she formulates messages about events. For example, there is a critically important distinction between the situation (A) in which a speaker has some information and knows that the hearer does not have the same information, and the situation (B) in which the speaker needs some information and has reason to expect that the hearer has the information that is needed. The situation (A) is one in which the speaker will ordinarily make a *statement* to the hearer, for example, "The cookies are on the table," and the situation (B) is one in which the speaker will ordinarily ask the hearer a *question,* for example, "Where are the cookies?" or "Are the cookies on the table?" (R. Lakoff, 1973).

Very often there are quite different sets of circumstances that determine how a speaker might use the language to accomplish the same goal. For example, depending on who the listener is, what the speaker knows about the listener, their relationship, and the situation, a speaker might say any of the following in order to gain the same end: "Close the window," "Please close the window when you get up," "The window's open," or "I'm awfully cold." There are certain situations for which there are already formulated routines for communication and the listener is not a variable, for example, answering the telephone, greetings, dinner table requests, and marketing. Far more often, however, a speaker needs to formulate new and different messages and necessarily makes judgments about the state of affairs and the listener in order to do so.

The form of an utterance will be influenced further by whether the objects, events, or relations that are referred to in the message are or are not present in the situation in which the utterance occurs. For example, whether the speaker says "The book is on the table" or "It is over there" will depend on whether the book and table are in the situation as well as whatever else either the speaker or the hearer has already said or otherwise knows about the book and its location.

The form of an utterance will vary depending on whether the utterance occurs as a response to something someone else has said or originates with the speaker's own intention. If the utterance responds to something someone else has said, it may confirm the intention of the other's utterance, it may expand on the information in the other's utterance, it may present an alternative to the message in the other's utterance, and so forth. The speaker may be more or less responsive to a prior utterance and may reproduce aspects of the prior utterance, depending on how he or she has processed the information in the utterance relative to individual needs. If the speaker's utterance originates with his or her own intention, then he or she has the options of making a statement, asking a question, or issuing a demand. All of these factors about situations and speakers and hearers contribute to both the form and the content of messages; to how people do things with words; and to how languages work.

THE INTEGRATION OF CONTENT, FORM, AND USE

Given the three components content, form, and use as a scheme for language description, one might inquire what else there is to consider. Their necessary interaction in development may be so obvious as to seem to make the assertion and their definitions unnecessary. The same or similar distinctions have certainly been made by others (see Cherry's 1957 review of similar categorizations). Nevertheless, linguistic theory in the years before the 1960s considered the form of language as the only object of study, and the goal of description could not include an account of meaning in messages. According to Bloomfield (1933), the realm of meaning embraced all possible events in the world and so was not a reasonable goal for linguistic inquiry. In contrast, Skinner's (1957) psychological explanation of verbal behavior centered on use and ignored form and content almost entirely. As a result, accounts of child language before the 1970s described form most often and use less often, but did not consider their interaction with meaning or with one another in any systematic way. By the same token, accounts of language disorders in children have been concerned almost exclusively with descriptions of form or use but rarely both and almost never in systematic conjunction with content or meaning.

For individuals using language and for children learning language, the components of content, form, and use come together in understanding and saying messages. Their intersection is schematized in Box I-5, where the three components together, in the center of the Venn diagram, represent language. While there can be one component in interaction with one or another component (e.g., see Chapter X), language is defined in this textbook as the necessary integration of all three. The integration of content/form/use is knowledge of language.

Knowledge of language is language "competence" (Chomsky, 1968), and

BOX I-5 THE INTERSECTION OF CONTENT, FORM, AND USE IN LANGUAGE

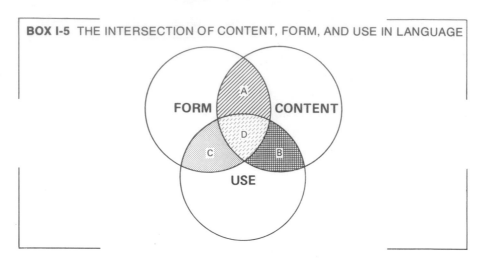

such competence or knowledge guides the behaviors of saying and under-standing. Knowledge of language, or competence, can be conceived of as a "plan" in the sense of a "hierarchical process in the organism that can control the order in which a sequence of operations is to be performed" (Miller, Galanter, and Pribram, 1960, p. 16). The mental plan that the child acquires is a system of rules—cognitive-linguistic rules for pairing sound (or movements) with meaning in messages, and social rules for pairing sound/meaning or movement/meaning connections with different situations. Children learn such rules of a mental plan in the course of development by inducing the integration of content/form/use in the language that they hear and the language that they use. At the same time that the behaviors of saying and understanding depend on a mental plan for action, the plan itself is influenced and shaped developmentally by the same behaviors. There is a mutual effect between behaviors and competence—children learn about language in the process of saying and understanding. (See Chapters VIII and IX.)

Thus, individuals have a plan that is knowledge of language, and they use that plan when they behave, that is, when they speak and understand messages. Language is knowledge of the integration of content/form/use, and such knowledge underlies the behaviors of speaking and understanding. Because language can be defined this way, it is possible to attempt to learn about an individual's knowledge of language by studying the individual's language behaviors. Learning language in the first place, and learning what someone else knows about language in the second place, require evidence. Children obtain evidence from behaving in certain ways and by observing the behaviors of others. The evidence that children obtain contributes to learning a plan for language. Similarly, the researcher, clinician, or teacher can obtain evidence about what children know by listening to and watching what children do. Issues involved in observing and describing children's language are discussed in Chapter II.

SUMMARY

This chapter presents a definition of language that provides a frame of reference for the discussion of language development and language disorders to follow. Language can be defined in different ways by different persons for different purposes. But, for this textbook, language is defined as knowledge of a code for representing ideas about the world through a conventional system of arbitrary signals for communication. Each of the key words in the definition—code, ideas, system, convention, and communication—is discussed more fully. It is seen that there are three basic dimensions to language defined in these terms. The first is language content, what individuals talk about or understand in messages. The second dimension is language form, the shape or sound of messages in terms of the elements in the message and the ways that the elements are combined. The third dimension is language use, the reasons why individuals speak and the ways in which speakers choose among alternative forms of a message according to what they know about the listener and the context.

The integration of content/form/use makes up language competence or knowledge. Such knowledge can be conceived of as a plan for the behaviors involved in speaking and understanding messages. Finally, it is pointed out that there is a mutual influence between the plan and the behaviors. At the same time that the plan directs the individual's behaviors, it is, itself, evolving and changing as a result of those behaviors. Children learn language as they use language, both to produce and understand messages.

SUGGESTED READINGS

Chomsky, N., *Language and mind.* New York: Harcourt Brace Jovanovich, Inc. 1972.

Halliday, M. A. K., *Explorations in the functions of language.* London: Edward Arnold, 1973.

Hockett, C. *A course in modern linguistics.* New York: Macmillan, 1958.

Lyons, J., *Introduction to theoretical linguistics.* London: Cambridge University Press, 1968.

Postal, P., Underlying and superficial linguistic structure. *Harvard Educational Review, 34,* 246–266, 1964.

Sapir, E., *Language.* New York: Harcourt, Brace, & World Inc., 1921.

Chapter II
DESCRIBING CHILDREN'S LANGUAGE

The integration of content/form/use for language is not an object or an event that children can observe directly. But children can observe language behaviors and the contexts of language behaviors. Children are active observers of regularities in behaviors and context, and the regularities that they observe in the environment lead them to form a succession of hypotheses about language that they can test with their own emerging comprehension and speech behaviors.

The task of *describing* child language is much the same as the children's task in learning language. The goal in studying child language is to describe what children know, and what children know is not directly observable. But one can observe children's behaviors and the different contexts in which their behaviors occur, and test hypotheses about the regularities in children's behaviors and the contexts of behaviors. In studying child language, it is necessary to describe the regularities in what children do in order to make inferences about what they know.

LEVELS OF DESCRIPTION OF CHILD LANGUAGE

There are three levels of description: the first level is obtaining the evidence to be described, the second level is interpreting the evidence in order to categorize it, and the third level is the formalization of the categorized evidence with a scheme that provides an hypothesis about children's knowledge. The basic requirements of each of these levels will be briefly presented before considering the important methodological issues at each level.

OBTAINING EVIDENCE

There are two principal options for obtaining evidence for the description of children's language. One option is to observe children's behavior in naturally occurring events and describe the content, form, and use of what the children do in naturalistic interactions, with a minimum of control and interference. A second option is to experimentally manipulate one or another aspect of one or another of the components of content, form, and use, and observe what children do as the result of such manipulation. The same set of assumptions apply with both naturalistic and experimental observations: one obtains evidence, interprets evidence in order to categorize it, and forms an hypothesis about what children know. The observation of children's behavior in naturalistic events is basic to the plan for describing language development and language disorders in this textbook, and therefore will receive primary emphasis in the following discussion of levels in the description of children's language.

Experimental Observation

Experimental studies are generally cross-sectional—different children are observed at different ages, and inferences about development are drawn from the different behaviors that are observed. Most experimental studies of

---

BOX II-1 AN EXAMPLE OF THE PROCEDURES USED IN AN EXPERIMENTAL
STUDY OF CHILD LANGUAGE (from Warden, 1976, in *RLDev*, p.
103)

Method

Twenty children, between the ages of 4 years 3 months and 4 years 9 months,
and 20 adults, average age 20 years, acted as subjects. Only native speakers
of English were used.

A farmyard scene was arranged on a table, using the following sets of
identical model animals: three horses, four cows, four pigs, four hens, four
ducks and four sheep. A portable tape-recorder was concealed under the
table to record the subjects' verbalizations.

Each subject was presented with four tasks. Two of these tasks (the
description tasks) required him to describe an action involving two model
animals, manipulated by the experimenter, in which one animal knocked the
other animal down: the other two tasks (the naming tasks) required the
subjects to name a previously unidentified animal indicated by the experimenter. The order of presentation of these four tasks was counterbalanced
using a simple ABBA design, with one half of the subjects receiving a
description task first (Group 1), and the other subjects (Group 2) receiving a
naming task first. As the purpose of the experiment was to discover whether
the subjects could use identifying expressions appropriately in the description tasks, a stratagem was necessary to ensure that such expressions were
required in the experimental context. When presenting these tasks to the
children, therefore, the experimenter blindfolded himself and manipulated
the animals from memory. The children were instructed as follows: "I'm
going to make some of the animals move about and do things, and I want you
to tell me what's happening. I'm going to put this mask on, so I won't see
anything, and I won't know what animals are moving or what they are doing. I
want you to tell me." It was hoped that this strategy would also induce the
children to describe the events fully, and not merely point to the referents.
The blindfold was not used with adult subjects, who were merely asked to
describe the events, but to imagine an audience who could not see them. In
the naming tasks, the experimenter picked up an animal and asked "What's
that?"

To perform appropriately on the four tasks, the subjects should use the
indefinite article in all their referring expressions. In the naming tasks, they
should respond to the question "What's that?" with a reply of the form "*a +
noun*" ; and in the description tasks, their responses to the instruction "Tell
me what's happening" should be of the form "A + noun is ——ing a + noun"
(e.g. "a cow is chasing a duck").

---

child language are studies of children's comprehension. Typically, a linguistic form is presented to children and they are asked to respond in some way. They might be expected to manipulate objects to correspond with the relations between the words in the sentence stimulus, for example, "Make the bear push the donkey" (in a study of action relations). The data that are observed consist of behavioral responses in relation to a presented nonlinguistic context and a related linguistic input.

Less often, experimental studies are attempts at manipulating or eliciting the speech that children produce. Such studies might include procedures that require the children to describe an event, complete a sentence, or imitate what the experimenter says. (See Chapter VIII for a discussion of elicited imitation as a research tool.) Here, the data that are observed consist of the children's utterances and can be interpreted only in the context of what the children were asked to say or by the context (i.e., a picture or object) that the children were asked to talk about. (See Berko, 1958, in *RLDev*, Warden, 1976, in *RLDev* and Box II-1.)

Naturalistic Observation

Although observations can be and sometimes are made of cross-sectional populations of different children being observed at different ages (see for example, deVilliers and deVilliers, 1973, in *RLDev,* and Smith, 1933, in *RLDev*), the observational research that provided the largest part of the information presented here has been longitudinal. The earliest longitudinal studies were parent diaries, of which Leopold (1939, in *RLDev*) is one of the most important examples. In a longitudinal research design, the behaviors that are observed at different times can more confidently be interpreted in terms of developmental change (Box II-2).

Description of children's language behavior may begin at the level of the anecdote—a single example or a few examples of behavior. Although a single instance of behavior may be interesting for one or another reason, a single instance or anecdote is never sufficient for inferences about patterns of regularity. Patterns of regularity are the ways in which behaviors are more or less similar to one another. A single instance of behavior may be important as an example of a dominant mode of behaving, or as an indication of some change in development, or it may be unimportant because it is an isolated instance that bears little or no relationship to anything else that the child does or is capable of doing. Describing language behavior necessarily consists of describing the interactions among separate behaviors in terms of their relative consistency with one another. Behaviors that are most consistent with one another (e.g., in terms of their syntactic structure, their meaning, their length, or the way they function for the individual) represent a regularity among behaviors. Other consistencies among behaviors represent other regularities, and the regularities

---

BOX II-2 AN EXAMPLE OF METHOD FROM AN OBSERVATIONAL LONGITU-
DINAL STUDY OF LANGUAGE DEVELOPMENT (from Brown, 1968,
in *RLDev*, p. 281–282)

Method

The subjects are three preschool children: Adam, Eve, and Sarah. The
parents of Adam and Eve have college degrees; Sarah's parents have high-
school degrees.

The research to be described here is carved out of a larger undertaking, a
longitudinal naturalistic study of the development of English grammar. The
principal data of the study are transcriptions of the child and his mother—
occasionally also his father—in conversation at home. For each child we have
at least 2 hrs of speech for every month, sometimes as much as 6 hrs.

The study does not cover the same chronological age range for the three
children; it does cover the same range in terms of linguistic development. At
the start of the study all three children were producing utterances whose
average length in morphemes ranges between 1.5 and 2.0. The upper bound
on utterance length for all the children was, at the starting point, 4 morphemes. We have used means and ranges of utterance length, simple
statistics external to the children's grammar, to mark out an initial developmental period on which our analyses have thus far focused. . . . The period
begins . . . when the mean utterance length was 1.75 morphemes and the
upper bound 4. It ends . . . when the mean was 4.0 and the upper bound 13.
. . . For this early period, utterance length is a fairly good index of general
grammatical level, a much better index than age . . . .

For the present research the following specific data were examined: all Wh
questions from all three children in all transcriptions . . . all child answers to
all Wh questions produced by parents in samples of 1400 utterances each . . .
for Adam all answers to Why questions in all samples.

---

themselves make up the *pattern* of behaviors. In analysis of behavior, in
order to describe behavior, one needs sufficient data to avoid emphasizing
unique or only marginally important behaviors at the expense of providing an
adequate account of the more strongly motivated and productive behaviors—of an individual child or groups of children.

A single instance or anecdote may be important then because it leads the
observer to observe other behaviors that can be compared with it. If the
original behavior bears no similarity to any other behavior, it can be
recorded as an exception or a marginal instance. If, on the other hand, the
original behavior is consistent with many other behaviors, the anecdote
assumes greater importance and can be used as an example. Thus
anecdotal behaviors can be important as an original guide to further

observation, and as examples of behaviors that turn out to be important because they predominate in a pattern of behaviors. Anecdotal evidence is only important or relevant if it assumes significance in relation to everything else that the individual does or can do.

Perhaps the most important single factor in obtaining evidence of child language and development is that what children do and what else goes on in the context is at least as important as what children say and what they hear. If only the child's utterances are recorded or transcribed, then it might be possible to describe something of what the child knows about language form, but the important interactions among content/form/use would be missed. There is very often a tendency in the literature to report lists of child utterances, perhaps categorized in some way. The assumption is that the meaning of the utterance is "transparent," and when it is not, then a translation or gloss of the utterance is provided. The problem is that such child utterances are very often interpreted from the adult's point of view. When information is also available from what the child tries to do or is doing, what the child sees is happening, or what the child is attending to in some other way, then there is more information available for understanding the child's intentions and meaning. Language behavior consists of utterances and signs in relation to some context. Even as children's language behavior becomes less and less concerned with the "here and now," they are still using language in situations that involve other persons most often. The context in which language is used, by the child and by others speaking to the child, is as important as what is actually said for understanding children's language behavior and making inferences about what children know.

There are then these two points to consider when obtaining evidence. Information from children's behavior and the context is as important as recording what children say or what is said to them. It is also necessary to obtain a sufficient amount of evidence so that inferences are not made and conclusions drawn on the basis of only one or a few instances.

CATEGORIZING EVIDENCE

The next level of description is the interpretation of behaviors for categorizing the patterns of regularity in the evidence that is obtained. A categorization or classification is a taxonomy—a presentation of the evidence according to similarities, regularities, and consistencies of one kind or another. There are possible taxonomies of language form, based on consistencies among the words or signs, structures, lengths, suprasegmental contours, or other surface features of children's utterances. Two examples of a taxonomy of language form are (1) grouping or listing children's utterances according to the number of words (single-word utterances, two-word utterances, three word utterances, etc.), and (2) grouping or listing utterances according to consistencies of word order (i.e., the occurrence of verb-object order ten times and object-verb order three times, or the occurrence of "here" as the first word seven times and as a final word in a phrase four times).

There are possible taxonomies of language content, according to the kinds of objects, relations between objects, relations between events or other ideas that children talk about. Examples of a taxonomy of language content or, more accurately, the interactions between content and form are: (1) grouping utterances according to whether they refer to moving objects or static objects that do not move; (2) grouping utterances in relation to a time line according to whether they refer to events that are in process at the time of the utterance or have just occurred or are about to occur; and (3) grouping utterances with a particular form and meaning, such as "no" (negation), according to subcategories of meaning such as nonexistence ("no pocket in there"), disappearance ("soup all gone"), rejection ("don't throw it"), and denial ("that's not scramble egg"). These are the kinds of negation described in Bloom (1970a).

There are possible taxonomies of language use, according to the functions of children's messages, or the patterns of discourse, or the different results

---

BOX II-3 CATEGORIZATION OF NEGATIVE UTTERANCES BY KATHRYN, 21 MONTHS OLD (from Bloom, 1970a, p. 185)

Nonexistence	Rejection	Denial
no pocket	no dirty soap	no dirty
no pocket in there	ə no chair	
no sock	no sock	
no fit (7)		
no zip		
no turn		
no close		
no window		
ə no		
no (11)	no (24)	no (3)

Note: Numbers in parentheses refer to the number of times the utterance type occurred in the text (tokens), discounting immediate repetitions.

Here negative utterances are presented according to the meaning of "no" in relation to the rest of the sentence, the semantic categories nonexistence (e.g., "no pocket" when there was no pocket); rejection (e.g.,"no dirty soap" when the soap was there and Kathryn pushed it away); and denial (e.g., "no truck" when Kathryn's mother handed her a car and called it a truck).

that are accomplished by children's messages. Examples of a taxonomy of language use are: (1) grouping utterances according to whether they appear to function for children as *comments* about what is happening, *reports* about what has happened in the past, *directions* or *requests* for some action, or *questions* for information or clarification; and (2) grouping utterances according to how they occur in discourse, that is, in response to what someone else says, or spontaneously without a prior utterance from someone else.

A taxonomy in the form of categorized lists of behavior is one form for presenting the regularities of behavior. That is, one can simply present the categories that result from the analysis, with a list of the behaviors observed within each category. As an example of an unquantified taxonomy, the description of semantic-syntactic development in Bloom (1970a) consisted of taxonomies in which all of the children's utterances were categorized and listed according to one or another criterion. For example, to describe the development of negation, the semantic categories of nonexistence, rejection, and denial were presented with all of a child's utterances simply listed within each of these categories as in Box II-3.

When taxonomies are quantified (i.e., each category presented as a proportion of all the behaviors observed), then the resulting description assumes additional power. As an example of a taxonomy with proportional values, the development of negative sentences in one child's language can be compared at different points in development. See Box II-4. The result of a taxonomy of proportions is the evidence it supplies of the relative importance of different categories, according to their relative frequencies, and a sequence of development in terms of increase in relative proportion, or stabilization of relative proportions from one observation to another.

FORMALIZING EVIDENCE

Once the taxonomy is achieved, then one can attempt to formalize the information about behavior that has been captured by the taxonomy—by hypothesizing the rules or rule system that appear to underlie the observed behaviors. Rules can be statements of procedures or descriptions of the

---

BOX II-4 PROPORTIONS OF UTTERANCES IN DIFFERENT CATEGORIES OF NEGATION IN THE DEVELOPMENT OF NEGATION

Kathryn, at Time I, produced 19 negative sentences, and .79 expressed nonexistence; .16 expressed rejection; .05 expressed denial. Twelve weeks later, at Time III, Kathryn produced 65 negative sentences, and .38 expressed nonexistence; .17 expressed rejection; .45 expressed denial. One can see the developmental changes from such a comparison—syntactic expression of nonexistence was learned before syntactic expression of denial.

conditions governing the occurrence of behaviors. Rules account for the behaviors that are observed and predict the behaviors that are possible although not observed. Although behaviors can be observed and categorized, the rules that are responsible for the behaviors can only be inferred and hypothesized. Rule systems are notoriously difficult to devise, but they are necessary for attempting to explain behavior. There are discovery procedures for arriving at the regularities in observations of behavior (e.g., Trager and Smith, 1957; Langacker, 1968) and manuals of field methods in anthropology and linguistics, but there are no discovery procedures for arriving at rules of grammar (Chomsky, 1965). The information about children's language development that was reported in Bloom (1970a) was tentatively formalized with generative transformational rules of grammar (Chomsky, 1965) for each child. Since 1970, however, there has been less of a consensus on models of grammar, and the later data from the same children that have been described and reported in, for example, Bloom, Lightbown, and Hood (1975), and Bloom, Miller, and Hood (1975, in *RLDev*) remain to be formalized.

There are, then, at least these three levels of description in the study of children's language behavior. One obtains evidence in order to observe and describe it. Once evidence is obtained, it is interpreted according to some scheme for categorizing consistencies or regularity. Once the patterns of regularity are identified, one can attempt to discover the rules or strategies in the plan that governs a child's language behavior. Although something like this chain of events may be the goal of studies of normal and disordered language development, there are differences among researchers and clinicians in orientation and approach to the problems that arise at each of these levels.

METHODOLOGICAL ISSUES IN DESCRIBING CHILDREN'S LANGUAGE

There is a central question to ask of studies that describe and attempt to explain child language: How does the evidence that is presented account for the resulting description or explanation? In observational studies, the question of accountability of evidence raises three methodological issues that correspond with the levels of description of children's language that have been discussed briefly so far. The first issue has to do with the first level, obtaining evidence, and the manner in which the original data of children's language behavior are represented and preserved as evidence for analysis. The second issue is interpretative and has to do with how the evidence is organized once it has been preserved—the issue of categories of analysis that are *derived from* the evidence versus categories of analysis that are *imposed on* the evidence. The first two issues are obviously related and mutually influential: how behavioral evidence is organized and interpreted is restricted by how the data are obtained and preserved in the first place. The third issue has to do with the means and methods for formalizing the results of an analysis of evidence. Although separating these issues is difficult, attempting to do so may be helpful in an effort to reconcile the requirements for the adequacy of both primary evidence and ultimate description. In the following sections, the issues of evidence, interpretation, and formalization will be discussed in general before the more particular issues of descriptions of child language are explored.

THE FIRST METHODOLOGICAL ISSUE: OBTAINING EVIDENCE

People observe and interpret children's behavior everyday by necessity, in order to interact with children, and they rarely think about it. But researchers, clinicians, and educators establish their distance from children's behavior in order to think about it, attempt to describe it and, hopefully, contribute to explaining it. Behaviors, then, constitute evidence.

Anthropologist Claude Levi-Strauss has articulated one law of evidence as follows:

> On the observational level, the main—one could say the only—rule is that all the facts would be carefully observed and described, without allowing any theoretical preconception to decide whether some are more important than others. (1963, p. 272)

An aspect of evidence accountability, then, would be the accuracy, completeness, and documentation with which behaviors are recorded, without regard to whatever preconceived expectations one might have of the data. However, as soon as one begins to think about behaviors, preconceptions will necessarily influence observations. Ethologist C. G. Beer has phrased the problem quite well: "for both logical and practical reasons, there can be no such thing as pure observation ... one's ideas evolve with one's research, reading and thinking ... trying to put oneself at sufficient distance for clear vision is like trying to leap over one's shadow" (1973, p. 49). Accordingly, Beer says, the evidence for description will invariably reflect the fact that one "has to start out with selection of one out of an infinite number of possible descriptive strategies, in accordance with whatever one's wits and experience offer as the best bet" (p. 54; see also Harris, 1964, pp. 17–18). There are then the primitive components of a behavior event to be observed and somehow represented or preserved so that one or another kind of interpretative operation can be performed on them. However, any description of behavior will be necessarily constrained by the process of observation, and the question for evidence accountability then becomes a matter of the degree of such constraint.

As soon as one begins to record behaviors, there is loss of information, and successive reductions of the data continue to restrict and limit their informative power. The original behavior, being a temporal event, only leaves a residue of information in the record that is made of it and the ultimate interpretation that is given to it. For example, once an event is recorded (whether recorded by hand or recorded by electronic audio or video tape recorder), something is necessarily left out of the record. The eye, the ear, and the hand can never preserve the detail, nuance, and complex circumstances of events. Recording behaviors by hand results in the greatest loss of information and constraint on observation. With very little distance between the occurrence of the event and the observation of the event, the record is narrowly constrained by the preconceptions and other limitations of the observer.

Even though something is left out of an electronic audio or video record (much more so in the former than the latter), the event is still preserved in large part so that repeated observations can be made. One can play a tape recording over and over, and hear and realize something more each time. The same recorded event can be observed by different observers. However, the process of transcription reduces mechanically recorded data further and provides another constraint on the available information; it is not possible to copy off the richness of tone and detail that can be preserved on tape. And as soon as one begins to categorize events for the purpose of description, other possible categories are automatically ignored: "description involves division and classification which exclude other possible divisions and classifications and hence other possible descriptions" (Beer, 1973, p. 53). However, depending on how accurate a record is made of the event in the first place and how accessible the record is for redivision and reclassification, it is possible to explore and evaluate successive schemes for categorization and description.

The loss of information in successive steps with data reduction through recording, transcribing, and categorizing is far less severe than the loss of information when behaviors are not recorded at all, and the only evidence that is obtained is the observer's interpretation of children's behaviors. There is a giant step of reduction when behaviors are interpreted directly, according to one or another preconception or system of analysis. The record then consists only of the interpretations; the behaviors themselves cease to exist altogether. When the data narrowly consist of only the interpretations of behavior, then it is no longer possible to examine the behavior events again for other interpretations that may be more relevant or more important for understanding how the behaviors functioned for the child. Coding events directly in the situations in which they occur, as they occur, can result in attention to aspects of behavior that are really not important aspects from the point of view of the child, or in missing the aspects of behaviors that would actually have turned out to be the really important variables. (See Bloom, 1974a for a discussion of these issues.)

The important evidence for understanding what children know about language is the regularity in the children's behavior, and regularities in behavior become apparent only with repeated observation. If a record is not made of the behaviors, they cannot be reexamined for the purpose of testing successive hypotheses about what the regularities in the behavior might be. This methodological issue is inseparably related to the second issue of derived versus imposed categorization: whether one obtains descriptive categories *from* the data, or imposes a predetermined categorization scheme *on* the data.

THE SECOND METHODOLOGICAL ISSUE: INTERPRETING EVIDENCE

Linguist Kenneth Pike distinguished between etic and emic levels in taxonomies that categorize behavior (a distinction that had been anticipated by Edward Sapir many years earlier):

> The principal differences between the etic and emic approaches to language and culture [lies in the difference between] . . . . units available in advance, versus [units] determined during analysis: etic units and classifications, based on prior broad sampling or surveys . . . may be available before one begins the analysis of a further particular language or culture . . . emic units of a language must be determined during the analysis of that language; they must be discovered, not predicted. . . . Hence, etic data provide access into the system—the starting point of analysis. They give tentative results, tentative units. The final analysis or presentation, however, would be in emic units. (1967, pp. 37–38)

Historically, the etic-emic distinction was made to apply to the study of phonology, where etic or phon*etic* units represent the purely phenomenological aspects of behavior such as the physiological (movement) and acoustic (sound) parameters of speech sounds.

Such phonetic units assume emic or phon*emic* status when they make a difference in the meaningfulness of words within a language. The phonetic [p] at the end of a word like "sip" in English may differ, depending on what follows after the word when it is spoken; some speakers may hold the [p], others may aspirate (explode) the [p]. But, regardless of whether the phoneme /p/ is exploded or aspirated or not the word is the same: "sip." The difference between the two sounds is phonetic—a physiological and acoustic difference that is not a meaningful difference in English; that is, "sip" with an aspirated /p/ and "sip" with an unaspirated /p/ are not two different words.[1] There are also phonetic differences between the phoneme /p/ and

---

[1] Brackets, [ ], indicate phonetic units; slashes, / /, indicate phonemes.

the phoneme /t/ that depend on where in the mouth the sounds are produced. But the phonetic difference between [p] and [t] is also a phonemic difference in English—"sip" and "sit" mean different things and are two different words. Thus, one may start out with three tentative etic units in describing stop consonants in English: aspirated [p], unaspirated [p], and unaspirated [t], but the result of an analysis of how these units function in the English language would be a description of two emic units /p/ and /t/. The difference between aspirated and unaspirated [p] is not important to the language. The etic-emic distinction has been extended to social and cultural analyses as well (see Harris, 1964, and Blurton-Jones, 1972, for discussions of the relevance of the etic-emic distinction to observational studies of behavior).

The goal of linguistic and behavioral analyses is an account of the regularities in the organization of behavior. To that end, one could begin with an *etic* scheme or tentative set of hypotheses that might have originated from one's observations and ideas (or some *a priori* classification). For example, the study of the development of Wh- questions (questions with "What," "Who," "Why," etc.) in children's speech that was reported by Brown (1968, in *RLDev*) was begun with ideas about questions that were influenced by current linguistic theory:

> Contemporary generative grammars of English, designed to represent the grammatical competence of adult native speakers, all employ transformational rules in the derivation of Wh- questions. The research to be described undertakes to determine whether or not there is evidence in the spontaneous speech of preschool children that such rules figure also in the child's competence." (p. 279)

Quite simply, Brown set out to describe the questions that preschool children use with the initial hypothesis that the kinds of rules that account for such questions in adult speech would be related to the rules that account for the questions the children used.

Brown might have only identified child questions that were consistent with forms of questions in adult speech, and reported the sequence in which children learn to use such question forms. Such a procedure of comparing the child behaviors with a set of existing categories (the different forms of adult Wh- questions) is a methodology that imposes an *etic* description on data. Such a methodology stops at the point of classifying behaviors according to a preconceived scheme for the interpretation and description of behaviors. However, Brown's analysis went much further than that.

Brown began with an etic categorization scheme as an initial hypothesis. The speech events in the data were divided and classified according to the similarities among them. The first division was to separate Wh- question utterances from all the other utterances; then the Wh- question utterances were divided according to kind of Wh- form ("What," "Where," "Why," etc.). At that point, Brown began to revise his original hypotheses because there were many more questions that did not fit into the original categories than did. In particular, Brown observed a very frequent form of child question, for example, "What John will read?" and "What his name is?" that, as he demonstrated, was not derived from the same rules for questions that adults know, but was not unrelated to such rules. Even questions that had a similar form as an adult question, for example, "What is that?" or "What dat?" turned out not to be the same structure as in the adult model.

Ultimately, Brown arrived at an inductive *emic* analysis that identified the relevant child language variables and their interactions in the child data. Such analysis involves successive hypothesis testing with the iterative process of division, classification, and evaluation of events, with resulting new hypotheses, and then redivision, reclassification, and reevaluation, until a reasonable account is obtained. Brown's final result (see *RLDev*) was a description of the structure of child Wh- questions, and an insightful explanation of the child structure. The explanation that Brown offered was related to both the adult structure and the patterns of discourse between parents and children that contributed to the process of development. Although Brown began with an hypothesis of categories from adult data, these were gradually revised, and the resulting descriptive categories came from the child data.

If one opts to derive the relevant categories from evidence through successive hypothesis-testing discovery procedures, then one is faced with the requirement of many data, and the number of subjects whose behaviors can be observed is limited. As a result, it is only possible to draw inferences about individuals, and the extent to which results can be generalized to groups of individuals may be limited. On the other hand, if one only imposes an etic system of analysis on evidence, then it may be possible to consider fewer data from larger numbers of subjects. However, the resulting account will always be limited to the original classification. When imposing a classification scheme on data, there is the risk of losing other important variables and interactions that are not included in the original scheme. The problems with such an approach were pointed out by Sapir (in Pike, 1967, p. 39):

> . . . the experiment of making a painstaking report (i.e., an etic one) of the actions of a group of natives engaged in some activity, say religions, to which [the experimenter] has not the cultural key (i.e., a knowledge of the emic system). If he is a skillful writer, he may succeed in giving a picturesque account of what he sees and hears, or thinks he sees and hears, but the chances of his being able to give a relation of what happens, in terms that would be intelligible and acceptable to the natives themselves, are practically

nil. He will be guilty of all manner of distortion; his emphasis will be constantly askew. He will find interesting what the natives take for granted as a casual kind of behavior worthy of no particular comment, and he will utterly fail to observe the crucial turning points in the course of action that give formal significance to the whole in the minds of those who do possess the key to its understanding. (*Selected Writings of Edward Sapir,* 1927, pp. 546–547)

The first two methodological issues cannot really be separated: (1) the large reduction of data that occurs when events are interpreted immediately in the situations in which they occur, as they occur, without otherwise recording the evidence, and (2) the use of a predetermined scheme of analysis that precludes the kind of hypothesis testing that might reveal other variables and hence, other possible analyses and more relevant conclusions.

To summarize, there are three possible methodologies available for interpretation in observational research. One is a strictly etic plan that imposes an *a priori* scheme of analysis on evidence and stops there. Whenever categories are made up in advance (e.g., categories of sentence patterns, or categories of speech functions) and children's sentences are examined and classified only according to how they fit into one or another category, the analysis follows an etic plan. Studies of comprehension are typically etic in that children's responses to a set of presented events are observed.

The second methodology is an etic to emic plan that starts out with the frame of reference or preconceptions of the observer and eventually reaches an emic account of the facts of behaviors that appears to be more relevant from the point of view of the subjects. When the observer sets out to describe children's behaviors, it is necessary to begin with some initial hypotheses or operating assumptions as a guide to observation. For example, in Brown's study of children's early questions, an initial assumption was that adult question forms were being learned by the children and would be used by them in their speech. The plan for analysis was to determine how the questions that were observed in the children's speech were related to each other and to adult question forms. The resulting emic description was an account of what these preschool children knew about Wh- question forms.

The third methodology is an etic to emic to etic plan that uses the resulting emic account as an etic set of hypotheses in order to investigate the behaviors of a larger group of children. For example, given the results of the etic to emic analysis reported by Brown, one could then use the account of the child structure of the Wh- questions of Brown's few subjects as an etic classification scheme and could determine whether the Wh- questions of another group of subjects could be categorized in similar ways (an etic to emic to etic analysis).

Two methodologies have been predominant in the study of children's language. One is an etic plan that describes children's language behaviors in terms of the adult model. The other is an etic to emic to etic plan that describes children's language in terms of child language.

Describing Children's Language in Terms of the Adult Model

In the course of development, children are not learning adult "parts of speech," and descriptions of the words that children use in terms of adult parts of speech can be misleading. Instead, children learn whatever forms they hear and see in conjunction with the regularly recurring experiences that are represented in memory. Thus, it is only coincidental that in the model of the adult language "cookie" and "sweater" are *nouns,* "see" and "put" are *verbs,* "there," "more," and "away" are *adverbs,* and "up" is a *preposition.* More important are the ideas, the elements of content that children represent with the words that they use. At some point in the description of the form of children's speech, however, it becomes useful to use the units or terms of description that are available from the target or model language. Thus, one can describe children's use of different phonemes, such as in the discrimination and production of /p/ and /b/, even though there has been no contrastive analysis to determine whether the children understand that /p/ and /b/ contrast the meanings of different words, for example, "pin" and "bin," Similarly, one can describe the words that children use as nouns and verbs only because we know them as nouns and verbs, recognizing that the words may not have achieved the grammatical status as parts of speech that they have in the target language. It is more important, for both description and explanation of children's language, that the children have learned the words that represent certain aspects of experience and have learned something of how such words can be combined in sentences, rather than that they have learned words that are nouns or verbs. Recognizing that, it makes little difference what we call the words.

On one level, then, it is possible to use adult category labels (such as phonemes and parts of speech) for describing the form of children's speech. Such terms for descriptive categories provide a meta-language for easy translation when comparing the resulting description with either a model of the adult language, or a model of child language.

On another level, describing child language in terms of the larger categories (i.e., grammar categories), of the adult language results more often in a description of child language in terms of what it is not instead of what it is. That is, if one only records children's development in terms of the successive appearance of adult sentence structures in their speech, then it would not be possible to know about those structures children use that are not also structures in the adult model. These leftover sentences or sentence structures might be quite acceptable as child structures, or they might be distortions of structures that reflect deviance or a disorder in development. Looking for adult structures in child speech may thus result in an undereval- uation of children's knowledge and capacities.

On still another level, the appearance of a sentence in a child's speech that has the form of an adult sentence does not necessarily mean that the underlying structure of the sentence is the same in both instances. Children may well use a sentence or even sentences that they have remembered from the adult speech that they have heard—but that sentence may be less representative of their knowledge of sentences than other utterances that are more frequent in their speech and that have no analog in the adult model. For example, a child who was 20 months, 2 weeks old with a mean length of utterance (*MLU*) of 1.19 morphemes, said "ə don't want baby," and dropped the doll he was holding. The utterance was a relatively well-formed sentence when compared with the adult model; however, it was the only instance of this form of negation in his speech. All of this child's other negative sentences were of the form "no more + *noun*," which is more characteristic of the form of negation in child language than it is characteristic of the form of negation in adult language (Bloom, 1970a). As another example, when *MLU* is approximately 2.5 morphemes, children use both nouns and pronouns in their speech but, although the form of their sentences may be similar to the form of adult sentences with shifting noun/pronoun reference, children at this point in development do not use either a noun or a pronoun for the same reasons adults do. Adults can use either a noun or a pronoun in a sentence according to what information the listener already has about the object that is being referred to. Children have yet to acquire the ability to switch from nouns to pronouns or pronouns to nouns according to the informational needs of the listener. Identifying adult structures in child speech can thus result in an overestimation as well as an underestimation of children's knowledge and capacities for language. (See Bloom, 1970b.)

Describing Children's Language in Terms of Child Language

A child's language behaviors can be described in terms of the sounds, words, and word combinations that were used in relation to the objects, events, and relationships that were being talked about. The resulting description of the language behavior of a particular child can then be compared with what is known about the language of other children—using an appropriate index for comparison. It is more appropriate to compare children according to the average length of their utterances (*MLU*) than to compare children on the basis of chronological age. Given an account of a child's speech behaviors, one can reasonably ask how these behaviors are similar to or different from the speech behaviors of other children who use utterances of similar length and from whom similar information is also available. However, it is necessary to keep in mind that even though *MLU* is a reasonable index for comparisons among children, it is only a gross index of language development. The use of *MLU* is reasonable up to a ceiling of a-bout four to five words, because the length of children's utterances increases with development. It is only a gross index of development because it presents no information about the structure of children's sentences, and there can be important differences in relative grammatical competence among children with the same average utterance length (Cazden, 1968). (See Box II-5 for procedures for calculating *MLU*.)

One can assume that children whose average utterance length is essentially similar or within a few decimal points may be using many of the same words and structures, talking about many of the same object and event relations, and using their speech in similar ways. But there will be differences between them as well. The similarities between them are evidence of regularity in development that corresponds to utterance length and provides some information about what the child who is being observed knows about language. Where there are differences between them, then one can look to the comparative or control child language model at earlier and later *MLU* points, with the assumption that there may not be a developmental correspondence with utterance length. However, when there are differences that persist after extending the comparative range of utterance length, then one might suspect that the child being observed is having some difficulty in learning language. (See Box II-6 for some relationships between *MLU* and age).

Such a chain of events, whereby a categorization that was derived from well-documented evidence from a few subjects is then applied or tested with evidence from a large number of subjects, is a reasonable goal for observational research. An an example, Cazden (1968) and then Brown (1973) described the acquisition of grammatical morphemes (inflections on nouns and verbs) in the speech of their Harvard preschool subjects. Their initial hypotheses came from what they, as investigators, knew about the noun and verb inflections in the adult model that the children were learning. The final result, however, was an account of what the children were learning—a longitudinal, emic account. Subsequently, deVilliers and deVilliers (1973, in *RLDev*) were able to use this emic account of child language that was obtained from longitudinal evidence as an etic plan to study the acquisition of grammatical morphemes in the speech of a larger, cross-sectional population of children.

The same kind of emic to etic methodology is the suggested goal for the plan for language disorders that is presented in this textbook. The first half of this book presents the evidence from normal language development that

---

BOX II-5 RULES FOR CALCULATING *MLU* (from Brown, 1973, p. 54)

1. Start with the second page of the transcription unless that page involves a recitation of some kind. In this latter case start with the first recitation-free stretch. Count the first 100 utterances satisfying the following rules.
2. Only fully transcribed utterances are used; none with blanks. Portions of utterances, entered in parentheses to indicate doubtful transcription, are used.*
3. Include all exact utterance repetitions (marked with a plus sign in records).* Stuttering is marked as repeated efforts at a single word; count the word once in the most complete form produced. In the few cases where a word is produced for emphasis or the like (*no, no, no*) count each occurrence.
4. Do not count such fillers as *mm* or *oh*, but do count *no, yeah,* and *hi.*
5. All compound words (two or more free morphemes), proper names, and ritualized reduplications count as single words. Examples: *birthday, racketyboom, choo-choo, quack-quack, night-night, pocketbook, see saw.* Justification is that no evidence that the constituent morphemes function as such for these children.
6. Count as one morpheme all irregular pasts of the verb (*got, did, went, saw*). Justification is that there is no evidence that the child relates these to present forms.
7. Count as one morpheme all diminutives (*doggie, mommie*) because these children at least do not seem to use the suffix productively. Diminutives are the standard forms used by the child.
8. Count as separate morphemes all auxiliaries (*is, have, will, can, must, would*). Also all catenatives: *gonna, wanna, hafta.* These latter counted as single morphemes rather than as going to or want to because evidence is that they function so for the children. Count as separate morphemes all inflections, for example, possessive (s), plural (s), third person singular (s), regular past (d), progressive (ing).

* These two procedures were not followed for the language samples of Allison, Eric, Gia, Kathryn, and Peter described in the studies that are discussed in this textbook: exact repetitions and doubtful transcriptions were not used. However, in connection with the data analysis for Bloom, Hood, and Lightbown (1974), *MLU* was calculated both ways—with and without immediate self repetitions—and there were no appreciable differences.

---

provided the goals of intervention that are presented in the second half of the book. The assumption is that this information will be useful as a set of hypotheses to use for observing and describing the language behavior of other children, who might or might not be expected to deviate in their development. The account of language development that is presented is an emic description of child language that has been culled from several studies

---

BOX II-6 AVERAGE VALUES FOR *MLU* FROM FOUR CHILDREN: ERIC, GIA, KATHRYN, AND PETER

Number of Speech Samples	Age (months, weeks)		MLU (morphemes)	
	Mean	Range	Mean	Range
7	20,2	19,1–21,3	1.17	1.04–1.34
4	25,1	24,2–25,2	2.54	2.30–2.83
7	29,2	28,1–31,2	3.23	2.63–3.64
4	35,1	34,2–36,0	3.62	3.05–4.23

Nelson (1973) reported a mean *MLU* of 1.91, range 1.03 to 3.37, for 18 children at 24 months, and a mean *MLU* of 3.23, range 1.80 to 4.46, for 16 of the same children at 30 months. Brown (1973) began data collection with two children after 24 months: at about 30 months, they ranged from 1.75 (Sarah) to 2.50 (Adam); at about 35 months, *MLU* was about 2.50 for both. Brown's third subject, Eve, had an *MLU* of about 3.0 at 24 months. While there is consistency in reported *MLU* means, there is obviously considerable variation among children of the same age.

---

of children's language behavior (some of which have been reprinted for reference in *RLDev*).

In an emic analysis one typically looks for the ways in which features of behavior are distributed among a large sample of behaviors. Such an analysis is a distributional analysis. The results of a distributional analysis are usually presented as a taxonomy of the regularities in the observed behaviors.

Distributional Analysis

Methodology in linguistics consists of discovery procedures—procedures of segmentation and classification of linguistic events, for the purposes of identifying the forms of linguistic units and their distribution in relation to each other. The form of a language unit is its shape or configuration, where it begins and where it ends. The distribution of a language unit consists of the language environments or linguistic contexts in which the unit has been observed, and in which it can be predicted to occur in other possible utterances. As an example of a distributional analysis to identify the form and distribution of language units, consider the following group of words in Kanuri, a language of Nigeria (Gleason, 1955, p. 24) with their English glosses.

(A)

gana	small	nəmgana	smallness
kura	big	nəmkura	bigness
kurugu	long	nəmkurugu	length
karite	excellent	nəmkarite	excellence
dibi	bad	nəmdibi	badness

It is not difficult to observe that there is one segment that occurs more frequently than the other segments, the segment "nəm-," which also (1) does not occur alone (as the other units do), and (2) occurs in prefix position relative to the other units. The meaning difference between words with and without "nəm-," is the difference between an attribute (adjective) and a state or quality (noun).

A similar analysis of the relative distribution of linguistic units is possible in child language. Consider the following 24 utterances spoken by a child, Kathryn, when she was 21 months old and her *MLU* was 1.32 morphemes.

(B)

nopocket	morecottagecheese	Mommydiaper	eatmeat
notruck	moresoap	Mommyopen	Wendyhair
nochair	morebook	Mommysock	sweaterchair
nosock	moremeat	Mommyiron	readbook
nooutside	moreraisin	Mommysock	bearraisin
noMommy	moremilk		tinyballs
			clowndance

In either list (A) or list (B) segmentation might proceed more easily if the person doing the analysis is a speaker of Kanuri or English, but one can easily observe the regularities in the form and distribution of linguistic units in both lists. When the 24 utterances in list (B) are segmented or divided into separate, smaller units, according to the relative frequency of different units, one can readily see that a small number of units occurs in the list frequently: "Mommy," "no," and "more," each occur six times; and others occur infrequently: "meat" and "sock" occur three times; "raisin," "chair," and "book" occur two times; the other 16 words occur only one time each. The units that occur most frequently, "Mommy," "no," and "more," occur as the first unit in the sequence; the units that occur two or three times are always the second unit, and the remaining units are really not separable as units on the basis of occurrence in more than one context. That is, one might guess that "eatmeat" and "sweaterchair" are each two units because "meat" and "chair" occur in other utterances as well. There is no indication in this sample, however, that "tinyballs," "clowndance," or "Wendyhair" are each more than just one unit. The distribution of the units in both languages could be described in terms of relative frequency and in terms of sentence position. The relative frequency and position of a word are its privileges of occurrence or its distribution relative to other words in the language.

Both the principles and procedures of distributional analysis have been described in detail by Gleason (1961) and Hockett (1958), among others. In addition to segmentation according to relative frequency and position, distributional analysis takes into account the difference in the meaning of utterances as well. Segmentation consists of the identification of those minimal units that make a difference in meaning between two larger units, so that the difference contrasts the one larger unit with the other. For example, in the pair pig/big, the minimal unit that contrasts the one word with the other (i.e., that establishes that the two words are different words) is the difference between /p/ and /b/, since the rest of the sound of the two words "-ig" is identical. A minimal pair is two units, with different meaning, that are acoustically different by virtue of only one phonological contrast (here the voiced/voiceless contrast between /b/ and /p/), so that one can attribute the difference in the meaning of the two words to the phonological contrast. Moreover, there are other minimal pairs with the same contrastive units: pin/bin; pie/bye; pearl/burl, and so forth. One can conclude that /p/ and /b/ are units that can make a difference in meaning between words, but do not, in themselves, have meaning. That is, pin, pie, and pearl do not share any element of meaning that could be attributed to the appearance of /p/ in each of them. Similarly, given the words pin, bin, kin, sin, din, fin, shin, and win, one can segment the "-in" on the basis of its frequency and position, but there is no consistency in meaning among all these words that could be attributed to the appearance of "-in" in each of them. However, there are units that do make a consistent difference in meaning between words, as with "nəm-" in list (A). And, in English, if one compares the words "unorganized," "uneducated," "undesirable," "unbecoming," and "undeveloped" with the words "organized," "educated," "desirable," "becoming," and "developed," it is clear that the unit "un-" makes a difference between each pair (unorganized/organized, etc.) and, moreover, makes the same meaningful difference for all of the pairs. One can conclude that "un-" is a meaningful linguistic element that is distributed in prefix position in certain words that are adjectives derived from verbs ("organized," "developed," etc., but not "organize," "develop," etc. and not "pretty," "big," "rich," etc.).

Contrastive analysis between units that make a difference in meaning but do not in themselves carry meaning, such as between /p/ and /b/, is the result of distributional analysis on the phonological level of language. Contrastive analysis that segments a unit that occurs within larger units and contributes its own meaning to each unit in which it occurs, such as "un-", is the result of distributional analysis on the morphological level of language.

In both kinds of distributional analysis, units are divided into segments according to their *form,* that is, the frequency of occurrence of the same form in different contexts, and their meaning or *content* (whether the occurrence of the form makes a difference in meaning between utterances with the form and without the form).

When distributional analysis has been applied to child language data, at the level of multiword utterances (e.g., see Braine, 1963a, in *RLDev;* Brown and Fraser, 1963; and Miller and Ervin, 1964), the emphasis was on the form of utterances only. These analyses were performed on much the same kind of child data as were presented in list (B), with the result that certain words in multiword utterances were segmented according to their distribution; they occurred frequently and in fixed position relative to other words. Meaning differences on the morphological level were presumed; that is, it was presumed that the units were different words with meanings that were somehow derived from the adult meaning of the same words. However, such distributional analyses were performed without considering the possible differences in meaning on the syntactic level, that is, without identifying the meaning of two-word phrases according to the meaning relations between the words.

Once the distribution of the forms in children's speech was observed and described in these earlier studies, it was possible to observe the semantic-syntactic meaning relation between the words. When the children's semantic intentions were taken into account (e.g., see Bloom, 1970a; Bowerman, 1973a; Brown, 1973; and Schlesinger, 1971), two kinds of distributions were observed. In one, the distributional analysis was similar to list (A), different phrases that shared the same unit, for example "more cottage cheese," "more soap," "more book," and "more meat" had the same meaning relation between the words, in this example, *recurrence,* or *another instance of.* In another kind of distribution, different phrases that did not share a unit, for example, "Mommy coat," "Daddy hat," and "Kathryn shoe," had the same meaning relation between the words, in this example, *possession.* More-over, the same phrase, for example, "Mommy sock," could have two different interpretations: "Mommy sock" referring to the possessive relation, Mommy ('s) sock, and "Mommy sock" referring to an agent-affected object relation, Mommy (is putting on) sock. Such distributional analyses were deeper semantic analyses in that they looked beyond the surface forms of the units that were combined. Using information from the children's behavior and the context, in addition to the words that were said, it was possible to make inferences about the underlying semantic-syntactic structure of their senten-ces. These studies will be discussed in greater detail in the chapters that follow. For now, it is important to understand how content and form interact in the distribution of words in children's sentences.

Implicit and Explicit Meaning in Messages

When judgements are made about the relation between form and content in a child's utterance, it is necessary to distinguish between what is actually encoded or represented in the message, and whatever else is also understood about the message. The goal of observation and description is to know what the child knows about language units and the combinations of language units for representing meaning in messages. There are other ways of conveying information about an event in addition to saying words; tone of voice, body posture, facial expression, and context all contribute information about the meaning of a message. Children can *talk about* complex states of affairs even though the form of their encoding is simple and limited, just as children can get meaning from a situation or understand something about an event, even though they cannot decode the linguistic signals that are used to encode the event. In describing child language, the meaning that is actually encoded in the message is the relevant evidence to use for inferring what a child knows about using *language elements* to represent information for some purpose or use. Similarly, tests of language comprehension evaluate the extent to which children analyze the linguistic units and the relations between linguistic units to arrive at understanding.

Several examples will illustrate the point. When a small girl hugs her teddy bear and says "bear," she is talking about the bear in relation to herself, but she is only encoding the name of the object in her utterance. She obviously knows she is hugging the bear, and she loves the bear; she may know she owns the bear; she may know about possession; and the listener/observer may know these things too from her behavior. Nevertheless, she has not encoded or represented either the action of hugging, the feeling of loving, or the notion of possession in her utterance, any more than she has encoded the information that the bear is brown and torn and dirty. If the child says "mine" in the same situation, the evidence is stronger for assuming that she is talking about possession, and the evidence is even stronger if she says "my bear." When Kathryn said "eat meat" as she reached for meat in the refrigerator, it was clear that she wanted to eat meat, but she did not encode that she wanted to; she encoded the relation between an action and an object (Bloom, 1970a). When Allison said "Mommy open" and gave Mommy a box of cookies after she was unable to open it, she only encoded the relation between an agent and an action. She certainly wanted Mommy to open the box; she knew Mommy was able to open the box, but she did not represent such information in her message (Bloom, 1973). It does not matter that the information that is intended by a child and explicitly coded in the child's messages is still not in adult form. Such child utterances as "eat meat" and "Mommy open" are child forms, not adult forms, but the children's semantic intention is clear and explicitly coded nonetheless. It is less clear but probable that Kathryn's and Allison's intentions also included *wanting* (to eat meat and for Mommy to open the box of cookies), but this information was not explicitly coded.

This distinction between the meaning *in* the message and the meaning *of* the message—the distinction between the implicit and explicit content of the message—is of considerable importance in understanding all aspects of communication: social and affective aspects as well as the conceptual aspects. More and more, as persons mature into adulthood, they use information from many sources—in the context and in memory—to communicate messages to one another. The operational rules that individuals follow to convey implicit as well as explicit meaning have been explored in studies of ethnomethodology (e.g., Garfinkel, 1967; Goffman, 1969; and Ervin-Tripp, 1972), and have begun to assume increasing importance in linguistic analysis, as well (e.g., Fillmore, 1975). They have to do with the use of language. (See Chapter VII.)

In order to attribute linguistic knowledge of the relations between content and form to children learning language, it is necessary to separate the information that is actually encoded by the units of the message from the information that may be presumed from the context or other nonlinguistic evidence—information about the interaction of content/form and information about the interaction of content/form/use. The plan for intervention that charts the relation between content and form according to sequence of development in the following chapters is based on this assumption. The content of a message may be inferred from the context. For example, when Kathryn said, "Mommy sock," the utterance, by itself, was ambiguous—the relation between the words could have had the meaning of *possessor object* or *agent affected object* (Bloom, 1970a). However, when she said, "Mommy sock," and held up her Mother's sock, the ambiguity between the two interpretations was resolved by the context. One could reasonably assume then that her message encoded the relation between something like possessor and object-possessed, even though there was not an *-s* to signal possession or a possessive pronoun in her utterance. But she did not, in the same utterance or even her next utterances, encode all of the information that was available from the context (the fact that she had found the sock, that she was holding the sock, that Mommy was not wearing the sock, etc.). Similarly, when Kathryn said, "Mommy sock," and Mommy was putting a sock on Kathryn, the utterance was, again, unambiguous because of the context. Even though there was not a verb in the utterance, the relation between the words was agent (Mommy) and affected object (sock).

There are levels of explicitness—including possessive *-s* or a verb ("put")—that would have made the meaning of the two "Mommy sock" messages even more explicit. The two instances of "Mommy sock" were less explicit because they were child forms, but the child's intentions were quite clear. In contrast, other information about the speech events, such as in the earlier examples of Kathryn wanting to eat meat or Allison wanting the box opened, may or may not have been implicit in the messages "eat meat" and "Mommy open." Such other information, however, was not coded in the messages at any level.

A description of the relation between content and form for inferring what children know about a linguistic code is limited to description of the words and the relations between the words that are actually said in messages. The results of such distributional analyses as have been described are typically presented as a taxonomy.

Taxonomic Descriptions

Once the regularities in a language are known, or at least, once it is possible to construct reasonable hypotheses as to what the regularities probably are, one can present the categorization of regularities in several ways. The taxonomic account can consist of an exhaustive list of all of the behaviors that were observed in each of the categories.

For example, the utterances in list (B) on p. 44 can be categorized according to (1) their form (all sentences with "more," all sentences with "no," all sentences with "Mommy," etc.); (2) the distribution of elements (all sentences with frequently occurring first-position words, that is, all sentences with "no," "more" and "Mommy," etc.); or (3) the distribution of the meaning relations between the elements (all sentences with the agent-object relation as in "bear raisin," "Mommy sock," etc.; the action-object relation as in "read book," "eat meat," etc.; and the recurrence relation as in all the utterances with "more," where the meaning relation and distribution of a form result in the same category). An example of such a taxonomy was presented in Box II-3 with a categorization of one child's negative sentences.

In addition to presenting a list of the behaviors observed in different categories, the relative distribution of behaviors in each category can be reported in terms of proportions, that is, the proportion of the behaviors that occurred in different categories. For example, in Box II-7 there is a taxonomy where the distribution of utterances that were spontaneous, imitated, or both spontaneous and imitated is presented in terms of proportions at different ages. In addition to a table of proportions as represented in Box II-7, developmental information could also be presented graphically, as in Box II-8.

Whether a taxonomy consists of lists of behaviors or the proportional distribution of behaviors, the taxonomy is the result of categorization of sounds, words, meaning relations, syntactic structures, and the like, and can represent information about the components of content, form, or use, or the interaction of these components. The resulting taxonomy can be compared

---

BOX II-7 AN EXAMPLE OF A PROPORTIONAL DISTRIBUTION OF DEVELOP-
MENTAL DATA (adapted from, Bloom, Hood, and Lightbown,1974).

Proportion of Syntactic Utterances that were Only Spontaneous, Only
Imitative, or Both Spontaneous and Imitative

Child	*M L U*	Age (Months and Weeks)	Spon-taneous	Imitative	Spontan-eous and Imitative
Peter	1.04	21,1	.34	.57	.09
	1.41	23,1	.57	.36	.07
	1.75	24,1	.57	.38	.05

BOX II-8 A GRAPHIC PRESENTATION OF DEVELOPMENTAL DATA (from
Bloom, Lightbown, and Hood, 1975)

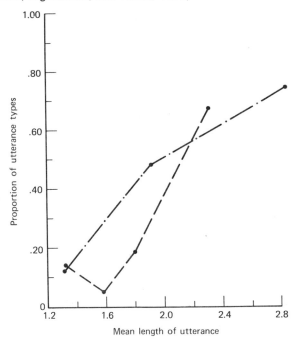

Here, the relative frequency or distribution of pronouns representing
possessor in possessive phrases, for example, "my pigtail," is plotted
developmentally in the language acquisition of two children, Kathryn and Gia.

with other taxonomies with the same variables—either for the same child or with children at the same level in development. Such taxonomic descriptions have abounded in child language research and were particularly prevalent in the 1930s, 1940s, and early 1950s in what came to be called "count studies."The study reported by Smith (1933a, in *RLDev*) is an early "count" study that looked at error data in children's speech. One can refer to McCarthy (1954a), Templin (1957), and Loban (1963) for examples of taxonomic descriptions in the child language literature. See also the theoretical discussion of "taxonomic grammar" in Fodor, Bever, and Garrett (1974).

A taxonomy consists of an account of the presumed regularities that are observed in language behaviors, regularities that provide evidence of what children know about language. Knowledge of language is generally presumed to consist of some kind of mental plan or system of rules. Thus, the taxonomic account presents the regularities in what children do, their behaviors, and such behaviors are the result of what children know. One can then hypothesize something about what a child knows, that is, something about the child's mental plan or rules of language that made it possible for such behaviors to occur. Hypotheses about the form of mental structures or rules of grammar are attempts at formalization that are intended to be explanatory. That is, a scheme of rules that can account for the behaviors or can predict the regularities among the behaviors is an hypothesis to explain either how the behaviors occurred or how the behaviors are related to one another. Formalizing the evidence from child language data, in an effort to understand children's mental plans, is the third methodological issue in describing child language.

The Third Methodological Issue: Formalizing Evidence

A formalization is an account of the mental plan whereby rules relate forms to content or meaning in language. Whereas a taxonomy presents the regularities that have been observed in language behaviors, a scheme of linguistic rules, on the other hand, is a set of formulas that can reproduce the regularities. A linguistic description includes a dictionary or lexicon, with the individual words and morphemes in the language that *stand for* elements of content, and a grammar, which is the scheme of rules that specify the ways in which categories of words and morphemes relate to one another (Box II-9).

All of the possible sentences of a language can, theoretically at least, be distilled or abstracted into a dictionary and a system of rules or grammar. Such a linguistic account—a dictionary plus a grammar—is a model or formalization of the plan of the language that will reproduce the sentences that are observed and will predict other sentences that are not observed but that are possible or permitted in the language. A linguistic description or

---

BOX II-9 PIVOT GRAMMAR

Braine (1963) used a distributional analysis of children's two-word sentences and, on the basis of the relative frequency of words and their positions in utterances, proposed three rules of grammar. The class of frequent words, for example, "no," and "more," that occurred in fixed position were called pivots, and the class of infrequent words that occurred in both positions (either first or last) were called x-words. The rules proposed by Braine were:

$$1.\ S \rightarrow P_1 + X$$
$$2.\ S \rightarrow X + P_2$$
$$3.\ S \rightarrow X + X$$

where P_1 and P_2 were mutually exclusive (two different groups of frequently occurring words, each occurring in either first or second position), and the rules for the three separate sentence types were unrelated to each other. Subsequently, a strong argument against pivot grammar was advanced by Bloom (1970a, 1971), Bowerman (1973), and Brown (1973), primarily because it failed to account for the semantics or content of sentences. Nonetheless, it is to Braine's lasting credit that the rules he proposed formalized certain distributional facts of child language, even though the grammar was not a generative one.

---

formalization of the facts of language is an hypothesis about underlying knowledge. A linguistic grammar is an hypothesis about mental grammar— an hypothesis about the real, actual rules that are not observable, but that form the mental plan that people have in their heads for knowing about sentences. (See Watt, 1970 and Bloom 1974b, for a discussion of the relation between linguistic grammar and mental grammar.)

In an ideal world one would hope to be able to use a set of etic discovery procedures to determine the emic patterns of regularity in language, and a set of formalization procedures to represent the emic information about patterns of regularity with a dictionary and grammar of that language. Historically, there have been different approaches to discovery and to formalization with different linguistic theories about language. There appears to be at least a tentative consensus in the present decade about levels of language description, and the consensus has emerged not only from linguistic descriptions of behavior, but from ethological descriptions (e.g., Beer, 1973) and sociological descriptions (e.g., Grimshaw, 1974). However, while it is clear that the levels of description consist of procedures for obtaining evidence, interpreting evidence, and formalizing the results of the interpretation of evidence, there is no consensus about which linguistic theory provides the best theory for determining rules of grammar.

A review of linguistic theory and methodology in linguistics is beyond the scope of this textbook (but see the readings suggested at the end of the chapter). The three linguistic theories that have been most influential on the study of child language and language development are generative transformational grammar, the semantic theories in general, and variation theory. Each of these will be discussed in more detail. These theories have influenced the study of child language because each of them provides insight into what the nature of the mental processes for speaking and understanding sentences might be. None of the theories has been entirely satisfactory. Variation theory presently combines aspects of generative transformational grammar and the semantic theories, and it appears to offer a very reasonable account of the facts of child language (as well as language in general). Because most linguistic theories analyze language behaviors at the level of the sentence (but this is changing with more and more attention to rules for discourse; e.g., Halliday and Hasan, 1975), it will first be helpful to define what a sentence is, in broad general terms, before discussing the linguistic theories.

A sentence is a sequence of units—words and grammatical morphemes. The words in a sentence are constituents, as in the string

$$a + b + c + d$$

where a, b, c, and d are constituents, and the plus sign indicates that they are connected in a particular order. However, because a, b, c, and d have no meaning, and there is no meaning relation between them in the string a + b + c + d, the plus sign simply indicates that they are added and the whole equals the sum of the parts. A sentence, on the other hand, is more than the sum of its parts. Each constituent in a sentence has meaning and takes on other meaning in relation to the other constituents. The constituents in a sentence like

"The small girl threw the ball"

relate to each other in different ways, some constituents, such as *small* and *girl* being more closely related to one another than to the other constituents, such as *threw* and *ball*. The relationships between *small* and *girl* and between *threw* and *ball* are immediate relationships, meaning that *small* and *girl* are in relation to one another with no intervening relationship. The constituents that are in immediate relationship to each other, such as *small* and *girl*, are immediate constituents. Thus, *small* and *girl* are immediate constituents, and *threw* and *ball* are immediate constituents. Furthermore, the constituent relation *small girl* and the constituent relation *threw ball* are also related to one another, at a higher level of constituent relationship. The constituent *small*, then, is not related to the constituent *threw* or the constituent *ball*, except as part of the higher-order relation between the immediate constituents *small* and *girl* (the sentence subject) and the immediate constituents *threw* and *ball* (the sentence predicate). "Sentences are not just linear sequences of elements, but are made up of 'layers' of *immediate constituents,* each lower level constituent being part of a higher level constituent" (Lyons, 1968, pp. 210–211). Such an analysis of a sentence into a hierarchy of "layers of constituents" can be represented graphically by bracketing or with a tree diagram; see Box II-10. The rules of grammar that children learn are semantic-syntactic rules for the constituent structure of sentences. Such rules are *semantic* rules, because constituents are combined according to the meaning relations between them; they are *syntactic* rules because constituents are combined according to rules of word order and hierarchical (subject-predicate) relationship.

Generative Transformational Grammar

Several attempts have been made to describe the sentences of children's language within the framework of one or another linguistic theory, and the

---

BOX II-10 A TREE DIAGRAM OF CONSTITUENT STRUCTURE

Given the sentence "The small girl threw the ball," one could bracket the immediate constituents like so: [(The (small girl) (threw (the ball)))], or present a tree diagram of the same constituent relationships:

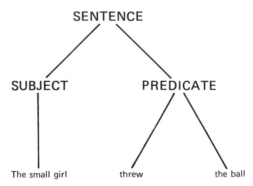

The words in the sentence are "the", "small", "girl", "threw", "the", and "ball". The words "the small girl" are constituents of one structure, the sentence-subject, and the words "threw" and "the ball" are immediate constituents of one structure, the predicate. Because the subject and the predicate are constituents of one another at a higher-level construction, the sentence is hierarchical. (See Lyons, 1968, pp. 21, ff., for a more explicit description of these relationships and the history of the representation of sentence relations in linguistic theory.)

influence of the theory of generative transformational grammar (Chomsky, 1957, 1965) was considerable in the 1960s. Because the generative notion had to do with the underlying knowledge that speakers have about the grammaticality of sentences, it was reasonable to hypothesize that the theory could describe and, possibly, even explain what children know in the course of language development. The theory is *generative* in that it has to do with the origin of sentences—the rules that speakers and hearers know for deriving sentence structures. The theory is *transformational* in that it has to do with the transformation of the underlying structure of a sentence, such as the relationships girl-throw-ball, into its different surface structures, such as "The girl threw the ball," "The ball was thrown by the girl," and "It was the ball that the girl threw."

Essentially, Chomsky had proposed that a grammar of a language is something more than a taxonomy of structures or sentence types such as declarative statements, imperatives, questions, and the like. Instead, the sentences that are possible in a language are related to one another according to their meaning. Following Harris (1957), transformational theory pointed out that there was a closer meaning relationship among such sentences as:

1. The girl threw the ball.
2. The ball was thrown by the girl.
3. Did the girl throw the ball?
4. Who threw the ball?
5. What did the girl throw?
6. It was the ball that the girl threw.

than among sentences that were all of the same *type,* for example, declaratives, interrogatives, or passives. That is, sentences 1 to 6 are more closely related to each other, as transforms of one another, even though each is a different sentence type, than are a group of simple active declarative sentences such as:

7. The girl hit the ball.
8. The rat ate the cheese.
9. The man swept the floor.

The theory of generative grammar (Chomsky, 1957, 1965) attempted to account for this relatedness among sentences in terms of an underlying system of rules. Certain rules in a generative grammar are basic, phrase structure rules that specify the semantic-syntactic relations among immediate constituents. The phrase structure rules would produce a single abstract structure that would be the underlying basis for sentences 1 to 6. Moreover, the same phrase structure rules underlie all of the indefinitely many utterances that are possible in a language and would generate different underlying structures for sentences 7 to 9. Another set of rules, transformations, would reorder and otherwise change the immediate constituents of the underlying phrase structure in order to specify the surface structure of the related active, passive, interrogative, and other forms, as in sentences 1 to 6.

The grammars proposed in Bloom (1970a), following Chomsky (1965), were offered as linguistic hypotheses about what three children knew about semantic-syntactic structure. The explicit assumption was made that one could describe the syntactic structure of utterances, the subject-predicate relation, only in terms of the underlying meaning that was encoded in or represented by what the children said. The meanings of the children's utterances, as inferred from accompanying contextual and behavioral information, were primary data for arriving at the rules of grammar which accounted for the structure of their sentences. It was assumed that syntax and semantics were mutually dependent and one could not be described or accounted for without the other.

The rules for the Gia grammar in Box II-11 work something like this. Each symbol on the right side of an equation stands for or represents a sentence constituent, where S is sentence, V is verb, NP is noun phrase, and VP is verb phrase. The arrow is the direction to "rewrite as." A sentence is derived by successively rewriting or replacing one of the symbols on the right side with a more explicit representation of the same constituent. Thus, in Rule 2, the VP (verb phrase) in Rule 1 is rewritten as a verb and a noun phrase; in Rule 3, the NP (noun phrase) in Rule 1 and Rule 2 is rewritten as either /ə/ plus a noun, or /ə/ plus a noun plus a noun, or just a noun. Parentheses indicate that the contained constituent is optional. The rules are mutually dependent: Rule 2 derives verb phrases that occur in sentences, and Rule 3 derives noun phrases that occur in verb phrases and also occur instead of verb phrases.

The lexicon feature rules specify the conditions for occurrence of different kinds of words. The transformational component is quite limited—there was no question, passive, or other transforms in Gia's language as yet. The optional transformation accounts for the different sentence positions of "away." The obligatory reduction transformation accounts for the fact that although three constituent relations (as between N and V, V and N, and N and N) were possible in the underlying structure of Gia's sentences, there were never more than two of these relations actually expressed in any one sentence. The format of these rules and the theory behind the rules are now outdated; nevertheless the grammar does represent or formalize something of what Gia knew about sentences when *MLU* was 1.3 morphemes.

Something like this generative chain of events underlies the ability of children to say and understand sentences. However, the grammar in Box II-

---

BOX II-11 A GRAMMAR FOR GIA, 20 MONTHS, 2 WEEKS OLD AND *MLU* 1.34
(adapted from Bloom, 1970a, p. 92)

Generative transformational grammars were proposed for the earliest word combinations by Eric, Gia, and Kathryn in Bloom (1970a). The following grammar was proposed for Gia, when the mean length of her utterances was 1.34 morphemes. The syntactic component of the tentative grammar for Gia, presented here consists of (1) the phrase structure, (2) lexicon feature rules, and (3) transformations (see text for further description and Bloom, 1970).

Phrase structure (where NP is noun phrase, VP is verb phrase, N is noun, Q is question, V is verb, and S is sentence):

1. $S \rightarrow N(Q) \begin{Bmatrix} NP \\ VP \end{Bmatrix}$

2. $VP \rightarrow V + NP$

3. $NP \rightarrow (\partial) (N) N$

Lexicon feature rules:

   i. $N \rightarrow [+N, \pm \text{ animate}]$

   ii. $[+\text{animate}] \rightarrow +[\_V]$

   iii. $Q \rightarrow [+\text{quantifier}]$

   iv. $[+\text{quantifier}] \rightarrow \text{more}$

   v. $V \rightarrow [+V]$

   vi. $[+V] \rightarrow \pm[\_NP]$

Transformations (where S.D. is structural description, the underlying structure, and S.C. is structural change, the transformation of the underlying form into the surface form; capital letters X, Y, Z represent major categories (or constituents), and lower case x with subscripts represents the order of positions of units in the original and transformed strings of units):

1. (T_1) Placement
   (optional)
   S.D.: away $+$ X
   S.C.: $x_1 - x_2 \Rightarrow x_2 - x_1$

2. (T_2) Reduction
   (obligatory)
   S.D.: $X - Y - Z$, where X, Y, Z are category symbols
   S.C.: $x_1 - x_2 - x_3 \Rightarrow x_i - x_j$, where $0 \lessgtr i < j \lessgtr 3$

The notation $0 \lessgtr i < j \lessgtr 3$ is a formula for specifying the restriction that two, one, or none of the constituents might occur, but if two occur they will be in the same order as they appear in the structural description. The number 3 refers to the subscript in the input side of the structural change; i and j are any two of the constituents with the restrictions that j is the constituent x_3 or x_2 or x_1, but i is the constituent x_2 or x_1 (if j is x_3) and the constituent x_1 (if j is x_2); 0 specifies the occurrence of zero or no constituents.

11 or others like it that can be proposed at one or another time in the course of development is only a linguistic hypothesis about the child's *knowledge* of rules of grammar. There is no way, obviously, of directly observing what the child's mental rules are like. Such attempts at formalization try to gain some understanding of what the child's rules might be like in order to gain an insight into what the child knows.

The Semantic Theories

The issue of semantics became a dominant concern in generative grammar after an original emphasis on syntax revealed that syntax was inseparable from underlying meaning. Innovations in semantic theory proposed that an underlying semantic basis was derivationally prior to the operation of rules of syntax (e.g., see Bierwisch, 1970; and Chafe, 1971; Fillmore, 1968; G. Lakoff, 1971; Leech, 1970; McCawley, 1968). Because semantics is the specification of meaning in language, and meaning derives from the mental representation of experience, the new descriptions of the semantic structure of language began to be used in accounts of early language development. Different investigators began looking among these new linguistic models for the "best theory" for representing what children know about language.

The semantic theories that seemed most attractive and most immediately relevant to child language data were case grammar, as proposed by Fillmore (1968), and the semantic theory of Chafe (1971). Noun forms characteristically predominate in the speech of children, and many two-word utterances include at least one noun as a constituent. The theories of Fillmore and Chafe accounted for the semantic structure of sentences in terms of the meanings of noun forms in relation to verb forms. Certain nouns are *agents* in relation to certain verbs; for example, "The *cat* spilled the milk" means that the cat caused the milk to spill; certain nouns are *patients* in relation to certain verbs; for example, "The *piece* (of puzzle) fits here" means that the puzzle piece is affected by an action as it is placed in position. Case grammar accounts for the semantic structure of sentences in terms of the meanings of noun forms, as specified by certain prepositions, in relation to verb forms. The semantics of early child language became the focus of research, and case grammar appeared to be most readily applicable to the semantics of child language (e.g., Bowerman, 1973a; Ingram, 1971; and Kernan, 1970). It was proposed that the basic grammatical relations subject-verb-complement, as in the sentences [(the cat) (spilled (the milk))] and [((the piece)(fits here))], where (the cat) and (the piece) are sentence subjects and (spilled (the milk)) and (fits (here)) are verb complements, were more explicitly described in case terms as the semantic relations agent-action and patient-location, respectively (Box II-12).

Thus, the need to include more explicitly semantic information led to more specifically semantic theories for the formalization of linguistic knowledge

---

BOX II-12 CASE GRAMMAR AND CHILD LANGUAGE. The following is part of a case grammar that was proposed for Seppo, a Finnish-speaking child, with *MLU* 1.42 (adapted from Bowerman, 1973, p. 198–200)

Deep Structure Rules

1. $S \left\{ \begin{array}{c} V(A)(O) \\ \left\{ \begin{array}{c} D \\ L \end{array} \right\} O \end{array} \right\}$

2. $\left\{ \begin{array}{c} A \\ O \\ D \\ L \end{array} \right\} \rightarrow N$

where V is verb and N is noun; (A) is the agentive case or instigator of the action; (D) is the dative case or the animate being affected by the action or state; (L) is the locative case or the location of the state or action; and (O) is the objective case, a semantically neutral case that is determined by the semantic interpretation of the verb, for example, things which are affected by the action or state identified by the verb.

Lexicon Feature Rules

i. N → [+N, ± animate, ± prolocative]

ii. [−animate] → [± vehicle]
   ⋮

Transformations

(T_1) Ordering (where elements on the left side of the equation are unordered) (obligatory)

      (a) V(A)(O) ⇒ (A) V (O)
      (b) D,O ⇒ D + O
      (c) L,O ⇒ O + L
      ⋮

Since all of Seppo's sentences consisted simply of propositions (P), the modality constituent (M), in case grammar with the rule S → M + P (Fillmore, 1968), is not included, because there were no operations such as negation, interrogation, or tense marking that applied to Seppo's sentences as a whole.

---

with case grammar rules. However, in addition to the syntax of any sentence (form), and in addition to the meaning of the sentence (content), there is also all of the other information that is necessary for actually speaking or understanding sentences (use). In speaking a sentence, the speaker needs to know about the context and the listener's prior knowledge—what the speaker says and how it is said depend on what he or she knows about the listener and about the context (e.g., see Fillmore, 1973; R. Lakoff, 1973; and Chapter VII).

Traditionally (within the paradigm of generative grammar), the use of language was an issue of *performance*, and performance was not relevant to formalization of linguistic knowledge or *competence*. Similarly, Fillmore (1975) has proposed that such information about context consists of an accumulation of situational "frames," which are the contextual criteria for determining whether a message can or cannot occur. Such frames, at least so far, appear to be discrete entities in their mental organization rather than connected by a rule system—a distinct departure from the generative notion. The fact remains, however, that more and more evidence has been accumulated to be formalized: evidence about the regularities in the use of language as well as regularities in the content/form of language. The more systematic the evidence about language use, the more apparent it has become that knowledge about the use of language is knowledge about language and a part of competence. The issue of formalizing rules of grammar that account for the integration of content/form/use in language competence has been dealt with in quantitative, probabilistic terms in variation theory. The variation paradigm uses *quantitative* information in that a rule of grammar is proposed to account for behaviors according to how frequently they occur. Such rules are *probabilistic* in that they are presented along with some value of probability that the rule will or will not apply in one or another context. Such rules are *variable* rules because they account for behaviors that may or may not occur, depending on factors in the linguistic and nonlinguistic environment that act either to favor or to constrain the operation of the rule.

The Variation Paradigm

The inclusion of evidence about the systematic variability of language in formal rules of grammar was suggested initially by Labov (1969), and it has been elaborated on since then by others including Bailey (1973) and Cedergren and Sankoff (1974). Labov (1969) pointed out that there are regularities in the ways that behaviors differ or are variable, in relation to factors in the linguistic and nonlinguistic context. For example, in nonstandard black English, the copula "to be" occurs as "is," "are," "was," or "were" in certain contexts, and does not occur or equals zero in other contexts.

Labov proposed that the concept of rules of grammar be extended in order to incorporate the quantitative evidence of the different frequencies with which forms occur in different nonlinguistic and linguistic contexts. Rules of grammar do not operate independently of the context; a rule operates in conjunction with constraints in the linguistic and nonlinguistic environment. The variable rules for grammars that Labov proposed included "the predicted relative frequency of a rule's operation . . . [as] an integral part" of a rule formula (Cedergren and Sankoff, 1974, p. 334; see also Sankoff and Cedergren, 1971; and Sankoff and Laberge, 1971).

The study of linguistic variation typically has been sociolinguistic in that it has been concerned with describing the effects of linguistic context (usually the preceding or following sounds with which a form occurs in a sentence) or extralinguistic factors that are sociologically or geographically determined, on different aspects of language use. For example, the occurrence of the relative pronoun "que" was observed to occur in the speech of adult Montreal French speakers with different frequencies according to the occupational level of the speaker. Professional-class speakers used "que" most often; working-class speakers used "que" least often (Cedergren and Sankoff, 1974). The source of linguistic variation in the child speech data that have been described so far in the literature are neither cultural nor social. Most of the studies of child language and development that have been reported in the literature have described the behavior of children from middle-class and generally college-educated parents. The variation that has been described includes variation among different subjects, such as the relative frequencies of nouns and pronouns in the sentences of different children, as described by Bloom (1970a), Bloom, Lightbown, and Hood (1975), Nelson (1975) and Ramer (1976), and different patterns of phonological development (Ferguson and Farwell, 1975). The variable lengths of child sentences (variation within the same subject) was described by Bloom (1970a), Bloom, Miller, and Hood (1975, in *RLDev*), and Brown (1973). These studies of child language variation will be described more fully in Chapter VI. Some intersubject variation in child language may be environmentally conditioned to the extent that it reflects differences in parent interaction styles (Nelson, 1973). More likely, variation in child speech is a function of individual cognitive development in interaction with a variety of different experiences that children have with aspects of the linguistic code (Box II-13).

Although both the kind of variation described in child language and its conditioning factors are different from those described in studies of adult sociolinguistic variation, the problems are very nearly the same. In both instances it is necessary to observe a large number of behaviors to be able to make inferences and to generalize about the regularities and variation in behaviors. However, in sociolinguistic studies one generalizes about a particular linguistic community; in child language one makes inferences about the linguistic knowledge of an individual child.

One consequence of Labov's variable rule model has been a reformulation of the competence/performance distinction. In the traditional view, competence consisted of a speaker's knowledge of language in the form of rules for those sentences that were most regular and consistent. The fluctuations or variation in the actual production and comprehension of speech (perform-

BOX II-13 VARIABLE RULES FOR CHILD LANGUAGE (adapted from Labov and Labov, 1976)

When children begin to ask Wh- questions, they frequently produce questions such as "What John will read?" and "Why John will read?" in which the subject noun phrase "John" and the verb auxiliary (tense marker and/or modal) "will" are not inverted, as they are in the adult question forms "What will John read?" and "Why will John read?" (Brown, 1968, in *RLDev*). Variable rules to account for the fact that inversion occurs at some times and not at others have been proposed by Labov and Labov (1976). They reported the following questions that were asked, among many others, by their 3-year-old subject, Jessie:

1. Does you have it or you?
2. Is peaches bigger than apricots?
3. How do babies get inside the mommies?
4. But how them buy their tents?
5. Where's Philadelphia?
6. Where this comes from?
7. What does sun do to snow?
8. What that means?
9. Why we are going down?
10. Why we can't wear sandals for walking in the wood?

Jessie's questions provided evidence of variation in her knowledge of the two adult transformation rules that account for Wh- questions:

(T_1) Wh-Fronting
        S.D.: X - Wh-NP - Y
        S.C.: 1   2   3 $\Rightarrow$ 2 1 3

(T_2) Inversion

$$\text{S.D.: } \begin{Bmatrix} Q \\ \text{Wh-NP} \end{Bmatrix} - \text{NP} - \text{Tense} - \begin{Bmatrix} \emptyset \\ \text{Modal} \\ \text{have} \\ \text{be} \end{Bmatrix} - \text{(Negative)} - \text{(Verb)} - \text{X}$$

    S.C.:   1   2   3   4   5   6 7
    $\Rightarrow$ 1 3 4 (5) 2 6 7

"The analysis indicated in (T_1) simply locates an item to be questioned. . . . The output of (T_1) is then subject to the more complex (T_2), which states that when a question word stands at the beginning of the sentence, the tense marker is attracted to that word; in doing so it must move around the subject noun phrase" (the NP, 2, in T_2). Labov and Labov concluded that Jessie knew (T_1), but that (T_2) had been learned for yes-no questions, as in (1) and (2) above and some Wh- questions but not others, as indicated in their formalization of the child variable rule:

$(T_2{}^1)$

$$S.D.: \begin{Bmatrix} Q \\ Wh\text{-}NP \end{Bmatrix} - NP - Tense - \begin{Bmatrix} \emptyset \\ Modal \\ have \\ be \end{Bmatrix} - (Negative) - (Verb) - X$$

+Manner
+Locative
+Concrete
+Temporal
+Reason

S.C.: 1   2   3   4   5   6 7
⇒   1 ⟨3 4 (5)⟩ 2 6 7

The angled brackets in the output of the rule indicate (1) that the process affects the bracketed elements variably (some of the time) rather than categorically (all of the time) and (2) the five syntactic features listed under Wh-NP are variable constraints in the linguistic environment that influence whether or not the rule applies to the bracketed elements. They are ordered vertically to indicate their relative strength: the rule applies most often if the Wh form is "how" (manner) as in questions 3 and 4 and least often if it is "why" (reason), as in questions 9 and 10. Parentheses, as in other generative rules, indicate optionality. Probability values are computed for each and are a part of the rule formula presented elsewhere.

ance) reflected competence interacting with and distorted by extralinguistic factors from the context and the individual's failures of memory, fatigue, distraction, and so forth. In contrast, the version of competence introduced by Labov and reinforced by others working within the variation paradigm includes the systematic variation in linguistic performance. He proposed that a speaker's knowledge includes both categorical rules (rules that always operate unequivocally and without variation) and variable rules (rules that operate only with particular probabilities that predict their use in different environments). Cedergren and Sankoff (1974) argued that the variation in the use of language is itself distributed in regular ways and that such regularities are a part of linguistic competence.

In conclusion, it has become more and more apparent that the data of child language provide different kinds of evidence about children's knowledge of language. As more and more evidence of the content, form, and use of language is accumulated, the formulation of rules of language needs to be extended to represent hypotheses about children's knowledge of grammar more completely. Writing rules of grammar is never an easy task, and there are no procedures for writing rules, which is why child language data are rarely formalized. However, formalization is always the more explicit and elegant (in the sense of simplicity and completeness) means of representing information about behavior and is, at least, a goal in levels of description (see Grimshaw, 1974).

SUMMARY

This chapter concerns goals, levels, and issues in describing children's language. The goal of description is to produce an account of what children know about language, so that children can be compared with some standard or model, and also compared with themselves at later times in development. Three levels of description are identified: obtaining evidence, interpreting evidence, and formalizing interpretations of evidence. Each of these levels of description is described and issues at each of the three levels are discussed more fully.

In order to describe what children know about language, it is necessary to observe children's language behavior. Children's language behavior includes what they say in relation to what they see and do in the context, and can be observed in naturalistic, everyday situations or in contrived, experimental situations. Obtaining evidence, then, is a matter of observing behaviors, and recording behaviors so that they can be observed again and again, and one or another scheme of analysis applied to them.

Interpreting evidence is discussed as a matter of finding the regularities or consistencies in children's behaviors, and several alternative kinds of interpretation plans are presented. One can begin with an *etic* plan—a set of initial hypotheses or assumptions about what the regularities might be—and compare a child's behaviors to see how well they fit. One can go on from there to describe behaviors that do fit as well as behaviors that are different and come up with an *emic* account of the patterns of regularity and variation that appear to be important for an individual child.

Finally, a formalization is an hypothesis about children's knowledge of language. Although there are no procedures available for formalizing evidence or writing grammars of children's language, there are different linguistic theories that have provided insights into what children's knowledge of language might consist of, and these were discussed. Children learn how content, form, and use are integrated in language, and their knowledge or plan for using language to speak and understand messages is reflected in the regularities and systematic variation that can be observed in their behavior. It follows that a linguistic theory that can account for both regularity and variation will be most likely to account for the facts of an individual child's language, and child language more generally.

SUGGESTED READINGS

In *Readings in Language Development*

Berko, J., The child's learning of English morphology. *Word, 14,* 150–177, 1958.

Braine, M. D. S., The ontogeny of English phrase structure: The first phase. *Language, 39,* 1–13, 1963.

de Villiers, J. and de Villiers, P. A cross-sectional study of the acquisition of grammatical morphemes in child speech. *Journal of Psycholinguistic Research,* 2, 267–278, 1973.

de Villiers, J., and de Villiers, P., Competence and performance in child language: Are children really competent to judge? *Journal of Child Language, 1,* 11–22, 1974.

Leopold, W., *Speech development of a bilingual child,* Vol. 1, Vocabulary growth in the first two years. Evanston, Illinois: Northwestern University Press, 14–37, 166–171, 1939.

Smith, M. Grammatical errors in the speech of preschool children. *Child Development, 4,* 183–190, 1933a.

Other Readings

Bauman, R. and Sherzer, J. (Eds.), Explorations in the ethnography of speaking. London: Cambridge University Press, 1974.

Beer, C. A view of birds. In A. Pick (Ed.), *The 1972 Minnesota symposium on child psychology.* Minneapolis, Minn.: University of Minnesota Press, 1973.

Blurton-Jones, N. (Ed.), *Ethological studies of child behavior.* London: Cambridge University Press, 1972.

McCarthy, D., Language development in children. In P. Mussen (Ed.), *Carmichael's manual of child psychology.* New York: John Wiley & Sons, 1954.

Sankoff, G., A quantitative paradigm for the study of communicative competence. In R. Bauman and J. Sherzer (Eds.), *Explorations in the ethnography of speaking.* London: Cambridge University Press, 1974.

Part 2
NORMAL LANGUAGE DEVELOPMENT

The development of language is the gradual and progressive integration of content, form, and use. The precursory capacities of infants that contribute to this development will be discussed in Chapter III. The available information about children's language and language development that bears on the development of the relations between content and form will be discussed in Chapters IV and V (the earlier development of vocabulary and structure) and Chapter VI (the later development of variation and complexity). The development of language use in relation to content and form will be taken up in Chapter VII, and the developmental relation between understanding and speaking will be discussed in Chapter VIII. Chapter IX will present a discussion of the processes that are involved in learning content/form relations.

Chapter III
ORIGINS OF LANGUAGE CONTENT, FORM, AND USE IN INFANCY

    Infants perceive and produce sounds (form); infants know about events in their immediate environments (content); at the same time, infants interact with other persons and objects in the context (use). What is the difference, then, in the interactions of content/form/use before and after the child begins to use words and, eventually, sentences, in the second year of life? The immediate difference between the early and later behaviors begins when infants begin to become conventionalized, that is, when they become aware of the mapping or coding conventions that organize the intersection of the content, form, and use components of language at the end of the first year. It appears that content, form, and use represent separate threads of development in the first year of infancy and begin to come together only in the second year as children learn words, sentences, and discourse (see Box III-1). Although infant behavior may be regular and consistent, the patterns of

BOX III-1 THE DEVELOPMENT OF THE PRECURSORS OF CONTENT, FORM, AND USE, AND THE CONTACT AMONG THESE COMPONENTS IN INFANCY, BEFORE THEY ARE INTEGRATED WITH ONE ANOTHER IN CONVENTIONAL WAYS FOR LANGUAGE.

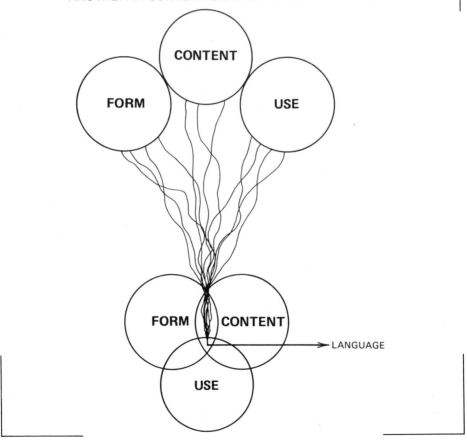

regularity and consistency do not coincide with *conventional* systems of reference in language and communication.

There are other differences between behaviors that are observed before and after the beginning organization of content, form, and use for conventional linguistic coding. For one, the infant behaviors that have been described before they become conventionalized relate to empirical events that are observable (i.e., sounds that can be heard and objects, events, and relations that can be seen). In contrast, the conventional mapping relation, although it uses observable events, is not itself directly observable; it represents an induction from experience. The induction about the coming together of content, form, and use in signs, words, phrases, and discourse is the essence of language development. Infants are apparently able to perceive and produce different features of the sounds of speech and to participate in visual and vocal interactions with others, but they are not able to bring these behaviors together in *conventional* ways.

Another difference is that infant communication in this first year *reflects* feelings and states more than it *intends* a representation of affect and changes in affect. That is, infants vocalize in connection with feelings of comfort and distress, and often there is someone to reciprocate and act to comfort or to share such feelings. One of the characteristics of cognition in infancy is the inability to separate personal movements from those that are seen and, similarly, to separate internal feelings from the external conditions that give rise to them (Piaget, 1954). It is in this sense that infants vocalize in relation to such internal states and external conditions and in response to them, but the vocalizations are not intended by the infants to represent such feelings.

Werner and Kaplan have described motor behavior similarly:

Before the child reaches a stage at which he clearly uses bodily movements to depict events, he already executes bodily patterns of movement that seem to be mimetic-depictive, but are, in fact, only *reactive* or *co-active*; that is, the infant does not represent an event but responds to it by changes in bodily posture or limb movement. Thus, for instance, the young infant may respond to the mother or father rocking back and forth by rocking movements of his own, or he may react to rhythmic sound patterns by moving his body in a corresponding rhythmical pattern. Such a response pattern does not truly imitate the model event [or represent the model event] depictively but is only a motor resonance of it or, at the best, co-active with it. (emphasis added, 1963, p. 87)

It seems apparent that infants begin to communicate information with vocalizations at a very early age. But infant vocalizations are not yet intended to depict or represent such feelings and affectual states so much as they are reactive and reflect such feelings that children have. The *intention* to communicate is another matter—one that involves the critical transition from knowledge about events in the world to knowledge about language for representing knowledge about the world. Two things loom large in this transition from vocalization that reflects to vocalization that intends to represent information about the child's feelings and knowledge: one is information about language—the conventional linguistic schemes that societies and cultures have evolved for sharing information among individuals; the other is information about persons and situations—the conventional pragmatic schemes that societies and cultures have evolved for regulating the exchange of information among persons. The first has to do with language form, and the second has to do with language use. Both have to do with language content.

It is not the case that infants learn sounds, intonation, stress, word order, and rules for interacting with other persons and then put these aspects of form together in connection with meaning; learning linguistic behaviors is not additive in infancy. Instead, it seems to be the case that the linguistic behaviors of infants are precursory behaviors or capacities that are slowly and only progressively assimilated and adapted to the *conventional* requirements of the linguistic and pragmatic schemes of language. Time is not wasted in infancy—children pay attention to what they see and hear, and acquire the capacities to include information about what they see and hear among their own behaviors. But it is not possible to see and hear the relation between sound and meaning—the rules, the conventions, or the grammar of language are not available directly in empirical events. Although children can shape their behavior to coincide with the empirical events that they see and hear, learning a linguistic code waits on the conceptual capacity for a linguistic induction, and such an induction is schematized by the interaction and overlap among content/form/use in the lower half of the figure in Box III-1.

Learning to represent information in messages is by no means an immediate induction nor an immediate insight—it evolves over a long period of time and is influenced by, as much as it influences, the continuing acquisition of the precursory capacities for linguistic behavior. One can talk, perhaps, of a "mapping insight"—the infant's realization of the relevance of his or her own capacities to the behaviors involved in linguistic coding. It is an insight that happens gradually, but it is an enormous inductive step in the child's development. The child's capacities are potentially suited for the task but need to be shaped by a process of successive coordinations of content, form, and use.

The development of language results from the interaction between the child and the context—specifically, the interaction among the child's changing needs and changing capacities, and the different situations in the environment. These interactions between the child and the context involve the processing of information whereby like events are related and generalizations are formed to be represented in memory. Some general aspects of information processing in infancy will be discussed in the next section. In the sections that follow, the precursors to language content, precursors to language form, and precursors to language use in infancy will be discussed.

PROCESSING INFORMATION ABOUT THE WORLD

The major task of infancy is to become aware that the myriad sights and sounds that infants see and hear have certain regularity and order. To that end, children begin, very early, to attend to moving objects and salient noises. Gradually they begin to build a record of their perceptual space—as a background against which they attend to objects that move and noises that appear. Eventually, they begin to discover that their bodies move and do things. Infants develop the capacities for learning language as they learn to see, hear, and do.

Attention is "the active selection of certain stimuli or certain aspects of experience, with consequent inhibition of all others" (Miller, 1962, p. 346). The importance of attention in development is all the more obvious when one considers that

> to deal with the whole visual input at once, and make discriminations based on any combination of features in the field, would require too large a brain, or too much previous experience to be plausible ... (attention) permits the perceiver to allot most of his cognitive resources to a suitably chosen part of the field. (Neisser, 1967, pp. 87–88)

Infant attention to the objects and noises that are in the environment guides and directs cognitive development. Cognitive development consists of the representation of experience: the reduction, transformation, and conceptual coding of information from the environment so that it can be kept in memory (Neisser, 1967). Information about objects and relations between objects are coded as schemas, and these schemas act to influence encounters with new and different events and are also influenced by encounters with new and different events (assimilation and accommodation, in Piaget's terms). Thus, at the same time that children's attention determines what it is that they learn from the environment, the accumulation of *experience* in memory also influences and directs what they attend to.

Conceptual coding of objects and relations between objects is not arbitrary and is certainly not conventional, since it goes on privately in the mind. Instead, the mental representation of information is conditioned by the nature of human mental capacities. Phylogenetically, over the history of generations, the organization of the nervous system has developed so as to make certain stimuli in the environment more salient than others. The evidence for this assumption is that from birth or shortly thereafter, infants selectively attend and are oriented to stimuli such as pattern and movement (Karmel and Maisel, 1975).

At the same time, the mental representation of information is conditioned by the nature of the child's intellect in interaction with the structure that exists in the child's external world. Objects, and the kinds of things that objects do, or that happen to objects, are essentially orderly and consistent, so that they are eventually predictable (J. Gibson, 1966; and E. Gibson, 1969). J. Gibson (1966) pointed out that the achievement of object permanence consists of the registering (or, in more contemporary terms, the coding or mental representation) of those features of the environment that are consistent from one event to another or consistent among the different objects that are encountered, and

> the registering of invariants is something that all nervous systems are geared to do, even those of the simplest animals . . . the human observer learns to detect what have been called the value or meanings of things, perceiving their distinctive features, putting them into categories and subcategories, noticing their similarities and differences. . . . All this discrimination, wonderful to say, has to be based entirely on the education of his attention to the subtleties of invariant stimulus information. (pp. 284–285)

Thus, "the human is a cognitive organism who directly senses only certain information from a highly structured world" (Salapatek, 1975, p. 133). The more experience infants have, the more their attention is drawn to the constancies and consistencies in the environment.

The processing of information about the environment begins at birth, but just how children gradually represent the information about the regularities in the environment in memory is still an unanswered question, but a question that has everything to do with language development. Such schemas or representations of experience in cognition eventually form the content of child language. Conceptual coding is the representation of information about objects and events in memory. Language is another form of coding, for representing information in messages. Children eventually learn to understand language and to use language that makes reference to what they know about objects and events in the world. Two factors that influence infants' attention to the constancies in the environment are movement and change. The result is the formation of categories of experience through identity and equivalence relations.

MOVEMENT AND CHANGE

A large factor that influences what information children process from the environment is the factor of change. Children's environments contain certain static arrays—the immediate confines of their cribs, their rooms, and their houses. Although static backgrounds do not move and change, children are continually moving with respect to their backgrounds. Children are picked up and put down, rocked and carried about, so that their own orientation changes with respect to the aspects of background that might otherwise be static. Children's movements in space result in the beginning mental representation of their spatial context, when objects are not independent from one another in the context.

At the same time, there are objects in a child's environment that also move and change in relation to the child. Most obviously, there are persons who come into and out of view and whose movements and changes affect the child's senses of seeing, hearing, and touching. Other objects in the environment also have this dynamic quality, for example, feeding bottles and blankets. A blanket appears to the child when the child is put down to rest and disappears when he or she is taken up for feeding and playing. The blanket is one of the first objects that a child can feel and smell and, moreover, its movements are integrated with the child's movements as the child turns and twists and begins to raise up, and so forth. The static spatial maps, for example, the crib, provide a background for the more salient objects that move, such as the blanket, and moving objects are gradually discriminated from their contexts and from one another.

Children might become aware that objects can exist independently from their spatial contexts through a process of remembering the location of very familiar particular objects that move or are otherwise involved in actions. Children can be aware of particular objects and their habitual locations from a very early age—before they begin to know any language at all—through movements that (1) bring such objects into and out of view, and (2) serve to emphasize or highlight an object in relation to a static background (e.g., see Bower, 1974; and Tronick, 1972). Several studies have reported that the earliest words children say and understand refer to moving objects (Huttenlocher, 1974; Leopold, 1939 in *RLDev*; and Nelson, 1973). Specific objects and then objects in general increase in salience in relation to their spatial contexts as children develop the capabilities for acting on objects in particular ways (Piaget, 1951, 1954; see also Gratch, 1975).

All of these experiences contribute to the process whereby information about objects and events is represented or coded in memory. Children's conceptual development depends on the ability to extract from the environment the aspects that are constant and predictable in relation to themselves and to one another. The central concern in this learning is with discovering the regularities in the environment and generalizing about events.

IDENTITY AND EQUIVALENCE

Certain events recur for children with comforting frequency—a mother's face, a bottle, and a blanket are a few of the most immediate objects that recur often for children. It is not at all clear how children know that the same object is the same object when it reappears, but the ability to identify recurring events as being similar is critical to being able to discover the regularities in the environment (e.g., see Hampshire, 1967), and is the basis for the processes of recognizing and identifying. There are two critical achievements in discovering regularities in the environment; the first is the realization of the *identity* of certain events, that an event (e.g., a mother's face or a blanket), that recurs is the *same* event; the second is the realization that certain events are of the same kind—that they have *equivalence.*

> When we encounter a common object—a hat, say—we either recognize that it is a hat, equivalent to millions of other hats, or we may recognize that it is Arthur's hat, a particular hat with its own identity, a hat we have seen many times before. To recognize that an object is a hat is to assign it to a class. To recognize Arthur's is to recognize an individual object. The class of all hats contains Arthur's hat as a member. (Miller, 1962, pp. 147–148)

The learning of language form, language content, and language use is bound to the learning of identity and equivalence relations. A critical problem in understanding the behaviors in infancy that are precursory to language learning is to define the dimensions that children use for establishing equivalence relations.

Children's eventual use of words (such as "car" or "more") or the understanding of a word used by someone else provide an index of their abilities to divide and classify events in the world. Although there are many cases where concepts can be identified with particular words, there is not a one-to-one correspondence between words and concepts. Concepts are not words; there are many concepts or properties of concepts that do not have names and, indeed, the same name can be applied to more than one concept (e.g., see Collins and Quillian, 1972). Also, children have many concepts before they learn words for these concepts.

However, words and signs are concepts. In addition to children's conceptual abilities for classifying and generalizing among objects and events in reality, there are the processes of division and classification of events for learning linguistic categories. Words have distinguishing physical and acoustic properties as well as distinguishing semantic and syntactic properties. Sounds have distinguishing acoustic and articulatory units that make meaningful differences between words. And there are grammatical concepts that include information about the ways in which combinations of words and sounds can represent relational meanings. Similarly, knowing how to use language depends on knowing about situations and being able to generalize among listeners in different contexts. The rest of this chapter will be concerned with the origins of such concept development and the behaviors of infants that are the precursors for the development of language content, language form, and language use.

PRECURSORS OF LANGUAGE CONTENT

The information about the regularities in the world that children acquire and remember consists of *object* concepts (information about the physical and functional features of different objects) and *relational* concepts (information about the ways in which objects from the same concept or from different concepts can relate to one another). Knowing about objects and about relations between objects begins in infancy. Piaget (1954, 1971) drew a distinction between figurative and operative knowing about objects. Figurative knowledge has a physical structure. As infants repeatedly see objects, they extract information about their physical appearance and form a mental copy or schema that allows them to recognize the object when they see it again. Operative knowledge has to do with children's actions and patterns of activity with objects through which they form mental representations or schemes for acting. The result of acting on things and with things, putting them here and putting them there, is that infants are able to see things in relation to one another and in relation to their own actions. The mental schemes that underlie infants' actions are repeatedly reorganized in the process of such activity. It is through such reorganized schemes that infants learn about relations among objects and, ultimately, the distinction between the actor and the object that is acted on (Gratch, 1975).

The result of this sensorimotor activity in infancy is that, sometime toward the end of the second year, children come to know about object permanence. Object permanence has been explained by Piaget as the knowing that objects exist in space and time, even when a child can no longer see them or act on them. Such knowledge involves knowing about objects and about relations among objects, and the object concepts and relational concepts eventually provide the content of children's language.

OBJECT PERMANENCE AND OBJECT CONCEPTS

The behaviors that Piaget observed and described (1951, 1954) have been observed since with many children. Once the behaviors were recognized and their importance was pointed out by Piaget, it became relatively easy for others to notice and appreciate how infant activity changes in the first 18 months. Observing how infants act with objects can provide insight into discovering the ways infants think about objects.

In the early months, infants act as though an object that is out of sight is also out of mind: when an object is hidden from view, they neither look after it nor search for it. Sometime toward the end of the first six months, babies will be able to remove an obstacle to uncover an object that has been only partly hidden from view. Although babies still will not search after or try to uncover an object that has been completely hidden by a cloth or a pillow, they will remove the cloth or pillow when part of the object (a bottle, for instance) can still be seen. At this point, the infants' behavior is evidence that the exposed part of an object is an index or indication of the whole object, and they can act to recover the part that is missing from view. Seeing the part of the object enables infants to remember the whole object.

In a series of experiments, Bower (1974) explored infants searching behaviors with respect to vanishing objects in the first 6 months, and confirmed many of the observations that had been reported by Piaget. Bower described how infants followed the path of a moving object with their eyes as the object disappeared behind a screen. He also measured acceleration of heart rate as an indication of either anticipation or surprise with the reappearance of objects from behind a screen. The result of a series of such experiments led Bower to conclude that infants as young as 2 to 4 months can track a moving object and anticipate its emergence from behind a screen. However, infants also continued to follow the path of a moving object after it had stopped moving. This led to the question of whether infants identify an object that disappears and then reappears as the same object, or another object. In another series of experiments, Bower demonstrated that infants could track any object that followed the same path of movement after disappearing behind a screen—even when the original object was replaced with an object that was entirely different perceptually. However, when the path of movement was changed, whether the object was the same object or not, infants appeared to be disturbed, and no longer tracked the object. It appeared, then, that the movement of the object or the tracking movement by 3-to 4-month-old infants is important in defining the identity of a moving object, and other features of objects are probably not taken into account.

After the first 6 months, infants are capable of finding a hidden object that had been entirely covered by a cloth or entirely hidden behind an obstacle such as a pillow. However, infants of 6 to 12 months continue to make a curious mistake. Imagine that an object has disappeared behind or under one obstacle and retrieved by the infant. If the same object is then hidden under a second obstacle—in full view of the child—then the child will proceed to search for the object in the place where it had first been found.

After the first birthday, infants no longer make the mistake of searching for an object in the first place where they had seen it hidden. As long as they see where an object disappears, they can search for it at that place and are no longer bound by their perceptions of the place of the original disappearance of the object. However, if the children see an object disappear, and the object is then hidden under a second obstacle but the children have not seen the second displacement, then they will not search for the object under the second obstacle when they fail to find it at the place where it originally disappeared. Piaget described this as a failure to take account of "invisible displacements." Although such tasks may seem to border on trickery, the fact is that by about the age of 18 months, children are able to succeed at recovering objects after invisible displacements. That is, even though they have not seen an object hidden or otherwise disappear, they will know to search for it and will not persist in searching for the object in the place where they had seen it disappear originally (Box III-2).

When children are able to search for objects that are hidden, then one can infer that they are able to think about objects that disappear or are no longer visible. This ability—to think about objects that are no longer perceptually present—is evidence that children have processed information from the environment (about objects) and transformed, coded, and stored that information so as to be able to remember and act on it. Bower has described children's behavior with respect to objects in the first 18 months in terms of rules for recognizing that an object is the same object, or rules for realizing how the factors of movement and place affect whether children realize an object is the same object or not. Whether one characterizes such behavior in terms of *rules* for knowing about objects, or in terms of *strategies* for dealing with objects, it is important to recognize that such infant behaviors as have been described by Piaget, Bower, and others are behaviors that occur with respect to objects in general. Behaviors such as search and tracking are the same behaviors, regardless of the perceptual properties of different objects. Children learn to watch after or to search for objects as different as bouncing balls and nursing bottles, cookies or toy fire engines. The achievement of object concept—the achievement of the recognition of the permanence of objects—is reflected in the fact that children come to have expectations about objects, in general, and to behave in similar ways with many different objects according to their expectations.

Concepts of Objects

At the same time that children develop strategies or rules for dealing with (1) *objects in general,* they also remember and think about (2) *particular objects,* such as Mommy, Daddy, bottle, and blanket, each of which consists of a class of one member in much the same way as the Empire State Building or Queen Elizabeth is each a class with one member, and (3) *classes of objects* that are perceptually and functionally equivalent, such as cookies, hats, bottles, and blankets. However, it is not at all clear that infants know that a particular object such as Daddy, Mommy, or the pet cat is indeed a "class of one" in contrast with objects that form classes with many members such as cookies and hats and cats in general. Children may remember information about objects in such a way that there are many Daddys, with each appearance being another instance of a Daddy. It is more likely, however, that the singular instances in their environment (their mothers, fathers, favorite blankets, bottles, and pet cats) are a stronger influence on infants to believe at first that there is only one cookie or only one hat and each instance of a cookie or a hat is a reappearance.

The task for children learning identity and equivalence relations, as in all

BOX III-2 EXAMPLES OF TASKS THAT CAN BE ADMINISTERED TO INFANTS IN ORDER TO TEST FOR KNOWLEDGE OF OBJECT PERMANENCE AND LEVEL OF SENSORIMOTOR DEVELOPMENT (from S. K. Escalona and H. C. Corman, Albert Einstein Scales of Sensorimotor Development).

Description of Task and Infant's Response	Score in terms of levels of progression in Piaget's Six Stages of Sensorimotor Intelligence
Visible Displacement—One Screen.	
Administration: Having secured the child's attention, object is placed on table, and slowly covered by pad.	
Response: Child finds object on two trials.	Stage IV; level 3
Visible Displacement—Two Screens.	
Administration: Immediately after child succeeded on previous item a second pad is placed on the table. Hide object under same screen, referred to as location A. After the child has found object under A, repeat the procedure, hiding object under second screen (location B).	
Response: Child searches only under A.	Stage IV; level 4
Response: Child searches first at location A, then at B.	Stage IV; level 5
Response: Child searches directly at B.	Stage V; level 1
Visible Displacement—Three Screens.	
Administration: Immediately after successful performance on previous task, a third screen (location C) is added to the field, and the object slowly hidden under it as before.	
Response: Child first searches under A or B, then goes to C.	Stage V; level 2
Response: Child searches directly under C.	Stage V; level 3
Visible Displacement—Random.	
Administration: While all three screens are in the field, the object is hidden under each of the three screens but never sequentially; Use the orders ACB, BCA, or BAC.	
Response: Child searches directly under correct screen on *three successive trials.*	Stage V; level 4

learning, involves processes of *generalization*, recognizing that different instances belong to the same concept, and *discrimination*, recognizing the perceptual and functional properties that cause members of the same concept to be different from one another. Children start out with the experience of a particular instance of Mommy or pet cat or nursing bottle, and they learn eventually that these object concepts expand to include other related instances and form a more general concept, such as the Mommys on the playground, the cats in the neighborhood, and so forth. Suppose that the family cat is small and grey and then suppose that the child comes across another object that also moves, has fur, tail, whiskers, and four feet but is black and white and large. Each time the two objects are seen, the child can either recognize them on the basis of different concepts—both of which share the common properties fur, tail, four feet, and whiskers; one concept also having the properties small and grey, the other concept also having the properties black and white and large. Other encounters with other objects may lead to other concepts but, eventually, there is the realization that certain properties are shared by these concepts and one concept emerges with the common properties fur, four feet, tail, and whiskers. That concept also includes, in addition to the common properties, another concept with the distinguishing features grey and small (see also Collins and Quillian, 1972).

The view that "some sort of memorial representation of the distinguishing and invariant features of a stimulus object is involved in differentiation of it from other objects or events in its absence" (E. Gibson, 1969, pp. 151–152) has come to predominate in discussions of the nature of object concepts. Gibson pointed out that terms such as "image," "schema," and "concept" all imply the idea of "a central tendency analogous to a composite photograph." She quoted Attneave (1957), who conceived of a schema as a "representation of the central tendency or communality of the class of objects in question" or a "prototype." Sapir (1921) spoke of an object concept as an "average" of one's experience with examplars, and Piaget (1954) spoke of "summary images." Knowing about objects, then, entails the mental representation of the invariant perceptual features among instances of objects—in terms of some sort of perceptual prototype. What we know about cats entails the information fur, four feet, tail, and whiskers, which form a composite or prototype *cat* in memory.

Learning object words that represent object concepts entails the ability to remember information about the object. That is, in order to recall the object when hearing a word, and in order to use a word to talk about the object, a child needs to know about the object. It is reasonable, then, to expect that children will learn the names of many objects only after they have achieved the sensorimotor landmark of learning about object permanence (see Bloom, 1973; Bates, 1976a, 1976b; and the study of early comprehension by

Huttenlocher, 1974). The exception to this assumption would appear to be the use of person names and names of objects that are closely and repeatedly associated with a child—such as a blanket, bottle, or favorite toy. In these instances, the child's conceptual information about the object is not a prototype, a schema formed after encounters with different exemplars. Instead, the child's conceptual information is a schema of the single object formed from different encounters with the same object. Representing information about object concepts is basic to representing information about word concepts.

The mental record of the child's active perception of invariancies in the environment is the object concept—having to do with the common behaviors that objects share in general, as well as the perceptual properties of particular objects. Such knowledge about objects becomes possible in the second year with the realization of the permanence of objects. The achievement of object permanence means that the child has succeeded in realizing that objects are separate from the sensorimotor activity or schemes in which they were experienced. That is, objects exist independently of the child and the child's movements with respect to them, and they also exist independently of the time and space contexts in which they appear. Thus, separating the object from the relationship between the child and the object, and from the relationship between objects and the time and place in which they occur, is at the heart of the achievement of object permanence.

OBJECT PERMANENCE AND RELATIONAL CONCEPTS

Objects, including persons, are related to one another and affect one another in consistent ways. Events that include the child also include objects in active and static relationship to one another and to the child. Thus, a second major factor that contributes to the content of language has to do with the concepts of relations between object concepts. Less systematic attention has been given to the concepts children form of the regularities in the ways that objects relate to one another than to the achievement of object concepts. The study of object permanence is the study of children's knowledge of objects. Although the relations between objects and between children and objects figure in an important way in how children come to know about objects, children also need to know about object relations, per se, and such knowing involves relational concepts. Most of the inferences about children's relational concepts have come through the study of children's later play; how children manipulate objects in play is seen as an index of what children understand about the relations between objects (e.g., Sinclair, 1970) and, eventually, children's language—where the assumption is that the semantic relations between words that are coded in children's messages reflect underlying conceptual relationships (Bloom, 1970a; Brown, 1973; and Greenfield, Smith, and Laufer, 1972).

Where do relational concepts originate? It is fairly clear that children do not learn the relations between objects through language, because children show that they already know something about the ways objects relate to each other long before they use linguistic forms to code such relations (e.g., Bloom, 1973; Halliday, 1975; Rocissano, 1975; and Sinclair, 1970).

Children need to have formed relational concepts as a necessary but not sufficient condition for learning the linguistic forms (words and multiword structures) that encode such concepts. There is no precise accounting of which relational concepts children form and in what kind of developmental order, but there is some information about the kind of intellectual activity in infancy that contributes to children's conceptual representations of relational information—mental activity that occurs in the interaction between infants and their contexts in the first 2 years.

Action and Locative Relations in Infancy

In describing the development of object permanence, Piaget convincingly demonstrated that infants learn to use the cues from the environment in regular ways that appear to be age determined. Infants, before the end of the first year and long before the beginning of multiword utterances at 18 to 22+ months, have demonstrated an awareness of relational cues from the environment for acting on objects. Piaget has given particular emphasis to environmental cues that figure in an important way in children's perceptions and activities that lead to the awareness of object permanence: in particular, the cues from movement and space.

When objects move, there is a source of movement, some actor, and an effect of the movement, which could be some change in location or other change in the mover or in some other object (or person). These relations between the originating source and the effect of movement is an action relation, and when some change in place is involved, the relation is locative. There are also relations among individual movements—regularities in activities that allow infants to generalize about certain movements (such as dropping or reaching). There are also static relations among objects and places, where no movement is involved.

Children discover the permanence of objects by observing the effect of movement on objects (e.g., that they appear, disappear, and recur). But, in addition to such general effects on objects, there are specific effects of specific movements (or no effect when there is no movement). There are objects that move (balls, bottles, and cats) and objects that typically do not move (sofas, bathtubs, and refrigerators). There are movements whereby children create effects (rolling over, splashing, and eating), and there are movements by others that affect children (stroking, rocking, and swinging). Movement is a dominant force in conceptual development in infancy, and there are regularities among movements by children and by others in relation to the context. What is not clear is at what point children extract the relevant variables within such events; at what point do they recognize the differences between a relation between themselves creating movement; themselves as recipients of the effect of movement; and objects affected by their movement or the movement of others. The task in conceptual development is to detect and mentally represent such regularities (conceptual coding). The conceptualization of the regularities among movement, the origin of movement, and the effect of movement is the development of relational concepts. ↵

Location and spatial relations also contribute in an important way to the discovery of object permanence. Most important, the critical behavior that distinguishes, for Piaget, children who are not aware of object permanence, children with growing awareness, and children with full awareness is the behavior of looking for an object in the place where it was last seen. At the fourth stage of sensorimotor intelligence, at about 8 to 10 months, children know to look for an object after they see it vanish behind a screen; this is a primitive relation between an object and the place where it was last seen. This object-place relation is a powerful one because, subsequently, children will continue to look for an object at the place where they first saw it disappear, even through they saw it moved again to a second place. According to Piaget (1954), eventually the failure in retrieving the object when looking at the first place teaches the infant to look for the object in the second place where it was hidden last (the realization of the relation of an object in successive places).

In studies by Harris (1975) and by Gratch, Appel, Evans, LeCompte, and Wright (1974), it was confirmed that a change of place was still a critical variable in the success of 9-to 10-month-olds in searching for a hidden object, but it was also demonstrated that the effect of a change in place interacted with memory. That is, the infants tended to "forget" where they had last seen the object placed if they could not look for it immediately. There are two explanations of the phenomenon: one is Piaget's explanation that children look to the first hiding place because that is where they had already experienced sensorimotor success in finding the object. The other explanation suggested by Harris (1975) and by Gratch et al. (1974) is that 9- to 10-month-old infants probably perceive (and code) the object in two successive places and can look in the second place if there is not a delay between hiding the object and looking for it.   Finally, Gratch et al. (1974) emphasized that, from other studies as well, it appears that "9-month old infants tend to have in mind the places of disappearing rather than the particular object which disappears," leading to a "memory hypothesis of object location" to explain the finding (p. 77).

Object permanence is the conservation of objects in "elementary spatial systems" (Piaget, 1960, p. 113), as children decenter themselves from the context and distinguish between their own movements and the movements of objects. "Parallel with this progress, a system of relations between objects themselves is constructed, such as the relation 'placed upon,' 'inside' or 'outside,' 'in front of' or 'behind' (with the correlating of different places with size constancy)" (Piaget, 1960, p. 115). Eventually sensorimotor intelligence, in contrast with perception, "goes beyond the perceptual field, anticipating relations which are to be perceived subsequently and reconstructing those which have been perceived previously" (Piaget, 1960, p. 112). An example is reported by Huttenlocher (1974) in a study of the early comprehension of object words by four children in the period from 10 to 19 months of age. At first, when asked "Where's the _____?," the children were able to locate objects that were not in view if the object occupied an habitual or fixed location (fish in a tank, cookies in the kitchen). Subsequently, they were able to locate objects in a temporary place, that were not in view (cookies that had been spilled in the living room earlier in the session). Huttenlocher concluded that information about the location of objects, as well as information about their properties, was retrieved by the children when they were asked to find the object. It appears that along with the perceptual properties and the movements related to objects, there is also information coded in memory about the locations of objects—in infants' formation of object concepts and relational concepts.

Instrumental Action

There are isolated examples in Piaget's descriptions of sensorimotor activity in the first year when infants appear to use one object (A) as a means of reaching a second object (B). Examples are a child pulling a pillow to reach an object that had been placed on the pillow, and pulling a string above a crib and causing a chime to ring. This coordination, among the child's movement, two objects, and the spatial context, is part of the exploration of objects, but there is a difference between these infancy behaviors and later exploratory behaviors in the second year. In the infancy examples, there was contiguity between the child, the intervening object (A), and the object (B). That is, the child fixes attention on the second object, and the first object is, in effect, a continuation or connection between the child and the desired object, instead of being a means to an end in the relation (AB).

Part of children's progress in learning the instrumental coordination between their own movement and two objects (AB) was outlined by Sinclair (1970) from observations of children's play. At first, until about 16 months, children's actions with respect to objects were nonspecific and limited to one object at a time. There were certain action patterns that children applied to almost any object, without regard for the attributes or functions of the object (e.g., mouthing, dropping, shaking, and throwing objects). In this same period, although not explicitly mentioned by Sinclair, children can act on two objects (e.g., bang two blocks together, drop a bead or block into a container, or remove an object from a container) in an apparent exploration of the contiguity of objects.

From about 16 to 19 months, children actively explored the function of individual objects, and their actions began to become object-specific as they took account of the different attributes and functions of objects (rolling a ball and eating with a spoon). At the same time, children also began to act on two objects that were not contiguous, where the first object (A) was used appropriately (i.e., according to its functional and attributive properties as an instrument), but not appropriately in relation to the object acted on (B) (dusting a doll's face with a feather duster and poking a doll's eye with a spoon). Finally, in the last half of the second year, children were observed to act on two noncontiguous objects simultaneously, where the first object was used in a conventional manner as an instrument in relation to the second object as a recipient (sweeping the floor with a broom, brushing hair with a brush, feeding a doll with a spoon).

There is progress in a sequence from actions with respect to objects in general, to action with respect to a single object according to its function and attributes, to actions with respect to a general relation between two objects, and to actions with a specific relation (instrumental) between two objects according to their functions and attributes. It is tempting to speculate on how the development of conceptual relations is related to the sequence in which children learn to use multiword utterances to code conceptual relations—whether, in particular, there is a recapitulation (what has been called *decalage* by Piaget) of the sequence of conceptual relations in children's later sequential development of language relations (Box III-3).

PRECURSORS OF LANGUAGE FORM

Linguistic coding is not arbitrary and not conventional in its formal mechanism, in that linguistic coding makes use of acoustic (or manual) signals because these are the sounds (or movements) that humans make. However, linguistic coding is arbitrary and conventional in its functional mechanism; that is, the uses to which the formal mechanism are put in representation are, in an important sense, independent from the events encoded in messages, and they evolve by way of tacit agreement among the members of a linguistic community. For example, the fact that words and manual signs are used to encode object concepts is not an arbitrary fact; the vocal mechanism and hands are very flexible parts of the anatomy. However, it is entirely arbitrary that the word "car" *stands for* cars, or that rising or falling intonation signal the difference between questions and statements. Children have to learn these facts of language, and they have to learn how their essentially

---

BOX III-3

The complexities of conceptual relations have only been touched on in this chapter, as the following would indicate:

The relations between concepts are as varied as concepts themselves; indeed relations are concepts. ... Even adjective concepts such as red or square differ in their relation to different concepts they modify. For example, green is related to grass in a different way than yellow is to canary, since the green penetrates the grass and the yellow is only superficial to the canary. Both relations are different from the relation of blue to sky, since the blue is only in the atmosphere of earth during the day. These examples illustrate that relations can be quite complex, even though the question of "what color is grass?" can be answered without getting into these complexities. (Collins and Quillian, 1972, p. 315)

Conceptual relations have their origin in the earliest experiences of infants, and they become progressively more complex through adulthood.

---

nonarbitrary resources, the movements and sounds they make, can be shaped to serve the arbitrary sound-meaning connections of language.

The idea is not new, that children know something of the form of language, but have to "relearn" the form of language when faced with the task of coding information. Roman Jakobson suggested in 1941 that features of the sounds that children babble in their vocalizations in the first year are then relearned as phonemic contrasts in the second year when they learn words. However, there is now evidence that in addition to phonology in vocalization, there are other aspects of communication that present the same phenomenon: sound production, suprasegmental intonation, speech perception, and syntax. With each, there is evidence of performance with a certain degree of facility from a startlingly early age, as children give evidence in their first years of knowing something about the *forms* (the sounds) of language. Yet these same behaviors, or behaviors derived from them, do not become *functional* for children so that they are integrated in a communication paradigm with content and use until much later, in the second year. The evidence of the precursors to linguistic form comes from both naturalistic and experimental observations of infant behavior.

SOUND PRODUCTION

There have traditionally been two separate views of how infant babbling relates to children's later behaviors; one view is that there is a continuity from babbling to later speech, and the other view is that there is a basic discontinuity. When learning theory has been used to explain the relation of babbling to later language learning, it has usually been proposed that infant vocalization provides the "stuff" of later speech, as one or another sound pattern gets reinforced and endures as part of children's repertoires of behaviors (e.g., Thorndike, 1943). On the other hand, Jakobson (1941, 1968), Lenneberg (1967), and others have pointed to the importance of maturation, with an essential discontinuity between early vocalization and the later more mature sounds of speech.

Much of the early research that attempted to describe infant vocalizations were intent on describing the origins of the sounds of adult speech (Irwin, 1947; Irwin and Chen, 1946; and Winitz, 1969); for that reason, infancy sounds were described according to how closely they resembled the phonemic sounds of adult language. However, when the fit was found to be less than exact, attention turned to describing the acoustic and articulatory patterns of infant sounds directly instead of comparatively (e.g., Wasz-Höckert, Lind, Vuorenkoski, Partanen, and Valanne, 1969; and Wolff, 1966). As a result, there exists a growing amount of evidence about the parameters of the sounds that infants make along with a consensus that there is little overlap between the sounds made in infancy and the sounds of speech. The sound patterns of infancy have been seen as biologically determined (e.g., Crystal, 1969; Lenneberg, 1967; and Lieberman, 1967), but coming more and more under self-control from the moment of birth. Because this is the aspect of infant vocalization that has received the greatest attention, it will not be discussed further here. (See Rees, 1972; Delack, 1977, in *RLDev*; and Oller, Wieman, Doyle, and Ross, 1976.)

INTONATION

A number of observers (e.g., Guillaume, 1927; Kaplan and Kaplan, 1971; Leopold, 1939; and Lewis, 1951) have emphasized the importance of intonation and stress variations as major factors in early vocalization. According to Lewis (1951), children respond to intonation before they respond to phonetic form, and will respond in the same way to adult utterances that have different phonetic form if the intonation contour is the same. To explain the transition from response on the basis of intonation to response on the basis of phonetic form, Lewis suggested that:

> the child responds affectively both to the intonational pattern of what he hears and to the situation in which he hears it. And at this very same time he hears a phonetic pattern, inextricably intertwined with the intonational pattern and—in many cases—linked expressively or onomatopoetically with the situation. Then his affective response fashions a new whole including the intonational pattern, the situation, and the phonetic pattern. When at last the phonetic pattern

acquires dominance so that irrespective of the intonational pattern it evokes the appropriate response from the child, we say that he has understood the conventional word. (p. 122)

In experimental studies with infants, Kaplan (1970) and Morse (1972) have reported the ability of infants (8 months old and 2 months old, respectively) to respond differently to changes in the intonation contour of acoustic signals (e.g., to distinguish between rising and falling intonation contours).

Intonation contours have often been identified in infants' vocalizations, and most often the descriptions of infant intonation contours have been in terms of comparisons with the sentence contours of adult speech. Thus, observers have "heard" statement, question, and exclamation contours in the vocalizations of infants, and have inferred a corresponding intention on the part of children to produce statements, questions, and exclamations (Menyuk, 1970). Other studies, however, have reported that even though different intonation contours occur in the vocalizations of infants and with early one-word and two-word utterances, such different contours that sound like statements or questions do not appear to signal meaningful differences; that is, they do not contrast different semantic intentions or grammatical structures (Lahey, 1972; Miller and Ervin, 1964; and Weir, 1964). Halliday (1975) reported a contrast between rising and falling intonation that appeared toward the end of the first year (at about 10 to 11 months) in the vocalization of his infant son, but it was not a contrast that exists in the adult language. Instead, the rising and falling contours were an idiosyncratic system that contrasted two general functions of vocalization that Halliday called pragmatic (rising) and mathetic (falling). (See Chapter VII.)

Most recently, Delack (1977, in *RLDev*) has reported results of a study of the vocalization of a group of 19 infants who were visited biweekly, beginning at 1 month and until they were about 1 year old. He observed seven different intonation contours in the recorded vocalizations, and these showed minimal developmental change in duration and frequency. The most prominent contour throughout was the rise-fall contour, and this was the only contour to show an appreciable increase in the time period.

In a study of the later development of a child from 17 to 22 months of age, Branigan (1976) observed that the rise-fall intonation contour was the most frequent pattern to occur with single words. It appears that the rise-fall contour of infant vocalization may be a more important parameter for later linguistic production (words) than the infant patterns that resemble the suprasegmental contours that characterize adult statements, questions, and exclamations. This result is another example of the difference between an etic plan (comparing infant intonation with adult intonation) and an emic plan (observing and describing infant behaviors directly).

SPEECH PERCEPTION

The studies of Eimas, Siqueland, Jusczyk, and Vigorito (1971, in *RLDev*), Moffitt (1971), Morse (1974), and others have demonstrated that very young infants are able to discriminate among certain acoustic (phonetic) parameters of speech sounds. In the study by Eimas et al. (1971, in *RLDev*), 1-month-old and 4-month-old infants were presented with two experimental conditions. In one condition, sounds from two different adult phoneme categories /p/ *and* /b/ were presented; in another condition, different sounds within the range of the same adult category /p/ *or* /b/ were presented. The stimuli were synthetically produced speech sounds, and changes in the infants' sucking behavior were measured as response. The result was that infants as young as 1 month were responsive to the speech stimuli and were able to perceive differences between the different adult phonemes—the difference between voiceless /p/ and voiced /b/. They did not discriminate (i.e., there was not a change in sucking behavior) when presented with differences in the same phoneme (variants of /p/ or variants of /b/). There have been a number of similar experiments with infant speech perception using different sounds and different response measures, and these studies are reviewed by Butterfield and Cairns (1974) and by Eimas (1974, 1975). It appears to be well-established that infants as young as 1 month have the ability to perceive and discriminate among different phonetic features of speech that are phonemic in the adult language.

Eimas and Corbit (1973) proposed that such perceptual capacities of infants derive from a system of "linguistic feature detectors" that begin to operate at birth and that are selectively and progressively adapted to the sounds of speech in the course of development. In studies of the development of bird songs, Marler (1976) has described the behaviors of very young birds and suggested that there are "auditory templates" that guide the learning of bird songs. Marler observed that in early bird song development there is a stage of "subsong," which he compared with infant babbling. Both bird subsong and infant babbling occur, he suggested, in the process whereby infants (bird or human) match vocal output to the auditory templates (or linguistic feature detectors, in the terms of Eimas and Corbit) that are progressively adapted to the speech sounds that are heard from the environment.

These abilities that have been described in infant production, perception, and intonation relate to the *form* of language. As Eimas (1975) pointed out, the fact that infants already have such linguistic feature detectors or auditory templates makes it easier for infants to learn the sounds of speech; at the least, infants do not first have to learn to discriminate speech sounds from nonspeech sounds. However, just how children's later language abilities relate to the early perceptual capacities of infants is far from clear (see

Butterfield and Cairns, 1974; and Eimas, 1975). For example, older children who are already learning language do not discriminate many of the same phonetic contrasts that young infants have been observed to discriminate. The voiced/voiceless distinction (the difference between [b] and [p]) that was discriminated by 1- to 4-month-old infants is one of the last discriminations made by 2-year-old children in speech sound discrimination tasks (Shvachkin, 1973; Garnica, 1973; and Graham and House, 1971). Thus, infants have such precursory capacities but need to learn how to use them for learning the relation between form and content.

SYNTAX

Just as infants present evidence that they know something of the sounds of speech before they use speech, so, too, have 1-year-old children demonstrated that they can know something about the syntax of speech before they are able to combine words in sentences.

In an observational study, using a videotape recording of a 16-month-old child, the use of consistent word order with an uninterpretable word /wídə/ was observed before other multiword utterances were productive in her speech (Bloom, 1973). This child produced two-word phrases with /wídə/ that indicated awareness of word order constraints and suprasegmental stress. In these phrases, the form /wídə/ was always in second position and, more important, /wídə/ appeared in combination with only a few of the child's more frequent words. Thus, /wídə/ occurred most often with "Mama," "Dada," "more," "no," and "uhoh." However, /wídə/ never occurred with other equally frequent words such as "up," "gone," "there," or "cookie." The combinations with /wídə/ occurred frequently and continued for a 3-week period. Her behavior was interpreted as evidence that she had learned something about word order—with /wídə/, which was consistently in second position, and with the few words that appeared with /wídə/, which were always in first position. However, /wídə/ was not interpretable. There was no semantic consistency in its use; it seemed to refer to anything and everything, and so it was concluded that it meant nothing.

Similar precursory behavior was observed also by Ramer (1976) in an observational study she reported with 12 children and in another study by Dore, Franklin, Miller, and Ramer (1976). Ramer described such behavior as the use of "pre-syntactic devices" that occur before children learn to use word order as a linguistic device to signal the meaning relations between words in sentences. Thus, speech perception, vocalizing, intonation, and the use of word order are precursory capacities that relate to the form of language. Such capacities have to be integrated with what children also know of content and use for the development of language. Just as infants begin to acquire the knowledge about the world in the development of cognition that later provides the content of language, infants are also learning aspects of the linguistic code that eventually, when integrated with language content, will make up the form of language. Similarly, there are behaviors in infancy that contribute to how children will eventually learn to use language.

PRECURSORS OF LANGUAGE USE

For a long time it has been generally acknowledged that the need for physical comfort is among the needs of infants, and infants' cries of discomfort have been recognized as among the earliest signs of communication. There has also been growing evidence that the social and affective needs of infants can influence their behaviors so that sounds of comfort and vocalizations that accompany positive affect are counted as signs of communication. There are three important aspects of such early signs of communication. The first is that early sounds and movements are the infant's own; they are discovered by the infant as he or she moves, twists, turns and breathes. They are remarkably similar from one infant to the next, because infants are physiologically similar to one another. Infants do not learn these sounds and movements from the environment; they discover them on their own.

The second aspect of early signs of communication in infancy is that the sounds and movements that are made by infants are part of the event being communicated. That is, infants' cries are, at the same time, indications of both discomfort and a part of discomfort; infants' satisfaction vocalizations are, at the same time, indications of satisfaction and a part of the feelings of comfort.

The third point is that these early behaviors in infancy inevitably have their developmental counterpart in children's later, more mature behaviors. Infancy behaviors are not forgotten or discarded; instead, they gradually evolve into more complex forms of communication, as already described with the origins of language content and the origins of language form.

These sounds and movements that infants make are different from the sounds of speech and the signs of sign language in two important ways: first, they result from children's movements and reflexes, and their form depends on children's physiological structures and functions; they are not learned from the environment. Second, the sounds and movements infants make are not intended to "stand for" or represent their feelings or experiences. Instead, they are, themselves, an integral part of experience. Toward the end of the first year, infants actually begin to reproduce an event consciously—in the apparent effort to recreate the event and make it happen again. Church (1961) gave several examples of what he called "concrete enactment," as children try to get others around them to participate. For example,

. . . to be picked up, he holds out his arms to an adult; to reinstate a round of merriment at the dinner table, he simulates laughter; to get an adult to operate a plaything, he hands it to the adult or moves the adult hand to the toy; to initiate the game in which the adult chases and catches him, he starts paddling away on all fours, looking back over his shoulder for the adult to follow. (1961, p. 58)

Such behaviors are a part of the content being communicated and the force of their communicativeness comes from adults who can recognize and respond to children's desires by participating in making the event happen again (see also Bates, Camiaoni, and Volterra 1975, for discussion of the development of intention to communicate in infancy).

INFANT COMMUNICATION

Early research by Rheingold, Gewitz, and Ross (1959) and by Weisberg (1963) had demonstrated that infants' vocalizations could be conditioned by social contact. Working with infants in institutions, it was found that at 3 months, vocalization increased as a function of a responding adult: "the speech of the infant, if only in a social situation, can be modified by a response from the environment which is contingent on his vocalizing" (Rheingold, et al., 1959, p. 72). Weisberg demonstrated that specifically human voice contact was the effective condition; the same result was not achieved by presenting infants with other contingent noises. Since that time, there has been a great deal of infant research that has demonstrated infants' sensitivity to social contact and to other aspects of the context. In research by Delack (1977, in *RLDev*) and by Lewis and Freedle (1973), differences in the amount as well as the quality of infant vocalizations have been observed as a function of where the infant is located, whether the infant is placed on the floor, in a tub, or on a lap, and whether there is an adult present or whether there is a familiar object such as a blanket or bottle. Such sensitivity to context has been described by these investigators as the genesis of the relation between sound and meaning in language, and it provides evidence of continuity from infant behavior to later behaviors. Indeed, observations through the microanalysis of sound films have revealed that the organization of neonate movements is synchronized with segmentation of adult speech as early as the first day of life (Condon and Sander, 1974).

In a study of the dyadic exchanges between mothers and their 3- to 4-month-old infants, Stern, Jaffe, Beebe, and Bennett (1975, in *RLDev*) observed that "infant vocalizations rarely occur (in a social situation) as an isolated motor act such as an adult can perform in speaking; rather, they occur as another element in the constellation of kinesic events that make up a communicative act" (p. 89). The mutual gaze between mothers and infants has been observed in several studies, and Bateson (1975) described such eye-to-eye contact as a "proto-conversation" between parents and children. In the microanalysis of dyadic gaze behaviors reported by Jaffe, Stern, and Peery (1973), a basic synchrony between mother and infant gazing was found to be an analogue of the rhythms of adult dialogue. There was a preponderance of mutual gazing in this earlier study by Stern and his colleagues, to which was added the later finding by Stern, Jaffe, Beebe, and Bennett (1975) that mothers and infants also vocalize in unison. "The nature of the interpersonal interaction and its emotional tone are communicated by the mutual and simultaneous performance of both gaze and vocalization" (p. 98), which are described further by Stern et al. as "quite special moments for the dyad."

By looking at each other and vocalizing together, or vocalizing in alternation, infants and caregivers are using primary forms of communication. Although these behaviors have been identified in a number of mother/infant pairs and can presumably be expected of any mother/infant pair, such communication is still highly personal. Infants and caregivers look at each other and vocalize in unison because looking and vocalizing are two behaviors that are available to infants almost immediately. They are behaviors that are available to infants, and the caregivers readily join in, communicating in a way that would probably not be impossible but would certainly be inappropriate with older children or with adults. Such interaction is an early instance in which caregivers modify their behavior according to the capacities of the infants they are interacting with, producing precisely the behaviors that are in tune with the infants' resources.

ORIGINS OF THE FUNCTIONS OF LANGUAGE

According to Halliday (1975), there is no form and there is no structure in such vocalizations, but there is expression and meaning in the functions that such vocalizations serve: "from the functional point of view, as soon as there are meaningful expressions there is language . . . before words and structures have evolved to take over the burden of realization" (p. 6). Children learn in infancy that vocalizations can perform certain functions for them, and even though these vocalizations do not conform to the sounds and structures of the adult model and are not conventional, they have meaning in the functions they serve for the children. In the period from 6 to 18 months, "using his voice is doing something . . . a form of action . . . which soon develops its own patterns and its own significant contexts" (Halliday, 1975, p. 10).

The first of two functions Halliday identified at 9 months in his son Nigel's development was the "interactional" or "me and you function of language" as the sounds and gestures of the child were used as he interacted with others in the environment. As has already been seen, this function has been identified as early as 3 to 4 months in infants interacting with their mothers. The second function at 9 months was the "personal function" whereby Nigel expressed "his awareness of himself"—personal feelings of interest, pleasure, disgust, and the like. By 10½ months, two more language functions could be identified, still without Nigel's using the forms and structures of conventional language but, instead, the sounds and movements of his own devices. The third and fourth functions were the "instrumental function," whereby the child satisfied material needs and obtained objects and help from those around him, and the related "regulatory function," whereby the child controlled the behavior of others—the "do as I tell you functions of language."

> The difference between [the regulatory] and the instrumental is that in the instrumental the focus is on the goods or services required and it does not matter who provides them, whereas regulatory utterances are directed towards a particular individual, and it is the behavior of that individual that is to be influenced. (Halliday, 1975, p. 19)

As children strive to perform such functions, they include more often among their own resources the sounds and movements that they hear and

---

BOX III-4 INTERACTION BETWEEN COMMUNICATION WITH AND WITHOUT THE INTENTION TO COMMUNICATE, AND COMMUNICATION WITH AND WITHOUT KNOWING THE CONVENTIONAL MEANS FOR COMMUNICATION

Period	Intention to Communicate	Conventional Coding of Ideas: Form/Content	Conventional Coding of Ideas and Use: Form/Content/Use
I	No	No	No
II	Yes	No	No
III	Yes	Yes	No
IV	Yes	Yes	Yes

In the beginning of infancy, I, children make known information about their needs and their internal states, but communication is neither intentional nor conventional. Subsequently, II, when infants begin to intend to communicate, they do not know the conventions for the form or the use of language in relation to content. Children appear to acquire, III, the code for representing ideas of content before they acquire, IV, the conventional rules for indicating function and using alternative language forms.

see others make. The primary forms of communication in early infancy include cries, vocalizing, smiles, and gazing; these are the early resources that infants have to use for meeting their physical and affective needs. While the physical and affective needs of children continue and become more socialized so, too, do children's resources for meeting these needs become progressively socialized as the second year begins. Children begin to use sounds and movements (words and gestures) that are more conventional and arbitrary than the intuitive sounds and movements of the primary behaviors of infancy (Box III-4). The continued development of language in the second year and until the third birthday will be described in the next two chapters.

SUMMARY

This chapter describes the behaviors of infancy that are continuous with the later development of the content/form/use of language. The three components of language begin as essentially separate threads of development in the first year of infancy, and are progressively coordinated until children induce the relationship between their own resources and needs, on the one hand, and the integration of content/form/use in the language in the environment, on the other hand. Language develops as a result of the interaction between the child and the context. As infants process information about the world, they are influenced by the factors of movement and change—both their own movements and those of other objects and persons. Children learn to perceive information about the regularities and consistencies in the context, and form concepts based on identity and equivalence relations among objects and movements.

The precursors of language content, form, and use were described. The precursors of language content or meaning have to do with what infants learn about objects and relations between objects. In particular, infants learn about the permanence of objects—the fact that objects exist apart from their own move- ments and actions, and apart from the time and space contexts in which they are perceived. Both the relation between object permanence and object concepts and between object permanence and relational concepts involving action and location are discussed. The precursors of language form are infant behaviors involving the perception and production of sounds and intonation contours and, later in the second year, the order of words. There appears to be a basic capacity that infants as young as 1 month have for tuning into the speech behaviors in the environment—linguistic feature detectors or auditory templates that enable them to discriminate between speech and nonspeech sounds and even between different categories of speech sounds. At the same time, infants are also sensitive to the social and affective aspects of the context, and the origins of language use begin in infants' earliest gazing and vocalizing exchanges with caregivers in the first few months. All of these infant behaviors are continuous with the eventual development of language that begins in the second year, but they are not linguistic behaviors. Language develops when the precursors of content, form, and use begin to be integrated with one another and with the conventional requirements of the language in the environment.

SUGGESTED READINGS

In *Readings in Language Development*

Delack, J., Aspects of infant speech development in the first year of life. *Canadian Journal of Linguistics, 21,* 17–37, 1976.

Eimas, P. D., Siqueland, E. R., Jusczyk, P., and Vigorito, J., Speech perception in infants. *Science, 171,* 303–306, 1971.

Halliday, M. A. K. A sociosemiotic perspective on language development. *Bulletin of the School of Oriental and African Studies,* University of London, Vol. XXXVII, Part 1, 60–81, 1974.

Stern, D., Jaffe, J., Beebe, B. & Bennett, S. Vocalizing in unison and in alternation: Two modes of communication within the mother-infant dyad. *In D. Aronson and R. Rieber (Eds.) Developmental psycholinguistics and communication disorders.* Annals of the New York Academy of Sciences, 263, 89–100, 1975.

Other Readings

Bates, E. *Language in context:* New York: Academic Press, 1976.

Bower, T. G. R., *Development in infancy.* San Francisco: W. H. Freeman & Co., 1974.

Cohen, L., and Salapatek, P. (Eds.), *Infant perception: From sensation to cognition,* Vols. I & II. New York: Academic Press, 1975.

Gratch, G., Appel, K., Evans, W., LeCompte, G., and Wright, N., Piaget's stage IV object concept error: Evidence of forgetting or object conception? *Child Development, 45,* 71–77, 1974.

Halliday, M. A. K. Learning how to mean: Explorations in the development of language. London: Edward Arnold, 1975.

Piaget, J., *The construction of reality in the child.* New York: Basic Books, 1954.

Piaget, J., *The psychology of intelligence.* Patterson, N.J.: Littlefield Adams, 1960.

Language content is what people talk about and what they understand of what other people say; it has to do with what people know about objects and events in the world, and the feelings and attitudes that they have about what they know. Developmentally, the content of children's language derives from information that is gradually stored in memory and from children's changing capacities to think and feel about surrounding objects and events. Thus, children's abilities for expression and comprehension of language depend on knowledge and situational context. The interaction between the two—knowledge and context—determines the content of language. The form of language is the shape, configuration, or external appearance of the representation of language content. Form has to do with the mode or manner of expression—the means whereby one individual can convey an element of content to another individual so that an element of experience can be shared.

There are, to be sure, many forms of representation. Elements of content can be conveyed or communicated from one individual to another in different ways. Pictures, diagrams, and maps are forms of representation; one certainly understands something about an object concept as a result of seeing a picture of the object; one can understand locative relations by reading maps or diagrams. Facial expressions and body postures convey information and are forms of representation.

The sounds that individuals can make with their vocal apparatus and the signs or gestures that can be made with the hands provide two forms of representation that differ from other forms of representation in several ways. A picture, a map, a facial grimace, or body posture are representational to the extent that the thing or relation being represented is also reproduced (as in the case of the picture or map), or is itself part of the content being represented, (as when tension of the body is, at once, a sign of tension and also part of being tense; a smile is a part of being happy as well as a sign that the smiler is happy). However, sounds in spoken language and movements in American Sign Language actually reproduce the thing or relation being represented only in certain cases: onomatopoeia and when order of mention follows order of events, in the case of sound languages; and iconicity and the specification of certain spatial relations in sign language. Otherwise, and most often, sound and sign languages are essentially arbitrary in the relations between signals and meaning (e.g., see Bellugi and Klima, 1976; and Frishberg, 1975), and children need to learn sound configurations or sign configurations that *stand for* elements of content.

In the second year, beginning some time after the first birthday, language learning is taken up with learning words. Some children may not begin to say words, although they may understand several or many words, until the end of the second year. Different children may use a vocabulary of single-word utterances for varying periods of time. Some may go through a fairly long period—8 to 10 months or more—when they say only one word at a time. This period in language development—the use of single-word utterances—will be discussed in this chapter as the development of vocabulary. However, it is not a discrete stage of development that begins when children first say or respond to a word and ends when children begin to combine words to say phrases. Instead, the single-word utterance period when children are 1 year old is continuous with the first year of infancy as the precursory behaviors of infancy begin to come together. The single-word utterance period is continuous with the later development of two-year-old children who combine words in phrases and sentences, in that there are precursors of both the content and the form of children's sentences in the use of single-word utterances before children actually say sentences.

Thus, although there is a single-word utterance period in development, it is not a separate stage of development with a beginning point and an end point. The single-word utterance period is not a time in which children merely accumulate more and more words. Vocabularies increase in this period, to be sure. However, there is also considerable developmental change in both the kinds of words that are used and in the ways in which words are used in the time between children's first and second birthdays. Saying one word at a time is only the tip of the iceberg, and describing children's language development in terms of the numbers of words they can say (or understand) is only a superficial description of form. It is even more important that in this period of time children are learning the sound patterns of words and the meanings of different kinds of words, and are learning to use words in relation to themselves and their activities in different ways.

PHONOLOGICAL DEVELOPMENT

How children learn the sound system of language has traditionally been a separate area of study, that is considered, most often, apart from semantic and syntactic learning. However, when one considers that the primary linguistic categories are phonological categories, in that knowing a word concept necessarily includes knowing one or more phonological units, then one cannot ignore phonology in studying content/form relations in lexical and grammatical development.[1]

Virtually all of the studies of phonological development until the 1970s took isolated phonemes or separate speech sounds as the units for analysis. Accordingly, norms for phonological development have traditionally been norms for speech sound production obtained with tests of articulation (e. g., Poole, 1934; and Templin, 1957). Similarly, studies of the relation between perception and production have been concerned with establishing the relation between auditory processing capacities and the acquisition of individual speech sounds (see, for example, Powers, 1957; and Winitz, 1969 for reviews of the literature). Virtually all of these studies tested children in the age range of 3 to 8 years. The general results were that the development of individual speech sounds or phonemes is correlated with age, that some sounds are mastered before others, and most of the sounds are produced correctly by the time children are 8 years old (Winitz, 1969).

Within the sequence of speech sounds that are mastered between 3 and 8

[1] This basic idea was pointed out to us by Harriet Klein, and the following discussion was based on her review of the literature in phonological development (Klein, 1978).

years of age, there is a tendency for sounds to be developmentally grouped according to features that they share, such as place and manner of articulation, nasality, and voicing. For this reason, other accounts of speech sound development have looked at the acquisition of distinctive features such as nasality, place of articulation, and friction, which are shared by groups of consonants (as described by Chomsky and Halle, 1968; Jakobson, 1941; and Jakobson and Halle, 1956). According to Menyuk (1968, 1972), there is a common sequential order in the mastery of the distinctive features of sounds among children speaking different languages (American English and Japanese).

In contrast with the idea that children learn phonology by learning one sound at a time, or successive distinctive features of sounds such as nasality, and the like, more recent studies have suggested that children do not learn individual sounds as such—they learn words and sounds according to the strategies or rules they acquire for learning words (Francescato, 1968). Thus, the emphasis for phonological learning has passed from the phoneme or speech sound as the unit of analysis, to the particular (and distinctve) features of groups of speech sounds as the units of analysis, to the word as the unit of analysis. Menn (1971) stressed the importance of the context of individual phonemes for learning words and suggested that the nature of the phonological rules that children learn depend on the first few words that they attempt to say. In more recent studies of developmental phonology, then, syllables and words have become units of analysis instead of phonemes or features of phoneme groups. There have been a number of observational studies that have described phonological rules (sometimes called processes or strategies) that account for the sound sequences that children produce as their earliest words, for example, Braine (1974), Ferguson et al. (1973), Ingram (1974), Smith (1973), Stampe (1969, 1972), and Waterson (1971)

According to Waterson (1971), children extract certain perceptual features of sounds from the words that they hear spoken by others, and the ability to abstract "some sort of schema in words or utterances" is a basic skill of linguistic perception. Thus, children acquire the sound pattern of language as they perceive the particular sound features in the words they are learning. Ingram (1974) adds that in addition to what a child perceives (and misperceives) of the adult system, the child's own production influences phonological development: "the child's word may have a certain syllable structure due to the syllable structure of the adult word and due to the constraints of his own [productive] system" (p.51). As an example, a child may produce the word [həfənt] for "elephant." In this example, the stress pattern in the model utterance determines, in part, the child's choice of syllables. In addition, an aspect of the child's own productive system— that a syllable cannot begin with a vowel—operates in conjunction with the stress pattern in the model utterance to determine how the child will attempt to produce the word.

It is not clear how children's perception of the model influences production, and with 1-, 2-, or 3- year-old children, perceptual capacities can only be inferred on the basis of patterns of production. Some investigations have cited evidence from children's production to support the claim that perception closely approximates the adult model (Smith, 1973; and Stampe, 1969, 1972). Others have been more inclined to view children's auditory skills as being developmentally determined (e. g., Braine, 1974) instead of being determined by the adult model, per se. Ferguson, Peizer, and Weeks (1973) raised the question of whether there is just one mental representation of a lexical item that underlies both the perception and production of the word. Perhaps there are two mental representations—one each for the perception and production of a word. All of these researchers agree that children learn phonology according to the features they perceive and discriminate in the words that they hear and attempt to say. Instead of learning one speech sound at a time, children learn the sounds of the language in context with one another. When a child tries to say a word, the position of a syllable in the word and syllable stress will interact with ease of perception or ease of production of the syllable to determine how the child tries to say the word (Klein, 1978). Such factors contribute to the regularities in the sound patterns of the model language that the child hears and stores in memory to use for saying words.

Children learn to combine the features of friction, nasality, and voicing with particular placement of the tongue and lips and movements of the jaw. It is generally agreed that children learn phonological rules for dealing with the variation that occurs when these features are combined in the different phonemic contexts of the words that the child hears and tries to say. Rules have been proposed by Ferguson et al. (1973), Ingram (1974), Menn (1971), Smith (1973), and others to account for children's production of phonological segments or syllabic sequences in different contexts and under different conditions. As a result, certain phonological processes have been identified as regularities in the ways in which children change the model in their attempts to produce it. There are reduction processes, where the child deletes a phoneme, for example, [ə:t] for "hurt," or deletes a syllable, for example, [aɪnd] for "behind" (examples, from Smith, 1973). There are processes whereby the child combines phonemes from two syllables into one syllable (coalescence), for example, [pæf] for "pacifier" (Menn, 1971). There are also assimilative processes, where one consonant influences another consonant, for example, [gɪk] for "kiss" and [bʌbəbæn] for "rubberband" (Smith, 1973), or one vowel influences another vowel. Finally, there is also reduplication, where both consonant and vowel assimilation occur, for example, [tɪtɪ] for "kitty" (Waterson, 1971). These four phonological processes—reduction, coalescence, assimilation, and reduplication—have been described most often in the literature, and children seem to vary in the extent to which they use one or another.

In sum, the phonological rules that the child learns and the phonological processes that characterize the child's attempts at reproducing words depend on the words that the child hears and chooses to learn . The words that children hear and attempt to reproduce guide them in discovering the relevant linguistic (phonological) categories in the dyadic exchange between child and adult.

WAYS OF KNOWING LINGUISTIC FORMS

Knowing a word entails the mental representation of a sound sequence in memory that can be recognized when it is heard and recalled so that it can be said. There are, in addition, at least, these four other levels of knowing a word. There is knowing a word in terms of its *referential sense*—as when the word "box" refers to the object box, the word "Mommy" refers to the object Mommy, and the word "open" refers to the action of opening. There is knowing a word in its *extended sense*—in terms of reference to not just a particular *box*, or the *opening* of only a particular box or only boxes, but in reference also to different boxes in different contexts, or opening doors, jars, and windows in addition to boxes, in different contexts. There is knowing a word in its *relational sense*—in terms of the meaning it assumes in relation to other words. Knowing "open" in relation to "box" is to know something of the relational meaning between words that refer to an action and an affected object. Furthermore, there is knowing a word in its *categorical sense*—the semantic categories of words that share some aspect of meaning—such as categories of nouns that refer to things that are perceptually and pragmatically alike (such as coins), things that can be acted on in similar ways (such as food or clothing), things that behave similarly (such as animals or fishes), and so forth. Finally, there is knowing a word in its *metalinguistic sense*—knowing that a word is a word, and that it is composed of sounds, talked about, written down, and so forth.

With these different levels of knowing a word (or sign) in mind, it is possible to recognize two common errors in observations of the acquisition of language form. There is, first, an error in the assumption that saying or responding to a word or a sign or a sentence is evidence that the child knows the word or sign or sentence. A second error is the assumption that *knowing* a word or a sign or a grammatical structure is the same in different contexts, regardless of use.

The use of a word in one context to refer to some object or event is some evidence that the child has made a necessary connection between a linguistic form (the word) and some element of experience (the object or event). However, knowing a word involves considerably more than that. Consider, for example, that many words refer not only to a particular instance of an object class in one context (such as "bottle" or "chair" or "Mommy"), but to the same object·in different contexts (such as Mommy feeding and Mommy walking into a room) and to other similar objects (such as different chairs, different bottles, and different Mommies). Thus, one aspect of *knowing* a word is knowing that the word stands for different objects or different events in many different contexts. Children learn this aspect of knowing a word by hearing the word and by using the word in many different contexts.

Another aspect of *knowing* a word is knowing that the word assumes an additional meaning in relation to other words. For example, "Mommy" in relation to "open" assumes a relational meaning relative to an action. In still another relation, "Mommy" in relation to "coat" can assume another relational meaning of *possessor*. Knowing words, then, entails knowing something of the relational meanings between words, where the referential sense of the word coexists with the additional relational meaning.

On still another level, knowing words entails knowing that words are related to one another because they share certain features of meaning. With respect to object words, there are certain semantic categories of words, for example, "coat," "hat," "shoe" or "meat," "raisin," and "cookie," that correspond with the natural categories of clothing or things to wear, and foods or things to eat. Such semantic categories are formed on the basis of their shared referential functions (as items of clothing or items of food) and also on the basis of their shared relational functions (as things persons wear or things persons eat). With respect to relational words such as verbs, there are semantic components that are shared by different verbs. Certain verbs refer to action events and form a category of action verbs; other verbs refer to states and form a category of stative verbs. Within such categories there are possible subcategories: among action verbs there is a subcategory of locative action verbs (e.g., "put," "go"), and a subcategory of causative verbs (e.g., "make," "help"); among stative verbs there is a subcategory of notice verbs (e.g., "see," "look," "hear," "listen"), and a subcategory of possession verbs (e.g., "have," "own," "keep," "possess").

Finally, because children use a word or a sign or a sentence in one situation or context, one cannot assume that they will be able to use the same word or sign or sentence structure in other contexts. There are indefinitely many tasks and situations in which children hear and need to speak, and the demands of different tasks and situations can vary in fundamental ways. To begin with, there are important differences between understanding and speaking (see Chapter VIII), and that assymetry is complicated further by the extent to which information from the context is available as support for understanding and speaking. At a minimum, there are critically important differences among the situations in which what children say or hear (1) represents an event in the observable context, (2) demands a mental representation of message meaning in the absence of an event in the context, or (3) relates to information that is contained in a prior message from someone else. These alternative states of affairs and their interactions with behaviors of understanding and speaking are explored at length in Chapter VIII.

The assumption that children *know* a word or a sign when they use the word or the sign in some context is an error. There are different ways of knowing words, and children learn the meanings and functions of words gradually, beginning at about 12 months of age and continuing well into the school years. None of the knowing that has been described so far is explicit in that children know that they know, or can reflect upon or talk about what they know. Such knowing is tacit and implicit, and the evidence of what children know comes from their language behaviors. It is not until the early school years that children acquire the metalinguistic capacity to talk about talking.

Different investigations of children's linguistic behavior have described the different ways in which children know words—according to how they use words at different times in development. Among the many studies that have described children's early referential words are the classic diary studies, including Leopold (1939, in *RLDev*) and also Bloom (1973), Clark (1973a), and Nelson (1973, 1974). Children's early use of words in a relational sense has been described by Bloom (1973), deLaguna (1963), Greenfield, Smith, and Laufer (1972), Guillaume (1927, in *RLDev*), and Ingram (1971). The ways in which children learn to combine words with different relational meanings have been described in many studies, including those by Bloom (1970a), Bowerman (1973a and b, in *RLDev*), Braine (1976), Brown (1973), Schaerlae-kens (1973), and Schlesinger (1971). And the evidence, at a somewhat later age, that children know that words can be semantically related because of elements of meaning that are shared among them has been described, for example, by Baron (1972), Bowerman (1974), Gentner (1975), and Rosch (1975).

VOCABULARY IN CHILD LANGUAGE: EARLY LEXICAL-SEMANTIC ISSUES

Although the words that children learn can be listed alphabetically, or chronologically in the order in which they appear in speech, they are not homogeneous—in terms of either the relation between form and use (how they are used) or the relation between content and form (their meaning).

The words that children learn differ in relative usefulness and underlying conceptualization. These differences are reflected in frequency and are important factors in describing the words that children learn. Children with vocabularies of 50 words will probably use a small core of these words, maybe eight or ten different words, with great frequency and in many different situations. Another, somewhat larger, group of words will occur less often but probably at least once a day or every two days, and the remaining words will occur rarely—perhaps only one or two times in several months. Consider a hypothetical child who knows only three words: "Mommy," "this," and "apple." The word "apple" occurs when the child eats or sees apples (or maybe also balls and oranges) and the child sees apples infrequently in comparison with all of the other objects that he or she sees. One object that is seen very frequently in many situations and in a rich and varied personal relationship is Mommy. Thus, relatively, "Mommy" is a word that can be used in more varied contexts with the frequently appearing object Mommy. The word "this" can be used in reference to a wide variety of objects that includes apples and possibly Mommy and maybe just about anything or anyone else. Thus, presented with the words "this," "Mommy," and "apple," the child will learn them according to whether he or she knows something about the events to which they refer and how useful they are.

THE DISTINCTION BETWEEN RELATIONAL AND SUBSTANTIVE WORDS

There are different kinds of information about objects. First, there is the information that all objects participate in similar behaviors that involve movement and relative location in space. Cats, cookies, hats, Mommies, and bottles come into and out of view and continue to exist even when they are no longer visible and when they can no longer be acted on by the child. At the same time, there is the second kind of information about the perceptual features of objects—the features that distinguish among objects that are different from one another—and the perceptual features that objects in a class of objects share with one another. In the first 2 years of life, children acquire rules or strategies for dealing with objects in general (object permanence), as well as the mental representation of different objects (object concepts, in terms of perceptual prototypes, schemas, summary representations, etc.). Both kinds of information are represented in children's early language. Certain words that children use have to do with the behaviors that are shared by many objects—relational words such as "there," "this," or "that" to indicate that something exists; "gone" or "away" to indicate disappearance; and "more" or "again" to indicate recurrence of objects. Other words that children use are substantive words that refer to particular objects such as "Mommy" and "blanket" (a favorite blanket), or classes of objects such as "ball," "cookie," and "car" (Box IV-1). (See Bloom, 1973 in *RLDev*; Leopold, 1939, in *RLDev*; and Nelson, 1973.)

Substantive Words

There are certain objects that are particular instances, such as Queen Elizabeth, the United States, the Empire State Building and, for young

BOX IV-1 DIALOGUE WITH ALLISON, 16 MONTHS OLD, REPRESENTING DIFFERENT WORDS CHILDREN USE (from Bloom, 1973, pp. 155–156). In this and all subsequent dialogues, the utterances spoken by the child appear on the right; the utterances spoken by an adult (parent or investigator most often) appear on the left; the material in parentheses on the left is description of relevant context. (See Appendix A for the conventions used for transcription.)

(Allison eating cookie, seems to be looking for something)	**cookie/ cookie**
Where's the cookie?	
(Allison holding out arms, gesturing)	**gone**
Gone	
(Allison sees cookie bag)	
	more
(Allison reaching for cookie bag)	**more cookie**
More cookie	
(Allison tries to get cookies out of bag; cannot; giving bag to Mommy)	**Mama!**
What darling?	
(Allison finally succeeds in getting cookie out of bag)	
	cookie

children just learning to talk, there are similar objects. That is, children know only one person as mother, one person as father, a bottle, a favorite blanket, and the like. There are other objects that occur as multiple instances—objects that look alike or behave similarly—so that they form a class of objects (e.g., dogs, houses, chairs, and girls). Each instance of an object such as the chair that I sit in, the chair in the living room, and the chair in the picture shares something with every other instance of the same class of objects. Thus, although there are wooden chairs, upholstered chairs, dining chairs, lounging chairs, and dental chairs, there is a summary object *chair* that must have been conceptualized so that the word "chair" could be learned and used in reference to separate instances. The concept of a chair would include the figurative information about what chairs look like—that a chair is an object with both a vertical and horizontal surface, four points of contact with a base (floor), and so on. The concept of a chair would also include functional information about what people do with chairs or how chairs are used.

Thus, in addition to specific persons and objects—each of which may be considered as a class or concept with only one instance—there are also object classes with several and, eventually, many objects as members, such as chairs, houses, and dogs. Although words in early child dictionaries such as "Mommy," "Daddy," "blanket," "bottle," "chair," and "cookie" are all *nouns* in that they name *things*, they refer to different underlying conceptualizations of particular objects or classes of objects. Certain words that children use make reference to single objects that are usually persons (e.g., "Mommy," "Daddy," "Baby") but may also be favored items such as a blanket, a pet, or a bottle (Box IV-2). Other words make reference to classes of objects that are similar according to perceptual and functional criteria, such as "apple," "chair," and "truck." The words that make reference to object concepts are substantive words, and are most often nouns in the adult model. The information about an object concept that is coded in memory includes information also about the ways that objects move and are affected by movement. The concept of an object includes information about the perceptual attributes of objects that distinguish among different object concepts and information about the movements that affect objects and that also distinguish among different object concepts. For example, balls are rolled and bounced, apples are rolled and eaten but not bounced, and

---

BOX IV-2 DIALOGUE WITH ALLISON, 19 MONTHS OLD, WITH USE OF PERSON NAMES FOR PARTICULAR OBJECTS AS SUBSTANTIVE WORDS (from Bloom, 1973, pp. 192–193)

	Mommy
What darling?	
	Daddy
Where's Daddy?	
	office
He's at the office	
(Allison squirming on chair)	**chair**
Is he on the chair?	
(Allison and Mommy laugh)	
That's silly/ is Daddy	
on the chair?	
(Allison looking at Mommy;	
crawling on chair)	**no**
No	
	Baby!
Baby's on the chair	

pudding is eaten but not rolled or bounced. Rosch, Mervis, Gray, Johnson, and Boyes-Braem (1976) suggested that the distinction between the perceptual attributes that distinguish among objects and the movements that can be made with the object (its function) is an artificial distinction in concept formation; the two kinds of information are not separable within the concept of the object. This view is consistent with Piaget's (1954) description of the importance of children's sensori-motor action patterns in the formation of object schemas.

Learning the meanings of substantive words entails the schematic representation of the perceptual information that distinguishes one class or kind of object (an object concept) from others. An instance (a particular cat) of an object class (cats in general) is recognized and named according to how close it is to the prototype object in memory. Rosch (1973) described "a 'core meaning' which consists of the 'clearest cases' (best examples) of the category, 'surrounded' by other category members of decreasing similarity to that core meaning" (p. 112). Although children undoubtedly know about objects in terms both of their perceptual attributes and their function, single-word utterances reflect a difference in the extent to which one or the other kind of information is coded in messages. Children use more different object names than they use names of attributes (words for size, color, etc.), and they also use more different object names than they use names of action (Goldin-Meadow, Seligman, and Gelman, 1976).

Relational Words

The words that children learn for representing movements or behaviors that can involve or affect different objects are function words or relational words because they make reference to relational concepts. There are many ways for objects to interact with one another, and several categorizations of the relations between objects are possible. There are the relations of a single object to itself—as in talking about its existence, nonexistence or disappearance; relations among the objects in a class that distinguish one from another according to relative size, color, or other attribute; action relations; locative relations; and relations within and among action and locative relation events. In the single-word utterance period, the relational words that appear most often in children's speech are the words that refer to reflexive object relations (Box IV-3).

A reflexive object relation is the relation of an object to itself or to an equivalent object from the same class, in subjective relation to children as they perceive the object and change in the object. For example, an object can exist, cease to exist, or disappear, and then the same object or one just like it can reappear or recur. The object is the same object or an equivalent object, and each event—the existence of the object, the disappearance of the object, the recurrence of the object—is a relation of the object to itself.

BOX IV-3 DIALOGUE WITH ALLISON, 16 MONTHS OLD, WITH USE OF WORDS REPRESENTING REFLEXIVE OBJECT RELATIONS (from Bloom, 1973, p. 166)

(Mommy picks up book; shows Allison back cover where there is no rabbit)	
Where's the rabbit?	
(Allison holding out arms, gesturing)	**gone**
Gone	
	more
(Allison looks away and then back)	
More/ where's _____	**gone**
He's gone	
(Allison takes book; turns it over so she can see rabbit)	
	there
There he is!	
(Allison turning book)	**turn**
Turn	
	- - -
(Allison drops book; trying to get on chair, grunting)	**up/ up/ up**

Reflexive object relations have to do with some action or behavior that is constant in many events—events that are otherwise perceptually different from one another. The word "more," for example, can refer to reading another book, eating another cookie, putting another label on a truck, another airplane passing overhead, or more milk in a cup. The milk in the cup, the airplane overhead, the label on the truck, the cookie, and the book all look different—they are each different objects in different contexts. But the different contexts in which the different objects appear (or in which children want them to appear) have a common element. In each context, there has already been an instance of the object, and the use of the word "more" makes reference to the fact of recurrence of the same object (or another instance of one just like it). Similarly, "this" refers to the fact that an object exists in the context; "gone" refers to the fact that an object has disappeared. Both existence and disappearance are facts that occur with many different objects in many different contexts, as with recurrence; what the contexts have in common in these instances is the fact that some object exists or some object has disappeared. There are words that children hear in relation to events that are themselves different in terms of what the objects in the event look like or how the objects are being used. However, there are constant features in these different events, and children come to recognize that constant feature of movement or behavior.

The relational words that refer to such behaviors of objects (e.g., "this," "there," "uh oh," "gone," "no more," "more," " 'nother," "again," or variants of any of these) tend to predominate early in the single-word utterance period of at least some children (Bloom, 1973; Corrigan, 1976; and Sinclair, 1970, in *RLDev*). Such relations of an object to itself (reflexive-object relations) present children with just those experiences that contribute to *object knowledge* and the realization that objects are permanent and continue to exist when they are gone from view. Children learn about objects by observing that an object continues to exist or reappears after it has disappeared from view. Sinclair (1970, in *RLDev*) related children's use of single-word utterances that represent ideas such as these to the development of children in the sensorimotor period as described by Piaget. She described the early words in this period as representing the "organizing activity" of children as they learn about the similar behaviors of many different objects, learning about objects in general. Object words, or what Sinclair called "denominational utterances," have to do with the knowledge of concepts of different objects, and come to predominate later in the single-word utterance period.

There are, essentially, four concepts of reflexive object relations: existence, nonexistence, disappearance, and recurrence.

Existence

Some object is in the context and has the child's attention, as the child either sees it, touches it, picks it up, or does something to it or with it. The child may say the name of the object, or may say some form of the demonstrative pronoun (e.g., "this," "that") or may use a routine what-question such as "What that?," even though the child may already know the name of the object. Brown (1973) called this "nomination."

Nonexistence

Some object does not exist in the context, or the child does not see it in the context, but there is some reason to expect it to be there or to look for it. The child may say something like "no," or "gone," or name the object with a rising intonation, "car↑" and look for it.

Disappearance

Some object has been in the context and then ceases to exist; the object may suddenly be hidden from view, may vanish or evaporate of its own accord (steam, bubbles bursting, a bus rounding a corner, an airplane flying past), or the child or someone else may have acted on it (breaking a bubble, tearing up a picture, eating an apple). Children may say the same words as for nonexistence or other negative words, such as "no," "gone," "no more," "all gone," "away," or "byebye" (in the sense of disappearance).

Recurrence

Some object exists in the context, and either (1) that object disappears and the same object or one equivalent to it in all respects reappears, or (2) another equivalent object is brought in relation to the first object as "another instance of" the object. Children may say "more," "again," or "another ('nother)."

Ideas such as these that have to do with concepts of the behavior of an object in relation to itself continue to be represented and to contribute to the meaning of the language of older children and adults. Children and adults certainly talk about objects that exist or do not exist, that disappear and that recur. These notions of language content are independent of the identity of particular objects, and so cut across age, culture, and social class. Baseball gloves, reading glasses, and screwdrivers disappear and recur, at a later age, just as balls, cookies, and nursing bottles disappear and recur for very young children. Piaget described how infants learn to "make interesting sights last" in the first year of life. The concept of recurrence is about making interesting sights last—finding *another instance* of something, obtaining *more* of something, doing an act *again*, regardless of what that act or something is—and is characteristic of much of human behavior.

Such words are very useful to children, referring as they can to many different objects and events, and they also refer to important conceptual notions that children acquire about the nature of objects and their own actions. Other words that children learn to use are also relational words with some constant feature or element of meaning that entails a relation between objects or between a child and some other object or movement—for example, "up," said as a child climbs up onto a chair, or picks up a doll, or pulls Mommy up from a chair. "There!" was said by Allison (Bloom, 1973) whenever she accomplished some act, such as getting a doll to sit on a toy truck, putting rubber animals in a parade line, stacking a tower of blocks; and "uh oh," was said whenever there was a sudden, fortuitous event, such as when she spilled her juice, the toy truck tilted over, or a cookie broke. Many verbs are also relational words; there is some constant feature in different events that may be some movement or some state of an object or objects. For example, the verb "put" occurs in situations in which different persons (such as Mommy, Daddy, Baby) act as agents in relation to different objects (such as a ball, a coat, a car) that are affected by the movement in different locations (such as the floor, a table, a room). The constant feature has to do with a transfer from one place to another. Similarly, the verb "run" occurs in situations in which there is the same movement—whether the object performing the movement is Mommy, the child, or the dog. Verbs occur relatively less frequently in the same presyntax period, and occur with increasing frequency after the beginning of multiword utterances and the acquisition of syntax (Box IV-4).

The lists of vocabulary words in Boxes IV-4 and IV-5 were made from videotaped samples of Allison's speech. Each observation lasted about 40 minutes. The first list of words was obtained when she was 16 months, 3 weeks old, about midway in the single-word utterance period; the second was obtained when she was 20 months, 3 weeks old, toward the end of the period, just as she was starting to use multiword utterances. Both lists include person names, relational words, and object words. Comparing the two lists, it is possible to see (1) an increase in the number of object words, (2) an increase in verbs, and (3) a decrease in the relative frequency of other relational words (Box IV-5).

THE DISTINCTION BETWEEN REFERENTIAL AND SOCIAL WORDS

Another distinction has been made in early, presyntax vocabularies by Nelson (1973), the distinction between words that do and do not make reference to objects, what Nelson called "referential" words, and "expressive" words. Referential words are general nouns; expressive words are everything else, and include forms that are social gestures or learned in social routines. The original distinction was based on the finding by Nelson that for some children, more than 50% of their first 50 words consisted of object referencing words, or nouns, whereas for other children, more than 50% of their first 50 words consisted of other words that were not nouns, including social gestures such as "Hi," "Bye-bye," and "Thank you." Nelson did not observe the relative frequencies with which the different words were used by the children nor how the children used the words; she recorded only mothers' reports that the children had said the word at least one time (Box IV-6). More first-born children were described by Nelson as "referential" and more later-born children were described as "expressive." Other researchers have reported similar kinds of observations that seem to support differences among children according to whether they use more names of objects or more social routine words (e.g., Dore, 1973).

There are several problems for the interpretation of this finding because of the nature of the research design. As discussed in Chapter II, how evidence is collected in the first place is the critical factor in determining the

BOX IV-4 Single-Word Utterances and their Frequency of Occurrence; Allison at 16 months, 3 weeks (from Bloom, 1973, p. 68)

all gone, 1	there, 30
away, 9	turn, 1
baby, 19	uh, 2
car, 2	uh oh, 7
chair, 14	up, 27
cookie, 15	wide, 1
cow, 3	
Dada, 4	
dirty, 2	
down, 22	
girl, 3	
gone, 19	
here, 1	
horse, 1	
Mama, 9	
mess, 2	
more, 24	
no, 21	
oh, 3	
pig, 6	
sit, 1	
stop, 1	

Most Frequent: there, 30
up, 27
more, 24
down, 22
no, 21
gone, 19
baby, 19

BOX IV-5 Single-Word Utterances and their Frequency of Occurrence; Allison at 20 months, 3 weeks (from Bloom, 1973, p. 104)

again, 1	doll, 5	moo, 1	skip, 2
ah, 2	down, 1	more, 13	snack, 2
all gone, 1	drive, 1	napkin, 3	sneeze, 1
Allison, 12	floor, 2	neck, 3	spill, 1
away, 4	floppy, 1	no, 20	table, 2
back, 1	funny, 1	nose, 1	talk, 1
black, 1	glass, 5	nudie, 1	there, 3
baby, 20	hair, 2	oh, 2	touch, 1
back, 3	hand, 1	on, 9	towel, 1
bag, 4	hat, 1	open, 1	town, 4
bath, 1	hello, 1	out, 1	toy, 2
Bloom, 2	help, 2	pat, 1	truck, 4
boom, 1	here, 1	play, 2	tumble, 2
box, 1	hi, 6	pin, 4	uh oh, 4
bye, 1	home, 4	police, 1	up, 11
car, 3	horse, 4	puppet, 10	walk, 1
chair, 4	juice, 2	rain, 1	wee, 4
clean, 6	lamb, 1	rest, 1	wipe, 1
coming, 3	lie down, 5	ride, 3	wiping, 7
cookie, 2	man, 2	rug, 1	wool, 1
cow, 7	mess, 1	running, 1	yummy, 4
cup, 5	mike, 3	school, 3	zip, 4
diaper, 11	mm, 8	scrub, 1	Most Frequent:
dirt, 1	mm hm, 1	sharp, 1	Mommy, 23
dirty, 5	Mommy, 23	sit, 6	baby, 20
			no, 20

114

BOX IV-6 TWO PATTERNS OF WORD ACQUISITION BY CATEGORY (adapted from Nelson, 1973, p. 22)

WORDS BY ACQUISITION ORDER

SUBJECT AND CATEGORY	1-10	11-20	21-30	31-40	41-50	Total
Rachel:						
Nominal specific	1	0	0	0	2	3
Nominal general	6	7	8	10	7	38
Action	1	1	1	0	1	4
Modifier	1	1	0	0	0	2
Personal-social	0	0	1	0	0	1
Function	1	0	0	0	0	1
Elizabeth:						
Nominal specific	4	1	1	0	1	7
Nominal general	1	3	2	6	5	17
Action	1	1	3	0	1	6
Modifier	1	0	2	3	0	6
Personal-social	2	5	1	1	3	12
Function	1	0	1	0	0	2

The two patterns of vocabulary acquisition described by Nelson (1973) are exemplified in the above table with two "extreme cases" of the result when the sample of 18 children "was divided along the lines of whether more or less than 50% of each 50-word vocabulary was in the general nominal category. ... The groups that resulted from this division were termed "referential" (R), implying a largely object-oriented language, and "expressive" (E), implying a more "self-oriented language" (from Nelson, 1973, p. 22). In Elizabeth's development, an "extreme case" of expressive vocabulary, general nominals were still most frequent ($n = 17$ or 34%); there were $n = 12$ or 24% personal-social words. The relative frequency of individual words or categories of words was not reported, that is, how often each word was used or how often the different kinds of words were used.

interpretation one can make of the evidence and what one can ultimately say about the behaviors. As a result, there is no way of knowing, in the study by Nelson (1973), how the different forms were used by the children—whether, for example, referential speech or expressive speech really dominated in terms of relative frequency of the different words and were, therefore, more or less important to the children's behaviors. Because the data consisted of parent reports, there is no way of evaluating possible bias in what was reported. Some parents may be more likely to pick up on a child's use of a social gesture; other parents may be more adept at discriminating referential words when these occur in contexts that contain the objects referred to, or some other cues that might facilitate both the child's production of the word and the mother's perception of the word.

However, there is indeed a distinction among words that are part of a social interaction exclusively, and other words that refer to ideas about the world. Other words beside nominals also refer to ideas about the world (such as relational words, including verbs). It appears that in addition to the relational/substantive classification, which would subsume "referential" words, there is a third classification of social routine words, such as "Hi," "Bye-bye," (as a greeting), "Thank you," and the like. Such words facilitate children's interactions with other persons and their consequent social development. Such words do not, however, underlie children's later development of grammatical structure. They do not occur as grammatical constituents when children eventually combine words. Although children may or may not differ in the extent to which they use social routine words as single-word utterances, all children combine referential (relational and substantive) words or proforms for such words (e.g., "it," "this," "there") when they begin to form sentences.

NARROW AND BROAD REFERENCE: OVEREXTENSION IN THE USE OF SINGLE WORDS

It is one of the most frequently documented facts of language development that as children begin to say recognizable words, they typically use words in contexts and in reference to objects and events that are inconsistent with adults' use of the same words. Children may often begin by saying a word in a highly restricted context—the context that corresponds most closely with an original experience of the word (underextension), for example, as reported in Bloom (1973), a child's use of the word "car" only when she was sitting on the window ledge and saw a moving car on the street below, and her use of the word "dog" only when she heard the sound of the identification tags of a neighborhood dog going by outside. These instances of narrow reference that have been reported anecdotally occur early, when children first begin to use words, and are the tentative beginning of the first word concepts (see also Anglin, 1975).

Once some connection between a linguistic form and some element of experience is made, the child typically begins to test the hypothesis about what the word *means* by attempting to use the word in different contexts. Consider, for example, the child who says "water" when in the bath, when holding a drinking glass filled with water, and when touching a pane of window glass; the child who calls all four-legged animals "dog;" the child who eats peas from the pod for the first time and then asks for another "book of peas." Saying "water" when touching a pane of window glass, calling a sheep a "dog," or calling a pea pod a "book of peas" are errors by the child when compared with the semantic domain within which the adult uses the same word. However, when viewed from the child's perspective, they are reasonable *guesses* about a relation between form and content in the effort to learn linguistic categories. In each case, the child has taken some preliminary information about what the word means (information that came from experience with hearing and saying the word before), and made a guess that the word might *fit* in a new situation. The child tests a hypothesis of the relation between content and form when encountering a new situation and guessing that one or another word might *fit*. This hypothesis testing continues throughout childhood (Brown, 1965) and manifests itself in different ways—particularly in the first 3 years when the child begins the process of matching form with content (Anglin, 1975; Bloom, 1973; Bowerman, 1976; Brown, 1965; Clark, 1973a; Greenfield, 1973; and Thomson and Chapman, 1977).

Such *mistakes* that children make as they try out the meaning of a word have been called *overextensions* in the literature. The term is an unfortunate one, based as it is on the adult use of a word or words as a standard. Of course, it is the adult meaning of the word that children are trying to learn, and how well they know the word can be judged only by how they use the word. However, it is possible to look at the ways in which children use words—when they begin to use a word and until they use the word in all and only the same contexts that adults might also use the word—and attempt to understand how word meanings are learned. When one does so, there appear to be at least two patterns of the ways children have of matching their own ideas of what a word means to a new situation in which they guess that the word might fit (what Brown, 1956, in *RLDev*, described as "the original word game").

In one pattern children seem to string together or *chain* an element or elements of one situation in which they heard or used the word before, with an element or elements in a new situation. An example of such a chained association is the child who says "water" when in the bath, then when holding a drinking glass filled with water, and then when touching a pane of glass. With such chained associations the meaning of the word is only loosely defined, and it changes each time the child attempts to use it.

In another pattern of matching words to new referents in learning the meanings of words, children seem to have in mind some fairly well-defined idea of what the word means. A child may name new instances, such as a sheep, according to how well it fits with the criteria in mind for the meaning of the word, such as "dog," that is said. Here the child's use of the word "dog" is based on a wholistic association—the meaning of the word includes information about dogs (such as *four feet*) that also applies to other objects such as cats, horses, and sheep, for which the child has not, as yet, learned other words.

These two patterns of *overextension* —chained associations and wholistic associations—will be discussed more fully in the following sections. Evidence of one or another kinds of *overextension* is not easy to come by. A complete record of everything a child said would be necessary in order to trace the development of the meaning of a word for an individual child. However, some children may not be as adventurous in trying out the meanings of words as other children, and some children may learn a word meaning and use the word consistently and appropriately without making the kinds of *mistakes* that are being described here. In any event, samples of a child's speech (such as an hour's tape recording) would probably not be

---

BOX IV-7 DIALOGUE WITH KATHRYN, 35 MONTHS OLD, LEARNING SOMETHING ABOUT THE MEANINGS OF THE WORDS "NURSE" AND "STEWARDESS"

(Lois and Kathryn are pretending to be on a plane to San Francisco)

	now why don't we shut the doors
Hm?	
	why don't you shut your ___
	- - -
	shut your door/ shut
	so no air can come in
I did	
	let's get ___/ ssh! ssh!/
	and nurses bring some ___
	some food
Who?	
	the __ the __ the __ the __ lady who
	lives in the airplane
Well what is her___	
who is the lady that lives	
in the airplane?	
What'd you call her?	
	a lady
Did you call her a nurse?	
or a stewardess?	
	a stewardess

helpful, since such words are not used frequently, especially when children first begin to say words. The evidence in the literature is anecdotal and consists of reports of examples by parents and investigators. In some instances (e.g., Brown, 1965; and Clark, 1973a) these reports have been brought together for discussion. Although the evidence is far from complete, it does appear that the kinds of chained associations that will be discussed below occur relatively early in the single-word utterance period, and wholistic associations appear to be a later development. However, something like each kind of association continues throughout childhood, and probably even adulthood, in the continuous process whereby the meaning of a word is acquired as the word is used or heard in different contexts (Box IV-7).

Chained Associations

The first time that a child hears a particular word is the original referent situation (or focussing event, Kates, 1974) for that word, and is the basis on which the child can begin to work out the meaning of the word. When children hear a word in the original referent situation and attempt to use the word in another situation, they will do so on the basis of the similarities or consistencies that they recognize in the two situations and in succeeding situations. There appear to be several ways in which children can build a chained association based on similarities between the original referent situation and succeeding situations in which they might use the word.

A chained association may happen if the child does not differentiate among the possible referents for a word when first hearing the word (Werner, 1948) (Box IV-8). If the child hears a word spoken, for example, when eating

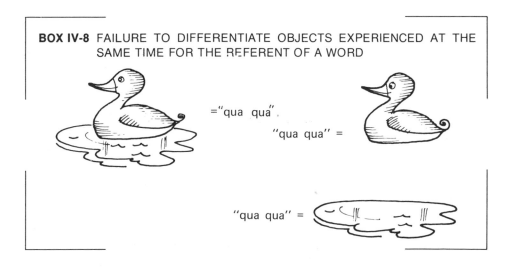

BOX IV-8 FAILURE TO DIFFERENTIATE OBJECTS EXPERIENCED AT THE SAME TIME FOR THE REFERENT OF A WORD

="qua qua",

"qua qua" =

"qua qua" =

a cookie, and then virtually the same situation presents itself, that is, the child is eating a cookie again, then the child's saying the word "cookie" is a good guess. However, suppose that the child is also drinking milk in the first situation when "cookie" was heard. If, at another time, when again drinking milk and there are no cookies, the child says "cookie," the word is a bad guess and someone will no doubt correct it (perhaps by providing a cookie). Werner (1948) reported that a child he observed used the word "qua-qua" to refer to both "duck" and "water," after hearing the word spoken in the context of the duck in the water. In such situations as these, the child has failed to differentiate among the possible referents of the word—hearing "cookie" in the context of milk and cookies, the child guesses that the word stands for both; hearing "qua-qua" when he sees a duck in the water, he guesses that "qua-qua" means "duck" and "qua-qua" also means "water" whenever he sees both or the other again. Werner suggested that since the child knows so few words, the objects that are experienced together when the child hears a word spoken are grouped together in the first concept of the meaning of the word. Subsequent use of the word when only a part of the original referent situation recurs is either applauded or corrected, depending on which part of the situation recurs. The referents of the word are associated because the child experienced them together in the original referent situation and did not differentiate between them for the meaning of the word.

There are other associations that children make for themselves, by chaining some aspect of an original referent situation to aspects of successive situations. There may be a shifting chain of associations in which each referent situation in turn provides a new association, a "chain complex" in which there is some consistency between situation A and situation B, and between situation B and situation C, but not necessarily between situation A and situation C (Vygotsky, 1962) (Box IV-9). For example, Guillaume (1927) described the following referents for "nenin" (breast), one of the first words used by his son at about 11 or 12 months: to ask for the breast; to ask also for a biscuit; in reference to the red button of a piece of clothing; the point of a bare elbow; an eye in a picture; and his mother's face in a photograph. In such a "chain complex," the child has associated different objects and events in different referent situations on the basis of either figurative features or functional features from the original referent situation. Associative figurative features are things that look alike (the button, eye, elbow, etc.); functional features are things that affect the child similarly (the breast and the biscuit).

Such associations from the original referent situation to succeeding situations are chained in the sense described by Vygotsky (1962). The child perceives something in a second situation that resembles the original situation in which the word was heard, and use of the word in the second situation may then lead to another association between some aspect of the

BOX IV-9 A CHAIN COMPLEX, IN WHICH SUCCEEDING REFERENCE SITUA-
TIONS PROVIDE NEW ASSOCIATIONS FOR THE MEANING OF A
WORD

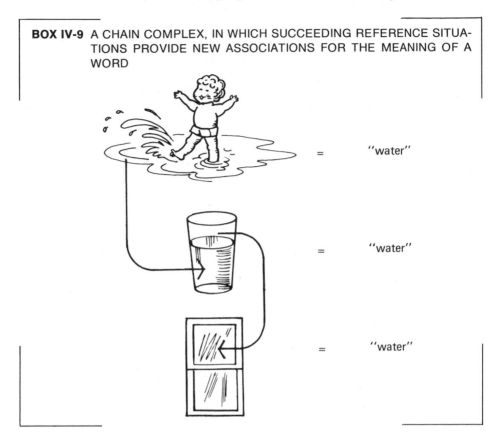

second situation and a subsequent situation, and so on. The use of "nenin"
was not confined to objects that were experienced together (as in the earlier
"qua-qua" example) but instead, was based on some perceptual/functional
commonality. In such a chain of associations there may be one or more
consistencies or common elements among the situations in which the child
uses the word, or they may form chains in which later associations are quite
far removed from the figurative and functional features of the original referent
situation.

Another kind of chained association is an association between some
feature of the original referent situation and a similar feature in succeeding
events, an "associative complex" (Vygotsky, 1962), where the children
connect a feature or features in the original referent situation with similar
features in succeeding events. The original feature or features do not define
a semantic field that overlaps with the semantic field in the adult meaning of
the word. That is, although one can recognize the features that children are

using as criteria for the meaning of a word, the same features are not those that would define the meaning of the word for adults in all the same situations. Here, the second, third, and fourth instance in which the word is used are all similar in some way to the first, but are not necessarily similar to each other. A number of examples of "associative complexes" were described by Bowerman (1974) in describing her daughter's use of words. The examples given by Bowerman were, with one exception, "moon," relational words, such as "kick," "giddiup," "nightnight," "close," "open," and "bump." For example, the original referent situation for "gi" (giddiup) was bouncing on a spring horse, at 14 months, 2 days. The word was subsequently said again, when bouncing on the horse ". . . as picks up tiny plastic horse, then tries to straddle it . . . as gets on toy tractor; as gets on trike . . . looking at horses on TV . . . as bounces on heels crouching in tub . . . as climbs into tiny chair . . . looking at hobby horse . . . bouncing astraddle on M[ommy]'s legs . . . etc.," (Box IV-10).

Such chained associations in the use of a word that have been described represent shifting connections among figurative, functional, and affective

BOX IV-10 AN ASSOCIATIVE COMPLEX, IN WHICH THE DIFFERENT INSTANCES IN WHICH A WORD IS USED ARE ALL SIMILAR IN SOME WAY TO THE FIRST INSTANCE, BUT ARE NOT NECESSARILY SIMILAR TO EACH OTHER (adapted from Bowerman, 1975)

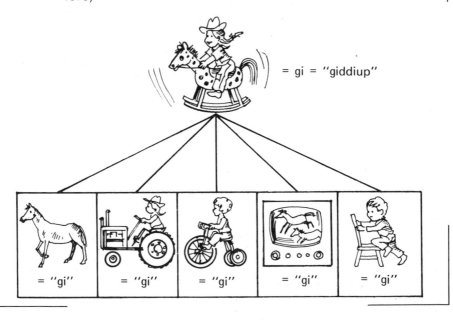

= gi = "giddiup"

= "gi"   = "gi"   = "gi"   = "gi"   = "gi"

features of otherwise diverse objects and events (a button, an elbow, photograph of a face, a biscuit, etc.). They appear to occur early, as children are learning object concepts and relational concepts as well as learning word concepts. Children's use of words in this period reflects the fact that word meanings are only tentatively defined. Children are their own "tutors" in the "original word game" in looking for the limits of the concept that define the meaning of the word (Brown, 1956, in *RLDev*). The use of such words in complexive and associative chaining patterns is a part of what Sinclair (1970, in *RLDev*) has called the child's "organizing activity" in the first half of the second year, as the child looks for evidence of consistency and regularity in the development of conceptual categories. Thus, children are acquiring word concepts as they acquire object concepts and relational concepts—and overextension reflects their hypotheses about the regularities in the environment, as well as their hypotheses about the meanings of words. They are learning the meanings of words by saying words in situations that they guess might contain the criterial element or elements of the original referent situation, or some previous referent situation. Such hypothesis testing contributes to stabilizing the underlying nonlinguistic, conceptual categories, as well as linguistic or word concepts.

Midway through the second year and more often in the last half of the second year after the achievement of object permanence, children's nonlinguistic conceptual categories are progressively more stable. When they use a word, their associations are defined more closely by the criterial features of the original referent situation. A classic example of generalizing the meaning of a word to new instances of the criterial referent is the description by Lewis (1959) of how his son learned the word "fafa" (flowers) from about 16 to 23 months (Box IV-11). The original referent situation was a bowl of yellow jonquils in the living room. The child said "fafa" the second time in the same situation as the original, in reference to the same bowl of yellow jonquils, demonstrating that he had formed an "identity category" for the word "flowers" (Brown, 1965, p. 311). However, when he again used the word, he used it to name another kind of flower, of another color, although still in a bowl, and had thus formed an "equivalence category" (Brown, 1965, p. 311). The child subsequently named pictures of flowers in a book and, by the time he was 23 months old, he was naming embroidered flowers and flowers made of sugar to decorate a biscuit. The child's use of criterial features to distinguish referents for "fafa" included the same range of phenomena to which the word "flower" can refer in adult use, and one can assume that he had learned a word concept "fafa" to map onto an already acquired object concept, which at 16 months included instances of only live flowers. Having the concept can guide the child to learn the word for the concept. Once having a word for the concept, the child plays the "original word game" to extend the concept when hearing the word in situations that

BOX IV-11 GENERALIZING THE MEANING OF A WORD TO NEW INSTANCES OF THE CRITERIAL REFERENT. HERE THE CHILD'S HYPOTHESIS ABOUT THE MEANING OF THE WORD IS GUIDED BY THE MENTAL REPRESENTATION OF THE CRITERIAL FEATURES OF THE OBJECT (from Lewis, 1959)

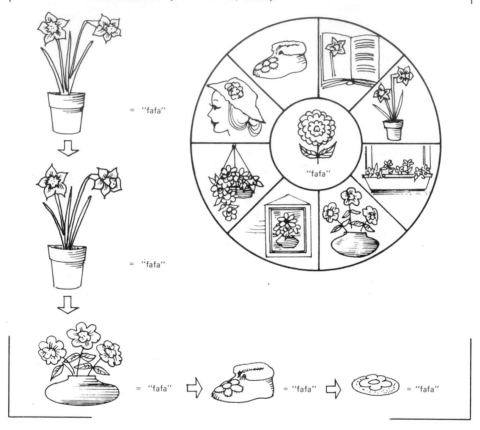

have the criterial features in a different form (sugar flowers and embroidered flowers). Here, the child's hypotheses of the criterial figurative and functional features of the original referent situation are fairly well-formed. The word is used in succeeding situations that are consistent with the mental representation (image, prototype, etc.) of the criterial features of the object to which the word referred in the original referent situation. Using a word in generalizing to new instances of an object in this way would appear to depend on the knowledge that objects endure and are permanent, as already discussed. Such correct applications of words mediate between overextensions that have been described as chained and overextensions that are wholistic.

Wholistic Associations

Once children begin to mentally represent classes of objects and events, their hypotheses about the meanings of words come from knowledge of objects. Instead of a shifting chain of associations whereby the meaning of the word is redefined each time the word is used, word meanings are more consistently defined by the properties of objects. The perceptual criteria (roundness, four-legs, texture, etc.) that determine whether an object belongs to an object concept also figure in defining the meanings of words. But object concepts are not words, and children have many more object concepts than they have words. When they do not have a word for an object concept, they very often form a wholistic association—using one word to refer to similar object concepts on the basis of some consistent property that the different objects share. For example, the words "dog," "cat," "horse," "cow," "goat," and "tiger" refer to objects that are all animate, with four legs, fur, and tails; as another example, the words "truck," "car," "fire engine," and "bus" refer to objects that move on the street and have wheels and motors that make noise. When children do not know the different words that refer to such objects, they may use one word to refer to several or all, for example, "dog" to refer to all four-legged animals or "truck" to refer to all vehicles.

When calling a horse a "dog," a child probably has a conceptual representation of an object "dog," but it is probably not true that the concept of dog also includes all of the perceptual features belonging to horses, cats, and sheep. The child appears to have learned a larger cognitive domain (four-legged animals), only part of which has been semantically represented (as "dog"). It seems entirely reasonable to adopt a strategy in which an already available word is used to represent different but related objects. It is almost as if the child were reasoning, *I know about dogs, that thing is not a dog, I don't know what to call it, but it is like a dog!* The words "sheep," "cat" and "horse" may be in the child's recognition vocabulary, that is, the child may be able to remember the object when hearing the name, even though the name is not recalled when the object is seen (Box IV-12). (See the discussion of overextension in speaking and understanding in Chapter VIII.)

In a comprehensive review of the diary literature that describes children's early words and the range of referents that have been observed in the overextension of words, Clark (1973a) described the perceptual criteria that appear to guide children in deciding whether or not to use a word (Box IV-13). Among the perceptual criteria that Clark observed were factors such as movement, texture, four-leggedness, shape, and size. Color was not a factor that seemed to guide the children in the diary literature in using words. That is, children often call different objects the same thing, such as "dog," because all the objects have four legs and fur, but there were no reports of

BOX IV-12 A WHOLISTIC ASSOCIATION, WHERE CHILDREN USE THE SAME WORD FOR DIFFERENTIATED BUT SEMANTICALLY RELATED CONCEPTS

= "dog"

= ?
("dog")

= ?
("dog")

children calling different objects (such as apples, valentines, and pencils) the same thing because they were all the same color. (But see Box IX-7).

At an earlier time, when children first begin to use words, the use of a word such as "dog" to refer to cats, sheep, and horses as well as dogs may have been the result of a failure to differentiate, that is, not knowing the difference between dogs and sheep and between dogs and cats (Box IV-14).

However, later in the single-word utterance period, when children know many object concepts (including a concept of dog, a concept of cat, and a concept of sheep), but know fewer words, they use the same word to refer to different objects because (1) they do not know enough words for recall, and (2) they recognize certain similarities among different object concepts.

BOX IV-13 SOME EXAMPLES OF OVEREXTENSION IN YOUNG CHILDREN'S SPEECH (from Clark, 1974, p. 112.)

Category	Word	First referent	Domain of overextension	Language
Shape	[mooi]	moon	→ cakes → round marks → on windows and in books → round shapes in books → tooling on leather book covers → postmarks (round) → letter O	English
	[buti]	ball	→ toy → radish → stone spheres at park entrance	Georgian
	[kotibaiz]	bars of cot (crib)	→ large toy abacus → toast rack with parallel bars → picture of building with columns on facade	English
	[tick-tick]	watch	→ clocks → all clocks and watches → gas-meter → fire-hose wound on spool → bathroom scales with round dial	
Size	[fly]	fly	→ specks of dirt → dust → all small insects → his own toes → crumbs of bread → small toad	English
	[bébé]	baby	→ other babies → all small statues → figures in small pictures and prints	French
Movement	[bird]	sparrows	→ cows → dogs → cats → any animal moving	English
Sound	[fafer]	sound of train (chemin de fer)	→ steaming coffee pot → anything that hissed or made a noise	French
Taste	[cola]	chocolate	→ sugar → tarts → grapes, figs, peaches	French
Texture	[va]	white plush dog	→ muffler → cat → father's fur coat	Russian

Wholistic associations provide evidence that children have begun to identify a larger semantic domain that is consistent with a superordinate semantic domain in the adult semantic system such as *animals* and *vehicles*. Although they do not use the word "quadriped" or "vehicle," the children have recognized that objects that are perceptually and functionally related in

BOX IV-14 FAILURE TO DIFFERENTIATE OBJECTS EXPERIENCED AT DIF-
FERENT TIMES FOR THE MEANING OF A WORD, AT AN EARLY
TIME IN DEVELOPMENT

their conceptual representation, are also semantically related in their linguistic representation. Although children most probably have differentiated among the particular object concepts or relational concepts to which they refer with the same word, the linguistic category or word concept is less differentiated, and the word may be used to refer to a "whole" semantic domain. Depending on the reaction of the listener to the child's guesses or hypothesis testing, the process of linguistic differentiation gradually results in learning more and more forms to represent such different content, which is manifest in the rapid growth in vocabulary that has often been described in the last half of the second year (e.g., McCarthy, 1954; Stern and Stern, 1907).

The process of hypothesis testing in learning new words continues with other content and other forms, well into the child's succeeding years. Bowerman (1974) described how the semantic domain of causal verbs was learned by her two daughters when they were 2 years old—the acquisition of such verbs as "break," "drop," and "kill" in which an agent causes something to happen. Other studies of lexical semantics with older children have been experimental studies of comprehension, in which children's semantic development has been described in terms of the strategies they use for understanding relational words such as "more" and "less" (Donaldson and Wales, 1970; Palermo, 1973; and Weiner, 1974); "same" and "different" (Donaldson and Wales, 1970; and Josephs, 1975); and "in," "on," and "under" (Clark, 1973b, in *RLDev*; and Kuczaj, 1975). By presenting children with an array of objects and asking them to do something with the objects, with a question or statement that contains the word being studied, it is possible to observe how they interpret the meaning of the word. There have been an increasing number of studies of comprehension of relational terms by 3-, 4- and 5-year-old children and by school-age children, with conflicting conclusions about the nature of children's semantic development. It has become quite clear, however, that children learn the meanings of words gradually, and how children interpret such words is influenced by many factors in the nonlinguistic as well as the linguistic context (see Clark, 1973b, in *RLDev*; and Kuczaj, 1975).

The increase in the number of different words at the end of the second year happens at about the same time or shortly before children begin to combine words with semantic relations between them. Just as the beginning of the single-word utterance period was continuous with development in infancy, and the precursory behaviors in infancy that contribute to the content, form, and use of words, the single-word utterance period is continuous at the other end with the development of grammar. The kinds of things that children are talking about with single words are the same kinds of ideas about objects and relations between objects that are encoded in their early multiword utterances. That is, children do not learn rules of word combination to express new ideas, but to use new forms (multiword utterances) to express the ideas they already have (Bloom, 1973; Greenfield, Smith, and Laufer, 1972; and Slobin, 1973, in *RLDev*). Furthermore, the same substantive words and relational words that children have so far been using one at a time begin to be combined with one another and with new words, particularly verbs. At first, such words may be said successively, but eventually they are joined together in different kinds of syntactic relation; this will be discussed in the next chapter. The combination of words in phrases and sentences sometime toward the end of the second year provides evidence that children are learning something about the structure of language.

SUMMARY

Most children begin to understand and say words in their second year, and they begin by saying only one word at a time. The period in which children use single-word utterances is a period of continuous developmental change—in both the kinds of words that children learn and in the ways that words are used. It is a period that is continuous with development in infancy, as the infant's precursory behaviors provide the resources for the inductions that the 1-year-old child makes about the integration of linguistic form with content and use. Within the period there are many levels or ways of knowing linguistic forms, and many factors that contribute to what a child knows about a word.

There are different kinds of words that children learn that make reference to different kinds of ideas that they have about objects and relations between objects. Certain words, substantive words, name object concepts—both particular objects that are only single instances (such as "Mommy") and classes of objects with many instances (such as "cookie"). Other words, relational words, refer across many classes of objects and have to do, in this period, very often with the relation of an object to itself—the fact that it exists, "there" or "this;" or disappears, "gone" or "away;" or reappears, "more." There are social words that children also learn in this period that include routines and greetings.

Children learn words gradually, by testing hypotheses of what a word means in the different situations in which they think that one or another word might *fit*. As a result, the use of a word is often inconsistent with the semantic domain the word might have in the adult model language—the child's frame of reference may be quite narrow and might be used to encode only a small part of the semantic domain, or the child's frame of reference may appear to be quite broad, leading to what has come to be called "overextension" in the use of a word. However, it has long been recognized in the child language literature that there are different ways in which children attempt to define a word by using it in new contexts, and several kinds of associations that children might make in defining a word were discussed.

Finally, the use of single-word utterances is continuous with the development of grammar and the linguistic inductions 2-year-old children make in learning the semantic and syntactic structure of multiword sentences. The words that children learn to use in the period represent the same kinds of ideas that are encoded in the content of multiword utterances, and the different kinds of words—particularly relational and substantive words—contribute to learning different aspects of linguistic structure in multiword utterances.

SUGGESTED READINGS

In *Readings in Language Development*

Bloom, L. The distinction between classes of single words. From *One word at a time: The use of single-word utterances before syntax.* The Hague: Mouton, 65–70, 1973.

Brown, R. The original word game. Appendix in J. Bruner, J. Goodnow, and G. Austin, *A study in Thinking*. New York: John Wiley & Sons, 1956

Clark, E. Non-linguistic strategies and the acquisition of word meanings. *Cognition, 2,* 161–182, 1973.

Guillaume, P. First stages of sentence formation in children's speech. Translated by E. Clark. In C. Ferguson and D. Slobin (Eds.), *Studies of child language development.* New York: Holt Rinehart and Winston, 240–251, 1973. Originally in *Journal de Psycholgie,* 1–25, 1927.

Leopold, W., *Speech development of a bilingual child,* Vol. 1 Vocabulary growth in the first two years. Evanston, Ill.: Northwestern University Press, 1939.

MacNamara, J. Cognitive bases of language learning in infants. *Psychological Review, 79,* 1–13, 1972.

Sinclair, H., The transition from sensory-motor behavior to symbolic activity. *Interchange, 1,* 119–126, 1970.

Other Readings

Bloom, L., *One word at a time: The use of single-word utterances before syntax.* The Hague: Mouton Publishers, 1973.

Clark, E., What's in a word? On the child's acquisition of semantics in his first language. In T. Moore (Ed.), *Cognitive development and the acquisition of language.* New York: Academic Press, 1973.

Dore, J. Holophrases, speech acts, and language universals. *Journal of Child Language, 2*, 21–40, 1975.

Ferguson, C., Peizer, D. and Weeks, T. Model-and-replica phonological grammar of a child's first words. *Lingua, 31,* 35–39, 1973.

Ingram, D. Phonological rules in young children. *Journal of Child Language, 1,* 97–106, 1974.

Menn, L. Phonotactic rules in beginning speech. *Lingua, 26*, 225–251, 1971.

Nelson, K., Structure and strategy in learning to talk. *Monographs of the Society for Research in Child Development, 38* (1 Serial No. 149), 1973.

Waterson, N. Child phonology: A prosodic view. *Journal of Linguistics, 7*, 179–211, 1971.

On several levels of description, the relation between content and form in child language is systematic, and, virtually from the beginning of the combination of words, children's language is structured. Structure is organization—a system whereby elements are interrelated or organized in relation to one another. There are several levels on which one can look for structure in child language and observe that children's language is systematic in the ways in which elements are interrelated. At the level of sentences, child language is systematic in the way in which words are combined in sentences. At the more general level of an individual child's competence with language, a child's language is systematic in the way in which the child's rules for language are related to one another. At the broader level of child language in general, there is systematicity in the way in which the regularities in the language of different children are related at one time, and change across time.

On one level, the level of sentences, elements are constituents (words, primarily), and sentence constituents are interrelated with one another according to rules of grammar that specify word order and the meaning relations between words. Structure implies predictability. Thus, knowing one part of a sentence, it is possible to predict what the other constituents of the sentence will be. For example, knowing that the sentence includes two nouns, one can predict that it will also contain a verb; knowing that the sentence contains a noun and a transitive verb, the occurrence of another noun can be predicted.

On another level, the level of the language competence of a particular child at a particular time, elements are the rules of language, and rules are interrelated so that knowledge of a sample of sentences will predict the other sentences that will or that can also occur. For example, if one hears a child say "Mommy read," "read book," "eat raisin," and "Daddy throw," it is possible to predict that other sentences with other nouns and verbs will occur. But if one hears another child say "read it," "throw this," "I eat," one might predict that pronouns instead of nouns will occur with other verbs.

On still another level, the extent to which the same rules are manifested in the language of different children is an indication of structure in child language in general. Finally, at the level of developmental change, elements are the changes that occur in language behavior at successive times. The extent to which different behaviors at different times are related to one another is an indication of structure in the development of language. Thus, evidence of structure in child language can be observed in the regularities in the language of individual children, in the language of different children, and in the language of children across time.

Language structure has to do with the relation between content and form: linguistic categories (words and relations between words), in relation to nonlinguistic categories (object concepts, and relational concepts). Although children's knowledge of objects and relations in the world is a major determining factor in their language learning, the ability to say sentences comes about as the result of several linguistic inductions about words and relations between words. The structure of children's language is, at once, both semantic and syntactic. On the semantic level, children's sentences encode content: reflexive object relations, which were already discussed at the single-word utterance level; and interclass and intraclass relations that involve actions, and states. On the syntactic level, the form of children's sentences gradually increases in length with different kinds of relations between constituents. The content of child language will be discussed first, and the development of form, from successive single-word utterances to sentences, will be discussed subsequently.

SEMANTICS IN CHILD LANGUAGE

The predominant content category in children's early speech has to do with the ways in which the different objects from different concepts—including persons—relate to one another through movements or actions (Bloom, Lightbown, and Hood, 1975; Bowerman, 1973a; and Brown, 1973). Children talk, overwhelmingly, about what they are just about to do, what they are doing or what they are trying to do, what they want other people to do and, less often, what they see other people doing. The action relations children talk about most often involve single objects—either in relation to themselves or to another person or animate being or simply an intransitive movement by an object that does not also involve another object, such as a doll dancing.

ACTION RELATIONS

Both transitive and intransitive action events are represented in children's sentences and single-word utterances before sentences appear in children's speech. Certain actions that children talk about involve the relation between an agent that brings about the action or "does" the action, and an object that is affected by the action. For example, all of the utterances "ride," "Gia ride," "ride bike," "Gia bike," and "Gia ride bike" are about the action and the relation between Gia (an agent) and the bike (an affected object). Other action events that do not involve an effect on a second object are intransitive relations between an actor that performs the action, and the action, such as "clown laugh" (Box V-1).

Except for special activities, such as "read" or "draw," the action names that children use tend to be the names of some of the most general actions that one can perform with objects—most general, because they are actions that can be performed with many different objects. The same verbs appeared over and over in the protocols of the speech of Eric, Gia, Kathryn, and Peter (such as "put" "make," "go," and "get,") and the most frequent verb was the pro-verb "do." The actions that children name most often are similar to the concepts of existence, nonexistence, disappearance, and recurrence; they are movements, behaviors, or functions that can affect many different objects.

Thus, the early action words that children use have considerable generality; that is, they are actions that are possible with many different actors, agents, and affected objects. It is possible to identify a hierarchy of actions according to how many different kinds of events with different objects can occur with the same actions. For example, children can get, make, put, and do many more different things than they can ride, eat, and open; they can

---

BOX V-1 DIALOGUE WITH KATHRYN, 24 MONTHS OLD, WITH EXAMPLES OF ACTION UTTERANCES

Did you see the toys I brought?

ə bring toys/ choo choo

Lois brought the choo choo train

Yes/ Lois brought the choo choo train.
(Kathryn reaching for bag)

ə want play with choo choo train/
ə want play with choo choo train/
(Kathryn taking out slide) want play/ what's this?

Oh you know what that is put down on floor// this/ ə do this

(Kathryn puts slide on floor; taking out two cars of train) do this/ ə want do this

(Kathryn trying to put train together) ə do this/ ə do this

OK/ you can do it/ you can do it/ look I'll show you how
(Lois puts it together; Kathryn searching in box) ə get ə more/ get ə more

no more choo choo train/ get truck

(Kathryn taking out truck) Kathryn truck/ where/ where
ə more choo choo train?

Inside/ it's in the box ə choo choo train ↑

(Kathryn taking out part of train) this ə choo choo train

---

ride, eat, throw, and open many more things than they can turn, blow, and cut. All of these actions, get, make, push, do, ride, eat, throw, open, turn, blow, and cut, are performed by children in relation to objects, but certain actions are more general than others; that is, they can affect more different objects and occur in more different situations.

Developmentally, action events become the single most important category in children's language. Although reflexive object relations are most frequent among children's earliest sentences, the action relations soon become more frequent. Eventually other categories of content, including the reflexive object relations, attribution and possession, are embedded as constituents in action relation sentences, for example, "ride my bike," and "eat chocolate cookie."

LOCATIVE RELATIONS

Children talk about the location of two objects in relation to one another long before they are able to specify the precise direction of the location through the use of relational words such as "to," "on," "in," "above," and "below." Children talk about *objects* that are located in relation to other objects that are *places*. Two major findings in the study of the language of Eric, Gia, Kathryn, and Peter have to do with the development of the content of locative expressions in the children's speech. The first was the fact that dynamic locative events (involving movement) were encoded before static spatial relations (where no movement occurred) (Bloom, Lightbown, and Hood, 1975). In dynamic locative events, the movement that brought about the spatial relation between two objects occurred within the speech event (locative action); for example:[1]

(Gia putting lamb in toy car)	lamb ə go car
(Eric carrying discs to his bed)	I put it down

In static locative events, an object was already located at the place at the time of the speech event (locative state); for example:

(Kathryn pointing to bananas on the refrigerator)	that ə banana up there
(Gia pointing to a picture of a baby in a basket)	baby basket
(Mommy's in the bathroom) Where's Mommy?	Mommy bathroom

The second result in the development of locative relations in the speech of Eric, Gia, Kathryn, and Peter was that there were three different categories of locative action relations between objects and places (Bloom, Miller, and Hood, 1975, in *RLDev*). Whereas the children always talked about an *object* (which could be a person) moving in the direction of (toward or away from) a *place*, there were three different kinds of movement relations: one in which a second object, an explicit *agent*, caused the affected object to move toward

---

[1] In this and all subsequent examples, the utterances spoken by the child appear on the right; the utterances spoken by an adult (parent or investigaor most often) appear on the left; the material in parentheses on the left is description of relevant context. (See Appendix A for the conventions used for transcription.)

the place (agent-locative action); one in which the object that moved was its own agent (mover-locative action); and one in which the object that moved was affected by an implicit agent (patient-locative action).

Locative Action and Locative State Events

Two of the four children used sentences that encoded locative action before they used sentences that encoded locative state. Both locative action and locative state were encoded at the same time in observations from the other two children, indicating that they either learned them together or the sequence of action before state happened in the time lapse before the sample in which both were observed. The children talked about objects moving in relation to places or locations more often than they talked about objects that were already located at places, and two of the children talked about locative action before they talked about locative state (Box V-2).

The distinction between "dynamic" and "static" aspects of events is represented in different ways in different languages. Almost all languages, however, have forms for representing the opposition between the "directional" aspect (locative action) and the "locative" aspect (locative state); see, for example, Leech (1970, pp. 198–201) and Lyons (1968, pp. 298, 397). The dynamic-static opposition for locative terms in pidgin and creole languages was explored by Traugott (1973), who concluded that the dynamic aspect appears to dominate in the course of the evolution of such languages. The dynamic aspect, locative action, also dominated in the language development of the children described here—appearing earlier and more frequently in their speech than locative state. This sequence appears to be an instance of the more basic dynamic-static distinction in languages in general (Box V-3).

BOX V-2 DIALOGUE WITH PETER, 26 MONTHS OLD, WITH EXAMPLES OF
LOCATIVE ACTION UTTERANCES

(Peter putting Patsy's barrette into his hair)	**put in my hair/put in my hair**
What?	**put in my hair my barrette**
Put in my hair my barrette?	**right/ put in my hair my barrette**
(Peter trying to put barrette in his hair)	**I put ən ən ə Patsy barrette/ take off my barrette/–––/ okay/**
(Peter turning to Patsy)	**can't do it Patsy**

BOX V-3 DIALOGUE WITH KATHRYN, 24 MONTHS OLD, WITH EXAMPLE OF
LOCATIVE STATE UTTERANCE

(Kathryn and Lois have been
looking at books)

  Let's see what's in this book/
  do you like this book?

(Kathryn pointing to shelf)   there's ə Humpty Dumpty up there

  Do you want the Humpty Dumpty
  book?   yes

Another explanation of the locative action, locative state sequence—which might not be unrelated to the fact that there is the same distinction in languages in general—has to do with the importance of movement and action in conceptual development. There are two other examples of the cycle of encoding action events before state events in language development in addition to the locative action, locative state sequence. The reflexive object relations—existence, disappearance, and recurrence—were action dependent in the single-word utterance period in that they appeared to occur in conjunction with the children's actions, their observations of the actions of others, and the movements of objects that bring objects into and out of view (Bloom, 1973). The peek-a-boo game is an example of a ritualized action sequence that involves existence, disappearance, and recurrence. Later, when the same reflexive object relations were encoded with multiword utterances, children referred to states of existence, nonexistence, and recurrence (another instance of) where no movement necessarily occurred to bring objects into and out of view, as well as to such relations in dynamic events.

In the second example, in the period when the children first used syntax, they encoded relations between persons and objects, and encoding most often preceded or accompanied an ongoing action or an intended action by the child, or by another person at the child's direction. Only after the children learned to encode person-object relations with the support of relevant action did they talk about states of objects or the states of persons, where their actions or the actions of others were not necessarily relevant to the content of the message. For example, attribution and possession and states of being such as "wanting" or "needing" were productive after action relations were productive in multiword utterances (Bloom, Lightbown, and Hood, 1975).

Movers, Agents, and Patients in Locative Action

There were three meanings of locative action utterances in the children's multiword utterances described in Bloom, Miller, and Hood (1975, in

RLDev). The children talked about objects moving toward places. Certain of the objects that were described as moving toward a place were, themselves, the agents of the movement: *movers,* that were both the affected object (the object that changed place) and the agent of the action; for example:

(Eric's mother preparing to
leave the house)   you go out little bit

(Kathryn crouching behind T.V.)   Kathryn sit down

Such events in which the mover and affected object were the same object were encoded in mover-locative action utterances (Box V-4).

In other locative action events, the object that changed place was moved by some other causative agent; such affected objects were the recipient of the action. There were two kinds of locative action events that involved two objects—one object that changed place and another object that caused the change of place. In patient-locative action utterances, a movement by an agent caused another object to change place, and the constituent before the

---

BOX V-4 DIALOGUE WITH ERIC, 25 MONTHS OLD, WITH EXAMPLES OF
MOVER-LOCATIVE ACTION UTTERANCES

(Eric and Lois are looking out
the window; pigeons on street
below; a man had just ridden by
on a bicycle)

                                                        bicycle!

   Bicycle/ who was riding a bicycle?   ə man riding/ ə pigeon riding
                                                      bicycle

   Pigeon riding bicycle!/I saw _____
   (Just then pigeon flew away)

                                                      pigeon left

   Pigeon left/ pigeon flew away
   (Rest of pigeons fly off)   pigeon flew away/ **many pigeon**
                                                    ə many pigeon fly away

                                                    no more pigeon/ no more pigeon/
                                                    no more pigeon

   No/ where'd they go?   go bye-bye/ pigeon/ **pigeon go**
                                                      bye-bye

   Yes/ where?/   **up in the air · ə pigeon**

verb or the subject of the sentence was the *patient*, the object that moved, and the agent was not specified; for example:

(Peter putting recording tape
in its box)   tape recorder goes in there

(Gia taking man and car to
bridge)   man go on bridge

In agent-locative action utterances, a movement by an agent caused another object to change place, and the constituent before the verb or the subject of the sentence was the *agent* of the action, and the affected object that was moved was part of the complement of the verb; for example:

(Gia bringing lambs to toy bag;
drops them into bag)   Gia away ə lamb

(Kathryn trying to reach gift
on table)   get it off

With agent-locative action, the relations among the objects in the event were the same as with patient-locative action: one object (a person) affected another object by causing it to change location. Although the semantic relations of agent-locative action sentences and patient-locative action sentences were the same, they were syntactically different: the affected object was mentioned after the agent-locative action verb, but the mention of the affected object preceded the patient-locative action verb.

The categories of locative action events developed sequentially, although the sequence was different for the four children: Gia and Peter learned agent-locative action first, Eric learned patient-locative action first, and Kathryn learned mover-locative action first. However, as the children matured, they became more similar to one another; when the mean length of their utterances was approximately 3.0 morphemes, agent-locative action was most frequent in the speech of Gia, Kathryn, and Peter, while patient-locative action was most frequent for Eric (Bloom, Miller, and Hood, 1975).

The locative constituent *place* that was entailed in locative action utterances is more specific than the locative case defined in the case grammar of Fillmore (1968) and referred to by Bowerman (1973b), Brown (1973), and others. According to Fillmore, the locative case "identifies the location or spatial orientation of the state or action identified by the verb" (p. 25). The locative constituent *place* in locative action utterances specified the *goal* of movement as some object or person was located at some place or moved to some place, which is what Fillmore referred to, somewhat ambiguously, as "orientation." The aspect of Fillmore's locative case that identifies "the location . . . of the state or action" is represented in the category action and place (see Table V-1, p. 160–161), in which place was not a complement constituent in an action relation (as was the goal in locative actions) but, instead, the place in which the nonlocative action or state (such as "write," "play," "build," "eat," "sleep," or "tired") occurred. With such simple actions and states, there is no necessity to specify place in order to complete the meaning of the verb. Developmentally, the category action plus place did not become productive until after locative action utterances were productive. That is, Eric, Gia, Kathryn, and Peter did not say action sentences such as "Those children doing *there*" (Kathryn) or *"orange chair* read ə book" (Gia) until after such locative action utterances as "put man ə *block*" (Kathryn) and "wrench go *there*" (Eric) were fully productive. Parisi (1974) reported the same sequence of development of locative action before action and place for Italian children (Bloom, Lightbown, and Hood, 1975).

STATE RELATIONS

The semantic relations of possession (an interclass relation with two objects related to one another) and attribution (an intraclass relation in which an object is distinguished from among other objects from the same class) are different from action relations (with and without location). They are static relations; states of being and not movement are coded. Similarly, the reflexive object relations discussed in Chapter IV (existence, nonexistence, and recurrence) are also static relations when they are events that do not occur as the result of or in connection with some movement. There is an important difference between the two, possession and attribution on the one hand and reflexive object relations on the other, in that the reflexive object relations begin in the single-word utterance period in the context of movement or change, and only subsequently are coded as states. One-year-old children talk primarily about the existence of moving objects; they talk about the nonexistence of objects that disappear; and they talk about the recurrence or reappearance of objects or events, or the appearance of a similar object or event (another instance).

Possession

Children recognize, very early, when a particular object is more often associated with or connected to one person than to other persons. The objects that come to be associated with particular persons form the domain of that person. Information about person-object domains is part of what children know about a person and about particular instances of an object concept. Such domains may be established on the basis of different criteria such as proximity (the clothes one wears or the chair one sits in), action (the briefcase one uses or the pipe one smokes), and the like.

In certain instances, the objects that are associated with particular persons are concepts that include only the single object—a class of one. A briefcase, a pipe, or a pair of eyeglasses, for example, may be the only instance of such objects that the child knows. In this case, the child identifies an object with a person, and most of what the child knows about the object (briefcase, pipe, eyeglasses, etc.) has to do with the person that is connected with or associated with the object. However, the information about the object is only a small part of what the child otherwise knows about the person. That is, the child knows a great deal about Mommy, what Mommy does, where Mommy is, and what objects are associated with Mommy. However, the fact that Mommy carries a briefcase or puts on eyeglasses may be the only information that the child has about the briefcase or the eyeglasses. Thus, among the child's single-word utterances in the second year, the child may *call* the briefcase "Mommy" or the eyeglasses "Mommy" or a certain chair "Daddy."

There are, however, many more object concepts that come to include many exemplars as members. The concept of hat includes information that allows children to recognize several objects of different sizes, different colors, and even different shapes as *hat*. In addition to distinguishing among objects from the same concept according to information about color or size, objects from the same concept are distinguishable according to the way in which they come to be associated with different persons. There is one hat that is different from another hat because it *belongs to* Mommy (or Daddy, or the child, etc.). Thus children come to encode different kinds of information about objects, including information about the person domains within which an object might exist.

Children's early reference to such person-object domains represents an intercategory relation of possession that identifies an object of one category (person) with an object of another category. Thus, when children talk about "Mommy(s) shoe," "Daddy(s) coat," or "baby(s) sock," they are talking about an object that can be identified in terms of its relation to another object. Eventually, children use such identifying information to contrast one object with another object from the same category, that is, to make the distinction among two or more objects of the same class according to the person to whom the object *belongs*, for example, "Daddy(s) hat" and "Mommy(s) hat." The concept of possession is another matter, however. The idea of possession is a much larger concept that entails information about the ideas of acquisition, loss, property, and so forth. Thus, although children speak about and understand relations between persons and objects that involve an awareness of association, that association is the possession concept in only a beginning sense.

Attribution

Certain relational concepts distinguish among the like objects from an object concept or class (Box V-5). All objects have attribute values; they all have shape, size, color and even temperature or felicity (whether or not the object is pleasing to see). For example, it is possible to distinguish among balls according to their size (big, tiny, fat), color (red, blue), texture (fuzzy, smooth), and firmness (hard, soft). Reference to the attribute values of an object in language is most often *contrastive*; one refers to the size of an object, the color of an object, or the prettiness or pleasantness of an object in order to contrast that object exemplar from the other objects that make up the object concept. Thus, to ask for "the red ball" is to distinguish that ball from other balls that might also be offered if one simply asked for "a ball."

In a semantic classification of adjectives, Huttenlocher and Higgins (1972) distinguished among (1) dichotomous attributes such as dead or alive, male or female; (2) attributes that are multidimensional, such as shape or color, and (3) the largest class of attributes, which consist of single continuous dimensions along which objects can be ordered relative to each other. There

---

BOX V-5 DIALOGUE WITH GIA, 23 MONTHS OLD, WITH EXAMPLES OF POSSESSION INDICATED BY * AND EXAMPLES OF ATTRIBUTION INDICATED BY **

Wanta play with the slide?
(Gia starting to get off chair)   my new book*,**/ new book**

New book? / where's a new book?
                                             library book**

Library book
(Gia gets off chair; going   my library book*,**/ Gia library
toward bedroom)   book*,**

                                             Gia buy book

(Running into bedroom;   Gia run/ Gia
Lois follows)

(Gia comes out with *Curious*
***George*, a library book)**

  Oh/ do you want to read that
  book?/ do you want to read that
  book?   yes
(Gia holding book)
  Ok, let's go
(Gia follows Lois to living room)
  What book is that?   Gia library book*,**

are different kinds of continuous dimensions. One dimension includes relative size, weight, or speed and is quantitative, with a ratio scale that involves some unit of measurement, such as inches, pounds, or miles per hour, and a zero point with no length, weight, or speed. There are also attributes of value and quality, for example, beauty, happiness, or goodness, where there is neither unit measurement nor a true zero point. Such attributes form an ordinal scale along which items are compared and ordered. There is also a third dimension of attributes such as, for example, temperature and intelligence, that involves some unit of measurement but lacks a true zero point, with the result that items are compared according to relative differences along an interval scale.

Developmentally, children begin to use adjectives as single-word utterances, and phrases with adjectives appear among their earliest multiword utterances. Among the attributes that have been specified in early single-word utterances between 16 to 21 months were, for example, "dirty," "funny," and "nudie" (Bloom, 1973). An older child who had begun to use multiword utterances, Kathryn, age 21 months and with an *MLU* of 1.32, said "tiny balls," "dirty sock," and "black hair" (Bloom, 1970a). However, references such as these to attribute values in early child speech is not contrastive. Kathryn did not say "tiny balls" to distinguish the balls hidden in a rattle from some larger balls; she did not say "dirty sock" to distinguish that sock from other, cleaner socks, and she did not say "black hair" to mark the difference between two persons, one of whom had black hair. The early attributive forms in the speech of children (see Bloom, Lightbown, and Hood, 1975) were used more in a nominal or absolute sense, in that a property was not attributed to an object so much as it was used to name or identify the object. Thus "tiny balls" are the objects inside of rattles and "nudie" was the name for a bare stomach.

In terms of relative frequency, the use of attributive forms is rare in single-word utterances and in children's earliest multiword utterances. The use of the adjective values described by Huttenlocher and Higgins (1972) in a contrastive sense (to distinguish among the members of an object class) is an even later development than their actual appearance in two- and three-word sentences.

Other State Relations

The developmental cycle of action and state in the development of reflexive object relations is recapitulated in the coding of verb relations. In early verb relations, actions precede states and locative action precedes locative state (Bloom, Lightbown, and Hood, 1975). In addition to locative states, which have already been discussed, there are other states represented in verb relations, such as knowing, wanting, having, and sleeping, and stative verbs that entail notice, such as seeing, looking, listening, watching, and hearing (sometimes referred to in the literature as verbs of perception). Such states are predicated of animate beings that can know, want, have, sleep, and so forth and also see, hear, listen, and so forth. When they first appear in children's sentences, the animate being or person affected is often the child, as in the following examples:

(Peter tapping paper on
which Lois had drawn a
house)   want ə house like that

(Kathryn pointing to
her overalls)   Kathryn have red pants

But others as person-affected are also talked about:

(Kathryn and Lois playing
in living room; Mommy is
in other room)   Mommy busy now

In addition to the stative verb relations that have been discussed, children learn to express state relations with the copula (some form of "to be," such as "is," "am," "are," "was," "were," etc.). In addition to their semantic structure as state relations, such object relations as existence, location, possession, and attribution are similar in their syntactic structure, which will be discussed in the second half of this chapter.

SYNTACTIC STRUCTURE IN CHILD LANGUAGE

Children progress through certain fairly well-defined steps in the development of the form of sentences: (1) *successive single-word utterances* occur in the transition from single-word to multiword utterances as children learn the semantic relations among words, when they hear words spoken and use single words in the context of events that they know about in a conceptual sense; (2) certain conceptual relations are coded with specifically relational words that are combined with substantive words in sentences that have *linear syntactic relationship*; and (3) certain other conceptual relations can also be coded with linear syntactic relations but are, eventually, mapped onto *hierarchical syntactic structures.* Eventually, children learn that syntactic structures (phrases or clauses) can be combined to express more than one relationship in a single sentence with *complex syntax.* Each of the first three of these developments will be taken up in the following sections. The development of the forms of complex syntax (and the content relations encoded by complex syntax) will be presented in Chapter VI.

SUCCESSIVE SINGLE-WORD UTTERANCES

Single-word utterances can most often be interpreted by an adult in relation to particular aspects of the topic and context of the event in which the word is said. Thus, a single-word utterance occurs as an element in a larger construct, the speech event, which consists of factors such as topic (what is talked about or referred to) and context (which includes speaker and hearer as well as objects, actions, and relations). In child speech events, factors that identify topics are almost always present in context. Children talk about what they see and what they do (in what has been called the "here and now") in a way that would be most strange for an adult. The redundancy between what children say and the context and behavior that go along with what they say allows one to identify what they are talking about more often than not. Events with separate single-word utterances, then, are distinguishable from one another by shifts in the topic and context with which the single words occur. However, when more than one utterance occurs without a shift in topic, there is reason to attribute a relationship between them and, indeed, to perceive them as *successive*.

When children first begin to say single words, they occur most often in speech events that include only one utterance that may be repeated many times. For example, trying to climb onto a chair, a child might say either "up" *or* "chair;" or picking up a cookie after having already eaten a cookie, a child might say "cookie" *or* "more." Eventually, children begin to say two different single-word utterances in the same speech event, and this later behavior—the use of successive single-word utterances—may come to predominate in children's presyntax speech, as happened with the children described by Bloom (1970a, 1973), Guillaume (1927 in *RLDev*), Leopold (1939), J. Smith (1970), and others; for example:

(Gia picking up her mother's slipper)	Mommy/ Mommy
What is that?	slipper
Slipper	Mommy
(Gia looking at a picture of a boy in a toy car)	go
Car	car/ ride

(Eric looking out the window at street
below; cars going by; children and adults
walking)   car/ see

See   car

Car   boy

(Allison took a pot from the shelf in the
stove and "stirred" with her hand)   cook/ baby

Is the baby cooking?   pot/ meat/

Successive single-word utterances have been perceived as separate utterances (instead of word combinations) because of relatively equal stress on the words, intervening pauses between the words, and falling or final pitch contour on each of the words.

One possible explanation of the occurrence of successive single-word utterances is that such speech is merely naming behavior. As children know more different words, they might be expected to use more than one word in the same speech event. However, all children expand their vocabularies in the second year, but not all children say successive single-word utterances to the same extent (Bloom, 1973). Furthermore, and more important, not all of the words named in succession are the names of *things*, for example, "see," "more," and "away."

Instead of simply naming objects, it appeared that the children in the above examples were talking about the relations in an event among persons and objects, as in "pot/meat," "Mommy/slipper," and "car/see." Their utterances were successive and related to one another because the children had perceived certain relationships in context and behavior. The lack of sentence prosody and the general unpredictability of the order in which successive single-word utterances were said corresponded with the observation that the semantic interpretation of such sequences was dependent on context. It was apparent that the children were aware of and could talk about things that go together, although they were apparently unable to code or specify the relations among them *linguistically*.

In the analysis of videotaped observations reported in Bloom (1973), a careful examination of the sequence of movements, in relation to what the child said in each of the speech events with successive single-word utterances, revealed two possible event structures with occurrence of such utterances. There appeared to be (1) events with *chained* successive utterances that occurred with successive movements (Box V-6), and (2) events with *wholistic* successive utterances, in which the entire situation appeared to be defined to begin with, and utterances were not tied to particular movements or shifts in context. The children appeared to have the whole goal in mind from the onset, and appeared to be talking about the complete scheme. Although both kinds of "structures" existed in each video sample, there appeared to be a progression in Allison's development from predominantly chained successive single-word utterances to wholistic successive single-word utterances in the period from 16 to 21 months (Box V-7).

Single-word utterances are apparently mapped onto successive movements first, and then, subsequently, successive single-word utterances are mapped onto the mental representation of a whole event (object or relation) in experience. Allison was saying only one word at a time throughout this period from 16 to 21 months, because she had not learned to coordinate and hold in mind at once the several notions underlying her separate utterances. But, further, she needed to learn the code for mapping her mental representations of the relations between objects and people onto the semantic-syntactic relations between words.

Although the use of successive single-word utterances does not characterize the speech of all children to the same extent, there is considerable support for the phenomenon of successive single-word utterances in the

---

BOX V-6 DIALOGUE WITH ALLISON, 16 MONTHS OLD: AN EXAMPLE OF CHAINED SUCCESSIVE SINGLE-WORD UTTERANCES (from Bloom, 1973, p 47)

(Allison reaching under chair; picking up cow)   cow/ cow/ cow

(Allison trying to put cow on chair on hind legs)   chair/ chair

   What's that?
(Allison giving cow to Mommy to help)   **Mama**
   What, darling?

Allison picked up the cow, saying "cow," tried to put it on the chair, saying "chair," and then turned for help, saying "Mama." Each of the utterances accompanied a particular movement relative to the total event. Single-word utterances in situations like this one appeared to accompany Allison's successive movements and (or) utterances or movements by someone else. Essentially, such successive single-word utterance events presented a *chaining* of utterances, each of which was somehow occasioned by a shift in context, where topic was held constant, as Allison noticed, remembered, or did something *new*. Such utterances were temporally chained and were related to one another only to the extent that they were accompaniments of movements that were temporally and schematically related to one another.

Box V-7 DIALOGUES WITH ALLISON, 21 MONTHS OLD: EXAMPLES OF WHOLISTIC SUCCESSIVE SINGLE-WORD UTTERANCES (from Bloom, 1973, p 51)

1. (Allison had been wiping her own bottom with a napkin; Allison goes to doll on Mommy's lap; wiping doll with napkin)
   Mommy baby

   (Allison giving doll to Mommy)
   Mommy/ wiping
   Mommy/ wiping

   (Mommy taking doll)
   wiping
   Wiping what?

   (Allison reaching for doll's bottom)
   here
   Here?

   (Allison wipes doll's bottom)

2. (Mommy had suggested taking off Allison's coat; Allison pointing to her neck)
   up/up

   What?
   neck/ up

   Neck?/ what do you want?/ what?
   neck

   What's on your neck?
   (Allison pointing to zipper and lifting up her chin)
   zip/ zip/ up

From her speech and behavior, and the context, it was clear that Allison wanted Mommy to wipe the doll's bottom and, in the second example, zip up her coat, and she appeared to have the whole picture in mind from the outset. In such events there was a distinct beginning and an end. One has the impression, particularly when watching a replay of the event, that the entire sequence of utterances was, essentially, predetermined by Allison's mental representation of the situation from the beginning.

literature—particularly in the diary studies where individual children were observed continuously. Leopold observed that two related one-word utterances were said in succession just before the emergence of two-word combinations in his daughter's speech. Guillaume (1927, in *RLDev*) gave perhaps the clearest account of the same behavior. He interpreted such successive single-words as separate holophrases, a series of word-sentences, each of which could stand as a sentence instead of as an element of a single statement. Whether each word in such a series is interpretable by an adult as a sentence or as an element of a sentence is unimportant. What is important is the impressive evidence of children's cognitive awareness of relationships among aspects of the situation and the obvious inability to code these relationships linguistically. It is also quite possible that when investigators have reported variable word order in children's early sentences (e.g., what Braine, 1976, described as a "groping pattern") they were really describing children who were producing successive instead of conjoined words—having learned the semantic relations between words but not syntactic rules for representing semantic relations.

The occurrence of successive single-word utterances marks a transition from the use of single words to multiword utterances. The content of children's successive single-word utterances—what they are talking about when they say several words in a speech event, but still say only one word at a time—is the same as the content of early multiword utterances. Children talk about objects and different kinds of relations among objects (including persons as objects). Just as there is continuity in language *content* in the transition from single words to syntax, there is continuity in language form as well, in the occurrence of word order with a meaningless form (/wídə/ in Bloom, 1973; Ramer, 1976; and Dore, Franklin, Miller, and Ramer, 1976) and in the similar rise-fall intonation contours that occur with successive single-word utterances and later multiword utterances (Branigan, 1976). Children begin to bring these separate aspects of language content and language form together in learning the semantic-syntactic structure of sentences some time toward the end of the second year and the beginning of the third year. The different kinds of words that children have learned to use as single words are combined with one another, and with other words (particularly verbs) that they have not yet used as single words, in the different kinds of syntactic relations that are described in the following sections.

LINEAR SYNTACTIC RELATIONSHIP

When a child says "more" and reaches for another cookie, it is reasonable to expect an eventual connection between the words "more" and "cookie" and, indeed, early word combinations such as "more cookie," "more airplane," and so on are among the earliest that children produce. When two-word utterances such as "more cookie" occur, the relational meaning between the words derives from the meaning of the separate words but, most particularly, from the meaning of the relational, function word, in this case, "more." Thus, certain relational meanings in early sentences are *functional* relations, where a constant form with specific meaning such as "more," "away," or "there" is combined with other words, and the meaning of the function word determines the meaning relation of the two words in each combination. Brown (1973) pointed out that such relations can be formalized (in the sense described in Chapter II), with the formula $f(x)$, a fixed value, f, combined with a variable (x) that can assume many values. That is, the same meaning, f, can combine with many different words (x), and the meaning of the relation $f(x)$ is determined by the meaning of the constant, f. There is no new meaning added to f or to (x). For example, in the phrases "more cookie," "more airplane," and "more cheese," there is the constant, f, "more," and the variable, (x), "cookie," "airplane," and "cheese," and the same meaning relation between the words, recurrence, which is also the meaning of "more."

Such word combinations are additive; that is, there is no new meaning other than the cumulative meaning of the two separate words when they are joined together. In the above phrases, the meaning relation between the word is recurrence; the meaning of "more" is recurrence and the meaning of "cookie," is unchanged. Similarly, in the phrase "cookie gone," the relational meaning between the words is disappearance and the meaning of "gone" is disappearance. The meaning of "cookie" is the same in both phrases, "more cookie" and "cookie gone." Because such word combinations are additive, and because the relational meaning of the phrase is determined by the meaning of one of the words, the structural relationship between them can be described as linear: the two words in the phrase are joined together, the meanings are added, and there is no new meaning as a result of their combination.

Furthermore, the linear word combinations with function words such as "more," "gone," "this," "there," and "no" are separate relations in that they do not share any meaning in relation to one another or in relation to other phrases that the child uses at the same time. The f words that enter into such functional, linear relations do not themselves form a class or category by virtue of some shared meaning with other words. That is, there is no common meaning among all the words "this," "there" (in the sense of existence), "more," "'nother," "no," "gone," and "away," that would be a criterion for assuming that they represent a category. They come together in a linguistic description of children's sentences because they share the same distribution (as discussed in Chapter II)—each as an f constant in relation to the same variable (x) words—but there is no evidence for presuming that children learn such function words as a *category* of words. Instead, each such f (x) relation is a separate relation that is unrelated to other word combinations that have different meaning relations. Children learn position rules for such f words, and each results in a separate semantic-syntactic "formula" (Braine, 1976).

The verb forms that children learn can be described in similar terms to some extent. Words such as "eat," "throw," "turn," and "push" can each be described as a constant, f, that can be combined with many variable (x) words such as "eat meat," "eat raisin," "eat nut," and "throw ball," "throw book," "throw raisin," and so forth. There are, however, important differences between verb forms and the functional forms such as "more" and "gone" that have been described. First, verb forms do not have fixed word order distribution, for example, "Mommy *eat*" and "*eat* meat" or "baby *turn*" and "*turn* button," and the like, occur. Second, when all the phrases with verb forms are compared, it turns out that (1) verbs do share meaning with one another according to how they relate to nouns in sentences, and categories of verbs that can be identified on the basis of shared meaning appear to be learned by children sequentially; (2) verbs do have fixed word-order position according to their semantic relations with nouns, for example, "Mommy eat," "baby eat," "horse eat," "Daddy turn," and "girl turn"; and (3) there are different relations between nouns and verbs, and these different semantic-syntactic relations are the immediate constituents of a higher level of structure (as discussed in Chapter II, and in Lyons, 1968). Thus, the structure of children's sentences with verbs is hierarchical, not linear.

HIERARCHICAL SYNTACTIC RELATIONSHIP

The verbs that children learn are, at once, both the result of their conceptual development—in that children learn the verbs that enable them to talk about what they know about, and the major determinant of the development of grammatical structure. The interclass relations that involved action and location were represented in the speech of Eric, Gia, Kathryn, and Peter with different categories of verbs. The children did not learn individual verbs and their relations to nouns one at a time. Instead, verbs appeared in the children's speech categorically—several verbs that had the same semantic-syntactic relations to succeeding and preceding nouns appeared at about the same time, and the different categories of verbs appeared in the children's speech one at a time.

The first semantic-syntactic category of verbs was simple action, then locative action, and then state (see Bloom, Lightbown, and Hood, 1975). Within the category of locative action one of the noun and verb constituent relations specified a place as the goal of an action, for example, "go *outside,*" or "put the lamb *here.*" There were three subcategories of locative action sentences according to whether the noun preceding the verb func-tioned as an agent of the action, a patient that was affected by the action, or a mover that was both agent and patient relative to the verb (see Bloom, Miller, and Hood, 1975, in *RLDev*).

There were also sentences in which the place in which an action happened was specified, for example, "*orange chair* read a book," or "Kathryn play *playpen,*" but the place was not the goal of the movement or an end point, but the location in which the entire event occurred. Thus, with the locative action verbs "put," "go," "fit," and "sit," the place constituent completed the meaning of the verb. With simple action verbs such as "eat," "read," "do," and "fix," the place constituent, if it occurred, functioned as an adverb does in the adult model language-it complemented the meaning of the whole sentence. Such simple action sentences with adverbial place (action and place) appeared in the children's speech after at least one category of locative action verbs became productive (Bloom, Lightbown, and Hood, 1975) (Box V-8).

The verbs that occurred most frequently in all four categories, with all four children, were the most general verbs, involving actions that could entail relations between many different objects. The verbs "get," "do," "make," "put," "take," "go," "sit," and "fit" occurred frequently. In contrast, infrequent verbs that occurred fewer than five times included "spill," "bake," "tickle," "wipe," "fold," "bounce," and "bump." Patient-locative action and mover-locative action utterances occurred with the same verbs. The events differed

---

BOX V-8 THE MOST FREQUENT VERBS THAT THE FOUR CHILDREN USED (adapted from Bloom, Miller, and Hood, 1975, in *RLDev*).

Rank Order of Most Frequent Verbs in Transitive Action and Three Locative Action Categories
(Data Combined for All Children)

Action		Agent-Locative Action		Mover-Locative Action		Patient-Locative Action	
Verb	Frequency^a	Verb	Frequency^b	Verb	Frequency^b	Verb	Frequency^b
get	252	put	287	go	132	go	285
do	169	take	48	sit	95	fit	65
make	132	away	26	go bye-		sit	34
read	86	turn	10	bye	28	fall	30
play	84	out	9	come	25	bye-bye	11
find	69	get	7	get	18	stand	6
eat	60	fit	7	fall	15		
fix	59	do	6	stand	11		
draw	52	dump	6	climb	9		
hold	50	sit	5	jump	7		
				move	6		
				away	5		

^{a} Includes verbs with frequencies of ≥50.
^{b} Includes verbs with frequencies of ≥5.

The transitive action verbs listed are only the verbs that occurred 50 times or more in the children's speech when the mean length of their utterances was about 2.5 morphemes. The locative action verbs are those that occurred 5 times or more in all of the samples from *MLU* 1.0 to *MLU* 3.0. Thus, the action verbs came from one speech sample from each of the children, when *MLU* was about 2.5; the locative action verbs came from several samples from each of the children.

only according to whether the object that changed location was also the agent of the action—the difference between "Mommy *go* store," when Mommy leaves to go to the store, and "lamb *go* here," as the child puts lamb into block.

Within each category of verbs, such as action, mover-locative action, and so forth, the meaning of the relation between a verb and noun, such as between action and place, or mover and action, is the same meaning, regardless of the individual lexical meaning of the verbs and nouns themselves. Children's sentences with verbs are not simply additive; that is, the combination of a noun and a verb results in some larger (superordinate) meaning that is more than only the individual meanings of the separate words. In addition to the inherent, lexical meaning of nominal forms such as "Mommy," "Daddy," "baby," "dog," and "Jane," such words also assume the relational meaning *agent* in relation to verbs such as "eat," "throw," and "push." Certain other nouns, for example, "toast," "horse," "ball," and "bridge," also assume the relational meaning *affected object*, or *patient,* in relation to verbs and in addition to their inherent lexical meaning. There are, then, nouns that function similarly in their relation to verbs and form categories such as agent, patient, place, affected object on the basis of such similar semantic-syntactic function.

Certain nouns relate to verbs as actors or agents of an action, certain other nouns relate to verbs as objects affected by an action, and still other nouns relate to verbs as the place that is the endpoint of some movement that changes the location of an object. Such semantic-syntactic relations between nouns and verbs are not separate relations. The relation between a verb and an agent noun such as "Daddy eat" is also related to the relation between that same verb and the object that is affected by the action, "eat raisin." The relation between the first relation (Y) ("Daddy eat") and the second relation (Z) ("eat raisin") is the superordinate relation (X) in the diagram below.

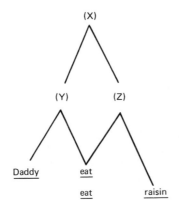

Categories of verbs such as action, mover-locative action, agent-locative action, and the like, are formed on the basis of the elements of meaning that the verbs share, and the same relations that the verbs have with categories of nouns or pronouns. Thus, the relation between a verb and an agent noun such as "Daddy eat" is the same relation as between a different verb from the same category and a different agent noun, such as "Mommy push." The relationship between "Mommy push" and "push swing" is the same superordinate relationship (X) as between "Daddy eat" and "eat raisin." The resulting structure is hierarchical in that the immediate constituent (Y) and the immediate constituent (Z) are both related, in turn, to the higher-order relation (X).

The constituent structures in hierarchical syntactic relationships can be called subject and predicate, if "subject" and "predicate" are defined in these terms, or the constituent structures can be called something else. Obviously, children do not know what adults know about sentence subjects and predicates, and using the same terms should not imply that they do. Children do not know the transformational rules that operate on subject and predicate constituents in adult grammar, and they do not know the distinctions between deep structure and surface structure subject/predicate relations as represented, for example, in the following sentences:

1. The girl pulled the wagon.
2. The wagon was pulled by the girl.
3. Pulling the wagon was what the girl did.
4. The girl pulling the wagon is my sister.

The same deep structure subject/predicate relation is contained in all of these sentences (the relations among girl-pull-wagon), but the surface structure subject/predicate is different in the four sentences.

Children learn that the same underlying deep structure can have different surface structures (transformations), as in sentences 1 to 4, only after they learn the relations in underlying deep structure. First, children learn that categories of nouns (or pronouns) relate to a category of verbs in regular ways. In the following sentences:

5. Bear eat meat.
6. Kathryn make a bridge.
7. Gia ride trike.
8. I do it.

the deep structure relations are all the same. The relation between the first noun and verb (subject) is related, in turn, to the relation between the verb and the second noun (predicate). With these sentences, all of which have the same kind of transitive action verb, the semantic-syntactic relations are the same: "bear," "Kathryn," "Gia," and "I" all have the same relation (agent) to the action verbs "eat," "make," "ride" and "do." In another set of sentences:

9. Lois read this book.
10. Mommy go outside.
11. Lamb go here (child moving lamb).
12. I put car right here.

the verbs are different and the semantic-syntactic relations are different (the differences among action and locative action verbs discussed above), but there is the same deep structure relation between the first noun-verb constituent relation (the subject) and the second verb-noun (or pronoun) constituent relation (the predicate complement).

Although children's knowledge of subject and predicate is not the same as the adult knowledge, neither is it the case that their knowledge is different. That is, children's early knowledge of the subject/predicate constituents in hierarchical structure is necessary but not sufficient knowledge about sentences. It is the beginning of the plan or scheme whereby sentences are created with the semantic relations that were formerly represented in successive single-word utterances, and the result of language development consists of progress toward filling in everything else that one needs to know of the linguistic scheme. Smith (1975) suggested "that young children have a general notion of subject and other grammatical relations that corresponds more or less to the traditional notions of subject, etc. . . . [and] may follow general rather than specific principles, especially with respect to word order . . . [and] only gradually differentiate between different types of relations" (pp. 313–314), in moving developmentally from general to particular linguistic concepts in the acquisition of grammar.

Knowledge of subject and predicate in children's early sentences consists of knowing (1) that semantic-syntactic categories of words are formed by word order and semantic relations between words, in addition to knowing (2) semantic relations between words, and (3) word order relations between words. The sentence subject in early sentences is a category of words that occurs semantically, with different meanings in relation to different categories of verbs, but occurs syntactically before the verb. The predicate in early sentences includes categories of words that occur semantically with entirely different meanings in relation to verbs, and occur syntactically after the verb. When subject and predicate are defined in these semantic-syntactic terms, then there seems to be little question that children know something about what adults know about grammatical categories. The requirement that children demonstrate most or all of the adult knowledge should not be necessary in order to describe children's grammatical categories in terms of a subject/predicate distinction.

The importance of hierarchical structure lies in the fact that children have learned to combine words with a semantic relation between them, where the semantic relation is not the same as the meaning of one of the words. That is, children have learned to use word order (syntax) in order to code semantic relations that are not already represented by an individual lexical item. Such hierarchical structure is evidence that children know more than the fact that words are ordered in sentences; they also know that categories of words are formed by word order. Thus, the verb relations with preceding nouns (sentence subject) and verb relations with succeeding nouns (sentence predicate) are parts of a larger superordinate structure (subject/predicate) instead of being separate formulas that are learned separately from one another, as was suggested by Bowerman (1973b, in *RLDev*) and Braine (1976).

The child speech data that were described in Bloom (1970a), Bloom, Lightbown, and Hood (1975), and Bloom, Miller, and Hood (1975, in *RLDev*) have been interpreted as evidence that knowledge of the basic grammatical relations between subject and predicate constituents underlies children's sentences with verb relations, whether or not both subject and predicate constituents actually occur in the same utterance. The claim is, quite simply, that when all the semantic relations agent-action, action-object, and agent-object occur productively in early two-word sentences, then the child knows the fuller constituent structure agent-action-object (in semantic terms) and subject-verb-complement (in syntactic terms), with semantics and syntax being inseparable. The fact is, however, that children's sentences are limited to two-word utterances until *MLU* reaches 2.0 morphemes long, and after that point, two-word utterances continue to occur.

Copular Structure

The copula "to be" has the forms "is," "are," "am," "was," "were," and so on, which may or may not be contractions (e.g., "it's," "I'm," "they're," or "Mommy's" [busy]). Four kinds of state relations that were discussed in the earlier description of semantic development can be expressed with the copula: existence, location, possession, and attribution. Sentences with these relations can take nominal subjects, such as "Mary is a girl" (existence/identity), "The sweaters are on the chair" (location), and "The dog is big" (attribution). Similarly, possessive state can be coded with a nominal subject and the verb "to have," as in "Daddy has shoes."

In stative utterances with these relations, the category of copular subjects can also be represented by different forms of demonstrative pronouns such as "this," "that," and "there," in sentences like "It's a book" or "That's a cow" (existence/identity); "There's the sweater" or "It's on the chair" (location);

"Those are mine" or "That's Mommy's" (possession); and "That's red" or "It's a big one" (attribution). Copular subjects actually precede the fully productive use of forms of the contracted and uncontracted copula (Brown, 1973). In Kathryn's speech at Time II (when MLU was 1.89 morphemes) there were 281 sentences with demonstrative pronouns, and only 88 of these included a form of the copula ("is" was used twice, both times with "this;" the others were "s" in variants of "that's" (e.g., "thas"). Examples of such sentences without the copula form were "this ə slide" and "that dogs" (existence), "this ə my" (possession) and "that Kathryn hair" (existence and possession).

The development of copular sentences (whether or not a form of the copula is included) parallels the development of the grammatical relation between subject and predicate. Once children present evidence that they know the subject-verb, verb-complement, and subject-complement relations with main verbs, then demonstrative pronouns ("this," "that," "there," etc.) with different semantic relations to the complement can be considered as copular subjects. The sentence complement can be either a nominative, an attributive ("big," "little," "green," "wet"), or possessive ("mine," "Mommy's," "yours") form. Until then, the early use of demonstrative pronouns to express existence is considered a functional relation. It appears that children learn the different forms of the copula as inflections (Brown, 1973) only after they learn the grammatical relations between subject and predicate.

Copular sentences are syntactically similar to sentences with main verbs in that different semantic relations can be embedded in the complement, as in "That's my dog" (embedded possession) or "There's another dog" (embedded recurrence). Similarly, main verbs (action, locative, notice verbs etc.) also begin to have complex complements with embedded relations, for example, "I throw a big ball," "She threw my ball," "Eat more cookies," and "I see more white horses."

So far language development has been described in the single-word utterance period (Chapter IV) and in the period of early sentences when *MLU* increases from essentially 1.0 to 2.0 morphemes (in the present chapter). Development in this period of early sentences will be summarized in the next section.

SEQUENCE OF DEVELOPMENT

The order in which children learn to talk about the categories that have been described so far in their multiword utterances was reported in Bloom, Lightbown, and Hood (1975); Table V-1 presents that information for the four children, Eric, Gia, Kathryn, and Peter. The categories that are presented in Table V-1 are remarkably similar to the kinds of semantic-syntactic relations that have been described in the speech of other American English children at the same point in development by Bowerman (1973a), Braine (1976),

Brown (1973), and Schlesinger (1971). There are certain kinds of things, like action and locative events, that children represent in sentences often, and certain other kinds of things, like instruments and recipients of action, that they represent rarely; and still other kinds of things, like emotional feelings or affective states, that they do not talk about at all. It is certainly true that 2-year-old children know about all of these things: they know about using instruments for eating, drawing, and hitting; they know about giving and showing things to other persons; and they know about feeling sad, angry, happy, or frustrated. The fact that children do not talk about these kinds of things in their early language may be taken as evidence that they do not know how to talk about them. In English, the grammatical structure for expressing the dative (indirect object or recipient of verbs such as "give" and "show") and the instrumentive ("with a fork" or "by a pencil") adds linguistic complexity to the predicate complement. Also, the forms that express feelings or emotions such as "sad," "angry," "frustrated," and "happy" are not so easily paired with any content that is easy to observe. For one reason, the tears, smile, or laughter that children see or feel are not, themselves, the emotions of sadness or cheer that they feel, but are, in fact, the means of expressing such emotions and affect.

Perhaps most important, however, is the fact that feelings or affective states are *overlaid* content and must always coexist (at least for young children) in connection with some real, tangible event; anger occurs along with having the T.V. shut off, having to take a bath, or being pushed off the swing; happiness occurs along with seeing Grandma and getting that hug and kiss, eating an ice cream cone, or sliding into a puddle; and frustration occurs along with not being able to open a box, reach the candy jar, or fit a piece into a puzzle. In short, it is the things and activities themselves that children talk about with their early words and sentences, and not how they feel about them. The feelings that children have are present from earliest infancy; in fact, feelings such as comfort, discomfort, and joy contributed to the content of infants' communication, as discussed in Chapter IV. But the content that children learn to talk about when they are learning language form and use has to do with the objects and events that happen and that bring about or change those feelings.

The Roman numerals in Table V-1 identify the successive samples of the children's speech behavior. The children were between 19 and 25 months in the time period covered here, and the mean length of their utterances increased from about 1.1 in the first sample to about 2.5 in the last sample. There were only three samples from Kathryn in this *MLU* period, because Kathryn was seen for the first time when *MLU* was somewhat higher (1.32) than the *MLU* for the other children at the time of their first samples. There were seven samples from Peter because Peter was seen more frequently, at

TABLE V-1

Proportion and Number of Different Semantic-Syntactic Relations in Each Sample[a] (from Bloom, Lightbown, and Hood 1975, p. 15)

Category	Eric					Gia				
	I	II	III	IV	V	I	II	III	IV	V
Action	.10 (1)	.18 (7)	.20 (22)	.16 (68)	.20 (219)	.06 (3)	.11 (23)	.35 (101)	.35 (173)	.32 (307)
Locative action		.03 (1)	.06 (7)	.09 (32)	.09 (96)	.06 (3)	.06 (12)	.12 (36)	.13 (67)	.09 (87)
Locative state		.03 (1)		.05 (21)	.02 (24)		.00 (1)	.04 (12)	.02 (10)	.03 (30)
State		.05 (2)	.09 (10)	.05 (20)	.07 (81)	.02 (1)		.03 (9)	.01 (4)	.03 (26)
Notice	.10 (1)	.03 (1)	.03 (3)	.01 (5)	.06 (69)		.01 (3)		.00 (2)	.01 (13)
Intention					.01 (16)			.01 (4)	.01 (4)	.14 (135)
Existence	.30 (3)	.15 (6)	.15 (16)	.07 (31)	.06 (64)	.23 (12)	.13 (26)	.06 (17)	.03 (13)	.03 (30)
Negation	.10 (1)	.15 (6)	.17 (18)	.05 (24)	.05 (56)	.02 (1)	.02 (4)	.01 (2)	.01 (7)	.04 (42)
Recurrence		.05 (2)	.07 (8)	.15 (65)	.03 (31)	.09 (5)	.20 (40)	.06 (18)	.02 (10)	.03 (24)
Possession			.03 (3)	.00 (2)	.02 (18)	.02 (1)	.03 (7)	.07 (19)	.08 (40)	.10 (91)
Attribution		.03 (1)	.05 (5)	.11 (46)	.10 (113)		.03 (6)	.05 (15)	.13 (67)	.10 (95)
Wh-question			.02 (2)	.00 (1)	.05 (54)				.01 (3)	.02 (19)
Place[b]		.05 (2)		.02 (9)	.02 (20)	.02 (1)	.01 (2)	.01 (2)	.01 (6)	.01 (8)
Action and place			.01 (1)	.01 (3)	.01 (7)		.03 (6)	.01 (2)	.02 (12)	.02 (15)
Dative				.02 (9)	.01 (14)				.01 (4)	.01 (5)
Instrument										.01 (5)
Other[c]	.10 (1)	.10 (4)	.02 (2)	.05 (22)	.08 (93)	.30 (16)	.13 (26)	.04 (11)	.06 (31)	.00 (4)
Equivocal					.00 (4)	.04 (2)	.02 (5)	.04 (11)	.02 (11)	.00 (2)
Anomalous/ undetermined	.30 (3)	.15 (6)	.10 (11)	.16 (66)	.12 (131)	.15 (8)	.20 (40)	.11 (33)	.07 (35)	.01 (12)
Total N of Relations	10	39	108	424	1110	53	201	292	499	950

[a] Proportions are rounded to nearest hundredth. Those less than .005 are given as .00.
[b] Multiword utterances that specified only place.
[c] Stereotype, routine, greeting, vocative, conjunction, affirmation, manner, and time.

shorter intervals. The sequence of development was based on the frequencies with which utterances occurred in the different categories. Both absolute frequencies (the actual number of utterances) and proportional frequencies (the relative frequency of a category) will be discussed. These data were also treated statistically, and the result of the statistical analysis is presented in Bloom, Lightbown, and Hood (1975, pp. 95–96). Only different utterance types are included in Table V-1; if the same utterance occurred more than one time, it was only counted one time. For example, Eric said "no more noise" more than 10 times as he played with a toy that made a squeaking noise when he twisted it, but "no more noise" was counted as only one of the six different negation utterance types that Eric produced at Time II.

Generally, the absolute frequencies of utterance types increased in all categories for each child across time. For the combined verb categories proportional frequency tended to increase as well, but for the combined categories existence, recurrence, and negation, proportional frequency

TABLE V-1—*(Continued)*

Kathryn			Peter						
I	II	III	I	II	III	IV	V	VI	VII
.24 (56)	.21 (174)	.24 (393)	.43 (3)	.40 (2)	.10 (7)	.23 (23)	.35 (28)	.14 (39)	.17 (81)
.06 (15)	.13 (108)	.12 (192)	.14 (1)		.06 (4)	.05 (4)	.17 (14)	.12 (33)	.15 (71)
.02 (4)	.05 (38)	.04 (67)			.03 (2)	.01 (1)		.05 (13)	.06 (30)
.04 (9)	.05 (38)	.06 (106)				.01 (1)	.01 (1)	.01 (4)	.04 (18)
.01 (3)	.01 (12)	.01 (20)			.03 (2)	.01 (1)		.02 (6)	.01 (3)
.02 (5)	.01 (11)	.07 (115)							.01 (7)
.04 (9)	.08 (68)	.07 (109)		.20 (1)	.07 (5)	.03 (2)	.05 (4)	.04 (10)	.07 (34)
.06 (14)	.05 (41)	.03 (54)			.04 (3)	.05 (4)	.02 (2)	.04 (10)	.02 (9)
.08 (19)	.03 (26)	.03 (44)	.14 (1)	.40 (2)	.24 (17)	.16 (13)	.12 (10)	.04 (12)	.06 (31)
.06 (15)	.06 (51)	.09 (141)			.07 (5)	.05 (4)	.01 (1)	.04 (12)	.06 (27)
.18 (41)	.09 (78)	.07 (116)	.29 (2)		.10 (7)	.18 (14)	.12 (10)	.16 (45)	.06 (31)
	.03 (23)	.07 (116)						.04 (12)	.03 (16)
	.02 (14)	.00 (3)			.10 (7)	.05 (4)	.05 (4)	.02 (6)	.04 (19)
	.00 (3)	.00 (8)							.01 (6)
.01 (2)	.01 (6)	.01 (10)							.01 (3)
	.00 (2)				.01 (1)				
.07 (26)	.06 (50)	.03 (58)			.03 (2)				.11 (56)
.01 (2)	.01 (11)	.00 (7)			.01 (1)			.18 (51)	
.09 (22)	.09 (79)	.05 (83)			.10 (7)	.11 (9)	.09 (7)	.10 (28)	.10 (48)
232	833	1642	7	5	70	80	81	281	490

tended to decrease. Thus, although there were always larger numbers of different utterances in each category as the children matured, utterances that made reference to interobject relations—the interactions between persons and objects or between objects—increased proportionally, while there was a proportional decrease in utterances that made reference to an object with respect to itself or its class (except for attributives). Given these proportional interactions, it was concluded that the categories of existence, nonexistence, and recurrence were an earlier development, and the verb categories were a later development for all of the children.

The category of possession accounted for .10 or less of the relations in each child's speech at each time and an average of .04 for all of the children in all of the data. However, this category tended to be less important in the early data and to increase developmentally with all of the children. The attribution category was different for different children; although absolute frequency tended to increase for all the children, no clear trend emerged for proportional frequencies. The verb categories in combination with the categories of possession, attribution, existence, negation, and recurrence accounted for an average of .77 of the semantic-syntactic relations in the utterances from all of the children.

Utterances in the categories dative and instrument emerged only in the later data, as can be seen in Table V-1. Even though the children were no doubt aware that (1) persons can be affected by certain actions that also involve other objects (e.g., as receivers), and (2) there are particular instruments for specific actions (e.g., pencils, crayons, spoons, keys), the children simply did not talk about these kinds of relations in their early syntactic utterances.

The sequence of development that was observed was as follows. The reflexive object relations existence, nonexistence, and recurrence preceded development of verb relations and the encoding of interobject relations. Within verb relations, action events (action and locative action) preceded state events (locative state, state, and notice), and action preceded locative action for two of the children. The categories of possession and attribution were variable among the children and appeared to be later developments for Eric and Peter. Other categories developed after the basic verb relations and included specification of instruments, the dative, wh- questions and, for Kathryn and Gia, matrix verbs (verbs that took another verb as a complement) such as "gonna" and "wanna" that indicated their intention to do something (e.g. "I gonna build this").

The important developments after *MLU* reached 2.0 morphemes were that (1) the full constituent structure (subject-verb-complement) became productive in a single, longer sentence; (2) the same semantic-syntactic categories that occurred in separate utterances when *MLU* was less than 2.0 began to be combined in a single sentence; and (3) other kinds of complexity, such as grammatical morphemes on nouns and verbs and the use of conjunctions, began to appear. These three developments were not just added on to what the child already knew. Instead the three developments interacted with each other, with resulting variation in children's sentences with increasing complexity. These two factors of child language, variation and complexity, become more and more important with later development.

Although the children were essentially similar to one another in the sequence of development of the semantic-syntactic categories—language content—there were differences among them in the form of their early sentences. In addition to intersubject variation, there was also variation within a particular child (intrasubject variation) in the course of development—particularly as the children learned more complex linguistic forms and more complex language use as *MLU* increased beyond 2.0. However, such variation has its own regularity, and the regularity in both intersubject and intrasubject variation make variation an important aspect of child language and development. Such variation among children learning language normally is an important factor to consider when evaluating children who are learning language with difficulty. It will be discussed in the next chapter.

SUMMARY

The content and form of children's sentences are described in the period beginning with the transition from single-word utterances until the mean length of multiword utterances increases up to about 2.5 morphemes. The semantic content of these early sentences consists of information about relations among objects—in particular, relations that involve actions and locations and persons, including the child and others. Action relations are predominant in the content that is represented in early sentences, being encoded in sentences before children learn to encode states that do not involve action. There are many kinds of things that children could talk about but, in fact, the categories of content represented in early sentences is quite circumscribed. The content of early sentences is also similar among the several children whose language development has been described in a number of studies in the literature.

The syntactic structure of early sentences evolves in fairly well-defined steps. Many children pass through a transitional period between using single-word utterances and using syntax in which they say several single words in succession. Such words are not linguistically connected or combined, but they are semantically related to one another in that they refer separately to related aspects of an event. The occurrence of successive single-word utterances provides evidence that children have certain conceptual notions about the ways that objects are related, even though they are not, as yet, able to encode such conceptual relations in the form of sentences.

When children do begin to combine words in sentences, there are two kinds of structures that appear to evolve out of the different kinds of words that children have learned and used, first as single words and then as single words said in succession. In one kind of structure, relational words that have a particular meaning are combined with other, substantive words, and the meaning relation between the words in combination is the same as the meaning of the relational word. Such combinations are described as having linear syntactic relationship. Other combinations of words result in a meaning relation that is not the same as the meaning of the individual words. These combinations involve categories of nouns, or pronouns, in relation to verbs. Such categories are described in terms of sentence subject and sentence predicate, with hierarchical syntactic relationship.

The sequence in which four children learned to encode semantic-syntactic categories in sentences is presented. On the basis of the relative (proportional) frequency with which utterances occurred in the different categories, it appeared that reflexive object relations (such as existence, nonexistence, and recurrence) preceded the encoding of interobject relations (with verb relations) for the four children. The categories of attribution and possession were more variable among the children (as to where they occurred in the sequence), but appeared, in general, to be a later development.

SUGGESTED READINGS

In *Readings in Language Development*

Braine, M. D. S., The ontogeny of English phrase structure: The first phase. *Language, 39,* 1–13, 1963.

Bloom, L., Miller, P., and Hood, L., Variation and reduction as aspects of competence in language development. In A. Pick (Ed.), *Minnesota symposia on child psychology, Vol. 9.* Minneapolis: The University of Minnesota Press, 1975.

Bowerman, M., Structural relationships in children's utterances: Syntactic or semantic? In T. Moore (Ed.), *Cognitive development and the acquisition of language.* New York: Academic Press, 1973.

Other Readings

Antinucci, F., and Parisi, D., Early language acquisition: A model and some data. In C. A. Ferguson and D. I. Slobin (Eds.), *Studies of child language development.* New York: Holt, Rinehart & Winston, 1973.

Bloom, L., *Language development: Form and function in emerging grammars.* Cambridge, Mass.: The M.I.T. Press, 1970.

Bloom, L., Lightbown, P., and Hood, L., Structure and variation in child language. *Monographs of the Society for Research in Child Development, 40,* (Serial No. 160), 1975.

Braine, M. D. S., Children's first word combinations. *Monographs of the Society for Research in Child Development, 41,* (Serial No. 164), 1976.

Brown, R., *A first language, the early stages* (Part 1). Cambridge, Mass.: Harvard University Press, 1973.

Dore, J., Franklin, M., Miller, R., & Ramer, A. Transitional phenomena in early language acquistion. *Journal of Child Language, 3,* 13–28, 1976.

Schlesinger, I. M., Production of utterances and language acquisition. In D. I. Slobin (Ed.), *The ontogenesis of grammar.* New York: Academic Press, 1971.

Development involves change over time: a child's behavior at Time 1 is different from the child's behavior at Time 2, and that difference or variation in language is an index of development. Such developmental variation in children's language is a fact that can be pretty much taken for granted; the task of describing language development includes description of behaviors at different times *plus* description of the ways that a child's behaviors are different or vary from one time to another. For a long time in the study of language development, this kind of developmental variation was described in terms of the developmental *norms* obtained from large groups of different children, of different ages, in cross-sectional studies (e.g., see McCarthy, 1954a; Smith, 1933a,b, in *RLDev*; and Templin, 1957). Developmental norms indicate how, for example, 2-year-old children in general are different from 3-year-old children in general.

The emphasis in child language research shifted away from cross-sectional studies of large numbers of children and toward the intensive, longitudinal study of a small number of children in the 1960s, in order to describe developmental change or variation in the *same* child over time (e.g., see the papers in Bellugi and Brown, 1964; and Bloom, 1970a). The emphasis in child language research was on describing the regularities in the language development of individual children. The norms of development were often conceived of in terms of *universals* of child language, with the assumption that individual children—from the same language community as well as from different language communities—would be more like one another in their development than they would be different (see Slobin, 1973, in *RLDev*).

The search for regularities in child language has produced some impressive results: children are remarkably similar to one another in the kinds of words they use, in the semantics of their early sentences, in their use of word order in early syntax, in acquisition of morphology and complex syntax, and in the ways that they use language. The regularities that have been described have been based on large numbers of observations of children's language behavior. The few exceptions to these regularities that have been reported, for example, in the use of word order (Braine, 1976), seem to make the regularities that much more impressive by comparison.

On the other hand, it soon became apparent that there are also important differences among children. A major result of the original study of Eric, Gia, and Kathryn was the fact that Gia and Kathryn were more similar to one another in the form of their early sentences than either one was to Eric (Bloom, 1970a). When the fourth subject, Peter, was added to the study, it soon became apparent that Peter and Eric were more similar to each other than either one was to Gia and Kathryn (Bloom, Lightbown, and Hood, 1975). The same individual differences or variation in the forms of early sentences that was described for Eric, Gia, and Kathryn in Bloom (1970a) has since been replicated in studies of other individual children by Nelson (1975) and Ramer (1976).

There are other interactions in child language data that point to the existence of substantial variation among children in their phonological development (Ferguson and Farwell, 1975), their lexical development (Clark and Garnica, 1974), and in their social use of speech (Dore, 1973; and Nelson, 1973). Indeed, the variation that has been reported has prompted a tendency to turn away from the pursuit of universals and norms in language development and to concentrate even more on describing individual capacities. For example, in their study of phonological development, Ferguson and Farwell suggested that

In order to gain a deeper understanding of phonological development and hence of phonology in general, some linguists at the present stage of the art might be well advised to turn away from the fascination of writing rules of maximum generality and consciseness for whole languages, and undertake instead highly detailed analysis of the idiosyncratic paths which particular children follow in learning to pronounce their languages. (1975, p. 438)

But, even if some children reach the target language sooner and some children travel different routes to the same goal, all of the children for whom data have been reported appear to have converged on the adult model from the beginning. That is, all of the variation that has been observed is consistent with variation that is also systematic, in some respect, in the target language.

Two kinds of variation in child language have been described briefly so far: the differences in child language at different times or at different ages—developmental variation, and individual differences among different children—intersubject variation. Another result of the longitudinal study of Eric, Gia, Kathryn, and Peter has been the fact that the development of each of the children was not linear; it did not proceed in a straight line with addition of more and more of the facts of language to each child's knowledge of language. Instead of being linear and additive, their development was *synergistic* (Bloom, 1976). Different aspects of language, and different aspects of the children's cognitive development and the context, combined with one another to influence the children's language behavior, with the result that there was variability within individual children—intrasubject variation (Bloom, Miller, and Hood, 1975, in *RLDev*). Deviant language development is still another kind of variation; in order to understand language development that is deviant, it is necessary to understand the range of intersubject and intrasubject variation in the language of children who are developing normally.

The variation that has been observed in children's language has its own regularity—it is not the case that individual children are all unique and different from one another. Instead, there are patterns of regularity in the variation among different children. And there are patterns of regularity in intrasubject variation also, so that the variability as well as the consistencies in children's behaviors are orderly and predictable. If regularity in variation is not immediately apparent, it may be that too few behaviors have been observed, too few children have been observed, or the analysis of the behaviors and the indexes used to compare behaviors may not be sufficiently sensitive.

There are, then, these two facts of child language: *regularity* and *variation.* Regularity has to do with the consistencies among a child's behaviors or among the behaviors of different children. Variation has to do with differences—differences among individual children, and differences in the behaviors of a single child—and variation is, itself, systematic and regular. It is also true that there are no absolutes in child language; there are almost always exceptions and some inconsistencies—what Labov (1969) referred to as free or residual variation, and what has often been referred to as "mistakes" in performance.

Intersubject variation and intrasubject variation in normal language development have been described in children's earliest sentences, and intrasubject variation has also been described in connection with the subsequent development of linguistic complexity (among other factors). Variation in child language will be described in this chapter first, after having just described early sentences in Chapter V, and before going on to describe the continued development of complexity in later language learning.

INTERSUBJECT VARIATION

The regularities in the ways in which children are different from one another is important in understanding how children learn the forms for encoding language content. The variable use of pronouns and nouns in early sentences will be discussed here in detail. Variation in phonological development is described, for example, by Ferguson and Farwell (1975), and variation in the strategies children use in understanding different linguistic forms as described, for example, by Clark and Garnica (1974) will be discussed more briefly.

PRONOMINAL AND NOMINAL STRATEGIES FOR EARLY SENTENCES

In the study of structure and variation in early sentences reported in Bloom, Lightbown, and Hood (1975, in *RLDev*), there was a clear distinction between two different linguistic forms for encoding the same semantic relations or content in the early multiword utterances of different children. (Box VI-1). Two children encoded relations between categories of words to represent the notions of action, location, and possession. For example, they used two categories of words to represent the two locative constituents affected object (such as "cup," "ball," "car"), and place (such as "box," "outside," "table"); for example, "put ball(in)box" and "put cookie(on)table." In contrast, two other children used a constant form (as with the functional relations described earlier) to encode these same notions: for example, "this one," "that" or "it" represented the affected object (Box VI-2); "I" represented the agent in action and locative events; "there" or "here" represented the place in locative events; and "my" represented the possessor, for example, "I make it," "put this one right here," and "this go there." The use of pronominal forms was not due to limitations in vocabulary. All of the children used similar numbers of nouns, and the two children who used pronouns primarily in relation to verbs also used many nominal forms as single word

BOX VI-1 DIALOGUE WITH ALLISON, 22 MONTHS OLD, SHOWING THE PATTERN OF PREDOMINANTLY NOMINAL REFERENCE IN ENCODING VERB RELATIONS IN EARLY SENTENCES. *MLU* IS 1.73 (from Bloom, 1973, pp. 235–236)

(Allison reaching for cookie box in bag)	there cookie/
There cookie (Allison takes out box of cookies)	
(Allison trying to open box of cookies)	baby eat/baby eat/ cookie//
(Allison holding box out to Mommy)	baby eat cookie
(Mommy doesn't take box)	
Yes/ you can have some cookies	
(Allison holding out box to Mommy)	Mommy
What?	
	open/Mommy open
Mommy open?	
(Mommy taking box of cookies)	box
Box	
	cookie
Okay	
(Mommy opens box; giving it to Allison)	
There	
(Allison taking and opening box)	eat cookies
Mm mm	
(Allison getting cookie out of box)	get out
Get out	
(Allison starting to eat cookie)	chocolate chip cookie
Chocolate chip cookie?/I think that's just a chocolate cookie	
(Allison eats cookie)	
(Allison reaching in box)	get Mommy cookie
Get Mommy cookie?	
(Allison gets cookie for Mommy; gives it to Mommy)	
Oh thank you (Mommy takes a bite) Mm	

BOX VI-2 DIALOGUE WITH PETER, 24 MONTHS OLD, SHOWING THE PAT-
TERN OF PREDOMINANTLY PRONOMINAL REFERENCE IN EN-
CODING VERB RELATIONS IN EARLY SENTENCES. *MLU* IS 1.75

(Peter and Lois playing with a take-apart car; Peter handing screwdriver to Lois)	broke this/ broke this/ broke this
What should I do with it? **broke this?** **(Peter pointing to bolt on car)**	fix it
(Lois fixing car)	
Fix it/ oh/ like this? **(Peter watching)**	like this ↑
(Peter trying to fix it)	like this ↓ / like this ↓
Right/ oh/ should I fix this?	fix this ↑
Right there	fix it/ this/ fix it

---

utterances, and in other semantic-syntactic relations such as recurrence, negation and attribution.

It was concluded that the first group of children, Gia and Kathryn, used a strategy of nominal reference and learned grammar in terms of category relationships, for example, the category affected object, with the nouns "ball," "cookie," and so on, and the category place, with the nouns "box," "table," and the like. The second group of children, Eric and Peter, used pronominal reference and learned grammar in terms of the relations between constant (pronominal) and variable (verb) forms. The children who started out with nominal reference later learned the pronoun forms for the categories agent, possessor, place and, to a lesser extent, affected object. The children who started out using pronouns predominantly used more and more nouns as *MLU* increased. Examples of these developmental interactions can be seen in Bloom, Lightbown, and Hood (1975, in *RLDev*). When *MLU* was about 2.5, the four children were similar to one another: the affected object was most often nominal, and the agent, possessor, and place were most often pronominal; see also Box II-9 and Box VI-9.

The same tendency toward a dominant pattern of either pronominal or nominal encoding in children's early multiword utterances was apparent in data reported in the literature by Nelson (1973) and Huxley (1970). As a result, Nelson (1975) reexamined her earlier data and subsequently reported an analysis that substantiated both the variation among different children and the developmental nominal/pronominal shift that had been reported by Bloom, Lightbown, and Hood (1975). Nelson interpreted the finding differently and concluded that children using predominantly pronouns were learning syntactic frames, whereas children using predominantly nouns were learning semantic relations between words. However, both groups of children were representing the same semantic relations in their speech, so that the distinction made by Nelson is not altogether clear. Ramer (1976) observed the same pattern of nominal/pronominal variation in the early sentences of a group of eight children whom she observed when the *MLU* was less than 2.0. Ramer discussed the fact that the eight children were also divided according to sex, as were the children described in Bloom (1970a) and Bloom, Lightbown, and Hood (1975). Kathryn and Gia and the four girls described by Ramer used categorical, nominal reference; Peter and Eric and the four boys in Ramer's study used a system of pronominal reference. This correlation is necessarily tentative, based on only 12 subjects, and there are contradictions in the literature. The subject of Halliday's (1975) study was a boy, Nigel, and he began with a categorical, nominal system (personal communication, M. Halliday). The subject in a study by Allen (1973) was a girl, and she used pronouns primarily.

In other studies, the same variation and shift was observed in the early language of French-speaking children in Paris by Lightbown (1973), and in a study by Schiff (1976) of the language development of hearing children born to deaf parents. However, the finding was substantiated in the language of only three of the five children studied by Schiff; two of the children did not have either a nominal or pronominal pattern in their early sentences. It was also the case that these two children acquired language most slowly—the *MLU* of their speech was less than 2.0 for a period of more than 10 months, which may indicate that they were acquiring language with difficulty. If so, it is not possible to know whether the difficulty was the result of or the cause of the fact that a dominant pronominal or nominal pattern was not characteristic of their speech with *MLU* less than 2.0. Interestingly, two of the three children who did have a predominant pattern used the nominal strategy with categories of nouns occurring in relation to verbs, even though the speech of their parents was extremely distorted with *MLU* less than 2.5 morphemes. It had been expected that a pronominal system with more constant forms would have been the easier system for these children to learn, because of the poor intelligibility of their parents' speech. The effect of parent input on determining whether children will use predominantly nouns or pronouns in their early sentences is an open question.

Finally, it must be stressed that in none of the above studies was the nominal/pronominal distinction absolute; it was only relative. That is, the children started out with *primarily* pronouns or *primarily* nouns. Furthermore, the first pronominal system that children learned was extremely limited, with no contrasts for either person or deictic reference. Initially, agents and possessors were first person only; the use of the pronouns "this" or "that" and "here" or "there" was not strictly motivated by deictic constraints in the contexts (such as whether objects were near or far from the child). Also, it is important to emphasize that the nominal/pronominal variation that has been observed is a variation in *form* only. The children in these studies have been similar to one another in the *content* of their messages. This variation in linguistic form with consistency in semantic content is similar to observations made by Slobin (1973, in *RLDev*) of acquisition by children learning different languages.

INTRASUBJECT VARIATION

Children are limited to essentially two-word sentences in the beginning of their use of syntax. Certain verbs that are intransitive (e.g., "jump," "sing," "run") have only a single constituent relation with an actor noun and appear among the earliest verbs. In the data reported by Bowerman (1973a) such verbs predominated in the speech of the three children she described. However, in the speech of other children described by Bloom, Miller, and Hood (1975), Brown (1973), Park (1970), and others, more verbs occurred that were transitive, with more than one sentence constituent being theoretically possible, that is, the relations subject-verb-complement. Early sentences with transitive verbs include the separate constituent relations subject-verb ("Mommy read"), verb-object ("read book" or "put pencil"), verb-place ("put chair"), subject-object ("Mommy book"), or object-place ("sweater chair"). Kathryn and Gia said sentences with all of these separate relations when the *MLU* of their utterances was less than 1.5, but they did not productively combine all of the constituent relations that were theoretically possible in a single sentence. That is, although they said "Mommy read" and "read book" and "Mommy book," they did not say "Mommy read book." Moreover, when all four children were able to produce sentences with the full constituent structure, for example, "Daddy go outside," "this lamb go in here," and "I put toys in box" and their *MLU* approached 3.0, two-word sentences, with only two-constituent relations, continued to occur. Brown (1973) reported the same development in the three children he studied: even after three- and four-word sentences were fully productive in the children's more mature speech, two-word sentences continued to occur.

When children produce two-word sentences, or only part of the constituent structure of a sentence, the realization of constituent relations, as between a verb and any of one or more nouns that are theoretically possible, is systematic, not random. The fact that children are limited to utterances that are only one or two words long in the beginning of their use of syntax was attributed to a process of reduction in Bloom (1970a). That is, because Kathryn and Gia produced all of the constituent relations separately, it was proposed that one or more constituents was deleted from the full underlying sentence structure (subject-verb-complement) in the occurrence of two-word sentences. The concept of reduction was modified in Bloom, Miller, and Hood (1975, in *RLDev*). The purpose of that study was to account for the fact that two-constituent relations (as between verb and object, subject and object, or subject and verb) continued to occur in the children's speech even as *MLU* approached 3.0 and the full constituent structure subject-verb-complement was frequent. The shorter sentences did not occur because the children could not say longer sentences; three-, four-, five-word, and longer sentences were actually quite frequent.

In the study reported in Bloom, Miller, and Hood (1975, in *RLDev*), all of the children's sentences with action and locative action verb relations were examined in the period with *MLU* less than 3.0. Two-constituent utterances were compared with three-constituent utterances in order to find out if there were differences between longer and shorter sentences that might explain why the shorter sentences occurred when longer sentences were theoretically possible. Because three-constituent sentences were being compared with two-constituent sentences when the full structure was theoretically possible, the sentences with intransitive verbs and imperative sentences were not included in the analysis. With intransitive verbs, the full structure includes only one relation (e.g., "bear jump") and with imperative sentences, the sentence subject is deleted in the adult model (e.g., "eat your lunch"). Longer sentences were compared with shorter sentences for differences in (1) extent of grammatical complexity (e.g., verb and noun inflections; negation; and embedding such semantic-syntactic relations as attribution, possession and recurrence in verb phrases); (2) *newness* of verbs and use of nominal or pronominal forms; and (3) the kind of accompanying discourse that provided the linguistic context of the utterance (Box VI-3).

The results were that grammatical complexity, lexical factors, and discourse factors operated with different effects: they (presumably along with still other factors that were not examined) either made it easier for longer sentences to occur by facilitating the full constituent structure, or they constrained or reduced the probability of realizing one or another constituent relation so that shorter sentences occurred. That is, when two-constituent utterances were compared with three-constituent utterances, it was found that the same factor (such as complexity, or how much the child knew about a word, or whether a noun or a pronoun was used, or whether there were prior related utterances) could have different effects on the length of sentences. The same factor, such as knowledge of words, could make it

BOX VI-3 DIALOGUE WITH KATHRYN, 24 MONTHS OLD, SHOWING THE VARIABLE LENGTH OF SENTENCES WHEN *MLU* IS 2.83

(Kathryn pointing to Daddy's
birthday gifts on dining
table)   that's Daddy's birthday

   Oh that's for Daddy/
want to go get that?

                                ə want ə go get it

   You want to get those/
alright.
(Kathryn turning toward table)   ə want ə get ə those birthday

   That's for Daddy's
birthday, Honey
(Kathryn going toward table)   ə want get there

   I wonder what they are
(Kathryn at table)   look/get//get

(Kathryn takes present from
table)

easier to say the full constituent structure (when the child knew the words well and had already used the words for some time), or harder to say the full constituent structure (as when the child used a relatively new word) (Box VI-4).

Briefly, only certain complexity was a constraining factor. For example, negation, two-part verbs, and embedded relations occurred significantly more often with two-constituent relations than with three-constituent relations. Discourse was a facilitating factor in that three constituents occurred significantly more often in context with a previous two-constituent utterance by the child or a contingent prompt or query from an adult. Lexical knowledge was either constraining or facilitating: old words occurred in three-constituent (subject-verb-complement) relations, while new words occurred more often with two-constituent relations. The results were interpreted within a framework of probabilistic grammar, and it was concluded that the variable length of children's sentences reflected systematic constraints and was not a matter of "lawless optionality," as had been suggested previously by Brown (1973). It was concluded that language acquisition is not strictly an accretive process whereby children add structure to structure or add one feature to another. Instead, it appears that the linguistic induction that children make in the transition from single words to syntax is an induction about the grammatical structure of sentences, and variable performance is a reflection of the mutual influence of different aspects of the children's knowledge of grammar, lexicon, and discourse.

The constituent relations in the children's sentences were more or less likely to be deleted or, conversely, more or less likely to be represented or realized, depending on (1) whether other complexity (such as attribution and negation) was added to the verb relations, (2) how well the children knew the verbs and nouns, and (3) the effects of discourse. That is, children learn the constituent structure of sentences, but the probabilities of realizing the different constituents (actually saying the words) varies according to the kind of other complexity that occurs in the sentence, what the children know about the semantic and syntactic properties or functions of different lexical items, or whether other discourse either supports or interferes with the

---

BOX VI-4 MATRIX OF THE INTERACTIONS AMONG LEXICAL, COMPLEXITY, AND DISCOURSE FACTORS THAT EITHER ACTED TO CONSTRAIN OR FACILITATE THE CONSTITUENT STRUCTURE OF SENTENCES (from Bloom, Miller, and Hood 1975, p. 45)

	L↓	L↑	D↑
C↓	1	2.5	4.5
L↓		2.5	4.5
L↑			6

The interaction of the three factors: C (complexity), L (lexicon), and D (discourse) was ranked according to their effects on realizing the full constituent structure, with 1 being the most constraining (↓) and 6 being the most facilitating (↑) conditions; this information is presented in the matrix. The full constituent structure (subject-verb-complement) occurred most often with old (well-known) words (L↑) and discourse support (D↑), and least often with new words (L ↓) and added complexity (C ↓).

BOX VI-5 THE RELATIVE FREQUENCY OF CONSTITUENTS IN SENTENCES WITH FOUR CATEGORIES OF VERBS (from Bloom, Miller, and Hood, 1975, p. 17–20, in *RLDev*)

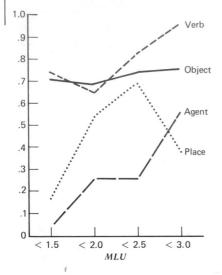

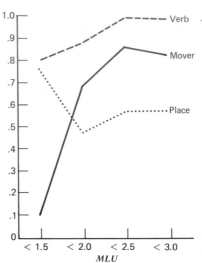

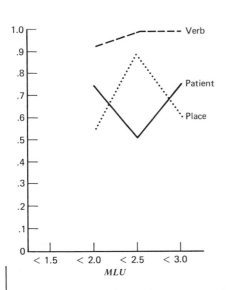

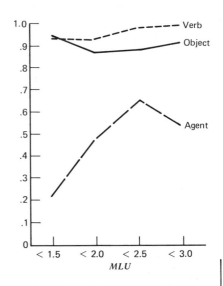

Apart from the verb, which was almost always the most frequent constituent, the constituent with the greatest probability of realization was most often the object that was affected by the action or was otherwise moved.

sentence. The probabilities of realizing constituents change, as the effects of such complexity, lexical factors, and discourse factors change in the course of development. In this view development from two-word sentences to three-word sentences consists of increased probability that sentence constituents are realized, instead of the addition of new rules or rule combinations in the grammar (Box VI-5).

As children continue to learn more and more about the structure of language, they learn new forms to represent content that has already been represented with simpler forms (see Bloom, 1970, in *RLDev*, regarding negation; and, more generally, Slobin, 1973, in *RLDev*; and Werner and Kaplan, 1963). They also learn new content and may either represent new content with old forms (as in the case of negation) or learn new forms as well. The continued development of structure—the development of more complex content/form relations—will be discussed in the rest of this chapter in terms of (1) subsystems of grammar such as grammatical morphemes, negation, and questions, and (2) complex syntax, or how children learn to coordinate their simpler sentences as clauses in more complex sentences.

LINGUISTIC COMPLEXITY AND RELATIONS WITHIN AND BETWEEN EVENTS

The study of the development of grammar, after the emergence of syntax, has been more fragmented than has the study of early sentences and single-word utterances. That is, there have been few attempts to describe children's later linguistic system as a whole by proposing a grammar of later child language in the way that grammars were proposed for early child language by, for example, Bloom (1970), Braine (1963, in *RLDev*), Bowerman (1973a), Brown (1973). Brown, Cazden, and Bellugi (1969) proposed a tentative grammar to account for the speech of one of their subjects, Adam, after the early stage of syntax in his speech. Gruber (1967) described the utterances of a somewhat older child in terms of topicalization, suggesting that utterances consisted largely of topic plus comment constructions. By and large, however, most accounts of the speech of older preschool children have focused on one or another of the particular subsystems of grammar, such as questions, negation, and grammatical morphemes.

There are two levels of content represented by the forms of grammatical subsystems and complex syntax: intraevent relations, or the relations within a single event, and interevent relations, or the relations between two or more events. Intraevent relations include aspects of an event such as whether or not the event is true (negation), the time that the event occurred, and the mood of the speaker toward the event. Such ideas about an event (intraevent relations) add information to the basic meaning of the message or, as Brown (1973) described it, provide the "tunings" or "modulations of meaning." The interevent relations between two events or conditions include, for example, coordinate, causality, conditionality, and sequential order. Again, such aspects of language content are relational concepts that are distinct from language topic; negation, mood, and time information can be added to whatever one is talking about (building houses, taking trips, cooking dinner, etc.). Causality, temporal, and coordinate relations are involved in riding bicycles, knitting sweaters, feeling sad, and the like. Thus, intra- and interevent relations are different from language topics; they are superordinate categories of language content, as are object knowledge and object relations which were discussed in Chapters I, III and IV. (see Box I-2). Causality, temporal, and coordinate relations as well as notions of negation, time, and mood are involved in action, locative, and possession events, and so forth.

INTRAEVENT RELATIONS

Four kinds of intraevent relations and the form of their encoding will be discussed in the acquisition of time language, grammatical morphemes, questions, and negation. Development in each of these consists of both learning new forms for representing content that had already been represented by earlier forms, or learning new content/form relations.

Time

When an event occurs is an invariant fact, but the information about when it occurs is variable relative to the time when the speaker chooses to speak about it, or the time when the listener hears about it. Thus, an event that happened at 3:30 p.m. on Wednesday, January 8, 1972 will be a recent event at 5:00 p.m. the same day, a less recent event the day after, and a long ago event in 1975. It may also have been an anticipated event before it happened at 3:00 on the same day, or earlier that morning or the day before. The time that an event occurs is represented in language in relation to the time of the occurrence of the message about the event.

One can speak of an event that is ongoing, that is, happening as one is talking about it or hearing it. One can speak of an event in the immediate past, having just happened, or in the distant past, having happened more than several minutes ago, several hours ago, several days ago, or several years ago (Box VI-6).

The semantic domain of *temporal* reference has intrigued philosophers and linguists for centuries. Psychologists have long been aware that the conceptual notion of nonpresent time and linguistic reference to past and future events are relatively late developments in the preschool years. For example, among the Wh- questions that children learn to ask, questions beginning with "when" are usually among the last to occur. It is not clear whether children learn time language first to talk about past or future events. On the one hand, one can have a conception of future events only in relation

---

BOX VI-6 DIALOGUE WITH KATHRYN, 33 MONTHS OLD, WITH EXAMPLES
OF EARLY TIME LANGUAGE

**(Kathryn had just woken up;
Mommy and Lois going into her
bedroom, Kathryn standing in
crib; she had not seen Lois
for 6 weeks)**

Hi

                                   hi

Hi Kathryn//
(Kathryn and Lois laughing)
**I haven't seen you in such a long
time**

                                 you came/ you come alot of days

I do come alot___

                                 you come again and again and again!

(Lois and Mommy laughing)

                                 **you come ə lots of weeks!/
again and again and again!**

(Lois and Mommy laughing)
I didn't come last week

                                 so you came this week

Right

---

to events already experienced. The ability to plan for and anticipate events
that are yet to be depends in a fairly obvious way on the memory or mental
organization of what one has already seen or done. On the other hand, 2-
year-old children typically comment on their *intentions*, that is, on what they
are about to do, more often than on what they have just done, with forms such
as "wanna," "gonna," and "have to" (Bloom, Lightbown, and Hood, 1975).
Cromer (1968) reported that the children studied by Roger Brown and his
colleagues made reference to future time more often than to past time in the
age range from 2 to 5 years. Other studies of the comprehension of temporal
reference have offered conflicting evidence. In a study of temporal decenter-
ing by Cromer (1971), subjects did better in *comprehending* past tense
sentences than future tense sentences, which is in essential agreement with
the findings of Clark's (1971) study of comprehension of "before" and "after."

The terms "before" and "after" are of particular interest because they
encode sequential time and are also linguistically polar opposites. In Clark's
experiments, 3- and 4-year-old children were more often correct in responding to items with "before" that to items with "after." Her interpretation of this

finding was not very different from the interpretation offered by Donaldson and Wales (1970) of results of their study of "more" and "less." Clark concluded that children learn the semantic dimension of time, and that the first binary division in the dimension has to do with plus prior and minus prior events. As with the studies of "more" and "less" and "same" and "different," children apparently learn the semantically positive terms, that is, "more," "same," and "before" first, and they *then* learn the semantically negative terms "less," "different," and "after."

Bever (1970) also found that subjects were better able to understand sentences with "before" instead of "after" when the terms preceded a subordinate clause. Bever concluded that the task was easiest for 4-year-old children when the order of mention corresponded to the order of occurrence, and that the first event in a series was psychologically more salient: both (1) "We sang songs, before we went to bed," and (2) "After we sang songs, we went to bed" were easier than (3) "Before we went to bed, we sang songs," or (4) "We went to bed after we sang songs." Amidon and Carey (1972) did not find a difference in comprehension of sentences with "before" and "after" by 5-year-old children. They suggested that difficulty in comprehension was due to syntactic instead of semantic complexity, depending on the location of the subordinate clause: items (1) and (4) were easier than items (2) and (3) because the subordinate clause followed the main clause (see also Clark, 1970 and 1971).

Most recently, Harner (1975, 1976) studied 2- to 4-year-old children's understanding of the notions of time in relation to the understanding of time language (verb tense and the terms "before," "after," "yesterday," and "tomorrow"). She found that (1) in linguistic reference to immediate past or future action, verb tense was better understood than "before" (*future* reference, e.g., "The girl before she jumps") and "after" (*past* reference, e.g., "The girl after she has jumped"); (2) in linguistic reference to more *remote* times, both past verb tense and "after" having future reference (e.g., "Toys for after this day") were understood better than future verb tense and "before" having past reference (e.g., "Toys from before this day"); and (3) 2-year-old children understood "yesterday" better than "tomorrow." There was, then, considerable variability in understanding linguistic reference to past and future events, depending on the particular linguistic form and the situation in which it was used. The terms "before" and "after" were used to refer to both past and future time, and each was better understood when used to refer to the next event or action following the present. Harner suggested that *both* "before" and "after" are better understood in the context of future time and action, instead of past time or action, and they are not initially understood as relationally ordered events with respect to each other.

Certain relational terms ("before-after," "more-less," "same-different," "inside-outside," etc.) have constant meanings, but their referential meanings shift with respect to the contexts in which they are used. Thus, for example, "before" means prior and "after" means subsequent in the ordering of two events or the aspects of a particular event; "more" means larger in amount and "less" means smaller in amount; "inside" means contained within a space and "outside" means excluded from a space. However, the same event A can occur both "before" an event B and "after" an event C; the same quantity X can be described (or referred to) as both "more" than another quantity Y and "less" than a third quantity Z; the same object can be referred to as both "inside" a building but "outside" a particular room. Such shifting reference no doubt presents a problem for children in learning the meaning of such words and presents no less a problem for a theoretical account of the acquisition of such meanings.

By far, the predominant linguistic forms that children learn when they begin to encode notions of time in their speech are the grammatical morphemes that are inflectional endings on verbs.

Grammatical Morphemes

Brown's account (1973) of the development of morpheme forms for the "modulation of meaning" expanded on the earlier study by Cazden (1968), that had described the noun and verb inflections in the speech of Brown's original three subjects, Adam, Eve, and Sarah. However, Brown compared these findings with other reports in the literature on the morphological development of children in the same age range (e.g., deVilliers and deVilliers, 1973, in *RLDev*; and Menyuk, 1969), and the result appears to be a fairly definitive account. He reported that the emergence of grammatical morphemes added to and intervening between the nouns and verbs in children's speech (e.g., "baby's meat," "rid*ing* trike") begins when *MLU* is between 2.0 and 2.5 morphemes. He pointed out that the "modulations" and "tunings" of meaning by grammatical morphemes cannot exist apart from the things and processes that are tuned; -*s* and -*ing* are meaningless by themselves. But it is still possible to talk about the things and processes without modulations, which is probably one reason why nouns and verbs such as "baby meat" and "ride trike" occur first in children's utterances, before they are modulated by the grammatical morphemes such as -*s* and -*ing*.

The grammatical morphemes that children begin to acquire in the beginning of the third year include new forms for encoding locative relations ("in" and "on") and the possessive inflection -*s* ("Daddy's coat"), both of which had been represented already by word order in the two- and three-word sentences. The new forms with new content that begin to be acquired include the plural inflection -*s* on nouns ("cats," "glasses," "dogs") and the articles "a" and "the." Perhaps most important is the beginning acquisition of the system of verb inflections and auxiliary verbs that indicate the time relations between the happening of an event and the occurrence of the utterance that talks about the event (Box VI-7).

Brown concluded that the various grammatical morphemes developed in a particular order over a period of 2 to 3 years. Although the rate of development was widely variant, this order appeared to be relatively constant among different children in different studies, as follows: present progressive, "in" and "on," plural, irregular past, possessive, uncontracted copula, and contracted auxiliary. The grammatical morphemes that were new forms to introduce new content into the children's speech—the verb endings and plural -s—predominated toward the end of the sequence. The grammatical morphemes that were new forms to represent content that was already being expressed—such as "in" and "on" and possessive -s—appeared toward the beginning of the sequence (Box VI-8).

BOX VI-7 DIALOGUE WITH KATHRYN, 33 MONTHS, THAT SHOWS HER BEGINNING ACQUISITION OF VERB INFLECTIONS AND AUXILIARY VERBS (the relevant forms are underlined)

I'm too hot

O.K.
(Kathryn taking off her sweater)

I's/I'm ə got too hot ___/I got too hot/ oh

I was sweating with that heat

I was sweating

if I got too hot I sweat

I got too ___/ I sweats

You sweat?

yes/ did you sweat?

No

why didn't you?

Because I wasn't wearing another sweater

oh/ why?

Because I just have one sweater on (Kathryn pointing to her own sweater)

well I have just two like this/ two sweaters

BOX VI-8 TABLE PRESENTING THE ORDER OF ACQUISITION OF 14 GRAM-
MATICAL MORPHEMES BY THE THREE CHILDREN, ADAM, EVE,
AND SARAH (from Brown, 1973, p. 271)

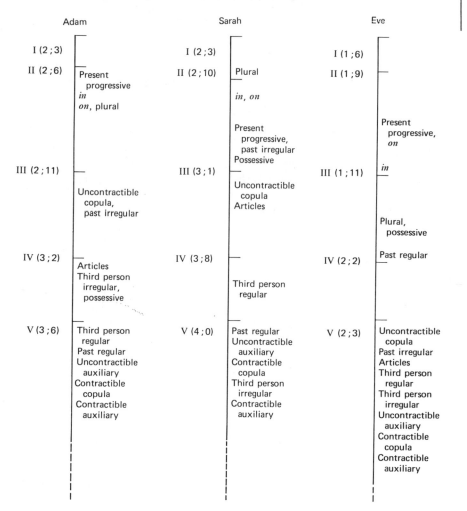

	Adam	Sarah	Eve
	I (2 ; 3)	I (2 ; 3)	I (1 ; 6)
	II (2 ; 6) Present progressive *in* *on*, plural	II (2 ; 10) Plural *in, on*	II (1 ; 9)

		Present
		  progressive,
		  past irregular
		Possessive
			Present
			  progressive,
			  on

	III (2 ; 11)
	Uncontractible
	  copula,
	  past irregular
		III (3 ; 1)
		Uncontractible
		  copula
		Articles
			III (1 ; 11) *in*

			Plural, possessive

	IV (3 ; 2)
	Articles
	Third person
	  irregular,
	  possessive
		IV (3 ; 8)
		Third person
		  regular
			IV (2 ; 2) Past regular

	V (3 ; 6)
	Third person
	  regular
	Past regular
	Uncontractible
	  auxiliary
	Contractible
	  copula
	Contractible
	  auxiliary
		V (4 ; 0)
		Past regular
		Uncontractible
		  auxiliary
		Contractible
		  copula
		Third person
		  irregular
		Contractible
		  auxiliary
			V (2 ; 3)
			Uncontractible
			  copula
			Past irregular
			Articles
			Third person
			  regular
			Third person
			  irregular
			Uncontractible
			  auxiliary
			Contractible
			  copula
			Contractible
			  auxiliary

The sequence of development of these grammatical morphemes for Adam,
Sarah, and Eve at five stages (Roman numerals) that were determined
according to *MLU* is shown here. The children's ages are given in parentheses at each stage. This sequence was also obtained in a later cross-sectional
study of the speech of 20 children by deVilliers and deVilliers (1973, in
RLDev).

In addition to encoding ideas about time, location, possession, and plurality, there are grammatical morphemes that are part of the verb auxiliary and represent or encode something about the mood of the speaker toward the event or toward the utterance about the event.

Mood

The attitudes that people have toward what they are saying can be represented in different ways, not only linguistically with grammatical devices such as questions versus statements or, for example, modal forms such as "should" or "must," but also with facial expression, body posture, and tone of voice. Lyons (1968, pp. 307–309) described three major linguistic modalities: the "unmarked" declarative (statements), the imperative (directions and commands), and the interrogative (questions). In their speech, children learn to use words and sentences that function to make statements, issue commands, and ask questions before they learn the different syntax forms that mark the distinctions among declarative, imperative, and interrogative utterances (see Chapter VII).

In addition to the major modalities, Lyons (1968) distinguished among three "scales" of modality that are relevant to the attitudes of the speaker. There is the scale of wish and intention, the scale of necessity and obligation, and the scale of certainty and possibility. These three scales obviously intersect with the major declarative, imperative, and interrogative modalities in communicating information about speakers' attitudes toward what they are saying. The first scale of wish and intention described by Lyons is also the first to be formally marked by modal forms in children's speech (with the catenatives "wanna" and "gonna") (Box VI-9). The third scale of certainty and possibility is marked first with the negative form "can't" and, subsequently, "can" and "can't" are used in contrasting situations (Bellugi, 1967; and Bloom, 1970a) (Box VI-10). The second scale of necessity and obligation is the last to be marked in children's speech. However, all three scales of attitude are represented or somehow indicated in what children say—probably from the very beginning of their efforts to communicate. One way or another, children indicate their intentions, wishes, and desires, a sense of necessity (if not obligation), and a sense of certainty or uncertainty. They gradually learn the different linguistic forms for such functions as they learn more about the structure of the modal system and forms of questions. Children learn the different syntactic forms of questions as they learn how to ask questions, as they learn in what kinds of situations to use different kinds of questions according to their needs in the situation and their attitude toward the listener.

Learning questions, perhaps more than any other grammatical subsystem, involves the intersection of content/form/use. Most child language studies, until recently, have described the form of children's questions, and these

BOX VI-9 DIALOGUE WITH ALLISON, 28 MONTHS OLD, SHOWING USE OF
CATENATIVE FORMS OF MOOD: WISH OR INTENTION (the relevant forms are underlined)

(Allison walks to Mommy, reaching up
for mike on Mommy's neck)

I **want** try that · that necklace

(Mommy taking mike off)
You want to try this
necklace? Okay
(Mommy putting mike on Allison)
You know what this is called?

something

See, it's a microphone/ there
(Allison taking mike off)
You don't want it?

I don't want it

(Mommy taking back mike)

no/
you want it on/ you have it on

How about a snack?/ how about a
snack?
(Allison climbing up on big chair)

I'm **gonna** sit on here

(Allison turning around, sitting up)

may I↑/ I **wanna** sit on here

You wanna sit on here?/
okay.
(Mommy looking in bag)
What do we have for the snack?

gonna have juice ə___

What?

cookies

What would you like to have?

apple juice

Apple juice/ all right.

oh I **don't want** drink it out cup/
ə **want** drink it out can

Oh, what did I say about that?
What did I say about drinking
it out of the can?
(Allison pointing, reaching to can on
table)
You want it?

Mommy I want it

(Allison pointing to can)
Aw, well, that's not such a good
idea honey.

I **want** drink it out can

This dialogue also shows Allison's use of pronominal forms in relation to
verbs, at a later point after the pronominal/nominal shift in expressing verb
relations; compare to Box VI-1.

BOX VI-10 DIALOGUE WITH ALLISON, 34 MONTHS OLD, TO SHOW USE OF FORMS OF MOOD IN THE THIRD SCALE OF CERTAINTY AND POSSIBILITY

(A baby and his father had just wandered into the TV studio)
  Maybe he'd like to see the truck?
(The baby touches the bus)
  He just decided which one he'd like to see
(Allison walking to baby)

(Allison picking up truck)
  Okay
(Allison putting truck down by the baby)
(Allison moving back to Mommy)

  Yes, I think he likes the truck.

he·he <u>may</u> want to play with the truck

maybe he'll play with the truck
he <u>can</u> play with the truck/
I <u>think</u> he'll play with the truck ↑

---

studies will be reviewed briefly. Other aspects of the context and use of questions will be taken up in Chapter VII.

Questions

Brown (1968, in *RLDev*) described the development of the form of Wh- questions from approximately 2 to 4 years of age. Brown was concerned primarily with tracing children's acquisition of the transformational rules that relate question forms to the corresponding affirmative statements that appear earlier in children's speech. He reported a developmental sequence in which an intervening syntactic structure occurred in the transition between a statement, such as "John will read the book," and a question, such as "What will John do?" or "What will John read?" The last two questions are acceptable in the adult model; that is, they are derived from the set of transformational rules that account for such forms in adult speech. Before the children in Brown's study produced questions such as these, in which (1) the subject "John" and the auxiliary verb "will" are *transposed*, as ". . . will John read?" and ". . . will John do?" , and (2) the Wh- word is *preposed*, as "What will John do?" and "What will John read?", they produced a form of question that occurs only in child language. The children's questions, "What John will do?," "What John will read?," "Why he play little tune?," and "Why not you see any?" include a preposed Wh- word, without transposing the subject and auxiliary verb (see Box II-15).

In this intervening stage in the development of question forms, the children were only preposing the Wh- words, "what," "why," "why not," and so on; they were not transposing the subject and the verbal auxiliary. Thus, in the course of development, the children seemed to learn and apply a preposing operation before a transposing operation. Both operations are basic in the adult system, so that the evidence indicated that the children were learning the grammatical structures that underlie adult Wh- questions, as described in the then current accounts of transformational grammar. However, there was evidently a systematic constraint on learning the operations that Wh- questions involve; the children preposed before they transposed. Brown offered several explanations of the sequence in learning how to ask Wh- questions that depended, primarily, on recurrent discourse patterns between mother and child.

Brown and Hanlon (1970) traced the development of tag and truncated questions in the speech of the same three children. They reported that such forms occurred in the children's speech in a particular order. Truncated answers ("he did" and "he didn't") occurred first and were frequent, appearing before truncated affirmative questions ("did he?"). Tag questions, for example, "We didn't have a ball, *did we*?" and "We had a ball, *didn't we*?" appeared later. In the order of emergence of syntactic forms in the children's speech, truncated and tag forms appeared after declarative, question, and negative sentences. The order of progression in Brown and Hanlon's terms, according to the adult grammar, is from "derivationally simple" constructions to those that are "derivationally complex", indicating that at least for some developmental sequences, complexity in adult gram- mar can predict order of emergence of structures or the relative difficulty with which they are learned.

Ervin-Tripp (1970) reported the sequence in which five children responded to different question forms addressed to them after the age of about 21 months; "where," "what," "whose," and "who" were responded to in appar- ently that sequence and before "why," "how," and "when." In a study by Soderbergh (1974), it was observed that the child being studied began to ask "what" questions herself, only after she was able to respond to "what" questions when others asked them. Hood (1977) observed eight children and described the development of the expression of causal relations. She found that the children first expressed causal relations in their own state- ments, before they responded appropriately to "why" questions. Except for a single child who asked "why?" as a single word question, the children did not ask "why" questions until after they were able to answer "why" questions appropriately. The result of Hood's analysis of the development of "why" questions complements the description of the development of tag questions that was reported by Brown and Hanlon and the description of the development of "what" questions that was reported by Soderbergh. It appears that children learn to ask particular kinds of questions only after they learn to respond to questions of the same kind, and they do not learn to ask and answer questions in general.

The investigations that have been restricted to describing the superficial syntactic form of children's questions and that have described development in terms of the changes in form over time have ignored the important differences among the conditions or states of affairs that can exist when individuals ask questions and make statements. Such differential, nonlinguistic conditions for making statements and asking different forms of questions is discussed in the description of the development of language use in Chapter VII.

Negation

Most of the events that people talk about are true—actual things that exist or happen, that persons can see, touch, hear, feel, and think about. Thus, most language consists of assertions that are, in effect, affirmations or statements of truth. Such affirmative statements are unmarked—that is, it is not necessary to mark a statement that is true, for instance, by saying "yes" as in "I want more milk, yes" or "Yes, that's a red ball," unless someone has questioned whether or not the event is true. If there is no reason to question the truth of an event (such as whether someone wants more milk, or a red ball exists), then there is no reason to say that the event is true—its truth is presumed or taken for granted.

Children start out talking about and understanding about true events—they understand and talk about objects that do exist and relationships that do exist, do occur, or might occur. However, as already discussed, a critical aspect of the environment that contributes to children's learning about the permanence or truth of objects and events is *change*—change that causes objects to disappear and events not to occur. When the content of language has to do with such events that do not exist or do not occur, then the language is marked for negation with some form of negation, such as "no," "not," or with the prefixes -*un, -dis,* and so on.

There are several kinds of negative events represented in children's language, and these have been identified in the meanings of early single words and subsequent sentences, and in different languages that have been studied developmentally, for example, French (de Boysson-Bardies, 1972), Italian (Volterra, 1971), German (Park, 1974), and Japanese (McNeill and McNeill, 1968). These categories of negation were described originally in children's sentences in Bloom (1970a), and have since been identified in children's single-word utterances by Belkin (1975). The categories of negation are nonexistence/disappearance, nonoccurrence, cessation, rejection, prohibition, and denial. All of them are represented in children's speech by single words, the word "no" most often, but their syntactic expression develops sequentially. The three categories of nonexistence, rejection, and denial appeared in sentences in that order in the development of the English-speaking children studied by Bloom.

Nonexistence and *disappearance* have already been discussed as reflexive object relations. Their development was parallel (coming in at about the same time) in the children studied by Bloom, Lightbown, and Hood (1975) and by Belkin (1975).

Related to the category nonexistence (and not distinguished in the analysis in Bloom, 1970a) are the negation categories involving movement or action events: *nonoccurrence,* when an action event does not occur as, for example:

(Kathryn, unable to turn a plastic screw
in washer)   no turn
(Gia, unable to fit a lamb into a block)   I can't put ə lamb in

and *cessation,* when a movement or action stops.

Rejection is a category of events in which some object or action or happening either exists in the context or is imminent or about to exist in the context, and is opposed by the child. Certain rejection events are things that the child does not want to do or to have, and the rejection may be paraphrased as "I don't want . . .," as in the following examples:

(Kathryn pushing away a worn piece of soap
in the bathtub, wanting to be washed with
new pink soap)   no dirty soap
(Gia pushing away lavaliere microphone)   I don't ə microphone.

Rejection events also included things that the child did not want others to do, and such rejection of what others are doing or about to do may be paraphrased as "Don't . . ." (the negative imperative), for example:

(Eric to Mommy after using the toilet)   no flush
(Gia taking Lois' book from the toy bag)   no take home

This difference between events that signaled rejection appeared also as a difference among Eric, Gia, and Kathryn in their acquisition of syntactic negation (described in Bloom, 1970a). Gia and Eric were similar to each other in that both learned the function and structure of the negative imperative first—rejecting an event that involved someone else as actor-agent, as in "no flush" and "no take home." In contrast, Kathryn learned syntactic expression of rejection first to express negation of her own desire or wish to have or do something, where she was the actor-agent, as in "no dirty soap."

Prohibition is a category related to rejection in that it involves the child's opposition to something someone else is doing or intends to do. Prohibition carried the added information that the opposed act is forbidden by authority. Children's earliest prohibitions are usually distant echoes of what they have probably heard their parents say to them (Belkin, 1975), such as "Don't play with matches." Except for these early stereotype prohibitions, the category develops later and is less frequent than events in the category of rejection.

Denial was the last category to become syntactically productive in the development of Kathryn, Eric, and Gia, described in Bloom (1970a), but the children studied by Belkin (1975) expressed denial in the single-word utterance period (with "no"). In denial events, children are negating the truth of a statement made by someone else, and children most often deny the truth about the identity of an object, for example,

(Mommy offering car to Kathryn) There's the truck

.   no truck

(Lois offering Kathryn yellow disc on a plate) Here's some scrambled egg

that not scramble

Syntactic denial probably appears in children's sentences after the other categories because of two reasons: it entails the children's holding two things in mind at the same time—the affirmative alternative (in the "no truck" example, the fact that the object Mommy held out to Kathryn was a car), and the false statement to be denied (McNeill and McNeill, 1968). But, also, denial is contingent on a statement from someone else—a more complex situation for formulating language than one in which the semantic intention originates within the child (see Chapter VIII). In sum, there was a clear progression in the development of different semantic categories of negation in the period from 19 to about 26 months of age in the speech of Kathryn, Eric, and Gia. All of the children used "no" as a single word to express rejection of something that they did not want to have or do. At the same time, however, multiword utterances with a negative marker, such as "no" or "no more", were comments on the disappearance, nonexistence, or nonoccurrence of an object or event that was somehow expected; for example, Kathryn said "no pocket" when there was no pocket in her mother's skirt (nonexistence), and Eric said "no more noise" when the vacuum cleaner was turned off (disappearance). Subsequently, after the productive syntactic expression of nonexistence, the children began to use multiword utterances with "no" to express rejection, for example, "no dirty soap" as Kathryn pushed away a sliver of worn soap, wanting to be washed with a new bar of pink soap. The third semantic category that developed after nonexistence and rejection was denial, for example, "no truck" (meaning "that's not a truck").

The three semantic categories appeared in the children's sentences in the order nonexistence, rejection, and denial, and there was a corresponding development in the form of their syntactic representation. Expression of nonexistence was elaborated in complexity, with variation in the form of the negative marker including "can't," "doesn't," and "not," before the elaboration of the expression of rejection. The form of utterances that signaled rejection increased in complexity before utterances expressing denial increased in complexity. A similar sequence of development was observed by McNeill and McNeill (1968) in the language of a Japanese-speaking child, which is particularly interesting inasmuch as the different semantic categories are marked in Japanese by particular grammatical morphemes.

In the study of negation by Bellugi (Bellugi, 1967; and Klima and Bellugi, 1966), three stages in the development of the syntactic form of children's negative utterances were described. In the first stage, Bellugi proposed that negation consisted of attaching a negative marker (such as "no" or "not") outside of a simple sentence, for example, "no drop mitten," or "no the sun shining." In the second stage, the negative marker appeared inside of the sentence, for example, "he no bite you." In the third stage, the negative sentences approximated the transformationally derived negative sentences in the adult model, for example, "Paul can't have one."

When both content and form were taken into account and the meaning relation between the negative marker and the rest of the utterance was considered in the analysis in Bloom (1970, in *RLDev*), it turned out that sentences in which "no" appeared before the sentence subject were not negative sentences at all. Instead, "no" before a sentence was anaphoric in relating back to something else either said or implied, and the sentence itself was actually an affirmative statement. Although the anaphoric "no" would be marked by a pause in adult speech, there was not a corresponding pause in the children's utterances. For example, "no Lois do it" occurred without pause between "no" and "Lois do it" and asserted that Lois was to connect the train cars. The "no" negated an alternative action; Kathryn had tried to connect the cars of the train, could not, and gave them to Lois, saying, "no Lois do it."

It was not the case, then, that the first negative sentences in the children's speech consisted of a negative marker attached outside of a sentence. When the negative marker appeared *outside* of a sentence (i.e., before the sentence subject), the sentence was actually affirmative (e.g., "Lois do it,").

When the negative marker occurred in a negative sentence, it occurred before the predicate, and the sentence did not ordinarily include a subject. Such truly negative sentences were generally among the most primitive sentences to occur in the children's speech, usually consisting of either an object noun or a verb. As discussed earlier in connection with variability in sentence length, there appeared to be a complexity limit on the children's sentences. The operation of negation within a sentence caused complexity and resulted in reduction, so that sentence subjects did not occur (Bloom, Miller, and Hood, 1975, in *RLDev*). Subsequently, in the further development of syntactic negation, when sentence subjects did occur in negative sentences, they preceded the negative marker, which appeared within the sentence before the verb.

In sum, the form of negation in the children's sentences was prepredicate in the Bloom analysis, as it is in the adult model as well (see Klima, 1964), and not presentence, as in the Bellugi analysis. Thus, negative sentences in the speech of the children described in Bloom (1970), although primitive, were more like the adult model than they were different. Similar results have also been reported in descriptions of the developmental syntax and semantics of negation in Italian (Volterra, 1971) and French (de Boysson-Bardies, 1972). The acquisition of the grammatical subsystem of negation provides one of the clearest cases of form following function in language development. Children learn new syntactic forms of negation to encode the content that they have already expressed in their speech with simpler forms (see Bloom, 1970, for discussion).

In the later development of more complex sentence relations, there is the same kind of relationship between form and function, for example, where two independent clauses that had previously occurred as separate sentences are conjoined with "and" and no new meaning or content is introduced. However, there is also the acquisition of new forms that do introduce new content. For example, when two clauses are combined in the sentence "Bend the man so he can sit," the relational meaning that results is causality, which is not coded by either of the clauses separately but only by their combination with each other and the connective form "so." These two aspects of later linguistic development—the learning of more complex linguistic form to represent content that children are already talking about with simpler forms, and the learning of more complex content/form relations—will be taken up in the next section.

EVENT RELATIONS AND COMPLEX SYNTAX

After *MLU* increases beyond 2.0, children begin to combine more than one semantic-syntactic relation in a single sentence and, by the time *MLU* increases beyond 3.0, children begin to use conjunctions and relative pronouns regularly for combining sentences as clauses in longer sentences.

At first, when *MLU* approaches 2.0, complexity is introduced when a semantic-syntactic relation such as recurrence, possession or attribution is embedded in verb relations, and sentences like "eat more egg," "that my teddy bear," and "put big balloon right here" appear. Sometime between 2 and 3 years of age, children begin to learn how to express more than one thought in a sentence with rules of grammar for conjoining and embedding two or more clauses in longer, complex sentences. There are several kinds of meaning relations expressed when children begin to combine two clauses, first as successive sentences and eventually as a single, complex sentence. Both the number of different kinds of clausal relations and the number of sentences with related clauses increase developmentally, beginning when *MLU* is about 3.0 morphemes (Box VI-11).

Most studies of complex sentences have described only the form of children's sentences. According to Limber (1973), the first type of complex construction he observed in the speech of children from approximately 18 months to 3 years of age was object complements, followed by relative

---

BOX VI-11 DIALOGUE WITH KATHRYN, 33 MONTHS OLD, WITH EXAMPLES OF COMPLEX SENTENCES

(Kathryn looking under her skirt)	I just have see
(Starting to get up) Why?	I'm gonna get some rubber pants
	because then I won't go tinkle in these pants so I'll get some rubber pants
Why?/ do you think you'll need them?	yes
Cause you'll know if you wanta go tinkling	but if I go tinkle in my pants·I have to get some of those rubber pants
Alright (Kathryn getting up)	okay
(Kathryn leaving living room)	I'll go get ə rubber ___/ I'll be right back
(Going into her bedroom)	the door is open so I can get in
(Coming back with them)	see I got some/ I found some

clauses and then coordinate and subordinate sentences with conjunctions. Other studies (e.g., Menyuk, 1969) have described the forms of the complex sentences of older preschool and school-age children.

Connective Forms

The conjunction "and" is the first connective form that children use according to the studies of English-speaking children reported by Beilin (1975), Bohn (1914), Clark (1970), Hood, Lahey, Lifter, and Bloom (1978), Jacobsen (1974), and Limber (1973), and studies of children learning languages other than English, for example, Swedish (Johansson and Sjölin, 1975), Italian (Clancy, 1974), and German (Werner and Kaplan, 1963.) Information concerning conjunctions other than "and" is much more limited and, for the most part, is based on data from children over 3 years of age, for example, Clark (1970) and Menyuk (1969).

The sequence in which the different connective forms were acquired by Eric, Gia, Kathryn, and Peter was reported in Hood, Lahey, Lifter, and Bloom (1977). The conjunction "and" was the first and most frequent connective the children used, which is consistent with observations in other studies. The sequence in which the other connectives appeared after "and" in the children's sentences from 2 to 3 years of age was as follows: "because," "what," "when," "but," "that," "if," and "so." This *sequence* of development in the period from 2 to 3 years of age is essentially similar to the relative *frequency* of different connectives that have been reported by other investigators who have observed 3- and 4-year-old children. Clark (1970) described the speech of 3½-year-old children and reported that "and," "and so," and "then" were more frequent than "when" and "because," which were, in turn, more frequent than "if." Chambaz, Leroy, and Messeant (1975) observed French-speaking children aged 3 to 6 years and reported that "parce que" ("because") was more frequent than "quand" ("when"). Menyuk (1969) reported that "because" was used more frequently than "so" and "if" by first-grade children. Thus, the sequence of acquisition of clausal connectives in the language development of Eric, Gia, Kathryn, and Peter in the year from 2 to 3 years of age, reflected the relative frequency with which the same connectives are reportedly used by older children.

Content Relations Between Clauses

The connective forms (conjunctions, relative pronouns and wh- adverbs) in the children's sentences were used to encode interevent relations and intraevent relations (as reported in Hood, Lahey, Lifter, and Bloom, 1977). With interevent relations there was a focus on two events, and with intraevent relations there was a focus on one event (with *event* defined simply as a happening or state of being). There were several kinds of intraevent and interevent relations, and these are represented in Box VI-12 as categories of content (the semantic relations between clauses.)

There were two kinds of interevent relations. In one type, *coordinate relations,* utterances referred to events and/or states that were bound together in space and/or time; each clause was meaningful by itself and independent of the other; and the two clauses together did not create a meaning that was different from the meaning of each of the clauses separately. Sometimes the same verb was used in both clauses or, if a second verb was not actually mentioned, the same verb as in the first clause was implied, for example:

(Peter pointing to and
touching furniture in doll
house)   that's full *and* that's full too

(Kathryn and Lois
sitting on floor)   I'm sitting here *and* you can sit
                                            there and rest

(Gia referring to two
different animals)   I put this on the train *and* this
                                            lamb on the train

In other coordinate sentences, there were different verbs in the two clauses, for example:

(Eric pointing to lamb)   that one is eating *and* now he's
                                            lying down

(Peter putting car in
bag)   I'm gonna put this away/ *then*
                                            I'm gonna ride my bike

(Kathryn and Lois playing
with bus)   now you drive *and* I be waiting
                                            over here

In the second kind of interevent relation, *superordinate,* the combination of the two clauses did result in a new meaning. There were essentially three kinds of new superordinant meanings. One was *causality,* where utterances expressed a dependency relation between two events and/or states, most often with one clause referring to an intended or ongoing action or state, and the other clause giving a reason for or result of it, for example: "she put a bandaid on her shoe *and* it maked it feel better;" "don't touch this camera *cause* it's broken;" and "I'm blowing on this *cause* it's hot."

BOX VI-12 CATEGORIZATION OF THE SEMANTIC RELATIONS IN COMPLEX
SENTENCES

Inter-event Relations		Intra-event Relations
COORDINATE **(NO NEW MEANING)**	**SUPERORDINATE** **(NEW MEANING)**	**SUBORDINATE** **(NO NEW MEANING)**
1. Same verb in two clauses 2. Different verb in two clauses	1. Causality 2. Antithesis 3. Time specification	1. Epistemic 2. Object specification 3. Notice complement 4. Other complement

---

A second superordinate meaning was *antithesis,* where utterances expressed a dependency relation between two events and/or states by means
of a contrast between them. Most often, the relationship between the clauses
was one of *opposition*, where one clause negated or opposed the other, or
exception, where one clause qualified or limited the other, for example: "I
gon' do this *but* this don't fits;" "it sound like a tunnel *buts* a bridge; and
"that train broke down *and* this train did not broke down."

The third superordinate meaning was *time specification,* where utterances
expressed a dependency relation between two events and/or states, where
the dependency was one of temporality, referring to one event or state
occurring prior to or simultaneous with the other, for example: "*when* I go out
I wanna blow bubbles here;," "I'm gonna put it in my room so I can see it
when I'm sleeping;" and "and I can't eat it *til* Mommy comes home."

There were four kinds of intraevent or *subordinate* relations referred to in
the children's sentences. No new sentence meaning was created by intraevent subordinate relations; instead, the two clauses merged to focus on one
referent. The first kind of subordinate relation was *epistemic*, where utterances coded certainty or uncertainty about a particular state of affairs. The
two clauses together focused on the object of certainty or uncertainty, for
example: "now I know *how* to take this off;" "I know *what* else is in it; " and "I
going see *if* there's more tape."

A second kind of subordinate relation was *object specification*. In this
subcategory of subordinate relations, the two clauses combined described
an object or person mentioned in the first clause. Most often, the person or
object was a predicate complement constituent, either object or place. The
most common types of object specification described the object or person
by function, place, or activity, for example: "a toilet *where* you poopoo"

(function); "this can go in a corner *where* sofa is" (place); and " the man *who* fixes the door" (activity).

The third category of utterances that referred to intraevent relations was *notice complement* utterances that served to call attention to a state or event. The joining of clauses, the first of which contained a notice verb, resulted in focus on the object of attention, which was the complement of the second clause most often, for example: "now look *what's* in here;" "watch *what* I'm doing;" and "look *what* my Mommy got me."

Finally, there were instances of complements other than notice complements (the *other complement* in Box VI-12), which simply did not fit the other patterns of event relations that were represented in complex sentences, for example: "that's *what* you can do;" "tell Iris *that* I wet my bed;" and "make sure *that* nothing happens to that train."

Developmentally, there were both similarities and differences among the children in the sequence in which the above categories of the content of complex sentences appeared in their speech. First, no content categories were productive for any of the children to begin with, with productivity defined as five or more different utterances in a category. Second, once complex sentences with connectives appeared and productivity was attained, several categories tended to be productive at the same time, but coordination (same verb) was the most frequent (and for Peter it was the first category that was productive). However, the children varied in their rate of acquiring productivity; Eric and Gia expressed several meaning relations at once, going from no productive categories in the first sample to five in the next. Kathryn and Peter, on the other hand, progressed more slowly, going from none in the first sample to one (Peter) or two (Kathryn) in the next. By the last sample, when they were about 36 months old, the children showed striking similarity in the relative frequency of utterances in the content categories. The rank order of the five most frequent categories in the last sample was the same for all four children, with the two exceptions that are noted:

1. Causality.
2. Epistemic for Eric and Peter; time specification for Gia; antithesis for Kathryn.
3. Coordination (different verb).
4. Coordination (same verb); reverse 3 and 4 for Eric.
5. Object specification.

In terms of the major categorization, the most frequent coordination was with different verbs in the two clauses; the most frequent superordinate relation was causality; and the most frequent subordinate relation was epistemic.

These results are in essential agreement with results reported by Clancy, Jacobsen, and Silva (1976) in a study of the acquisition of conjunctions in English, German, Italian, and Turkish. In all four languages, juxtaposition without, and later with, a surface connective expressed four basic kinds of relationships: coordination, sequence, antithesis, and causality. Coordination was the first to emerge in all languages; the order of the remaining relationships was variable. Although Clancy et al. referred to semantic relations expressed both with and without connectives, and the above results report on only sentences that expressed these relations *with* connectives, the kinds of relations observed and their sequence are similar to the results reported by Hood, *et al*. That is, coordination occurred before superordinance (causality and antithesis) which occurred before subordinance. Sequence was not directly applicable to any of the relations observed in the present study; it seemed to encompass both coordination and time specification.

Thus, the later development of complex syntax was characterized by the use of an increasing number of different connective forms and an increasing number of different semantic relations between clauses. The first and most frequent connective was "and," which was used in the beginning to connect clauses with a variety of different meaning relations, but the meaning of coordination was predominant. There was a gradual decrease in the occurrence of "and" as the children learned other connective forms to express different meaning relations, and "and" was used to express coordination primarily. The children's utterances gradually increased in length as a function of learning new, more complex forms to encode those categories of content that were already represented in their earlier, more primitive utterances, but also because the children learned to express new, more complex ideas and more complex relations between ideas.

SUMMARY

This chapter describes two important aspects of children's language—variation and complexity. First, there is considerable variation in language development. Language development does not proceed in a straight line, and children do not add words to their vocabularies and do not add structures or rules to their grammar in any simple way. Instead, there is a synergistic coming together of children's knowledge of many different aspects of language content, form, and use. The result is that children are different from one another in important ways, and the language behavior of the same child varies in important ways.

Both the intersubject variation and intrasubject variation that are described have their own regularity and are systematic, not random. Many studies have reported differences among children in how fast they learn one or another linguistic form. However, there are also important differences among children and variation within individual children in more substantive aspects of language development. Recognizing and understanding such variation in normal child language is important for attempting to recognize and understand deviant language development which is, in effect, another form of variation in child language.

Second, a major factor that contributes to variation in child language is the development of increasing complexity in children's sentences. As children's sentences get longer, they begin to get more and more complex. At first, children combine the semantic-syntactic relations that had appeared in their earliest utterances with one another. Eventually, children learn to combine two simple sentences and join them with a connective form, as in sentences like "bend the man so he can sit." Between these two developments, beginning when *MLU* is about 2.0 and continuing until *MLU* is longer than 4.0, children are learning several subsystems of grammar. In particular, the development of grammatical morphemes on nouns and verbs, questions, and negation are discussed in this chapter. The acquisition of the subsystems of grammatical morphemes, questions, negation, and complex syntax continues over a long period of time, and these intersect with one another and with other aspects of language form, content, and use that children are also learning.

SUGGESTED READINGS

In *Readings in Language Development*

Bloom, L., Lightbown, P., and Hood, L., Pronominal and nominal variation in child language, In *Structure and variation in child language. Monographs of the Society for Research in Child Development, 40,* (Serial No. 160), pp. 18–24, 1975.

Bloom, L., Miller, P., and Hood, L., Variation and reduction as aspects of competence in language development. In A. Pick (Ed.), *Minnesota symposia on child psychology, Vol. 9.* Minneapolis: The University of Minnesota Press, 1975.

Brown, R., The development of Wh- questions in child speech. *Journal of Verbal Learning and Verbal Behavior, 7,* 279–290, 1968.

de Villiers, J. and de Villiers, P. A cross-sectional study of the acquisition of grammatical morphemes in child speech. *Journal of Psycholinguistic Research, 2,* 267–278, 1973.

Slobin, D. Cognitive prerequisites for the development of grammar. In C. Ferguson and D. Slobin (Eds.), *Studies of child language development.* New York: Holt, Rinehart & Winston, 1973.

Other Readings

Bloom, L., Semantic and syntactic development of early sentence negation. From Lois Bloom, *Language development: Form and function in emerging grammars.* Cambridge, Mass.: The M.I.T. Press, pp.170–221, 1970

Brown, R., *A first language, the early stages* (Part 2). Cambridge, Mass.: Harvard University Press, 1973.

Cazden, C., The acquisition of noun and verb inflections. *Child Development, 39,* 433–438, 1968.

Clark, E., How young children describe events in time. In G. B. Flores d'Arcais and W. J. M. Levelt (Eds.), Advances in psycholinguistics. New York. American Elsevier, 1970.

Clark, E & Garnica, O. K. Is he coming or going? On the acquisition of deictic verbs. *Journal of Verbal Learning and Verbal Behavior, 13,* 559–572, 1974.

Ferguson, C. A. & Farwell, C. B. Words and Sounds in early language acquisition. *Language, 51,* 419–439, 1975.

Hood, L., Lahey, M., Lifter, K., and Bloom, L., Observational, descriptive methodology in studying child language: Preliminary results on the development of complex sentences. In G. P. Sackett (Ed.), *Observing behavior, Vol. I: Theory and application in mental retardation.* Baltimore: University Park Press, 1978.

Nelson. K. The nominal shift in semantic-syntactic development. *Cognitive Psychology, 7,* 461–479, 1975.

Ramer, A., Syntactic styles in emerging language. *Journal of Child Language, 3,* 49–62, 1976.

Chapter VII
DEVELOPMENT OF LANGUAGE USE IN RELATION TO CONTENT AND FORM

Languages exist because of the functions they serve; therefore, how children learn to use language for such different purposes as to get and give information and initiate and monitor interactions with others is a major aspect of their development. The success of messages depends on the very delicate interplay among an individual's needs, expectancies, and capacities in relation to the needs, expectancies, and capacities of others, all of whom are in situations in which they have greater or lesser control over the course of events according to many different circumstances. These are the issues that have come to the forefront in the recent coming together of linguistics, anthropology, philosophy, psychology, and sociology in a new social dimension of linguistics that has as its general domain the *use* of language.

Within the general domain of language use, there are several subdomains that are essentially related to one another. All of these subdomains consider aspects of language and context, but at different levels of analysis and with different emphases. There are (1) the acts that are performed with words (Austin, 1962; Dore, 1977, Garvey, 1975, in *RLDev*; Searle, 1969; and the papers in Cole and Morgan, 1975); (2) the functions that speech acts or speech events serve in meeting the needs of individuals (Ervin-Tripp, 1977; Halliday, 1970, 1975; Hymes, 1964; Jakobson, 1960; and Schnelle, 1971); (3) the understanding and use of information that is not explicit in the literal meaning of a message, that is, conversational implicature (Grice, 1975), and presupposition and entailment (Gordon and G. Lakoff, 1975); and (4) the necessity for using information from the listener and the context for deciding among alternative forms of messages such as definite and indefinite reference, pronominalization, different forms of requests and questions, and the like (Ervin-Tripp, 1964, 1970; Maratsos, 1974; Shatz, 1977; Sacks, 1972; Garfinkel, 1967; Fillmore, 1975; Warden, 1976, in *RLDev*; and, especially, Halliday and Hasan, 1975). A wider perspective of language use that combines some or all of these subdomains is taken in ethnographic studies of speech communities (Abrahams, 1974; and Phillips, 1974) and descriptions of children's development of "communicative competence" by, for example, Bates (1976a), Bruner (1975), and Ryan (1974).

Just as with the development of language form and content, the development of language use results from the interaction between children and contexts—specifically, children's changing needs in relation to the changing situations in their environments. Children learn any number of behaviors for meeting the needs that arise both within themselves and as a result of one or another context in which they find themselves. Some of these behaviors may be almost fortuitously arrived at: something that the child does *works* in one or another situation. Other behaviors have been contrived by societies and children must observe these in order to learn them. The use of language is a decision-making process: individuals decide which resources will meet a particular need in a given context. Developmentally, children's needs change, just as they acquire new resources for meeting changing needs in different contexts.

It is possible to hypothesize three chronological levels in the development of language use. The first level, in infancy, is the level of *primary forms.* Infants' needs are basically physiological and affective, and their resources are biologically determined or fortuitously contrived, and adapted only gradually to differences in the context. The same behavior, (e.g., crying or whimpering) can be used to meet several needs, regardless of the situation. Eventually, at the second level of *conventional forms*, decision making comes to involve conventional means as children's movements and vocalizations become more consistent with those around them, and their needs continue to become more social in addition to having to do with physical states and feelings. Bruner (1975) has emphasized the importance of the coordinated actions between infants and their caregivers in the transition to conventional behavior. "Language acquisition occurs in the context of an 'action dialogue' in which joint action is being undertaken by infant and adult" (pp. 55–56). At this second level children have learned sounds and gestures, and the same form can be used in different ways. Children may use the same word or word combination to refer to different events, for example, "Mommy" or "Mommy open" when Mommy is opening (or unable to open, or has just opened) a door, a box, or a jar. Or children may use the same word or word combination for different purposes, such as to get Mommy to open something, to announce that Mommy has opened something, or to stop Mommy from opening something.

As children learn more about the code, they also develop conceptually and socially so that they can begin to make inferences about situations and interpret the effects of different forms of messages on different listeners. At a third level of *conventional use*, they learn that there are alternative means or forms for achieving the same purpose, according to differences in the situational context. For example, to get water, one can issue a command, "Give me a drink;" make a statement, "I want water" or, less directly, "I'm thirsty;" and ask a question, "Is there any water?" (e.g., Ervin-Tripp, 1977; and Garvey, 1975).

The first of these levels in the development of language use, the origins of language use in infancy, was discussed in Chapter III. The second and third levels will be discussed in this chapter in relation to the development of form and content—in terms of how children begin to use conventional forms of sound and movement for communication toward the end of the first year, and how children learn to use conventions of use for deciding among alternative forms of messages according to the requirements of the listener and the situation, in the second and third years.

The two interweaving threads that converge and expand in the development of language use are *function* (Halliday, 1975) and *alternation* (Ervin-Tripp, 1972). The functions of language can be served by alternative forms of messages, and children need to acquire such different resources or alternative forms for meeting their communication needs. That is, children must learn the rules of language use for deciding which forms to use in different contexts, for learning when and how to say what to whom. It is not enough, for example, for children to learn to refer to an object by its name ("bus") or a pronoun ("it"); they must learn both forms of alternative reference (and others) and must also learn when it is acceptable to use one or the other form and when it is not. It is acceptable to say "It's coming" when standing at the bus stop, but the same phrase would not be acceptable somewhere else unless the listener had some other way of knowing what "it" referred to.

TRANSITION FROM THE ORIGINS OF USE IN INFANCY TO CONVENTIONS OF USE

Communication in infancy is neither intentional nor conventional; that is, infants' means of communicating are, at once, both a part of the need being communicated and the consequence of the infants' physiological response to one or another interaction with the environment. Only gradually do infants progress to communicating with *intention* to communicate in the second half of the first year. Although still unable to use the conventions of language, infants come to know that their behavior can influence the behavior of others, and they behave with the intention of achieving that influence. Ultimately, in the second year, infants begin to learn the sounds and signs in the context that are part of language, and communication becomes both intentional and *conventional.* An infant's progress, then, is from earliest communication (i.e., without intention and without convention), to intentional communication that is not conventional to, eventually, communication that is intentional and that uses conventional means. (See also the description of the origins of language use or "pragmatics" in Bates, 1976a).

Infants begin to discover the arbitrary and conventional facts about language toward the end of the first year and begin to use gestures and to make sounds that are similar to the gestures and sounds that they see and hear others make. However, as emphasized by Piaget (1954), the fact that children use the forms of social convention (speech and gestures) is not evidence that they are capable of the social or rational thought from which such conventions originate. Piaget described "the practical character of the acts of sensorimotor intelligence and their search for success or satisfaction . . . the child does not at first succeed in reflecting in words and concepts the procedures that he already knows how to carry out in acts" (1954, pp. 406-407). Thus, children perform social gestures and produce social (conventional) sounds as new means or resources for meeting their needs, without awareness of their origin or social significance. Children's early gestures and early words are used at first subjectively as extensions of the individual and personal sensorimotor acts of younger infants.

GESTURES AND WORDS

The first gestures of infants that are consistent with the gestures of the community include showing, giving, and pointing. Pointing, as a communicative gesture that involves a recipient, emerges out of the earlier pointing behavior that does not involve a recipient—the sensorimotor act through which infants explore the distance between themselves and external objects, and figure-ground relationships (Werner and Kaplan, 1963). Observations of two infants by Bates, Camaioni, and Volterra (1975) confirmed this progression from subjective, sensorimotor pointing that served a cognitive function to communicative pointing that involved a recipient—where children use the object as a means to obtain attention from an adult. The developmental sequence of the earliest communicative gestures used by the infants studied by Bates et al. (1975) was, first, showing objects to an adult, and, then, both giving objects to an adult and pointing out objects to an adult. They described these gestures as "proto-declaratives," since they function "to direct the adult's attention to some event or object in the world" and the infants' first labeling words eventually occurred with the same showing, giving, and pointing behaviors. (See, also, deLaguna, 1963, p. 99.)

Children's overextension in the use of words as they learn words has already been discussed in the earlier chapters having to do with the development of language content/form. However, Piaget has offered an explanation of the early overextension of words that is a corollary to the appearance of the communicative pointing gesture after children are observed to use pointing for more subjective cognitive function (as described in Werner and Kaplan, 1963; and by Bates et al., 1975).

As described by Piaget (1962), children's words are used only partially according to the objective criteria (i.e., according to the perceptual similarity of objects in a class) that define a word's meaning for adult speakers. Piaget described true concepts as formed according to the qualities or properties of objects that form classes or sets of objects, and systems of classes, "whether or not the child himself and his own activity are also involved" (p. 218). By contrast, the early use of words derives more from sensorimotor intelligence, as objects are assimilated to the child's point of view, and words are used subjectively, according to the point of view of the child. It is in this sense that Piaget suggested that the "first verbal schemas are intermediary between the schemas of the sensory-motor intelligence and conceptual schemas" (p. 218).

Early words and early gestures may be used, then, for their subjective, cognitive function before they are used for communicative function. The account by Piaget accords well with other descriptions of the transition from the primary forms of infancy to the conventional forms that are beginning to be used in the second year (e.g., the first communicative gestures that have already been described) and Halliday's (1975) description of the early interactional, personal, and heuristic functions of vocalization in the period from 9 to about 17 or 18 months. Similarly, Dore (1975) described children's early "speech acts" in the second year as serving affective and cognitive functions before the more intentionally communicative functions. Bruner (1975) has underscored the importance of the social-cognitive interaction between infants and caregivers in "passage from pre-speech communication to language" (p. 1). Eventually, the gestures and words that children use and continue to learn occur less and less often as a part of the event being communicated—as children begin to dissociate their use of the word from themselves and their subjective, personal interactions in the situation—and begin to occur more often as representational or symbolic with the intention to communicate to some other person. However, this later use of linguistic forms with the intention to communicate never replaces the earlier subjective and personal use of linguistic forms; the two continue to coexist in children's use of language, depending on the functions that language serves for them.

FUNCTIONS OF LANGUAGE

A useful distinction among the functions of language has been captured by Halliday (1974, in *RLDev*) in the distinction between the "mathetic" and "pragmatic" functions of language (Box VII-1). The use of linguistic form with a mathetic function is the use of language for learning about the world. It has its origins in the earlier "personal" and "heuristic" functions (see Chapter III) that have been identified by Halliday, as well as the earlier cognitive use of gesture described by Werner and Kaplan (1963) and the subjective overex-

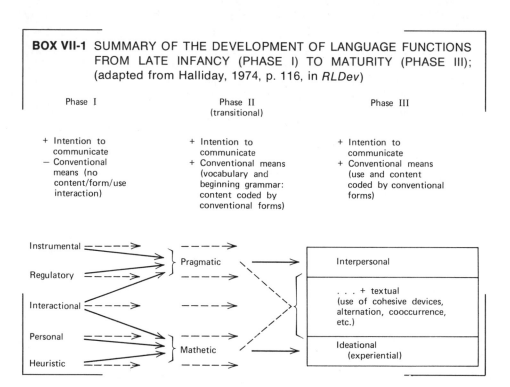

BOX VII-1 SUMMARY OF THE DEVELOPMENT OF LANGUAGE FUNCTIONS FROM LATE INFANCY (PHASE I) TO MATURITY (PHASE III); (adapted from Halliday, 1974, p. 116, in *RLDev*)

Phase I

Phase II
(transitional)

Phase III

+ Intention to communicate
− Conventional means (no content/form/use interaction)

+ Intention to communicate
+ Conventional means (vocabulary and beginning grammar: content coded by conventional forms)

+ Intention to communicate
+ Conventional means (use and content coded by conventional forms)

Instrumental

Regulatory

Interactional

Personal

Heuristic

Pragmatic

Mathetic

Interpersonal

. . . + textual
(use of cohesive devices, alternation, cooccurrence, etc.)

Ideational
(experiential)

tension of words described by Piaget (1962). The "heuristic" function appeared after the personal, regulatory, interactional and instrumental functions, at about 13–14 months in Nigel's development. It was characterized by the use of vocalization to explore the environment; at the very earliest stage, the heuristic use was the demand for a name of something, but it eventually developed into the whole range of child questions. In its earliest manifestations, the mathetic function is characteristic of children's sensorimotor behaviors as they learn about themselves in relation to objects in the world.

BOX VII-2 DIALOGUE WITH PETER, 25 MONTHS OLD, THAT IS AN EXAMPLE OF MATHETIC LANGUAGE, WITH HIS SPEECH HAVING PERSONAL AND HEURISTIC FUNCTIONS

(Peter sits on couch
watching Lois; Lois knocks
barrels off train)
   The barrels fell off
   the train

                        [həi]↑

   The barrels fell off
   the train

                        [həi]↑

   They fell down

          fell off the train ↑ /they fell down ↑

   Mmhm/ you heard
   me/ you just pretended

          barrels fell the train ↑

   Mmhm/ the barrels
   fell off the train

          barrels fell- - -train ↑

   Mmhm
(Lois knocks barrels
off train, Peter laughs)
   What happened?

          barrels fell the down the train

   That's right
(Peter watching Lois)   **barrels ə fell the train ↑**
   Not yet/ I'm putting
   them back on the train/
   oop (one fell off)

Here Peter appears to be concentrating on the action of the barrels in relation to the train and, just as important, with the forms of language that represent what happens when the barrels fall *down* and *off* the train.

In later and progressively more mature manifestations of the mathetic function, children use language to represent what they see and hear around them as they learn about the relations of objects in their environment apart from their relations to themselves (Box VII-2).

The pragmatic use of words has its origins in the earlier "instrumental" and "regulatory" functions described by Halliday, whereby children attempt to satisfy their material needs and regulate the behaviors of other persons around them (Box VII-3). (see Chapter III.) There is, then, a process of "functional generalization" (Halliday, 1974, in *RLDev*, p. 28) as children use words and structures they are learning in both pragmatic contexts that have instrumental and regulatory functions and in mathetic contexts that serve personal and heuristic functions. The interaction function, already well documented at 3 to 4 months of age (Bateson, 1975; Stern, 1971; and Stern, Jaffee, Beebe, and Bennett (1975, in *RLDev*) obviously contributes to both the mathetic and pragmatic uses of language (Box VII-4). Halliday pointed out that the functions of language can be identified separately for individual utterances when they first appear. However, already in the second year, both pragmatic and mathetic functions are served by the same utterance.

BOX VII-3 DIALOGUE WITH ALLISON, 19 MONTHS OLD, THAT IS AN EARLY EXAMPLE OF PRAGMATIC LANGUAGE HAVING BOTH INSTRU-MENTAL AND REGULATORY FUNCTIONS

(Allison offering cookie to Mommy)	**Mommy**
Oh, thank you	
(Mommy taking cookie)	**cookie**
Thank you	
(Allison looking at cups)	**juice**
Juice?	
Shall we have some juice?	
(Mommy shaking juice can)	
(Allison pointing inside cup)	**cup**
(Allison picks up one cup;	
picking up second cup;	**Mommy/**
holding it to Mommy)	**juice**
Mommy juice	
(Allison putting cup down)	**no**
(Allison shaking own cup)	**baby!**
Baby	
(Allison picking up Mommy's cup	**Mommy/**
looking inside cup)	**juice**

BOX VII-4 DIALOGUE WITH KATHRYN, 35 MONTHS OLD, THAT IS A LATER EXAMPLE OF PRAGMATIC LANGUAGE HAVING REGULATORY FUNCTION

(Kathryn has just done a somersault)

    I'm waiting for you to do one

> why don't you do one?
>
> but you·you have·you have to do one first

(Lois tries; laughs)
    I can't

> - - -
>
> I'll show you how/
> watch/
> - - - a somersault

    What?

> watch

(Kathryn does one)
(Lois laughs)
    Yes
(Kathryn laughs)

> see that ↑
>
> now can you try one ↑ /
> cause I teached you how/
> I'm a teacher

    You teached me how
    you're a teacher

> watch/ uh//

(Lois does one)
(Lois laughs)
    Yes/

> you see ↑ / you did it!
>
> you can go/ can you go back?

(Laughing) No I can't
    go back

> why?

Because I'm too old//
    (laughs) I'm too old/
    and now I'm exhausted

> why?

    Because I did a somersault

> I'm not

    You're not?
(Kathryn laughs)
    You're not what?

> I'm not exhausted

(Kathryn and Lois laugh)
    You're a funny-oney

> no/I'm a teacher

    Oh is that what you are? oh

> a cinderella teacher

(Kathryn does somersault)
(Kathryn and Lois laugh)

FUNCTIONS OF LANGUAGE AND ACTS OF SPEAKING

There is a difference between messages that state, describe, or report information that is either true or false, and performative messages that are part of doing an action (Austin, 1962). Expanding on the work of Austin, Searle (1970) pointed out that "notions of referring and predicating [can be detached] from the notions of such complete speech acts as asserting, questioning, commanding, etc., and the justification for this separation lies in the fact that the same reference and predication can occur in the performance of different complete speech acts" (p. 23). For example, reference to *sweeping the floor* can be made in the act of asserting "He is sweeping the floor," the act of questioning "Has the floor been swept?", or the act of commanding "Sweep the floor!" Acts such as asserting, questioning, and commanding were called "illocutionary acts" by Austin. Thus, in addition to the act of uttering a sentence (or making a sign or gesture), which is called the "locutionary act," speakers perform "illocutionary acts" when they ask a question, make a promise, or give an order. Some verbs in English that denote illocutionary acts are "describe," "assert," "criticize," and "apologize." The correlary of the illocutionary act that is performed by the speaker is what Austin termed the "perlocutionary act," which is the consequence or effect that speech acts have on the actions, thoughts, and beliefs of hearers. Some verbs in English that denote perlocutionary acts are "convince," "scare," "inspire," and "enlighten."

For a particular sentence, then, one can describe (1) its propositional meaning or content (what is referred to or predicated), (2) a locutionary act (the fact that someone says the utterance or makes the sign or gesture), (3) an illocutionary act (the intent the speaker has to affect the situation), and (4) a perlocutionary act (the effect the utterance has for the hearer). Speech act theory accounts for some of the same linguistic facts of language as does transformational theory (Chomsky, 1957, 1965); the sentences "He is sweeping the floor," "Has the floor been swept?" and "Sweep the floor!" are all transforms of the same underlying structure with the semantic relations among *someone, sweep,* and *floor.* But, whereas transformational theory focussed on the *forms* by which meanings or propositions could be expressed, speech act theory focussed on the *use* of expressions in the situations of speech events. As a result, speech act theory is often referred to as a theory of "communication" or "communicative competence" in studies of children's use of language (e.g., Bates, 1976a; Dore, 1975; Garvey, 1975a, in *RLDev*; Schnelle, 1971; and Shatz, 1977).

Schnelle distinguished three kinds of speech acts in which children act in relation toward adults, and enumerated several instances of each. There are (1) "affectively and voluntarily determined acts" (p. 184) such as those in which the child expresses bodily and psychic feelings, or satisfaction or disatisfaction with situations, or expresses wishes or requests to an adult. There are (2) "role-determined speech acts" (p. 184) such as those in which the child calls the adult, expresses love for the adult, requests expressions of love from the adult, expresses thankfulness, affiliation, happiness about, approval or discomfort about punishment or rebuke, and so on. And there are (3) "informational speech acts" (p. 185) such as when the child calls attention to a situation, an event or an act, asks for additional information with respect to a given situation, reports a situation to the adult that had been experienced earlier, or expresses thoughts or evaluations of a situation to an adult.

Speakers of a language do things with words—they accomplish certain acts with their messages apart from representing the information that is the content of their messages. Some speech acts are highly ritualistic, and the same function is achieved by the same or similar forms in different contexts (e.g., performing a marriage, opening a session in court, toasts and introductions). Other speech acts are more varied with respect to the contexts in which they occur and with respect to the form and content of messages (acts of requesting, promising, warning, prohibiting, apologizing, etc.). Acts of requesting, for example, have the same function but can vary in the form of the request according to the context in which it occurs. Obviously, there are certain specialized speech acts that most individuals never learn because they are particular to an occupation or vocation (performing a marriage, opening a session in court, making a sales pitch, etc.). However, other speech acts, (acts of requesting, greeting, promising, warning, apologizing, prohibiting, etc.) are far more general and are presumed to be within the competence of most if not all adult speakers.

Children appear to learn to use those speech acts first that have the least variation in linguistic form and the fewest degrees of contextual freedom, such as greetings, in which the same or similar forms occur in the same kinds of context. Such speech acts can be learned as routines with the same form, such as a greeting ("Hi" and "Byebye"), a transfer ("Thank you"), an apology ("sorry"), or a prohibition ("no" or "don't") occurring in similar contexts. Such words with such speech act functions have been observed in the early vocabularies of children (Gruber, 1973; Ingram, 1971; Bates, 1971; Antinucci and Parisi, 1973; Dore, 1975; Nelson, 1974; and Parisi and Antinucci, 1970). In contrast, speech acts that entail different message content in different contexts, such as requesting an action, requesting permission, warning, inviting, or promising, are a later development; they usually appear in the later preschool years (ages three to five years) but continue to develop and change into adulthood as the individual encounters new and different contexts.

It is necessary to recognize that even though such routines as have been described occur in children's behavior, and they can be characterized as performative messages in that they accomplish some act, they do not meet the strict conditions on performatives that were described by Austin (1962). According to Austin, there are "felicity" conditions for the performance of speech acts and, in order for performatives to be "felicitous" or "happy," (1) accepted conventional procedures for performing the act must exist; (2) there must be appropriate persons participating in the speech act; (3) the procedures must be executed completely and correctly by the participants (speaker and listener); (4) the participants must have the appropriate thoughts and feelings (motivations and satisfactions) about the acts; and (5) the participants must follow through or conduct themselves accordingly. These conditions require knowledge of a set of linguistic conventions for indicating the functions of speech acts, and the conventional devices typically include variations in word order, stress, intonation contour, and verb mood, as well as a set of performative verbs (e.g., "promise," "apologize," and "warn") (Searle, 1969). The speech acts of adults entail both intention to act and knowledge of convention.

The routines or stereotype expressions that young children learn to use in particular contexts, on the other hand, entail little or no variation in linguistic form, but they can be successful in maintaining social exchange between the participants. In the study of adult-child discourse reported in Bloom, Rocissano, and Hood (1976), such social routines were comparatively rare and did not change in frequency in the period from about 20 to 36 months. In contrast, routines were frequent in exchanges between peers reported by Keenan (1974), who described the interactions between her twin sons at 29 months of age, and by Garvey and Hogan (1973) who described peer play and conversations between 3- to 5-year-old children.

The distinction that has been made between the routines and limited speech act performatives in children's speech, and the more varied and complex speech acts that are possible in the mature language and increasingly identified in the speech of preschool children, is consistent with a distinction made by Bernstein (1964a, 1964b, 1972, and elsewhere) citing the work of Hughlings Jackson. Bernstein pointed out the differences between "highly coded" utterances that are restricted and limited in their form in different social contexts and "now coded" speech that is elaborate and newly created to fit different reference requirements. Highly coded speech is easily predictable and limited in explicit content; it is social but impersonal, for example, "What are you doing?", "Where are you going?" In contrast, elaborated, now-coded speech is unpredictable and the representation of explicit content is facilitated because speech is formulated for each particular situation, for example, "Why are you holding the spoon that way?" or "Did you go downtown to see your brother?" According to Bernstein, individuals naturally shift from one type of speech to another, depending on the context of social situations, and there are situations that are dominated more by one than by another type of speech. In particular, Bernstein cited the peer group as one in which a restricted code is more probable than an elaborated code (see the above references to the work of Keenan and Garvey and Hogan). Other social situations in which restricted expression or routines are acceptable are, for example, the exchanges in which goods are transferred or something is being demonstrated.

Although highly coded, restricted routines are characteristic of children's early speech acts, there is increasing use of more varied forms that are adapted to situational differences in the preschool years, as children learn more about varying the forms of messages according to the demands of the situation for achieving one or another purpose or function. There are different messages having the same content but different form that accomplish the same purpose in different contexts—as when the child gets a cookie after saying "Will you give me a cookie?", "I want a cookie," or "I wish I had a cookie".

Garvey (1975, in *RLDev*) pointed out that "there is a large family of social gestures whereby one person attempts to influence the behavior or attitude of another. This family, which we will call *interventions,* includes suggestions, invitations, prohibitions, requests for permission, and the request for action" (p. 44). Garvey chose to study the use of requests for action by 3- to 5-year-old peer dyads primarily because responses to requests are readily observable and involve "important dimensions of interpersonal understanding" in that "the desires or needs of one person are to be satisfied through or in conflict with the desires or needs of another person" (p. 45). The request function has its origins in the early instrumental and regulatory functions that were identified by Halliday (1975) before the age of 12 months. The general category of requests was the most frequently identified category of speech acts in the study by Garvey, and requests for action was the most frequent individual speech act type in the speech of a group of 3-year-old children observed by Dore (1975). The ability of 3- to 5-year-old children to use and respond to different forms of requests for action is a major accomplishment in the development of language use.

There were four forms of requests for action identified by Garvey: (1) *direct requests* (the imperative form), for example, "Leave it alone;" (2) *indirect requests* in which the content of the request (who is to do what) is embedded in matrix sentences with "want," such as "I want you to come;" (3) *indirect requests* in which the content of the request is embedded either in matrix sentences that indicate some general condition of the participant or some condition of the act such as its necessity, for example, "You have to open the door" or, in imperative matrix sentences, for example, "See if you can open the door;" and (4) *inferred requests* in which the actual content of the request for action is not expressed but the speaker indicates "a desire for some state of affairs" without specifying an action, for example, "That door should be open," "Is there any coffee?," or "I want some coffee." Direct requests were most frequent, included eight different meaning factors (see *RLDev*), and were used equally often and with equal success by both groups of younger dyads (age 3 years, 6 months to 4 years, 4 months; *MLU* = 4.76) and older (age 4 years, 7 months to 5 years, 7 months (*MLU* = 6.18). Indirect requests were used far less frequently and were used on the average twice as often by the older dyads than by the younger dyads. Inferred requests were rare. Garvey concluded that the "interpersonal meanings" in the children's requests depended on the perception of nonlinguistic conditions—as speaker and hearer interpret the situation and each other's behavior—but also depend on a shared understanding (a convention) of how their beliefs and attitudes about one another can be represented with alternative linguistic forms.

The rules for alternation involve choosing a linguistic form for representing some content to achieve some end. Making such linguistic decisions requires that the speaker be able to make judgments about the situation and about the social status of the listener, as well as judgments about what the listener already knows and needs to know. Thus, the ability to take the listener into account when formulating messages is a major requirement for the development of language use.

CONVENTIONS FOR ALTERNATION IN LANGUAGE USE

Acquiring the ability to decide when one or another social situation requires or expects one or another kind of speech, or one or another means of performing the same speech act, is learning when to say what to whom, and is a part of children's learning words and structures for expressing content/ form relations. The resources of a speaker of a language include rules for *alternation*—rules for determining which forms of the language are required and are appropriate in one or another context—as well as rules for *cooccurrence*—rules for determining what other behaviors are also required or desirable given the selection of one or another alternant (Ervin-Tripp, 1972; Gumperz, 1972; and Jakobson, 1957).

> If one looks to the places in conversation where an object (including persons) or activity is identified (or as I shall call it, 'formulated'), then one can notice that there is a set of alternative formulations for each such object or activity, all the formulations being, in some sense, correct (i.e., each allowing under some circumstance 'retrieval' of the same referent). Furthermore, that the selections made at each spot are 'fitted' to each other, or 'go together.' Rather than saying 'they fit the topic,' or are 'appropriate to the topic,' it may be preferable to say that in their co-selection, they, at least in part, 'constitute' the topic. (Schegloff, 1972, pp. 95–96)

The use of language, then, has to do with processes of *alternation,* the paradigmatic choice of one of a number of possible alternatives, and syntagmatic *cooccurrence,* the subsequent selections that are required given the choice of one or another alternant.

When children begin to use the conventional words and structures of the adult language, according to Halliday, they mark the distinction between the pragmatic and mathetic uses of linguistic forms in their speech in a way that is idiosyncratic and characteristic only of child language. The distinction Halliday noted was explicit: pragmatic utterances were spoken with a rising intonation and mathetic utterances were spoken with a falling intonation in the first half of Nigel's second year. Differences in the intonation contours of children's single-word utterances were also reported by Dore (1973), who identified three contexts, labeling, asking, and calling, which corresponded with the three contours falling, rising, and abrupt rising-falling. However, the consistent use of intonation to differentiate among children's intentions has been questioned (Bloom, 1973) and it appears that rising intonation may occur with mathetic functions as well, just as falling intonation may occur with pragmatic functions. In an analysis of the different contexts in which Eric, Gia, Kathryn, and Peter used the two intonation contours, it was found that both contours were used frequently in almost all contexts. In only one context, *search for missing objects* was rising intonation used consistently— and *search* is consistent with the pragmatic function defined by Halliday (Bloom and Hood, in progress).

The contrast between rising and falling intonation, if it is a consistently motivated distinction, is one of the very few ways in which children distinguish among different purposes or among different contexts for the same purpose. The same word and the same structure occur in different contexts for different purposes, such as to make a comment or issue a command, and for the same purpose, such as a request for action in different circumstances. In addition to intonation, children depend on other information in the context (such as gestures and other facial and body behaviors, to distinguish between one or another communicative intention) instead of using different lexical or syntactic forms of messages. Similarly, adults interpret what children intend by what they say by paying attention to the (1) "accompaniments of the utterance . . . such as pointing, searching, playing with specific objects, refusing," the (2) "circumstances of the utterance such as the presence or absence of particular objects or people, the relation of these to the child, any immediately preceding events or speech," and the (3) "aspects of the utterance such as intonation patterns, which are variously interpreted as insistence, protest, pleasure, request, etc." (Ryan, 1974, p. 201).

Thus, to get someone to open a box, a child might point to a closed box, clutch at the box to try to open it, whine, cry, and put an adult's hands on the box, but will still say "Mommy open box" (or any one or two of the same words). On the other hand, when seeing Mommy open the box, the child might smile or laugh but, again, will say "Mommy open box." The child cannot, as yet, say such different messages as "Will you open the box?", "You can open the box," or "The box needs to be opened." Children use conventional forms that function as questions, comments, reports, or commands, and they can indicate these different functions by varying prosody to some extent, and using gesture, facial expression, and the like. But they have yet to learn that there are different forms that represent the same information and achieve the same end result, and that there is a conventional system of rules for deciding among such alternative forms according to the context.

Thus, children acquire linguistic schemes for the relations between form and content, and they discover the situational constraints that govern the use of the different linguistic schemes that require the use of alternative linguistic forms (see Bates, 1976a; Cazden, 1970; Garvey, 1975; and Ryan, 1974). This is the third stage in the development of language use—having acquired some knowledge of the functions of language and the correspondences between form and content in language, children begin to acquire the capacity to change the form of messages according to the different ways in which they need to use messages. The learning of the social conventions for the uses of language begins in the third year, but continues through adulthood. Language use involves changing needs in changing contexts. Just as there is a fixed number of linguistic items (words) and rules of grammar that allow for the production and understanding of indefinitely many sentences, there is also apparently a fixed number of language functions, but indefinitely many contexts, situations, or environments in which language is used with these functions. The contexts for the use of language change throughout the life span—from earliest childhood, through the school years, into adulthood with family and occupational contexts, and, eventually, into old age, which may include contexts of loneliness and illness.

The early development of the use of language for meeting different needs in different contexts will be discussed here in terms of (1) the use of presuppositions and the role of the listener, (2) conversational discourse between speakers, and (3) alternative forms of reference, deixis, and ellipsis.

PRESUPPOSITION AND THE ROLE OF THE LISTENER

"Speaking in social life [is an] adaptive and creative practice" (Bauman and Sherzer, 1974, p. 12) that requires, for its success, the existence of shared knowledge, and the ability to make judgments about the capacities and needs of listeners in different social situations. As a result, there is considerable variety in the forms that messages can take, as speakers adapt the form and content of their messages according to what they presuppose the listener already knows and what they judge the listener needs to know in order to understand and respond. The egocentricism of children has been often underscored in descriptions of their behavior and in explanations of their thinking, and the assumption that usually follows is that egocentricity precludes children from taking the listener into account in a speaking situation. The distinction made by Piaget (1924, 1955) between egocentric and social speech in the language development of children from 2 to 6 years was based on his observations that children tend to talk more in "collective monologues" than they provide "adapted information" or issue commands. Since the distinction was made by Piaget, it has been followed by attempts either to prove or disprove the conclusion that the egocentricity of children prevents them from understanding and using the point of view of the listener in conversation (see McCarthy, 1954a; and Glucksberg, Krauss, and Higgins, 1975).

Although the speech of young children is generally conceded to be more creative than it is adaptive, there has been some evidence that children can and do differ in their ways of speaking to different kinds of listeners. Smith (1933b, in *RLDev*) observed that children from 2 to 5 years old ask significantly more questions when they are interacting with an adult than when they are interacting with other children of the same age. Moreover, when children asked questions in situations where they were interacting with a peer, they typically directed their questions to an adult who was also in the room.

A study by Shatz and Gelman (1973) demonstrated that 4-year-old children talked differently to younger, 2-year-old children than to 4-year-old children or to adults. Among the modifications in the speech of the 4-year-old children was the use of direct, unmodified imperatives to 2-year-olds in contrast with the use of embedded imperatives with adults, and the use of more concrete verbs in the here and now to 2-year-olds in contrast with the use of abstract verbs (e.g., "know," "remember," "guess") with adults. The 4-year-old children talked to other 4-year-old children more in the way they talked to adults than in the way they talked to 2-year-old children. There were factors that even operated to influence the talk by 4-year-olds to different 2-year-olds, such as the younger children's levels of linguistic development, physical size, cognitive development, and capacities for attention. Shatz and Gelman suggested that such factors are used by the older children as feedback for monitoring what they say.

In a longitudinal study of the language development of normal-hearing children who were born to deaf parents, Schiff (1976) observed that the 2-year-old subjects modified their speech according to whether they were talking to their deaf mothers or to a visiting hearing adult. The children used more oral language and longer utterances with the hearing adult than with their deaf mothers, and used more manual signing and deaflike distortions in their speech to their deaf mothers than to the hearing adult. Thus, as young as 2 years of age, these normal-hearing children were able to adapt their speech to the needs of their listeners, according to whether they were speaking with their deaf mothers or a hearing adult.

In a study of children's code switching, Berko-Gleason (1973) pointed out that the earliest listener-adapted variation to be observed in language development is between talking and not talking in infancy, as infants can be observed to vocalize, "Say bye-bye," and the like, to members of the family, but they become silent in the presence of strangers. Another stylistic variation she has observed in children under 4 years of age is the use of whining only with parents or parent figures, and an often abrupt switch to whining when a parent appears. Older children were observed using high-pitched "baby talk" intonation and telegraphic speech (without the use of grammatical morphemes) when speaking with 2-year-olds, and 6- and 8-year-old girls were observed using prescriptive and didactically adult formalisms (e.g., "Now you just carry them home and don't run" and "You share them") (p. 164).

In discussing sociolinguistic rules for alternation, Ervin-Tripp (1972) presented an analysis of American rules of address (expanded from an earlier account of forms of address in American English by Brown and Ford, 1964). The parameters that interacted in this formal scheme to determine how adult speakers decided on forms of address included age, status-marked situations (courtroom, faculty meeting, Congress), name known or unknown, friend, colleague, or kin, rank or hierarchy within a working group, sex (married or unmarried), and identify (according to occupation or courtesy, e.g., doctor or professor). It appears from the research that was cited that among these distinctions, only age and kin or not kin are parameters that influence the alternation of forms of address in speech by young children.

So far, studies of alternation in children's speech have described the changes in the form of utterances primarily. There is also evidence that children can vary the content that is represented in alternative messages according to their perceptions of the knowledge of the listener (Maratsos, 1973; and Menig-Peterson, 1975). Maratsos asked 3- and 4-year-old children to talk about toys to a listener who was presented to them as being blind and to a listener with normal vision. The children were much more explicit in their messages to the "blind" listeners than to the listeners who could see. In the study by Menig-Peterson, 3- and 4-year-old children were asked to talk about an experience to adults under two conditions, one condition when the adult had also participated in the experienced events one week earlier, and the other condition when the adult was naive about the events. The children made more references to the earlier event and introduced more information about the event to the naive listener, than to the knowledgeable listener.

Thus, children between 3 and 4 years of age can modify both the form and content of their speech according to what they presume that their listener knows. However, children learn to make such judgments about the informational needs of the listener only gradually.

Initially, children do not distinguish among different kinds of utterances according to different conditions in the environment. There are certain conditions that determine the kinds of utterances that speakers use, according to the extent to which speaker and listener share information about a topic (R. Lakoff, 1973). In one such condition, speakers do not ordinarily tell their listeners what they already know, and *statements* (as opposed to questions) occur when the speaker has some information and can presume that the listener does not (e.g., "They have a blue car"). When the speaker does not have some information and has reason to believe that the listener does, he or she will typically ask a *question* (e.g., "What color is their car?"). On the other hand, when the speaker assumes that he or she and the listener may already share some information, the assumptions can be verified with a *tag question* ("They have a blue car, *don't they*?").

However, children typically tell their listeners what they already know, as indicated by the preponderance of statements that are comments on the here and now in children's early speech. When children begin to ask questions, they typically already know the answer to the questions (Lewis, 1938; and Bloom and Hood, in progress), and do not appear to be using question forms to *question,* so much as they are simply engaging in the act of *asking* (a distinction made by Mishler, 1975). It has been suggested (Bloom, 1974b) that children's ability to recognize such different conditions of *use* as outlined by Lakoff will be a factor contributing to the acquisition of the linguistic rules for different statement and question *forms*. The sequence of development from statements, questions, tag questions and, finally, negative questions (Brown and Hanlon, 1970) may be determined at least in part by the sequence in which children learn to make judgments about the required listener conditions.

The situation is a controlling variable in other ways for determining the amount, the topic, and the form of messages in discourse (e.g., Bates, 1971; Cazden, 1970; and Shatz, 1974). Children have been observed to talk more often and to use longer utterances when they originated the topic of conversation (Cooperman, cited in Cazden, 1970; and Freedle, Lewis, and Weiner, 1974). Differences in the initiation of topics and in the complexity of the linguistic form of utterances of 2- to 4-year-old children have been observed in situations that differ according to the activity, the participants, and the extent to which the children can control the events that are happening (Bates, 1971; and Shatz, 1974). Initially, according to Corsaro (n.d.) 2-year-old children are more concerned with their own intent with respect to the topic than with the intent of and participation by a listener.

Mishler (1975) explored the conditions imposed by the authority relationships between speakers (adults speaking to children, children speaking to adults, and children speaking to children) as determiners of different kinds of discourse exchanges.

DISCOURSE DEVELOPMENT

A major result of children's increasing ability to understand the needs and resources of listeners is progress in the development of discourse. Adult discourse has been described traditionally in terms of the occurrence of shared elements in successive messages (Harris, 1964), which creates a texting or cohesion in the linguistic exchanges between speakers (Halliday and Hasan, 1975). Such linguistic accounts of the shared form of messages in discourse have been augmented by description of shared content (topic) in messages (e.g., Fillmore, 1975), by sociological studies of regulation of social interaction through discourse (Sacks, 1972; and Schegloff, 1972), and by philosophical studies of the logical postulates of conversation (Grice, 1975; and Gordon and G. Lakoff, 1975).

The rules that speakers and listeners use for initiating and maintaining the topic of conversation result in the maintenance of regularity and reciprocity between speakers. Speakers depend on feedback from their listeners and *mutual monitoring* for maintaining their part in the reciprocity of conversation. Speakers must know whether listeners are paying attention in the first place and, if they are paying attention, whether they understand the message, and when and if they intend to respond to the message (Goffman, 1969). The signals and rules that adults use for taking turns at speaking in conversations were described by Duncan (1972). The use of head nods and indicators such as "hm" and "uh huh" were described by Dittman (1972) in the conversational exchanges of school-age children. Garvey (1975b) has described the quite systematic use of repetition and contingent queries (e.g., "What?", *"Where* did he go?") in the interactions between 3- to 5-year-old peer dyads; Keenan (1974) described the use of repetition and utterance completion that regulated the reciprocity of discourse between her 29-month-old twin sons; and Keller-Cohen (1977) described the use of repetition for cohesion in the development of discourse by children learning a second language. Corsaro (n.d.) described several aspects of reciprocity in discourse that children learn to recognize and use; these are acts and responses for initiation, contribution, maintenance, and termination of discourse, and they involve the initiation of topics, topic-relevant responses, topic shifts, and topic termination (see also Keenan and Schieffelin, 1975).

Such techniques for feedback and monitoring the give and take between speakers *frame* conversations; they provide a skeletal structure for discourse. Children begin to learn these aspects of communication before their third birthdays. One of the earliest techniques for monitoring discourse exchanges begins when children seek to establish that someone is listening before they begin to talk. The use of the vocative (calling someone's name) to gain the attention of a listener before continuing with an utterance has been observed often among 2-year-olds, and young children may repeat the vocative "Mommy, Mommy, Mommy . . ." 10 or more times before getting assurance from the listener to proceed with what they want to say. Another technique for monitoring the listener's attention and interest consists of tag queries such as "right?", "O.K.?", and the like, which have their counterpart in adult queries such as "Do you understand?", "Get it?", and "What do you think?" Children also need to learn rules for turn-taking, for sequencing contributions to discourse, and for acknowledging and agreeing with linguistic and nonlinguistic contributions to the topic (Corsaro, n.d.). Such techniques contribute to framing a conversation so that speaker and listener can cooperate with one another in regulating the exchange of information.

The exchange of information, for varied purposes, is at the heart of discourse and depends on the ability to produce utterances that are semantically related to prior utterances from another speaker. This ability increases substantially from 2 to 3 years of age (Bloom, Rocissano, and Hood, 1976; and Corsaro, n.d.). Children learn to share the information in prior messages in different ways. In certain instances, information about a topic is shared because the speakers are both talking about the same event in the context; such successive utterances are semantically related because of *contextual contingency*.

Adult: I can't get the bolt off

                        need a screwdriver

In other instances, semantically related utterances share the same topic and also share some aspects of linguistic form and so are also *linguistically contingent* on prior adult utterances.

Adult: I see two

                        I see two bus come here

In the longitudinal study of the development of discourse from 2 to 3 years of age by Bloom, Rocissano, and Hood (1976, in *RLDev*), child utterances that were contextually contingent did not change in relative frequency. The important developmental change was a sharp increase in the relative frequency of child utterances that were linguistically related to prior adult utterances. The children were learning to share the topic of a previous utterance and add new information relative to the topic by producing linguistically contingent utterances that shared the same verb relation as in the adult utterance. They either replaced a Wh-constituent, added a subject-verb-complement constituent, or modified a subject-verb-complement constituent that was already stated in the prior adult utterance. For example:

Adult: What's in your hand?

book (Wh- replacement)

Adult: Mommy sit

Mommy stool
(addition of complement
constituent)

Adult: Let's take the shoes out

doll shoes (modification
within complement)

Linguistically contingent child utterances occurred more often after a question than after a statement from the adults. There was also an increase in the proportion of adult utterances that were questions. Although linguistic contingency always occurred more often after questions than after statements, the developmental increase in linguistic contingency was greater with statements than with questions. These two findings (that the adults asked proportionately more questions over time and that linguistic contingency increased more in response to statements than in response to questions) resulted in an equilibrium between adult questions and statements on the one hand and the kinds of contingent responses produced by the children on the other hand. The proportion of linguistically contingent child utterances that occurred after adult questions remained the same in the period from 2 to 3 years of age. The other categories of child discourse that were observed—contextual contingency, imitation, and no response—were also constant functions in relation to the occurrence of questions and nonquestions in the speech of the adults. The proportion of child utterances in each of these categories that occurred after questions did not change in the period from 2 to 3 years. This balance between adult and child messages provided evidence that discourse between adults and children is quite systematic in the course of development.

Regardless of the source of contingency between semantically related messages (whether contextual or linguistic), the children's utterances either *expanded* the prior adult utterance, for example,

Adult: I'll put my scarf on first
(getting ready to leave)   home

or provided an *alternative* to the adult utterance, for example,

Adult: Shall we sit on the sofa
and read my book?
(going to orange chair)   orange chair read book

Expansions were more frequent than alternatives and similar kinds of expansions or alternatives have been observed repeatedly in child discourse (e.g., Corsaro, n.d.; Garvey, 1975a; Keenan, 1974; and others).

With both kinds of contingent responses—expansions and alternatives—there was development in the ways in which information given in the prior adult message was marked in the children's utterance as the same information as viewed from the children's own orientation. There were changes in form (*shifting reference,* for example, from "you" in the adult message to "I" in the child message or from a noun to a pronoun); use of forms to point out or otherwise indicate the relative orientations of speaker and listener (*deixis,* for example, the use of "this" and "that," here" and "there"); and the elimination of redundant elements (*grammatical ellipsis,* for example, leaving out the words "you" and "going" in the question "Where're you going?" when responding "to the store"). Part of the children's development of discourse, then, consisted of learning the conventions for shifting reference, deixis, and ellipsis in communication.

SHIFTING REFERENCE, DEIXIS, AND ELLIPSIS

One of the difficulties in learning language has to do with the fact that there are many words in the language that are not stable in reference, because their use depends on the orientation of the speaker—and orientation varies among speakers and within situations. Jesperson (1924) called such words "shifters," and he gave as examples nouns such as kinship terms, for example, "Daddy," where Daddy to one child is not Daddy to another child, and "home," where my home is not your home. He described a young child who, having been told that Grandma was at home, insisted strongly that Grandma was not at home because Grandma was at Grandpa's house. Other words also differ in their use, depending on the point of view of the speaker and listener in the context of the speech event and in relation to the content of the message—in particular the class of personal pronouns, "I"/"You;" demonstrative pronouns, "this"/"that," "here"/"there;" certain verbs, "go"/ "come," "bring"/"take;" and the morphological processes on verbs that signal person, time, aspect, and so on. All shifters have a general or lexical meaning, for example, "I" means something like "self" or "ego," and "come" means "to arrive" but, in addition, they also have an "indexical meaning" (Jakobson, 1957) or a "deictic function" (Fillmore, 1973) in that they point out or indicate the relations between the participants of a speech event and the content of the message.

Jakobson (1957) proposed a classification scheme for the analysis of the relations between lexical and indexical (or deictic) meaning, with two basic distinctions: a distinction between an event and its participants, and a second distinction between the speech about the event and its content (p. 492). There are *events* and *participants* on the one hand and the *content* and forms of *speech* on the other. These interact with one another so that there is the content event (E^c) or what is being talked about, and there is the speech event (E^s) or the occurrence of a message about the content event. There are, also, the participants in the content event (P^c) and the participants in speech events (P^s).

As an example, consider that there are two persons, *David* and *Joan*, who are the participants in the event *going to the store*:

$$[(David) (Joan) (go) (store)] = E^c \text{ or the content event,}$$

and

$$(David) \text{ and } (Joan) = P^c \text{ or the participants in the content event}$$

A message about the event might be:

$$\text{"I'll go to the store with you"} = E^s \text{ or the speech event,}$$

with

$$\text{"I" and "you"} = P^s \text{ or the participants (speaker and hearer) in the speech event}$$

One can talk about either events or participants or talk about the relations among them. Certain linguistic forms, then, can refer to the participants themselves (P^c) David and Joan, or to the relation between participants and the content event being talked about (P^cE^c) David and Joan going to the store. Other linguistic forms can refer to the content event iself (E^c) going to the store, or its relation to other content events (E^cE^c), for example, going to the store after doing the dishes, or going to the store and buying a book. The linguistic forms that are "shifters" would be used when there is reference to either the speech event (E^s) itself or the participants in the speech event (P^s), in relation to content events or content participants. In the above example "I'll go to the store with you," "I" and "you" are shifters. They indicate speaker and hearer roles (P^s) in relation to the event and the participants in the event or the relation (P^s)/(E^cP^c).

The capacity for shifting reference is one aspect of the more general process of alternation. Alternation is the use of one of several possible forms that share the same essential meaning or referential function, but differ according to relations between content events and speech events, or even between speech events. For example, "this" is used instead of "that" if the speaker is talking about a near object, that is, "I want *this* (not *that* one over there)," and "bring" is used instead of "take" if the recipient is also the speaker, that is, "Please bring the book to me." Anaphoric reference means that something in one message refers back to something in a prior message, or is a shared reference between speech events. For example, "it" is used instead of a noun if the referent has already been named in a prior speech event, as in the two messages "I see the *book*" and "Give *it* to me." The definite article "the" is used instead of the indefinite "a" if the object has already been specified, for example, "Did you see 'Gone with the Wind'?"/ "No, but I read *the* book."

It is relatively easy to talk about events in the world (actions, relations), participants in events in the world (objects, persons), and the relations between events and participants. The participants and events of language content provide what Brown (1973) has called the "building blocks" of early sentences: the forms (single words and structures) that represent such content are learned first. It is considerably more complicated to talk about or otherwise take account of the relations between the events and participants in content, on the one hand, and speech events and participants in speech events on the other. As a consequence, the forms that Jesperson (1924) and Jakobson (1957) called "shifters" and the capacity for alternation among them appear later in the speech of children and are learned through trials and tribulations over a very long period of time.

The appearance of shifting reference in children's speech has been documented in children's use of pronouns (Bloom, Lightbown, and Hood, 1975; Huxley, 1966; Sharpless, 1974; and Tanz, 1976); definite and indefinite articles (Brown, 1973; Maratsos, 1974; and Warden, 1976, in *RLDev*); recoding in discourse (Bloom, Rocissano, and Hood, 1976); deictic verbs, that is, "come"/"go;" "bring"/"take" (Clark and Garnica, 1974; and Richards, 1976); kinship terms (Haviland and Clark, 1974; and Piaget, 1928); and in the use of certain antonymous adjectives, such as "same"/"different" (Donaldson and Wales, 1970; and Josephs, 1975). With each of these kinds of alternation, acquisition continues often well into the school years and involves the very complex interplay between children's opportunities for using and hearing others use shifting reference and their linguistic, conceptual, and social development. As a result, none of the existing studies are complete; at best they document the earliest stages when children begin to use alternative forms to take account of the shifting relations between the content event that is encoded in messages and the participants and context of the speech event.

There appear to be two different kinds of sequence in which children can learn to use alternative forms for indicating the relations between content events and speech events (E^c/E^s). In one sequence, children might learn the different forms that are possible only after they learn the relevant distinctions that such words encode and the reasons for choosing between them. In such a sequence one could say that *form follows function* in development. There is another sequence in which *function follows form* in development, as children learn a number of alternative forms before they learn the relevant distinctions for using one or the other alternant and rules for choosing among them. So far the evidence seems to indicate that one or the other of the two sequences are characteristic of the development of different classes of alternants. The acquisition of form seems to follow the understanding of function as children acquire the system of personal pronouns, the ability to recode aspects of a prior utterance in producing contingent discourse, and pairs of deictic verbs. In contrast, function appears to follow the acquisition of alternative forms when children learn shifting nominal/pronominal reference, shifting definite/indefinite reference, and rules for ellipsis.

Personal Pronouns

Children appear to learn different personal pronoun forms for the grammatical functions that they already know (e.g. sentence subject and object of the verb) as they learn the relevant relations between participants in the content event (P^c) and participants in the speech event (P^s) for person, number, case, and gender distinctions. Huxley (1970) described the acquisition of personal pronouns in the spontaneous speech of two children. In spite of the fact that one child started out with a predominantly nominal strategy (using nouns in relation to verbs) and the other child started with a predominantly pronominal strategy (using pronouns in relation to verbs), the apparent sequence of development was similar for the two children (using five instances as a criterion for assuming that the child knew something about using each pronoun). The sequence for the child who was predominantly pronominal to begin with was:

$$
\begin{array}{ccc}
& \text{"you"(sb)} & \\
\text{"I"(sb)} & \text{"she"(sb)} & \text{"we"(sb)} \\
\text{"it"(sb)} \rightarrow \text{"them" (ob)} \rightarrow & \text{"they"(sb)} \rightarrow & \text{"you"(ob)} \\
\text{"it"(ob)} & \text{"me"(ob)} &
\end{array}
$$

The sequence for the child who apparently learned pronouns as a substitution system after having first learned nouns was:

$$
\begin{array}{c}
\text{"I"(sb)} \\
\text{"it"(ob)} \rightarrow \text{"them" (ob)} \rightarrow \text{"you"(sb)} \rightarrow \text{"they"(sb)} \\
\text{"it"(sb)}
\end{array}
$$

Both children learned "it" (ob) as one of their first pronouns, learned "I" (sb), "it" (sb and ob), and "you" (sb) before learning "you" (ob) or "we" (sb), and learned "them" (ob) before "they" (sb). The pronouns "us," "he," and "him" were rare.

Recoding

As children learn to participate in discourse—to produce utterances that share the same topic with preceding utterances by someone else—there are several kinds of formal relations between successive messages. The earliest kinds of linguistic contingency that were described in Bloom, Rocissano, and Hood (1976) were instances in which children either repeated part or all of the prior utterance:

Adult: She might pinch her fingers

pinch her fingers,

or added something to a prior utterance:

Adult: Put this on with a pin

sharp

After a period of time in which the children either repeated or added but did not do both in the same sentence, they began to both repeat and add in the same sentence:

Adult: I didn't bring the
choochoo train today

bring choochoo
train tomorrow

The sequence then was repeat *or* add, and then repeat *and* add.

During this same period, for example, when the children responded to an adult utterance, they sometimes responded by repeating all or part of the prior adult message and changing its form without adding to or changing its meaning. The ways in which these recodings occurred indicated that the children were learning to switch pronominal forms for anaphoric deixis (to change the form of a message as a signal that the second speaker was now encoding the message but from his or her own perspective). The earliest recoding (*MLU* < 2.0) were predominantly shifts from the nominal coding of predicate objects (in the adult utterance) to pronouns (in the child utterance). For example:

Adult: I see the truck

see it

Subsequently, when *MLU* was between 2.0 and 2.75, there was pronominal shift for agents from "you" (in adult utterance) to "I" (in child utterance). When *MLU* approached 4.0 (in the last samples at 36 months), there was deictic shift for objects, "this" and "that," and place, "here" and "there." These results were described in Bloom, Rocissano, and Hood (1976) as one way in which the children maintained the topic and cohesion in conversation. The children did not use all kinds of recoding when they began to recode. Instead, there was a sequence in the appearance of different forms of recoding with different functions.

Deictic Verbs

A study by Clark and Garnica (1974) described how children learn verbs that have deictic function, such as the pairs "come"/"go" and "bring"/"take." Using a comprehension task, it was found that the meaning of "come" and "bring" was understood by the youngest children (6 and 7 years old) as well as by the oldest children (8 and 9 years old), but "go" and "take" were apparently not understood by the youngest children. Only the 9-year-old children appeared to understand the four words equally well. "Acquisition consists of the child working out which combinations of rules relating goal, speaker and addressees are appropriate for each deictic verb" (p. 569). It appears that the direction of movement toward the goal in relation to the participants in speech events was the major factor in these children's comprehension performance, and the two verbs "come" and "bring" with the same direction of movement were learned before their semantic counterparts "go and "take," which had another direction of movement.

However, using a production task in an experimental study with children 4 years to 7 years, 7 months old, Richards (1976) observed considerably earlier ages of acquisition for these same verbs. She reported that the pair "bring"/"take" were acquired later than the pair "come"/"go." She concluded that "acquisition of these verbs involves mapping the appropriate words onto preconceived features of situations, rather than the abstraction of the semantic features underlying each verb" (p. 655). Thus, it appears that children acquire verbs that are situationally related, as "come" and "go" are both related to the movement of *persons* toward or away from some goal, and "bring" and "take" are both related to the movement of some other *object* toward or away from some goal, instead of acquiring the verbs that share the feature *toward* (as "come" and "bring") separate from the verbs that share the feature *away from* (as "go" and "take").

There is no well-documented evidence about children's use of these same verbs with deictic function in their speech. The verbs "go" and "come" are used in their nondeictic sense as general verbs of motion in the speech of 2-year-old children, and "go" is far more frequent than "come" (Bloom, Miller, and Hood, 1975, in *RLDev*). "Take" occurs stereotypically, as in "Take a ride," at the same age, but there is no evidence of how "take" and "bring" are used subsequently.

Nominal/Pronominal Coding

When children begin to combine words for their earliest sentences with *MLU* less than 2.0, there appear to be two alternative strategies available to them. As discussed in Chapter VI, children can encode the semantic-syntactic relations between verbs and nouns, or between verbs and pro-nouns, and it appears to be the case that many, if not most, children use either one or the other strategy (Bloom, Lightbown, and Hood, 1975; Huxley, 1970; Nelson, 1975; and Ramer, 1976). When *MLU* passed 2.0, there was a shift—from nominal to pronominal coding for the children who had earlier combined verbs with nouns, and from pronominal to nominal coding for the children who had earlier combined verbs with pronouns (Bloom, Lightbown, and Hood, 1975). When *MLU* was about 2.5, the children knew that it was possible to use both nouns and pronouns in relation to verbs (i.e., to refer to themselves by name and "I," to refer to a car as "car" and "it," "this," or "that," and to refer to a place as "table" and "here," or "right there").

Pronominalization is a cohesive device in the adult language whereby a proform is substituted for a lexical item or word in order to continue reference to some object or event. There are basically two ways in which pronouns can be used: gesturally and anaphorically. Pronouns are used *gesturally*, to point out or otherwise indicate an object, action, or person of reference as when someone says "Give *it* to me" and reaches for the candy. Children's early use of pronouns appears to by primarily gestural. Anaphoric pronouns refer back to some object that has already been mentioned by one of the discourse participants, as in "There's some candy on the table. Will you get *it* for me?" (See Box VII-4.)

Even though the children in Bloom, Lightbown, and Hood (1975) used both nominal and pronominal forms when *MLU* was about 2.5, they did not provide evidence that the use of one or the other alternative (nouns or pronouns) was motivated by the requirements of the situation and the relation between content events and speech events (E^c/E^s). The children typically used nouns, even when it was clear from the nonlinguistic context or prior linguistic context what was being talked about, and they typically used pronouns gesturally when there was no information available to the listener about the identify of the referent from linguistic or nonlinguistic context. The children learned nouns and pronouns as alternative forms, after having learned each system separately and before they learned how contextual constraints govern the anaphoric use of one or another linguistic form. Although they acquired the forms or the *capacity* for alternative reference when they were about 2 years old, there was no evidence that they knew the rules for the alternative *use* of the different forms (Bloom, Lightbown, and Hood, 1975).

Experimental research with older children, however, has demonstrated that 3-year-old children understand the use of the pronoun "it" when it is used anaphorically in sequences of sentences such as "There is a box with five marbles. Give *it* to me" (Chipman and de Dardel, 1974; and Tanz, 1976). Tanz also reported that 3-year-old children understand the difference between definite ("it") and indefinite ("some") references to quantity. Sometime between 2 and 3 years, then, children learn such distinctions. It remains to be studied how they learn to mark these distinctions in their own speech (Box VII-4).

BOX VII-4 DIALOGUE WITH KATHRYN, 35 MONTHS OLD, WITH EXAMPLES OF SHIFTING NOMINAL/PROMINAL REFERENCE THAT IS MOTIVATED BY THE COHESION REQUIREMENTS OF DISCOURSE. When both speakers are referring to the same object or event, once it has been named by one of the participants in discourse (or otherwise pointed out), then one or the other participant can use a prominal form, without losing information, to refer to it

(Kathryn and Lois were pretending they were in an airplane, being served by a stewardess)

Oh/ well she's gonna bring us some food//
Oh what would you like?

some fruit

Some fruit? mm/ Okay/ what kind of fruit?
(Kathryn laughs)

chocolate fruit!

Chocolate fruit!
Oh
(Kathryn laughs)
I never saw chocolate fruit
(Kathryn laughs)

here she ___she comes and she's bringing it// well___there's some people behind us/ and she's gonna give them/ but then she'll come around and see me and you/ and and/ she'll say "would you like some food?" and we say "oh yes we want chocolate food"

Definite/Indefinite Articles

The indefinite article "a" (or "an") and the definite article "the" are forms of discourse that depend on the relationship between speaker and listener for their meaning (Brown, 1973; and Maratsos, 1974). One would say "I saw the horse go by" if the listener already had some referent or some knowledge of a particular horse. If reference was being made to just any horse, one would say "I saw a horse go by."

Brown used a criterion of acquisition of grammatical morphemes that required the use of a particular form (such as the use of definite articles for specific reference, or the use of indefinite articles for nonspecific reference) in 90% of the contexts that required its use. Using this criterion with his observational data from three children, Brown reported "when the doubtful cases are excluded and separate acquisition points tentatively identified for *a* and *the* these are within a sample or so of one another, and so it seems that the definite-nondefinite articles are acquired as a system" (p. 351). However, before the point of criterion, "the child's use of articles cannot support any inferences about his control of semantic and grammatical rules" (p. 355). It seems, then, that both article forms "a" and "the" are used, perhaps more or less indiscriminantly, before children learn the relationship between speaker and listener that governs their conventional use to signal the distinction between specific and nonspecific reference. Brown appeared to leave this question open.

In an experimental study, Maratsos (1974) used story-telling tasks with 3- and 4-year-old children to examine their use of definite and indefinite articles for specific and nonspecific reference. According to Maratsos, the children were able to differentiate indefinite noun phrases with nonspecific reference from indefinite noun phrases with specific reference. However, when it was necessary for the children to keep track of the listener's referential knowledge, they did less well.

In a follow-up study, Warden (1976, in *RLDev*) observed children's use of definite and indefinite articles in different contexts. In one experiment (see Box II-1) he established that 4-year-old children consistently used the indefinite article "a" in a naming task (shown an animal and asked "What's that?"), but used definite articles in a description task (shown a cow chasing a duck and asked to "tell me what's happening"). Adults in the same experiment used the indefinite article in the naming task and in the description task as well. In two other experiments Warden examined children's ability to use the indefinite article to introduce a new referent into a discourse context, and to use the defnite article to refer to a referent that had already been introduced. Warden argued that

> A speaker's ability to use the articles appropriately can be revealed most clearly when he is allowed to provide the verbal context for his referring expressions, rather than being constrained to respond to a verbal context imposed on him by an experimenter, as in Maratsos' studies. (p. 11)

In Warden's study, children under 5 years used definite reference predominantly in both contexts, failing to take account of their audience's different knowledge of the referent in the two contexts. Children did not consistently use indefinite expressions to introduce new referents until sometime betwen 5 and 9 years of age. Warden pointed out that

> The physical presence of both referents and audience may have encouraged the use of definite references, particularly by young children. It may be that

young children would use identifying expressions (with indefinite articles) more readily in contexts where either the referents are absent (e.g., recounting of a prior event) or the audience is absent (e.g., a telephone conversation). (p. 112)

Both the study by Maratsos and the study by Warden provide evidence of how children might learn to take account of linguistic context in learning to use definite and indefinite articles. Just how children also learn to take account of differential cues from the nonlinguistic context remains to be determined.

Grammatical Ellipsis

Halliday and Hasan (1976) described substitution (alternation) and ellipsis as two types of cohesion relations between parts of a text (or discourse). In substitution, one item is replaced by another item (such as a noun by a pronoun or an indefinite article by a definite article). In ellipsis an item is omitted or, put another way, one item is "replaced by nothing" (p. 88).

An important means for providing cohesion in texts of naturally occurring discourse is the elimination of redundancy through ellipsis. For example, the second utterance in the discourse sequence between one speaker, "The girl's in the truck," and a second speaker, "The boy's in the truck," is typically reduced in natural language to "The boy is, too." Similarly, an answer to the question "Who's riding the bike?" is "My sister is riding the bike," which could be reduced to "My sister is riding," "My sister is," or "My sister." Grammatical ellipsis consists of the regular deletion of one or more sentence constituents (subject-verb-complement) that is redundant with a prior message. Its occurrence provides evidence that the speaker is able to take account of prior linguistic reference by themselves and others in order to eliminate the redundant elements in their speech.

Children's early sentences are fragmented in that major sentence constituents (subject-verb-complement) are regularly omitted (Bloom, 1970; Bloom, Miller, and Hood, 1975, in *RLDev*; Bowerman, 1973b in *RLDev*; Brown, 1973; Park, 1974; and others). According to Brown (1973), children have knowledge of the fuller constituent structure when they produce partial constituent relations (i.e., subject-verb, verb-object, and subject-object), but they do not have adequate knowledge of rules of discourse to know when to say either the full constituent structure or only a fragment. Not yet knowing the rules of discourse, children overgeneralize from the elliptical and truncated adult speech that they hear and form the impression that it does not matter how much of a full sentence one says.

Other factors were described in Bloom, Miller, and Hood (1975, in *RLDev*) that contributed to an explanation of the variable length of children's sentences and the fact that two constituent relations occur regularly long after children clearly demonstrate the capacity to express three constituent relations in sentences. One factor that was specifically tested in that study was whether the occurrence of partial sentences in the children's speech when *MLU* was less than 2.5 was the systematic result of an effort to take account of prior linguistic reference and eliminate redundancy between messages that follow one another. In order to explore whether ellipsis was a regularly occurring grammatical process, the relation between child utterances and preceding adult utterances (adjacent adult-child utterance pairs) was examined whenever a transitive action or locative action relation was expressed.

All the child utterances with these verbs that were adjacent to a preceding adult utterance were classified as contingent or noncontingent. A contingent utterance was linguistically and/or semantically related to the preceding adult utterance. A necessary but not sufficient condition for ellipsis is that the elliptical utterance be contingent on a previous utterance. If the proportion of contingency in two-constituent sentences is greater than in three-constituent sentences, then one might conclude that the children were using ellipsis in responding to adult speech. However, although the proportion of contingent utterances increased developmentally for the four children from *MLU* of 1.0 to 2.5, the frequency of contingency was not different between two- and three-constituent sentences.

As another test, contingent action utterances in the last sample from each child, when *MLU* was about 2.5, were examined directly to determine (1) if the two-constituent utterances were elliptical, for example,

Adult: **What are you looking for?**

> **look for my pencil**

and (2) if the three-constituent utterances occurred in an elliptical condition (i.e., where the child utterance was at least partially redundant), for example,

Adult: **What are you gonna do?**

> **I'm gonna fix it**

For Kathryn and Eric there were more three-constituent sentences in elliptical conditions, whereas for Peter and Gia the opposite was found. However, none of these differences were significant (by chi-square test). It was concluded that grammatical ellipsis, as it operates in adult speech, was not yet productive in the children's speech and could not be a factor accounting for the variable length of utterances. In contrast, the important conclusion that followed from the several analyses of discourse variation was that discourse (i.e., discourse defined in terms of the preceding related utterances by the child or an adult) often influenced the length of the children's utterances by providing memory support to facilitate the occurrence of longer three-constituent sentences. These were very often redundant, because the children tended both to repeat part of the preceding utterance and to add something to it. In addition to learning how to produce longer utterances with full constituent structure, children also need to learn how to use the linguistic context to produce shorter utterances in the linguistic contexts where fragments of sentences are acceptable. Thus, children produce partial utterances long before they know about the conventions or rules that govern the permitted occurrence of partial (elliptical) utterances to provide cohesion or texting in discourse. Children need to *learn* how to use grammatical ellipsis.

Children must acquire specifically linguistic abilities for producing and interpreting grammatical sentences (the coding relations between content and form) for making reference to objects and events in the world. But children also must acquire specifically social and cognitive abilities to become competent members of the linguistic community, knowing not only what may be said, but also knowing what should and should not be said, and when, where, and to whom (Hymes, 1964).

Most of what has been discussed about language development so far has been concerned with what children learn to say; what children understand from language has been touched on only briefly because research into the first 3 years of child language has been concerned primarily with production, for reasons that will be discussed presently. The developmental relationship between understanding and speaking will be discussed in the next chapter.

SUMMARY

Two principal aspects of language use are described in this chapter. One has to do with the functions of language—why people use language and the kinds of things that people do with language. The other aspect of language use has to do with the conventions of alternation—the rules that speakers of a language know for deciding which forms, among the alternative forms of messages that are available, can be used to achieve one or another goal or function. The beginnings of communication are described, and it is pointed out that infants start out with neither the intention to communicate nor the conventional means of language to use for communicating. Gradually, however, infants' sounds and movements evolve into early words and gestures in the transition from subjective and cognitive behavior to more social and communicative behavior.

The functions of language are the reasons why people speak, and these undergo their own development. Halliday (1975) identified several "social-semiotic" functions of communication in infancy that appear to evolve into the two broad and general functions that he labelled "pragmatic" and "mathetic," the former concerned with achieving practical gain, contact and interaction with others, and the latter concerned with gaining knowledge about the world. The pragmatic and mathetic functions of language each develop, in turn, into several more specific regulatory and other functions. The functions of language as conceived by Jakobson, Halliday, and others are personal concerns of the individual in contact with the environment. Others (e.g., Austin and Searle) have conceived of the functions of language in the more social and pragmatic terms of "speech acts." Speech acts were discussed in this chapter as being either highly constrained and limited in both form and context (such as with greetings, exchange of goods, and the even more ritualistic speech acts of opening a session of court or pledging allegiance to the flag) or more flexible and variable in forms and contexts (such as with speech acts that request, promise, and prohibit). It appears that children begin using speech acts that are highly constrained in form and context, such as in greetings "Hi" and "Bye bye," or in exchange situations with "Thank you;" they progress gradually in learning more variable forms of requests, and the like, that are appropriate in different contexts.

There are different forms of language that can achieve the same purpose, and children learn to choose among these alternative forms according to the needs or requirements of the situation. In particular, children learn how to infer what their listeners already know and need to know and to take these needs into account in deciding on the forms of messages. Perhaps the most important result of such learning is the ability to participate in conversation, or discourse—to know how to use the information from a prior message to produce a contingent message. In particular, children learn about conditions for shifting reference—which includes the use of personal pronouns, deictic verbs, and definite and indefinite articles— and grammatical ellipsis for avoiding the repetition of redundant elements in the cohesion relations between messages. All this learning begins in the child's third year, but continues well into the school years.

SUGGESTED READINGS

In *Readings in Language Development*

Garvey, C., Requests and responses in children's speech. *Journal of Child Language, 2,* 41–63, 1975.

Halliday, M. A. K., A sociosemiotic perspective on language development. *Bulletin of the School of Oriental and African Studies, 37,* 60–81, 1974.

Smith, M., The influence of age, sex, and situation on the frequency, form and function of questions asked by preschool children. *Child Development, 4,* 201–213, 1933b.

Warden, D., The influence of context on children's use of identifying expressions and references. *British Journal of Psychology, 67,* 101–112, 1976.

Other Readings

Bates, E., Pragmatics and sociolinguistics in child language. In D. Morehead and A. Morehead (Eds.), *Normal and deficient child language.* Baltimore: University Park Press, 1976.

Bloom, L., Rocissano, L., and Hood, L., Adult-child discourse: Developmental interaction between information processing and linguistic knowledge. *Cognitive Psychology, 8,* 521–552, 1976.

Clark, E., and Garnica, O., Is he coming or going? On the acquisition of deictic verbs. *Journal of Verbal Learning and Verbal Behavior, 13,* 559–572, 1974.

Dore, J., Holophrases, speech acts, and language universals. *Journal of Child Language, 2,* 21–40, 1975.

Halliday, M. A. K., *Learning how to mean—Explorations in the development of language.* London: Edward Arnold, 1975.

Hymes, D. (Ed.), *Language in culture and society.* New York: Harper & Row, 1964.

Maratsos, M., Preschool children's use of definite and indefinite articles. *Child Development, 45,* 446–455, 1974.

Richards, M., Come and go reconsidered: Children's use of deictic verbs in contrived situations. *Journal of Verbal Learning and Verbal Behavior, 15,* 655–665, 1976.

Schnelle, H., Language communication with children—toward a theory of language use. In Y. Bar-Hillel (Ed.), *Pragmatics of natural languages.* New York: Humanities Press, pp. 174–193, 1971.

The relationship between understanding and speaking has barely been touched on in the study of child language. Children's early speech has received far more attention than children's early understanding, largely because of the difficulties involved in measuring comprehension and not because of a lack of interest. A major problem in evaluating comprehension is that children's responses are multidetermined—what children do depends on many things in addition to what they hear. In contrast, child speech can be written down or otherwise recorded and, if nothing else, simply reported or described. However, there has also been an unfortunate tendency to take comprehension for granted, in the light of what little anecdotal and experimental evidence about comprehension has been reported. The result is that the prevailing view of the developmental relationship between the two is, quite simply, that comprehension necessarily precedes production at every step along the way. However, as awareness about the processes involved in speech development has increased, there has been a growing interest in comprehension development, and deeper questions than whether the one precedes the other have begun to emerge. In particular, one would like to know more about the factors that contribute to understanding messages, how such factors relate to producing messages, and the relation of both to linguistic and cognitive development.

Inasmuch as communication depends on the extent to which the semantic intention of the speaker matches the semantic interpretation of the listener, the knowledge that each has could not be independent. Thus, it is most probably not the case that understanding and speaking develop separately, with children learning different *rules* for each. Because it is necessary to process words and semantic-syntactic structures in order to learn them, the production of speech might appear to be dependent on the prior development of comprehension. But, while it is most probably not the case that speaking and understanding are altogether separate developments, it is by no means clear that speech and understanding represent just two different modes of the same development.

The hypothesis that will be proposed here is that the two represent mutually dependent but different underlying processes, with a resulting shifting of influence between them in the course of language development. In short, it will be suggested that the developmental gap between comprehension and speaking probably varies among different children and at different times, and that the gap may be more apparent than real.

Before describing some of the factors that contribute to the understanding and speaking of messages and the relation between understanding and speaking in development, it will be helpful to review how their interaction has been described in diaries or case histories of development and in recent psycholinguistic studies of young children. As will be seen, there is most often a strong assumption of a necessary temporal priority in the relation between comprehension and speech development. For example, according to McNeill, "children probably add new information to their competence mainly by comprehending speech" (1970, p. 102). Observations of small children both by experimenters and by parents have almost always produced the strong impression that children respond to much more language than they can actually say themselves. However, it also happens that there has always been a certain amount of skepticism in the early diaries about the nature of children's comprehension and exactly what it is in speech events that children are responding to when they appear to understand what is said. More recently, there has been growing skepticism about linguistic comprehension in the psycholinguistic literature, as well.

THE COMPREHENSION-PRODUCTION GAP

Lewis (1963) described the beginning of comprehension in terms of the affective coalescence of intonation contour, phonetic form, and situation into "a new whole," which is, presumably, the primitive mental representation of semantic information linking acoustic linguistic events (intonation and phonetic patterns) with visually perceptual, nonlinguistic (situational) events. With respect to the relation between comprehension and emerging speech, Lewis noted a 1-month lapse between understanding reference to objects and the clear use of words for objective reference (at 17 months), for example, "ba" (bath), "ba" (button), and "ha" (honey). Lewis did not, however, relate the early influence of intonation for emerging comprehension to the use of intonation in early speech.

Spitz (1957) described the early development of awareness of prohibitive "no" as a first semantic notion. His explanation of its emergence was based on the exaggerated and often abrupt change in emphasis and affect in mothers' speech that accompanies the stern "no" and headshake as their children start to crawl about and investigate. Spitz described the beginning of comprehension in the association between "no" and a set of events or behaviors that have been defined for children by their mothers as "prohibited." In this case, children need to associate the acoustic event with events that transcend the perceptual properties of different objects. Thus plants, electric wires, knives, and matches share common reference, even though they look quite different, because they have been associated with "no" and the accompanying prohibiting behavior from an adult. Although prohibitive "no" is often reported in the diary studies as responded to by children in their first year, there have been no reports of prohibitive "no" in children's earliest speech. Indeed, the use of the prohibitive "no" other than stereotypic use develops after the use of "no" to signal the other semantic notions of nonexistence, disappearance, rejection, and denial (Belkin, 1975; and Bloom, 1970, 1973).

Leopold (1939, in *RLDev*) reported that the beginning of his daughter Hildegard's comprehension was at 8 months and was, at first, limited to:

> her own name . . . [which] usually induced her to turn her head expectantly toward the speaker. There was no doubt that she referred these sounds in some way to herself. . . . In the second half of the ninth month she took a decisive step forward: both speaking and understanding began [although] it was speaking in a very rudimentary sense. (p. 21)

Subsequently the word "Daddy" and prohibitive "no, no . . . made her pay attention, stop crying, and look around." Leopold reported that understanding increased rapidly thereafter while progress in speaking was slight. However, the earliest words that were understood—her name, "Daddy," and "no, no"—were not among the first words in Hildegard's subsequent speech. Some time toward the end of their first year, then, children may indicate recognition of an association between an acoustic event, a word, and an object by a shift of gaze toward the object or by an arrest of attention.

Children may also recognize the relation between a word and some behavior or association among different objects and events (such as in the context of prohibition). Although speech recognition is often reported to precede speech production, early recognized words are not usually the same words that are later spoken.

Even though the first words that a child says are not necessarily the same words that are first understood, there are similarities as well as differences between early production and early comprehension. For one, children respond initially to hearing names of particular objects or persons (such as the child who recognized the word "birds" in reference only to the birds in a mobile, or "music" only in reference to a particular record player; Bloom, 1973). Similarly, the words that children first learn to say often make reference to only a particular instance of an object or event (underextension) For another, children recognize behaviors that different objects can share. Among the earliest words that children say are words like "more" to specify another instance or recurrence of an object or event; "gone" to comment on the disappearance or nonexistence of objects; and "up" for different objects that can go *up*. Saying the words "more," "gone" and "up" are similar to children's early comprehension of prohibitive "no," because the same word is ascribed to referents with different figurative properties. Thus children seem to learn words in reference across perceptually different objects, such as "no," "more," and "gone" for both comprehension and production. More important than a continuum in development from understanding to talking is the fact that both result from similar kinds of influences.

It is not the case that production depends on prior comprehension for each instance in which a word is used. There have been reports of overextension of reference for the words that children say, where a word is used in situations that seem to share a common element for the child, but not necessarily for adults (Bloom, 1973; Clark, 1973a; see Chapter IV). For example, Werner (1948) described a child's use of "afta" to designate a drinking glass, a pane of glass, a window, and also the contents of a glass. The child did not understand the word used in each situation before using it himself; there is little likelihood that he heard the word in the same situations, but that did not keep him from using it. Although it is necessary to hear a word in order to say it in the first place, a child may well learn to understand the word by learning how to use it—that is, by generalizing or associating properties of the situation in which the word was first heard, to new situations.

The reports of children's overextension in the literature have most often been anecdotal descriptions of children's speaking in naturalistic situations. More recently, there has been some question as to whether children also overextend in comprehension as well. Huttenlocher (1974) tested four 1-year-old children's understanding of object words by asking "Where is

_____?" She reported that there were no instances of "overgeneralization;" the children "did not respond to a word unless they knew its referent" (p. 357). However, there were instances in which children confused the words that were within the same "cognitive-semantic domains," such as facial features ("Where is your nose?") and foods. Huttenlocher suggested that these errors occur because the word schemas within a domain are mentally stored together and so are easily confused. It seems, however, that such confusability may be partly an explanation instead of a refutation of overextension in comprehension (and production) in some instances. What is not clear is how this explanation (confusion of word schemas) and another explanation (insufficient or imprecise word schemas) can be decided on from the evidence. Such confusion errors that Huttenlocher described for comprehension are similar to many of the overextensions that have been described for children's production (see Clark, 1973a). In a study that required children to point to pictures and name pictures, Thomson and Chapman (1977) tested five children aged 21 to 27 months. They found that some words were overextended in both comprehension (picture pointing) and production (picture naming).

FROM SINGLE WORDS TO SENTENCES

Once children are well into the use of single-word utterances in the second year, the question of related development in comprehension assumes a different form. The question in the second year of development is whether or not children process the syntax of sentences that they hear in order to understand sentences, even though they themselves say only one word at a time. The prevailing assumption has been that children do understand a great deal more than they are actually able to say in this period of time, and such presumed understanding is often used as an argument for the claim that single-word utterances are holophrastic or "one-word sentences."

Children between 1 and 2 years of age do appear to understand a great deal that is said to them and often seem to respond appropriately to complex statements and directions. But the directions and statements they respond to so readily refer to their immediate environment more often than not. Utterances in the speech of mothers addressed to their children are frequently redundant in relation to context and behavior, and language learning no doubt depends on the relationship between the speech children hear and what they see and do. For example, the statement, "Will is going down the slide," spoken to a child who has been playing with Will on the playground would be likely to cause the child to look for Will or look toward the slide. If children do not understand sentences that refer to relations among objects and events that are not immediately available, then the extent to which they analyze the semantic-syntactic structure for understanding is certainly questionable. Thus, the same statement "Will is going down the slide" or the question "Is Will going down the slide?" would most probably draw a blank if the child hears it at the dinner table or while taking a bath.

Leopold (1939) pointed out that comprehension during the period when speech is limited to single words depends primarily on children being able to recognize the highly stressed and salient words in an utterance. Adults speaking to children help them to understand by repeating key words and exaggerating stress. Guillaume (1927) vividly described the elaborations through gesture, emphasis, and repetition that are used to help very young children understand what is said to them. For example, "Give Grandma a kiss. Grandma. Give her a *kiss*. Give *Grandma* a kiss," with pointing and pursing the lips and maybe even turning the child's head toward Grandma would most probably produce the desired result. Although such a description may seem somewhat extreme, cues such as repetition, exaggeration, pointing, and gesture come to be automatic for the adult, and children no doubt come to look for such cues and use them for getting meaning from the stream of speech that they hear.

The cues of repetition, exaggeration, pointing, and gesture are also present in children's own behavior in the second year, but it is not at all clear how such behaviors relate to children's perception of such cues by others. One would like to know how children's movements augment their speech, and whether the interactions between expressive movements and speech relate to children's perception of combined gestural and auditory cues from adults. The important issue in relating development in comprehension to development in speaking is the relation between a child's mental schemas for processing such linguistic and nonlinguistic cues, on the one hand, and the mental processes that result in utterances, on the other hand.

One investigation that attempted to tap children's understanding during the single-word utterance period was reported by Shipley, Smith, and Gleitman (1969, in *RLDev*) using data from two groups of children: one group used only single-word utterances; the second group used telegraphic two- and three-word sentences. Children were presented with commands that directed them to act on an object in their immediate presence. The commands were varied as (1) single words (e.g., "ball"); (2) telegraphic (e.g., "throw ball"), or (3) well formed ("Throw me the ball"). The first finding that was reported was that children who used only single-word utterances themselves responded most often to single-word commands, providing no support for the idea that comprehension exceeds production in this period of development. Moreover, the tasks did not evaluate whether or not the children analyzed the structure of the sentences, inasmuch as merely touching the ball or picking up the ball was accepted as a positive response.

The second finding reported by Shipley, Smith, and Gleitman (1969, in *RLDev*) was that the older children who were using two- and three-word utterances preferred to respond to well-formed commands instead of to telegraphic or single-word commands. However, this second result cannot be taken as evidence that comprehension exceeds production if the well-formed commands manifested the same structure represented in the children's own telegraphic (i.e., reduced) utterances. It has been pointed out that early two- and three-word utterances are often reductions of more complete underlying structures (Bloom, 1970a; and Bloom, Miller, and Hood, 1975, in *RLDev*). For example, the actual utterances "read book" and "Mommy book" would have the fuller underlying structure *Mommy read book* given (1) the relevant nonlinguistic state of affairs (Mommy reading, or about to, or supposed to read a book), and (2) evidence elsewhere in a large enough corpus of utterances that the child understands the linguistic relations between agent (of an action) and object (affected by the action).

There seems to be an asymmetry between understanding words and understanding relations between words in the transition from using single-word utterances to using longer, structured speech toward the end of the second year. On the one hand, a child needs to understand something of the semantics of a word in order to respond to the word when it is spoken by someone else. For example, in order to recognize the association between the acoustic event "milk" and the substance *milk* that is available and offered with regularity in the daily routine, the child must have perceived and mentally represented, however primitively, the acoustic configuration of the word. On the other hand, the child does not need to know or to understand the semantic-syntactic relations between words, (i.e., the *structure* of sentences) in order to respond when someone talks about the actual relations between "Mommy" and "book," between "baby" and "milk," or between "ball" and "floor," when (1) the individual words are already understood, and (2) such objects and relations occur along with the utterances that make reference to them.

When a sentence is redundant with respect to the context in which it occurs, then the amount of information that children need to get from the linguistic message is probably minimal. On the other hand, knowledge of semantic constraints and knowledge of syntax are necessary for understanding linguistic messages that do not refer to the contexts in which they occur. In such utterances, the *meaning* is in the linguistic message alone. There is, then, another assymetry between understanding multiword utterances and speaking multiword utterances. Children do not have to process syntax to understand reference to relations in immediate events, but children do need to learn something about the syntax of the language and semantic constraints in order to talk about such relations in any coherent way. Thus, knowing a word and knowing a grammar, and understanding structured speech and using structured speech, apparently represent different mental capacities. It may be misleading to consider that such capacities develop in linear temporal relation, with comprehension simply preceding production.

PSYCHOLINGUISTIC TASKS TO COMPARE COMPREHENSION AND PRODUCTION

Several different experimental attempts have been made to investigate the relationship between understanding and speaking in the course of development. Three procedures that will be considered here are (1) the imitation-comprehension-production (ICP) tasks devised by Fraser, Bellugi, and Brown (1963); (2) training tasks; and (3) the use of elicited imitation.

In the Fraser, Bellugi, and Brown ICP tasks, 3-year-old children were presented with pairs of pictures that portrayed 10 different grammatical relationships, for example, the relationship between subject and direct object. Each pair of pictures presented two contrasting representations of a relationship, for example, a *girl* pushing a *boy*, and a *boy* pushing a *girl*. The investigator presented each pair to the children, saying, "Here are two pictures, one of a boy pushing a girl, and the other of a girl pushing a boy." In the imitation task the children were asked to repeat one or the other sentence, "The boy is pushing the girl" or "The girl is pushing the boy." In the comprehension task the children were asked to point to the picture that goes with one of the sentences, for example, "Show me the picture of the girl pushing the boy." In the production task, the children were asked to say a sentence for one of the pictures. The results of the experiment were that imitation was easiest and production was most difficult, leading Fraser, Bellugi, and Brown to conclude that imitation precedes comprehension and comprehension precedes production in the course of language development. Subsequently, Lovell and Dixon (1967) repeated the ICP tasks with 2-year-old children, with the same results and apparent confirmation of the conclusion that children are able to imitate and then understand certain linguistic structures before they use them.

There are several problems in accepting the results of the ICP test. For one, in the production task, the children have already heard the sentence in the introduction to the instructions "Here are two pictures, one of a boy pushing a girl, and the other of a girl pushing a boy," which may have given some linguistic support to the children for making up their own sentences. Imitation was the easiest task, but it was also the case that the length of the sentences presented for imitation was always within the children's auditory memory span. Children have difficulty repeating sentences that exceed memory span even when they themselves are able to produce the same sentences spontaneously at a different time, as will be seen subsequently in the discussion of elicited imitation.

Baird (1972) and Fernald (1972) have challenged both the methodology and the conclusions of the ICP test. Fernald pointed out that the response possibilities were not equated for the comprehension and production tasks and, in part, favored higher scores for comprehension. In pointing to a picture in the comprehension task, the children could be either right or wrong, depending on which picture they chose, and their chances of being right was 50 percent. However, in the production task, Fraser, Bellugi, and Brown had more stringent requirements for a correct response, and the children had much less chance of being right. Fernald repeated the experiment but equated the response possibilities for both comprehension and production (see Box VIII-1). When looking at only the correct or incorrect responses in both tasks, comprehension and production were essentially the same.

Keeny and Wolfe (1972) tested the production, imitation, and comprehension of subject-verb agreement for number in English sentences by 46 3- and 4-year-old children (e.g., "The bird *is* singing" versus "The birds *are* singing"). Production of subject-verb agreement was evaluated in the children's spontaneous speech; 94% of 906 utterances were correct for "be." More than 50% of the sentences had pronouns instead of nouns as subjects. The authors concluded from this sample that the children reliably inflected verbs for number agreement in their spontaneous speech. In the imitation task, sentence stimuli were either grammatical or ungrammatical (for subject-verb agreement) and did not exceed memory span, for example, "The bird is singing." Verbatim responses were scored; 83% of the grammatical sentences were repeated verbatim. However, in 93% of the ungrammatical sentences not repeated verbatim, the children corrected the noun and verb inflection, again demonstrating that they knew the rule for producing subject-verb agreement in sentences.

BOX VIII-1 AN EXAMPLE OF DEFFERENCES IN SCORING PRODUCTION IN THE ICP TASKS

In the ICP tasks, a child is shown a pair of pictures and told "One of these pictures is called 'The boy draws' and the other is called 'The boys draw.'" He or she is then asked to "Tell me the name of this one" (pointed to by the examiner). In the scoring by Fraser, et al., the response was counted as correct only if the noun was produced without the inflection -s plus the verb with the inflection -s for the first picture, and the noun with -s plus the verb without inflection for the second picture. In the Fernald scoring, the response was counted as correct if the child produced only the noun without the -s for the first picture and the noun with the -s for the second picture. In this way the same minimal contrast (boy/boys) that the child used for comprehension was also required for production.

The results of three comprehension tests in the Keeney and Wolfe experiments were not so clear cut. In one of the comprehension tests, the verbal test, children were presented with either a spoken singular or plural verb and asked to say a subject-noun that agreed in number; results of this test indicated that the children were responding to the verb number inflection in that they most often produced subject-nouns in agreement. In the second and third tests, the children were asked to point to one of a pair of pictures that represented a bird or birds, acting out either a full spoken sentence in one test, or only the spoken verb of a sentence in the other (verbal) test. In responding to full sentences, the children were most often right (apparently responding to the noun number) but, in responding to the verb alone, they were not. Based on the results of this experiment, Keeney and Wolfe concluded that the children did not understand the relation between verb inflections for number and the meaning of singular or plural, even though they could produce subject-verb agreement for number in their speech. They concluded that production does indeed precede comprehension in reference to inflection for verb number.

One might indeed question whether the verb inflection adding -s to a verb, actually means singular versus plural to children, apart from noun (or pronoun) number. Expecting children to recognize its quasisemantic function may be a metalinguistic task that is beyond their capabilities at 3 and 4 years. The fact that the inflection was fully productive in their spontaneous speech was evidence that they had learned a syntactic rule that they could not identify. Such learning may reflect a certain integrity of the linguistic system as children are learning it. That is, learning one aspect of the system may well necessarily entail knowing related aspects, so that knowing plural rules for nouns and speaking sentences will predict the use of verb agreement. In this case, as with lexical items, using a linguistic form may be a means of learning it.

In a study by Lahey (1974), there is support for the idea that children may incorporate surface features of the language into their speech before they fully understand the underlying meaning distinctions that such forms represent. Lahey compared 4- and 5-year-old children's comprehension of coordinate, center-embedded relative clause, and right-branching relative clause sentences under four conditions of presentation: (1) with both prosody and syntactic markers, (2) with markers but without prosody, (3) with prosody but without markers, and (4) with neither prosody nor markers. The children were asked to act out sentences such as "The cow hit the pig that chased the deer" with toy animals; the number of semantic-syntactic relationships that were acted out was scored.

Lahey reported that center-embedded sentences, for example, "The cow that hit the pig chased the sheep," were easier to understand than right-branching sentences, such as, "The cow hit the pig that chased the sheep," which were the most difficult to understand. This was in contrast to the report by Menyuk (1969) that more nursery school children *produced* right-branching sentences than center-embedded sentences. Furthermore, scores for center-embedded sentences were significantly lower when prosody was eliminated (and the sentences were spoken as a list of words) but syntactic markers were present. Lahey concluded that word order was the major linguistic cue, rather than syntactic markers, that the children used to process the sentences presented to them, even though they were at the age when children are reported to produce many syntactic markers in their spontaneous speech. Some of the children in the study spontaneously reproduced the sentences as they acted them out and either repeated the marker or supplied it when it was missing but, nevertheless, did not demonstrate the relationship that was marked by the relative pronoun by acting it out.

Two studies compared the ability of younger children to respond to word-order variations in comprehension tasks with their ability to use word order in their own speech. Wetstone and Friedlander (1973) reported that children who used two- and three-word utterances with consistent word order responded equally well to normal word order and varied word order in questions and directions presented to them. Chapman and Miller (1975, in *RLDev*) used object manipulation to compare children's comprehension and production of subject-object order in semantically reversible sentences with animate and inanimate subjects and objects, for example, "The dog is chasing the boy," and "The car is pushing the truck." They reported that children used appropriate subject-object order in speaking significantly more often than in responding to subject-object cues in a comprehension task.

Of particular interest in the Chapman and Miller study was the result that the two younger groups of children (with *MLU* less than 2.5 morphemes) responded correctly at less than chance level to sentences with an inanimate subject and an animate object, indicating that they were responding to the animacy of the nouns more often than they responded to word order to determine the relationship of each noun to the verb. However, when Chapman and Miller analyzed the children's responses in their production task to determine how often inanimate subjects and animate objects were encoded, they found conflicting results. The children with the shortest *MLU* (average 1.8) and longest *MLU* (average 2.9) tended to encode the object and the subject regardless of whether they were animate or inanimate. They encoded the object more than twice as often, no doubt because the question they were responding to was some form of "What . . . doing?" Chapman and Miller interpreted these production results to mean that "the child's encoding strategies bear no obvious direct relation to his decoding strategies in early stages of language acquisition" (p. 367). Alternatively, one might also question to what extent elicited production in an experimental task such as

Chapman and Miller used bears a direct relation to children's spontaneous production in naturalistic situations. The factors that contribute to the children's behaviors are different in the different situations.

The comprehension result in the Chapman and Miller study is consistent with other reports that animate nouns predominate as sentence subjects in children's early sentences (Bloom, 1970a; Bowerman, 1973a; and Brown, Cazden, and Bellugi, 1969). It appears that semantic-syntactic knowledge of verbs influences comprehension and production similarly in early development. The semantics of verbs determines the selectional restrictions on nouns as subjects and objects, and the verbs that predominate in early grammar are the verbs that allow reference to people doing things and inanimate objects being acted on. Eventually, children need to learn that (1) the semantic-syntactic restrictions with verbs such as "hit, chase, bump, push, pull, and carry" (the verbs used in the Chapman and Miller tasks) can be relaxed to specify inanimate agents and effect on animate objects, and (2) word order can override certain selectional restrictions of verbs as a stronger linguistic device. Again, as with lexical items and grammatical morphemes, using word order may be a means of learning more about its grammatical function as children actively apply their knowledge to new situations and thereby expand on it.

TRAINING TASKS

In a study by Guess (1969) two severely retarded boys, each 13 years old and with reported mental ages of 4.5 years, were trained for the acquisition of the plural morpheme. When trained to understand the forms, the subjects did not generalize to expressive use at the same time. Subsequently, after being trained to use the plural forms correctly, successful reversed receptive training did not generalize to reversed expressive use. Guess concluded that the subjects' ability to learn to understand the plural morpheme was independent of their ability to learn to use it.

In a follow-up study, Guess and Baer (1973) trained four retarded subjects concurrently in both comprehension and production of different allomorphs, either /s/ or /z/, of the plural morpheme. Subjects were trained to understand one plural form and to produce a different plural form. The findings indicated that even when trained concurrently both to understand and to use the plural morpheme so that new, untrained stimuli were responded to correctly, three of the four retarded subjects exhibited partial or no generalization of performance from comprehension to production or *vice versa* with the same plural allomorph. As Guess and Baer pointed out, other studies have used a learning paradigm to demonstrate the effectiveness of training in one modality (production or comprehension) for facilitating performance in the other, for example, studies of articulation (Winitz and Preisler, 1965; and Mann and Baer, 1971).

The issue with respect to the relation between understanding a speech form and using a speech form in the process of learning the form has to do with the many variables that interact to affect understanding and speaking. On the one hand, one might well question how it is possible for an individual to use a linguistic structure or form without knowing something about it. However, the important fact is that both understanding and speaking a linguistic form—whether a particular word, a grammatical morpheme, or a syntactic structure—depend on a great many variables, both linguistic and nonlinguistic. The studies by Guess and by Guess and Baer compared the effects of specific training for auditory discrimination and expression of a grammatical form; their results indicated that there was little mutual influence between the two kinds of performance within the contingencies of the reinforcement paradigm. In the experimental situation, the contingencies of reward might be strong enough to preclude any behavior that is not directly reinforced. Even though subjects included new instances within the response category (when they supplied the learned morphemes to novel words), the variables that defined the response behavior were necessarily constrained. It is not clear what the subjects knew that led them to say or respond to the plural morpheme.

In a naturalistic situation, children might respond to the form when they hear it, but what they understand of the form might depend heavily on the situation in which it is heard, or on the state of affairs to which it refers. By the same token, children's use of a particular form cannot be taken as unequivocal evidence that they know the form so that they can understand and use it in unlimited reference and in any situation. This fact becomes quite important when one considers children's performance in elicited imitation tasks.

ELICITED IMITATION

An important limitation in studies of speech output has to do with the constraints of topic and context as influences on the grammatical structures or words that children use. That is, what children say depends on what they are talking about. One must obtain large samples of speech in order to be assured of some degree of representation of a child's linguistic knowledge. But the time involved in collecting and processing large speech samples has limited the number of children that can be studied in this way, so that other techniques for tapping children's knowledge are necessary. One such technique is to have children repeat phrases and sentences that contain the linguistic form being studied. The underlying rationale for presenting such sentences to children to imitate has been that children will process sentences that exceed auditory memory span according to what they know about the structure of sentences. As a result, it has been argued that (1) one can tell how much is understood of the original sentence by looking at how much of the meaning of the original sentence is preserved in a child's repetition of it, and (2) the child's repetition will provide evidence of coding abilities for production. The underlying premise in elicited imitation tasks, then, is that if a sentence is too long for children to hold in memory, they will process the meaning of the sentence, and their imitation of it, although shorter and inexact, will provide some evidence of (1) the extent to which they understood it, and (2) what they know about speaking such sentences.

The technique has been used with different research questions in mind. Menyuk (1963) had children imitate well-formed (by adult standards) sentences and utterances, produced by children, that did not conform to the model adult language. Others have compared imitations of standard English and black English sentences by black speakers (e.g., Labov, 1968) or by black and white speakers (e.g., Baratz, 1969). Rodd and Braine (1971) attempted to assess the ability of 2-year-old children to repeat a variety of phrase structures.

In order to explore further the relation between spontaneous speaking and elicitied imitation, Peter was asked to play a repetition game. Peter had already been identified as an imitator in natural speech: an average of one third of his utterance types consisted of repetitions of something spoken by someone else (Bloom, Hood, and Lightbown, 1974 in *RLDev*). Thus, Peter imitated easily in naturalistic situations, and he played the game when presented with sentences to elicit imitation. The following exchanges took place between an adult investigator and Peter, age 32 months, 2 weeks, as they played "Simple Simon says:"[1]

Simple Simon Says	*Peter*
1. This is a big balloon.	This a big balloon.
2. This is broken.	What's broken?
3. This is broken.	That's broken.
4. I'm trying to get this cow in here.	Cow in here.
5. I'm gonna get the cow to drink some milk.	Get the cow to drink milk.
6. You made him stand up over there.	Stand up there.

These sentences were among a list of 14 sentences presented to Peter. He readily attempted to repeat all but two: "That is not bigger," and "What's that on your leg?"

Looking at his responses to sentences 1 to 6, one might conclude that (1)

---

[1] From data collected in collaboration with Patsy Lightbown and Lois Hood. The numbered utterances on the left were presented by an adult investigator for Peter to repeat.

Peter probably understands but cannot produce the copula "is," as in sentences 1 to 3, and (2) Peter may or may not understand, but he cannot produce causal connectives such as "gonna," "trying," and "made" in sentences 4 to 6. However, all of the 14 sentences presented to Peter for imitation had actually been produced by Peter spontaneously the preceding day, as follows:

Speech Event	*Peter*
2 and 3. (Peter showing airplane with broken tail to investigator)	This is broken.
4. (Peter trying to get a colt's feet to fit into a barrel)	I'm trying to get *this* cow in here.
5. (Peter, holding the cow, going to the toy bag to get barrels)	I'm gonna get the cow to drink some milk.
(Peter returning with the barrels)	I'm gonna get the cow to drink some milk.
6. (Peter trying to get investigator to spread an animal's legs so that it will stand in a spot he had cleared for it)	You made him stand up over there.

It seems that, given the support of contextual events and his own behavior, Peter's spontaneous speaking ability exceeded his ability to imitate sentences presented to him for imitation. When asked to reproduce sentences that did not relate to immediate context and behavior, he could not produce the very same utterances he himself had produced with such support. In pointing out that their subject also could not reproduce the same sentence she herself had said earlier, Slobin and Welsh (1973) suggested that intention, in addition to context, contributed to the support for the production of messages.

Intention to speak and contextual support for the utterance are two factors contributing to production performance that are missing in elicited imitation performance and in most comprehension tasks. Thus, a child's saying a sentence originates with (1) an internal state of knowing, needing, or intending, (2) a referent in context and behavior, and (3) linguistic knowledge about structure and semantic constraints. In responding to a sentence that is heard in the certain absence of condition 1 and the possible absence of condition 2, the child can depend only on condition 3. Talking and understanding are clearly different behaviors and seem to involve something more than simply a temporal relation in the course of their development.

BETWEEN UNDERSTANDING AND SPEAKING

A disparity between perception and production has been presumed for a long time in speech and psychology as well as in art, and various attempts have been made to understand and explain it (e.g., see the papers in Olson and Pagliuso, 1968). Among the most often quoted examples of the difference between perception and production is the fact that children are able to recognize geometric shapes long before they can reproduce them. Adults can recognize and appreciate a work of art but few, indeed, can reproduce one. Some small children can hear the difference between "light" and "white," yet they cannot say the words differently themselves, saying "white wight," and individuals learning a second language often understand more than they can say.

There are several asymmetries between understanding and speaking that are similar to the asymmetries in other domains that involve perception and production tasks. Among the explanations of the disparity between perception and production that have been offered, there is reference to memory factors affecting recognition and recall (Mandler, 1967); the knowledge of extra details or attributes that is needed for reproduction as opposed to recognition (Maccoby and Bee, 1965); and the intervening mental reconstruction of an image as the basis for reproduction (Piaget and Inhelder, 1971). Such explanations have not been explicitly extended to young children learning language, but they may contribute to an exploration of the developmental relationship among understanding, talking, and thinking. The memory load for saying a sentence is presumably greater than for understanding, in that individuals need to recall the necessary words and their connections to say them, but these linguistic facts are immediately available to them when they hear them spoken by someone else. Children can experience a sentence as more or less independent of its parts—for instance, they can understand only the lexical items and their individual semantic constraints—but saying sentences involves bringing together the elements (units and structure) to form a whole.

According to Piaget and Inhelder (1971), in recognizing a word or a sentence, children relate what they hear to existing perceptual schemas, but saying the word or sentence involves contructing an intervening representation in the form of a "symbolic image." In Piaget and Inhelder's view, the latter is more difficult. This last point is most critical—mental representation of the meaning of messages is basic to both understanding and speaking. It is not clear how representational images relate to either the acoustic signals that children hear or the speech that they produce. Both seem to involve the construction of schemas, but at different levels of complexity. The relative cognitive complexity, and hence the relative difficulty between speaking and understanding, is different or varies according to different relations between children and their contexts. Furthermore, even within one or another modality—speaking or understanding—there are different task demands, depending on the interaction between the child and context. Contrary to the view of Piaget and Inhelder (1971) referred to above, it may well be the case that in certain child/context interactions the mental representation that gives rise to an utterance is cognitively less complex than the search for an "existing" perceptual schema that is triggered by hearing speech (Box VIII-2).

One might consider that in the course of development, both linguistic events (A) and nonlinguistic events (B) provide input that is perceived and organized at (C) in Box VIII-2. What children know of language—that is, the information that allows them both to understand and to produce messages— is represented in (C). Whether one speaks of images, concepts, or schemas, there is necessarily some form of mental representation of the meaning of messages in (C). There is not a one-to-one relation between (A) and (B), that is, between linguistic facts, on the one hand, and items and events in the real world, on the other hand. Instead, there is a necessary internal mental representation of experience that is coded or mapped by language.

What are some of the factors that may be involved in producing and understanding messages in the course of language development, given the basic premise that language does not code reality directly but, instead, language codes individuals' intervening mental representation or their *experience* of reality? The question is an enormously complicated one, and there does not yet seem to be existing evidence that will lead directly to an answer.

With respect to producing messages, it has been observed repeatedly (e.g., Leopold, 1939; Brown and Bellugi, 1964; and Bloom, 1970a) that children typically talk about what they are doing or what they can see in the immediate *here and now* in which their utterances occur. Thus, children

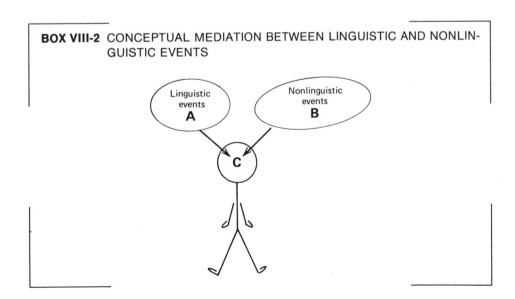

BOX VIII-2 CONCEPTUAL MEDIATION BETWEEN LINGUISTIC AND NONLINGUISTIC EVENTS

Linguistic events
A

Nonlinguistic events
B

C

might climb on a tricycle and announce "ride trike," or fit a peg into a hole and comment "this fit" or "no fit" (if it does not). Child utterances are redundant with respect to the context in which they occur, and to which they also refer, more often than not. Adults, in marked contrast, do not ordinarily talk about what they see or what they are doing in talking to other adults, when listeners are there to see for themselves. In adult discourse, an utterance that bears no relation to the perceivable situation can elicit an appropriate response that also does not relate to what the speakers see or here or do at the same time.

Egocentricity is often invoked to account for the fact that children seem not to take into account the information that is already available to the listener or, indeed, to take the listener into account at all. A second point that can be made is that caregivers' speech to children is probably no less redundant and, indeed, language learning probably depends on the fact that mothers will not typically discuss finances or an argument with a friend when they talk to their children. Instead, when a young child comes into a room with a ball, the typical comment might be "You've got a ball," "That's your red ball," or "Do you have a ball?" Thus, it might be argued that children talk in the *here and now* because their parents talk in the *here and now* to them. However, both the fact that children are centered on their own actions and perceptions when they produce messages (i.e., their egocentricity) and the fact that caretakers' speech to children is also redundant with respect to context may well be related to another cause: that young children are strongly dependent on the support of nonlinguistic context for both producing and understanding messages. However, it is not the immediate context *per se* that supports children's messages or that enables them to decode messages from others; instead, it is their mental representation of the circumstances and events in nonlinguistic contexts.

There are at least three components in (C) that interact with one another as the child produces messages and understands messages. There is, first of all, the child's immediate *consciousness*—what the child thinks about when in the process of perceiving an utterance or producing an utterance. The child's consciousness is influenced by what is attended to in the context, as well as by the second component that contributes to the meaning of messages—the child's *memory* or conceptual information about the world. In order to understand a message, the child needs to process the information in the message in relation to what is already known. In order to produce a message, the child forms a semantic intention on the basis of information from memory in interaction with information from the context. Finally, the child needs to know some scheme for *linguistic processing*, a lexicon and rules of grammar, in order to process linguistic forms to extract meaning from messages, and to use linguistic forms to represent information in messages. These three aspects of children's thinking—consciousness,

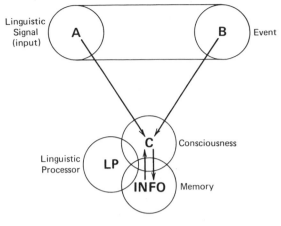

FIGURE VIII-1

memory, and linguistic processing mechanism—interact differently in the different states of affairs in the contexts in which messages occur.

In Figure VIII-1, the interaction that is schematized is one in which a linguistic signal (A) encodes or maps onto an event (B). In early development, when utterances occur in the *here and now,* success in understanding the message in (A) would depend on the extent to which the nonlinguistic relations are understood in (B), with the immediate perceptual representation of the event in consciousness as the source of the child's information at (C). The linguistic signal may function simply to call attention or focus the child on the event, and extent of understanding would be relatively independent of the complexity of the signal, with limited linguistic processing at LP.

Similarly, in Figure VIII-2, the child is again presented with an event (B), but it is the child who produces the linguistic signal (A) relative to event (B), as output. Here, the success of the child's producing the message depends, again, on the immediate perceptual representation of the event (B) for content, but also on the ability to use a linguistic processor for the form of coding the information represented in (C). Given the states of affairs represented in Figures VIII-1 and VIII-2, comprehension may well exceed or at least be equal to production, depending on the extent to which the linguistic processing mechanism is necessary. In both, the same information about event (B) is available at (C), but linguistic processing appears to be necessary for producing messages about events, but not necessary for understanding such messages when these relate to immediately perceived events. But, if understanding is easier than talking, it is important to recognize that understanding can be largely nonlinguistic which, at least at this early stage of development, would seem to close the comprehension-production gap.

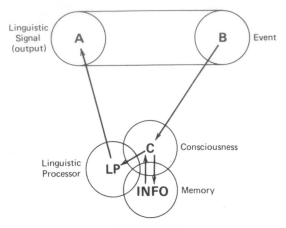

FIGURE VIII-2

This appears to be a plausible account of at least part of the relation between understanding and speaking in the period when children say only one word at a time—given the information referred to earlier and other accounts as well (Bloom, 1973). That is, children in the single-word utterance period say only one word at a time because they do not yet know a linguistic code for representing information through semantic-syntactic relations between words. The fact that children are limited to single-word utterances is evidence that they do not know enough about semantic-syntactic structure to say sentences; how much they know of semantic-syntactic structure for understanding sentences remains to be determined.

What of the relation between understanding and speaking when children are using multiword utterances? The conditions in Figures VIII-1 and VIII-2 continue to prevail; that is, there is still the perceptual representation of immediate events in consciousness at (C) to support both encoding and decoding. It can now be assumed that the child's linguistic knowledge is more complex and functions to provide information from the linguistic signal that the child receives, in addition to determining the form of the child's messages. Here the relation between comprehension and production is less clear-cut. The assumption that production itself is evidence of comprehension has been tested in a number of studies, with similar results.

In the study by Wetstone and Friedlander (1973) children who themselves used consistent syntactic word order in saying sentences were unperturbed when presented with sentences with scrambled syntax for comprehension. The results reported by Chapman and Miller (1975, in *RLDev*) suggested that comprehension during early development of grammar depends on lexical decoding, with semantic relations between words cued by the relations between objects in event contexts at the same time that children are using knowledge of syntax (word order) to say sentences. In a study by de Villiers and de Villiers (1974, in *RLDev*), children performed differently in tasks that required their saying sentences, understanding sentences, and making judgments regarding the relative acceptability (well-formedness) of sentences. The authors concluded that these three kinds of behavior do not develop at the same time. Of the children that they studied, the younger children were able to say sentences with consistent word order between constituents but, at the same time, they responded to directions with irreversible relations the same way regardless of the order of the constituents (e.g., girl eat apple, eat apple girl, apple girl eat). Older children objected to unacceptable word order. The ability to make judgments about the grammaticality of sentences was demonstrated only by children who were even older than the first two groups. Such experimental studies as these that present children with specific tasks for comprehension, production, or judgment of sentences are different from naturally occurring situations in which children understand and speak according to their own needs and motivation. Nevertheless, they do provide evidence that comprehension and production tasks are tapping different aspects of children's knowledge about language.

From the beginning and increasingly through to adulthood, messages are produced and understood by the child without the support of an encoded event in the context being available to the child's consciousness at (C). In fact, it seems that the major task for the child in the course of language development is the ability to speak and understand messages that are independent of external situations or internal affectual and need states (Chomsky, 1966). Language has its greatest power when it conveys information that is not otherwise available to the listener. Although the achievement of the ability to use a linguistic code relatively independent of context appears to be the major task of language development in the school years, it has its beginnings in the early preschool years, when children begin to learn language.

With respect to understanding that is independent of the situation in which it occurs, consider Figure VIII-3 where there is no corresponding event in context. Here, the linguistic signal must be processed at LP, the linguistic processor, first. As the signal is processed, there is little or no support in the immediate context for representing the information in the message. The linguistic signal is the source of information about the message. Therefore, information from the LP must be compared with what the child already knows (INFO in cognitive memory) in order to obtain a mental representation of the content of the message at (C) and thereby understand it.

Speaking that is independent of the situation in which it occurs is schematized in Figure VIII-4. Here, the mental representation at (C) origi-

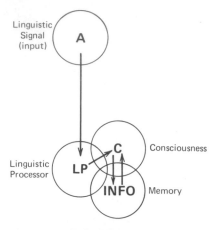

Linguistic Signal (input)

A

LP — Linguistic Processor

C — Consciousness

INFO — Memory

FIGURE VIII-3

nates internally, from the information in cognitive memory (INFO). Thus, the utterance codes what the child already knows. The LP receives the information for the form of the message, from a mental representation, image, or schema in (C).

Comparing the child speech represented in Figure VIII-4, where there is no external event (B), with the child speech represented in Figure VIII-2, where there is an external event (B), one can see that where there is an external event to be talked about, message content is more immediately accessible at (C) to the LP for the form of the output. Although there is necessary

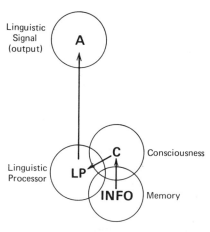

Linguistic Signal (output)

A

LP — Linguistic Processor

C — Consciousness

INFO — Memory

FIGURE VIII-4

interaction between (C) and stored INFO in order for the child to know what is in (B), the mental representation for the content of the message is in the immediate perception. Similarly, one can compare understanding in Figure VIII-3, where there is no event (B), with understanding in Figure VIII-1, where there is an external event (B) that interacts with the message (A).

In this account, one can see how young children's speech occurs most often in relation to immediately perceived events, and children apparently understand speech about immediately perceived events. Figures VIII-1 and VIII-2 do not explain speech and understanding in the *here and now*; they offer no new information, but simply schematize interactions for speaking and understanding.

Comparing speaking and understanding, it is not difficult to understand why comprehension in Figure VIII-1, where there is an external event (B), would be easier than where there is not an external event, as in comprehension in Figure VIII-3 and speaking in Figure VIII-4. However, the comparison that may be more pertinent to the language development evidence that has been discussed is between understanding and speaking in the absence of an external event (B), the comparison between events in Figures VIII-3 and VIII-4. When the information for the content of the child's message at (C) originates with some idea from memory, speaking may well be easier than understanding. In order to understand the content of a message that the child hears, the mental representation at (C) depends on the more complicated task of extracting information from the external signal (through the LP) and relating that information to what the child already knows in memory.

A still more complicated state of affairs occurs when the child says something in response to a prior utterance from someone else. Here the information for the content of the child's responding message originates from what is understood of the input message from someone else in relation to what is already known. When children need to obtain information from a prior linguistic signal, relate that information to existing knowledge, and form a contingent semantic intention, they are participating in discourse. Contingent discourse is both the goal in language development and a means whereby children learn language. (See Bloom, Rocissano, and Hood, 1976.)

Piaget and Inhelder (1971) argued that the need for constructing the mental image or schema makes production difficult. It would certainly make production in the absence of an event (B) more difficult than production given an external event to talk about. But it also appears that creating the mental representation as input to linguistic encoding for speaking may be cognitively less complex than deriving a mental representation as a result of linguistic decoding in comprehending. The argument is, essentially, that what individuals know about an event will determine their ability both to speak and to understand messages that code that event. Furthermore, either the event in actual context or the mentally represented event in consciousness will be a richer source of information about messages for children than a linguistic signal alone.

FACTORS THAT CONTRIBUTE TO UNDERSTANDING MESSAGES

There are many sources of information that children can use for understanding messages. Although there have been several experimental efforts to isolate children's comprehension of linguistic form alone (e.g., Wetstone and Friedlander, 1973; de Villiers and de Villiers, 1974, in *RLDev*; and Chapman and Miller, 1975, in *RLDev*), children naturally do not need to depend on only linguistic form for comprehension any more than they learn only linguistic form for speaking. Understanding is accomplished by the intersection of various cues from the context, both linguistic and nonlinguistic, in

---

BOX VIII-3 CHILDREN'S RESPONSE STRATEGIES DURING THE SENSORI-MOTOR AND PREOPERATIONAL PERIODS IN DEVELOPMENT; AGES GIVEN ARE ONLY APPROXIMATE (adapted from Chapman, 1977)

Nonlinguistic Response Strategies, Sensorimotor Stage IV (8 to 12 months). There are a number of ways in which infants' actions can give the impression that they understand what is said. However, these response strategies are strongly tied to the context with, at first, no dependence on the words that the children hear.

Child, when someone says something:

1. Look at objects that the speaker looks at.
2. Act on object that you notice.
3. Imitate the ongoing action that you see.

Comprehension Strategies, Sensorimotor Stage V (12 to 18 months), with beginning *lexical* understanding.

Child, when someone says something:

1. Attend to the object mentioned and. . . .
2. Give evidence that you've noticed the object mentioned.
3. Do what you usually do with the object, or in the situation.

Comprehension Strategies, Sensorimotor Stage VI (18–24 months), with lexical comprehension in conjunction with context to determine sentence meaning.

Child, when someone says something:

1. Locate the objects mentioned and. . . .
2. Give evidence of that you noticed the object mentioned
3. Do what you usually do in the situation:
   a. put objects into containers.
   b. use objects in conventional ways.

   or

4. Act on objects in the way mentioned:
   a. with self-as-agent.
   b. choose handier object as an instrument.

Comprehension Strategies, Early Preoperations (2 to 4 years), with lexical comprehension and context or past experience to determine sentence meaning.

Child, when someone says something:

1. Do what you usually do in the situation:
   a. probable location strategy: locate an object in its usual place.
   b. probable event strategy: interpret reference to events as they usually occur.
2. Supply missing information (e.g., "in the chair" in response to "How does he sit?" or "Where does he sit?" or "Why does he sit?", etc.).

Comprehension Strategies, Late Preoperations and Concrete Operations (4 to 11 years), with lexical and syntactic comprehension for simple structures; the use of context and overgeneralized syntactic strategies; and past experience influencing the interpretation of complex sentence meaning.

Child, when someone says something:

1. Word order strategy: noun-verb-noun interpreted as *actor-action-object*
2. Order of mention strategy: interpret temporal order relations as matching order of mention (e.g., with "before" and "after").
3. Probable relations in events strategy: interpret relations in events as they usually occur.

interaction with prior knowledge. Early in language development, children's comprehension is determined by, at least: the semantics of individual lexical items; children's underlying cognitive structures or awareness of relations among persons and objects (such as the relation of possession) or among objects (such as the relation of location); cues from the facial expression, gaze, and gestures of the speaker; and cues from events in the context. The structural relationship between words or the grammar of the sentence is just one of the factors that can contribute to understanding messages, particularly in early language.

Several experimental studies have demonstrated that what children know about an event will influence how they interpret a message about the event. Given the same linguistic message, children will have greater or lesser difficulty interpreting it, depending on what they already know about the state of affairs encoded in the message. In a series of experiments, Huttenlocher, with Eisenberg, Strauss, and Weiner, (1968a, 1968b, 1971) has demonstrated that messages such as "The red truck pushes the green truck" will be responded to with varying delay, depending on whether one or the other or neither of the objects is already placed in a three-space track or ladder. Thus, children's ability to determine the relationship between two nouns in a sentence is determined in part by how the corresponding objects appear to them in the situation in which the sentence occurs.

The kinds of information that children use and the extent to which they use different kinds of information change with development. That is, very young children may not understand messages so much as have strategies for responding to messages (Chapman, 1977). Such strategies change as a function of age and experience in speaking and understanding. In the early years, response strategies are very often nonlinguistic and are based on event probabilities (e.g., Bever, 1970; Clark, 1973b, in *RLDev*; and Strohner and Nelson, 1974). Experimental studies of the comprehension of 2- and 3-year-old children have demonstrated that the strategies they use in responding to directions do not depend on processing syntactic information from messages. Chapman (1977) reviewed and synthesized the literature on children's comprehension. She presented a longitudinal account of the strategies that children might use for responding to messages at different sensorimotor stages in development in the first 2 years and in the early preoperational period in cognitive development from 2 to 4 years of age (see Box VIII-3).

It was not until the age of 5 years in the study by Strohner and Nelson (1974) that children were able to use syntactic information to interpret sentences correctly. It is well known, however, that long before the age of 5 years, children are using complex syntax for formulating their own messages (Brown, Cazden, and Bellugi, 1969; Hood, Lahey, Lifter, and Bloom, 1978; and Menyuk, 1969). The relation between using syntax in speaking and using syntactic information for understanding is not well understood.

Perhaps the most forceful evidence of children's development of more strictly linguistic processing comes from their increasing participation in discourse—where successive utterances between children and other speakers share the same topic. One such observation is the developmental increase in linguistic contingency, as child utterances come more and more to share the same verb relation and add new information to prior adult utterances (Bloom, Rocissano, and Hood, 1976). Another kind of evidence that children are processing the forms and structure of prior messages in order to respond is the use of "contingent queries," as described in the speech of 3- to 5-year-old children by Garvey (1975b). Garvey reported that children use queries such as "What?", "Hm?", and "Who did it?" in their conversations, and that such queries are quite systematic as regulators for the flow of conversation between speakers, providing feedback and continuity. However, it was also the case that the children invariably used contingent queries when they had not heard or understood some portion of the preceding message, and the queries functioned to aid them in processing the message. Such evidence indicates that 3- to 5-year-old children are depending more on the linguistic form of the message they hear for understanding than on the other linguistic and nonlinguistic cues that appeared to contribute more to understanding at an earlier age.

CONCLUSION

Earlier it was said that the major achievement in language development is the ability to use a linguistic code independently of the situational contexts in which utterances occur. In attempting to explain the development away from dependence on context, it is necessary to recognize the continual development of increasingly more complex systems of mental representation of both linguistic and nonlinguistic information. Also, it is clear that even in adults, context continues to be important. Research by Johnson, Bransford, and Solomon (1973), Bransford and Johnson (1972), and Bransford and Nitsch (1977) has demonstrated how the availability of context and prior knowledge can influence comprehension and recall of linguistic messages by adults. Adults understood more from hearing a prose passage when provided with an overt context, and they attempted to mentally create situational contexts when they heard the prose passage alone.

The assumption that children necessarily understand a word or a structure before being able to produce it (Ingram, 1974) is no longer warranted when one considers that children cannot have heard a linguistic form in all of the possible circumstances of its use, and yet, nevertheless, invariably use the linguistic form in entirely new situations. Children do not say words and sentences in only those situations in which they originally heard them. Although they no doubt recognize the connections among a linguistic form, the context in which it is understood, and the context in which it is said, it seems quite reasonable that saying linguistic forms in new contexts will contribute to learning more about linguistic forms for understanding them in other contexts. R. Clark, Hutcheson, and Van Buren (1974) reported a case history of a child who used many wholly learned, unanalyzed phrases among his early multiword utterances; they concluded that "production might be viewed as a central mechanism of linguistic change, rather than a process lagging behind comprehension" (pp. 39–40).

There are, then, several sources of the variability in speaking and understanding performance that have been observed in development. The performance of a particular child will differ to the extent to which learning and maturation have influenced development in any of the component systems: the mechanism for linguistic processing, cognitive memory, and capacities for the mental representation of information in consciousness. The relationship between understanding and speaking in language development is probably never a static one but, instead, shifts and varies according to the experience of the individual child and his or her developing linguistic and cognitive capacities.

SUMMARY

Until this point, most of what has been presented has been concerned with the content/form/use of children's speaking. This chapter is about the interaction between children's understanding and speaking in the course of development. To begin with, children's understanding has been largely taken for granted in the study of language development. The assumption has been that children simply learn to understand everything they learn to say, but only sooner; that is, comprehension precedes production. However, a closer look at the evidence reported in observational studies of children's language reveals that the gap between understanding and speaking is often more apparent than real. In the use of single-word utterances, and in the transition from single-word to multiword utterances, there is not a simple one-to-one relation between understanding and speaking. The words that children first learn to understand and respond to are not, necessarily, the first words that they learn to say. Moreover, there are different factors that contribute to understanding and speaking, and each represents different mental capacities.

Several kinds of psychological tasks that have been used to compare children's comprehension and production are discussed, particularly the comparison of imitation, comprehension, and production, training studies, and studies of elicited imitation. With each of these tasks, the results could be interpreted in various ways with respect to the relation between understanding and speaking. Several training studies have resulted in little crossover from one modality to another. In elicited imitation tasks, the fact that the spontaneous semantic intention as well as contextual support for utterances are missing could lead to misinterpreting a child's behavior as evidence of what the child knows about language. These two factors—semantic intention and support from the context—are seen as particularly important in differentiating between the behaviors that contribute to understanding and speaking.

The final portion of the chapter concerns a discussion of the different linguistic and nonlinguistic factors that contribute to producing and understanding messages. It is seen how children's attention to (1) events in the context interacted with (2) information in memory to represent the (3) meaning of messages in consciousness. Moreover, such interaction between components is different for the processes of understanding and speaking, and such differences undergo change in the course of development.

SUGGESTED READINGS

In *Readings in Language Development*

Chapman, R., and Miller, J., Early two and three word utterances: Does production precede comprehension. *Journal of Speech and Hearing Research,* 18, 355–371, 1975.

de Villiers, J., and de Villiers, P., Competence and performance in child language: Are children really competent to judge? *Journal of Child Language, 1,* 11–22, 1974.

Shipley, E., Smith, C., and Gleitman, L., A study in the acquisition of language: Free responses to commands. *Language, 45,* 322–342, 1969.

Other Readings

Bransford, J. and Johnson, M. Contextual prerequisites for understanding: Some investigations of comprehension and recall. *Journal of Verbal Learning and Verbal Behavior, 11,* 717–726, 1972.

Chapman, R. S., Discussion summary—Developmental relationship between receptive and expressive language. In R. L. Schiefelbusch and L. L. Lloyd (Eds.), *Language perspectives—Acquisition, retardation, and intervention*. Baltimore: University Park Press, 1974.

Huttenlocher, J., The origins of language comprehension. In R. L. Solso (Ed.), *Theories in cognitive psychology*. New York: Halsted, 1974.

Wetstone, H., and Friedlander, B., The effect of word order on young children's responses to simple questions and commands. *Child Development, 44,* 734–740, 1973.

Chapter IX
LANGUAGE DEVELOPMENT AS AN ACTIVE PROCESS

Language development is the result of the child's interaction with the context—an active process whereby the relation between linguistic categories (form) and nonlinguistic categories (content and use) are learned. The general question having to do with the relative influence of biological and environmental factors on language learning will be taken up first. Then the issue of contact between linguistic and nonlinguistic categories will be discussed. The rest of the chapter will be taken up with description and discussion of the particular processes that are involved in children's imitation, development of discourse, and the caregiver input that children receive from the environment for language learning. A full discussion of the processes that contribute to language development is not possible here. Discussion of the basic capacities and specific abilities that underlie language learning is presented in Chapter XIX.

In the early 1960s, an important theoretical conflict dominated attempts at the explanation of language development. On the one hand, the child was seen as the ever-changing product of maturation. On biological grounds (e.g., Lenneberg, 1967) and on linguistic grounds (Chomsky, 1965; Fodor, 1966; and McNeill, 1966, 1970), children could not escape their fate— barring physical or mental complications, they could not help but learn to talk. Part of children's genetic makeup included a linguistic sensing mechanism that was more than merely the capacity for learning language. The mechanism itself, a "language acquisition device," consisted of information about language—at the least, information about the aspects of properties of language that are shared by all languages. Such a view placed heavy

266

emphasis on the child—children learned to talk because they were biologi-cally prepared for it or linguistically preprogrammed to do so.

In contrast to what came to be called the nativist view, other theorists (most notably, Braine, 1963b, 1965, 1971a; Jenkins and Palermo, 1964; and Staats, 1971) placed heavy emphasis on the influence of the environment in shaping and controlling children's learning. In this view, children learned the linguistic behaviors that were presented and then reinforced by the environ-ment. But, just as with the nativist view, the child's role in this environmenta-list view was, again, essentially a *passive* one—learning language was largely determined by language experience and by the ways in which individuals in the environment respond and react to what children say and do.

The argument between those who hold that language is innate and acquisition is the product of maturation and those who believe that language is learned and shaped by forces in the environment is a historical argument that has long been debated by philosophers and linguists. (E.g., see the discussion in Jakobson, 1941, 1968). The debate was revived most recently with Chomsky's critique in 1959 of Skinner's *Verbal Behavior* (1957). Since that time, a great deal has been written, and one can follow the argument in, for example, Bellugi and Brown (1964), Smith and Miller (1966), Lyons and Wales (1966), Jakobovits and Miron (1967), Dixon and Horton (1968), Reed (1971), and Slobin (1971). As the dust has settled, it has become clear that neither explanation could be entirely correct. Most recently, attempts to explain language development emphasized the active participation of the child, in terms of the child's strategies for actively interacting with linguistic and nonlinguistic aspects of the environment in the course of development (e.g., Bever, 1970; Bloom, 1973; Bloom, Lightbown, and Hood, 1975; Clark, 1973, in *RLDev*; Slobin, 1973, in *RLDev*; and Watt, 1970).

In contrast to both the nativist view and the behavioral (environmentalist) view, both of which saw the child as essentially passive with respect to the forces of destiny and circumstance that prevail to influence language learning, the view presented here is of the child as an active seeker and processor of new information, selectively paying attention to the environ-ment.

CONTACT BETWEEN LINGUISTIC AND NONLINGUISTIC CATEGORIES

In the "original word game" described by Brown (1956, in *RLDev*), children are confronted with an environment that is quite complex and that can presumably be divided up in different ways; the question exists of knowing what attributes of objects and events are relevant for forming nonlinguistic (conceptual) categories. At the same time, parents present their children with linguistic forms, and Brown suggested that the opportunity to see the connection between a linguistic form and the features of the environment to which it refers guides the child in learning the relevant attributes of the environment for forming nonlinguistic categories. As an example, Brown pointed out that, conceivably, children might be able to categorize the attributes of a group of coins and make divisions among them—perhaps according to those that are dull and those that are shiny. Classification schemes could be revealed "by giving some equivalent response to the shiny range and another response to the dull range . . . he might call one group dimes and the other pennies, or he might kiss the one group and throw the others away" (p. 287). Someone in the environment, a "tutor," could progressively correct the classifications until the child knew the different categories of coins. There is an important alternative, however—the tutor could provide the child with the names for the coins to begin with, which would provide the categorization scheme for the coins directly (Box IX-1).

Given the linguistic categorization, that is, the words "pennies," "nickels," "dimes," and "quarters" paired with the appropriate objects, the child would learn to ignore the difference between dull and shiny coins and to sort according to size. However, the child might already have arrived at the nonlinguistic categorization of the same objects based on size, sorted them as small, bigger, biggest, and then learned the names "dimes," "nickels," and "quarters." There is still another possibility: given the decimal concept of 100 parts and the division of 1, 5, 10, and 25 parts, one could then learn the names for different numbers of parts or fractions of 100. It seems reasonable to expect either the first or second of these possibilities to happen with children. Although the third possibility is most often the way that foreign visitors learn the American coin system, it is almost certainly not the way that children learn the names for coins. The point is that the relations between linguistic categories and nonlinguistic categories do not necessarily move in only one direction in development.

BOX IX-1 POSSIBLE SCHEMES FOR SORTING COINS

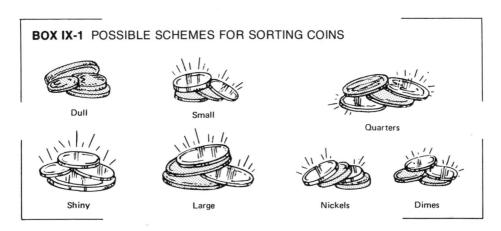

Dull   Small   Quarters

Shiny   Large   Nickels   Dimes

The issue here is the extent to which children learn about objects and events in the world through the language that they hear (see also Church, 1961), or the extent to which children use what they already know about objects and events in the world in order to learn language. It has been pointed out by Bloom (1970, 1973, 1974b), Cromer (1974), Leonard (1974), MacNamara (1971, in *RLDev*), Nelson (1974), Piaget (1970), Sinclair (1973), and others that children learn their first words and sentence structures after they have acquired relevant conceptual distinctions that are coded by such words and structures. For example, in the description of negation in Bloom (1970), it was seen that children learned the different forms of negative sentences (linguistic categories) only after they had already learned different meanings of negation (nonlinguistic categories).

In an ideal world, one would like to be able to determine empirically just when children *have* a concept, in relation to precisely when they can recognize a word and when they can say the word. But, if one considers that object concepts and word concepts evolve continuously and are not all or nothing categorizations, it becomes clear that there is more of a mutual influence between acquiring linguistic categories and acquiring nonlinguistic categories than a simple temporal or causal relation between them. When children know something of an object concept or a relational concept, hearing a word can direct them to the limits of the concept that define the meaning of the word. Similarly, hearing a word can guide children to discover the relevant aspects of their experience that define the limits of the concepts. Children can have a concept of cookie and a concept of recurrence, but hearing the word "cookie" and hearing the word "more," and, also, saying the words as well, can help to direct them toward new instances of each of the concepts and so contribute to the formation of linguistic *and* nonlinguistic categories.

The behaviors of understanding and saying messages are, themselves, the means whereby the iinguistic categories and rules of the language plan are learned. Just as with learning about an object or a relation between objects, a word or a sign and rules for the combination and use of words and signs are not a one-time learning experience. Situations or speech events have certain constant properties, but they are never precisely the same in all or any respects. For example, a child might have seen the pet dog before, but the dog's position, location, speed of movement, kind of movement, sounds, and so on, can vary in both large and subtle ways. In each new event in which the dog appears, the child needs to have processed some new information from the context (such as the movement or position or shape of the dog in that context), and compared it with some existing knowledge (the previous experiences the child has had of the same or similar dogs in earlier contexts) in order to recognize the object *dog*. Similarly, every time that a child hears a word or a sentence, says a word or a sentence, or sees or makes a manual sign, is somehow unique and different from every other instance of the same word, sentence, or sign. Everytime the child hears the word "dog" or says the word "dog," something more about the meaning of the word "dog" can be learned. Children learn the aspects of language continually, adding to their mental plans for language everytime they use language (see Box IX-2).

The mental plan that is knowledge of language is controlled and affected by the more general cognitive processes of attention and memory. There has been much consideration given to the cognitive factors that underlie the development of language. According to McNeill (1970), Slobin (1973, in *RLDev*), and others following Chomsky (1965), "some part [of language competence] is specifically linguistic" (McNeill, 1970, p. 75), instead of being but one aspect of cognition in general. Others, for example, Bruner

---

BOX IX-2 DIALOGUE WITH ERIC, 31 MONTHS OLD, SHOWING HOW A CHILD MIGHT LEARN SOMETHING ABOUT THE MEANING OF A WORD, HERE THE WORDS "WRENCH" AND "STOOL"

(Babysitter is preparing Eric's lunch)
I see your Mommy's frying pan/ I can't reach that way up there

   oh you need__/
   you need a wrench ·to ·get up/
   you need ·a stool to climb up and you need a wrench

That's right/that's right

Lois: What is a wrench for?

   it's called a plier

Lois: What does she need that for?
(Eric pointing to the cabinet, which does not have a lock)

   'cause for the cabinet is locked

   it's up in the air/you can't reach it

Learning might have occurred here in two possible ways—not only by having to think about the word "wrench" in response to Lois' questions, but also by saying the word originally.

(1975) and Greenfield, Nelson, and Saltzman (1972), have explored the ways in which other behaviors are similar to language behaviors as manifestations of a more generalized cognitive function. Bruner described the reciprocal play and exchanges between caregivers and children; Greenfield and her colleagues described the schemes that very young children use when playing with nesting cups. Miller, Galanter, and Pribram (1960) had suggested that

> We might speak metaphorically of a general grammar of behavior, meaning that the grammar of a language . . . that is built around hierarchical plans and their various transformations . . . was only one example of a general pattern of control that could be exemplified in many other realms of behavior. (p. 155)

According to Bever (1970), Schlesinger (1974), and others, language is what it is because of the nature of mental capacities; languages of the world are similar and have universal properties in common because persons everywhere have similar cognitive capacities.

It is an open question, which may or may not be resolved eventually, whether a mental plan for language is similar in structure and function to the rest of an individual's cognition as a part of some general mental capacity or is, instead, some separate mental capacity that is both similar and different in essential ways from the rest of cognition. Nevertheless, it seems clear that children have a mental plan for speaking and understanding messages. The mental plan, or knowledge of language, consists of some basic information in memory about contact between linguistic and nonlinguistic categories, and some set of principles or strategies for using and adding to this information in different contexts. Bever (1970) proposed that children operate with knowledge of certain "basic linguistic capacities" in conjunction with "processing strategies," and Slobin (1973, in *RLDev*) described "operating principles" that children use to process and learn language to speak and understand.

The balance of influence between linguistic and nonlinguistic categories is most probably a shifting one in the course of development. Knowing something about words and sentence structures is knowing something about the relations between form (linguistic categories) and content and use (nonlinguistic categories). Children know something about the relations among content/form/use when they begin to use words and sentences, but they also learn more about words and sentences as they hear them and use them in new contexts. One process whereby children learn about linguistic and nonlinguistic categories is in the dyadic exchange between children and adults. Brown and Bellugi (1964) observed two processes that occur in the dyadic exchanges between parents and children that help in the child's induction of the linguistic system. One process has to do with adults' imitation of what children say, at the same time expanding what the child says. Thus, if the child says "eat doughnut," an adult might typically respond, "Oh, you want to eat your doughnut now," or "Sure you can eat the doughnut." The second process has to do with children's imitation of what adults say, at the same time reducing what the adult says. Thus, if an adult says "Do you want to eat your doughnut?", the child might typically respond "eat doughnut." Exchanges between parents and children have been explored in the study of children's imitations of the adult model, the development of discourse, and the linguistic input that caregivers supply to children.

IMITATION

The tendency that children often have to repeat the speech they hear has been observed over and over again. However, there has not been a consensus in the literature as to whether imitation is important or, if imitation is important, in what ways imitation contributes to language learning. One prevailing assumption has been that children need to repeat the speech that they hear in order to learn it. For example, according to Jespersen, "one thing which plays a great role in children's acquisition of language, and especially in their early attempts to form sentences, is Echoism: the fact that children echo what is said to them" (1922, p. 135). Kirkpatrick (1909) and others believed that children are virtually compelled to imitate and that they imitate not only what they themselves have seen or done previously, but also totally novel behavior. Bloch (1921), Guillaume (1968), Lewis (1951), and others described a critical stage of imitation that comes between the stage of comprehension and the beginning of speech. Other early observers, on the other hand, such as Meumann (1903) and Thorndike (1913), discounted the importance of imitation for language development altogether.

Behavioral psychologists who are interested in language learning have seen imitation as a necessary precondition for reinforcement and learning (e.g., Mowrer, 1960; and Staats, 1971) or a combination of imitation and reinforcement as relevant to language learning (Sherman, 1971). Psycholinguists and linguists influenced by generative transformational grammar, on the other hand, have argued that the most important information about a sentence is in its underlying structure, so that repeating surface structure, or what is actually heard would not be helpful to the child (e.g., McNeill, 1966; and Slobin, 1968). In support of the transformationalist claim that imitation cannot be important, Lenneberg (1967) pointed out that it was possible to learn language without being able to speak at all, as in the case of individuals with paralysis of the speech musculature·who, nevertheless, understand speech.

There have been few studies that actually compared the spontaneous and imitative utterances in the speech of children to provide empirical support for one or another view of the importance of imitation. One such study that was motivated by the conflict between behaviorist and transformationalist views of imitation was reported by Ervin-Tripp (1964). In that study, speech samples of five children were examined. Rules of word order were presented to account for the children's utterances that were spontaneous (i.e., without a preceding model), and then the children's imitative utterances were examined to determine whether they "fit" the rules that accounted for the spontaneous utterances. Ervin-Tripp reported that for one child, imitative utterances were less complex (shorter and with fewer grammatical markers), but for the other four children there was virtually no difference between their imitative and spontaneous utterances. The conclusion that was offered was that imitative speech was not "grammatically progressive" and therefore not an important factor in the children's grammatical development.

There were other reports that raised some skepticism about this conclusion, however. For example, Bloom (1970a), Brown (reported in Slobin, 1968), and Slobin (1968, 1974) observed children in the early stages of syntactic development and suggested that children seemed to be imitating speech that was just somewhat more advanced than the speech that they tended to use spontaneously. In a study of children's responses to commands (Shipley, Smith, and Gleitman, 1969), it was reported that children who were just beginning to use multiword utterances were more likely to imitate part or all of a command presented to them if it contained a nonsense word (not, necessarily, imitating the nonsense word). Shipley et al. concluded that imitation may contribute to learning vocabulary, as suggested by earlier observers of children's language as well, but left open the question of whether imitation contributed to syntactic learning.

There has been, then, considerable disagreement about whether imitation is a process for language learning, some conflict about the relative importance of imitation for lexical or syntactic learning, and no information about just how imitation might function if, indeed, it is a process in language learning. In order to help clarify such issues, a comparison was made between the imitative and spontaneous speech of Kathryn, Eric, Gia, and Peter (and two other children) by Bloom, Hood, and Lightbown (1974, in *RLDev*). That study was observational (as was the study by Ervin-Tripp); children were observed in naturalistic situations at home. Imitation was defined as follows. An utterance by the child was considered to be imitative of an adult model utterance if the child repeated all or part of a preceding adult utterance, and did not change the model utterance in any way except to leave something out. The children were not asked to imitate; that is, their imitation, when it occurred, was not elicited. It is important to keep this distinction in mind, because of the large number of child language studies that have used elicited imitation as a research technique (see chapter VIII for a discussion of elicited imitation).

The children differed in the extent to which they imitated: two children imitated frequently (see Box IX-3), two other children imitated only rarely (see Box IX-4), and the children were generally quite consistent with respect to whether or not they imitated in the time period of the study. With respect to lexical and grammatical factors, the children did not imitate the words or syntactic structures that appeared most frequently in their spontaneous speech, and they did not imitate words or structures that were entirely absent from their spontaneous speech. Instead, the children imitated the words and structures that had just begun to appear in their spontaneous speech. The words and structures that were imitated at one time were no longer imitated at a later time, after they had become productive in spontaneous speech

---

BOX IX-3 DIALOGUE WITH PETER, 24 MONTHS OLD

(Peter pointing to tape recorder light)	light/light/light
Patsy: Light?/do you remember how to <u>turn the light on</u>?	
(Peter touching light button)	uh huh/
Patsy: You sure do/ yep	
	I <u>turn the light on</u>
Patsy: Well, you have to pull it	
Lois: That's right	
(Peter has light on)	that's right/
	look at that!/ look at that!
Patsy: <u>Look</u> at that <u>light</u>	
	look at light
Patsy: Look at light	
(Peter pointing to lamp)	light there
Patsy: Uh huh/ there's another light	
(Peter pointing to over-head light)	light ə hall
Patsy: Light <u>in</u> the hall	
	light <u>in</u> ə hall
Patsy: Uh huh/ there's a light in the hall	

Peter and Patsy are talking about lights; the light in the tape recorder, the lamp, and overhead in the hallway. Peter, who imitated more than the other children, tends to repeat part or all of what Patsy says. In the final pair of utterances, Patsy imitates Peter, and Peter repeats her fuller utterance with "in."

BOX IX-4 DIALOGUE WITH GIA, 22 MONTHS OLD

(Gia sits with puzzle in its
case on her lap)
  You like that puzzle
  don't you? (Pointing to
baby on puzzle board)   **baby in**
  Baby in, yes/ the baby
  is in
(Gia laughing)   **ə baby**

(Holding board in its plas-
tic case out to Mommy)   **back/ Gia back ə baby**
  Gia back?/ put the baby back?
                                              yes

  Let's take it <u>out</u> and then
  you can put the baby back
(Mommy takes puzzle
from case)
(Gia taking baby out)   **baby <u>out</u>**

Gia and Mommy are talking about a puzzle with famly figures in it. The puzzle is still in its plastic case. Gia, who imitated rarely, tends not to repeat what Mommy says. It is not clear here what Gia means by "back;" perhaps she wanted to take the pieces out and then put them back or, perhaps, she was not clear on the meanings of "back" and "out." In the final pair of utterances, Gia uses the word "out" that Mommy had used, in an utterance similar to her own first utterance in the sequence.

(see Box IX-5). It was concluded, on the basis of these kinds of interactions in the speech of the children who imitated, that imitation is evidence of an active processing of model utterances, relative to the contexts in which they occur, for information about the relation between form and content (linguistic and nonlinguistic categories) for language learning. Because the children only imitated forms that they themselves had already started to produce to some limited extent, it is apparent that they had already learned something about the linguistic form and something about the content being encoded by the form already. Part of the "original word game" includes imitating linguistic forms, as the child makes contact between linguistic categories (form) and nonlinguistic categories (content).

The question that remained was what happened when the children did not imitate. What other kinds of contingency were possible between child

BOX IX-5 EXAMPLE OF DEVELOPMENTAL INTERACTION BETWEEN SPON-
TANEOUS AND IMITATIVE SPEECH, PETER, 22 TO 25 MONTHS
OLD (from Bloom, Hood, and Lightbown, 1974)

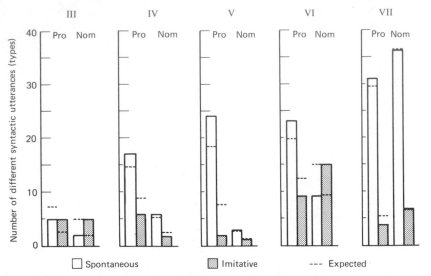

Action-on-*Affected-Object*. Peter, Times III to VII.

This figure shows the interaction between imitative and spontaneous
occurrence of Peter's sentences with transitive action verbs and object
complements. When such sentences first appeared (Time III), they were
imitative most often. Three weeks later, imitation was less than the amount
expected, given the proportion of Peter's speech that was imitative overall.
(The dotted lines indicate the expected levels of imitation.) Imitation increased again when Peter began to substitute nouns for pronouns in the
same kinds of sentences (Time VI). Again, 3 weeks later, utterances with
pronouns and nouns as objects of transitive action verbs were primarily
spontaneous.

utterances and preceding adult utterances, and how do other kinds of
discourse relations contribute to the processes whereby children learn
content/form/use relations?

DISCOURSE

The answers to the above questions are not immediately apparent. On the
one hand, it is obvious that conversation between children and caregivers
would be a medium for the contact between linguistic categories and

nonlinguistic categories that is necessary for language learning. Given that imitation reflects such contact and contributes to language learning, it is reasonable to expect that other kinds of discourse would as well. There have been several suggestions that such is the case (e.g., Brown and Bellugi, 1964; Brown, Cazden, and Bellugi, 1969; Greenfield, Smith and Laufer, 1972; and Slobin, 1968). On the other hand, however, there have not been empirical demonstrations of precisely *how* discourse contributes to language development.

The development of discourse has already been discussed in Chapter VII as an aspect of the development of language use. In the study of the development of discourse reported in Bloom, Rocissano, and Hood (1976), different kinds of contingency between prior adult utterances and child utterances were observed. All contingent utterances were, by definition, semantically related to the prior adult utterances. However, in certain instances, semantic relationship was a function of the context, where both child and adult were talking about the same thing. In other instances, utterances were semantically related because they were also linguistically related to the prior adult utterances, with continuity between the form of the adult utterance and the form of the child utterance. Such linguistic contingency, most often, consisted of the child utterance sharing the same verb relation with the prior adult utterance. That is, whether the child actually repeated the same verb or not, the utterance was one that would *fit into* the prior adult utterance—either to supply a missing constituent, replace a constituent, or expand a constituent (see Box IX-6).

These findings about the relations between child and adult utterances complement the earlier studies (Bloom, Lightbown, and Hood, 1975; and Bloom, Miller and Hood, 1975, in *RLDev*), which demonstrated the importance of verbs in the children's linguistic development. Because verb

---

BOX IX-6 DIALOGUE WITH ERIC, 33 MONTHS OLD, THAT SHOWS VERB RELATIONS IN LINGUISTIC CONTINGENCY

(Eric sets wire man down in very awkward position, with legs twisted around the body)

Hm/does that man stand?

> **yeh**
> **he pretending himself is ə beetle**

(Lois and Eric laugh)
He <u>looks like</u> a beetle

> **he <u>looks like</u> ə bumblebee**

relations figure so prominently in the children's developing discourse patterns, it seems reasonable to assume that the children were either learning systems of verbs and verb relations through discourse, or they were learning how to participate in discourse by using what they knew of the verb system and verb relations. Either one or both of these assumptions may be true. In a related finding (Bloom, Miller, and Hood, 1975, in *RLDev*), it was easier for children to produce a sentence with three constituents (a subject, a verb, and a complement) after they themselves had already produced a sentence with only two of the constituents, for example, "close it/I close it;" and "get a button/I'm gonna get a button." Hearing a word or sentence (spoken by someone else or the child) can provide support for the child in the effort to say the same word or an extension of that sentence. In addition, then, to the social and pragmatic functions of discourse (see Chapter VII), children's early discourse, which includes imitation, appears to be a process whereby children learn the relations between linguistic form and content. The speech that is addressed to children is, obviously, the key factor in such a process.

CAREGIVER INPUT FOR LEARNING LANGUAGE

By far, most of what has been described about linguistic interactions between children and adults has centered on the linguistic input that children receive for learning language. The impetus for the studies that have looked at children's linguistic environment came from the attempt by transformational linguists to minimize the importance of the environment for language learning. Chomsky (1965) pointed to the errors of performance in adult speech (the false starts, circumlocutions, break-offs, etc.) and reasoned that language learning would be a superhuman task if children had only to depend on deformations of language that are presented to them in the environment. How could children learn the regularities of language, if they needed to filter out all of the noisy interference from mistakes in performance?

The answer to the question came quickly, and it was not a surprise to find out that, indeed, parents' speech to children provides an ideal model to children for language learning. In its simplicity and redundancy, the speech that is spoken to children is an admirable presentation of form in relation to content; in its flexibility, speech to children is well-tuned to the child's needs in different contexts, and it is progressively modulated to the child's developing capacities.

In most of the studies of mothers' speech to children, the broad, general characteristics of utterances have been described and reported, for example, by Broen (1972), Nelson (1973), Newport (1976), Phillips (1973), Sachs, Brown, and Salerno (1972), and Snow (1972, in *RLDev*). The major result of these studies has been the consensus that the utterances that children hear from their mothers are short, simple, and redundant, with many questions and directives, on the one hand, and, on the other hand, few morphological inflections, syntactic complexities, and nonfluencies (see Box IX-7). Mothers' speech is generally pitched higher, with an exaggerated intonation pattern to young children. However, it is not just mothers who speak this way; young children also modify their speech in similar ways when they speak to

---

BOX IX-7 DIALOGUE WITH KATHRYN, 21 MONTHS OLD, THAT PROVIDES AN EXAMPLE OF SOME OF THE CHARACTERISTICS OF CARE-GIVERS' SPEECH TO CHILDREN THAT HAVE BEEN DESCRIBED IN STUDIES OF THE LANGUAGE INPUT THAT CHILDREN RECEIVE DURING DEVELOPMENT

(Kathryn picks up a red bean bag in shape of a frog)

Santa Claus

Santa Claus? (Mommy laughs) That's a frog, Honey/ that's not Santa Claus/ that's a frog/ red frog

frog

See the red frog?/ that's a red frog

(Kathryn puts frog on car)

sits

Yes, he's sitting down/ that's right

∂^n- - - car

(Kathryn starts to pull bean-bag's hair)   ə hair
Yes, he's got his hair there/ don't pull out his hair/ ow/ ouch/ ouch/ ouch
(Kathryn pulling beanbag hair and laughing)
Ouch what are you doing? what did you do?/ what did you do?/ what did you do?/ poor beanbag

younger children (Berko-Gleason, 1973; and Shatz and Gelman, 1973), as do adults who are not parents (Sachs, Brown, and Salerno, 1972; and Snow, 1972, in *RLDev*). The speech that young children hear from virtually all directions, then, is scaled down, simplified, and repetitive.

Other studies concentrated on describing particular features of caregivers' speech. For example, Holzmann (1972) studied the forms and frequency of questions in mothers' speech, and she reported that from 15% to 33% of the mothers' utterances she studied were questions; this result is consistent with other studies (e.g., Nelson, 1973; and Newport, 1976). Broen (1972) described imperatives and copula ("to be") sentences with demonstratives either to name an object or to ask the name of an object; she concluded that there is a strong tendency for parents to identify objects and feelings when they talk to children.

Overwhelmingly, studies of linguistic input have documented that parents talk to their children about their immediate context—about what the children are seeing and doing in the "here and now" (Brown, Cazden, and Bellugi, 1969; Ling and Ling, 1974; Nelson, 1973; Phillips, 1973; Söderbergh, 1974; and others). The fact that parents' comments to children refer to what the child is already attending to, or directs the child's attention to something in the context, is the *sine qua non* of the language learning process, and it would be hard to imagine the "original word game" if such were not the case. Indeed, if speech addressed to children did not make sense relative to events in the context, then it would, quite simply, make no sense at all—such speech could not be a model for learning. Even if the form of caregivers' speech is seriously distorted in other ways, as is the speech of deaf parents to their hearing children, it can still provide a model for learning the relation between content and form as long as form is presented in a context in which the relevant content exists (Schiff, 1976). This mutual attention between parents and children to the pairing of linguistic content and form is preceded by a mutual attention between parents and children to action and event sequences in infancy, in which language may play little or no part (Bruner, 1975).

These interactions between parents and children have been described as teaching behaviors; for example, Snow (1972) described caregivers' speech as "a set of 'language lessons'" (p. 561). Characteristics of caregivers' speech such as expansions and redundancy (repeating and rephrasing messages until some response or recognition occurs) are effective teaching aids. And parents use other prompts and prodding, ask rhetorical questions, and answer their own questions (e.g., Moerk, 1975; Söderbergh, 1974; and Seitz and Stewart, 1975). However, it appears that parents rarely correct their children, except for errors of fact (Brown, Cazden, and Bellugi, 1969) and less often for phonological and grammatical errors (Moerk, 1975) (see Box IX-8). Thus, it appears that parents are most aware of the content of their

---

BOX IX-8 DIALOGUE WITH GIA, 27 MONTHS OLD, THAT PROVIDES AN
EXAMPLE OF PARENT CORRECTING CONTENT INSTEAD OF
FORM

**(Mommy gave Gia a bottle of
milk for lunch; milk was fresh;
Gia pushing bottle away)**

> it old

It's old?

> yes

It's not old

> it's old

**It's not old
(Mommy picks up Gia's bib;
starts to put it on her; bib
is soiled)**

> that old

**It's not old/ Well if you
didn't spill all your food over
it it wouldn't be old.**

---

children's speech and provide children with a model of the relations
between content and form (Box IX-9).

However, studies of the input that children receive for language learning
have been limited, almost exclusively, to descriptions of the superficial form
of speech. While the obvious fact that parents talk to children in the here and
now has been well substantiated, there has been little description of the
content of caregivers' speech. Instead, parents' speech has been described
with many of the same measures of children's language that were used in the
early *count* studies of the 1930s and 1940s (summarized in McCarthy,

---

BOX IX-9 DIALOGUE WITH GIA, 27 MONTHS OLD, THAT PROVIDES AN
EXAMPLE OF PARENT ACCEPTING CONTENT AND IGNORING
(I.E., NOT CORRECTING) FORM

**(Mommy had told Lois that Gia
was not wearing a diaper)**

> **I made the sissy little bit**

Yes you did.

1954a), such as mean length, kinds of sentences, completeness of sentences, numbers of words, or numbers of parts of speech.

Recently, Snow (1974) reported a semantic analysis of Dutch mothers'
speech to their children in which she looked for the same semantic relations
that have been described in children's early two-word sentences. She found
that the same "semantic relations provide a very adequate description of the
content of mothers' speech," not only at a time when the children's speech
(which apparently was not analyzed) was apparently Stage 1 speech (when
the same semantic relations were presumably represented), but also later,
with more mature children. This result should not be so surprising; as
pointed out earlier (Chapters I and V), the content categories or semantic
relations in early children's speech (action, possession, recurrence, etc.)
would be expected as well in the speech of older preschool children,
school-age children, and adults. That is, even adults talk to adults about
action events, locative events, and possession as well as existence, disappearance, and recurrence. Description of semantics alone, just as earlier
studies of syntax alone, is less informative than description of semantic-
syntactic relationship. As presented in the sequence of development of
content/form interaction in Chapter V, content categories—the meaning or
semantic relations in child utterances—do not change developmentally,
except that new categories are added. What does change in the children's
speech is the interaction between content/form. That is, the same kinds of
content are presented in more complex forms. One would expect, then, that
it is the interaction between content/form in adult speech that is important for
input as well. Furthermore, Shatz and Gelman (1973) and Newport (1976)
pointed out that the communication needs between parents and children in
the situation, and the functions of their utterances, will also result in
simplification and redundancy of input. The interaction among content/form/
use is the critical factor that makes adults' speech to children the elegant
model for learning that it is.

Potentially, the most important finding in studies of adult input is the
flexibility of caregivers' speech that results in gradual but consistent
modifications in the model as children learn more about language. Not only
do adults talk differently to children than they talk to other adults, but it
appears that they talk differently to children of different ages, according to
how much they have learned about language (Broen, 1972; Moerk, 1975;
Nelson, 1973; and Phillips, 1973). For example, the adults in the study by
Nelson (1973) produced more expansions and imitations of their children's
speech at 24 months than at 13 months (median age). In the study by
Phillips (1973), it was reported that mothers used more different words and
more different parts of speech per utterance, and more "abstract" vocabulary
words with 8-month-old children who knew little if any language than with
18-month-old children who were learning words and first-word combinations.

The general assumption that caregivers modulate their speech to children as a function of linguistic maturity (instead of age alone) was questioned by Newport (1976), who did not observe parents using more complex speech with more linguistically mature children. However, her measures of the children's linguistic maturity were similar to the measures used by Phillips, who found differences. Since in both studies the measures of linguistic maturity were superficial, and the ranges in each of these measures in the Newport study tended to be quite limited (e.g., words per verb ranged from 1.0 to 1.48; noun phrase per utterance ranged from 0.80 to 1.47; and morphemes per noun phrase ranged from 1.0 to 1.46), they may not have provided a sensitive index of the linguistic maturity of the children. The fact that correlations between structural complexity in caregivers speech and children's linguistic maturity were not found is not necessarily evidence that such correlations do not exist.

In the adult-child discourse in Bloom, Rocissano, and Hood (1976), there were differences in the adult speech to the children between 24 and 36 months of age, and these differences appeared to reflect the developmental changes that were observed in the children's speech. For example, the adults asked proportionately more questions as the children's linguistically contingent responses to adult questions increased. In responding to the children, the adults tended to repeat what the children said less frequently, and to ask Wh- questions for expansion more frequently. In the study of causality by Hood (1977), it was observed that adults did not ask causal questions (with "Why") until after the children had begun to use causal statements in their own speech. Thus, whether or not adults are using longer and more complex speech because children are older and are also using longer and more complex speech may be less important than the fact that adults are sensitive to many different kinds of signals that children give out—signals about what they already know or are learning, and signals about what they are ready to learn. Such sensitivity between the active seeking of the child and the responsive monitoring of the parent is as important to the social and affective mutuality between children and parents, in the course of development, as it is to learning the relations between language content, language form, and language use.

SUMMARY

The material that has been presented so far is concerned with description of children's language behaviors—in the effort to describe *what* it is that children learn when they learn language. This chapter concludes the half of the book that considers normal language development with discussion of some of the things that contribute to *how* children learn language. Although the emphasis on *what* instead of *how* may seem disproportionate, the fact is that much more information exists about what children learn than exists for explaining how such learning takes place.

The literature in child language contains many theoretical accounts that attempt to explain language development; these are discussed here in terms of the relative importance that has been given to either biological or environmental factors in such theoretical statements. Neither the position of biological or innate determinism nor the position of environmental determinism could be entirely correct. Both factors come together in the child's interaction with the context, and the child matures as an active seeker after new information.

Language development occurs in the process of contact between linguistic categories (language form) and nonlinguistic categories (content and use). The question of the relative influence of the one over the other—which has been asked in the traditional literature in terms of the larger question of the relation between language and thought—is discussed. There is a mutual influence between children's conceptual development (nonlinguistic object concepts and relational concepts) and the linguistic categories (linguistic word concepts and structure) of the language that they hear.

The child learns a plan for language (knowledge or competence) that guides behaviors of speaking and understanding but, at the same time, the child adds to the mental plan for language everytime language is used to speak or understand. Processes whereby children makes contact between linguistic categories and nonlinguistic categories are discussed. One process is imitation; children imitate the words and structures they are currently learning when they repeat all or part of the speech that they hear. In addition to imitation, other kinds of discourse contribute to how children learn relations among the content/form/use of language. Of considerable importance to imitation and discourse is, naturally, the kind of speech that children hear. The speech addressed to children is their major input for learning and is described here as a well-tuned model of contact between linguistic and nonlinguistic categories.

SUGGESTED READINGS

In *Readings in Language Development*

Bloom, L., Hood, L., and Lightbown, P., Imitation in language development: If, when and why? *Cognitive Psychology, 6,* 380–420, 1974.

Brown, R., The original word game. Appendix in J. Bruner, J. Goodnow, and G. Austin, *A study in thinking.* New York: John Wiley & Sons, 1956, pp. 284–291.

MacNamara, J., Cognitive bases of language learning in infants. *Psychological Review, 79,* 1–13, 1972.

Slobin, D., Cognitive prerequisites for the development of grammar. In C. A. Ferguson and D. I. Slobin (Eds.), *Studies of child language development.* New York: Holt, Rinehart, & Winston, 1973.

Snow, C., Mother's speech to children learning language. *Child Development, 43,* 549–565, 1972.

Other Readings

Bever, T., The cognitive basis of linguistic structure. In J. Hayes (Ed.), *Cognition and the development of language.* New York: John Wiley & Sons, 1970.

Bloom, L., Rocissano, L., and Hood, L., Adult-child discourse: Developmental interaction between information processing and linguistic knowledge. *Cognitive Psychology, 8,* 521–552, 1976.

Brown, R., and Bellugi, U., Three processes in the child's acquisition of syntax. *Harvard Educational Review, 34,* 133–151, 1964.

Cromer, R., The development of language and cognition: The cognition hypothesis. In B. Foss (Ed.), *New perspectives in child development.* New York: Penguin Education, 1974.

Guillaume, P., *Imitation in children.* Chicago: University of Chicago Press, 1968.

Shatz, M., and Gelman, R., The development of communication skills: Modifications in the speech of young children as a function of listener. *Monographs of the Society for Research in Child Development, 38,* Serial No. 152, 1973

Snow, C. E., and Ferguson, C. A. (Eds.), *Talking to children: Language input and acquisition.* London, England: Cambridge University Press, 1977.

Part 3
DEVIANT LANGUAGE DEVELOPMENT

Although most children learn their native language in a relatively short period of time and without instruction, there are other children who have considerable difficulty; they learn language only with much help or they never learn language at all. These children are the concern of their parents and of specialists in the fields of speech pathology, audiology, education, psychology, and medicine. The language development of these children is the focus of the remaining chapters.

The following three chapters are concerned with defining, describing, and identifying language disorders in children just as Part 1 was concerned with ways of defining and describing normal language development.

Chapter X defines and describes language disorders in terms of content/form/use interactions and illustrates dysfunctions that may occur in each interaction. Chapter XI discusses the issues involved in describing deviant language—issues that relate to obtaining and interpreting evidence for the purpose of either clinical assessment or determining qualitative differences. A discussion of differences between normal and deviant language is also included. Finally, Chapter XII discusses means of identifying children with deviant language development.

287

It is possible to approach the study of children who do not develop language normally from a number of different points of view. One might concentrate on the reasons why a child, or groups of children that are similar in certain ways, do not learn language easily. In this case the terminology used to define and describe the children's difficulties would most likely relate to etiological considerations.

On the other hand, one might focus on the language itself—regardless of etiology. It is our purpose to focus first on the language of children who are not learning language normally—to define and describe language disorders for the purpose of facilitating language learning. The definition and descriptions of language disorders will thus be similar to the definition and descriptions of language and normal language development that have already been presented in Part 1.

LANGUAGE DISORDERS

There is currently no consensus on the definition of the terms used to describe the child, or the language of the child, who is not learning language normally. The terminology currently used includes *deviant* language, language *disorder*, language *disability*, and *delayed* language.

Some professionals use these terms as though a language disorder were a diagnostic entity instead of a descriptive term. When this is the case, the terms refer to a child who is having difficulty learning language but apparently not because of intellectual, sensory, or emotional problems. Etiology is either unknown or is presumed to be neurological. (See Kleffner, 1973; and Morehead, 1975).

Other professionals use the terms *deviant, disordered*, or *disability* as descriptive terms to refer to language development that is unlike that of normal development—not only in time of onset and rate of development but in the actual behaviors learned and the sequence in which they are learned. (See Chapter XI for a discussion of this point.)

Although both designations—language disorder as a diagnostic entity or as a description of qualitative differences from normal development—are ultimately important for the understanding of children who have difficulty learning language, such distinctions are often difficult to make. There is a need for a descriptive term that can include both quantitative and qualitative differences in language development. The terms disordered and deviant suggest difference or upset from normal function; they are used here as terms of general description without considering language disorder as a diagnostic entity and without considering the nature of the differences. The term disability will not be used because it suggests an incapacity and thus is *more* specific than the terms disordered or deviant. Other more descriptive terms can be used if the nature of the difference is focussed on.

Thus, the term *language disorder* will be used here as a broad term to describe certain behaviors, or the lack of certain other behaviors, in a child that are different from the behaviors that might be expected considering the child's chronological age. The term language disorder is used as a descriptive label in that it refers to a description of behavior; the term will not be used to refer to a diagnostic entity that could explain the behavior, in the way that such terms as dysarthria or acquired aphasia would explain or otherwise account for other kinds of behavior. A language disorder, as defined in these terms, is often identified by persons who encounter the child interacting in many situations that demand talking and understanding. The different behaviors that might be noticed are varied and include: little or no talking, little or no understanding of instructions, any unusual use of words or phrases, or grammatical mistakes in sentences that interfere with communication. Thus we can use the term language disorder to refer to any disruption in the learning of a native language—that is, in the learning or use of the conventional system of arbitrary signals used by persons in the environment as a code for representing ideas about the world for communication.

The key words that were elaborated for defining language in Chapter I also represent the key elements in defining a language disorder: ideas, code, conventional system, and communication. Children with a language disorder may have a problem in formulating *ideas* or conceptualizing information about the world; they may have difficulty in learning a *code* for representing what they know about the world; they may be able to learn a code that does not match the *conventional* system used in the linguistic community; they may have learned something about the world and something about the conventional code, but are unable to *use* the code in speaking or understanding in certain contexts or for certain purposes; or they may develop ideas, the conventional code, and the use of the code, but later than their peers, or with dysfunctions in the interactions among the components.

Language involves the interactions among content/form/use schematized in the Venn diagram in Figure X-1. Form refers to the conventional system of signals—the dictionary of sounds and words, along with the rules for combining the dictionary items so as to form phrases and sentences. *Content* refers to the ideas about objects and events in the world that are coded by language. *Use* refers to the contexts in which language can be used and the functions for which it is used. Normal language development has been described as the successful interaction among the three, as represented in area D. Disordered language development can be described as any disruption within a component *or* in the interaction among the components.

Difference from normal development can be described according to the way in which these components interact with one another. It is possible to focus on disruption within individual components and among components, but it should be kept in mind that these descriptions do not represent diagnostic categories; they, too, are simply broad descriptions that are helpful in emphasizing the way language functions as a system and the ways in which that system can be disrupted. As such, they serve to remind us that language learning and language disorders involve more than difficulty learning form—words and sentences. These descriptions are not specific enough to lead directly to intervention, because they do not specify the particular kinds of behaviors within each of the components and the interactions among components that need to be learned. They can be used, however, to indicate how a language disorder deviates from normal language. Thus, the descriptions are more specific than the generic term language disorder.

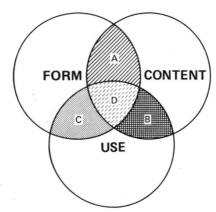

FIGURE X-1
The Interaction of Content/Form/Use in Language.

DEVELOPMENTAL DELAY

In the description of a language disorder the area D in Figure X-1 can represent normal sequence of development within each component and with their interactions, but beginning later than expected or proceeding slower than expected. That is, the child uses the same forms to talk of the same ideas in the same contexts and for the same purposes as the child with normal development. Such language would follow an expected sequence but would be delayed, either in onset or rate of development, or in both onset and rate. Although such problems are included under the broad descriptive label of language disorders, they are also referred to as language delay or maturational lag.

Other language behaviors that can be described as a language disorder differ in the extent to which a component may be disrupted, or in the extent to which there is disruption in the interaction among the components. In the following discussion, some of these possible disruptions will be explored and schematized to show the result of separation of one or another of the components or of their weak interaction. The other components or interactions may not be entirely intact and well functioning, but they represent more intact skills than are available in the separated or weakest component.

DISORDERS OF FORM

The partial overlay of content and use, B, with the separation of form, schematized in Figure X-2, represents children whose ideas about the world of objects and events and abilities to communicate these ideas are more intact than their knowledge of the linguistic system for representing and communicating these ideas.

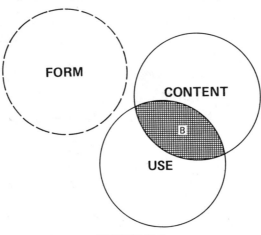

FIGURE X-2
Disruption in the Form of Langauge.

Such children may use gestures or primitive forms for communicating ideas, but they have difficulty learning the conventional system of arbitrary signals for coding and communicating. Boxes X-1 and X-2 present dialogues with children that illustrate a primary weakness in the knowledge they have of linguistic form for coding ideas of the world, but well-developed ideas of the world that they communicate in many contexts for many functions.

Word-finding difficulty that is occasionally observed in children and often reported in adult aphasia is another disruption in the interaction between form and content. Such children circumlocute or talk around the idea they are trying to communicate, having difficulty in recalling the form that

---

BOX X-1 DIALOGUE WITH CINDY, 7 YEARS OLD. EXAMPLES OF A DISOR-
DER HAVING TO DO WITH LANGUAGE FORM

Cindy reported to her therapist an incident that happened at home the previous day.

(Cindy pointing to the tape recorder)   uh/uh

(Pointing over shoulder)   **home**

                                                 Buh/ (her name for her brother)

**(Cindy slides arm over table and down
toward the floor points to
tape recorder and to floor;
frowns; wagging finger)**   **Mama/Mama**

Cindy communicated an event that had happened in the past by using gestures and a limited number of single words. On another occasion, Cindy met her therapist in the hall.

                                                 hi/

**(Cindy points to self, then pointing
down hall)**   **milk/**

In this latter example, Cindy communicated about an event in the immediate future; she was on her way to obtain milk for lunch. In both examples, it is evident that Cindy was communicating ideas, but only through gestures and limited linguistic form. Cindy is a child who knows about many objects and events in the world, and readily attempts to communicate her ideas, but she is having difficulty learning the necessary words and combinations of words to represent what she knows more fully.

BOX X-2 DIALOGUE WITH FRANK, 6 YEARS OLD. AN EXAMPLE OF A DISORDER HAVING TO DO WITH LANGUAGE FORM

(Frank walked into the clinician's office)

                                        hi/ doing

I'm typing   help ↑
No, thank you, I'm all
through/ I have to teach now

                                        teach ↑

Yes   where

Over in that white building
                                        oh/

(Pointing to pencil sharpener)   that

You know/ what's
it for?
                                        pencil/sharp

Right, it's a pencil
sharpener

(Walking out door)   bye

Frank communicates well but generally with only one- and two-word utterances.

---

represents what they are trying to say. Use, in such instances, is well integrated with content, but the form for representing content is not available.

There are few who would quarrel with labeling children such as those illustrated in Boxes X-1 and X-2 as having a language disorder. Their problem is with the linguistic dimension of language; both the conceptual and interactional dimensions are intact.

DISORDERS OF CONTENT

Other children who do not learn language normally appear to be weakest in conceptual development—in the development of ideas of the world that make up the content of language. The language of *some* of these children is best illustrated by Figure X-1; it is similar to normal development but is slower to develop. One might read the transcripts of such a child and say

"Why do you say this child has difficulty with language? This child is like many 2- or 4-year-old children I've met." The problem is, of course, that the child is not 2 or 3 years old, but perhaps 5 or 8 years old.

Other children with disruption in conceptual development may exhibit language behaviors better represented by Figure X-3; that is, the development of form/use interactions may be more advanced than the interactions with content. Although the language development of blind children is yet to be thoroughly described, some young blind children appear to exhibit development of form/use interactions that far exceed their development of content. Lacking visual input, certain sensori-motor concepts develop more slowly than the ability to develop social interactions and concepts of form. Such children are often echolalic and speak in grammatically well-formed sentences that appear in advance of their ideas. Children with visual impairments may well use form as a means of learning about the content of language. (See the discussion of the "original word game" in Chapter IX, and Brown, 1956, in *RLDev*).

The language behaviors of many hydrocephalic children may also be represented by Figure X-3. These children have been characterized as hyperverbal, with "cocktail party speech" (Schwartz, 1974; and Swisher and Pinsker, 1971). Cocktail party speech appears to be an example of well-developed form (with well-developed articulation, intonation, and stress patterns) that is used for social interactions but with weak conceptual underpinnings. According to Schwartz, the language of the hydrocephalic child follows normal developmental milestones in terms of form but is superficial and irrelevant in content. It often appears they do not know the

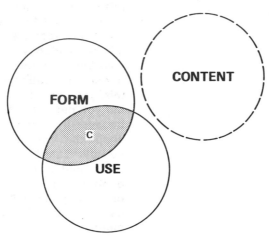

FIGURE X-3
Disruption in the Content of Language.

meaning of what they say. (For an example, see Box X-3.) Unlike the children characterized by Figure X-2, such children know about form and the creation of complex sentences; unlike the children to be discussed next that are represented by Figure X-4, such children do use form as a means of social interaction and to refer to present contexts. Such children reportedly give many commands, ask many questions, and are extremely sociable. The language used seems to serve interpersonal functions; in fact, some have been described as verbally aggressive.

It is unusual to find the pattern illustrated in Figure X-3 simply because conceptual development is necessary both for learning about form and learning about using form as a means for social interaction. When conceptual development is weak, the influence is generally obvious in all components and their interaction. Because of this, some would say that these children do not have a *language* disorder but, instead, have a conceptual disorder. On the other hand, one could say they have both a language disorder and a conceptual disorder, and, in fact, it is not always clear that the disorder of content may not be improved by knowledge of form—that is, learning form may aid in the development of concepts.

As described above, however, there are occasional children for whom

---

BOX X-3 AN EXAMPLE OF A DISORDER IN CONTENT FROM A 6-YEAR-OLD HYDROCEPHALIC CHILD (from Schwartz, 1974, pp. 466–467)

(Shown a button and asked to tell about it)

this is a button/ it has two holes in it/ it's like a lady has/ it has a shape/ it is round/ this is a button/ you put it on your blouse or an apron·in case an apron has a button/ that's big like this/ you can roll it and throw it but you never smash a window/ because if you have a button or a shape that goes on the wall or if you take it and hang it on the dress that would be very nice/ would you do that for me?/ if you have a dress or a coat you can hang it on or you can keep it out to take it to the store.

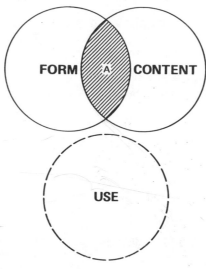

FIGURE X-4
Disruption in the Use of Language.

content is the weakest interaction and, although these children may have some forms and may use them to communicate they, too, may be described as having a language disorder if the content of their utterances is different from that expected based on their knowledge of form and use, and based on their chronological age. Parents, educators, and clinicians are interested in studying and in facilitating the language development of children whose conceptual development is slower than or different from normal.

DISORDERS OF USE

Some children give evidence of content/form interactions that are more intact than use, as schematized in Figure X-4. With these children, learning the system to code ideas appears to be less of a problem than using the system for communication. The overlay of form and content, A, represents knowledge of the conventional system as a code for meanings, and it is a more intact interaction than the use of the code either in terms of context or purpose. Examples of this disruption in language use are difficult to present because continual interaction with such children is usually needed before the nature of the disruption becomes apparent. Although similar isolated examples can occur with all children, the repeated occurrence of such behavior causes these children to stand out from their peers. Examples are presented in Box X-4 and Box X-5, with the warning that these behaviors must be considered in the light of the frequency with which they appear in

BOX X-4 DIALOGUE WITH GEORGE, 10 YEARS OLD. AN EXAMPLE OF A
DISORDER IN THE USE OF LANGUAGE. (We are indebted to R.
Connelly for providing this example.)

(George and clinician enter clinic
room and look out at falling snow)

Look at that snow It's
all on the grass

you're not going outside

No, I'm not going out-
side/ are you going outside?

no

(George no longer directing gaze
toward therapist)

that's okay/yeah/I can
stay inside with Joe/
yeah/okay I can stay
inside with Joe/okay/
I do some work inside
with Joe/oh I can work
with Joe/Joe big Joe
gonna stay inside/Jane
gonna go outside/he
gone yeah/I can stay in-
side with Joe/okay/I'll
do some work with Joe
cut-color-create[1] inside/
okay/Jane's gonna go
out

Who are you talking to?
(Pause) George?

to (---) self

you can stay inside with
Joe/yeah/Jane's got
boots/gonna stay inside
with Joe

Are you talking to me?

okay I can stay inside
with Joe/okay

[1] Cut-color-create is the name of one of the classroom activities. Joe is a student aide, Jane is the
teacher.

BOX X-5 DIALOGUE WITH MARK, 10 YEARS OLD. AN EXAMPLE OF A DISORDER IN THE USE OF LANGUAGE. (We are indebted to L. Weber for providing this example)

(Mark and his teacher are talking)

> **Mom used to take me to McDonalds February 1974/she used to put me up in the --- at 1 :30/ and I went to the doctors' office at 2 :45**

What kind of things do you eat when you go to McDonalds?

> **a hamburger/a Big Mac/ quarter pounder/soft drinks/and french fries/ I never go to McDonald's for breakfast you know**

Why not?

> **why well you know/I used to sleep in New York/ in the Catskill Mountain/ I used to go to a motel/I don't know where I ate breakfast/you know RD's roast beef sandwich/that restaurant was in Pennsylvania but it's in New Jersey/it's now in New York on the way to New York City/ Manhattan**

the children's daily behavior. Such children's use of language is more often intrapersonal than interpersonal; they talk about something that is out of context and either ramble repetitively or tangentially associate ideas without regard for the listener. Again, it is the frequency of such instances and the frequency of intrapersonal communications that make such language different in use from that of the child's peers.

Other children with disruptions in use rarely verbalize even if questioned or prodded. When prodded into speaking, their productions indicate a greater knowledge of the code than their general use would suggest.

DISTORTED INTERACTIONS OF CONTENT/FORM/USE

There are children who use forms to communicate ideas but the forms are inappropriate both to the context and to the meaning they apparently intend to convey. There is an inability to use linguistic form to represent meaning that is relevant to the content or context of the situation. There is some development within each component, but the interactions among them are distorted. Such children may utter stereotyped utterances, producing complex sentences with sophisticated grammatical markings, but produce few utterances that are meaningful, except in a very gross way, to the situation. Although use is limited, the utterances may be used to get attention, to make requests, or as a response to another's utterance, and thus are used for communication. These children may, in an unusual way, be communicating an idea, thus suggesting some interaction of content and use. It is, however, the weak interactions among content/form/use that are particularly outstanding, as illustrated in Figure X-5. It appears that these children have learned complete utterances in response to certain situations or ideas without knowing the semantic-syntactic relations that are represented within the sentences that they can use. Examples can be found in Box X-6.

Thus the distortion of content/form/use interactions characterizes the children who, unlike those described by Figure X-2, produce sophisticated examples of the conventional signal system; unlike those described by Figure X-3, may have complex ideas of the world but do not code these ideas appropriately; and, unlike those described by Figure X-4, use forms for interpersonal interaction. In a distorted interaction disorder, messages are well formed and are used for specific purposes in the situation. There is, however, a contradiction between the content of a message and its use and

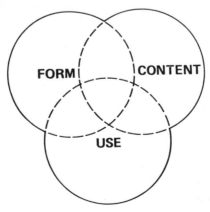

FIGURE X-5
Disruption in the interaction among components.

BOX X-6 EXAMPLES OF DISTORTED INTERACTIONS OF CONTENT/FORM/
USE

From Cunningham, (1968, pp. 231, 237, in *RLDis*)
A child, named Thomas, using words spoken at some prior time by an adult,
requests ice cream by saying:

> **you want some ice
> cream, Thomas?/
> yes, you may.**

Another boy, repeating what had been said by a house mother when dinner
was demanded at the wrong time, requests dinner by saying:

> **daresay she'd throw me
> out if I gave it to you
> now.**

In each of these examples forms were used for the purpose of obtaining
something. Each child had an idea he attempted to communicate, and the
forms used were grammatically correct. However, there was a mismatch
between the content of the form that was used, the content of the idea being
expressed and the function of the utterance. These children had apparently
remembered large segments of form, one or two complete sentences,
associated with an idea or situation, and had learned that such forms could
be used to interact with the environment. Further examples support the idea
that form and content are globally associated with some function.

From Kanner (1973, p. 165)

   (A child, Fred, given a gift)   **you say thank you**

From Rutter (1966, p. 60)

   (When wanting someone to go away)   **see you in a fortnight**

   (When meaning no)   **don't you want it**

From Cunningham (1968, p. 237)

   (Hitting the interviewer)   **be a good boy**

   (Eating plasticine chips)   **you mustn't eat the chips**

All of these utterances appear to have been associated with a similar
situation in some past experience.

between the content of the message and its form, while some element of content relates the message to the situation in which it occurs.

SEPARATION OF CONTENT, FORM, AND USE

There are children whose linguistic behavior is a fragmentation of content/form/use such that none of the components appear to interact with another. Such children use stereotypic speech with utterances that have little or no relation to the situations in which they occur or to any recognizable content. For example, these children may recite radio and television commercials or news and sports broadcasts without apparent connection to external stimuli in the situation and with no apparent function other than perhaps to establish or maintain some communication contact. In such situations, content, form, and use are separate from one another, as represented in Figure X-6. An example of similar behavior with a nonstereotypic utterance can be found in Box X-7. It may be that in instances of such nonstereotypic utterances, content and form are interacting, but the content is unrelated to the external environment. Kanner (1946, *in RLDis*) pointed out that some apparently irrelevant utterances can be traced back to an earlier experience and are in some idiosyncratic way associated with the present context. A child standing in the clinic room says "Don't throw the dog off the balcony" when there is no dog or balcony in view. The utterance had been spoken to him 3 years before by his mother, who was tired of retrieving a toy dog the child had repeatedly thrown from a hotel balcony. According to Kanner, the child

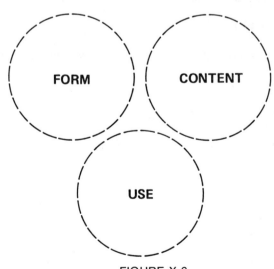

FIGURE X-6
The Separate Components Without Interaction.

BOX X-7 AN EXAMPLE OF SEPARATION OF THE COMPO-
NENTS OF CONTENT, FORM, AND USE (from
Cunningham, 1968, p. 237, in *RLDis*).

(Looking at a watch)   **there's the doors/**
                                  make the doors/
                                  there's the east

---

uttered the expression whenever he was tempted to throw anything. Such associations may be true for other behaviors that are nonstereotypic but appear to have no interaction among the three dimensions of content, form, and use. Again, it is the prevalence of such behaviors and not the isolated occurrence of examples of the behaviors that mark them as different from the language behaviors of peers.

SUMMARY

The term language disorders is used here to describe language behaviors that are different from those expected considering a child's chronological age. The many descriptions presented emphasize that language disorders encompass many different kinds of disruption in the integration of content, form, and use. Thus, the term is not only a description of the behavior of children who have difficulty learning the form of language (disorders of form), but also describes children who can talk easily and readily but who say nothing (disorders of content), or talk to no one (disorders of use), as well as children who use forms to communicate ideas but not in the conventional manner (distorted interactions of content/form/use) or who utter forms with no apparent meaning or purpose (separation of content/form/use). In addition to the behavior interactions that are described here, there are other behaviors that cannot be so neatly schematized, but that stand out nevertheless as different from expected behaviors.

This view of language disorders has resulted in an emphasis on the need to describe what children do, and what they have difficulty in doing, in order to understand possible disruptions in the development of the system. To plan the goals of an effective program for treatment and education, these descriptions must be further refined and placed within a framework, such as a developmental sequence that specifies the sequence of goals.

It is possible to approach the study of deviant language development from a number of different points of view. The reasons why some children do not learn language as their peers do might be considered important, or one might focus on the nature of the language behaviors themselves. The various approaches that have influenced the ways in which children with language disorders have been most typically characterized, for clinical and educational reasons, can be grouped according to their focus: (1) a categorical orientation; (2) a specific abilities orientation; and (3) a linguistic orientation.

ORIENTATIONS TO LANGUAGE DISORDERS

A *categorical orientation* to language disorders in children concentrates on classifying certain syndromes of behavior that categorize the whole individual, based on a limited number of behavioral manifestations. Thus, they can be considered molar or global categories. They are clinical categories based on possible precipitating factors such as mental retardation, emotional disturbance, neurological impairment, and hearing impairment. Within this orientation the description of language disorders and of children with language disorders focusses on the categories—on the precipitating factors and symptoms related to each category. Intervention is then guided by the categorical placement and the related etiological considerations. This orientation is further discussed in Chapter XVIII.

In contrast to the global categories formed by the categorical orientation, other approaches have formed more molecular categories; that is, they have categorized behaviors instead of whole individuals. Some of these approaches have attempted to identify and describe the abilities that are necessary for the learning and use of language in order to diagnose and remediate abilities that may be considered defective. The molecular categories of abilities that are considered necessary for learning and using language include aspects of language processing such as those involved in memory, discrimination, and association. The child with a language disorder has been described in terms of the relative strengths and weaknesses of certain processes or abilities. Intervention has been geared to remediating or strengthening the abilities that are considered missing or weak, in order to improve language; in this sense the orientation is also etiological. This orientation is referred to here as a *specific abilities orientation* and is discussed further in Chapter XIX.

Other approaches with a different, primarily *linguistic orientation*, have formed molecular categories to describe the language of the child with a language disorder. Such categories also describe the behaviors of individuals instead of describing the individual as a whole. The description of language disorders and of the child with a language disorder has been based on descriptions of language, and intervention has concentrated on teaching language. The behavior to be changed is described and taught; therefore these approaches, combined and referred to here as a linguistic orientation, are not etiological but are symptom oriented.

Each orientation has contributed important information; each has had its limitations. The orientation that is most relevant to describing deviant language behavior and development is the linguistic orientation; it will be described further in this chapter, and it provides a framework for the major portion of this book.

Rapid developments in linguistic theory and heightened interest in the study of language development spurred the growth of linguistic approaches to language disorders in children. Developments in the field of linguistics—particularly the introduction of the theory of generative transformational grammar (Chomsky, 1957, 1965)—provided more sophisticated techniques for describing language than had previously been available. The sophistication and interest generated by these ideas were first applied to the study of normal language development (as discussed in Chapter II), and later to the study of deviant language development. The study of language disorders involves the same levels of description and methodological issues as the study of normal language development: obtaining evidence to be described, interpreting the evidence in order to categorize it, and formalizing the interpretations with a scheme that provides a hypothesis about the child's knowledge. (See Chapter II for a discussion of these issues.) The study of deviant language development has paralleled the study of normal language development using similar observational techniques, taxonomies for describing, formalization procedures and, to a degree, a similar goal.

OBJECTIVES OF DESCRIPTION

The goal of studying both normal and deviant language development has been to describe what a child or group of children knows about language, and to compare that knowledge with some standard or model. The difference lies in the ultimate objective of that comparison. In most cases the ultimate objective of describing deviant language is either to identify children with a language disorder or to plan educational intervention. A related third objective is to determine whether differences between deviant and normal language development are mainly *quantitative* (later onset and slower rate of development) or *qualitative* (different content/form/use interactions or different sequences in their development). This latter objective is usually met by comparing the language of a group of children who are in some way similar (often having been assigned a similar categorical label such as mentally retarded, deaf, emotionally disturbed, etc.) to a normal population. The results of this comparison are used to define clinical syndromes and to support or reject hypotheses about the interrelationship of language learning and other factors (intelligence, perceptual processing, etc.). In contrast, the first two objectives are most common when describing the language of a particular child, and the results are applied to decisions concerning language intervention.

A PLAN FOR ASSESSMENT

Intervention geared to facilitating the language learning of children who have a language disorder must be adapted to each child according to what the child needs to know about language and how the child can best learn language. Describing a child's language behavior for the purpose of identifying a problem or for planning intervention is referred to as assessment. Assessment is carried out before intervention is begun, so that the educational program begins immediately with the most appropriate and reasonable goals and procedures for facilitating language learning. Assessment continues during intervention in order to chart progress, establish new goals, and make necessary changes in procedures.

To be most efficient and useful, persons involved in assessment must operate with a *plan*. An overall plan for assessment differs from a specific program or set of procedures. Although a program specifies certain techniques, and perhaps their order of application, a plan stresses the objectives of assessment and categorizes procedural techniques that might be useful for reaching each objective. An overall plan is needed if the assessor is to evaluate the usefulness of new testing instruments that appear on the market and the new observational methods that are mentioned in the literature. Because children are different in the way that they can respond to procedural techniques, one cannot become bound to a limited set of testing instruments or procedures. In addition, a *plan* of assessment focussing on the goals and purposes of any technique or test instrument in general may help to avoid the tendency to collect large quantities of information with one or another instrument, without need or use for that information. Too often the instruments of assessment have dominated the clinical and educational description of language, resulting in the collection of unnecessary or unusable information.

All information about a child may be interesting, but the information obtained from assessment should bear directly on identifying whether there is a problem, or on determining the goals and procedures for intervention. In the process of assessment, the clinician must be continually aware of the purpose of each technique that is used. That awareness extends to the information that can be expected and also to the reason why that information is needed. The answer to all perplexing problems in assessment is not always to search for another instrument, but to determine why more information is needed, specify what that information is and, only then, to be concerned with the procedures for obtaining that information.

A plan for clinical assessment, entails certain objectives:

1. To determine whether there is a problem that needs further assessment and intervention.

2. To determine the goals of intervention—to indicate what the child needs to

learn, and what the child should be able to learn—in terms of the content/form/use of language.

3. To suggest procedures of intervention—to indicate the factors that need to be taken into account for the child to be able to learn language skills most effectively.

Each objective of assessment determines the information that is needed to reach that objective; the information that is needed in turn determines the techniques to be used to obtain the information. Thus, the objectives of assessment lead to the information needed, and the information needed leads to the techniques, as schematized in Box XI-1. The objectives are outlined in Table XI-1 with the information needed to reach the objectives.

In order to determine the existence of a problem and to determine the

TABLE XI-1
Objectives of and Information from Assessment

Objectives *Why* Use a Procedure	Information Needed *What* the Relevant Procedure Will Produce
1. To determine the existence of a problem	A comparison of language behavior with language behaviors of children of comparable age
2. To determine the goals of intervention	A description of the content/form/use of the child's language behavior
3. To plan procedures of intervention	
a. To reduce effect of maintaining factors	Amount and type of language exposure in the environment; social and cognitive development; sensory acuity; general health
b. To determine the role others can play	Description of home and school environment
c. To provide motivators and reinforcers	Child's interests, likes, and dislikes; child's social interactions
d. To plan structure of intervention sessions	Child's attention span and degree of distractibility in different contexts
e. To plan methods of presenting input	Sensory acuity and association of meaning with the signal
	Reactions to variations in acoustic signals, such as rate, intensity, and prosody
	Response to different modalities, in combination and alone
f. To determine the form of the output signal	Oral motor capabilities; ability to make auditory-vocal associations

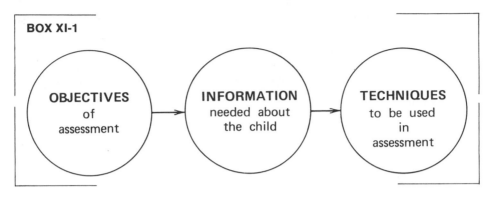

BOX XI-1

OBJECTIVES of assessment → INFORMATION needed about the child → TECHNIQUES to be used in assessment

goals of intervention, information is needed about the child's language itself: how the child uses the conventional system of signals to represent what the child knows about the world; what aspects of the system the child uses (form); what ideas of the world the child communicates (content); the purposes for which the child uses the system and how the child chooses among alternative means in different contexts (use). To determine the existence of a problem, given the definition in Chapter X, a child's language will be compared with norms for other children of the same age. To determine the goals of intervention, given a developmental approach, a child's language performance will be compared with the developmental sequence of content/form/use. The lack of behaviors and the behaviors that follow in sequence after the observed behaviors provide the goals of intervention; the goals of intervention form the content of the intervention program.

In addition to information about a child's language behavior, it is also necessary to obtain information about the situations and conditions that would help the child to learn more about language. Are there factors interfering with language learning that can be changed? What aspects of the child's environment can be used to assist language learning? What conditions favor the child's language performance? Under what conditions does the child learn best? What conditions tend to disrupt the child? What interests the child? What seems to motivate and what appears to reinforce the child? This information leads to suggestions about the procedures for intervention, the third objective of assessment. Thus, the information needed from assessment includes both a description of the child's current language performance, and a description of whatever factors may influence the child's learning new language behaviors.

In order to plan the most effective procedures for intervention, it is necessary to know: the role that the family and school might play in the intervention program; the most advantageous structure for an intervention program (e.g., a highly structured one-to-one relationship, or a low-structured group experiential program); the necessity for manipulating the input signal (amplifying the signal, supplementing the signal with another sensory modality, etc.); the maintaining factors that might be eliminated; and both the topics and reinforcers that might best motivate the child to change language behaviors. Certainly no one set of intervention procedures is applicable to all children, just as no one set of intervention goals is appropriate to all children.

Given the objectives of assessment and the information needed to reach these objectives, we are left with the problem of how to obtain this information—how to collect evidence about the child and about the child's language and how to interpret the evidence that is obtained. Evidence of a child's knowledge of language is influenced by complex interactions among the child, the observer-describer, the contexts of observation, and the language behavior to be described (see Box XI-2). For example, the observer-describer brings to the observation certain preconceived ideas that influence what is observed and how it is described. In addition, when the observer is a part of the situation, the observer's personality and interactional patterns will influence the behavior of the child. Labov (1970) reported that the familiarity of observers and interactional patterns influenced the language sample obtained—only small restricted samples were obtained from many children when in the context of strange adults, while richer

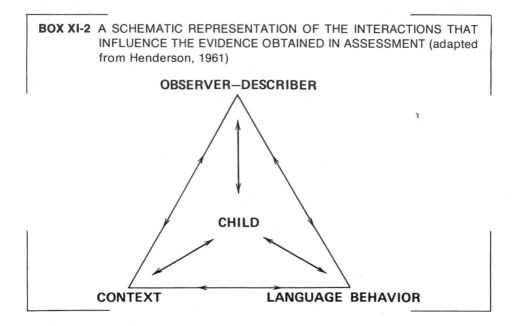

BOX XI-2 A SCHEMATIC REPRESENTATION OF THE INTERACTIONS THAT INFLUENCE THE EVIDENCE OBTAINED IN ASSESSMENT (adapted from Henderson, 1961)

OBSERVER–DESCRIBER

CHILD

CONTEXT   **LANGUAGE BEHAVIOR**

and longer samples were obtained in peer-peer interaction. The context of observation also influences what language behaviors are observed (Cazden, 1970). Longhurst and Grubb (1974) reported that low structured settings elicited samples that were more complex and longer than samples obtained in highly structured settings. Further discussion of these and other interactions is included in this chapter and in Chapter XVI.

OBTAINING THE EVIDENCE

Two major considerations involved in obtaining evidence about deviant language development are the observer, who chooses the behaviors to describe, and the context in which the language behavior is observed. Both considerations were discussed in Chapter II and are discussed further in the following sections.

OBSERVER

Basically, all assessment techniques are observations under various conditions. Information from assessment is influenced by the acuteness and accuracy of the observer.

To be an acute and accurate observer involves a number of factors; the most important factor is an understanding of the behavior being observed. While anyone could observe and describe the comings and goings of a group of birds, undoubtedly most observers would miss many important aspects of the birds' performance because of a limited knowledge of the meaning and relative importance of the different movements and sounds of birds. Some observers might describe the color of the feathers, the speed of flight, the excitement and wariness of the birds, and the different noises that they make. All of these are important observations, but they are not the same observations that an ethologist might make. Similarly, many individuals hear and enjoy operatic singers and can describe their voices, but most descriptions probably would not help the singer who wished to improve singing skills. Thus, it is possible to observe a child talking and interacting with someone else, and describe many important and interesting aspects of the situation, but not provide the information that is necessary for understanding what the child knows or for changing the child's behavior.

The first requirement for observation is to know the behavior you are observing and to have a framework for describing the observed behavior. To provide a description of a child's language performance that will be useful for describing what the child knows about language in comparison with the normal child, or for planning intervention that will facilitate language learning, one needs to understand language and its normal development in terms of content/form/use. Part 1 provided information to help in understanding language and its normal development—the framework for describing deviant language behavior advocated in Part 4 is a developmental framework that includes aspects of the content/form/use of language.

If the observer must know the behavior being observed, can one use other nontrained observers (as parents or teachers) to obtain information about a child's language? In the example given earlier about the observations of birds, the ethologist could request that others keep track of the number of times and the different directions from which the bird approaches the nest. This limited set of observations could be recorded without a full understanding of the behaviors of birds, and could provide the ethologist with information relevant to the description of birds. So, also, it is possible to solicit information from unsophisticated observers about the content/form/use of language if one asks specific questions of the parent or teacher. In many instances teachers and parents can be quickly trained to keep a record of particular behaviors in school and home settings. In this way the speech pathologist obtains relevant information by imposing a framework for observation on others who interact with the child.

In addition to observations about language, other specialists can provide different kinds of information that is important to planning the procedures of intervention—information that is beyond the expertise of the language specialists and requires different points of view and knowledge of different behaviors. For example, the medical person might provide information on the possibility of seizures; the educational specialist could contribute information on learning styles, and topics in which to embed language training; the psychologist might describe social interactional patterns; and the audiologist might suggest the need for a specific type of amplification. The usefulness of such reported observations is dependent on the assessor's skill in (1) soliciting the information that is most applicable to the purposes of assessment, and (2) interpreting the accuracy and relevance of the reports of others. Too often reports are requested from other professionals, without specification of the kind of information that is wanted, and are filed, but never referred to again. If the goals of assessment and the information that is needed to reach these goals are kept in mind, then one will not be asking for a "psychologist's report" or a "neurologist's report" but, instead, will be asking for *particular information* from the psychologist or neurologist. One will be tapping the thinking of other professionals to assist in planning intervention. In addition to other professionals, a child's family is a rich source of many kinds of information relevant to the goals and procedures of intervention, but much of this information is also lost if it is not solicited with its relationship to intervention kept in mind. There are, then, two sources of information about the child: the observations that are made directly and the observations that are reported by other professionals or those in close contact with the child.

CONTEXT

In addition to the observer, another consideration in obtaining evidence is the setting in which the observation occurs. As noted before, a variety of settings is desirable for generating useful hypotheses about interventon. How might settings vary? The first thought that comes to mind is the *familiarity* of the setting to the child. The familiarity of the actual physical location may be an influential variable for some children, but it cannot always be controlled. The ideal arrangement would be to see the child at home as well as in a new situation. A more important, and generally controllable, variable may be the familiarity of the individuals who interact with the child in the observation session. When possible, one should attempt to observe the child with family, friend, or teacher, not only as part of the observation session itself, but also in the waiting room, hallway, or cafeteria. Children typically interact in everyday situations with persons they know best, so that every opportunity should be taken to observe the child in contexts that are familiar and representative of daily life.

In addition to the influence of context on the amount of data obtained (i.e., the number of utterances), the context may also actually affect the type of language behavior observed (e.g., the use of particular semantic-syntactic structures). The load on the language system for encoding and decoding information in messages varies with the availability, in the mind of the speaker or hearer, of a *mental* representation (conceptualization) of the ideas of the world that are being coded (see Bloom, 1974c, and Chapter VIII for discussion of this point). Speaking about events in the here and now may be easier than talking about events that are removed in space and time from the utterances. Listening to a speaker without the support of a present event may demand more of the language coding system than talking about an event that is represented in consciousness from memory. Thus, the language used by a child to talk about a ball game played the day before (or any event in which the child is involved or that is uppermost in mind) may be different from the language that is used in other situations in which experiences are tapped that might not be so easily retrievable from memory (e.g., when the child is asked to tell about an object, to describe what might be done given some hypothetical situation, to listen and answer questions about a story, to act out, recall, or imitate verbal comments or directions, or even to tell a story about a static picture that is not necessarily familiar).

Many assessment contexts tap these latter language situations and rarely pay as much attention to utterances that may be precipitated by what the child might be thinking about—the child's own mental representations. Such contexts tend to be highly structured; the child is moved from task to task, and little consideration may be given to the ways in which tasks may influence one another by influencing the child's mental state. It is often rare that the child is able to use ongoing events in these contexts to support the representations about the messages to be encoded or decoded. Less structured situations tend to allow the most support for spontaneous speech,either from mental representations in consciousness or from ongoing events.

As with the study of normal language development, the techniques used in obtaining evidence include observation in naturalistic interactions and observation of responses to the experimental manipulation of one or another of the components of content, form, and use. The difference between these two techniques can be thought of in terms of the degree of structure imposed by the observer. In the naturalistic observation the imposition of structure is minimal; this type of observation, when applied clinically, is referred to as *obtaining a naturalistic language sample*. In the observation of responses to experimental manipulation the imposition of structure by the observer is high; this type of observation, when applied clinically, is referred to as *standardized testing*. In addition, there are observations that fall somewhere on the continuum between high and low imposition of structure that are referred to here as *nonstandardized elicitations*.

Standardized Testing

Highly structured observations are strictly etic—that is, they use preset categories for description and thus do not allow for other interpretations. The observational techniques reported in the literature and used in many clinics and schools have emphasized highly structured observations and immediate evaluation of the data—often all that is recorded is the number of right or wrong responses. Standardized testing has been the most common means of obtaining evidence about deviant language for clinical purposes (see language assessment procedures, for example, in Berry, 1969; Myers and Hammill, 1969; Carrow, 1972; and Irwin and Marge, 1972). The highest degree of structure is imposed on a situation with the administration of a standardized test. In order to compare children's responses to particular tasks, it is necessary for the observer to keep constant as many of the situational variables as possible. To reduce the number of variables and keep the situation constant, many things need to be determined in advance, such as directions, the methods for presenting materials, the time devoted to certain tasks, and responses to the child's questions. By controlling the situation in this way, the differences between the ways children respond to the task are more likely to be attributable to differences between children themselves than to differences in the situation. The structured situation generally provides information that is relevant for comparing children with respect to language behaviors.

Such a situation makes it difficult to determine what a child knows about language as a system to be used for communication. Observations of a child in highly structured situations are most advantageous when one has need to know how a child responds and behaves in a formalized context, and if the child's responses are similar to the responses of other children who are exposed to the same contexts. Highly structured observations are less useful when one wishes to determine what language system a child has and how it is used in order to plan for an intervention program or to specify qualitative differences between deviant and normal language. For these objectives a less structured situation is more helpful.

Naturalistic Observation (Language Sample)

The situation where the observer imposes the least amount of structure can be described as a naturalistic setting—it is a setting that is common, or natural, for the child. If language is the behavior to be observed, then the setting should be not only familiar or natural to the child but also one in which the child has the opportunity to interact verbally—to direct interactions and activities—both as an initiator and as a responder, and to talk about topics that are of interest and that are easily retrievable from the child's memory. Although a structured setting is also a natural part of at least the school child's daily life, and perhaps the home life of some children, it does not afford enough opportunities for the child to direct interactions and activities to make it useful for sampling language behaviors. Since language is a form of communication and essentially a social interaction, its use can only be described in a social context—ideally one that is representative of the child's usual interactions. Some homes, school playgrounds, lunchrooms, or classrooms (during a free activity period) may be used as settings for naturalistic observations in a relaxed structure. In lieu of an actual visit to the child's natural environment (at home or at school), one might attempt to recreate a relaxed naturalistic type setting within the clinic or educational facilities that are available to the observer, using appropriate toys and the parent or assessor as interactor.

Low structured observations allow for both etic and emic interpretations if the process of observation does not involve severe data restriction before the observations are recorded. To understand how the language of the child with a language disorder is both similar to and different from the language of the child with normal language development, and to best describe what the child knows about language, low structured observations offer most flexibility in interpretation. Recently, low structured observations have been frequently recommended as an assessment procedure (e.g., see Crystal, Fletcher, and Garman, 1976; Engler, Hannah, and Longhurst, 1973; Lee, 1974; Tyack and Gottsleben, 1974; and Chapter XVI), and have been used as a means of obtaining evidence about qualitative differences (e.g., Cunningham, 1968, in *RLDis*; Lackner, 1968; in *RLDis*; Menyuk, 1964b;

Morehead and Ingram, 1973, in *RLDis*; and Shapiro, Roberts, and Fish, 1970). Information from the language sample obtained in a low structured observation can be supplemented with information obtained through non-standardized elicitation.

Nonstandardized Elicitation

Midway between high and low degrees of observer-imposed structure are situations where responses are elicited in a nonstandardized manner. The situation is similar to the low structured observation except that the assessor takes a more active role in manipulating the context to elicit particular responses. The observer may suggest certain tasks and probe responses to these tasks, but the child's responses and interests determine the exact procedures that are used. Thus, children might be asked to describe what they are doing, to give directions to puppets, or to respond with actions to certain linguistic input. All these are carried out in a play context and, unlike standardized elicitations, use topics and objects that the child has chosen. Unlike the low structured observation, the assessor intervenes in the play and attempts to elicit particular content/form/use interactions; the interactions have been determined in advance, but the procedures for eliciting interactions evolve in the situations as they happen, and the child has the support of ongoing events. The use of such techniques is discussed in Chapter XVII.

The function of nonstandardized elicitations is to observe some aspect of the child's language performance, and not to compare the child's responses with those of other children. The tasks may vary from tasks, on the one hand, in which the stimuli and directions have been largely worked out in advance, to more informal tasks, on the other hand, that are devised and revised during the assessment session according to the responses of the child. It is possible to devise a series of tasks that are not object or action specific and thus are adaptable to many contexts and the interests of many different children. Such tasks can be used to probe various content/form interactions, and to probe various uses of language. The nonstandardized elicitation of responses is most useful for testing hypotheses about a child's language in order to plan the goals of intervention; such elicitation is less useful for comparing children with one another. This type of situation is also helpful for determining procedures for intervention, particularly in regard to how responses might best be learned by a particular child. A situation that is least structured provides the opportunity to observe the child's spontaneous behaviors, and is the best situation for forming hypotheses to test subsequently with more structured elicitation procedures. Both kinds of information—from a language sample and from the elicitation procedures that are based on the information in the language sample—are used to form hypotheses for goals of intervention.

In conclusion, the evidence obtained about deviant language is influenced by the observer's knowledge of the behavior to be observed, the variety of contexts observed, and the degree of structure imposed on the contexts by the observer. The objectives of observation influence decisions about how to obtain data and also influence how the data are interpreted.

INTERPRETING THE EVIDENCE

To place the obtained evidence in some meaningful perspective, it must be categorized in relation to a model or standard of comparison, and it must be presented in a frame of reference that is relevant to the objective of comparison. Such activities have to do with forming taxonomies and presenting the taxonomies once they have been formed.

FORMING TAXONOMIES

A taxonomy is a categorization of the behaviors that are observed. In the study of deviant language the taxonomies of form are usually etic and are based on the adult language or on emic descriptions of normal language development.

Taxonomies of Form

The formal characteristics of language structure, as outlined for the adult speaker by the science of linguistics, have most often provided the taxonomies used to describe the form of deviant language. There is not, however, a set of accepted or standardized categories. Both the theory of generative transformational grammar and procedures of structural linguistics have been drawn on. The emphasis in each has varied with the preferences of individual researchers and clinicians, and the resulting categories of description have been different. For example, Menyuk (1964b) described differences in the sentences produced by children with and without a language disorder according to grammatical transformations (being influenced by the theory of generative transformational grammar), while others (Dever and Bauman, 1974; and Engler, Hannah, and Longhurst, 1973) recommended use of tagmemic or structural categories (being influenced by procedures from structural linguistics). Although the names of the categories may vary, most categories of form have represented one or another application of linguistic theory to the description of the structural characteristics of language form.

When the linguistic system of the adult language has served as the model for comparison, using low structured observations, the children's behaviors have been described in terms of their approximation to the adult model (e.g., the sentence types, transformations or grammatical parts of speech, and features that are included, omitted, substituted, or incorrectly placed in their speech). Box XI-3 is an illustration of the use of sentence types from the

BOX XI-3 FREQUENCY OF SENTENCE TYPES IN THE 1000 SENTENCE SAMPLES FOR EACH RETARDED CHILD (from Lackner, 1968, in *RLDis*)

MENTAL AGE OF RETARDED CHILDREN (YEARS AND MONTHS)	CHRONOLOGICAL AGE OF RETARDED CHILDREN (YEARS AND MONTHS)	SENTENCE TYPE						
		DECLARATIVE	NEGATIVE	QUESTION	NEGATIVE QUESTION	PASSIVE	NEGATIVE PASSIVE	NEGATIVE PASSIVE QUESTION
2,3	6,5	563	275	162				
2,11	13,1	517	293	171	19			
3,3	7,10	516	337	99	37	11		
4,9	16,2	430	393	127	41	9		
8,10	14,4	438	351	119	45	24	18	5

These data illustrate the increasing use of adult sentence types as mental age increases.

adult model as a means of describing deviant language development; Box XI-4 illustrates an analysis based on adult parts of speech. Often the language of such children is described in terms of what is lacking—what the child must learn in order to become a fluent speaker. Parents, teachers, and the clinicians and educators who are unsophisticated in linguistic analysis commonly use descriptions such as "the child confuses pronouns," "the child does not speak in complete sentences," and so on. The descriptions of language behavior that have been used by speech pathologists in the past concentrated on quantifying such adult-based descriptions through such measures as the length complexity index, which assigned points to speech structures according to their complexity and completeness when compared with the adult model (see Johnson, Darley, and Spriesterbach, 1963, for

---

BOX XI-4 GRAMMATICAL STRUCTURE OF RESPONSES BY MATCHED PAIRS OF MONGOL/NON-MONGOL PATIENTS TO TWO FORMS OF INTERVIEW (N = 11 PAIRS) (from Mein, 1961, p. 57)

PART OF SPEECH	CONVERSATION MEAN PERCENT		PICTURE DESCRIPTION MEAN PERCENT	
	MONGOL	NON-MONGOL	MONGOL	NON-MONGOL
Verbs	19.36	20.27	5.55	7.64
Nouns	31.91	26.91	66.73	50.55
Adjectives	10.00	10.36	8.09	10.36
Adverbs	6.09	6.55	1.27	3.36
Prepositions	7.36	7.82	2.00	3.64
Pronouns	9.64	11.00	2.18	3.09
Articles	7.00	6.18	7.73	12.91
Conjunctions	2.73	3.64	5.91	8.18
Miscellaneous	5.91	7.27	0.55	0.27

These data were based on an analysis of language samples collected in two contexts—a conversational interview and description of pictures. The two populations were matched on the basis of sex, chronological age (mean was 20 years, 9 months for mongols and 20 years, 5 months for nonmongols), and mental age (mean was 4 years, 6 months for mongols and 4 years, 7 months for nonmongols).

As might be expected, the percentage of nouns was higher for both populations when the subjects were describing pictures and a greater variety of word types was used in the conversational context. This analysis showed few differences between the groups except for the relatively higher percentage of nouns for the mongols in both contexts and a lower percentage of articles in the picture description context.

BOX XI-5 COMPARISON BETWEEN THE NORMAL AND DEVIANT LANGUAGE USERS IN TERMS OF THE NUMBER OF CHILDREN USING EACH STRUCTURE AND THE FREQUENCY WITH WHICH EACH STRUCTURE WAS USED. N = NORMAL SPEAKERS; D = DEVIANT SPEAKERS (from Leonard, 1972, p. 433)

STRUCTURE	NUMBER OF CHILDREN USING STRUCTURES			MEAN FREQUENCY			STANDARD DEVIATION		
	N	D	p[a]	N	D		N	D	p
Negation (He is *not* smiling.)	7	2	ns[b]	2.44	0.67		1.59	1.66	0.05
Contraction (She's happy.)	9	8	ns	17.67	8.78		6.33	6.34	0.01
Auxiliary *be* (The lion *is* jumping up.)	9	8	ns	22.00	7.78		6.48	5.83	0.001
Adjective (The *big* bear likes her.)	9	5	ns	6.78	1.44		4.21	1.59	0.01
Infinitival complement (I want to *sing*.)	9	9	ns	14.56	5.89		6.88	6.47	0.05
Indefinite pronoun (*It* was gone.)	9	8	ns	15.11	7.00		8.30	5.79	0.05
Personal pronoun (The ghost saw *them*.)	9	9	ns	30.56	16.00		12.70	10.09	0.05

Main verb (The plane *flies* funny.)	9	9	ns	51.00	22.89	7.25	11.01	0.001
Secondary verb (He wants the boy *to sing*.)	9	8	ns	18.00	5.44	6.78	6.62	0.01
Conjunction[c] (I want it *but* I won't get it.)	9	6	ns	7.00	2.44	5.17	2.46	0.05
Verb-phrase omission (That funny.)	5	9	ns	1.00	11.78	1.32	8.60	0.01
Noun-phrase omission (Wanna go.)	3	9	ns	0.44	5.22	0.73	4.55	0.01
Article omission (Ghost is gonna scare us.)	4	9	ns	0.78	3.22	0.97	2.39	0.05
Inversion verb number (There's the bears!)	8	5	ns	2.22	0.56	1.09	0.53	0.01

[a] p = probability of this result occurring by chance alone; in other words, significance level.
[b] ns = not significant.
[c] Lee and Canter (1971) conjunction classification.

Language samples were based on children's responses to pictures following a predetermined set of prompts by the interviewer. Data were analyzed according to structures defined by Menyuk (1964b) and by Lee and Canter (1971). Normal and deviant children were compared in terms of the number of children who used a structure and in terms of the frequency with which each structure was used. The table reports differences found between the groups on structures used by at least 50% of one of the groups. Results indicate there are differences between the populations in the frequency with which certain structures were used and not in terms of the number of children who used a structure.

procedures). Children with language disorders have also been compared with normal children in terms of their relative approximations to the adult model, as illustrated in Box XI-5 (see also Menyuk, 1964b).

Highly structured observations designed for clinical assessment (i.e., standardized tests) have also most often been based on adult models of form. Since most tests elicit only one or perhaps two responses of a particular type of form, or content/form interaction, responses can usually only be categorized according to such domains of form as vocabulary, phonology, or some aspect of syntax. (See Chapter XII for an example of such categorization of tests to elicit language form.) Responses are occasionally clustered in a further subdivision of form as adjectives, articles, and so forth. (See Carrow, 1968, 1974.) In all cases tabulations are made of the number of correct and incorrect responses—correctness determined by conformity to the adult model.

Highly structured observations (experimental studies) made for the purpose of determining qualitative differences between normal and deviant language can more often be categorized according to a particular form type, as questions, (e.g., Quigley, Smith, and Wilbur, 1974) or conjoined sentences (e.g., Wilbur, Quigley, and Montanelli, 1975) or content/form interactions (e.g., Jarvella and Lubinsky's study of deaf children's use of language to describe temporal order, 1975, in *RLDis*). Responses are, again, usually based on the adult model, and the number of children using a particular correct or incorrect form is reported. (See Brannon, 1968, in *RLDis*).

When child language has served as the basis for forming taxonomies, the categories have been taken from the emic descriptions of child language that have emerged from the longitudinal studies that were reported in Part 2 (e.g., Bloom, 1970a; Bloom, Lightbown, and Hood, 1975; and Brown, 1973). The language of the language-disordered child is then described in terms of its similarity to the normal child at a similar point in language learning, for example, types of two-word combinations that may never appear alone in the adult model but that are used by children first learning to combine words. This use of child language represents an emic to etic approach, as discussed in Chapter II, and it is the approach outlined in Chapter XVI.

Taxonomies of Content

In a first report on the taxonomies of the content of deviant language, Leonard, Bolders, and Miller (1976, in *RLDis*) described and compared semantic relations expressed in the two-word utterances of normal and language-disordered children. Their descriptions were influenced by Fillmore's case grammar (1968), which was based on the adult speaker, with adaptations based on studies of normal child language; their comparisons indicated no differences between the populations when matched by *MLU* (see Box XI-6). Similarly, Freedman and Carpenter (1976) described and

BOX XI-6 AN EXAMPLE OF A TAXONOMY OF LANGUAGE CONTENT, WITH THE MEAN FREQUENCY OF UTTERANCES USED TO EXPRESS EACH SEMANTIC RELATION PRESENTED HERE BY AGE AND MEAN LENGTH OF UTTERANCE.[a] (adapted from Leonard, Bolders, and Miller, 1976 in *RLDis*)

SEMANTIC RELATION	3-YEAR OLD N[b]	3-YEAR OLD LD[c]	5-YEAR OLD N	5-YEAR OLD LD	MLU 5.03 N	MLU 4.97 LD
Essive + locative	3.90[d]	10.00[d]	2.20[d]	11.20[d]	4.43	5.14
Verb + agentive	3.70[d]	10.40[d]	7.70	10.40[d]	5.00	9.86
Locative + designated	3.00	3.70	1.80	2.10	3.86	3.57
Attributive + designated	3.00	1.50	2.30	1.50	4.29	3.14
Verb + agentive + locative	6.50	7.20	9.60	6.30	6.86	7.43
Verb + agentive + objective	3.60	4.10	6.40	3.60	3.00	5.43
Verb + agentive + dative	1.70	2.60	3.00	2.00	—	—
Utterances that reflected more complex semantic rules but were not used twice by half of the subjects	10.40[e]	2.10[e]	9.30[e]	1.50[e]		

[a] Data were based on a sample of 50 utterances. Only semantic relations that occurred at least two times by at least half of the children in each group were included.
[b] N = normal.
[c] LD = language disordered.
[d] Least significant difference < .05
[e] Least significant difference < .001

compared the number of different semantic relations expressed in the two-word utterances of four normal and four language-impaired children. Their descriptions were based on the taxonomies of content that evolved in the studies of normal child language by, in particular, Bloom (1970a) and Schlesinger (1971) and as summarized by Brown (1973); their comparisons again showed few differences when children were matched by *MLU*; the one significant difference was that the language-impaired children used a greater proportion of different utterances to code *existence* than the normal children.

Taxonomies of content/form interactions have also been suggested for clinical assessment to provide information about the goals of language intervention. The taxonomies used have been based on child language as a model; that is, they evolved from the study of normal development (as did the categories used by Freedman and Carpenter, 1976). The categories described by Brown (1973) for two-word utterances have been suggested for the categorization of utterances obtained in free play (MacDonald and Nichols, 1974) and for utterances obtained by elicitation (MacDonald and Blott, 1974). A more extended taxonomy of content/form interactions, based on the study of normal child language, is presented in Part 4 as a plan for language development goals.

Taxonomies of content have been used less often in highly structured clinical observations or experimental studies of language-disordered children. Recently Duchan and Erickson (1976) compared normal and retarded children on their comprehension of various semantic relations (agent-action, action-object, possession, and locative) presented with varying forms (including utterances without function forms, that is, telegraphic utterances; utterances containing nonsense forms inserted for function forms; and utterances with function forms as in the adult model). They found no differences between the two groups, who were at the same level of language learning (as determined by *MLU*).

Taxonomies of Use

Taxonomies of use applied to low structured observations have most frequently related to communicativeness and the relevance of utterances to context. For example, Shapiro, Chiarandini, and Fish (1974, in *RLDis*) divided utterances into communicative and noncommunicative. Cunningham (1968, in *RLDis*) classified utterances as egocentric utterances, to include categories such as echoes and inappropriate remarks, and socialized utterances, to include categories such as giving information and answering or asking questions. Although Cunningham's first level of categorization was influenced by Piaget's (1955) study of child language and the distinction between egocentric and social speech, the basis of the subcategories is not clear. Kanner (1946, in *RLDis)* combined aspects of use with content/form.

PRESENTING TAXONOMIES

Taxonomies may be presented in a number of ways. In some analyses a frequency count has been made of utterances in each category (Engler, Hannah, and Longhurst, 1973; and Lackner, 1968, in *RLDis*, in Box XI-3), of the number of children producing each category (Menyuk, 1964b; and Leonard, 1972, in Box XI-5), of the proportion of utterances in a category (Mein, 1961, in Box XI-4), and of the variety of utterances within a category (Freedman and Carpenter, 1976). In other studies a weight has been assigned to each sentence based on the categories included in that sentence (Lee and Canter, 1971; and Lee, 1974, discussed in Chapter XVI), while in others the child has been assigned to a particular level according to the average length of utterances produced (Morehead and Ingram, 1973, in

RLDis; and Leonard, Bolders, and Miller, 1976 in *RLDis*) and the categories found at that level have been listed (e.g., Johnston and Schery, 1976, in Box XI-7).

To know, however, that a child produced six utterances that were classified as negatives, or responded correctly to 22 out of 60 utterances, or that 10 children produced an utterance type is not meaningful until placed in some frame of reference that compares the categorization to some standard or population. Neither quantifying responses according to taxonomies nor listing utterances by taxonomy is meaningful unless the information is placed in a context or perspective that relates to the original purpose of the observation.

PRESENTING TAXONOMIES FOR CLINICAL ASSESSMENT

Taxonomies derived from observations of a particular child in order to identify a language disorder or to plan intervention may be placed in meaningful context by three approaches: (1) norm referencing—comparison with a group; (2) criterion referencing—comparison with a predetermined standard of performance; or (3) communication referencing—comparison with some concept of communicative behavior that is not predetermined— that is, without defined norms or standards of performance. Each provides important but different information. The approach used in reporting observations varies with the objective or purpose of observing. It is important to understand the value of each type of reference when describing observations and when reading descriptions of observations.

Norm-Referenced Descriptions

Norm-referenced descriptions compare the behaviors of one child with behaviors of other children. Norm-referenced descriptions may be reported as standard scores that reflect a child's standing relative to peers (e.g., percentile rank, which represents the percent of children who scored lower than this child). These comparisons are based on results of the same task administered to a large number of children of the same age or grade level.

Or norm-referenced descriptions may be reported as an age-equivalent score where the age score reflects the average age of children with similar language behaviors. These equivalent scores may be based on developmental milestones of language (such as age of first word, two-word combinations, or full sentences) or on a quantitative scoring of responses on language-related tasks (such as selecting the picture representing vocabulary items or syntactic structure presented to the child). (See Chapter XII for a discussion and evaluation of differences between equivalent scores and standard scores.) Norms can also be used as a reference point to report the results of observations of others. For example, the *Vineland Social Maturity Scale* (Doll, 1965) and the *Verbal Language Development Scale* (Mecham,

1958) are two scales that use parent interviews to solicit information about a child and provide the means for comparing that information with norms, resulting in a social maturity quotient and a language age, respectively.

Sometimes informal observations are reported in terms of norm-referenced descriptions, for example, a teacher or parent may report that a child

---

BOX XI-7 LANGUAGE LEVELS AND A TAXONOMY OF FORM

TABLE 1

Mean values for summary language measures by level (from Johnston and Schery, 1976)

LEVEL	N	MEAN-WORDS-PER-UTTERANCE	MEAN-MORPHEMES-PER-UTTERANCE	MEAN-WORDS/MEAN-MORPHEMES
1	10	2.29	2.58	0.890
2	17	2.78	2.95	0.944
3	51	3.67	4.05	0.907
4	76	4.59	5.12	0.895
5	133	6.19	6.97	0.894

TABLE 2

Language level (Johnston and Schery criteria) at which each morpheme was used at all and acquired (90%) by 50% of the subjects at that level in three research studies (from Johnston and Schery, 1976)

	USE AT ALL	90% USE IN OBLIGATORY CONTEXTS		
	J&S	J&S	DEVILLIERS	BROWN
Plural -s	1	2	1	1
In	1	2	2	1
On	2	3	2	1
-ing	1	3	2	2
Irreg. past	1	1.4	—[a]	2
Article	1	4	4	3
Copula uncontracted	3	5	4	2
Possessive -s	5	+[b]	—	3
Aux. "be" uncontracted	4	5	—	3
Past -ed	4	5	4	3
3rd person -s	4	5	4	3
Aux. "be" contracted	3	5	—	(4)[c]
Copula contracted	1	+[b]	3	(4)
Irreg. 3rd person	5	5	—	(4)

[a] Dashes indicate insufficient data.
[b] Did not reach criteria at any level.
[c] Numbers in parentheses are probable.

Johnston and Schery (1976) reported on the use of grammatical morphemes by 287 language-disordered children, aged 3 years, 10 months to 16 years, 2 months. The data were based on 100-utterance language samples obtained and analyzed by teachers under the guidance of the authors. Children were grouped by language level—based on utterance length, as outlined in Table 1. Results were then compared with two previously reported studies in normal language development. The language-disordered children acquired (i.e., they used the morphemes in obligatory contexts 90% of the time) the morphemes in much the same order as the normal children, but this acquisition was at a later level of development, that is, when their *MLU* was higher than that reported for normal children.

behaves like a 3-year-old, or that the child's language behaviors are most like those of a 1-year-old. Or, more specifically, one might report that a child has not yet given evidence of producing two-word combinations, as might be expected of a 2-year-old child. Since norm-referenced reports of observations are comparisons of a child with other children, they best serve the function of determining the existence of a problem—of describing how a particular child's language behaviors relate to peer language behaviors. Norm-referenced reports are helpful for determining *who* might be considered for intervention, but they are less helpful for determining the goal and procedures for intervention.

Criterion-Referenced Descriptions

In lieu of, or in addition to, a normative reference, observations can be reported in terms of an operational criterion of performance. References related to criteria of performance have become important in educational technology, since interest has focussed on students' mastery of operationally defined instructional objectives. Tests designed to measure achievement in these terms have been called *criterion-referenced* tests; they compare the performance of a child or group of children to a preset standard or criterion. The difference between criterion-referenced and norm-referenced tests and the application of criterion-referenced instruments have been reported by B. Bloom, Hastings, and Madaus (1971); Glaser and Nitko, (1971); Gorth and Hambleton, (1972); and Popham and Husek, (1969). The purpose of criterion-referenced measures is to provide information about the performance of individuals or groups of individuals relative to certain tasks or goals. It is particularly relevant as a means of reassessing behaviors during intervention to determine the effectiveness of a program and the need to establish new goals. Normative scores cannot be used for this same purpose, because normative reference points are not defined with respect to the behaviors that are being observed but, instead, with respect to how many other children behaved in the same way. The norm-referenced score gives certain comparative information but gives no information about the nature of the child's own behavior or its relevance to some specified skill. As such, normative scores do not directly relate to the kind of information that is needed for planning the specific goals of intervention.

In order to use criterion reference as a means of reporting taxonomies, a criterion of performance must be established beforehand—a criterion that indicates competence or productivity of that behavior in the child's repertoire of behaviors. Examples of such operational criteria have been used in the study of normal language development. One instance of a particular behavior or a single production of an utterance type cannot be considered adequate evidence that a child has mastered the rule that underlies the form. However, if one observes several instances of a behavior in different situations, there is more than a single instance to use as evidence for inferring knowledge of the rules or other conceptual organization that was responsible for the utterance. For example, if a child says "no juice," "no bath," "no get dressed," "no ball," in situations where the child was rejecting these objects or activities, one could reasonably conclude that the child knew a rule for negation, and that rule specified that "no," a negative marker, could be juxtaposed with other, different words, in different situations that presented the same meaning content of rejection. Suppose that, at the same time, the child also said "don't do that" only once. Although one could conclude that the child knew something about the content of negation and the form of negative utterances ("no" plus a word), there is less evidence that the child also *knows* the contracted negative particle "don't" until it occurs in more different situations, and with different words ("don't eat it," "don't touch," etc.).

Bloom (1970a) set the criterion for *productivity* of a semantic-syntactic relation in an observational study in terms of an absolute frequency criterion: the use of five or more different multiword utterances that represented a particular structure or semantic-syntactic relation in the course of five hours or more of observation. The use of a criterion of at least five utterances was initially an arbitrary decision, but it was supported as an indication of rule-governed behavior when the sequence of development that resulted using the absolute frequency criterion was compared with the sequence obtained using proportional measures (a relative instead of an absolute measure) (Bloom, Lightbown, and Hood, 1975).

Brown (1973) set the criterion for the *acquisition* of various grammatical morphemes at 90% occurrence in contexts in which the morpheme would be obligatory for adult speakers (see also, Johnston and Schery, 1976, in Box XI-7 for an application of this criterion to language disorders). Such a criterion, that compares the child behavior with expected adult behavior, represents a standard of performance based on an extrinsic measure—the adult model. Brown counted the number of times that a morpheme (e.g., plural -s) was obligatory (i.e., the number of required contexts) in a sample of language, and then counted the number of times the child produced the morpheme in order to compute a proportion of morpheme use. With either the frequency measure or the proportional measure, the behavior was specified and a quantitative criterion was set in advance. These are examples of criterion-referenced descriptions—a description in relation to a preset standard of performance.

Both the frequency criterion and the proportional analysis that are cited here represent measures of the child speech data that make comparisons of the child's behaviors with a standard of performance for that behavior. A teacher in a classroom may use a criterion of 80 or 90% correct responses on a math test to decide that a child has learned a particular skill and is ready to move on to the next level. (Contrast this with grades given in many college courses that are *curved* and are therefore a norm-referenced comparison of a student with other students in the class.) An experimental psychologist may decide that 30 seconds of eye contact will be a criterion for attending behavior. The American Cancer Society considers that a patient is cured who is cancer free for five years after surgery for removal of a malignant growth. All of these criterion-referenced observations compare observations with preset quantitative criteria. The observation is not reported as a comparison with other children, but as a measure of the child's own behavior in relation to a preestablished standard, which may have been derived from experience with other individuals. The purpose of the observation is not to determine how well the child does in comparison with others, but how well a certain behavior is established. Criterion-referenced observations are most helpful in initial assessment to determine the initial goals of intervention programs and in reassessment to determine when those goals have been reached and when new goals should be established.

Communication-Referenced Descriptions

When descriptions make reference to the general communication behavior of the child without considering either norms or standards of performance that are previously defined, this description will be referred to as *communication-referenced* description. The criterion or standard of performance is not well defined and is not set in advance but, unquestionably, some expectation is implied—otherwise the behavior would not have been described. For example, the teacher describes a child to the speech pathologist as a child who smiles a lot and who frequently touches other children's hair. The teacher may not have had a list of behaviors that included smiling and touching hair, yet, when asked about Mary's mode of communicating with others, these behaviors become relevant to the description. The criterion related to contact or communication—the standard or specific behaviors that de-

---

BOX XI-8

Nancy was taken from her wheelchair and seated on the floor facing the interviewer. She immediately swiveled so she faced the opposite direction. When turned to face the interviewer, she repeatedly swiveled herself until a box of toys was placed in front of her. Facing the box, she remained in position and picked out toys from the box. She handled each without looking at it, and then dropped it to pick up another. Occasionally, she emitted the sounds /f/ or a nasalized /a/.

---

fined the domain of description—was not specified, and many descriptions of the language-disordered child fit into precisely this type of criterion reference. This kind of description is called communication-referenced description to distinguish it from the use of criterion reference that relates to a well-defined standard of performance.[1] Communication-referenced descriptions obtained through clinical assessment are rarely quantified and include any behaviors that the observer feels are relevant to describing a child's communication. (See Box XI-8 for an example.)

An important point to reiterate here is that taxonomies should record the regularities and consistencies that are to be found among all of the different behaviors a child (or adult) may present. Isolated instances of behavior, although no doubt interesting and possibly important, are less important than a larger number of behaviors that share common elements or features. Regularities should emerge in almost any sample of behavior, and they may well be different for different children, and even different for the same child at different times in the course of development. Although differences among behaviors are important (see the discussion of variation in child language in Chapter VI), the structure of the child's communication behavior is most important for determining goals of intervention. The structure of behavior is revealed in the patterns of regularity that can be observed. The description of patterns of behaviors may lead to intervention goals and eventually to criteria for measuring achievement of those goals, so that a preset standard of performance that is criterion-referenced may eventually result from communication-referenced descriptions.

Assessment Objectives in Relation to Context and Description

Observations, for the purpose of identifying a child with a language disorder and for planning intervention, are generally reported in all three frames of reference: norm reference, criterion reference, and communication

---

[1] What is here called communication referenced seems close to what Hively (1974) referred to as "domain referenced."

reference. Each has a particular function. Norm-referenced descriptions help to determine the existence of a problem; criterion-referenced descriptions help to determine what will be taught in planning the goals of intervention; communication-referenced goals are generally descriptive and may lead to goals of therapy or to procedures. The structure of different contexts and the types of reference most often used to reach each objective of assessment are summarized in Table XI-2.

Information obtained from standardized observations is usually reported in reference to normative data (as a language age, percentile rank, etc.), but other forms of reference can be used. For example, many reports of standardized observations comment on the child's behavior within the domain of a structured task (the child's attention span, frustration level, dependence on the examiner, etc.,) and thus provide communication-referenced description that may be useful to planning the procedures of intervention. In addition, some clinicians try to use responses to particular items on tests to determine goals of intervention, that is, as a hypothesis about the child's knowledge of that structure. For example, if the child responded correctly to an item that demanded the production of plural -s, but failed an item that demanded the production of possessive -s, one might conclude that the plural -s morpheme does not need to be taught but that learning the possessive -s morpheme should be a goal of intervention. It is not, however, advisable to use test data in this way.

Research by Dever (1972) and by Prutting, Gallagher, and Mulac (1975, in

TABLE XI-2

Reference used to Report Observations According to the Structure Imposed by the Observor and the Objective of Assessment

Objective of Assessment	Degree of Structure Imposed by the Observer and Most Useful Reference for Descriptions High--→Low		
	Standardized Elicited Response	Nonstandardized Elicited Response	Relaxed Structure Nonelicited Response
Determine existence of a problem	Norm-referenced		Norm-referenced
Plan goals of intervention		Criterion-referenced	Criterion-referenced Communication-referenced
Plan procedure of intervention		Criterion-referenced	Criterion-referenced Communication-referenced

RLDis) has indicated that responses to highly structured elicitations are not predictive of productions in free speech. Determining goals of intervention from item analyses of standardized tests is, therefore, of questionable value and is usually not necessary when information from low structured and nonstandardized elicitation can be obtained. Thus, in Table XI-2, standardized elicited responses are listed as being most often norm-referenced and used to determine the existence of a problem. For example, a report might read: "Mary scored below the tenth percentile in both the tests of vocabulary and the tests of syntax that were administered. These scores suggest a language disorder, and she has been referred for further assessment in order to plan intervention."

Observations of situations that fall at the low end of the continuum of observer-imposed structure—naturalistic situations—are generally reported in communication-referenced terms and criterion-referenced terms and are used to plan goals and procedures of intervention. Communication-referenced reports of these naturalistic situations attempt to give a total picture of the communication behaviors that are observed. The communication forms may or may not be linguistic (e.g., they may include gesture) and they may or may not relate to the adult or child model of language discussed previously. The purpose of the description is to describe what it is the child does and to hypothesize what the child knows about communication in general. Norm-referenced descriptions of naturalistic observations generally refer to the developmental milestones (first words, single words, two-word phrases, simple sentences, etc.), and not scores, language ages, or quotients. Such descriptions can be used to determine the existence of a problem.

The criterion-referenced descriptions of low structured observations can vary and can be similar to the criterion used for describing elicitation responses. One might, for example, go over a transcript of a recorded naturalistic observation and compute the productivity of different taxonomies of content/form interactions (e.g., reporting that the *-ing* was used 60% of the time it was obligatory, or agents were mentioned in 20% of the agent-action-object relations). Otherwise, one might describe an observation in a naturalistic setting with a particular criterion in mind to begin with, looking for, for example, *X* number of instances of possession or action-object utterances. A relaxed structure, or naturalistic setting, lends itself equally well to communication- or criterion-referenced descriptions and provides information relevant to the goals and procedures of therapy. It can also aid in determining if there is a problem by reference to developmental milestones. Thus, in Table XI-2, all forms of reference are listed in this column. Most often, the communication-referenced descriptions that are obtained through naturalistic observation lead to hypotheses about the child's communication behavior, which may be then tested by criterion-referenced descriptions of the behavior, elicitation of responses from the child, and solicitation of reported observations.

Nonstandardized elicited responses are most often used to plan goals and procedures of intervention and are most often criterion-referenced. An assessor may design situations to elicit a particular content/form interaction (such as plurals). Although such situations can be communication-referenced, in a manner similar to that discussed for low structure, this and norm-referenced descriptions are rarely used. Thus only criterion reference is listed in the column headed nonstandardized elicited response.

Ongoing Versus Initial Assessment

Most of what has been said about assessment applies to either the initial contact with a child or at any stage during intervention; however, there are some differences between initial and ongoing assessment. The focus of ongoing assessment is planning goals and procedures of intervention. One is less concerned with comparing a child's behavior with that of other children and more interested in comparing a child's behavior to a standard of performance relative to the mastery of the immediate goals that one has set for intervention. Throughout intervention, goals are constantly changed; as one is reached, another is established. Ongoing assessment is important to determine whether a goal has been reached and which goal is appropriate next. An additional aspect of ongoing assessment is the constant evaluation of the effectiveness of procedures used for facilitating language development. Procedures are changed based on this assessment.

A great deal of ongoing assessment takes place within the intervention setting, but other settings must also be observed if goals include, as they should, the use of language outside the intervention structure. The variety of settings for ongoing assessment includes both low and intermediate structure, rarely high structure, and the descriptions used to report observations include both criterion- and communication-referenced descriptions, rarely norm-referenced descriptions. As with initial assessment, both direct and reported observations are important.

Thus, the issues in clinical assessment revolve around the objectives of such assessment and include: (1) the method of obtaining evidence (including the observer and the context of observation); (2) the aspect of language described (content, form, or use); (3) the model used as a standard (adult language or child language); and (4) the frame of reference in which the evidence is reported (norm-, criterion-, or communication-referenced description.) Different decisions concerning each of these issues may influence the selection of children for whom intervention is considered appropriate, the ease with which goals of intervention are planned and, finally, what the goals will be (i.e., what the child will be taught). Many of these same issues relate to research directed toward determining whether deviant language is qualitatively different from normal language.

PRESENTING TAXONOMIES TO DETERMINE QUALITATIVE DIFFERENCES

Conflicting evidence has been reported about the nature of differences between deviant and normal language. Some researchers report qualitative differences while others report only quantitative differences. There are, however, differences in research methodology—in the method of obtaining evidence, in the model of comparison, in the aspect of language described, in the population of language-disordered children studied, and in the criteria used for matching the language-disordered children with normal children. These differences are discussed below as variables that may affect conclusions about qualitative or quantitative differences.

In the first application of the concepts of generative transformational grammar to the study of language disorders, Menyuk (1964b) reported differences between a group of normal children and a group of language-disordered children, matched according to chronological age. When the two groups were compared according to their use of adult structures, there were more children who omitted aspects of structures in the disordered group and fewer children who used transformations. According to Menyuk, the structures used by children with a language disorder that were not also found in the adult model were unlike the nonadult structures used by a younger child she had observed who developed language normally. Menyuk concluded that the system learned by children with a language disorder was qualitatively different and not just delayed.

Leonard (1972) compared 50- utterance language samples from two populations matched for age, vocabulary test scores, and socioeconomic class—one group of normal children and one group diagnosed as language disordered. His taxonomies for analysis were similar to Menyuk's (i.e., transformational categories derived from the adult model). Leonard concurred with the findings of Menyuk, and reported differences between the groups in the *frequency* with which each category was used in the children's speech (see Box XI-5 for a summary of this comparison). Both Menyuk and Leonard looked only at linguistic form without regard for semantic intention and used a model based on comparisons with the adult model; they both concluded that the language differences between normal and disordered populations were qualitative.

The opposite conclusion (that differences were only quantitative and not qualitative) was drawn by Morehead and Ingram (1973, in *RLDis*), Lackner (1968, in *RLDis*), and Johnston and Schery (1976). Johnston and Schery, using Brown's (1973) and deVillier and deVillier's (1973, *in RLDev*) descriptions of the sequence of the acquisition of grammatical morphemes in normal children, found no differences in the "structural aspects of grammatical morphology." The language-disordered children "learned the same forms in much the same order, and with the same general relationship to overall language development level as indexed by sentence length" (pp. 256–257). The difference found related to rate of acquisition—there was a longer interval between the first production of a morpheme and its general application (see Box XI-7).

The conclusions of Morehead and Ingram and of Lackner were based on grammars written to account for regularities in their data and were presented as hypothetical accounts of what the children knew about language (a formalization of evidence as discussed in Chapter II). Lackner (1968, in *RLDis*) collected language samples and responses to imitation and comprehension tasks from a population of mentally retarded children and wrote a grammar (influenced by Chomsky, 1957, 1965) for each child that could generate sentences that the children spontaneously used and forms that they could understand. He concluded that "the grammars of the retarded children appear to be subsets of an adult grammar" (p. 311), and not rules that were qualitatively different from the adult model. Structures generated by the grammars were presented to five normal children from 2 years, 8 months to 5 years, 9 months in comprehension and imitation tasks. According to Lackner, an ordering was maintained "between the complexity of the grammars and the mental ages of the retarded children, and the chronological ages of the normal children" suggesting "that the language behaviors of normal and retarded children are not qualitatively different, that both groups follow similar developmental trends" (p. 309). In addition to this analysis, Lackner looked at the use of adult sentence types and found an increase in types used with increased mental age (see Box XI-3).

Morehead and Ingram (1973, in *RLDis*) studied two groups of children, one with normal development and the other diagnosed as language disordered, matched according to linguistic level (as determined by *MLU*). Also influenced by Chomsky (1957, 1965), they wrote grammars for the language samples they obtained from both groups. Based on a comparison of these grammars, they concluded that the differences between the groups were primarily related to time of onset and rate of development of rules of language, and not in the types of rules the children used. They also noted, as did Leonard (1972), that certain constructions were used more or less frequently by the two groups.

The two studies, by Lackner and by Morehead and Ingram, looked only at linguistic form (although Morehead and Ingram reported using context to analyze forms); both tried to discover a system and write a grammar that would account for the utterances and predict future utterances; both used naturalistic low-structured contexts to collect data (although Lackner supplemented these data with information elicited through imitation and comprehension tasks); and both tried to discover a system and write a grammar that would account for the utterances and predict future utterances instead of looking for the presence or absence of adult categories in their data. Morehead and Ingram, in fact, made direct comparisons with the language of normal children at a similar stage of development.

However, another study based on comparisons with child language (Lee, 1966) concurred with Menyuk's conclusion that language disorders represent qualitative differences, not just delay. Lee (1966) used sentence types that were reported to have occurred in studies of child language (described by McNeill, 1966) as the standard for comparing one language sample from a boy with a language disorder with one language sample from a boy with normal language development. (This type of analysis is discussed in Chapter XVI.) She observed that certain structures (i.e., certain linguistic forms) that were described by McNeill were not present in the sample from the child with a language disorder, and she suggested that the absence of such structures may impede the child's further syntactic development. Unfortunately, the method of obtaining evidence for each child differed, a fact that may have accounted for some of the differences (see Bloom, 1967). Keeping the method of obtaining evidence constant, Morehead and Ingram (1973, *RLDis*) found no such differences.

Similarly, Leonard, Bolders, and Miller (1976, in *RLDis*) and Freedman and Carpenter (1976) controlled the method of obtaining evidence and found no difference in the *content* of normal and language-disordered children matched according to *MLU*. Freedman and Carpenter found not only the same content categories in both populations, but also the same degree of diversity in the use of different utterances within each category. Leonard et al. wrote rules to describe content and, while no differences were found when children were matched by *MLU*, they did find qualitative differences when children were matched on the basis of chronological age (see Box XI-6). Thus, when *MLU* is used as a means of matching, fewer differences have been reported in descriptions of content and form—or in the comprehension of content and form interactions (Duchan and Erickson, 1976)—suggesting that the criterion for matching populations may be another important variable.

Cunningham (1968, in *RLDis*) compared two groups (one diagnosed as emotionally disturbed, the other as mentally retarded) who were similar in chronological age, mental age, and average sentence length. He found differences in taxonomies of *use* derived both from child observation (Piaget, 1955) and from the adult model. An additional variable, then, may be the aspect of language that is categorized. (Interactions among content/form/use have not been used for comparison.)

Other comparisons of deviant language with normal language development have used highly structured experimental techniques that were developed by researchers for eliciting responses in the study of normal language development. The most widely adapted tasks have been Berko's (1958, in *RLDev*) tasks for eliciting grammatical morphemes with nonsense words and pictures. Children with language disorders typically have performed similarly to the normal children tested by Berko, although their development has been later and slower. The evidence from these studies supports the idea of delay instead of qualitative difference in the development of the morphemes tested.

The question of whether the language development of children with language disorders is different from normal or only delayed in comparison with normal development is far from settled. The question is not a simple one. At least four major issues emerge: (1) how the evidence is obtained; (2) whether the taxonomies are based on the adult model or on a child model of language; (3) whether the taxonomies are of content, form, or use; and (4) whether the criterion for matching the normal and language-disordered children is chronological age, mental age, or some measure of language level (*MLU*).

No one has yet studied the interactions of content/form/use, but clinical experience and the literature on language disorders suggest that both delay and qualitative differences may exist (see Chapter X for examples). More descriptive studies of the longitudinal development of individual children are needed in order to provide the hypotheses that can be tested with larger populations of children. Certainly more information is needed about the development of content/form/use interactions in the language of the language-disordered child. The linguistic orientation has provided the most informative descriptions of the language of the language-disordered child so far, but it has represented only a beginning.

Writing rules to account for the regularities found in data, as was done by Lackner (1968, in *RLDis*) and Morehead and Ingram (1973, in *RLDis*), is the most elegant means of presentation, but it is time consuming and rarely done. Since differences have been reported in the frequency with which certain utterance types are used by language-disordered children in comparison with normal populations (Leonard, 1972; and Morehead and Ingram, 1973, in *RLDis*), the use of variable rules that account for the systematic interaction of content/form/use may be the best way to describe differences between normal and deviant language (for a discussion of variable rules, see Chapter II). While the rules of content or form alone may be the same, their interaction and the contexts that govern when they are applied may differ.

Describing deviant language either for clinical assessment or to determine qualitative differences involves similar problems. Both the clinician and the researcher must consider the influence of procedure for obtaining samples of language behavior, the model used to describe and compare the obtained behavior, and the aspect of language considered (content, form, or use). The clinician also must consider the purposes of each observation. In the initial contact with a child, the first object is to determine the existence of a problem—the objective considered in the next chapter.

SUMMARY

This chapter concerns the objectives of describing deviant language, obtaining evidence of deviant language, and interpreting that evidence. Most important, it is concerned with the interrelationships of these factors. It is pointed out that the objectives of description determine both the methods of obtaining evidence and the way that evidence is described and interpreted; that the method of obtaining evidence can limit the way it can be categorized and interpreted; and that the way evidence is categorized further limits conclusions that can be drawn.

The context for obtaining evidence is discussed in terms of the degree of structure imposed by the observer. Structure ranges from standardized testing (high structure) to observations of the child in play or during daily activities (low structure). Different contexts provide different information that is useful for different purposes. Information obtained from any context must be categorized and presented in comparison to some standard or model. Categories discussed include the content, form, and use of language and their interactions, while the standard of comparison is either the adult model or a child model of language. Both the categories used and the model of comparison may influence plans for intervention (what will be taught) and conclusions about qualitative versus quantitative differences between normal and deviant language. An additional influence on the latter is the population used for comparison and how it is matched with the language disordered population.

Differences in type of comparison (frame of reference) are also discussed and related to the objectives of clinical assessment: norm reference for identification of a language disorder, and criterion or communication reference for planning intervention. It is concluded that methodological issues relate directly to the purpose of description and include: method of obtaining evidence, the aspect of language described, and the model and means of comparison in interpreting the evidence.

SUGGESTED READINGS

In *Readings in Language Disorders*

Brannon, J., Linguistic word classes in the spoken language of normal, hard-of-hearing and deaf children. *Journal of Speech and Hearing Research, 11,* 279-287, 1968.

Cunningham, M., A comparison of the language of psychotic and non-psychotic children who are mentally retarded. *Journal of Child Psychology and Psychiatry, 9,* 229–244, 1968.

Kanner, L., Irrelevant and metaphorical language in early infantile autism. *American Journal of Psychiatry, 103,* 242-266, 1946.

Lackner, J. R., A developmental study of language behavior in retarded children. *Neuropsychologia, 6,* 301–320, 1968. Reprinted in D. Morehead and A. E. Morehead (Eds.), *Normal and deficient child language*, Baltimore: University Park Press, pp. 181–208, 1976.

Leonard, L., Bolders, J., and Miller, J., An examination of the semantic relations reflected in the language usage of normal and language-disordered children. *Journal of Speech and Hearing Research, 19,* 371–392, 1976.

Morehead, D. M., and Ingram, D., The development of base syntax in normal and linguistically deviant children. *Journal of Speech and Hearing Research, 16,* 330–352, 1973.

Prutting, C., Gallagher, T., and Mulac, A., The expressive portion of the N.S.S.T. compared to a spontaneous language sample. *Journal of Speech and Hearing Disorders, 40,* 40–49, 1975.

Shapiro, T., Chiarandini, I., and Fish, B., Thirty severely disturbed children: Evaluation of their language development for classification and prognosis. *Archives of General Psychiatry, 30,* 819–825, 1974.

Other Readings

Cazden, C. B., The neglected situation in child language research and education. In F. Williams (Ed.), *Language and poverty, perspectives on a theme.* Chicago: Markham, 1970.

Dever, R., A comparison of the results of a revised version of Berko's test of morphology with the free speech of mentally retarded children. *Journal of Speech and Hearing Research, 15,* 169–178, 1972.

Gorth, W., and Hambleton, R., Measurement considerations for criterion-referenced testing and special education. *Journal of Special Education, 6,* 303–314, 1972.

Johnston, J. R., and Schery, T. K., The use of grammatical morphemes by children with communication disorders. In D. M. Morehead and A. E. Morehead (Eds.), *Normal and deficient child language.* Baltimore: University Park Press, pp. 239–258, 1976.

Leonard, L., What is deviant language? *Journal of Speech and Hearing Disorders, 37,* 427–447, 1972.

Menyuk, P., Comparison of grammar of children with functionally deviant and normal speech. *Journal of Speech and Hearing Research, 7,* 109–121, 1964.

Chapter XII
IDENTIFYING CHILDREN WITH LANGUAGE DISORDERS

As pointed out in the previous chapter, the objectives of language assessment are: (1) to determine the existence of a language problem; (2) given the existence of a language problem, to plan goals of intervention; and (3) given the goals of intervention, to plan the procedures for an intervention program. Each objective requires different kinds of information, and different techniques are often required in order to obtain the different kinds of information that are needed. In order to provide a *plan* for assessment with a focus on these objectives, the chapters on assessment will discuss procedures as they relate to each specific objective and to the kinds of information needed to reach each objective.

The first objective of assessment is to determine whether a child has a language disorder—a problem with learning or using the conventional system of signals used by people in the environment as a code for representing ideas about the world for the purpose of communication. It is often possible to determine that a child has a language problem after brief informal observation. The child's language skills may be either so severely delayed or so different from the language skills of peers that even the most unsophisticated observer would know that there is something wrong. The children who can be readily identified as having a language disorder are often referred for professional assessment by their families. When the family has already decided that there is a problem, confirmation of the language disorder may take only a short observation, and elaborate assessment procedures or standardized language tests may not be necessary to achieve this first objective. The objective of assessment then shifts to determining the goals and procedures for an intervention program that will best meet this child's needs.

On the other hand, there are children who are referred for assessment to find out whether a language problem might account for some other behaviors that have been observed—in particular, a failure to learn to read or otherwise to achieve in school. Language differences or delays in language development may not be so easily observed in children whose language development has not attracted attention until it was associated with difficulties with school language behaviors. Therefore standardized norm-referenced descriptions may be needed to determine the existence of a language problem. Before a battery of tests is administered, school records should be checked to see if any information is already available on language performance—information that was obtained as a part of another evaluation of the child's learning problem. In addition, reported observations of the child's language and learning problems, and at least a short direct observation of the child's language behavior in a low-structured setting, should precede the administration of standardized instruments. The information that can be obtained from these reported and direct observations, in addition to whatever information might already be available from the school records, will aid in determining what further specific information is needed. By using these other sources of information, it may be possible to avoid wasting time in administering tests that provide unessential or redundant information. For example, if a child has been given an intelligence test that includes vocabulary as a subtest, another vocabulary test may not be needed, unless there is reason to believe that the child might respond differently to the different tasks used on each test (e.g., picture identification, in contrast to telling what a word means) or to the domain of words tested (e.g., Spanish versus English, or verbs versus nouns).

Thus, before subjecting the child to a battery of tests, the assessor should have the purpose of the assessment clearly in mind to be assured of obtaining the information that is needed to achieve this purpose. If the information is already available from other sources, it need not be duplicated. When there is insufficient information available about the existence of a language problem, it will be necessary to obtain information about a child's language skills as compared with those of peers. The techniques that can be used to obtain this information are presented here and are discussed in terms of the degree of structure they impose on the observation setting.

LOW STRUCTURED OBSERVATIONS

The techniques reported here can be used to examine the language behavior of the child in settings that are familiar and comfortable and that involve as little manipulation of language behavior as possible. Information can be obtained either indirectly from reports by those who have observed the child, and from the persons who live with the child or who interact with the child frequently, or information can be obtained from observation of the child directly.

REPORTED OBSERVATIONS

Reported observations come from two sources: (1) other professional persons who have seen the child during other assessment or intervention procedures, and (2) persons who are closely associated with the child in everyday environments, such as the child's parent, caregiver, or teacher. Both sources of reported observations, if properly tapped, can supply a wealth of information that is pertinent to all the objectives of language assessment. (See Table XII-1).

When looking at what other professionals have reported about the child's behavior, one can search for communication-referenced descriptions of the child's language. If the child's language behavior is different in any way from the language behavior of peers, it will usually evoke some comment in psychological, medical, or educational reports. These comments provide important information that can be helpful for identifying a language disorder and, possibly, additional information that might indicate whether the problem is related to interactions among the content/form/use of language.

An even richer source of information than that provided by other professionals is the information that can be reported by persons who are with the child daily, either in school or at home. By interviewing parents and teachers, one can obtain descriptions of the child and of the language the child uses in the most relaxed and familiar everyday environments. Interviewing can begin by encouraging parents and teachers to describe the child's language behavior in their own words and from their own point of view. The questions asked by the interviewer should, at first, be general enough to encourage spontaneous descriptions; the questions that follow can be narrowed, with more specific aims in mind, after a broad picture has been presented. The specific questions that are asked will best be derived from the general report that was given initially. These further questions will be asked to clarify, with examples, the information that was reported spontaneously, and to obtain information that was not reported. After a direct observation has been made, a follow-up interview can be used to confirm that the behaviors observed were representative of the child's behaviors generally and to obtain information on behaviors that were expected but not actually observed.

In addition to the assessment interview, parents can be asked to keep a diary or log of certain communication behaviors that take place in the home and to report these to the assessor. For example, parents can be asked to observe and report examples of the forms the child typically uses to talk about action events or possession, or to report examples of the child's use of language to obtain objects in the environment, or how objects are obtained if language is not used. When requesting such examples, it is important to specify clearly the kind of information that is requested and to stress the need for descriptions—reports of the child's utterances and descriptions of context—instead of evaluations—judgments of "good" or "bad" behaviors. To solicit information about how the child uses language to obtain objects, one might present a number of possible contexts and ask how the child would typically respond to each. For example, if the child wants a cracker or item of food that is not within reach and not in sight, what might the child do and say? If the child wants an object that another child or adult is holding and that is readily visible, what might the child do and say? Do these response patterns ever vary? If so, how? Are the responses described prompted in any way by an adult or another child? These reported examples complement the information that is obtained from direct observation of the child's behavior in unstructured settings, and the information gained from behavior elicited by more structured procedures.

The use of parents as informants can provide a rich and important source of information, but this depends on the willingness and the ability of the parent to cooperate. Unquestionably there are some who cannot, or will not, report reliable information; fortunately, they are not the majority. The cooperation of a parent or teacher and the usefulness of the information that they can provide will depend on the sensitivity and care with which the interview is conducted. Although there is, necessarily, some question about the accuracy of reported information obtained from even the most cooperative informant, most informants can give meaningful information if the instructions and information requested are clearly specified. In any case, the information provided by informants can only be used to supplement information from direct observation of the child. Interview information cannot be the sole source of information about the child. The greatest values of reported observations are that they provide information from a wider variety of settings than can be tapped in direct assessment procedures, and they can include

TABLE XII-I

Information To Be Obtained from Reported Naturalistic Observations, and the Relevance of Reported Information to the Objectives of Language Assessment

Information To Be Obtained	Objective of Assessment: To Determine		
	Existence of Language Problem	Goals of Intervention	Procedures for Intervention
Historical			
Age at which language milestones reached	X		
Age at which other developmental milestones reached			X
Changes that have occurred in language behavior in the past, and correlated environmental or physical factors			X
Description of current language behaviors			
General comparison with peers	X		
Amount of verbalizations—how much the child talks	X	X	
Intelligibility of speech—how well the child is understood	X	X	
Comprehension of the language of others—how much the child understands of what others say with accompanying context and without relevant context	X	X	X
Use			
Functions for which language is used (demand, comment, question, tell stories, etc.)	X	X	X
Contexts of referents talked about (here and now, self-actions, etc.)	X	X	X
Form			
Kinds of words used (e.g., nouns, pronouns) and the variety of different words used	X	X	
Typical length of utterances	X	X	
Relative completeness of sentences	X	X	
Variety of sentence structures (e.g., statements, questions)	X	X	
Variety and appropriateness of morphological endings	X	X	

TABLE XII-I—*(Continued)*

Information To Be Obtained	Objective of Assessment: To Determine		
	Existence of Language Problem	Goals of Intervention	Procedures for Intervention
Other forms of communication (e.g., gestures and manual signs)	X	X	X
Content—what the child communicates			
Kinds of objects	X	X	X
Kinds of events	X	X	X
Kinds of states and feelings	X	X	X
Kinds of relationships between objects	X	X	X
Kinds of relationships between people, or people and objects	X	X	X
Kinds of relationships between events	X	X	X
Description of nonlinguistic behaviors			
Social interactions with:			
Children			X
Adults			X
Preferred activities, foods, etc.			X
Medical history			
Current medication, contraindications to activities, possibilities of seizures, etc.			X
Motor skills (coordination for running, catching, drawing, etc.)			X
Attention to sound, both verbal and nonverbal			X
Span of attention to preferred and nonpreferred activities			X
Factors that interfere with attention			X
Description of environment			
Availability of others to assist in intervention			X
Factors that may be interfering with language growth (e.g., lack of peers, lack of stimulation, bilingualism)			X
Home setting			X
School setting			X

information about the child's behavior in settings that are most natural to the child. Reported observations can enrich and supplement direct observation, but major decisions about the goals and procedures of intervention are not made on the basis of information from this source alone.

DIRECT OBSERVATIONS

If it is not possible to visit the child's own natural and unstructured environment, it is necessary to create a setting within the clinical or educational environment that is as relaxed and naturalistic for the child as possible (See Chapter XVI). When a child is referred by a parent or teacher and is described as having a language disorder, the direct observation of the child for the purpose of collecting a language sample provides both a means of confirming that report and a means of obtaining descriptive information about the child's language behaviors. The interviews with parents or teachers before the direct observation would have pointed out the particular behaviors that have been noticed by others, and these behaviors might be the first behaviors to look for when observing the child. The comments from the child's parent or teacher might, for example, be an initial etic scheme that directs the observer's attention in the observation session to aspects of content/form/use.

Information from low-structured direct observations can be norm-referenced in order to identify a language disorder. A number of analyses and indices can be used: age-equivalent scores can be computed based on the average length of utterances (see *MLU* scores in Box II-6, and procedures in Box II-5, and McCarthy, 1954a) or for a length-complexity index (see norms and procedures in Johnson, Darley, and Spriesterbach, 1963); and percentile ranks can be obtained based on developmental sentence scoring (for norms and procedures, see Lee, 1974). These procedures are particularly relevant when the assessor is most interested in obtaining a language sample for descriptive purposes, but also needs quantitative verification of a language problem (thus the same data can be used for both), or when quantitative verification of a language problem is needed and the child will not respond in a formal standardized test situation.

If during the first part of the observation it is obvious that a problem exists, the remainder of the session should be used to obtain descriptive information—information that will be relevant to the goals of intervention. However, if it appears that there is not a language disorder, it is often important to pursue a description of the child's language behaviors anyway, if parents or teachers are concerned about the child's language development. The information about what the child does know about language and the hypotheses about what the child will most probably learn next are important for parent counseling, in order to establish realistic expectations for the child's development and to facilitate the learning process. Most parents are reassured when they have something positive to do to facilitate language development and when they have information on what aspects of language are probably going to emerge next. Parents are less often reassured when they are only given a language age or told that the child will eventually talk normally.

The situation is somewhat different when a child is referred for assessment of language behavior as a part of a general team evaluation, because the presenting problem is a behavioral problem, a hearing problem, a learning problem, or some problem other than a language problem. If a short observation of a child who has been referred for a problem other than a language disorder does not suggest language behaviors that are obviously different from peers in the language community, one might want to terminate temporarily the naturalistic session and begin some standardized norm-referenced observations. Since there is no need to calm a concerned parent, descriptions of the child's behavior may be less relevant than comparisons. In addition, evaluation teams who need to make decisions regarding the child's education are often more interested in norm-referenced descriptions than criterion-referenced descriptions.

Naturalistic observations allow the assessor to view a sample of the child's communication behavior in order to compare the child's behavior with information about normal language development and the communicative behavior of children of the same age. A naturalistic setting with relaxed structure can provide the context for observing dysfunctions in the interactions of content/form/use. The same kinds of information may not be as obvious in a situation in which the observer imposes a high degree of structure. Observations of the child's language behavior in a relaxed structure will provide information to determine or confirm the existence of a problem, while also providing the most important information relevant to determining the goals of intervention. (See Chapter XVI for information on the use of relaxed settings.)

In conclusion, the initial information to be obtained when determining if there is a language disorder is best obtained from both reported observations and direct observations of language behavior in a low-structured context. Using the information from these observations, comparisons can be made with the language behaviors of similarly aged children. Some comparisons are made using the traditional developmental milestones (age of first word, combinations of words, sentences). Other comparisons involve the interactions of content/form/use, and lead to hunches or hypotheses about possible dysfunctions in these components or in the interactions among them. Most professional persons would probably agree that a child with a 2-year delay in progress through early developmental milestones should receive some help to facilitate the development of language skills. The evaluation of shorter delays, however, and the possibility of qualitative differences in a child's language behavior are more difficult to delineate. There are no established quantitative indexes for making these comparisons between the language behavior of children who develop normally and the behavior of children who present a language disorder.

Many observations of children who do not develop language normally, and familiarity with descriptions of normal language development, will lead the observer to acquire sensitive intuitions about the existence of a language disorder and about the nature of the language disorder. In many situations, persons making the assessment and the referral source are willing to act on such intuitions, so that assessment can proceed immediately to determine what the child is ready to learn and how learning language might best be facilitated. In other situations, the referring source would like more quantitative comparison with other children; the assessor is not confident of intuitions about the child's problem; or there is not enough information available for comparing the child's behavior with peer behavior—either because it could not be obtained from the child or because comparison data do not exist for children developing language normally. In such instances, the assessor may turn to standardized norm-referenced observation to determine the existence of a problem.

STANDARDIZED ELICITATIONS

Formal elicitation techniques that provide norm-referenced results generally have standardized administration procedures. There are many published tests, scales, and instruments currently available. In order to use the information that can be obtained with such instruments effectively—whether the instruments are currently available or will be published in the future—it is important to know how to analyze and use the information about the child's knowledge of language that can be obtained from each. At times children will come for assessment with records of test scores that were obtained previously or that were obtained in another context. It is important to know if these test scores can be used to determine the existence of a language problem or to provide other information about the child's language. At other times the assessor will be searching for a standardized test that will provide information relevant to determining the existence of a problem. What kind of information will best supplement the information obtained from observations in low-structured settings? Which instruments will provide that type of information? In this section some means of evaluating current tests and scales are discussed in relation to the information they provide about the content/form/use of language, to enable clinicians and educators (1) to decide *whether* to use such instruments, and (2) to determine *how* to use the information that the instruments provide. Before discussing the information about language that is available from different standardized measurement instruments, it is necessary to consider certain prerequisites to using test information.

MEASUREMENT

To use norm-referenced standardized tests effectively, one should be familiar with the science and practice of *measurement*. One should have an understanding of: norming procedures; measures of central tendency (mean, median, and mode); measures of variability (standard deviation); concepts of reliability (standard error of measurement); and concepts of validity (whether the tests provide the desired information). In addition to this information on measurement, the assessor must consider the relevance of the population that was used in developing the norms to the individual being tested (e.g., a test normed on a population that speaks black dialect may not help in identifying a language disorder in a child whose native language is not that black dialect but standard English dialect, and vice versa). Such discussions are beyond the scope of this textbook. If the reader is not familiar with this information and will be using standardized test scores, he or she should consider reading a textbook about such information (e.g., Cronbach, 1970).

One consideration in the use of any standardized test information, a consideration that is important to the goals and scope of this textbook, is the type of norm reference used to report results—equivalent scores or standard scores. The raw score in a test, usually representing the number of correct responses, has no meaning by itself. With norm-referenced reports the raw score is described in relation to the raw scores other people obtained who have taken the test. The raw score can be reported in terms of other children who are in the *same* population as the child being tested (e.g., children of the same age or in the same grade) and is then referred to as a *standard score*; or the raw score can be reported in terms of *other* populations who have taken the test (e.g., children of other ages or in other grades) and is then called an *equivalent score*.

A standard score, therefore, tells us how a child responded in relation to other children of the same population. If the child and the population with which the child is to be compared are the same (e.g., 5 years of age), and if the group of 5-year olds is representative of all 5-year olds, the scores can be converted in terms of a standard score. Standard scores relate directly to a theoretical distribution of scores on a normal curve, and may be reported as percentile ranks, stanines, deviation IQ, or other scaled scores. Each can be described in terms of the number of standard deviations (S.D.) from the mean of the population of such children. (See Box XII-1 and Addendum p. 367.)

If we accept that what 68% of what a population does is 'normal,' we can identify deviant language as behavior which is not within one standard deviation (S.D.) of the mean. Children who score above (+) one S.D. will be considered as having superior language skills; those who score below (−) one S.D. will be considered as having below average or poor language skills.

Alternatively, one could define normal as what 95% of the population does

BOX XII-1 STANDARD SCORES, PERCENTILES, AND AREAS UNDER THE NORMAL CURVE (with permission of the Psychological Corporation). See p. 367 for discussion of this table.

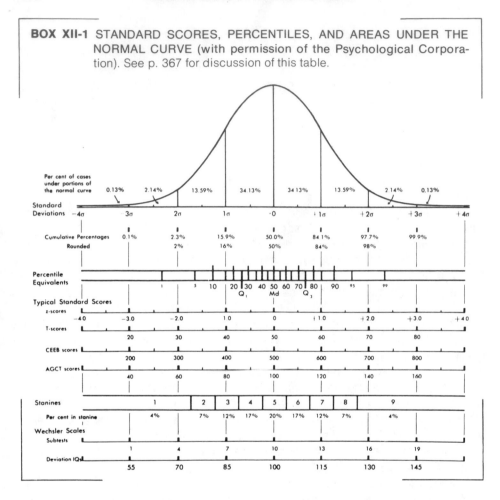

and identify deviant language as behavior that is not within 2 S.D. of the mean. The latter standard (−2 S.D.) is used to identify mental retardation (Grossman, 1973). Using the first definition of normality, 16% of all children could theoretically be identified as having difficulty learning language; with the second definition, 2.5% of all children could be so identified. Individual tests often include recommendations for cut-off scores; for example, Lee (1970) suggested the tenth percentile, which is somewhere between −1 and −2 S.D. (see Box XII-1 to identify where it falls). Since identification by such means is only a first step in assessment—a step that is followed by more in-depth descriptions of both language behaviors and other factors that will influence learning language—decisions about intervention are not made on test scores alone. Taking the narrow view of normal (within ±1 S.D.) may bring some children for further assessment for whom no recommendation is made about improving language skills. On the other hand, the broader definition of normal (within ±2 S.D.) may mean that some children, who could benefit from recommendations or direct help, will be missed. As long as identification is seen as a search for children who may benefit from intervention and not as the discovery of some entity (see Chapters X and XVIII for further discussion of labeling), the narrow definition of normal may be most useful.

The important difference between standard scores and equivalent scores is that results on language tests that are reported in standard scores can be converted to standard deviation units, and test results can be described relative to deviance from the average performance of children of the same age. On the other hand, equivalent scores do not compare raw scores with other children of the same age (or, in fact, with any population of which the child is a member), and therefore cannot so readily be used to identify children with a language disorder. Equivalent scores transform raw scores to language age, mental age, or grade equivalency, which represent measures of central tendency for age or grade. A language age of 4 years on a test tells us that the raw score received by a child was the same as the median, or mean, score achieved by a group of 4-year-olds. If the child who has received this score is also 4 or is under 4 years of age, we know that performance is at least average and that the child does not have a language disorder. If, however, the child is over 4 years, we do not know that language is not within normal range, because we have no information on the variability of performance within each age range; we do not know, for example, how many 5-year-olds also received that score. It is quite possible and very often probable that the normal distribution of scores for 4- and 5-year-olds overlap, so that more than 16% (−1 S.D.) of the 5-year-olds received a raw score equal to or less than the mean of 4-year-olds. Obviously, as the distance between actual age and age-equivalent scores increases, the likelihood of overlap between the two ages decreases. We do not know at what point this happens, however, unless variability measures (S.D.) are reported.

Take, for example, a hypothetical child, Bill, age 5 years, 9 months, who has taken the *Illinois Test of Psycholinguistic Abilities* (ITPA) (Kirk, McCarthy, and Kirk, 1968), which has tables for converting raw scores to standard scores and age equivalent scores. The standard score that represents the mean raw score is 36, and 1 S.D. is 6 points (comparable to Wechsler mean of 100, and S.D. of 15 plotted on the figure in Box XII-1). Let us say that Bill obtained a raw score of 15 on each of the three subtests listed below. Given this raw score, age-equivalent scores would be as listed below; given his chronological age, the standard scores would be as listed below:

	Age Equivalent	Standard Score (Mean = 36) (S.D. = 6)
1. Auditory reception	4 years, 3 months	28 (>−1 S.D.)
2. Auditory sequencing	4 years, 5 months	31 (<−1 S.D.)
3. Auditory association	4 years, 11 months	26 (>−1 S.D.)

While the age equivalent on test 3 was higher than on test 2, the standard score on test 3 was lowest. This means that he more closely approximated the mean of children his age on test 2 than on test 3 and that this closer approximation is not reflected in the age-equivalent scores.

Since the purpose of norm-referenced descriptions is to identify children who are not learning or using language as well as their peers, it follows that the type of score that is most applicable for this purpose is the standard score, which directly compares the child with a peer group. Therefore, measures that report only age-equivalent scores are less useful for this purpose than measures that report standard scores. The type of norm-referenced report that is used in a testing instrument should be an important consideration in selecting tests to be used in assessment.

INFORMATION ABOUT LANGUAGE IN STANDARDIZED TESTS

In addition to the type of norm reference, each test must be evaluated in terms of the information it provides about language. By virtue of the fact that language necessarily involves the interdependence among content, form, and use, instruments that measure language skills cover more than one aspect of language. By categorizing the instruments according to content, and form, as in Table XII-2, it is suggested that the information available from the test is primarily organized with respect to a particular aspect of language, although it may give other information or tap other skills. Tests of linguistic form can again be grouped according to which component of form is stressed (lexicon, syntax, or phonology). From test scores one can obtain norm-referenced information about form—general linguistic skills having to do with lexical, syntactic, and phonological performance; and content—knowledge about objects and events in the world that may or may not be coded by language; but little information about use—the ability to use language in different contexts for different purposes. In Table XII-2 some tests have been grouped according to the principal information that can be provided by each (a reference for each is listed in the table, and an abstract of many of them can be found in Cicciarelli, Broen, and Siegel, 1976; and Irwin, Moore, and Rampp, 1972; see, also, Appendix C). The purpose of the table and the following discussion is to enable persons using the tests or using the resulting test scores to understand what information the test provides about language. No attempt is made here to evaluate each instrument (in terms of reliability, validity, normative population, etc.). For an evaluation of such instruments, see *Mental Measurement Yearbook* (Buros, 1972).

Assessment of General Language Skills

The first category listed in Table XII-2 includes instruments that cover a number of language skills and aim to answer the general question: Is the language performance of the child comparable to that of age peers? The developmental language scales have been compiled from more general developmental scales and profiles, and behaviors are usually categorized according to age; age equivalent scores are the result. The usual procedure is for the assessor to interview a person who is familiar with the child or to observe the child directly and check for the presence or absence of each behavior. The norms usually consist of a point count, where a total number of points is based on the number of behaviors that are either reported or observed. The behaviors that have been tapped are varied and cover linguistic responses as well as nonlinguistic behaviors such as block building, drawing, or motor responses. Each aspect of language included in the task is covered in just enough depth to comment on the child's overall language performance in only the most general terms.

Some language development tests are based on developmental milestones obtained from profiles of development, but obtain information by eliciting behavior from the child instead of relying on reported or observed information. Some of these tests attempt to separate the language skills to be covered and comment on the relative age-equivalent norms of different skills. The amount of information that is obtained with any of these language development scales or tests is limited, and the primary goal in administering the scale is to obtain a general measure of performance.

A last source of information on general language performance is the verbal portions of intelligence tests. Low verbal intelligence scores can be used to support the hypothesis that a child's language behavior is not comparable to that of peers. It is not suggested that one administer an intelligence test to determine the existence of a language problem, but the information from intelligence testing is often available to the language specialist and might be used to support or question other data.

A measure of general language performance is most useful when there is some uncertainty about how the general language behavior of the child compares with peers. A norm-referenced description of the child's language might be in order if the comparative question could not be answered during direct observation in a low-structured setting, and there is some question

TABLE XII-2

Published Norm-Referenced Measures for Evaluating Language Behavior, Presented According to Information Each Provides about Language[a]

Information Available	Measures with Norms	Type of Norm Reference	
		Equivalent Score	Standard Score
GENERAL LANGUAGE PERFORMANCE	*Developmental scales* (solicited reported observation)		
	Verbal Language Development Scale (Mecham, 1958, 1971)	x	
	REEL—Receptive-Expressive Emergent Language Scale (Bzoch and League, 1971)	x	
	Communicative Evaluation Chart from Infancy to Five Years (Anderson, Miles and Matheny, 1963)	x	
	Tests (direct observation and elicitations)		
	Preschool Language Scale (Zimmerman, Steiner, and Evatt, 1969)	x	
	Utah Test of Language Development (Mecham, Joy, and Jones, 1967)	x	
	Houston Test of Language Development (Crabtree, 1958)	x	
	Intelligence Tests		
	McCarthy Scale of Children's Ability—Verbal (McCarthy, 1974)		x
	Wechsler Intelligence Scale for Children—Verbal (Wechsler, 1949)		x
	Wechsler PreSchool and Primary Scale of Intelligence—Verbal (Wechsler, 1967)		x
CONTENT/ FORM Lexicon and Syntax Receptive			
	Test for Auditory Comprehension of Language (Carrow, 1973)		x

TABLE XII-2—*(Continued)*

Information Available	Measures with Norms	Type of Norm Reference	
		Equivalent. Score	Standard Score
Lexicon			
Receptive	Peabody Picture Vocabulary Test (Dunn, 1959, 1965)		x
	Full Range Vocabulary Test (Ammons and Ammons, 1948)	x	
	Stanford-Binet Vocabulary Subtest (Terman and Merrill, 1960)	x	
	ITPA Auditory Reception Subtest (Kirk, McCarthy, and Kirk, 1968)		x
	Boehm Test of Basic Concepts (Boehm, 1969)		x
Expressive	Wechsler Vocabulary Subtest (Wechsler, 1949)		x
	ITPA Verbal Expression Subtest (Kirk, et al., 1968)		x
Syntax			
Receptive	M.Y. Test of Grammatical Competence (Miller and Yoder, 1972c)	x	
	Northwestern Syntax Screening Test (Lee, 1971)		x
	Assessment of Children's Language Comprehension (Foster, Giddan, and Stark, 1969, 1973)	x	
Expressive	Berry-Talbot-Exploratory Test of Grammar (Berry, 1966)	x	
	Northwestern Syntax Screening Test (Lee, 1971)		x
	ITPA-Grammatical Closure (Kirk, et al., 1968)		x
Phonology			
Receptive	Wepman Auditory Discrimination Test (Wepman, 1958)	x	
	Goldman-Fristoe-Woodcock Test of Auditory Discrimination (Goldman, Fristoe, and Woodcock, 1969)		x
Expressive	Developmental Articulation Test (Hejna, 1959)	x	
	Templin-Darley Screening Test (Templin and Darley, 1969)		x

TABLE XII-2—(Continued)

Information Available	Measures with Norms	Type of Norm Reference	
		Equivalent Score	Standard Score
CONTENT	ITPA: (Kirk, McCarthy, and Kirk, 1968)		
	Visual Reception		x
	Visual Association		x
	Manual Expression		x
	Goodenough-Harris Drawing Test (Harris, 1963)		x
	Leiter International Performance Scale (Arthur, 1952)	x	
	Wechsler Performance Intelligence Scale (Wechsler, 1949, 1967)		x
	Picture Arrangement		x
	Picture Completion		x
	Object Assembly		x
	Piagetian Sensori-Motor Scale (Corman and Escalona 1969; Uzgiris and Hunt, 1975)	x	

[a] These and other instruments are referenced in Appendix C.

that the child's language behavior might be inadequate and related to other problems. A quick means of obtaining a norm-referenced description is the administration of one of the general language scales or tests. Most of these measures of general language performance are normed for only preschool children and are only reported as age-equivalent scores. For school-age children verbal intelligence measures probably provide the best general index of language skills, but they are more time consuming to use and must be administered by a psychologist. However, many children who are referred for language evaluation have previously been given an intelligence test, and the verbal scores reported can be used to estimate the possible existence of a problem. Most, but not all, measures of intelligence are reported in standard scores.

A general measure of language performance is least useful if it is already known that there is a general problem with language, and it is necessary to determine which aspects of language are affected or how the problem relates to some other problem that the child presents. If one already knows that there is a general problem, but needs to know which aspects of language are affected with respect to norm-referenced standards, then instruments under content/form or content assessment might be considered.

Content/Form Assessment

The second category in Table XII-2 presents some of the available instruments that provide information about a child's knowledge of content/form interactions and answer questions about how the child compares with age peers on responses demanding knowledge of language. Subcategories under content/form in Table XII-2 are instruments that measure the child's acquisition of lexicon, syntax, and phonology. Each subcategory is further subdivided to separate measures that are receptive and stress decoding of the linguistic signal, from measures that look at expressive language and stress linguistic encoding. A test has been included as a lexical test in Table XII-2 if the response that is expected from the child is primarily dependent on the understanding or the use of a single word. A test has been included as a syntactic test in Table XII-2 if the responses that are expected from the child are primarily dependent on the understanding and use of syntactic structures that present linguistic items in one or another relation to each other. For example, a test is a measure of syntax when each item used in the sentence stimuli is also pictured or otherwise presented to the child, so that the test is not to recognize the appropriate referents for the words but, instead, to demonstrate the *relationships* among the referents. A test has been included as a phonological test in Table XII-2 if it taps the child's knowledge of the sound system more than knowledge of word meaning or syntax (e.g., if words within the child's vocabulary are used to elicit production or discrimination responses).

There are important differences among the tests within each of these categories—differences that probably account for the fact that different results may be obtained when two tests within a category are administered to the same child. Some differences can be related to the different tasks that are used to measure performance. Some tests use visual stimuli to elicit responses; others use auditory stimuli, motor stimuli, or some combination of all three. Some tests have only a limited or closed set of responses from which the child can choose, while other tests are more open ended. Other differences can relate to the variety of language behaviors that are sampled within a category. For example, some vocabulary tests are concerned mostly with nouns (*Peabody Picture Vocabulary Test*; Dunn, 1959, 1965), while other tests tap the child's understanding of relational words (*Boehm Test of Basic Concepts*; Boehm, 1969) and others test verbs and the semantic features of words that can be used with them (the auditory reception subtest of the ITPA, Kirk et. al. 1968). The grammatical closure subtest of the ITPA taps only grammatical morphemes and, in particular, tests the plural morpheme with many items, while the *Northwestern Syntax Screening Test* (Lee, 1970, in *RLDis*) covers a broader range of syntactic structures, but usually taps only one instance of each structure. Consequently, different norm-referenced scores can result from tests listed under the same category in Table XII-2, either because of the different behaviors tested or the different tasks used to test the behavior.

If test results are available from another source before assessment, the results should certainly be analyzed in terms of what they say about the content/form/use of the child's language. In this way, the results can be used to decide what should be observed or elicited in direct observations. A difficult question is when to administer such specific measures if they have not already been administered. Vocabulary measures, if not previously administered to the child, are perhaps the most efficient way of determining if a child has a problem learning the lexicon. Comparative information about lexical development is difficult to obtain from naturalistic observation, more difficult to obtain than information about syntax or phonology. Standardized elicitation of syntax and phonology might be called for (1) when a child has not said very much during a low-structured observation; (2) when it is necessary to have norm-referenced information on receptive performance in these areas; or (3) when a general language deficit has been reported, and one is interested in determining whether the deficit involves syntax and/or phonology. Norm-referenced observations reported in standard scores are helpful in giving such information to determine the existence of a problem. Norm-referenced reports of any type are less helpful in describing *what* the child *knows* and planning *what* to *teach* a child.

Content Assessment

The third category of tests listed in Table XII-2 includes tests that tap the concepts that language codes—the content of language. It is possible to obtain certain information about the child's cognitive development without directly tapping language skills. A test is included in this category if: (1) the test gives information about the child's capacities for representational thought and ability to act on represented information (in the mind) as opposed to empirical information (in the context); (2) the test does not require that the child respond to much verbal instruction, nor that the child interact verbally with the examiner in order to complete the task; and (3) completion of the tasks does not require that the child verbalize the answers but, instead, the scoring reflects nonverbal solutions. If most of these tasks are successfully completed by the child, then it is possible to conclude that the child is able to mentally represent aspects of the world that are not also perceptually present in the situation, and to perform actions that are contingent on these mental representations. Although the tasks in such tests are not direct measures of the content that is coded by language, age appropriate scores with these measures can suggest that the child's concepts of the world, and the ideas that are coded by language, are most likely intact. However, low scores do not also indicate that the reverse is true; task variables, motivation, and many other factors can account for negative results with the use of any task to measure behavior.

Norm-referenced information obtained from the tests that fit into this category can assist in determining if there is a problem in the content component of language. The assessment of cognition is usually the responsibility of those trained in psychometrics. However, the *Illinois Test of Psycholinguistic Abilities*; (Kirk et al., 1968) and the *McCarthy Scales* (1974) are commonly administered by the speech pathologist or learning disabilities specialist and include information relevant to language content. When the results of these tests or of intelligence tests are available, the assessor should know their relevance to language.

Although a description of what the child does or does not know about language is more interesting and relevant than intelligence test scores, there are times when one wishes to determine the relative strength or weakness of content as a component in relation to content/form interactions. Norm-referenced descriptions based on intelligence tests can do this more efficiently and precisely than criterion- or communication-referenced descriptions, and such tests are also often necessary for placing a child in one or another educational program. Content assessment for planning remediation, however, is best geared to criterion- and communication-referenced descriptions that can be related to goals such as those outlined in Chapter XIV.

Use Assessment

Determining the existence of a problem with language use is particularly difficult using standardized norm-referenced descriptions, because use is automatically constrained in any standardized test situation. The only use of language that is usually measured by standardized tests is the ability to manipulate verbal symbols in order to solve problems, to analyze relationships between symbols (as are represented by analogies), or to talk about or operate on linguistic forms (as in word analysis). A child who does poorly with such standardized measures of language use might, on the other hand, use language effectively for social interaction and for solving problems about familiar things. In addition, tests that require information that has had to be learned by the child through verbal interaction, such as the number of miles from New York to Chicago (as asked on the Information subtest of the WISC, Wechsler, 1949), tell us something about the child's ability to learn through language (if it can be assumed that the child has been exposed to this information). On the whole, however, standardized observations and norm-referenced descriptions are generally an unsatisfactory measure of a child's ability to use language for the exchange of information and ideas with another person. Use can best be assessed through criterion- and communi- cation-referenced descriptions of behavior in low-structured settings; there- fore, measures of use are not included in Table XII-2.

CONSIDERATIONS IN TEST SELECTION

There are many factors to consider when selecting a testing instrument to be used in the assessment of a particular child's language (see also Emerick and Hatten, 1974). Three of these have been considered at length in this and the previous chapter.

1. If the purpose of description is identification, is it to identify overall language knowledge or knowledge of a particular aspect of language knowledge?
2. Does the test provide information about (a) overall language knowledge, (b) content/form interactions (vocabulary, morphological inflections, function words, word order, complex sentences, etc.), or (c) content? Is this informa- tion relevant to the purpose of description?
3. Is the population on which the test was normed representative of the population of which the child is a member? That is, are the norms appropriate for the child? (a) Some tests are normed on children from a restricted geographic area, such as a small midwestern city; a particular social class; a particular dialect pattern; or a narrow range of intelligence. Is the population relevant to the child? (b) Some tests tell only what the average score is for children of different ages or grades (equivalent scores) and not the distribu- tion of scores for children of the same population (standard scores). Which is most relevant to the purpose of description?

In addition, there are other considerations that each clinician must take into account. A few are listed here.

1. If the purpose is not identification, will the test provide information leading to goals or procedures of intervention?
2. Is the information supplied necessary or needed?
3. Can the information supplied be obtained in any other way? If so, is this method of obtaining it the best, considering the stress on the child, the time it takes, and the quality of the information that is obtained?
4. Is the test material appropriate for the child's age, intelligence, interests, motor ability, behavior patterns, and the like, in terms of level, range of difficulty, directions, and tasks?
5. Will the test cause the child or parent to feel badly about the problem, and possibly create further problems?
6. Is the test reliable? That is, can the same results be obtained by different examiners or by the same examiner at different times?

7. Has the test been validated? Are the reports of validity appropriate to the purpose of assessment and the information needed?

8. Is the test familiar to the assessor? Will it be easy to administer, score, and interpret?

Much of this information can come only from a careful study of the test manuals, items, and materials. There is no one test or set of tests that is right for all children or for all assessors. Each professional must be aware of instruments that are available and must choose among them or reject them according to considerations such as those listed above.

USING NORM-REFERENCED TESTS OF CONTENT, FORM, AND USE

An example of how the information from tests that have been discussed in this chapter might be used is illustrated in Tables XII-3 and XII-4. The standard or scaled scores from different tests are apt to be reported differently. In this table an attempt has been made to equate the scores from different tests in terms of a normal curve so that the results from different tests can be compared; in other words, it converts all scores to z scores, as was illustrated in Box XII-1. For clinical purposes such equation is useful, but it should be kept in mind that each test was normed on different populations, and the comparisons are only as good as the degree to which these populations resemble each other.

The commonly used language measures that report results in standard scores are listed in Tables XII-3 and XII-4. The tests are listed in the column on the left according to information they provide about language. The remaining columns present the scores obtained by a child in terms of standard deviations. Scores that are below 2 or 3 S.D.s below the mean are referred to as low and suggest a language disorder. Scores within 1 S.D. of the mean are considered normal (recall that ±1 S.D. includes 68% of the population). Scores between −1 and −2 S.D. suggest the need for further assessment. Scores that are equal to 2 or 3 S.D. above the mean are considered high and are presented on the right.

The test scores that are presented in Table XII-3 are the actual test scores of a child named Danny who was seen and tested regularly by a child study team over a period of time. The analyses of these test results indicated a problem with general language skills and weakness in form involving both syntax and phonology, but not vocabulary. The child's knowledge of vocabulary, (i.e. score on the *Peabody* and a subtest of the ITPA) was similar to that of other children his age; that is, scores fell within ±1 S.D. This discrepancy in performance with different aspects of language form demonstrates the danger of inferring knowledge of one aspect of form from behavior with another. For example, a vocabulary test cannot be used as an estimate of other language skills. Information about the purposes for which the child

TABLE XII-3
Using and Comparing Publisher's Norm-Referenced Scores for
Standardized Tests of Language
CHILD'S NAME: Danny

Tests	Scores Presented According to Deviation from the Mean[a]						
	−3 S.D.[b]	−2 S.D.	−1 S.D.	Mean	+1 S.D.	+2 S.D.	+3 S.D.
GENERAL							
McCarthy Verbal Scale							
Standard Score	20	30	40	50	60	70	80
Wechsler Intelligence Scale for Children— Verbal							
Standard Score	55	70 [76][c]	85	100	115	130	145
Stanford-Binet							
Standard Score	52	68	84	100	116	132	148
CONTENT/FORM KNOWLEDGE							
General—(Vocabulary and Syntax)							
Test for Auditory Comprehension of Language							
Percentile	.1	2	16	50	84	98	99.9
Lexicon: Receptive							
Peabody Picture Vocabulary Test							
Percentile	.1	2	16	[48] 50 (53)[d]	84	98	99.9
Illinois Test of Psycholinguistic Abilities- Auditory Reception[e]							
Standard Score	18	24	30 [33]	36	42	48	54

Lexicon: Expressive Weschler Intelligence Scale for Children— Vocabulary Standard Score	1	4	7	10	13	16	19
Illinois Test of Psycholinguistic Abilities— Verbal Expression Standard Score	**18**	**24**	**30** (32)	36	42	48	54
Syntax: Receptive Northwestern Syntax Screening Test Percentile		**10**	25	75	90		
Syntax: Expressive Northwestern Syntax Screening Test Percentile		(10)	25	75	90		
Illinois Test of Psycholinguistic Abilities- Grammatical Closure Standard Score	**18**	**24** (25)	**30**	36	42	48	54
Phonology: Receptive Goldman-Fristoe-Woodcock Test of Auditory Discrimination Percentile	**.1**	**2**	**16**	50	84	98	99.9
FORM (Syntax: Expressive) Carrow Elicited Language Inventory Percentile	**.1**	**2**	**16**	50	84	98	99.9

[a] Scores ≤ −1 S.D. suggest the need for further assessment (such scores are presented here to the left of the line and in bold type).

[b] S.D. = Standard Deviation.

[c] Numbers enclosed in a square represent scores obtained by Danny at 5 years of age.

[d] Numbers enclosed in a circle represent scores obtained by Danny at 6 years of age.

[e] The auditory reception subtest also involves the use of word order, an aspect of syntax, so that low scores cannot be interpreted as indicating a problem with only vocabulary.

TABLE XII-4
Using and Comparing Publisher's Norm-Referenced Scores for
Standardized Tests (Content)
CHILD'S NAME: Danny

Tests	Scores Presented According to Deviation from the Mean[a]						
	−3 S.D.[b]	−2 S.D.	−1 S.D.	Mean	+1 S.D.	+2 S.D.	+3 S.D.
CONTENT							
Wechsler Intelligence Scale for Children—Performance							
Standard Score	55	70	85	100	115[c]	130	145
Wechsler Intelligence Scale for Children—Picture Arrangement							
Standard Score	1	4	7	10 11	13	16	19
Wechsler Intelligence Scale for Children—Picture Completion							
Standard Score	1	4	7	10	13	16	19

Wechsler Intelligence Scale for Children—Object Assembly Standard Score	**1**	**4**	**7**	10	13 [15]	16	19
Wechsler Intelligence Scale for Children—Coding Standard Score	**1**	**4**	**7**	10	13	16	19
Illinois Test of Psycholinguistic Abilities—Visual Reception Standard Score	**18**	**24**	**30**	[35] 36	42	48	54
Illinois Test of Psycholinguistic Abilities—Visual Association Standard Score	**18**	**24**	**30** [32]	36	42	48	54
Illinois Test of Psycholinguistic Abilities—Manual Expression Standard Score	**18**	**24**	**30**	36	42	58	54

a Scores ≤ −1 S.D. suggest the need for further assessment (such scores are presented here to the left of the line and in bold type).

b S.D. = Standard Deviation.

c Numbers enclosed in a square represent scores obtained by Danny at 5 years of age.

used language and the contexts in which he used language was not available through these standardized tests. This analysis is presented to demonstrate how standardized test information can be used to answer the question: Is there a problem with the content/form interactions of language? Some estimate of dysfunction in the content component can be obtained by scores on tests of conceptual knowledge that are nonverbal. Results plotted in Table XII-4 suggest Danny had no dysfunction in this component.

Obviously, it was not necessary to obtain all of this information in order to determine the existence of a problem. It is equally obvious that no further norm-referenced description was needed for this child in order to determine the existence of a problem. Even given all these scores, it is still not possible to know what the child knows or does not know about language. It is only possible to know how this child responded to certain tasks in relationship to how other children his age have responded. Additional norm-referenced descriptions would only provide more of the same information. What is needed now is information that will help to determine what it is the child is ready to learn—information for determining the goals of intervention. Such information is not available from all of the information in Tables XII-3 and XII-4. Just as the speech pathologist needs more than a cut-off score on an articulation screening test to plan what sounds to teach, so the speech pathologist needs more than norm-referenced language scores to plan language intervention. To plan articulation goals, an inventory of a child's production of phonemes in various contexts—an inventory that describes how the child produces these phonemes—is needed, and to plan language goals the speech pathologist needs an inventory of language skills in various contexts. Only with such a description is it possible to know *what* to teach the child.

SUMMARY

If the objective of assessment is to identify a language disorder (i.e., to determine if the child's language skills are appropriate for the child's age), then the descriptions of language behavior that are most relevant are norm-referenced descriptions. The norms that are used for the purpose of determining if there is a language disorder may be based on developmental milestones or scores from a standardized test. The settings that are used can vary from low to high structure, depending on the child's reaction to each and the degree and type of deviation from normal language that is suspected or first observed.

It is suggested that reported observations and direct observations in a relaxed, low-structured setting precede the administration of standardized tests. This order helps one to decide selectively what information is needed and thus which, if any, standardized tests might be appropriate.

A number of factors that should be considered in the selection of standardized instruments are discussed. First, the point is made that standard scores are better for identifying a language disorder than equivalent scores. Second, it is suggested that the information available in tests can be described in terms of content/form interactions, content alone, or general measures of language performance. Last, it is pointed out that one cannot measure most aspects of use with standardized instruments.

After a problem has been identified, the task is to plan intervention. Planning intervention involves describing a child's language instead of comparing a child's response to language tasks with other children.

SUGGESTED READINGS

In *Readings in Language Disorders*

Lee, L., A screening test for syntax development. *Journal of Speech and Hearing Disorders, 35,* 103–112, 1970.

Other Readings

Cronbach, L., *Essentials of psychological testing*. New York: Harper & Row, 1970.
Uzgiris, I. C., and Hunt, J. Mc. V., *Assessment in infancy*. Urbana, Ill.: University of Illinois Press, 1975.

ADDENDUM RE: BOX XII-1, PAGE 350

The relationship of the various scores to the theoretical distribution of scores as represented by the normal curve is presented in Box XII-1. Note that the midpoint on the chart represents the mean, or average, score — the 50th percentile and the fifth stanine. On the Wechsler scales of intelligence, this score is reported as 10, if it is based upon a subtest, or 100 if it is based upon an entire scale. Tracing a score from the bottom of Box XII-1, a child with a 70 I.Q. on the entire Wechsler, or a score of 4 on one of its subtests, has scored below the fifth percentile. (That is, 95% of children the same age who took the test as a part of the original normative population, achieved higher scores.) Each of the scores is based upon the relationship of a score to the mean, and the other scores of the children who were a part of the original normative population. In this case, the child's score was 2 standard deviations below the mean — hence a z score of -2. The percent of a normally distributed population that scores between the mean and one standard deviation is 34.13%.

Part 4
GOALS OF LANGUAGE LEARNING BASED ON NORMAL DEVELOPMENT

In this section the information about the sequence of normal development that was presented in Part 2 is applied to a plan for facilitating language learning in the language-disordered child. The plan consists of a sequence of language behaviors that are the content/form/use interactions in language learning. Chapter XIII presents the underlying assumptions for the plan, an outline of the plan, and a discussion of alternatives. Chapters XIV and XV present the plan for language learning in detail. The goals of early language learning are discussed in Chapter XIV, and the goals of later language learning are discussed in Chapter XV.

Chapter XIII
A PLAN FOR
LANGUAGE
LEARNING:
ASSUMPTIONS
AND ALTERNATIVES

Once it has been determined that a child is not learning or using language as well as children of the same age (i.e., once a language disorder has been identified), the next objective of assessment is to determine the goals of intervention. Goals of language intervention are the specific language behaviors the clinician or teacher expects that a child will demonstrate after selected intervention procedures. For example, a language goal might be to produce two-word utterances (form) about action events (content) by naming both the action and the object acted on (e.g., "eat cookie," "throw ball"), as the child asks someone else to perform the action (use). One might further specify the frequency with which these forms are to be used before the goal is considered to have been met, for example, 50% of the time that the child talks about action events.

The most general goal of an intervention program is the long-term goal—to communicate effectively with language in different daily situations. In the interim, in the course of a child's participation in an intervention program, there is a continuous process of (1) setting immediate, more specific goals, (2) evaluating progress toward the goal, and (3) revising the goal as progress and learning occur, or where progress does not occur.

The more immediate goals of an intervention program are the expectations that one has for the child within a specific period of time, perhaps one month at a time. The goals that are set for the child must be realistic—goals that relate to the child's current performance and abilities with language. Goals should not be determined by what is missing from the child's language in comparison with adult language as a model; what the child already knows should determine the goals.

In order to determine goals that are reasonable and suited to the needs of a particular child, one must have a plan that provides: (1) a means of describing specific language behaviors that are part of language learning; (2) a sequence in which these specific language behaviors can best be learned; and (3) a means of determining which of these language behaviors are already a part of a particular child's language system.

Without a format for describing language, it is impossible to specify what behaviors are already a part of a child's system or what behaviors must be learned. The behaviors to be described include the content of children's language, the linguistic forms they produce, and the way in which they use these forms to talk about ideas of the world and to interact with other persons. Without a sequence of the behaviors to be learned one is left with random or intuitive guesses about which behaviors to teach first. Without a means of determining what a child already knows about language it would be impossible to utilize a plan efficiently. This plan is based on a set of assumptions about language and about facilitating language learning in the language-disordered child. The plan is presented here and is discussed more fully in the two chapters that follow. The present chapter concludes with a discussion of alternative plans, based on different assumptions.

ASSUMPTIONS THAT UNDERLIE THE PLAN FOR LANGUAGE LEARNING

The basic assumptions that underlie this plan for language learning have to do, first, with the notion that language involves interactions among the three components of content/form/use; second, with an emphasis on linguistic behaviors regardless of the cause of the disorder; third, with the use of information about normal language development as the basis for the sequence of the goals of intervention; and fourth, with the expression of goals in terms of language production explicitly and language comprehension only implicitly.

A THREE-DIMENSIONAL APPROACH

A first basic assumption is that the form of utterances—words and syntactic structures—is only one of the important components of language. Cognitive notions underlie utterances; that is, children talk because they have something to say. Form alone, apart from the underlying meaning it codes, is empty. The semantic intentions or meaning of children's utterances recur with great frequency; that is, they underlie many utterances. These intentions originate in the child's experience—in the conceptual representation of the world of objects and events. In early language development it seems clear the child does not learn sounds, words, and syntactic structures and then find meanings for these forms; instead, it appears that children learn about objects and events and then search for the forms to code various aspects of their experience. Therefore the plan does not present forms before or in isolation from the meanings the forms represent. Learning a language depends on prior conceptual representations of experience. In addition learning a language involves more than learning a code; it involves learning to use that code in varying contexts and for varying purposes. Goals of intervention and assessment must include information about the interactions among content/form/use.

A LINGUISTIC APPROACH

The second assumption is that a plan for language intervention should provide information about language as the basis for evaluating and facilitating a child's progress in the development of language—information about content/form/use interactions—regardless of the cause of the language disorder. The language that the child needs to learn is determined by the child's language performance, and not by the underlying emotional, intellectual, or physiological bases of the language disorder. Some, who view language behavior as a symptom of one or another kind of pathology, would argue that the goal of assessment and the content of an intervention program should be directly related to the underlying basis of the language problem before being concerned with the language behavior itself. One might respond that language may well be the underlying basis of certain emotional and intellectual problems and should be considered prior to or concurrent with consideration of these other problems. Such rhetoric obscures the basic problem that cause-effect relations between two correlated behaviors are often impossible to determine.

The current view of most professional persons concerned with special education and communication disorders is that any remediable problem a child presents should receive attention; no one problem should wait upon remediation of another problem unless strong evidence exists that one cannot be remediated in the presence of the other. Usually help can be given in several areas simultaneously by one or several professional persons with different kinds of competence. For the speech pathologist, information about behaviors other than language behaviors may aid in determining *how* a child can be taught, but it is the information about language behavior that determines *what* needs to be learned. The plan presented here is thus oriented to the language code and to language use as the basis of a language intervention program. It is concerned with the *learning* and the *use* of a conventional system of arbitrary signals to code ideas about the world and is thus a *linguistic* approach.

A DEVELOPMENTAL APPROACH

The third basic assumption is that the most reasonable and practical hypotheses on which to base intervention goals are to be derived from what is known about normal language development. Both conceptual development and linguistic development have built-in systems of priorities; what happens at any point in the development of either is important in influencing subsequent development. Knowledge of one part of either system will predict information about other parts, and one cannot ignore such sequential dependencies in progressing from one stage to another in language development. With respect to form, children will characteristically learn and use certain, particular words that will relate in an important way to the phrase structures they can be expected to learn and use subsequently. In turn, certain early two- and three-word phrases will be necessary antecedents to the more complex sentence structures that will be used subsequently. What may appear to be the simplest and most fundamental phrase structure in adult sentences may not necessarily be the first structure learned by children. For example, it is less conceptually complex for children to know and code the relations between agent, action, and object than to know and code notions such as plurality or the relative size or color of objects. It is suggested, therefore, that success in teaching the language system will depend on respect for certain priorities—both linguistic and cognitive priorities—in the course of development. The plan suggested here takes such priorities into account and is thus a *developmental* approach.

It can be argued that information on normal development is not appropriate for planning intervention programs for the child with a language disorder.

Since the child is, by definition, not learning language as a normal child would, it is in fact the normal learning process that has failed. Does not a developmental approach just provide the child with more of the same experience, and does not the child need something different from the normal model? To be sure, the child with a language disorder has not learned language as the normal child has, but the use of developmental information does not imply that the experiences provided will be the same experiences with which the child has already failed. However, some children may indeed need *more* of just the same experience with which they have difficulty. It is reasonable that more of the same input that is received by the 2-year-old learning language would help the older child who is performing with the language skills of a 2-year-old. As pointed out in Chapter IX, parents provide elegant models for language learning. Both the content and the form of their input to the child learning language is different from that to the more linguistically sophisticated child or to adults.

Although we are not aware of data to support our intuition, our clinical experience suggests that adults do not continue the same simple input about the here and now when talking to the older child who has the linguistic skills of a 2-year-old child. The difference in chronological age apparently influences the linguistic input to the child in the direction of more complex forms about events in the past or future (e.g., questions such as, "What did you do yesterday?", "Remember the last time you were here?", "Next week when you come. . . ."). More of the same, then, refers to more of the same environment the child may have received at a younger age but is possibly not receiving at present. The approach to intervention is developmental in that it takes into account the level of the child's language development, regardless of chronological age, for planning input.

Another objection to a developmental approach is that precisely because the child with a language disorder is older than the normal child learning language, his or her ideas about the world are probably not the same. Therefore the older child should not be expected to use language with the same content/form/use as is represented in the language behavior of a younger child. However, as discussed in Chapter I, the content of a linguistic code has to do with meaning relations that can be considered independent from specific topics or situations. Older children talk about the existence, nonexistence, and recurrence (language content) of baseball cards and pizza (specific topics of content), just as younger children talk about the same content with respect to topics such as choo-choo trains. Similarly, with respect to other content categories such as action, location, possession, and attribution, the topics can vary with age level, but the linguistic content is the same, regardless of topic. Indeed, nonexistence, recurrence, action, location, state, possession, and so forth, are the content categories represented in adult speech as well. (See Chapter I as well as Fillmore, 1968; Chafe, 1971; and Leach, 1970.)

The current choice for planning a program for assessment and intervention is between the available information about *normal language development* and *adult intuitions* about which linguistic forms (words and structures) are simplest, easiest to learn, easiest to teach, and most important. The use of clinical intuition for planning assessment and intervention has resulted in several easily recognized clichés in programs for children with language disorders. One such cliché is the widespread practice of teaching children to label objects and then teaching children to combine words. This procedure is contradicted by all the data on language development. At even the single-word level, children talk about *relations* between objects and events in their environment instead of only labeling objects. Indeed, not only the presyntax child, but also older children and adults, talk about *relations* between objects and events more often than identifying the names of objects.

A second cliché in language intervention programs that has resulted from reliance on adult intuition instead of on information about language and language development has been the emphasis on coding attribution and plurality. Children with language disorders are, typically, taught names of objects such as "ball" and "book" and then taught "balls," "books," "big ball," "red ball," "new book," and "two books." Such phrases *seem* simple, but the evidence suggests that they are cognitively and linguistically more complex than action and locative relations, which appear earlier and more frequently in normal language development.

Consideration of developmental information indicates that the normal child learning to talk is efficient both in terms of the information selected to code and the forms selected for representing this information. The coding of action relations ("throw ball," "push car") not only more closely approximates the basic structure of English sentences (subject-verb-complement) than attribution ("red ball"), but it appears to be the kind of information more often communicated by adults and older children as well. Many factors may account for the normal sequence of development—cognitive development is only one factor. Thus, the plan certainly recognizes that the older child is cognitively and emotionally different from the 2-year-old learning to talk, and such differences will be important in influencing the topics ("balls" or "baseball cards") that the child chooses to talk about. At the same time, the child needs to learn the linguistic code for representing the common properties and relations that many different objects share. Thus, information about normal language development can provide the most reasonable hypotheses for language assessment and intervention, until evidence to the contrary is available. (See Lahey, 1978; and Ruder and Smith, 1974, for further discussion of this issue.)

A PRODUCTION APPROACH

The goals to be presented here relate to the production of linguistic forms to code meanings for different functions and in different contexts. The reason for listing goals for production instead of or along with goals for comprehension is simply because more is known about the development of children's production of content/form/use interactions than is known about the development of children's comprehension of these interactions. Contrary to the expectations of many, comprehension does not always precede production. (See Chapter VIII for a discussion of the relationship between production and comprehension.) A sequence of development related to comprehension cannot yet be even approximated. The absence of comprehension goals is *not* to be interpreted to mean that comprehension is unimportant or ignored in the plan. In intervention, all content/form interactions are presented in a context that represents the meaning relation being coded. Input is stressed throughout. Thus, comprehension is being facilitated at the same time as production. Production, however, is used as the measure of progress and as the behavior by which the sequence of goals is determined.

A PLAN FOR LANGUAGE LEARNING: GOALS OF CONTENT/ FORM

The goals of content/form will be discussed here; the goals of content/form/ use interactions will be presented in the sections that follow. The goals of language intervention consist of categories of linguistic forms that code the ideas that children have of certain regularities in the world. Those ideas are not the only knowledge that children have of the world, but these are the ideas that are coded with the earliest linguistic forms.[1]

CONTENT OF DIFFERENT FORMS

The meaning categories that are presented in the plan were derived from the spontaneous speech of children with normal language development. (See Chapters IV, V, and VI for a full discussion.) The categories include the relationships among objects and events and are not topic specific. (See Chapter I for a review of this distinction between topic and content.) These categories are presented in the tree diagram in Box XIII-1, according to the kind of knowledge they include: knowledge of objects and classes of objects; knowledge about relations of objects of the same class (intraclass relations), and of objects of different classes (interclass relations); and knowledge of relations of an event to the utterance or speaker (intraevent

[1] For some children some goals of content (which deal with learning about regularities in the world), some goals of use (which deal with encouraging interpersonal communication) and some goals of form (which deal with actually making linguistic forms, either signs or vocalizations) may need to precede the plan. Some of these behaviors that are precursors of content/form/use interactions in normal language development are outlined in Chapter XIV.

BOX XIII-1 CATEGORIES OF CONTENT

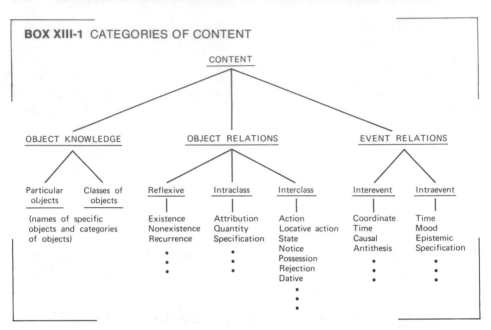

relations) and of relations between two events (interevent relations). All of the categories presented in the plan are defined in Appendix B and examples are included in Chapters XIV and XV—most have been discussed in Chapters IV, V, and VI.

It is important to remember that the categories represent regularities between content and form and are not intended to represent all that the child actually means. Thus, when a child locates an object and says "sweater chair," the utterance is categorized as locative action, but when the child points to the sweater that is on the chair and says the same words, "sweater chair," the utterance is categorized as locative state. It is not possible to know whether the child meant action in one instance and state in the other, but it is possible to categorize regularities between context and form (in this case action versus state events).

There are certainly alternative ways of categorizing what children talk about; the categories presented as language goals have evolved out of recent research in language development that has described the content of children's utterances. Certain additional kinds of utterances have been noted, as vocatives (calling someone), instrument (one object used to act on another object, as "He cut the cake with a *knife*"), affirmation ("yes," "OK"), comparatives ("more than," "bigger," etc.), greetings ("Hi," "Good morning"), routines and stereotypes ("Thank you," etc.), and comitive ("Go with me"), but these have not been included in the chart. These were not included in the plan for language intervention because they either:

1. Have not been reported in the speech of most children before the age of 3 years.
2. Did not manifest systematic developmental change.
3. Did not represent meaningful relations (e.g., routines and stereotypes).

FORM IN RELATION TO CONTENT

Some of the descriptions of form included in the plan have evolved from research in language development, such as the distinction between linear and hierarchical relations in early two-word combinations. Other descriptions of form, such as words for parts of speech, have been borrowed from the adult model for convenience of description. The plan describes form both in terms of these descriptive categories and in terms of specific lexical items or inflections such as *can't* or *-ing*. The categories and lexical items that are used in the plan are presented in Box XIII-2 according to the superordinate categories of morphology and syntax.

PHASES OF CONTENT/FORM INTERACTION

The interaction of language content (meaning) with linguistic form (words and structures) has been presented as successive phases of development. The phases present a developmental sequence of the way children code ideas of the world with linguistic forms.

The boundaries of the first five phases were determined by mean length of utterance (*MLU*) values. (See Box II-5 for directions for computing *MLU*.) This measure has been found to be a convenient index of linguistic development in the early stages of language development—until *MLU* of 3.0. It is also the measure that was used to equate subjects in the studies of normal children on which the developmental sequence was based. Behaviors in each phase represent the interactions found in samples of normal child language with the following *MLU* values: less than 1.2 in Phase 1; less than 1.5 in Phase 2; less than 2.0 in Phase 3; less than 2.5 in Phase 4; and less than 3.0 in Phase 5.

After *MLU* of 3.0, there was less regularity in the relation between *MLU* and language behaviors among Eric, Gia, Kathryn, and Peter. For this reason, the samples of language behavior data were used in a different way in order to determine phase levels 6 to 8. The language behaviors presented in Phase 6 represent the interactions found in the first two samples from Eric, Gia, Kathryn, and Peter after each had reached an *MLU* of 3.0. For example, for Gia, the samples of Phase 6 behaviors were obtained when Gia was 28 months, 1 week and 29 months, 3 weeks old and her *MLU* was 3.07 and 3.64, respectively. The language behaviors presented in Phase 7 were obtained from the next two samples, that is, the third and fourth samples after *MLU*

BOX XIII-2 CATEGORIES OF FORM AND SOME SPECIFIC FORMS

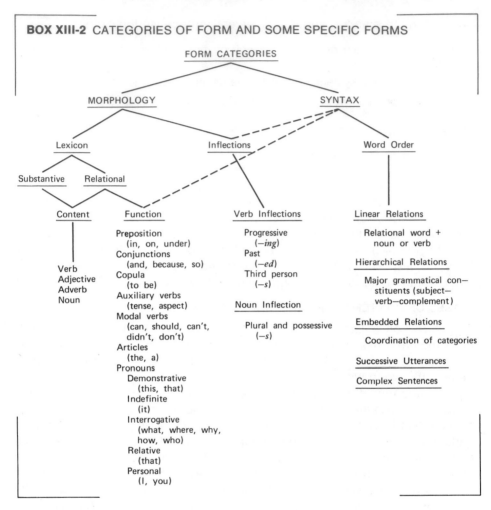

reached 3.0, and the behaviors presented in Phase 8 were obtained from all the remaining samples, after *MLU* reached 3.0.

The information about order relations, grammatical morphemes, and complex sentences represents a consensus in the early child language literature, and the principal sources have been Bloom (1970a, 1973); Bloom, Lightbown, and Hood (1975); Bloom, Miller, and Hood (1975, in *RLDev*); Bowerman (1973a); Brown (1973); Clancy, Jakobsen, and Silva (1976); de Villiers and de Villiers (1973, in *RLDev*); Hood (1977); Hood, Lahey, Lifter, and Bloom (1977); Limber (1973); Ramer (1976); and Schlesinger (1971). In contrast, other aspects of development have not received the same attention in research, and the corresponding information that is presented in the plan is necessarily more tentative. The coordination of categories that begins in

Phase 3 for example has not been studied in depth, and the sequence suggested here is the result of preliminary analyses of the original transcriptions of the language samples from Eric, Gia, Kathryn, and Peter.

Each phase presents the appearance of new language skills—that is, the *productive* use (five different utterances) of a specified form for talking about particular ideas; it was *not* based on the children's *mastery* of these interactions. Thus the increased use of these interactions continues to be a goal in succeeding phases. Information about the expected sequence of eventual mastery is available only for grammatical morphemes (Brown, 1973; see Box VI-8; and de Villiers and de Villiers, 1973, in *RLDev*) but even that is not specified by content category. Thus, complete mastery is not a part of the plan, and all of the phases should be viewed as a flow of behavior.

The phase boundaries are arbitrary and are used to help focus thinking and organize the material; they are not demarcations or entities that exist within the child, nor do they represent clear-cut differences in behavior. Although behaviors listed as new interactions in one phase are developing, those behaviors in a previous phase are continuing to be used, and behaviors in a following phase may begin to appear.

In the plan outlined in Box XIII-3 the columns represent the content categories (defined in Appendix B). The number and type of content categories follow a developmental sequence. Although only 9 categories are needed to describe the content of utterances in Phases 1 and 2, at least 21 categories are needed to represent the content of children's language in Phases 7 and 8. This increase in categories is schematically represented by the steplike increase in the number of columns. The rows represent the sequence of development from first interactions of content and form in Phase 1, at the top of the chart, to later developments in Phase 8.

The forms used to code the categories are described in the boxes at the intersections of the columns and rows. Thus the description of form listed in a box represents the type of form that has become productive to code the content listed at the top of the column. The changes in form within a column from row to row represent developmental change in how children talk about the same ideas.

In addition to noting the use of a single-word or multiword combination to code a content category, the use of specific forms (such as certain lexical items, grammatical morphemes, or question words) are noted at the appropriate phase. The language development of children includes more than the coding of particular content categories; it also includes the coordination of one or more categories in a single utterance; for example, the utterance "read my book" includes the coordination of action with possession. Such coordinations are marked by the sign "+" and the category that is embedded. For example, in Phase 3, in the first column marked "Existence," the

BOX XIII-3 A PLAN FOR LANGUAGE DEVELOPMENT GOALS: CONTENT/FORM

PHASE	EXISTENCE	NONEXISTENCE	RECURRENCE	REJECTION	DENIAL	ATTRIBUTION	POSSESSION	ACTION	LOCATIVE ACTION	LOCATIVE STATE
1	SW	SW	SW	SW	(SW)	(SW)	(SW)	SW	SW	
2	R + S	R + S S + R	R + S S + R			(Adj + N)	$\left(\begin{bmatrix} N \\ P \end{bmatrix} + N\right)$	2 Const	2 Const V + Prep Prep + N	
3	(+Attri-bution)					(+ Exist-ence)		3 Const	3 Const	2–3 Const
4	+Recur-rence +Posses-sion "a"	+Action	+Exist-ence +Action	(R + S)		+Action	+Existence	+Attribution* +Place +Non-existence* +Recurrence* +Intention −ing	+Intention	+Wh-Q +Prep
5	+ Wh-Q +Copula	"can't" "didn't" "not" (+Locative Action)	(+State)	"don't" +Action	R + S "not"	(+State)	−'s +Action +Locative Action	+Irregular past +Possession* +Rejection* +Place and Intention +Possession and Intention	V + Prep* +Possession (+Nonexistence*) Patient +3rd Per −s Mover −ing	
6		(+Locative Action)			+Locative Action	(+State)		+Attribution* (+Recurrence*)		
7							(+Wh-Q)			
8										

KEY

sw	= single word utterance	( )	= optional goal—C/F can be postponed until a later phase
R	= relational word		
S	= substantive word	[ ]	= either one or other of the bracketed forms
N	= noun	*	= first productions may be with two instead of three constituents
V	= verb		
P	= pronoun	+	= coordination of two or more categories
Prep	= preposition		
Const	= major grammatical constituents (Subject—Verb—Complement)		
Pers	= person		

	STATE	QUANTITY	NOTICE	TIME	COORDINATE	CAUSALITY	DATIVE	SPECIFIER	EPISTEMIC	MOOD	ANTITHESIS
3	2–3 Const	(−s) (numbers)									
4			2–3 Const	−ing +Action Intention +Action +Locative Action							
5	(+Attribution) (+Recurrence)	"some" "many" "all"		−ing +Locative Action- Mover Irregular Past +Action 3rd Pers −s +Locative Action- Patient	SUCCESSIVE CLAUSES Intraclausal "and" (Interclausal "and")		N + N	"this/that"			
6	(+Possession)			"now"		("and")	+Prep "to" "for"	"the"			
7					"and then"	"because" "so"			("what")	"can"	"and" ("but")
8			Complement "what"	Time Specification "when" Progressive "be" Past -ed 3rd Pers −s		+Wh-Q		Relative Clause "that" "where"		["should"] ["have to"]	

entry "+ Attribution" indicates that attribution, such as "dirty ball," is coordinated with existence, such as "that ball," to form utterances such as "that dirty ball." Empty boxes do not mean that the child has ceased to code a particular content category but, instead, that *no new forms* are used; the child codes the category with the same forms used in previous phases.

There is an important limitation (by design) in the plan that needs to be pointed out and underlined at the outset, and then again as the plan is used. The interactions represented here have to do with only the meaning of the actual linguistic elements and the relations between linguistic elements that are used by the child. In a particular situation, there will often be many different aspects and nuances of an event that will be communicated in various ways—through voice tone, gesture, facial expression, and eye gaze. However, the focus on the interaction of form with content has to do with only the meaning of linguistic elements in relation to one another. The major issue is how children use linguistic form to represent or code meaning. Any meanings that are conveyed by other mechanisms are certainly important, but do not contribute to an understanding of what children know about the linguistic code for representing information about objects and events in the world. For example, if a child says, "go outside," it may be quite clear that the child has the *intention* to go outside (the child might get a coat, run to the door, etc.). However, with the utterance "go outside" only the relation between a locative action and place has been coded, and not any of the accompanying aspects of the event—such as *intending* to go outside, or *who* will go outside. Similarly, if the child says "sweater chair" while carrying a sweater to the chair, only the relation between an object (sweater) and a place (chair) has been coded in a locative action event. The event is a locative action event because the relation between "sweater" and "chair" is dynamic (includes movement) and involves a change in location (to the chair). But the child has *not coded* the actual movement (putting or carrying) and has not coded intention, any more than the facts that the sweater is green and handknitted by Grandmother, or that the chair is Mommy's usual reading chair. (See the discussion of implicit and explicit meaning in messages in Chapter II.)

Although the utterance may be categorized as a locative action utterance because it includes two major grammatical constituents of locative action utterances (object-place) in a locative action event, the child is not given credit for coding the locative action itself. Likewise, if two utterances are juxtaposed and the relationship between them is temporal (e.g., the child says "put here/sit down" while putting the sweater on the chair and sitting on it), she or he will be credited with talking *about* sequential events with successive utterances, but not with coding the temporal sequence, as with "and" or "and then." The plan, then, quite literally presents the interaction between form and meaning: the issue at question has to do with how much of the child's semantic intention actually gets translated (represented or coded) by the child's knowledge of language, in an actual utterance.

It is also important to reiterate that a goal represents the productive use of an interaction and not complete learning. A goal may be considered attained if the child is able to spontaneously use a form to code a particular content category without prompting and in a few contexts that were not used in training. It is not expected that the child will immediately use the content/ form interaction in all possible contexts. Increasing the frequency of the interactions is an ongoing goal. Thus, while the child is expected to use two-word utterances to code action relations before completing Phase 2, it is expected that single-word utterances will still be used to code the same relations. Plural -s is presented in Phase 3, but it is expected that the child will continue to omit this morpheme in many contexts until well into Phase 4. (Note the plural morpheme is not used in obligatory contexts 90% of the time until an *MLU* of 2.25; Brown, 1973.) Thus a goal does not mean that complete learning of that interaction should occur in a phase, but that productive use of the new interaction should be established before moving to a new phase. Goals from previous phases continue to remain as goals until complete learning is accomplished. Such a pattern reflects the normal course of language learning.

Certain behaviors have been placed in parentheses to indicate either their infrequent use or variability among children in the sequence of acquisition. Such behaviors should be considered as optional in their phase placement; that is, they may be delayed until a later phase.

With the exception of connectives, modal verbs, and a few grammatical morphemes, actual lexical items are not listed because the items selected will vary with topic, and appropriate topics will differ greatly among children. Some criteria for selection are discussed in Chapter XXI. Growth in vocabulary is a continual goal. Although it is not represented on the chart, it is expected that new lexical items will be gradually and continually incorporated into the program. The rate at which new items are added and specific lexical items selected will vary with the individual child's rate of learning, interests, and the context.

Verb categories (action, locative action, notice, state) in many phases are marked by the number of constituents included in the utterance—constituents defined as the major grammatical constituents of subject-verb-complement. (Note that complement can include two constituents, object and place, in locative categories.) Embeddings within a verb category, marked with a + and the name of the category (e.g., possession), indicate the presence of at least two constituents plus the embedded category; when an embedding is marked with an asterisk it indicates that the inclusion of this complexity within the utterance may result in a reduction of the full three-term constituent structure (subject-verb-complement) to two terms—usually by omission of the subject. (Recall also, that this reduction of constituent structure is likely to occur with the introduction of new lexical items. See Chapter VI for a discussion of factors influencing reduction.) The development at each phase is discussed with examples in Chapters XIV and XV.

It is particularly important to stress that the plan is a clinical tool—a plan for the goals of language learning—and was not designed as a means for determining qualitative differences between normal and deviant language. The sequence is based on the study of normal development, both research reported and in progress, but there is variability both within and among children, some of which is noted on the chart either by parentheses, brackets, or asterisks. The plan is an hypothesis about the sequence in which content/form can best be learned through intervention, and not a list of behaviors that are the correct behaviors for a particular *MLU*. If a language-disordered child with an *MLU* of 2.75 is missing behaviors that are listed in Phases 3 and 4 but has some behaviors that are listed in Phase 6, this suggests only that those missing behaviors in Phases 3 and 4 should be goals of intervention before other behaviors listed in later phases. The plan should *not* be used to describe the child's language as qualitatively different. If the intent of describing the child's language is to determine if qualitative differences exist, comparisons should be made with the original research on which the plan was based. (See Chapter XI for a discussion of determining qualitative differences.)

A PLAN FOR LANGUAGE LEARNING: GOALS OF CONTENT/ FORM/USE

Knowledge of the language code has been described as content/form interactions, while skills involved in using the language code have been referred to as content/form/use interactions. Goals for facilitating language learning must take into consideration both the contexts in which the content/ form interactions are used, that is, the situations in which children speak or sign, and the purpose or functions for which they speak or sign.

The use of language can be considered from a number of perspectives. For the purpose of outlining some developmental aspects of use that can serve as goals, two factors will be considered: the context of the speech event and the function of the utterance (i.e., the desired result). Each of these factors is further dichotomized. Contexts are dichotomized into linguistic and nonlinguistic contexts, and functions are dichotomized into intrapersonal (mathetic) and interpersonal (pragmatic) functions. Some of the elements of each are schematized in Box XIII-4. These distinctions are important because they change developmentally. Nonlinguistic context also includes the child's growing awareness of the need to adapt messages to the listener— eventually through the use of alternative forms to code the same content for the same use.

BOX XIII-4 CATEGORIES OF USE

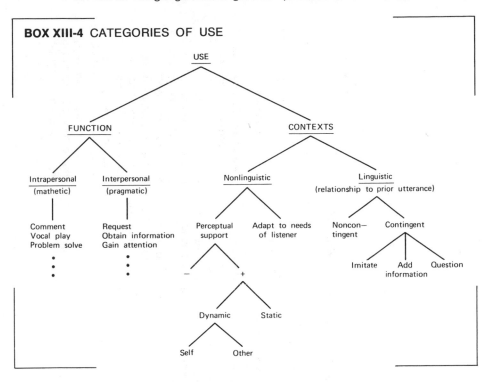

Observations of children learning language without difficulty suggest that there are developmental aspects of learning to use messages that parallel the learning of content/form interactions presented earlier. A summary of certain aspects of use are outlined on the use chart (Box XIII-5) according to the phases of development presented in the section on goals related to content/form interactions. The rows again represent developmental sequence. Phases have been grouped when differences in use have not been found among the phases. The columns refer to the contexts in which, and the functions for which, messages are produced. The first column concerns the functions of language—the purpose for which the child produces the language he or she knows. Considered under context are both the nonlinguistic and the linguistic contexts in which language is used. Nonlinguistic contexts include the child's growing ability to talk about objects that are not within the perceptual field and about events in which the child is not a participant. Last, nonlinguistic context includes the growing adaptation to the different needs of different listeners. Linguistic context, on the other hand, includes the child's changing responses to the linguistic input of others—the development of discourse.

BOX-XIII-5 A PLAN FOR LANGUAGE DEVELOPMENT GOALS: CONTENT/FORM/USE

USE

FUNCTION	CONTEXT		Linguistic
	Nonlinguistic		
	Perceptual Support	Other	Relationship to Verbalizations of Others
P H A S E S 1 Intrapersonal (mathetic) 2 Comment (most frequent)— Vocal play 3 Interpersonal (pragmatic) Regulate other's actions Obtain objects Call attention to self or objects Social interaction—routines	Communicates about objects and events that are present (+Here+Now)	Most utterances about a. What child is about to do b. What child wants others to do c. What child is doing	Majority of utterances follow the verbalizations of others although not usually contingent on them Imitation appears more after nonquestions than questions of others When utterances are related to (contingent on) others' verbalizations: most likely related by virtue of meaning and context—not linguistic structure (e.g., "Let's build a house", "Get block")

4 **5** As above, plus Interpersonal Obtain information (identity-location) (Note: Many questions are asked that are not to obtain information, but rather may serve a mathetic function)	Increasing number of utterances about Immediate past Imminent future	Increasing number of utterances about what others are doing	Number of spontaneous utterances increases although they are not the most frequent Other utterances tend to be more often contingent on others' verbalizations, as expansions that are linguistically related, in that they continue the same verb relation as in the other's utterance (e.g., "Let's build a house," "build it right here")
6 **7** **8** As above, plus Interpersonal Obtain information about or clarification of another's utterance (Increase in interpersonal function)	Increased distancing from referent (−Here−Now)	*Listener* Gradual adaptation to listener differences and communicative needs	Spontaneous utterances now greater than adjacent utterances; imitation is rare Adjacent utterances are mostly contingent and communicate new information

The information in these two presentations of goals for language learning, one with the goals of content/form and the other with the goals of content/form/use, is further described, with examples, in the next two chapters. In Chapters XVI and XVII, procedures for determining which of these behaviors a child already knows are discussed.

ALTERNATIVE PLANS

There are a number of alternative plans for facilitating language learning based on other assumptions. A few that are based on a linguistic approach are discussed below. These alternative plans differ from the plan presented here in that either the sequence of goals is not specified or is different, or in that all three dimensions of language (content, form, and use) are not taken into account.

THE SEQUENCING OF LANGUAGE BEHAVIORS

As noted earlier, the sequence of language goals within many language programs has been determined primarily by adult intuition. Those forms that adults (clinicians, teachers, parents) felt were most important for the child to learn, or easiest for the child to learn, have been taught first. It is now apparent that the intuitions that adults may have about the relative simplicity or importance of different words or syntactic structures do not agree with the kinds of words and sentence relations that young children normally use when they first learn to talk.

Adult intuitions about language learning have similarly resulted in pre-scriptions for teaching the correct adult model of a sentence instead of approximations to that model, for fear of allowing incorrect productions to become established. Thus, when teaching sentences like "The boy is chasing the cow," each morpheme (as *the, is, -ing*) is given equal weight. A child might be taught to imitate the entire sentence, often by chaining the words in sequence (the—the boy—the boy is—etc.) or backward (cow—the cow—chasing the cow), or by selecting the new feature (e.g., "is") and chaining from that (*is—is* chasing—, boy *is* chasing—, etc.). However, in the normal process of learning language, the basic grammatical relations (such as between "boy" and "chase," and between "chase" and "cow") are expressed long before the articles ("the"), auxiliaries ("is"), or morphologi-cal inflections (*-ing*) are added. The normal child learning language is most likely to say "chase cow" and then "boy chase cow" before learning "chasing cow" or "the boy chase the cow." It would seem reasonable that the more appropriate hypotheses to use in planning the goals of an intervention program ought to come from the information that is available about sequential development in normal language acquisition. It is certainly conceivable that the use of adult intuitions to prescribe a sequence of treatment goals may have partly accounted for the fact that spontaneous and creative use of language is often reported not to occur with intervention programs.

The use of information from normal language development to sequence the behaviors to be taught in a language intervention program has been recommended by Lee (1966, 1974), Miller and Yoder (1972a, 1974), and Rees (1972b) and has been applied by W. A. Bricker (1972), Bricker and Bricker (1970, 1974), Crystal, Fletcher, and Garman (1976), Eisenson (1972), Harris and Taenzer (1976), Leonard (1975b), MacDonald and Blott (1974), Miller and Yoder (1972b), and Stremel and Waryas (1974). There has been, however, considerable variation in the developmental data that have been used and the extent to which developmental data have been applied in conjunction with adult intuitions. For example, Stremel and Waryas (1974) move from an initial vocabulary of a few nouns and verbs to the following sequence:

1. Noun + verb (subject + verb) and verb + noun (verb + object) (when the object constituent may include object, location, adverb, and where the verb may include state), then
2. Noun + verb + noun, then
3. Noun + verb (-*ing*) + noun.

These are taught before possession, attribution, existence, or negation relations in two-word utterances, as contrary to plans presented here and by Ingram and Eisenson (1972). Ingram and Eisenson presented two goals of coordination:

1. Verb + *in* + adjective + noun.
2. Verb + *in* + possessive + noun.

before goals that include three constituents (subject-verb-object), contrary to the plans here and by Stremel and Waryas. The developmental data from which some of the sequences were derived are not clear, nor is it clear how much the sequences were influenced by adult intuitions. Most programs have focussed on early syntactic constructions—unquestionably because this is the stage of normal development that has received the most attention by researchers and about which the most is known. In addition, a few have applied the earlier developmental data that are available to children's preverbal behaviors (Bricker and Bricker, 1974; and Eisenson, 1972) and single-word utterances (Miller and Yoder, 1974).

CONSIDERATION OF THE THREE DIMENSIONS OF LANGUAGE

Goals also vary in the extent to which they emphasize form alone, or linguistic forms in interaction with content. Recent research on language development has repeatedly emphasized the importance of semantics in language learning (e.g., Bloom, 1970a, 1971, 1973; Bloom, Lightbown, and Hood, 1975; Brown, 1973; and Bowerman, 1973a; Greenfield, Smith, and Laufer, 1972; Schlesinger, 1971, 1974). As a result, the emphasis on semantics in language teaching programs has become more apparent. Nevertheless, many goals appear more oriented to linguistic forms than to informational content. Many programs still present single-word utterance development in terms of the number of nouns or verbs to be learned and present syntactic development in terms of the combinations of parts of speech (e.g., noun-verb or preposition-noun combinations). Semantics is brought into such programs when the meanings that are coded by the forms are mentioned, and the necessity of teaching linguistic forms in meaningful context is stressed (Stremel and Waryas, 1974; and Eisenson, 1972). The content of language has generally been considered only to the extent that linguistic forms are never empty—words and structures necessarily have referents. The problem is that there have been few attempts to organize the *content* and *use* of language in the same way that linguistic forms have been organized and presented. There is, however, a recent trend in this direction (Miller and Yoder, 1974; MacDonald and Blott, 1974; and the plan presented in this chapter and elaborated on in Chapters XIV and XV).

Development of the use of language has remained the weakest part of all language programs, perhaps because information on how normal children learn to use language is sparse. Programs include commenting and demands (or tacts and mands in Skinnerian terms), labeling, responding to questions, and in some cases asking questions, but there has been no attempt to present a developmental sequence of these uses of language. The ability to talk about objects and events that are removed in time and space from the immediate situation has rarely been programmed; the ability to distinguish between the child or another person as the agent of an action has rarely been programmed; the ability to respond to the verbalizations of others, taking into account the form or content of the input stimulus, has rarely been programmed. The approach that is outlined here has made a first attempt at considering some of these variables in the use of language. Obviously, additions will be made as new information is gained.

There has been a shift in the ways in which the goals in language programs have been sequenced—away from sequences determined by adult intuitions of relative simplicity and ease of learning and toward sequences based, at least to some extent, on what is known about the normal sequence of development. There has been a corresponding shift, influenced also by information about normal development, from consideration of linguistic form alone to an increasing emphasis on the ideas coded by linguistic forms. There is more and more apparent awareness that the functional use of the language code deserves more attention if the language that is taught to children is not to result in only stereotypic and limited use in specific stimulus situations. Unquestionably, any program that is directed to teaching language will probably increase the use of these behaviors to some extent and in some way. It is the efficiency of teaching different behaviors to children that may vary, in addition to the kinds of goals that are eventually achieved. The ultimate goal of any language program is to develop language skills that will enable a child to be linguistically creative and to use language as a means of representing and exchanging ideas. Although most language programs have achieved some success toward reaching these goals, there has been an expanding interest and enthusiasm for more refined use of developmental data to bring even greater success.

Any program is but a first hypothesis about the language behaviors that are goals and about the sequence in which they can be expected to develop. Further information about normal development, facilitating language learning, and the influence of environmental and physical factors on language learning will need to be incorporated into any sequence of goals for language learning. The plan proposed here is, thus, an hypothesis based on currently available data about normal language development. The assumptions and overall design of the plan may not change, but the specifics of the plan will continue to be adapted to new information.

SUMMARY

The plan for language learning presented in this chapter is based on four assumptions—assumptions about language in general, and about facilitating language development in the language-disordered child in particular. These assumptions are that: (1) language is three-dimensional and includes content/form/use interactions; (2) the goals of language intervention should be based first on linguistic behavior and not on etiology or correlates of the language disorder; (3) the best hypotheses for determining the goals of an intervention program currently come from information about normal development; and (4) goals are best described in terms of the child's productions, since developmental information about comprehension is not yet available.

The plan is presented in two parts; the first outlines the goals related to the interactions of content with form, and the second outlines the goals related to the interactions of use with content and form. A number of alternative plans, based on alternative assumptions, are discussed. Differences among these alternative plans and the plan presented here include the dimensions of language that are incorporated and the sequence of goals.

SUGGESTED READINGS

Other Readings about Assumptions:

Engelmann, S., How to construct effective language programs for the poverty child. In F. Williams (Ed.), *Language and poverty*. Chicago: Markham Publishing Co., 1970.

Miller, J., and Yoder, D., On developing the content for a language teaching program. *Mental retardation*, *10*, 9–11, 1972.

Rees, N., Bases of decision in language training. *Journal of Speech and Hearing Disorders, 38,* 98–110, 1972.

Ruder, K., and Smith, M., Issues in language training. In R. Schiefelbusch and L. L. Lloyd (Eds.), *Language perspectives: Acquisition, retardation and intervention*. Baltimore: University Park Press, 1974.

Other Plans of Intervention:

Crystal, D., Fletcher, P., and Garman, M., *The grammatical analysis of language disability: A procedure for assessment and remediation*. London: Arnold, 1976.

Gray, B. B., and Ryan, B., *A language training program for the non-language child*. Champaign, Ill.: Research Press, 1973.

Ingram, D., and Eisenson, J., Therapeutic approaches in congenitally aphasic children. In. J. Eisenson (Ed.), *Aphasia in children*. New York: Harper & Row, 1972.

Lee, L., *Developmental sentence analysis*. Evanston, Ill.: Northwestern University Press, 1974.

MacDonald, J. D., and Blott, J. P., Environmental language intervention: The rationale for a diagnostic and training strategy through rules, context and generalizations. *Journal of Speech and Hearing Disorders, 39,* 244–257, 1974.

Miller, J., and Yoder, D., An ontogenetic language teaching strategy for retarded children. In R. Schiefelbusch and L. Lloyd (Eds.), *Language perspectives: Acquisition, retardation and intervention*. Baltimore: University Park Press, 1974.

Stremel, K., and Waryas, C., A behavioral psycholinguistic approach to language training. In L. McReynolds (Ed.), *Developing systematic procedures for training children's language*. American Speech and Hearing Association Monograph #18, 1974.

Chapter XIV
GOALS OF EARLY LANGUAGE LEARNING

The goals of early language learning presented in this chapter are Phases 1, 2, and 3 of the plan that was outlined in Chapter XIII, along with certain of the precursors of language learning that were discussed in Chapter III. In normal language development, children demonstrate evidence of having categorized some of the regularities in their linguistic and nonlinguistic environment before they show evidence of having induced the conventional interactions among language content/form/use. Certain of these precursory behaviors are listed here as goals of early language learning. They are goals that should occur with the goals for Phase 1 for children who are *prelinguistic* in that they have not yet begun to use words or signs. Although these precursory behaviors develop normally before the behaviors listed in Phase 1, it is not clear that each of these behaviors must be established *before* Phase 1 behaviors are learned—that is, that each is a *prerequisite* to learning about the interactions of content/form/use; and second, the behaviors listed as precursors continue to develop throughout the early stages of language learning. The emphasis placed on precursory goals in an intervention program would vary with different children according to their individual readiness to learn Phase 1 goals.

PRECURSORY GOALS OF LANGUAGE USE

Infants communicate with others throughout their first year of life and, in the latter part of the first year, communication becomes more and more intentional. Precursory goals of language use have to do with communication; children learn to communicate *before* they learn and *as* they are learning the content and the conventional forms for communication. The precursory goals of language use include reciprocal gazing, regulating the behaviors of others, and calling attention to objects and events.

Reciprocal Gaze Patterns

Reciprocal gaze is an early form of interpersonal communication between caregivers and children. Such gazing usually takes place in a more general context of interpersonal exchange such as smiling, touching, feeding, and vocalizing (see Chapter III). It is not expected that the child will sit still and maintain eye contact in the absence of other activity, instead, the goal is the frequent exchange of gaze in the context of other interpersonal activities such as greeting, showing, giving, and pointing.

Regulating the Behaviors of Others

In the latter part of the first year of life infants attempt (and generally succeed to some extent) to manipulate the behavior of others. The infant, without linguistic forms, requests attention and assistance and objects, by gesture, facial expression, and nonlinguistic vocalization. All attempts to communicate with another should be rewarded in the early stages of language learning, even though the child does not use the appropriate content/form interactions. There is no evidence to support the notion that inhibiting a child's nonlinguistic attempts at communication will enhance the learning of content/form/use interactions; in fact, the opposite may be true. Children learn to communicate before they learn the conventional forms for communication.

Calling Attention to Objects and Events

After children have begun to engage in reciprocal gaze and, after they have begun to regulate the behaviors of others, they should be encouraged to direct the attention of others to objects or events, first by showing and giving an object to an adult, and then by pointing to objects.

These goals, which represent some of the normal child's behaviors that precede the learning of content/form/use interactions, are suggested as goals of early language learning that go along with goals of Phase 1. However, they are behaviors that continue to develop throughout the pre-school years and can be encouraged along with all language learning activities in the contexts of an intervention program.

PRECURSORY GOALS OF LANGUAGE CONTENT

Certain nonverbal behaviors precede the development of linguistic behaviors and reflect the development of the cognitive skills that are prerequisite to language development or representational thinking (i.e., the ability to represent something in mind when it is not present). Representational thought is important, not just for talking about things that are not present, but for the formation of categories that words represent. A noun, for example, does not only refer to a particular object, but to a class of objects that come together as a class because of certain properties and functions that they share. In order to form such a class so that a linguistic form can be learned in relation to it, it is necessary to have some sort of mental schema or representation of the relevant objects that were experienced in the past. Some of the behaviors that give evidence of developing representational thought are presented below with the contexts in which their development might be observed and encouraged in the course of an intervention program.

Language training for a child with the apparent cognitive skills of a 6- to 8-month-old infant would begin with the goals and procedures in this phase of the intervention program.

The behaviors listed here will continue to develop into the subsequent phases, with other nonlinguistic behaviors that emerge subsequently. At this point in development and, correspondingly, at this point in an intervention program, it is *not expected* that the child will use or understand speech. However, the child will be spoken to about what he or she is doing, is about to do, and appears to want others to do. The prelinguistic goals of intervention have to do with the behaviors of the child and play with objects.

SPECIFIC GOALS FOR REFLEXIVE OBJECT RELATIONS AND INTRACLASS RELATIONS

Certain goals that are preliminary to the interaction between content/form have to do with the formation of the concept of self, the child as perceiver and actor, and the formation of categories of objects. Objects within a category relate to one another or a single object relates to itself, as objects appear, disappear, and recur in the child's perceptions and activities. Similarly, children come to realize themselves as constant factors in various events that involve their own movements as well as the movements of other persons and objects. The realization of such constancy of self and permanence of objects is a necessary precondition for the eventual use of a linguistic form in relation to self or in relation to objects.

Each general goal presented below will be elaborated in terms of more specific subgoals that represent particular behaviors that contribute to reaching the more general goal.

Searching for Objects That Disappear: Recurrence

In early infancy, the disappearance of an object causes no more than a fleeting glance in the direction of its disappearance. The child acts as though the object does not exist unless it is within the perceptual field. A more prolonged search by the child requires that the object be mentally represented, and there are several activities that can be directed toward that goal. The first requirement is to have an object or person that has strong interest value for the child, such as a favorite toy or food (Box XIV-1).

An object may be removed from sight slowly so that the child can follow its path. Initially the object or person can be only partly hidden, generally in the same location. As the child is successful in such search activities, the process of hiding can gradually become more complex with complete disappearance, more rapid rate of disappearance, and new locations.

BOX XIV-1 AN EXAMPLE OF FACILITATION IN AN EXCHANGE BETWEEN THE NINETEENTH-CENTURY TEACHER JEAN-MARC-GASPARD ITARD AND HIS PUPIL, VICTOR, "THE WILD BOY OF AVEYRON." ITARD USED TASKS RELATED TO OBJECT PERMANENCE AS A MEANS OF ENCOURAGING SOCIAL INTERACTIONS WITH VICTOR, WHEN GAMES MORE APPROPRIATE FOR HIS AGE FAILED TO HOLD HIS ATTENTION. THIS ILLUSTRATES HOW DIFFERENT GOALS CAN BE FACILITATED SIMULTANEOUSLY WITH SIMILAR ACTIVITIES (from Itard, 1962, p. 21)

Here is one, for example, which I often arranged for him at the end of the meal when I took him to dine with me in town. I placed before him without any symmetrical order, and upside down, several little silver cups, under one of which was placed a chestnut. Quite sure of having attracted his attention, I raised them one after the other excepting that which covered the nut. After having thus shown him that they contained nothing, and having replaced them in the same order, I invited him by signs to seek in his turn. The first cup under which he searched was precisely the one under which I had hidden the little reward due to him. Thus far, there was only a feeble effort of memory. But I made the game insensibly more complicated. Thus after having by the same procedure hidden another chestnut, I changed the order of all the cups, slowly, however, so that in this general inversion he was able, although with difficulty, to follow with his eyes and with his attention the one which hid the precious object. I did more; I placed nuts under two or three of the cups and his attention, although divided between these three objects, still followed them none the less in their respective changes, and directed his first searches towards them. Moreover, I had a further aim in mind. This judgment was after all only a calculation of greediness. To render his attention in some measure less like an animal's, I took away from this amusement everything which had connection with his appetite, and put under the cups only such objects as could not be eaten. The result was almost as satisfactory and this exercise became no more than a simple game of cups, not without advantage in provoking attention, judgment, and steadiness in his gaze.

Ultimately, other objects may be placed as obstacles in the search, such that the child will have to displace the obstacle object in order to reach the hidden object that is the object of search. (See Box III-2.)

The subgoals are presented here sequentially and were derived from the descriptions of the development of object permanence by Piaget (1954):

1. To gaze in the direction of a moving object, visually tracking its movements.

2. To gaze at a moving object and look for its reappearance after it disappears behind an obstacle (such as a screen).

3. To gaze at a moving object that is then partially hidden by a stationary object (or screen) and actively search for it when it fails to reappear from behind the stationary object.

4. To gaze at a moving object that is then entirely hidden by a stationary object (or screen) and actively search for it when it fails to reappear from behind the screen.

5. To watch as an object is first hidden behind one obstacle and then a second obstacle, and then actively search for the object behind the second obstacle.

6. To actively search for an object behind a second obstacle, where the child has not seen the object hidden the second time.

Causing Objects to Disappear

The child has come to discover that objects exist even after they have disappeared, by first watching them reappear and then actively searching for them after they have disappeared in order to cause them to reappear. Such relations of an object to itself is, in this way, brought into relation to the child's movements. The child's actions on the objects again affirms for the child that objects are permanent events when the child causes objects to disappear. Such observations as these have been derived from Piaget's (1954) descriptions of child behavior in the period of sensorimotor intelligence before the age of 2 years, but they are most simply affirmed by observing two of the most popular of infant play behaviors: playing peek-a-boo and playing with a jack-in-the-box.

With each of these subgoals, the child first watches someone else perform the action and then the child repeats the action. After each disappearance, the child is expected to retrieve the object (recurrence), as in the previous goal to search for objects that disappear. Subgoals are:

1. To drop objects into a box and cover the box each time.
2. To drop two different objects into two boxes.
3. To hide an object under a cloth on the table or behind a screen.
4. To hide an object under the table or under a chair.
5. To hide several objects in the same place.
6. To hide several objects in different places.

When the child searched for an object or made objects disappear, there was a relation between the object and the child that was, in effect, an intercategory relation (between two objects, one of which was the child). There are subsequent goals related to the development of content in language that have to do with certain other ways that objects relate to one another.

SPECIFIC GOALS FOR INTERCLASS RELATIONS

There are relationships between objects or between objects and persons that are understood by the child before these same relations are coded by language, (i.e., before the interaction of content with form). As children become aware of such intercategory relations between objects, they may already be using words to talk about earlier intracategory content relations (i.e., to name objects or comment on their existence, disappearance, and recurrence). The predominant relation between objects that forms a major content or meaning category in the subsequent development of language is the action relation.

Acting on Different Objects in Similar Ways (Nonspecific Play)

There are certain actions that can be performed on objects regardless of the different perceptual properties or different functions that different objects might have. For example, children learn that objects with different tastes and textures can, nevertheless, be mouthed and many objects can be eaten. Many kinds of objects can be dropped, thrown, or banged. This kind of play with objects, where different objects are manipulated in the same way, was described as an important step in children's development of play in the second year by Sinclair (1970, in *RLDev*). Subgoals are:

1. To watch as different objects (such as a ball, a brush, a piece of paper, a crayon, a book, a shoe, a hat) are, for example (1) dropped to the floor, (2) banged on a table, (3) put into a box, (4) rubbed along the floor, and (5) patted with a hand.

2. To perform the same movements and actions with different objects, after watching them performed by someone else.

Acting on Different Objects in Prescribed Ways (Object-Specific Play)

There are certain actions that can be performed with only certain objects, depending on the perceptual properties and functions that different objects have and that distinguish among them. For example, children learn that a ball can be rolled, but a book, a shoe, or a hat cannot; a hat goes on a head, but a ball or a book do not; a piece of paper can be crumpled, but a ball or a shoe cannot; a crayon can make marks on paper, but a ball or a shoe cannot; a cookie can be eaten, but a ball or a shoe cannot (Box XIV-2). Subgoals are:

1. To watch as two different objects (such as a ball and a brush, or a piece of paper and a rubber band) are first manipulated in the same way. Examples: rolling both the ball and the brush, then brushing hair with both the ball and

---

BOX XIV-2

The distinction between object-specific play, where the child's manipulation of an object is different according to the properties of the object, and nonspecific play, where the child treats objects in similar ways regardless of the differences among them, was described by Sinclair (1970, in *RLDev*) in her description of the normal development of patterns of play in the second year of life. The same distinction has also been made by Bricker and Bricker (1974) in an early language intervention program that has stressed the importance of learning the nonlinguistic behaviors that are preliminary to learning language behaviors in development. They reported a comparison between two groups of 2-year-old children playing with objects, one a group of mentally retarded children and the other a group of children developing normally. The retarded children used more nonspecific play behaviors, while the normally developing children used more object-specific play.

---

the brush; crumpling both the piece of paper and the rubber band, then stretching both the paper and the rubber band. The differences between the different objects in the same tasks should be exaggerated with facial expression and the like.

2. To perform the same movements with two different objects as in Subgoal 1, after watching them performed by someone else.
3. To choose an object (among a group of two, then three, then four objects, etc.) and perform appropriate action, such as crumpling paper, rolling a ball, brushing hair, and the like.

Acting on Two Objects in Relation to Each Other

Actions thus far have consisted of movements by the child to affect a single object in a particular way. Two or more objects can be brought into relation to one another with respect to a specific action. Such interobject relations can be those (1) in which one object acts on another object (with the child or another person as the agent making the action occur), or (2) locative actions in which the child or another person causes one object to be changed from one place to another place. Subgoals are:

1. To watch someone else cause one object to act on a second object. Examples: a doll riding a horse; an animal riding in a truck; a doll drinking from a bottle, or a cup; a bird pecking at some "food" in a dish; a monkey swinging from a tree; and a puppet rolling a ball.
2. To perform the same movements that cause one object to act on a second object, as in Subgoal 1.
3. To watch someone else change the location of an object from one place to

another place. Examples: moving a doll from one room in a toy house to another; moving a hat from one doll to another; and moving a ribbon from around one animal to around another.

4. To perform the same movements that cause one object to change from one place to another place.

The goals that have been presented so far have to do with objects, and the ways that objects (including persons as objects) can be related to one another. Children learn such things about objects without knowing the words or linguistic structures to use in talking about, or understanding when others talk about, objects and object relations. The interaction of content/form is the knowledge of the words and the linguistic structures that code or represent such objects and object relations.

PRECURSORY GOALS OF LANGUAGE FORM

Before learning the words and the linguistic structures that code or represent the content of language, normal children also display evidence of some knowledge of form. Infants, for example, vocalize frequently, and their later vocalizations include some of the segmental and suprasegmental features of the adult language. Thus, production of the linguistic signal should be a goal related to early language learning. It is again stressed, however, that while the child is not expected to have learned words or signs at this point, the context of facilitating these goals should involve input that is meaningful. Goals of form follow.

Imitating Movement and Vocalization

The imitation of body movement and sound vocalization can eventually lead to the movements and sounds that provide the forms of language. The goals of imitation are not only goals of form, but are also related to both content and use. In order to imitate the child must attend to and respond to another person—an aspect of use. And the movements and sounds that the child imitates are often meaningful to the child and to the context in which they occur—aspects of content.

At first, one may be able to instigate behavior by the child, either motor or vocal behavior, by copying the child immediately after the behavior has been produced. When this can be accomplished, then the time delay between the child's original action and copying the child's action can be carefully increased, until it is relatively easy to stimulate the child to imitate any action that is a part of the usual repertoire, even if it has not occurred for a long period of time. Eventually some of the child's behaviors can be combined in ways in which they have not been combined before—so that it is possible to form a novel pattern made up of behaviors already familiar to the child. At the same time, new behaviors that are somewhat similar to old behaviors might be attempted, as the child is presented with more new behaviors.

The following subgoals are presented sequentially and were derived from the descriptions of the development of imitation by Piaget (1962).

1. To imitate body movements that the child has already made, and can see himself or herself make.

2. To imitate vocalizations that the child has already made.

3. To imitate body movements that the child has made, but that the child cannot see himself or herself make.

4. To imitate vocalizations and body movements that the child may not have made, where the body movements are those that the child can see himself or herself make.

5. To imitate new models that the child may not have made, where the movements are those that the child cannot see himself or herself make.

Producing the Linguistic Signal (Either Sign or Vocalization) in Varying Degrees of Approximation to the Adult Model

First goals would be simply an attempt to produce the word or sign in relation to the goals of content and use. Only gradually would one expect the child to approximate more closely both the suprasegmental and the segmental features of the model (i.e., to say the word or make the sign more clearly and precisely). It is important to emphasize that exact reproductions are not expected until the child has achieved the behaviors listed in the eight phases of content/form/use interactions. Just how phonological, syntactic, and lexical development correlate with one another in normal development is not known, but many normal children, for example, have not mastered the phonemes of the adult language until the age of 7 years (Poole, 1934; and Templin, 1957), when their language skills are well beyond the skills in Phase 8. It is also important to reiterate that the facilitation of this goal should *not* include imitation of the linguistic signal outside of a meaningful context; for most children the production of forms should be encouraged in the context of related content and use. (See Chapter XXI.)

GOALS OF CONTENT/FORM/USE: PHASES 1, 2, AND 3

The first phases of language learning that are presented here represent the behaviors that have been described for normal children with *MLU* less than 2.0. Presented first are the goals of use that interact with content/form in Phases 1, 2, and 3.

GOALS OF USE THAT INTERACT WITH CONTENT/FORM: PHASES 1, 2, AND 3

When normal children begin to use a conventional system of forms to code ideas, they typically talk about objects and events that are in the immediate environment. Events talked about tend to be events in which the child is a participant or in which the child wishes someone else to participate; the child rarely talks about what others are doing. Many utterances follow, or are adjacent to, those of another, but they are often not related to the previous utterance. When related they may be imitations, or related by virtue of the nonlinguistic context both speakers are sharing. Although the interpersonal functions of gaining attention and requesting or demanding are present, a common function is the intrapersonal function of commenting. The goals, as presented in Chapter XIII for this period, are outlined below.

1. *Function*. To produce utterances for the purpose of:
   a. Commenting about objects and ongoing events.
   b. Vocal play.
   c. Regulating others—getting others to do things.
   d. Obtaining objects.
   e. Calling attention to self or objects.
   f. Social interaction and social rituals.
2. *Context—Nonlinguistic*. To produce utterances:
   a. About objects and events that are ongoing or present.
   b. About the child's own dynamic interaction with the environment: what the child is about to do; what the child wants others to do; and what the child is doing.
3. *Context—Linguistic*. To produce utterances:
   a. Following the utterances of other persons, but not necessarily contingent on the utterances of others.
   b. Following the utterance of another and related to that prior utterance by the nonlinguistic context both share.

GOALS OF CONTENT/FORM: PHASES 1, 2, AND 3

The content/form interactions that characterize the early phases of language learning outlined in Chapter XIII are elaborated on in this section. Each phase is presented separately and each goal within the phase is listed, followed by examples taken from the language samples of Allison, Eric, Gia, Kathryn, and Peter when their *MLU* was within the limit of the phase presented.

Phase 1: Single-Word Utterances

The stage when children use single-word utterances has long been recognized as the first of the linguistic "developmental milestones," but it has received little attention in terms of the underlying cognitive notions or meanings until recently. As a consequence, clinicians have concentrated on teaching children to name objects—to acquire a vocabulary of nouns. It is now apparent that naming is only a small part of what young children are doing in this period when they are able to say only one word at a time. In fact, there is evidence to indicate that naming may be a relatively late development in the single-word utterance period and that for many children the words that are used most often and most consistently in this period of time are not names of objects. More important, the view of single-word utterances as primarily and simply naming behavior ignores the different underlying meanings represented by single words that come to be expressed with more and more elaborate forms in later phases.

The single-word utterances that the child uses express certain basic ideas about the environment. At this phase linguistic *form* first intersects with *content*. Children begin to learn the code for representing what they know in order to understand and produce single-word forms. These underlying cognitive notions reflect what the child has learned about the world—that persons, objects, and events exist, disappear, and recur; and that persons and objects are acted on and are located in space. These notions of the world make up most of the content or meaning of the first utterances that, in this phase, are in the form of single words.

The utterances described within this phase are presyntactic. A few combinations of words may occur, such as "all gone," but they are considered as single unanalyzed units. Toward the end of Phase I, many children begin to use series of one-word utterances, single words said in succession but not combined as phrases ("man, car, drive, garage"). Such successive single words tend to refer to different aspects or to relationships among aspects of a situation. They are semantically related to one another by virtue of the child's conceptualization and mental representation of the behavior and context with which they occur. Children, however, do not use syntax to code such relationships; the order in which such words occur successively varies and is not predictable.

The first behaviors presented within this phase consist of relational words and person names. As noted in Chapter IV, relational words occur early in the single-word utterance period and are used frequently throughout. Last, substantive words (i.e., nouns) complete the presentation of Phase I. Nouns are used in contexts similar to contexts that elicit relational words. Thus the child might be looking for an object that has disappeared and name the object "ball," or might point to one ball and say "ball" and then point to a second and say "ball." Children also reject objects by naming them, often accompanied by a negative headshake or whine.

In this phase where linguistic form first intersects with content it is important to emphasize that the meaning of a word depends on the underlying more basic mental representation of an aspect of experience. Words cannot be learned and cannot be used apart from the element of experience that they code or represent. In the course of intervention, a child will be helped to acquire different underlying concepts as new words are presented in appropriate contexts. But the child may well learn or already know something about the meaning of a word without being able to say it or recognize the word after hearing it (i.e. know that things can disappear, "gone," and that they can recur, "more"). One needs to look for such evidence of awareness. Accordingly, some nonlinguistic forms as gestures may be used to aid the child in learning to express and understand the linguistic form. They should not be suppressed but; instead, should be encouraged as a supplement to the linguistic form.

Behaviors that are used least frequently or were not used by all children in this phase are placed in parentheses and noted as *Optional Goal*. These behaviors may be held until the next phase (Box XIV-3).

Box XIV-3 GOALS OF CONTENT/FORM INTERACTIONS INTRODUCED IN PHASE 1

Content Category	by	Form
To code:		
Existence		Single-word utterances; relational words and later object names
Examples:		
(Allison showing a picture to someone)		*there*
(Allison pointing toward the photographer)		*man*
Nonexistence[a,b]		Single-word utterances; relational words
Examples:		
(Gia reads book; closing it)		*no more*
(Gia sees a fly land on Lois's leg; flies away)		*leg/ all gone*
(Allison looks at picture of girl; turns picture over so she can't see girl)		*no*
Recurrence[a]		Single-word utterances; relational words
Examples:		
(Peter drinks all the milk in his glass)		*more*
(Allison takes broken cookie from bag; puts it down; reaching in bag for another cookie)		*more*

Rejection[a,b]   Single-word utterances; relational
                                                     words

Examples:
  (Lois starts to put blocks away;
  Gia stopping her)   *no*

  (Eric is playing with his toy
  vacuum cleaner; Mother wants him
  to show Lois his new truck which
  makes noise)
  Make noise with the truck   *no*

(Denial)[a,b,c]   Single-word utterances; relational
                                                     words (used less frequently than
                                                     previous categories)

Examples:
  (Allison puts calf on floor)
  Is that the lamb?   *no*

  (Eric has his toy telephone)
  Is that Lois's telephone?   *no*

(Attribution)[d]   Single-word utterances; relational
                                                     words as adjectives (frequency of
                                                     use is variable—less frequent with
                                                     some children than others)

Examples:
  (Peter eating lunch; touching his
  spoon which is warm)   *hot*

  (Mommy and Allison give doll a
  "bath" in a paper cup; Allison
  takes doll from Mommy; looking
  at it)   *clean*

(Possession)[a]   Single-word utterances; name of
                                                     possessor or pronoun (use in this
                                                     phase variable among children; if
                                                     coded, it may be by naming the
                                                     person associated with an object, or
                                                     by a pronoun)

Examples:
  (Gia holding up Mommy's telephone
  book)   *də Mommy*

  (Peter picks up blocks; holding
  them to his chest)   *mine*

Action[a]	Single-word utterances; relational words as verbs
Examples:	
(Peter opening flap of tape recorder case)	*open*
(Allison turning book over from front cover to back cover)	*turn*
(Allison trying to put horse on chair and can't do it; giving it to Mommy)	*help/horse/help*
Locative Action[a]	Single-word utterances; relational words as verbs or prepositions
Examples:	
(Allison trying to get on chair)	*up*
(Peter reaching out to his stool)	*sit*
(Allison stepping out of truck)	*out*

[a] In addition to the behaviors listed here, object names are used in many situations: for example, naming the object acted on, located, possessed, noticed, wanted, etc. They are not listed under content because the relational meaning of such words is not clear. Their use in these contexts should, however, be encouraged.

[b] Some children do not have negation utterances early in this phase.

[c] Parentheses indicate that goal is optional in this phase.

[d] Attributes rarely refer to color or shape.

Phase 2: Emerging Semantic-Syntactic Relations

Once the child has begun to express many basic notions in the form of single words, he or she progresses to an elaboration of the form in which these very same notions are expressed. The distinguishing feature of Phase 2 is the elaboration of the linguistic representation—increased complexity of utterances. This is the phase familiarly referred to as the "two-word stage" and, indeed, this is a true description of the form of the utterances; children now combine two words in one utterance.

It is not the case, however, that the child has simply matured to the point where he or she can actually produce two words together and so simply joins together any two words that he or she has often heard expressed together in the speech of others. If that were the case, then language learning would be a matter of learning sequences of words that are commonly heard together without particular motivation for the sequence. Considerable argument has been advanced against this view, as pointed out in Chapter V. The intersection of particular words and the *order* in which these words occur is motivated by the *relationship* between the words that codes the conceptual notion or meaning the child intends to express. The child's two-word utterances at this point are, for the most part, syntactic. Order of words is now used to code the relationship between the words, but there appears to be a limit to only two words at a time. This limit holds even though the child is able to code a number of different and often intersecting relationships (such as, action-object, agent-action, agent-object).

Two elaborations in form develop during this phase. One that has been discussed is the combination of words into ordered relationship—the use of word order as the first expression of syntax. A second elaboration is the increase in the number of different words to express the same relationships—more topics are coded within a relationship—that is, more objects and actions are talked about. Thus the child uses longer utterances and more words to talk about the same content categories that were talked about in Phase 1. However, the same notions are still often expressed in single-word utterances or in a series of single words. (See Chapter V.)

Children in this phase may show a preference for nominal or pronominal forms for agent and object of action or locative action, place in locative action, and for possessor. Such individual preference should be encouraged during this phase (Box XIV-4).

Box XIV-4 GOALS OF CONTENT/FORM INTERACTIONS INTRODUCED IN PHASE 2

Content Category	by	Form

To code:
  Existence   Two-word utterances—relational word plus object name

    Examples:
    (Lois just put mike on Kathryn)   *this necklace*

    (Gia pointing to picture of rabbit)   *ə rabbit*

  Nonexistence   Two-word utterances—relational word plus object name

    Examples:
    (Kathryn searching for pocket in Mommy's skirt; there is no pocket)   *no pocket*

    (Kathryn picking up clean sock; then picking up dirty sock)   *no dirty/ this dirty*

    (Eric heard an airplane outside a few minutes previous)   *no more airplane*

Recurrence	Two-word utterances—relational word plus object name

Examples:
(Mommy is giving Kathryn a bath; finishes lathering her)	*more soap*
(Peter pointing out window at street light; pointing at another one)	*light/ more light*
(Eric twists wheels; stops; twisting wheels again)	*no more noise/ more noise*

Rejection	No new behaviors (still use of single word as in Phase 1)

Denial	No new behaviors (still use of single word as in Phase 1)

(Attribution)[a]	Two-word utterances—adjective plus noun (used infrequently by some children—generally is a small proportion of syntactic utterances at this phase)

Examples:
(Mommy is about to put freshly washed overalls on Kathryn; Kathryn had spilled something on them the day before)	*dirty pants*
(Peter looking at tape recorder buttons)	*tape recorder button*

(Possession)	Two-word utterances—noun plus noun, pronoun plus noun (used infrequently in this phase by most children)

Examples:
(Kathryn has pair of Mommy's socks)	*Mommy sock*
(Gia pointing to hat on her doll)	*dolly hat*

Action (agent-action-object relations)	Two-word utterances—verb plus noun or pronoun, and pronoun or noun plus verb are most common (preference for either nouns or pronouns is likely)

Examples:
(Eric reaching for cup of juice)	*ə eat juice*

(Gia riding her tike bike)	*ride this*
(Gia carrying book to Mommy)	*read ə book*
Locative Action (agent-action-object-place relations)	Two-word utterances—verb plus noun or pronoun, and pronoun or noun plus verb are most common (most often the object is named with either the place or the action; noun or pronoun preference is likely)
Examples: *(Gia takes handful of snapshots to desk)*	*away picture*
(Kathryn trying to climb on chair)	*up Kathryn*
(Kathryn putting sweater on chair)	*sweater chair*

ᵃ Parentheses indicate that goal is optional in the phase.

Phase 3: Further Semantic-Syntactic Development

In this phase there is continued development in the use of word order to express semantic relationships. Three term relationships are expressed; for example, the basic frame of the sentence, subject-verb-complement, becomes productive to express agent-action-object relationships. Three of the four terms of agent-locative action relations (agent-action-object-place) or the three terms of other locative action relations (patient-action-place; mover-action-place) become productive. Meaning categories of attribution and existence are coordinated with each other. The grammatical morpheme -s becomes productive to code plurality but is not yet used in most instances that are considered obligatory in the adult model. Number words may also be added, usually the number "two". Other numbers may be spoken, but they are often inaccurate in referring to actual quantity. In addition to these further developments of form, some new meaning categories are coded: locative state, state, and quantity. Continued development of more lexical items to express the same meaning categories presented in earlier phases is a part of this and every succeeding phase. The nominal/pronominal preferences noted in Phase 2 may continue through this phase (Box XIV-5). (See Chapter VI for further discussion of this phase of development.)

Following the productive use of the behaviors in these phases, the child learns new behaviors characteristic of later phases, but continues to develop the frequency with which the behaviors of Phases 1, 2, and 3 are used. The later phases are discussed in the following chapter.

Box XIV-5 GOALS OF CONTENT/FORM INTERACTIONS INTRODUCED IN PHASE 3[a]

Content Category	by	Form

To code:

Existence

Two- and three-word utterances generally coding the two constituents, subject-complement; coordinated with Attribution for some; frequent use of /ə/ as an apparent article; occasional use of contracted copula but not productive with most children

Examples:
(Kathryn pointing to picture in magazine) — *that ə funny man*

(Eric holding yellow disc) — *that's yellow one*

Nonexistence

Two-word utterances; no new behaviors (same as Phase 2)

Recurrence

Two-word utterances; no new behaviors (same as Phase 2)

Rejection

Single-word utterances; (some children start to use two-word utterances but single-word utterances more common, as in Phase 1)

Denial

No new behaviors; single-word utterances (same as Phase 1)

(Attribution)[b]

Two- and three-word utterances; *coordinated* with Existence; simple attribution is most common (see Existence for examples)

Possession

Two-word utterances; no new behaviors (same as Phase 2)

Action

Three constituents: subject-verb-complement; generally the most frequent relation expressed; pronominal/nominal preferences still exist (either nouns or pronouns can occur)

Example:
(Eric stacking blocks)   *I do it*

*(Gia holding book
out to Mommy)*   *Mommy open that*

*(Kathryn opening
book to first page)*   *Kathryn read this*

Locative Action   Three constituents: subject-verb-complement (object and/or place); used frequently; pronominal/nominal preferences still exist (either nouns or pronouns can occur)

Examples:
(Eric putting man on train)   *man sit train*

(Gia putting lamb on toy car)   *lamb ə go car*

*(Kathryn pushing lamb through
windows of doll house)*   *lamb go in there*

Locative state[c]   Two- and three-word utterances often including two constituents of the subject-verb-complement (usually object and place are mentioned) pronominal/nominal preference may exist

Examples:
(Eric points to toys on shelf)   *ə dolly up here*

*(Gia points to picture of a baby
in a basket)*   *baby basket*

*(Gia pointing to baby figure on form
board)*   *baby in*

State[c]   Two or three constituents of the subject-verb-complement; proniminal/nominal preference may exist

Examples:
(Eric tries to take book from Lois; whines)   *I want book*

*(Eric pointing to photograph of himself
sleeping)*   *baby sleep*

(Gia reaching for Daddy figure)   *Gia want Daddy*

(Quantity)[c]   Plural -*s* and/or a number word, such as "two"

Examples:

(Peter looking out window; to one then another chimney)	two buildings
(Kathryn pointing to library books on piano)	Mommy library books
(Eric pointing to two calves)	two cow

[a] The greatest proportion of utterances are about action and locative action. Utterances about state, locative state, and possession are a small proportion of the total utterances. The proportion of utterances about attribution varies among individual children.

[b] Parentheses indicate that goal is optional in this phase.

[c] New category.

SUMMARY

In normal language learning certain behaviors precede the interaction of language content/form/use. Some of these behaviors are precursory goals for the development of language use and include reciprocal gazing, regulating the behaviors of others, and calling attention to objects and events. Other precursory goals are related to development of content—behaviors that demonstrate an increased ability to represent something in mind when it is not present. Certain other behaviors are precursory goals for the development of language form— primarily the behaviors that are involved in the ability to imitate movements and vocalizations that are related to the form of linguistic signals. These early behaviors are suggested as early goals of language learning that should precede or be concurrent with Phase 1 of the plan.

The early phases of the plan for language learning are presented as goals for language learning. Phase 1 marks the first intersection between content/form/ use—the single-word utterance stage, while Phases 2 and 3 represent the emergence of syntax—the use of word order to code meaning relations. In this period children talk about objects and events that are present and that they themselves are involved in. Many utterances are comments without apparent interpersonal function; others are used to regulate the environment.

The goals of later language learning presented in this chapter are Phases 4 to 8 of the plan that was outlined in Chapter XIII. The content/form goals include the emergence of morphological inflections, the embedding of certain content categories in verb-complement relations, and the development of complex sentences. The content/form/use goals include an increase in the number of utterances that are produced without perceptual support from the nonlinguistic context; that are linguistically related to the utterances of others; that are more and more adapted to the needs of a listener; and that are used to obtain information.

These developmental changes are presented in two parts: first, those that occur in Phases 4 and 5, and then those that occur in Phases 6, 7, and 8, as defined in Chapter XIII.

GOALS OF CONTENT/FORM/USE: PHASES 4 AND 5
GOALS OF USE THAT INTERACT WITH CONTENT/FORM: PHASES 4 AND 5

In Phases 4 and 5 there is an increasing number of utterances about objects and events that are not present in the nonlinguistic context. Although the child is beginning to talk about objects and events without immediate perceptual support, it is important to note that the child is rarely talking about events that have occurred days or weeks ago or that will occur days or weeks in the future. Instead, when children are not talking about the "here and now," they are usually talking about something that has just been experienced, perhaps minutes before, or that they are planning to do or want to happen in the next few minutes. In contrast to the earlier phases, the children are also beginning to talk about the actions of others and not only about their own actions or what they want others to do. The use of language in these new nonlinguistic contexts (i.e., without immediate perceptual support and about others' actions) increases in later phases.

Accompanying the changed use of language in nonlinguistic contexts is a changing response to linguistic contexts. First, there is an increase in the number of utterances that do not follow the utterances of another (i.e., utterances that are nonadjacent). The number of these spontaneous utterances increases in comparison with the earlier phases, but they still number less than half of the total number of utterances produced by children at this point in development. The adjacent utterances are now, however, more often likely to be linguistically contingent on the prior utterance. Although more likely to be contingent, they are less likely to be imitations; but instead, they tend to add information to the same verb relation that was expressed in the prior utterance. Many of these linguistically contingent utterances that add information are appropriate answers to questions.[1]

At this point in development children themselves begin to ask increasing numbers of questions—questions about location and identity primarily. Not all of these questions appear to function as a means of obtaining new information, because the child often already knows the information requested. There is, however, a gradual increase in the use of questions to obtain new information. Almost all questions are related to context and not to the prior utterance of another (i.e., children rarely respond to the utterances of another with a contingent question). (See Chapter VII.)

The goals, then, of use that interact with content and form in these phases

---

[5] Note that the content of questions asked to children varies over time and appears to depend on the content the children themselves talk about, thus children are rarely asked questions about causality until they themselves begin to talk about causality. Linguistically contingent responses may not occur to questions about content the child is not talking about in other situations.

relate to function, nonlinguistic context, and linguistic context:

1. *Goals Related to Function:*
   a. To increase the number of utterances that serve the interpersonal functions listed for Phases 1, 2, and 3 (e.g., to obtain objects; to regulate the actions of others; to call attention to self or objects and events in the environment).
   b. To produce utterances in order to obtain information about identity or location of objects related to present context.
2. *Goals Related to Nonlinguistic Context:*
   a. To produce utterances about events that have just happened or are about to happen.
   b. To produce utterances about persons and objects that are not perceptually present but are expected to be or have just previously been present.
   c. To produce utterances about what other persons are doing.
3. *Goals Related to Linguistic Context:*
   a. To increase the number of utterances that are initiated by the child—that are nonadjacent to the utterances of another.
   b. To increase the linguistic contingency of adjacent utterances; that is, to produce a greater number of utterances that are related to both the form and content of the utterances of others.

Each of these goals of use is an important part of development within these phases and should cooccur with the goals of content/form interactions.

GOALS OF CONTENT/FORM INTERACTIONS: PHASES 4 AND 5
Phase 4: Embedded Relations and Grammatical Morphemes

In Phases 1, 2, and 3 the child learned the first intersections of content/form in the single-word utterance period (Phase 1) and then moved to the first syntactic coding of semantic relations with the use of word order. Each of these achievements continues to develop in later phases—both vocabulary and the number of utterances that use word order as a means of expressing semantic relations increase.

Although behaviors learned in Phases 1, 2, and 3 continue to develop, there are new behaviors that emerge and mark this fourth phase. For one, there is the addition of two new content categories—notice, which forms another major verb relation (along with action, locative action, locative state, and state) and time, which is embedded within the verb relation categories of action and locative action. The previously established category of rejection is now syntactically coded and a number of the previously established content categories are now coordinated. Attribution, nonexistence, recurrence, and place (previously expressed only as a constituent of locative relations) are now coordinated with action verb relations; and recurrence and possession are embedded within existence utterances.

When this embedding intervenes between the major constituents of action (as do attribution, nonexistence, and recurrence), there may be a tendency to produce only two of the three constituents—probably verb and complement. (See Chapter VI.)

Finally, Phase 4 marks the emergence, but not mastery, of a number of grammatical morphemes. The indefinite article "a" appears in existence utterances along with the demonstrative pronoun (previously one or the other had been the frequent form); the present progressive verb inflection -ing becomes productive in action verbs; the prepositions "in" and "on" are used in locative state utterances; the modal verbs "wanna" and "gonna" become productive as a means of expressing intended action or locative action; and the interrogative pronoun "where" is used to ask questions about location.

Box XV-1 includes specific examples of the new behaviors that become productive in this phase.

Phase 5: Successive Related Utterances

Phase 5 is marked by the coding of four new categories of content. One category of content, coordinate, refers to the cooccurrence of objects or events in time and space or to the sequential occurrence of two events; causality refers to cause-effect relations that generally include the child's motivation; dative refers to the indirect object or recipient; and, finally, specification points out or describes a particular object or event in contrast to another. A new form that emerges in this phase is the juxtapositon of successive, related utterances that are related to one another by cooccurrence, sequential occurrence, or cause-effect relationship. The juxtaposed utterances may or may not be connected by a conjunction—if a conjunction is used it is generally "and."

Grammatical morphemes, which became productive in Phase 4, are used more frequently and at least one emerges in a new context—the present progressive -ing is now productive with mover-locative action relations in addition to action. At the same time, new grammatical morphemes emerge: possessive -s; third person -s verb inflection in patient-locative action utterances; and irregular past with some action verbs. The interrogative pronouns "what" and, less frequently, "who," are used to question identity; the negative modal verbs become productive; the copula is used more frequently with existence; and prepositions occur in locative action utterances that include the verb.

As with Phase 4, there is increased coordination of content categories; most are embedded in action and locative action utterances and two are embedded in state utterances. There is an increasing number of syntactic utterances—particularly three constituent utterances and utterances with embedded relations—and a corresponding decrease in the number of single-word utterances. Children also talk more and there is an increase in

Box XV-1 GOALS OF CONTENT/FORM INTERACTIONS INTRODUCED IN PHASE 4

Content Category	by	Form

To code:

Existence   Coordinated with Possession and Recurrence; inclusion of demonstrative pronoun and "a"

   Examples:
      Possession and Existence
        (Gia sitting on her bike)   *this ə my bike*

        (Peter looking at Patsy's pen on floor)   *that's ə Patsy's pen*

      Recurrence and Existence
        *(Gia takes clown from toy bag; taking
        out second one)*   *this another clown*

Nonexistence   Coordinated with Action (see Action for examples)

Recurrence   Coordinated with Existence and Action (see Existence and Action for examples)

(Rejection)[a]   Two- and three-word utterances; not frequently used and not productive yet by all children

   Examples:
      *(Kathryn finds bear book; puts it down;
      picking up slide)*   *no bear book*

      *(Gia has been holding lamb; throwing it
      on the floor)*   *no want that*

Denial   No new behaviors; single-word utterances (same as Phase 1)

Attribution   Coordinated with Action (see Action for examples)

Possession   Coordinated with Existence (see Existence for examples)

Action   Coordinated with Place, Attribution, Recurrence, Intention, Nonexistence and *-ing*; simple coding of action continues to be used frequently with increasing use of three constituents; coordinations are productive but infrequently used and when produced it is likely that one constituent (most often the subject) will be deleted if coordination is marked with footnote *b*.

Examples:
Action and Nonexistence[b]
(*Gia tries to put lamb in block; can't*)   *can't do dit*
Action and Recurrence[b]
(*Gia bringing a man to Lois*)   *man read another book*

(*Peter draws circle, which he calls "hole",
drawing another one*)   *write it nother hole*
Action and *-ing* (auxilliary is rarely present)
(*Peter drawing*)   *I writing circles*

(*Gia riding tankcar*)   *I riding tankcar*
Action and Intention
(*Gia going to door*)   *I'm open door*

(*Peter drawing*)   *gonna make it man/
house*
Action and Attribution[b]
(*Peter tries to draw a tree*)   *make ə big tree*

(*Gia painting with black paint*)   *I draw red man/
I draw black man*
Action and Place
(*Gia scribbles on toy pan*)   *I write my pan*

(*Peter holding box of recording tape;
pointing to tape recorder*)   *there's ə tape go
round right there*

Locative Action   Simple coding is frequently used, with increasing use of three constituents; Coordinated with Intention

Examples:
Locative Action and Intention
(*Peter pointing to screws on tire of car;
then starts to unscrew tire*)   *gonna take ə wheel
out*

(*Gia pointing out window*)   *I wanna go outside*

Locative State   Use of prepositions "in", "on"; Wh-questions; this category is less frequently coded than Action and Locative Action

Examples:
(*Peter noticing piece of masking tape on
car*)   *tape on truck*

Locative State and Wh-Questions
(Peter noticing train car is missing a
plastic disc)   *where is it*

(Gia looking around for car driver)   *where man go*

State	Increased use of two- and three-word utterances; no new behaviors (same as Phase 3); still used infrequently
Quantity	Plural *-s* used most of time when required
Notice[c]	Two- and three-word utterances ("look" used with "ə" or "at")

Examples:
(child shouts in hall outside; Gia listens)   *I hear Kevin*

(Gia pointing to rabbit in a picture)   *ooh look at the*
                                                       rabbit

(Lois drew a screwdriver on Peter's paper;
Peter gets toy screwdriver and puts it on
paper next to drawing)   *look at that*

Time[c]	Intention with Action and Locative Action; *-ing* with Action; Intention may be coded by modals as "wanna", "gonna", "have to", or the contraction "I'm"; *-ing* form is most often used without the auxilliary "to be" (see Action and Locative Action for examples)

[a] When a content category is in parentheses, it indicates the goal is optional in this phase.
[b] May result in omission of the subject.
[c] New category.

the number of utterances produced by a child in a half hour or hour sample and as well as different lexical items used.

It is also at this point that pronominal/nominal preferences begin to disappear; pronouns are used by children who have not yet used them and nouns are used more frequently by children who had preferred pronouns. Thus, the child who has used only person names for agent begins to say the personal pronouns (first "I" and "you," then "he" and "she"); the child who has used only nouns for spatial locations now uses "there." In contrast, the child who has depended heavily on such pronominal forms now uses the nominal form (as person, object, or place name), particularly when the form is a part of the complement—as the object of an action or a location. (See Chapter VI.)

Examples of new behaviors that become productive within this phase are in Box XV-2.

Box XV-2 GOALS OF CONTENT/FORM INTERACTIONS INTRODUCED IN PHASE 5

Content Category	by	Form

To code:
  Existence   Copula, generally in the contracted form; Wh-questions

    Examples:
    (Kathryn picks up her new book)   *that's a book*

    (Eric holding out
    piece of puzzle to
    Lois)   *what's this*

  Nonexistence   "Not", "can't", "didn't"; coordinated with Locative Action (see Locative Action for examples)

    Examples:
    (Gia trying to get a toy)   *I can't reach*

    (Gia looking in the bag)   *it's not in the bag*

  (Recurrence)[a]   Coordinated with State (see State for examples)

  Rejection   "Don't"; coordinated with Action (see Action for examples)

  Denial   Two- and three-word utterances; at first with "no" and later using "not"

    Examples:
    (Peter pointing to barrels)   *there's the bolt*
    Barrels   *barrels/ not bolts*

    (Mommy to Kathryn) You're just tired   *I not tired*

  (Attribution)   Coordinated with State (see State for examples)

Possession   Coordinated with Action, Locative
                                                 Action (see Action and Locative
                                                 Action for examples); also, -s
                                                 inflection becomes productive but is
                                                 not always used

Examples:
  (Kathryn pointing to gifts for Daddy)   that's Daddy's
                                                       birthday

  (Lois picks up one of Gia's blocks; Gia
  reaching for it)   that's my's

Action   Irregular past; coordinated with
                                                 Rejection[b]; coordinated with
                                                 Possession[b]; coordinated with
                                                 Intention and Possession[b];
                                                 coordinated with Intention and Place

Examples:
  Action and Irregular Past
    (putting figures in truck)   I did that one
      Yes
    (putting another figure in)   and now do this me

    (Eric went to the zoo yesterday; he is
    telling Lois about it)   I fed ə ducky
  Action and Rejection[b]
    (Lois scatters Gia's blocks)   don't touch my
                                                       blocks

    (Mommy to Kathryn) Do you want to go to
      the bathroom?   no/I not go in bath-
                                                       room/I did tinkle

  Action and Possession[b]
    (Kathryn and Lois are reading a book;
    referring to picture)
      Daddy's hanging up the clothes.

                                                     Mommy hangs my
                                                       socks up

  Action and Intention and Possession[b]
    (Gia has washcloth; then pretends to
    wash hands)   I going wash my
                                                       hands
  Action and Intention and Place
    (Peter has train)

                                                     I wanna write the
                                                       choo choo train

    (Gia reaching for microphone)   I want touch here

Locative Action   Verb plus "in", verb plus "on"[b];
                                                 Coordinated with Nonexistence (rare

	but productive with some children)[b]; Coordinated with Possession[b]; Patient plus third person -s; Mover plus -ing

Examples:
Verb plus Preposition[b]
  (Kathryn putting discs on her lap)   put this on my lap

  (Patsy is holding Peter's baby sister
  Jenny; Jenny begins to cry)   put her down in the
                                           cradle

(Locative Action and Nonexistence)[b]
  (Daddy left; Mommy stayed)   not going away

  (Eric tries to sit on high stack of blocks)   and ə no sit down
Locative Action and Possession[b]
  (Peter trying to put Patsy's barette in his   put in my hair my
  hair)   barette/
                                           I put on ə Patsy
                                           barette

  (Lois takes her sweater off)   you putting your
                                           sweater on

Patient-Locative Action and Third Person -s
  (Eric assembling a train)   and that goes
                                           here

  (Gia putting puzzle piece in)   this fits
Mover-Locative Action and -ing
  (Eric opening door)   I going

  (Gia going to door)
    I'll see ya later/ where're you going?
                                           I going out to
                                           playground.

Locative State   No new behaviors

State   Coordinated with Attribution and
                                           Recurrence
Examples:
  (State and Recurrence)
    (Lois and Kathryn are pretending to have   I want some more
    lunch)   egg

    (Peter had eaten some pretzels; running   I want some more
    back to kitchen)   pretzels Mommy
  (State and Attribution)
    (Gia gets her new sand pail and shovel;
    showing it to Lois)   I got new pail

    (Kathryn holding red disc)   Kathryn want red
                                           one

Quantity   "some," "many," "all"
  Examples:
    (Eric pointing to pieces of clay)   *look/see/see clay/*
                                                                   two clay/many clay/
                                                                     1-2-3-4/2-3-3-3/look

    (Kathryn pretending to drink)   *I have some orange juice*

    (Kathryn looking at picture of moths)   *all these in there*

Notice   No new behaviors; same as Phase 4

Time   Irregular past tense plus Action verbs; *-ing* plus Mover-Locative Action; Third person *-s* plus Patient-Locative Action; (see Action and Locative-Action for examples)

Coordinate[c]   Successive utterances; intraclausal "and" and then interclausal "and"
  Examples:
    Successive Utterances
      (Kathryn pretending to have a stove)   *that be the stove/ want cook it/ I dump out this way/ stir it*

    Conjoin Objects—Intraclausal
      (Gia throwing papers on floor and stepping on them)   *I wanta fix the book and stand on this and this and this*

      (Peter telling Lois about trip)   *going to see Nanna and Bill and Jack*

    (Interclausal-Same Verb)
      (Gia looking at a book)   *look/ there's a bear having a birthday party and there's a buzz*

    (Interclausal—Different Verb)
      (Eric taking girl out)   *and the little girl goes out ə the bathtub*
      (puting little girl in dining room)   *and eats*

Causality[c]   Successive utterances with an implicit causal relationship between them; they may occasionally be conjoined with "and"
  Examples:
    (Peter gets ink on his hands)   *dirty hands/ hafta wash əm*

(Eric's train is stopped by a pile of blocks)		*choo choo train can't go anyplace/ fix dat/*
(Gia trying to unbutton pocket of doll's dress; there is a handkerchief inside the pocket)		*I want ə handkerchief/ unbutton it/*

Dative[c]   Three- and four-word utterances; prepositions are usually missing

Examples:

(Lois arrives at front door; Eric runs to open it)	*open door Mrs. Bloom*
(Lois pretends to eat)	*you get some Kathryn*

Specifier[c]   "this" and "that" used contrastively to specify which object; commonly used with State

Examples:

(Gia pointing to her brush on shelf)	*I want that brush*
(Eric standing in front of chest under which discs had rolled)	*I need that blue*

[a] When a content category is in parentheses, it indicates that goal is optional in this phase.
[b] May result in omission of the subject.
[c] New category.

GOALS OF CONTENT/FORM/USE: PHASES 6, 7, AND 8
GOALS OF USE THAT INTERACT WITH CONTENT/FORM: PHASES 6, 7, AND 8

As children become more proficient with more sophisticated forms to code more ideas, they also use the code in a wider variety of contexts, with increasing adaptation to the needs of the listener and for more interpersonal functions. There is increasing reference to the activities of others, to objects and events that are further removed in time from the context of the utterance. Adaptations to listener needs are evidenced by changes in tone of voice and sentence structure, when talking to infants, and the early use of alternative forms that take into account differences in context. For example, the children can use first and second person singular pronouns correctly to shift reference from speaker to hearer; they appropriately code definite and indefinite reference with the articles "a" and "the;" and they occasionally use ellipsis for cohesion and to avoid redundancy in discourse.

In addition, there is a marked increase in the number of spontaneous (nonadjacent) utterances so that now nonadjacent utterances are more frequent than adjacent utterances. The adjacent utterances that do occur are now primarily contingent on both the linguistic form and the semantic content of the prior utterance. There has been a decline in the number of utterances that are imitations of prior utterances—imitations are now rare. There is also a marked increase in the number of utterances that add information to prior utterances, and in the number of questions children ask. Questions are occasionally contingent on prior utterances:

The goals of use, then, that interact with content/form in these phases relate to function and nonlinguistic and linguistic contexts.

1. *Goals Related to Function:*
   a. To further increase the number of utterances that serve interpersonal functions—for example, questions.
2. *Goals Related to Nonlinguistic Context:*
   a. To increase the number of utterances that refer to objects and events that are removed from the present context.
   b. To produce utterances about objects and events that are increasingly further removed in time from the present context.
   c. To produce utterances with increased adaptation to the listener.
      (1) Shifting references (e.g., speaker/hearer distinction in pronouns).
      (2) Definite/indefinite articles.
      (3) Ellipsis based on shared information.
3. *Goals Related to Linguistic Context:*
   a. To reduce the number of imitated utterances.
   b. To respond to the utterances of others with contingent utterances that add information to the prior utterance (as by elaboration, explanation).
   c. To obtain further information about or clarification of another's utterance.
   d. To increase the number of nonadjacent utterances.

GOALS OF CONTENT/FORM INTERACTIONS: PHASES 6, 7, AND 8
Phase 6: Complex Sentences

It is in this phase, with *MLU* now over 3.0, that sentences are connected to each other as clauses with a conjunction (generally "and"). The relationship between these clauses is most often coordinate; that is, no new meaning is created by joining them with the conjunction "and." At first, many include the same verb in both sentences and mark the cooccurrence of objects and events. There is increasing use of different verbs in each sentence but, when children first conjoin utterances with different verbs, the relationship between events is generally sequential and the utterances are produced as the events take place (i.e., the child codes event$_1$ as it happens *and* then codes event$_2$ as it happens, connecting each utterance with "and").

Later, in Phase 6, a number of sentences coding sequential events have a potential cause-effect relationship between them. Such utterances may be considered intermediary between coordinate and causal and can be described as precausal. They are included here under causal and make up the major portion of causal utterances in this phase. In addition to the use of

---

Box XV-3 GOALS OF CONTENT/FORM INTERACTIONS INTRODUCED IN PHASE 6

Content Category	by	Form
To code:		
Existence		No new behaviors (same as Phase 5)
Nonexistence		No new behaviors (same as Phase 5)
(Recurrence)[a]		Coordinated with Locative Action (see Locative Action for examples)
Rejection		No new behaviors (same as Phase 5)
Denial		No new behaviors (same as Phase 5)
Attribution[b]		Coordinated with Locative Action (see Locative Action for examples)
(Possession)		Coordinated with State—infrequently used (see State for examples)
Action		No new behaviors (same as Phase 5)
Locative Action		Coordinated with Attribution[b]; coordinated with Recurrence[b]; (both are rarely used)

Examples:
Locative Action and Attribution[b]

(Gia sliding wheels down a slide)	*here goes a green wheel/there goes a green wheel*
(Eric looking for something to put in a dump car)	
What are you looking for?	*I put a little thing in it*
(Locative Action and Recurrence)[b]	
(Eric putting lambs on the train)	*I get more lamb in the train*

(Lois puts doll's sock on Kathryn's big toe)	*put 'nother/ put 'nother one*

Locative State   No new behaviors (same as Phase 4)

(State)   Coordinated with Possession; rarely used

Examples
(Mother asks Eric if he wants supper)

yeh

(to Lois he says)

you come back/you come next year/I want my supper

(Mother returning from store; Gia expected her to buy furniture)   *I wan ·I wan my my table and chair*

(Kathryn speaking of her mother)   *she has a bandaid on her toe*

Quantity   No new behaviors (same as Phase 5)

Notice   No new behaviors (same as Phase 4)

Time   ''now''
Examples:
(Kathryn can't tie the shoe; gives it to Lois)   *now/ your turn*
(Lois starts)   *now my turn*

Causality   Use of ''and'' to conjoin clauses
Examples:
(Gia eating cake)   *I want spoon ·and I going take it*

(Eric rubbing his knee)   *I fall down on a choo choo train/ and my knee hurt*

Dative   ''to,'' ''for''
Examples:
(Gia gets stool for Lois)   *this is a stool for you*

(Eric takes form board in case from toy bag; handing it to Lois)   *will you open these for me*

Specifier   "the" used to indicate specificity
  Example:
    (Kathryn picking up crayon box)   *let's put these in the box*

---

[a] When a content category is in parentheses, it indicates the goal is optional in this phase.
[b] May result in omission of the subject.

syntactic connectives, there is an increasing number of successive utterances without connectives.

There is also further development of grammatical morphemes and further coordination of content categories. New grammatical morphemes that emerge are the article "the" used to specify definite reference, and the use of the prepositions "to" and "for" to code dative. Attribution and recurrence are embedded within locative action utterances and possession is embedded within state utterances. Examples are presented in Box XV-3.

Phase 7: Syntactic Connectives and Modal Verbs

This phase marks an increase in the number of complex sentences, in the number of relationships expressed by complex sentences, and in the specification of the relationships between clauses. Causal relationships are now more commonly coded by "because" or "so," and sequential relationships are sometimes coded by "and then." One new interclausal relation expressed is antithesis, which may be coded by "and" or "but." A second new interclausal relation to emerge is epistemic, referring to the child's state

---

Box XV-4 GOALS OF CONTENT/FORM INTERACTIONS INTRODUCED IN PHASE 7

Content Category	**by**	**Form**
		No new behaviors in any categories except:
To code: **(Action)**[a]		Wh- questions used infrequently and not by all children to question agent, or object of an action, or the action itself

Examples:
*(Peter takes broken airplane from toy bag
and brings it to Patsy)*

who broke it

(Peter rolls discs down slide)

*now what should we
do with əm*

(Lois puts train together; Gia watching)

what you doing

*(Kathryn and Lois looking at picture of
boy feeding elephant peanuts)*

*what's the boy
feeding*

Coordinate

"and then" used to conjoin clauses
representing sequential events

Examples:
*(Lois and Eric pretending it's
lunchtime for the children)*

*let the Mommy into
the frigerator
and get some
pineapple yogurt
and then she
come out*

Causality

"because" and "so" used as
conjunctions

Examples:
*(Lois and Patsy are
ready to leave)*

*I wanna come with
you/cause I got
shoes on and I'm
ready to go*

(Gia at her bookcase)

*let's all take all the
books out so we
can read them*

*(Kathryn giving bend-
able girl to Lois)*

*you bend her over
okay/so I can put
her on this
rocking chair so
she can rock*

*(Lois follows Kathryn
into bathroom)*

*you stay away cause
I hafta go in there*

(Epistemic)[b]   Complement constructions
    Examples:
      (Peter getting another crayon out)
                                      look at this one
        What color is that?
                                      I don't know what
                                      color.

Mood[b]   "can" is used late in the phase to
                                      code possibility and permission
    Examples:
      (Kathryn dragging bag)
      I'll come help you
                                        I can do it

      (Gia showing Lois her bedroom)   *that's a __/ and this*
                                        is my bed/even---
                                        pajamas///I can
                                        only have the
                                        nightie when I go
                                        to sleep

Antithesis[b]
    Example:
      (Eric looking at a book)   *the butterflies saw*
                                        the bumble
                                        bees here ·but
                                        they ǝ not
                                        coming out.

---

[a] When a content category is in parentheses, it indicates the goal is optional in this phase.
[b] New category.

---

of knowledge about something ("know what," "don't know what," etc.). It is an optional goal in this phase; although it is quite frequent with some children, it does not appear until the next phase for others.

Another new relation is mood, an intraclausal relation that is coded by a modal verb. The mood coded is most generally *possibility* and is usually coded with "can." Additionally, some children ask questions about actions, the agent of an action, or the objects of an action. (See Box XV-4.)

Phase 8: Relative Clauses

Three new interclausal relations are coded, both with and without connectives. Specification now includes object specification—at times with juxtaposed successive utterances and at times by use of a relative clause and the relative pronoun "that" or "where;" predicate complement constructions are

---

Box XV-5 GOALS OF CONTENT/FORM INTERACTIONS INTRODUCED IN PHASE 8

Content Category	by	Form
		No changes in any categories except:

To code:
Notice   Complement constructions
  Examples:
    (Kathryn jumping on a board)   *watch what I'm doing*

    (Kathryn running)   *see how fast I can run*

Time   Third person -*s*; regular past -*ed*; auxilliary "to be;" conjunction "when;"

  Examples:
    Third Person -*s*
      (Kathryn trying to put girl doll on chair)   *you try to put that girl on here because she keeps falling off/ okay*

      (Lois to Gia) What does Mommy do when Daddy goes to work?
                                                she sweeps

    Regular Past
      (Lois picking up Kathryn's blocks)   *well I dumped all these blocks out and made a big big mess*

      (Eric looking at a book)
        This animal you can't see/ why?
                                                because is all covered up

        Why?
                                                because the zoo-keeper closed it

    Auxilliary "to be"
      (Eric looking at a book)
                                                and the bunny rabbits are sleeping and everybody's sleeping

(Kathryn looking at a book)
  What are the others doing?

                                             oh, they're eating/
                                               and this little girl
                                               is having milk/

  How about that dog?   he isn't having any
                                               food

(Kathryn scratched her head)
  What is the trouble?
                                             I was scratching my
                                               head

    Time Specification   "when" as conjunction
      *(Eric looking at a picture of a girl   crayons/see it tells
      coloring)*   you when you
                                                 want to be pink
                                                 you change pink
                                                 but when you
                                                 want to be
                                                 change red ·when
                                                 you want to
                                                 change red ·go
                                                 ahead and take
                                                 red/ and when
                                                 you to take
                                                 red ·take it/and
                                                 then you want to
                                                 take ·white

      (Gia playing with Lois's toys)   we can__when__
                                                 when__ when
                                                 you come to my
                                                 house I let you
                                                 play with your
                                                 toys

  Causality   Wh- questions
    Examples:
      (Kathryn pointing to Lois's shoes)
                                             why'd you bring
                                               these shoes

      To cover my feet
                                             Why

      Cause they were cold
                                             Why

      Cause it's cold outside
      (Patsy playing with Peter moves
      microphone)   why are you putting
                                               it right there

Specification	Two clauses: conjoined, juxtaposed, or subordinated
Examples:	
(Kathryn looking at picture of fishing rod)	*it looks like a fishing thing and you fish with it*
(Kathryn talking about a scoop)	
	it's just a thing that I hold.
Mood	A variety of modal verbs for obligatory mood and, occassionally, permission
Examples:	
(Kathryn taking a hot dish from oven, then putting it down)	*I better get a pot holder because I might burn my hands*
(Eric wants dolls to sit in chair)	*they should sit down in a chair*
(Kathryn and Lois having a tea party)	*well I hafta get that knife so I can cut the cake*

used, particularly to focus attention on a state or event; and time specification is coded by subordinate clauses and the connective "when."

This last phase is also marked by further development of grammatical morphemes. The past tense regular inflection *-ed* becomes productive, but is still often omitted; the third person singular *-s* inflection is now occasionally used in other verb categories; and the auxiliary "to be" is used productively with present progressive verbs, although still often omitted. New modals are used to code mood, often to code obligation, including forms such as "should," "must," or "have to." Children now begin to use causal questions with "why." (See Box XV-5.)

SUMMARY

This chapter is concerned with the goals of later language learning—with elaborating the behaviors outlined in Chapter XIII as the goals of content/form/use in Phases 4 to 8. Goals of use that interact with content/form include an increasing number of utterances that (1) are produced without the perceptual support of nonlinguistic context or the child's own activities; (2) are nonadjacent (i.e., do not follow the utterance of another); (3) use alternative forms that require adaptation to the listener; and (4) are used to obtain information.

There is concurrent growth in the number of content categories that are coded with linguistic form. In Phase 4, 14 content categories account for most of the content expressed by forms while, in Phase 8, at least 21 categories are needed to describe what children talk about.

Finally, there are changes in the forms used to code other content categories. Phases 4, 5, and 6 include the embedding of two content categories within one utterance—as the embedding of attribution within utterances coding action relations. Additionally, grammatical morphemes begin to appear in Phase 4. Phase 5 marks the appearance of many juxtaposed successive sentences that, while meaningfully related to each other, are not usually connected syntactically. In Phase 6 some of these successive sentences are connected with "and" to form complex sentences; and in the last two phases there is further use of syntactic connectives to form other complex sentences, with more specification of the semantic relationships between the clauses. Modal verbs are also used productively in Phases 7 and 8 to code mood, and there is continued development of grammatical morphemes in Phase 8.

Certainly there are other developments that occur during this period—developments that have not yet been described in a manner that is useful for a plan for language learning, but that could be incorporated in such a plan as additional information becomes available.

As pointed out in Chapter XIII, there are three parts to the plan for language development goals: first, a description of the language behaviors that are a part of language learning; second, a sequence of these behaviors based on normal development, which represents an hypothesis about the order in which they can best be learned in order to reach the ultimate goal of communicative use of linguistic behaviors; and third, a means for determining which behaviors, or rules, are already an established part of the child's language system and which are yet to be learned. Both a description of language behavior, in terms of content/form/use interactions, and a sequence for presenting these behaviors, based on normal development, were presented in Chapters XIII, XIV, and XV. In order to select the behaviors that are the most appropriate goals for each individual child, some techniques for determining which content/form/use interactions the child already has established and which the child has yet to learn will be considered in this and the next chapter. Although the procedures discussed may be applied to alternative plans, they will be considered and applied here primarily in terms of the sequence of content/form/use interactions presented in Chapters XIII, XIV, and XV. Thus, the information presented in Chapters XIII, XIV, and XV together with the information presented in this and the following chapter provide a means of describing language behaviors, determining which behaviors a child knows, and deciding which behaviors a child is ready to learn—information that is necessary for planning the goals of intervention.

Too often, in assessment, there is a tendency to focus on what a child does not know—what the child must learn. In order to plan goals that are determined by a developmental model it is equally important to describe what the child does know; only by knowing what the child does know are we able to hypothesize what the child is ready to learn. To determine what behaviors are a part of a child's language system, it is necessary to observe the child's language behaviors, obtain a record of the observations, analyze the observed behaviors according to content/form/use interactions, and set a criterion for deciding that the observed behaviors are the result of the child's language system and not unique utterances. This chapter includes discussion of each of these points as applied to direct observations that are low structured. More highly structured observations are discussed in Chapter XVII.

USING LOW STRUCTURED OBSERVATIONS

Following the identification of a language disorder, direct observations should be made of the child in settings that are representative of the child's daily life, and reported observations should be obtained from people who are in contact with the child in normal life activities. These direct and reported observations provide the first bases for descriptions of the child's language system—descriptions that can be supplemented later with information obtained from some means of nonstandardized elicitation. Thus, a sample of the child's language behaviors obtained in a low structured setting can be used to generate hypotheses about the child's language system; elicitation tasks can then be used to test some of these hypotheses and fill in missing information. The combined use of information from low structured observations and elicitation tasks provides the most complete picture of the child's content/form/use interactions. The use of direct observations is discussed here.

The problems with using low structured observations to obtain information about language behavior are primarily related to the time involved in obtaining and analyzing such samples, and to the extent to which the sample of language can be considered representative of the child's language behavior in general. Critics of this method of obtaining evidence feel that the length of time that is needed to obtain, record, and analyze samples of language behavior is impractical for the average clinician. Certainly, the time that is involved in obtaining and analyzing language samples is not brief. However, it is also true that the traditional diagnostic procedures, which include the administration and scoring of numerous standardized measures, take considerable time. More seriously, while the administration and scoring of standardized tests of language behavior can take as much, or more, time as the analysis of a language sample, such standardized tests have not been able to provide the rich information that is potentially available in a representative language sample, that is, information about what kinds of ideas the child can code and how the child can use the linguistic code in interpersonal situations.

The second problem—whether the sampled behaviors are truly representative of what the child knows—is not unique to language samples but, instead, is a problem with samples of any behavior. Observing a child using language in a naturalistic setting may well be more representative of what the child actually *does*, than is the highly constrained sample of the behavior collected with formal elicitation techniques under unreal conditions (see Chapters II and XI, as well as Bersoff, 1971). Both criticisms—the time it takes to obtain a sample of language behaviors, and the extent to which the sample is representative of the child's language behavior in general—have, however, limited the use of a language sample as an assessment technique to those clinicians who have been specifically trained with such procedures, or who are particularly interested in a linguistic orientation to childhood language disorders.

Planning direct low structured observations involves consideration of a number of factors: context of the observation, length of observation, method of transcribing; and method of analysis. Each is discussed below.

CONTEXTS OF OBSERVATIONS

As pointed out in Chapter XI, the more varied the contexts in which the child is observed, the better the chance of obtaining information that is representative of the child's knowledge of language. When possible, therefore, the child should be observed in a number of situations. In school, a child might be observed in a classroom setting, playing with a friend, and in direct interaction with the assessor; in a clinic, the direct observations might include interactions with the assessor as well as interactions with a member of the family and with another child; and in the home, the child might be observed interacting with family and friends. If there is time for only one direct observation, care should be taken to arrange a setting that will allow for the largest and most representative sample possible. Since the goal of this observation is to find out what the child *does* (i.e., what language the child uses), adult intrusions and interactions should be as relaxed and as natural as possible and should not be designed to test the child or to elicit specific words or linguistic structures. There will be time after the direct observation in the low structured context to attempt to elicit behaviors that have not yet been observed.

The most frequently suggested sampling contexts have focussed on describing pictures, talking about toys, or responding to probes by an interviewer (Engler, Hannah, and Longhurst, 1973; Lee, 1974; and Tyack and Gottsleben, 1974). Describing pictures seems to be a strain for many children, particularly young children who tend to label objects in a picture, thereby limiting the content/form/use interactions that can be observed. These same children respond more naturally and more spontaneously when simply presented with a few objects and activities.

Longhurst and Grubb (1974) and Longhurst and File (ms.) investigated the effect of various contexts on the language sample obtained. They found that less structured conversational settings elicited more language and more complex language than structured, task-oriented settings or pictures, and that pictures were least effective. Lee (1974) also reported that younger normal children used more spontaneous speech when presented with toys than with pictures or stories. Although Lee reported that older normal children tended to talk more in response to pictures and the retelling of a familiar story than they did when presented with toys to play with, it has been our experience that a greater number and variety of language behaviors may be obtained when conversation revolves around some concrete activity (e.g., construction toys, science experiments, or art projects) and the child is allowed to talk about the activities in any way. This is particularly important for children who are in the early stages of language development, regardless of age.

Although questions are a part of any adult-child interaction, they alone cannot be counted on to elicit the major portion of a language sample from children in the early stages of language development. This is particularly true if the questions are not related to ongoing here-and-now activities. When questions are used, they should be open-ended and not of the yes-no or what's-its-name variety, which tend to elicit single-word responses. Since many children in the early stages of language learning do not comprehend the more complex question forms that elicit longer utterances (such as "how does" "what would happen if," or even directions such as "tell me about,"), the usefulness of questions is limited even when they do refer to ongoing events. In adult-child interactions in normal language development, adults ordinarily ask children questions that are consistent with the child's level of development. For example, adults do not ask "where" or "why" questions until the time when children talk about location or causality in their own spontaneous speech. (See Chapters VII and IX for discussions of this and related issues.)

LENGTH OF OBSERVATIONS

The minimum length of observation or the minimum number of utterances that should be obtained in a clinical sample has not been agreed on. Many have suggested 50 to 100 different utterances as a sample for clinical analyses (Lee, 1974; and Tyack and Gottsleben, 1974). The minimum length of sample necessary to obtain reliability on a measure of the mean length of utterance within a sample is 50 utterances (Darley and Moll, 1960; and McCarthy, 1930). The length of a clinical sample is limited by time pressures surrounding busy clinicians and the difficulties involved in eliciting speech from the language-disordered child. Too few utterances, however, make it impossible to say much about the child's language in terms of content/form/ use. A sample of 200 or more different utterances would provide a better data base, although undoubtedly this number may be unrealistic for many children in a clinical situation. In reality, the time that is available probably sets the limit on size of sample. Most diagnostic sessions are limited to 1 hour per visit, both for purposes of scheduling and for reasons relating to a child's interest span. If a child does not use much spontaneous speech in $\frac{1}{4}$ to $\frac{1}{2}$ hour of observation, it is probably better to switch situations than to continue the same observation for a longer time. With a very talkative child, a full 1-hour session may not be needed for the low structured direct observation, and the extra time may be used for eliciting particular responses. Generally one should attempt to record a minimum of $\frac{1}{2}$ hour of direct observations. The $\frac{1}{2}$ hour may involve more than one setting and can be obtained over a period of days if necessary—in fact, such variety is probably advantageous.

RECORDING AND TRANSCRIBING OBSERVATIONS

The three generally used means of recording clinical language samples are videotaping, audiotaping, and handwritten notes. Many clinics and schools have ready access to video tape equipment and use it routinely to record both diagnostic and therapy sessions. This method of recording is ideal because it can provide a record of context, facial expressions, and body movement as well as speech. Videotapes can be transcribed to include all speech, context, body movement, and the like.[1]

Next in preference, after videotaping, is an audiotaped recording of direct observations. This method is far less expensive, less obtrusive in the environment, and the equipment is generally more portable, but audio recordings only provide a record of vocal interactions. Many experimenters and clinicians have managed to overcome this limitation in a number of ways. Some record much information about context in side comments that are spoken softly into the recorder, or by comments to the child that mention context (e.g., the child says "help me" and the clinician responds "help you? you can't get the toy box open?"). These methods of describing the context help in the recall of the situation during transcription. Most observers, however, have found that hand notes taken during the observation are necessary in order to get good contextual data. These notes are coordinated with the vocal utterances as the tapes are transcribed.

In both audio and video recording, clinicians and experimenters have found it useful to repeat many of the child's comments during the interactions in order to clarify what may not be intelligible when listening to the tapes. This repetition should be limited, however, if it becomes a source of annoyance or even of interest to the child. Audiotapes must be transcribed soon after taping by someone who was present at the observation in order to recall context and to coordinate context with utterances.

A last method of recording observations that is frequently used, but is less accurate, is the hand transcription of utterances and contexts as the interactions take place. This method is most useful in situations where it is difficult to audio or video record (e.g., on the playground or in the cafeteria, and when background noise may be too great to obtain clear voice recordings with ordinary recording equipment). The method is most effective with children who speak little and with children who speak primarily in single-word utterances; it is less effective with the child who uses more language, particularly the child who speaks in more than three-word utterances, because of the limitations in the amount of information that can be written in a period of time. However, if hand transcription is the only method

---

[1] The transcription conventions that have been developed by Bloom and her research assistants for transcribing videotapes and audiotapes are included in Appendix A.

of transcription feasible, information on every third or fourth utterance can be recorded and can be helpful. The major problem with on-the-spot hand transcriptions is accuracy (e.g., determining if there really was an -s inflection attached to a word).

With practice obtained from carefully transcribing many audio- and videotapes, some clinicians have found direct on-site hand transcribing an effective way of obtaining information that otherwise would be lost—either because of time or because of situational limitations. Some speech pathologists do all assessment in the classroom (e.g., Taenzer, Harris, and Bass, 1975; and Taenzer, Bass, and Kise, 1974) by following the child and writing down as many utterances as possible and coding some aspects of context in order to determine content and use. Obviously, much information is lost by this technique but, by collecting hundreds of utterances in continual ongoing assessment, some clinicians (e.g., Taenzer, et al., 1975) have been able to describe children's language effectively in terms of the goals outlined in the previous chapters.

Hand notes may also be used to supplement information from recorded observations, for example, by recording utterances and context from *show and tell* or *freeplay* in the classroom and from hallway conversations. When observations are geared to a specific question, as a particular content/form interaction or a certain aspect of use, recorded information is particularly useful. Given a specific category or utterance type to record, the observer does not have to take notes on *all* utterances and contexts. Belkin (1975) found that trained observers agreed well with transcriptions of audiotapes when they were asked to hand record children's negation utterances in direct, low structured observations. In an unpublished pilot project[2] trained observers were able to hand record examples of action utterances that correlated highly with the action utterances transcribed from a videotape of the same observation.

Thus, the use of handwritten notes as a method of recording behavior does offer possibilities to the overscheduled clinician who feels that taperecorded observations are an impossible burden and thus language samples are an impossible assessment procedure. Video- or audiotaped observations are the preferred methods of recording language samples, but recording utterances and context by on-site hand notes is better than no sample at all and worthy of consideration if the limitations are fully recognized. Certainly for the student and the clinician who are inexperienced in language sampling and analysis, experience with tape recording and carefully transcribing language samples should precede reliance on hand notes. Audio or video recordings are also a necessity for the child who is not readily intelligible,

---

[2] Carried out in collaboration with S. Gozenbach at Montclair State College in 1975.

thus allowing opportunities for repeated replay of utterances for transcription.

ANALYZING TRANSCRIPTIONS OF DIRECT OBSERVATIONS

The analyses that are generally suggested for clinical application are comparative analyses, in essence *etic* analyses that are intended to describe the behaviors of the language-disordered child in relation to a predetermined taxonomy of language behaviors.

The taxonomies used may categorize language content, form, or use or may categorize interactions among these components. No matter what aspect of language is the focus of the taxonomies, or which particular taxonomies are selected, the clinician must have a criterion for deciding how many examples of a particular behavior will be necessary as evidence that a goal or aspect of language is a productive part of the child's language system or has been learned.

CRITERIA OF PRODUCTIVITY AND ACHIEVEMENT

Goals of learning generally include criteria of acquisition as well as descriptions of the behaviors to be learned. In terms of language behaviors, a criterion can be one of productivity or one of achievement. Meeting a criterion of *productivity* would provide evidence that a behavior is systematic and the product of the child's language system. Meeting a criterion of *achievement* would provide evidence that a behavior is used most of the time that it is expected to be used according to some standard of expectation—generally in terms of adult language usage (which is the ultimate goal of language learning).

Several different utterances of a form category to code a content category can be taken as evidence that a content/form interaction has been established and is part of the child's productive language system. A specified number of different utterance types can be used as a criterion reference (see Chapter XI)—a standard of performance that can be used in describing the child's performance in relation to the goals of content/form interactions (Chapters XIII, XIV, and XV). For example, if a child produces over five different utterances using verb-object to code action, it is assumed that the utterances are derived from knowledge of a linguistic rule. If only one or two different utterances were produced, if the same token such as "hit Eric" was uttered five times, or if utterances obtained were exactly the utterances taught in the same situation, one could not be as confident that a rule for this content/form interaction was established. A criterion of five different utterance types was arbitrarily set by Bloom (1970a) as a criterion for assuming that a form/content interaction was productive in 5 to 8 hours of sampling normal children's developing language. Since clinical samples used for clinical language assessment are generally ½ to 1 hour long, the criterion will be necessarily fewer. It would seem that four different examples (utterance types) in 1 hour may be taken as strong evidence (and three examples as perhaps weak evidence) that a content/form interaction is established. Of course, if there are fewer or no occurrences of a behavior, there is still the possibility that the behavior would have occurred if the assessment sample had been longer.

Proportional measures can be used as an estimate of achievement. The number of utterances using a particular content/form interaction (such as subject-verb-complement to code action) can be compared to the total number of utterances which code action where three constituents would be expected in the adult model. Although an interaction may be considered established, or productive, based on the production of four different utterances, low proportional frequency may suggest that the interaction should be included as a goal in order to increase the frequency of production.

FORM ANALYSIS

There are many taxonomies currently used in the analyses of clinical language samples. Most of them involve categorizing the forms the child produces according to linguistic categories (Crystal, Fletcher, and Garman, 1976; Engler, Hannah, and Longhurst, 1973; Lee, 1974; Streng, 1972; and Tyack and Gottsleben, 1974). For example, Engler et al. and Streng have provided a means of describing utterances in terms of basic sentence types and modifications of these types. Sentence types are determined by the structure of the verb phrase; one category includes intransitive verbs, another includes transitive verbs, and another includes copula or linking verbs. Modifications of these sentence types are also categorized and include questions, imperatives, and embedding of sentences. When such an analysis is completed, the clinician has a sophisticated linguistic description of the forms the child used in terms of forms of the adult model. The clinician knows which forms the child needs to learn in order to become a proficient speaker of the native language. What is not clear from the resulting analyses is how to sort these forms to determine which forms to teach first (i.e., to determine a sequence of goals). What is also lacking is information on the meaning relations the child can encode (content) and the way the child can use the forms (use).

The first of these problems, the sequence in which the forms should be taught, is handled by Tyack and Gottsleben (1974) and by Lee (1974). Each presents analyses and sequences of form that are based on information about normal language development. Lee has presented two levels of analysis: one for presentences that do not include a subject and verb, called developmental sentence types (DST); and one for complete sentences (i.e., utterances that include a subject and verb), called developmental sentence scoring (DSS).

Lee's Developmental Sentence Analysis

The DSS provides normative data and can be used to identify a language disorder based on a language sample. In addition, the DSS provides a developmental sequence of eight grammatical forms as used in sentences containing a subject and a predicate: indefinite pronouns; personal pronouns; main verb elaborations, including, infinitives and gerunds; negative forms; conjunctions; interrogative reversals; and Wh- question forms. This developmental sequence is broken down into eight levels and provides a sequence both within and among the eight grammatical features. Goals can thus be easily determined for teaching these eight grammatical features in sentences that include both a subject and a predicate. Unfortunately, the intermediary steps are not specified. The sequence of particular features was based on their production in essentially complete sentences. It is not clear that the sequence presented would be the same if these forms were sequenced based on their production in less complete sentences, nor is it clear what intermediary behaviors would be expected and encouraged. Thus, while using developmental data to sequence forms, the language behaviors described and the sequence of goals are, in essence, based on an adult model—the production of forms in complete sentences.

Many grammatical features are not included in the DSS analysis. It is implied that certain form types such as articles, plurals, and possessives are developed early and so probably would be goals comparable to other first level goals. The sequence of adverbs, prepositions, embedded sentences, and other features is not discussed and so would have to be determined by other information. Finally, information on content and use is not included. Nonetheless, the information, while limited in these ways, does provide a means of describing a language sample and an hypothesis for sequencing these language behaviors for children in later stages of language learning.

The DST, on the other hand, involves earlier stages of language development and is divided into three levels—single words, two-word combinations, and constructions (utterances over two words that do not include both a subject and a verb). Within these levels there are two subcategories for inclusion of elaborations or modifications such as plural, possessive, conjunction, or question. Utterances at each level are then placed in one of five categories: (1) *noun phrase elaborations*, including the addition of articles, adjective plus noun, and even noun phrase plus noun phrase (as in "Daddy____ball" where the verb is deleted); (2) *designative utterances*, which appear to be primarily identity statements and eventually include the copula; (3) *descriptive statements* that also eventually include a linking verb;

(4) *verbal elaborations* of both transitive and intransitive verbs (but not linking verbs); and (5) *fragments* that are neither noun phrases nor one of the above three categories but are utterances that need *both* a subject and a verb to become a sentence. Goals are not as clearly derived from the DST analysis as the DSS, nor is it clear how the transition is made between these levels and complete sentences. For example, plurals occur at the single-word level as well as at other levels, yet it seems unlikely that plurals in single words would be a goal before the use of word order for combining two words; subject-verb-object combinations are not included in the DST analysis, but phrases such as "my big car" or "some more truck" do occur and, again, it seems unlikely that such phrases would be goals before subject-verb-object combinations. The DST analysis, then, does not seem to lead readily to a sequence of developmental goals but, instead, provides a means of describing the form of certain presentence utterances that occur in normal development.

Lee's developmental sentence analysis (DST and DSS) is presented in Tables XVI-1 and XVI-2 for 100 different utterances from a 4½-year-old boy named Tommy. Utterances in each DST category can be described by level and by sentence elaborations and sentence modifications within each level. Elaborations include plurals, which Tommy used once; articles, which he used quite frequently; possessive inflection, which he used only once; and verb elaborations, which he did not use. Descriptions of sentence modification include pronouns—indefinite and possessive pronouns, which were used occasionally, and second and third person pronouns, which were not used at all in this sample; negation—no negation examples were used in this sample; questions, which were used four times; and conjunctions, which were not found in this analysis.

In addition to the above description of sentence elaborations and modifications, the summary of DST would note the number of utterances in each category as an indication of the variety of sentence types used by the child. In the present analysis many examples were found in each category.

A summary of DSS analysis would comment on the analyses of each grammatical feature. Indefinite pronouns were present at both the first and third levels. Also at the first level were personal pronouns, including first and second person pronouns, but none were in the objective case. Most main verbs that Tommy used were uninflected, including many copulas but few auxilliaries, and were also at the first level; secondary verbs were rarely found in this sample. Negatives were used only twice, once as a stereotype "I don't know;" conjunctions did not occur; interrogative reversals were present with the copula; and second level Wh- questions were found, including the forms "where" and "what," but not "who" or "how many."

By comparing these behaviors with the sequence on the DSS chart, the

TABLE XVI-1
DST Analysis

Tommy	CA: 4,5	MLU 2.75	Single Words: 26	Two-word Combinations: 20	Constructions: 21	Sentences 33

	Noun	Designator	Descriptive Item	Verb	Vocabulary Item
Single words	dolly chair door upstairs Daddy supper Mommy outside kitchen window downstairs	here there	quiet tired over	look kiss eat close	hah yeah oh oh woops hi oops

	Noun Phrases	Designative Elaboration	Predicative Elaboration	Verbal Elaboration	Fragments
Two-word combinations	one dolly a dolly a baby Daddy Mommy	s'e little this mom this dolly that Daddy	window out it outside where dolly where Mommy	gonna sleep open window gonna eat gonna hide see window	that way this way good night Daddy
Constructions	two more toys	it a bed there a little bed dat my Daddy	chair in the room garage in a house Mommy over there Mommy in this bed where the bed where mommy's bed	in come in house put in the hou/ garage gonna eat supper wake up Daddy n sleep in this room go in that way	in the room in the house in the room in this way in the bed in the kitchen

TABLE XVI-2
DSS Analysis

DSS Score 3.6

Tommy

	Indefinite Pronoun	Personal Pronoun	Main Verb	Secondary Verb	Negative	Conjunction	Interrogative Reversal	Wh-Questions	Sentence Point	Total
I got some	3	1	1						1	6
I got dolly		1	1						1	3
he tired		2	—						0	2
Mommy sleeping			—						0	0
Daddy sleeping			—						0	0
Daddy's hungry			1						1	2
that's dad	1		1						1	3
Daddy going up			—						—	0
Daddy go in this one	1,3	2	2						—	4
where'd she go			2				6	2	1	13
where's Daddy			1				1	2	1	5
where's Mom			1				1	2	1	5

Utterance							Total
um she eat supper	2					—	2
when we eat	3		5			—	8
there's my mommy	1	1				1	3
dolly fall		—				—	0
Mommy sit down there		—				—	0
Dolly goin to bed		—				—	0
Daddy go in this bed	3	2				1	6
we're going to bed	3	1				1	5
what's this		1	2	1		1	5
Mommy go in this	1	1				1	3
this is the homework	1	4			4	1	10
I don't know		1			4	1	2
there's mommy now	1	4				1	10
I don't see a garage	1	4			4	1	13
where'd go	1	1	2	6	4	1	13
there's a bed		1				1	2
there's the Mommy's bed		1				1	2
this it is the bed	—	1				—	1
there's table		1				1	2
that's my mommy	1	1				1	4
there's daddy	1	1				1	2

following goals were derived. Goals for first level behaviors included:

1. Increase the use of subject-predicate sentences (since so few occurred).
2. Increase the use of the copula (since so many were omitted on DST).
3. Develop verb elaboration *is* and *-ing*.
4. Develop the use of negatives *no* and *not* plus verb.
5. Develop first person pronouns in the objective case.

And, as later goals, develop:

6. "Wanna" and "gonna" as secondary verbs.
7. Irregular past with main verb.
8. *-s* and *-ed* inflections on main verb.
9. Other forms of "to be" with auxilliary and copula.
10. Third person pronouns in possessive and objective cases.
11. Wh- question forms "who," "how many," "how much," "what-do," "what-for."

Tyack and Gottsleben's Language Sample Analysis

Tyack and Gottsleben (1974) suggested analyzing 100 different multimorpheme utterances. Their transcription sheets include the child's utterances and underneath a gloss, based on context, of what the utterance would be in the adult model. Each utterance is marked according to syntactic structure. All function words and morphological inflections that are included in the child's utterance are circled. A check is placed in the location where obligatory forms have been omitted. For example:

Noun + Verb + Noun	(Syntactic Structure)
Daddy go√ (in) this bed.	(Child's Utterance)
The daddy goes in this bed.	(Adult Gloss)

The total number of words is divided by the total number of morphemes to compute a word-morpheme index. This index is used to place the child at a developmental linguistic level derived from the cross-sectional study of normal language development by Morehead and Ingram (1973, in *RLDis*). The forms found at each level by Morehead and Ingram provide the sequence of goals and the categories for analysis.

A score sheet, which lists forms by linguistic level, is used to analyze the transcriptions. Omissions, substitutions, and inclusion of function words, morphological inflections, and basic construction types are noted on the score sheet beside the expected linguistic level. Finally, the score sheet is analyzed according to the forms (function words, morphological inflections) and construction (sentence) types that are mastered (i.e., 90% correct use in obligatory contexts). No minimum number of utterances or contexts is necessary, thus, no criterion of productivity is included.

The forms and construction types that are not yet mastered but that are expected at linguistic levels below the child's assigned level (as determined by the word-morpheme index) become the goals of intervention. The first goals arc the forms that the child used inconsistently (less than 90% of the time in obligatory contexts), and second goals are the forms that did not appear at all. If there is no obligatory context for forms or constructions that are expected below the assigned linguistic level, pictures or other situations outside of the sampling situation are used to elicit them. The language sample that was used to illustrate DST and DSS was analyzed according to the method suggested by Tyack and Gottsleben. Tommy had a word morpheme index of 3.0, which placed him at the third linguistic level. The analysis of constructions showed multiple examples of all constructions expected for Levels 1 and 2. On Level 3 there were many examples of the "noun + is + noun or adjective" construction, but there were also many examples where the copula was missing. In addition, there were few examples of "modal + verb + noun" or the "noun + verb + noun + noun" constructions that are expected at Level 3. The analysis of function words and morphological inflections showed no evidence of Level 1 modal verbs "want" and "wanna" or of the verb particle "up." On Level 2, there was no evidence of the use of the pronoun "me" and inconsistent use of articles, plurals, and -ing. Last, the omitted forms at Level 3 included "them," "with," "these," plural "/-əz/," "is" auxiliary, and the modal "hafta." The only form used inconsistently at this level was the copula "is." Goals for Tommy, using this analysis of the first 100 different utterances, would be to teach:

1. Consistent use of articles "a" and "the."
2. Consistent use of plural -s.
3. Consistent use of present progressive -ing.
4. "Want" and "wanna" as modals.
5. "Up" as a particle.
6. "Me."
7. Consistent use of "is" in noun + is + noun/adjective constructions.
8. The construction modal + verb + noun.
9. The construction noun + verb + noun + noun (i.e., inclusion of object and prepositional phrase in a complete sentence).
10. "No" and "not."
11. "What" as question form in subject position.

Note that the two different analyses concluded with many similar goals for this child; the copula, -ing, "me," "wanna," and the question "what." There are also some differences that are probably not contradictory. It is not clear where Lee would consider plurals and articles but probably, similar to Tyack and Gottsleben, they would be early goals. The goals from DSS of third person, -s, and of past tense inflections, however, would be later goals in the Tyack and Gottsleben sequence. Intermediary structures such as "modal + verb + noun" are not considered by Lee. Thus, when goals of form are derived from developmental sequences, different procedures of analysis can result in similar goals. Differences that do result may be the result of differences in the means of obtaining the developmental data (e.g., Lee's data for the DSS sequence were cross-sectional and utterances that were not essentially complete sentences, with both subject and predicate if expected in the adult model, were excluded in determining the sequence of grammatical features.)

Muma's Cooccurring and Restricted Structure Procedure

Muma (1973) has suggested a further refinement of form analysis that can help in specifying the goals of intervention—the cooccurring and restricted structure procedure (CORS). The analysis compares the grammatical contexts in which certain grammatical systems (such as adverbial, verb auxiliary, negation, pronouns, etc.) that the child is in the process of learning are produced. The contexts in which restricted forms (nonadult forms) occur are compared with the contexts in which the adult model forms occur. The system chosen for CORS analysis (the target system) is one that the child uses often, sometimes in restricted fashion and sometimes as it occurs in the adult model. Thus, structures used inconsistently, according to any form analysis, would qualify if the structures occurred frequently. The purpose of the analysis is to see if the restricted structures tend to occur in particular grammatical contexts (as sentence types, or with certain sentence modifications), while the adult forms occur in other grammatical contexts, that is, to explain the inconsistencies or variation in terms of the cooccurrence of the restricted structures with other structures. This information could then help in planning which systems to teach and the grammatical contexts in which the form would be taught.

One example given by Muma is the occurrence of a restricted form (omission, substitution, or redundancy) of the subject noun phrase when any complexity is added to that phrase (such as modification of the noun). A CORS analysis is illustrated in Box XVI-1.

CONTENT/FORM ANALYSIS

The procedures just described have classified utterances by form. When goals of intervention are derived from such analyses, they relate to learning the forms of language. Learning form is certainly a part of language

BOX XVI-1 CORS ANALYSIS—UTTERANCES WHERE SUBJECT IS OBLIGATORY

Inclusion of Subject		Omission of Subject (restricted structure)
this mom	she eat supper	gonna eat supper
this is the homework	I get money	eat right in the house
this it is the bed	chair in the room	get ə coke
that daddy	dolly fall	eat hot dogs
there's table	Mommy sit down there	buy milk
that's dad	dolly/ we're go in	drink it
that's my mommy	to bed	get money
this ə phone	Mommy in this bed	eat carrot
there ə little bed	my baby upstairs	here go again
there's ə bed	Daddy going up	in come in house
there's the mommy's	Daddy go in this one	go in that way
bed	I don't know	put in the house/
there's daddy	Mommy sleeping	garage
there's mommy now	Daddy sleeping	want pop pop
there's my mommy	Daddy's hungry	
it ə bed	I got some	
he tired	I got dolly	
here it is	I want hot dog	
there it is	you got my two	
it outside	dollars	
	I want carrot	
	I don't see ən ə	
	garage	
	Mommy over there	

To illustrate a CORS analysis using Tommy's language sample, sentence subjects were selected as a target system. They fit the criteria for selection in that they were obligatory in many contexts and used in both a restricted and adult manner. The above utterances are those where a subject was obligatory (they do not include questions, imperatives, and elliptical responses).

Both sentences that contain the copula, where the copula subject is a demonstrative pronoun (e.g., "this," "that," "there") and sentences with main verbs are included. One pattern of grammatical cooccurrence that differentiates restricted forms from the adult forms is the inclusion of copula subjects. As a matter of fact, they are always included. (See the first column.) Main verbs, on the other hand, may or may not cooccur with sentence subjects. The lexical item omitted in the restricted forms was generally "I," yet "I" occurred in other utterances that did not differ in complexity; the predicate of both adult and restricted forms of sentences with main verbs included complexity. Thus, the CORS analysis cannot completely account for the inconsistent inclusion of sentence subject. One can, however, account for the restricted structures when content is also considered, as will be discussed later. Although the concept of CORS is important, the restriction of such analysis to form alone may weaken its effectiveness.

intervention but, as stressed throughout this book, form is only relevant when related to content and use. If goals of intervention are to include content/form/use interactions, then analyses that lead to goals must include all three. In this section we will present a procedure for the analysis of content/form interactions and, in a later section, a procedure for analysis of use interacting with content/form will be presented.

It is possible to superimpose content interactions on the form classification systems that have just been discussed. For example, under Lee's (1974) DST Verbal Elaboration Category, one could subcategorize content categories of action, locative action, and internal state. Sentence types, as presented by either Streng (1972), Tyack and Gottsleben (1974), or Engler et al. (1973), or sentences listed for Lee's DSS could be subcategorized according to the semantic relations between the verb and the nouns, and the resulting analyses could be reported as content/form interactions.

Another approach is to begin with a classification of content in children's messages using the framework presented in the first part of this book. This focus has intuitive appeal for those who feel that children learn forms to talk about content in early language learning. After a content categorization is obtained, the forms that the child used for talking about each category can be described with a resulting description of content/form interactions. These procedures differ from the other language sample analyses discussed here in that another component, *content*, is added and that content is the prime focus—the *first* level of categorization.

In order to lead directly to the goals of intervention the categories of content/form interactions used are those listed in Chapters XIII, XIV, and XV under goals of language learning. The objective here is to determine which of these content/form interactions are already a part of the child's language system and which have yet to be learned. The interactions that are not yet a part of the child's system will become goals of intervention and the sequence in which they will be presented is determined by the sequence of phases (a concept similar to linguistic level). Goals in earlier phases (Phases 1 and 2, for instance) will generally precede goals in later phases (such as Phases 5 and 6).

To describe the procedure for determining the content/form goals of intervention, the language sample of Tommy, that was analyzed and discussed earlier for form alone, was analyzed again. This time all utterances (over 175) obtained during the ½ hour observation were considered. At first Tommy played with a dollhouse; later he played with a telephone, toy fruit, and trains.

Categorizing Content of Verb Relations

In analyzing Tommy's utterances, the first level of analysis concerned *multiword* syntactic utterances. These utterances were *first* categorized according to the categories of the verb relations because eventually all other categories become coordinated with the verb categories. To categorize an utterance as an example of *syntactic* coding of a verb relation, at least two of the major constituents of subject-verb-complement (SVC) must be present. There is, however, one exception. Sentences that express state can include the categories of existence, possession, and attribution. When such sentences contain the copula, the copula subject can be a demonstrative pronoun ("this," "that," "there," etc.). If the *only* examples of SVC are copular subjects with demonstrative pronouns, these are not categorized as verb relations, since they are often early-learned routines and are not evidence of knowledge of grammatical relations. (See Chapter V.) The term complement is used here in its traditional sense and includes any constituents that complete the verb—the object affected by the action, the place in locative utterances, and the predicate nominative or adjective. Note that locative utterances may have two obligatory constituents within the complement: object and place.

To determine the appropriate verb category for each utterance, both the form of the utterance and the context in which it was spoken were used (see Chapters XIV and XV for descriptions and examples of all content categories and Chapter II for a discussion of explicit versus implicit meaning). For example, if Tommy said "dolly sit down" as he sat the doll, it was categorized as locative action, but the same utterance would be categorized as locative state if he had referred to the fact that a doll was already sitting in a chair. Thus, utterances such as "put coat," "coat chair" "mommy put," "mommy coat," or "mommy chair" (referring to mommy putting her coat on the chair) would have been categorized as locative action. If the utterance included another content category in addition to the two constituents of a verb relation—such as "put my coat," "coat big chair"—these utterances, if spoken in the context above, would also be categorized as locative action. So far, the categorization only applies to the semantics of the verb relation in multiword utterances that included two major constituents of a verb relation. Multiword utterances that were simple codings of other categories—such as "Bobby car" (possession), "big car" (attribution), "no car" (nonexistence, denial, or rejection), and "two new coats" (attribution and quantity)—as well as single-word utterances, were categorized separately and will be discussed later.

Before starting analyses, every intelligible utterance on the transcript was numbered for easy reference back to the transcript. All utterances that included two constituents (including object and place in locative utterances) of a verb relation were placed with their number on a worksheet that represented that relation. Only different utterances (examples of utterance *types*) were recorded on these sheets. If the same utterance was repeated a number of times it was written once (different comments about use may be included, however). The frequency of occurrence (the number of *tokens*) was stated in parentheses beside the utterance. All available utterances with two constituents were categorized.

It is important to note that a lot of time was not spent on a few isolated utterances that were difficult to categorize; if in doubt about action versus locative action, the utterance would have been placed on the action sheet and starred to note uncertainty. All other utterances that fit more than one category were called *equivocal* and were listed separately, noting the possible categories in which they might be placed. Utterances that were semantically anomalous were written on a separate sheet marked undetermined or anomalous.

Tables XVI-3 to XVI-8 present the utterances in Tommy's language sample that contained at least two major constituents of a verb relation. (Demonstrative pronouns plus noun were considered two constituents here, since examples of subject-verb-complement were found in other verb categories.) Each table represents a different verb relation (noted on the top of the sheet as content category). The utterances were listed in the left column. The next 8 columns, marked Form Analysis, were used to note the presence or absence of the major constituents (this analysis will be discussed next). The last two columns were used to make comments on both the context and function of the utterances (to be discussed in a later section about use). The information in the form columns was summarized below each column (also discussed in the next section). Finally, the bottom third of the table was used to note the coordination of other categories with each verb relation (also to be discussed).

Describing Form and the Coordination of Content Categories

Form analysis focussed on the major grammatical constituents of subject-verb-complement (SVC)—recall that the copula is here considered as the verb. The purpose of this analysis was to determine the number of constituents that were included in order to determine whether the category was *productive* at Phase 2 or 3, and to compare the number included with the number expected in the model language to determine *achievement*. Last, the particular constituents omitted were noted and often described. For example, in Table XVI-4, the first utterance "she eat supper" included the three expected constituents of SVC, and so a 3 was placed in the column for inclusion of three constituents and in the column for three constituents expected. In contrast, the second utterance "gonna eat supper" included only two constituents where three were expected. A 2 was placed in the column for inclusion of two constituents and a 3 was placed in the column for three constituents expected. An 0 was placed under S in the column for expected constituents omitted to note that it was the subject that was omitted. Under comments "-Agent, Other" describes the omitted subject as an agent of an action who was other than Tommy himself.

Each column was totaled to determine whether two or three constituents were productive in Tommy's language. Again using Table XVI-4 as an example, there were 14 examples of action expressed with two constituents, certainly meeting the criterion of productivity, but only two examples of the inclusion of three constituents. From these totals it is apparent that the content category action was productive at Phase 2 (with two constituent utterances) but not at Phase 3 (where three constituent utterances would be expected). It was further noted that the constituent omitted was usually the subject in utterances most often referring to Tommy himself as the agent of an action.

In order to determine whether Tommy coordinated content categories and embedded other content in action utterances with at least two constituents, any other content category that was represented in an utterance was underlined. For example, in Table XVI-4 "gonna" was underlined in the second utterance "gonna eat supper," as an example of intention. Some of the content categories that could be coordinated with action utterances are listed in the lower part of the table. Intention has been included under Time (see the chart in Chapter XIII) and so the utterance number and the word "Intention" were written under Time. All of the lexical items underlined in each table represent coordinated content categories listed at the bottom of the table.

Plotting goals for Verb Categories

The information about verb categories was then summarized according to the sequential goals presented in Chapters XIII, XIV, and XV (see Table XVI-9). In Table XVI-9 the six verb relations are presented with the forms used to code each, along with coordinated categories, according to the phases outlined in Chapters XIII, XIV, and XV. The actual number of utterances was written on the line in front of the possible forms or coordinations. Thus the action row states that 14 utterances included only two constituents (SVC), while 2 utterances included three constituents. In addition, there was one coordination with intention, one with place, one with -*ing*, and two with Wh-questions.

When evidence of proportional occurrence in expected contexts was available, it was written in parentheses (as here 3 constituents were included 20% of the time they were expected). When the number of utterances exceeded four and the percent of inclusion in expected contexts approximated 90%, that interaction was not considered as a goal of intervention. However, behaviors in the next two phases beyond that interaction, or nonproductive behaviors in earlier phases, were potential goals.

TABLE XVI-3
Language Sample Analysis Worksheet

CONTENT CATEGORY Existence   CHILD'S NAME Tommy   DATE OF SAMPLE _____

	Form Analysis								Use Analysis	
	Subject-Verb-Complement Constituents				Expected Constituents Omitted					
	Included		Expected							
Utterances[a]	2	3+	2	3+	S	V	C	Comments	Context	Function
17 what's this		3							Ch-I	Obtain Information
18 it ə bed	2			3		0		-Copula	R-Q+	
26 this mom	2			3		0		-Copula	Ch-I	Comment
37 this is the homework		3		3					Ch-I	Comment
60 this it is the bed		3		3					Ch-I	Comment
61 this dolly	2			3		0		-Copula	Ch-I	Comment
77 that daddy	2			3		0		-Copula	R-Q+ point	
79 there's table		3		3					Ch-I	Comment
84 that's dad		3		3					R-S+	
99 that my daddy	2			3		0		-Copula	R-Q-	
100 that's my mommy		3		3					Ch-I	Comment
111 this ə phone	2			3		0		-Copula	Ch-I	Comment
157 what's your name		3		3					Ch-I	Ritual

Frequency of utterances (to
determine productivity)　　6　7　13　6

Proportion of utterances with
expected constituents in-
cluded (to determine
achievement)　　→　→　→

$$7 \div 13 = \underline{.54}$$

Coordinated categories (utterances that include two constituents plus another content category)

Nonexistence	Rejection	Denial	Recurrence	Attribution	Possession	Quantity	Time	Mood	Dative	Specification	Causality	Conjunction	Wh-Question	Place	"a"
					$\frac{my}{100}$					$\frac{the}{37}$			$\frac{what}{17}$		18
					99					60			157		111
					$\frac{your}{157}$										

[a] Numbers in front of utterances refer to number of utterance on the transcript.

TABLE XVI-4
Language Sample Analysis Worksheet

CONTENT CATEGORY __Action__ CHILD'S NAME __Tommy__ DATE OF SAMPLE _____

	Form Analysis								Use Analysis	
	Subject-Verb-Complement Constituents				Expected Constituents Omitted					
	Included		Expected							
Utterances[a]	2	3+	2	3+	S	V	C	Comments	Context	Function
27 she eat supper		3		3					Ch-I	Pretend
88 gonna eat supper	2			3	0			-Agent, Other	Ch-I Negate	with head nod
93 when we eat	2		2						Ch-I	Ritual, Pretend
112 eat hot dogs	2			3	0			-Agent, Other	R–Q+	Pretend
115 eat right in the house	2			3	0			-Agent, Other	Ch-I	Comment
118 say yes	2		2						Ch-I	Demand
119 who calling	2		2						Ch-I	Ritual
128 get a coke	2			3	0			-Agent, Self	Ch-I	Pretend
129 I get money		3		3					Ch-I	Pretend
145 buy milk	2			3	0			-Agent, Self	R–Q–	Pretend
146 drink it	2			3	0			-Agent, Self	Ch-I	Pretend
149 get money	2			3	0			-Agent, Self	Ch-I	Pretend
155 eat carrot	2			3	0			-Agent, Self	Ch-I	Comment
164 give money back	2		2						Ch-I	Demand
167 give me that	2		2						Ch-I	Demand
174 help me	2		2						Ch-I	Demand

Frequency of utterances (to determine productivity)   14   2   6   10   8

Proportion of utterances with expected constituents in-cluded (to determine achievement)   2 ÷ 10 = .20

Coordinated categories (utterances that include two constituents plus another content category)

Nonexistence	Rejection	Denial	Recurrence	Attribution	Possession	Quantity	Time	Mood	Dative	Specification	Causality	Conjunction	Wh-Question	Place
						-s 112	-ing 119		167				who 119	115
							Inten- tion 88						when 93	

[a] Numbers in front of utterances refer to number of utterance on the transcript.

463

TABLE XVI-5
Language Sample Analysis Worksheet

CONTENT CATEGORY Locative Action   CHILD'S NAME Tommy   DATE OF SAMPLE _____

	Form Analysis								Use Analysis	
	Subject-Verb-Complement Constituents				Expected Constituents Omitted					
	Included		Expected							
Utterances[a]	2	3+	2	3+	S	V	C	Comments	Context	Function
3 an come in house	2			3	0			-Patient	R-S+	
19 chair in the room[b]	2			3/4	?	0		-Verb (maybe -Agent)	Ch-I	Comment
22 there a little bed	2			3		0		-Copula	Ch-I	Comment
23 there's the Mommy's bed		3		3					Ch-I	Comment
25 dolly fall (2)	2		2						R-Q+	
30 go in that way	2			3	0				R-Q+	
41 mommy sit down there		3		3					R-S+	Comment
43 there's daddy (2)		3		3					Ch-I	Comment
47 my baby upstairs[b]	2			3/4	?	0		-Verb (maybe -Agent)	Ch-I	Comment
71 put in the hou_s/c garage	2			4	0		0	-Agent, Self -Object	R-Q+	
72 it outside	2			3		0		-Copula	Ch-I	Comment
75 there's my mommy		3		3					Ch-I	Comment
81 we're goin to bed[b]		3		3					Ch-I	Comment
87 mommy in this bed[b]	2			3/4	?	0		-Verb (maybe -Agent)	Ch-I	Comment
101 daddy going up	2		2						Ch-I	Comment
102 daddy go in this one		3		3					Ch-I	Comment
150 there it is		3		3					Ch-I	Comment

464

Frequency of utterances (to determine productivity)   10   7   2   15   3   5   1

Proportion of utterances with expected constituents included (to determine achievement).   7 ÷ 15 = .47

Coordinated categories (utterances that include two constituents plus another content category)

Nonexistence	Rejection	Denial	Recurrence	Attribution	Possession	Quantity	Time	Mood	Dative	Specification	Causality	Conjunction	Wh-Question	Place	Verb plus preposition
				22	$\frac{my}{47}$ 75		$\frac{-ing}{81}$ 101			$\frac{the}{19}$ 23					$\frac{in}{3}$ 30
					$\frac{-s}{23}$		$\frac{ed-}{(aux.)}$ 81			$\frac{that}{30}$					71
										$\frac{this}{87}$ 100					$\frac{to}{102}$ 81

[a] Numbers in front of utterances refer to number of utterance on the transcript.

[b] These three utterances were, in fact, ambiguous in terms of form description. They could have been interpreted as including two constituents of the complement (object-place) with subject (as agent) and verb deleted. ("I put *mommy in this bed*") instead of as including subject-complement constituents with the subject as patient and verb deleted ("*mommy goes in this bed*").

TABLE XVI-6
Language Sample Analysis Worksheet

CONTENT CATEGORY __Locative State__ CHILD'S NAME __Tommy__ DATE OF SAMPLE _____

	Form Analysis								Use Analysis	
	Subject-Verb-Complement Constituents				Expected Constituents Omitted					
	Included		Expected							
Utterances[a]	2	3+	2	3+	S	V	C	Comments	Context	Function
13 there's a bed		3							R-Q+	Comment
34 where dolly (2)	2			3		0		-Copula	Ch-I	Tease
36 where's mom		3							R-Q-	Tease
39 where'd she go		3							R-Q-	Tease
40 where's daddy (2)		3							R-S+	Tease
51 there is	2			3			0		R-Q-	
56 where the bed	2			3		0		-Copula	Ch-I	Obtain information
59 where mommy's bed	2			3		0		-Copula	Ch-I	Obtain information
62 there's mommy now		3							Ch-I	Comment
73 where'd go	2			3	0				Ch-I	Obtain information
78 Mommy over there	2			3		0		-Copula	R-Q+	
107 where the phone	2			3		0		-Copula	Ch-I	Obtain information
121 is daddy here		3							R-S	Ritual
139 here it is		3							R-Q+	
175 where the train is		3							Ch-I	Obtain information

466

Frequency of utterances (to
determine productivity)   7   8   15   1   5   1

Proportion of utterances
with expected constitu-
ents included (to deter-
mine achievement)   8 ÷ 15 = $\underline{.53}$

Coordinated categories (utterances that include two constituents plus another content category)

Nonexistence	Rejection	Denial	Recurrence	Attribution	Possession	Quantity	Time	Mood	Dative	Specification	Causality	Conjunction	Wh-Question	Place
					$\underline{\text{-s}}$		$\underline{\text{now}}$			$\underline{\text{the}}$			$\underline{\text{where}}$	
					59		62			56			34	
										107			36	
										175			39	
													40	
													56	
													59	
													73	
													107	
													175	

[a] Numbers in front of utterances refer to number of utterance on the transcript.

TABLE XVI-7
Language Sample Analysis Worksheet
Verb Category

CONTENT CATEGORY State   CHILD'S NAME Tommy   DATE OF SAMPLE

	Form Analysis								Use Analysis	
	Subject-Verb-Complement Constituents				Expected Constituents Omitted					
	Included		Expected		S	V	C	Comments	Context	Function
Utterances[a]	2	3+	2	3+						
Internal State										
21 I don't know	2		2						R-Q+	
50 he tired	2			3		0		-Copula-	Ch I	Comment
52 mommy sleeping	2		2						R-Q-	Reason
53 daddy sleeping	2		2						R-Q+	
90 daddy's hungry		3		3					R-S-	
125 want pop pop	2			3	0			-Self	Ch-I pretend	Request
134 I want hot dog		3		3					Ch-I pretend	Request
154 I want carrot		3		3					R-S+	Comment
Possessive State										
42 I got some		3		3					R-Q+	
44 I got dolly		3		3					R-Q-	
132 you got my 2 dollars		3		3					Ch-I pretend	Obtain information
137 got any money	2		2						Ch-I pretend	Obtain information
Attributive State										
14 so little	2			3	0				R-Q+	

468

Frequency of utterances (to determine productivity) 7 6 4 9 2 1

Proportion of utterances with expected constituents included (to determine achievement)

$$6 \div 9 = .66$$

Coordinated categories (utterances that include two constituents plus another content category)

Nonexistence	Rejection	Denial	Recurrence	Attribution	Possession	Quantity	Time	Mood	Dative	Specification	Causality	Conjunction	Wh-Question	Place
don't 21					my 132	some 42 any 137 -s 132 two 132	-ing 52 53							

a Numbers in front of utterances refer to number of utterance on the transcript.

TABLE XVI-8
Language Sample Analysis Worksheet

CHILD'S NAME Tommy   DATE OF SAMPLE _____

CONTENT CATEGORY Notice

	Form Analysis								Use Analysis	
	Subject-Verb-Complement Constituents				**Expected Constituents Omitted**					
	Included		Expected						Context	Function
Utterances[a]	2	3+	2	3+	S	V	C	Comments		
1 I <u>don't</u> see a garage		3		3					Ch-I	Comment
97 see window	2		2						Ch-I	Call attention
Frequency of utterances (to determine productivity)	1	1	1	1						
Proportion of utterances with expected constituents included (to determine achievement).	↓ 1	↓ ÷	1	= *1.0*						

Coordinated categories (utterances that include two constituents plus another content category)

Nonexistence   Rejection   Denial   Recurrence   Attribution   Possession   Quantity   Time   Mood   Dative   Specification   Causality   Conjunction   Wh- Question   Place

$\dfrac{\text{don't}}{1}$

[a] Numbers in front of utterances refer to number of utterance on the transcript.

470

Based on this analysis, goals for Tommy included Phase 3 and Phase 4 behaviors. Two of the goals involved increasing the frequency of the production of three constituents to code action and locative action. To specify these goals further, the semantic role of the individual constituents (SVC) used and omitted was examined in each category (see Chapter V for a definition of these roles). In the action category Tommy usually talked about what he was doing and omitted naming himself as agent—subject as self-agent was most often the deleted constituent. The subject of locative action sentences was included more often than the subject of action sentences—47% versus 20%. These subjects of locative action did not, however, code agent of the action but, instead, patient. They referred to the object he was locating as in utterance 87 on Table XVI-5, "mommy in this bed," as he put the mommy doll on the bed.[3] The most often deleted constituent in locative action was the verb, and second most frequent was the subject. The object was rarely deleted, and the place was never deleted. The goal of increasing the use of three constituents could now be stated more specifically in terms of content:

1. To increase the use of subjects as agents of actions.
2. To increase the use of verbs in syntactic utterances that code locative actions.

Thus, these two goals of content/form include, as did the previous analyses of form according to Lee (1974) and Tyack and Gottsleben (1974), increasing the use of subject-verb-complement sentences, but here the goal is stated in terms of both content and form. The constituent that was missing was seen to vary with the semantics of the verb relation and could be described according to content. Note that this analysis accounts for the inconsistent use of subject that could not be accounted for using the CORS analysis (Muma, 1973 and Box XVI-1), which focussed only on form.

Other goals for action and locative action involved the coordination of other categories with the verb relations. They are listed here as further goals, but they may be superceded, in terms of sequence, by the further analysis of these coordinated categories. For example, if a category, such as attribution, was not productive (i.e., was not coded syntactically at least four times) in the sample, the simple syntactic coding of attribution—a Phase 2 behavior—would become a goal before the coordination of attribution with action—a Phase 4 behavior. With this in mind, the next goals for the verb relations of action and locative action were as follows:

3. To coordinate intention—"gonna", "wanna"—within action and locative action utterances.

---

[3] The interpretation of these utterances as two constituents of the complement instead of patient-place would not alter the fact that agent was the semantic role of deleted subjects.

TABLE XVI-9
Results of Verb Category Analysis
Phases of Content/Form Interaction
(Forms Used and Coordinations of Categories)

CHILD'S NAME *Tommy*

Verb Relations	1	2	3	Phases of Content/Form Interaction 4	5	6	7	8
Action	—sw (verb)	*14* 2-Const	*2* 3-Const (20%)	*1* Place / *1* Intent / — Rec / — Attrib / — Nonexist / *1* –ing	— Intent + Poss / — Reject / — Intent + Place / — Irregular past		(*2* Wh-Q)	
Locative Action	—sw (prep or verb)	*10* 2-Const	*7* 3-Const (47%)	— Intent	*5* V +Prep / *2* –ing / *3* Poss / (— Nonexist) / — 3rd Pers –s	*1* Attrib / (— Rec)		

Locative state

            $\frac{7}{8}$ 2-Const   — Prep

            $\underline{8}$ 3-Const $\underline{9}$ Wh-Q

            (53%)

State

            $\frac{7}{6}$ 2-Const   (— Attrib)   ($\underline{1}$ Poss)

            $\underline{6}$ 3-Const   (— Rec)

            (66%)

Notice

                    $\underline{2}$ 2-3-Const   — Compl

Existence   — sw $\underline{13}$ 2 words   (— Attrib) $\underline{2}$ "a" $\underline{2}$ Wh-Q

                                        $\underline{\ }$ Rec $\underline{7}$ Copula

                                        $\underline{3}$ Poss

KEY

sw	= single word utterance	Reject	= rejection
Const	= constituent	Prep	= preposition
	(subject-verb-complement)	Compl	= complement
Intent	= intention	Pers	= person
Rec	= recurrence	Nonexist	= nonexistence
Attrib	= attribution	( )	= goal optional in this phase
Poss	= possession	(%)	= percent of expected occurrence
Wh-Q	= wh-questions	V	= verb

473

4. To coordinate recurrence—"again", "more"—within action utterances.
5. To coordinate attribution within action utterances.
6. To coordinate place within action utterances.
7. To coordinate nonexistence within action utterances.
8. To coordinate present progressive -*ing* with action.

Goals for locative state included use of the prepositional phrase to indicate static location of objects as a part of the complement (e.g., "the doll is *on the bed*") using both "in" and "on":

9. To use prepositions "in" and "on" to talk of static location.

Last, goals for existence included:

10. To coordinate attribution within existence utterances ("that's a big bed").[4]
11. To coordinate recurrence within existence utterances ("that's another man").
12. To coordinate possession within existence utterances ("that's my doll").

The missing constituent in existence and locative state categories was generally the copula verb, which was productive but not used in 90% of expected contexts. It would become a goal after Phase 3 and 4 behaviors have been reached. There were no goals for state at this time, but goals for notice would include:

13. To increase the use of notice verbs and coding notice with two or three constituents.

Once having completed the analysis of content/form interactions that specifically related to verb categories, the remaining categories were analyzed.

Tabulating Remaining Categories

The remaining utterances were categorized on a separate sheet (see Table XVI-10). First, the number of times these categories were coordinated with all verb relations was obtained by totaling the columns on the verb category sheets and placing the number, (with the form used when it influenced phase placement), in the first column of Table XVI-10. If the total

---

[4] Recall that some goals are listed in Chapters XIII, XIV, and XV as optional goals and are marked in Table XVI-9 in parentheses. In this analysis, these included the coordination of attribution with existence. The decision to work on these behaviors would be determined by the frequency with which these relations were coded in two-word utterances; by the ease with which the child acquired them; and by the intuitive discretion of the clinician. Optional merely suggests that they can be postponed for a phase or two and that lack of progress on these goals would not inhibit movement to other coordinations, which may be goals of a later level.

number of coordinations exceeded the criterion of four, the particular category was considered productive at the two-word level. For example, the *possessive* was used three times in locative action, three times in existence, once in locative state, and once in state, for a total of eight instances. Since the number of coordinations exceeded the number for establishing productivity of possession with two words, and there was no way of establishing the expected context for the use of possession, the transcript was not searched for further examples. Next the number of utterances coding possession was entered in Table XVI-11 which, like Table XVI-9, lists content/form interactions by phase but, *unlike* Table XVI-9, lists only forms that are *not* specified in the plan in terms of their coordination with a verb relation. Tommy had a total of 8 utterances which included two words to code possession and so was given credit for productivity of the content/form interaction in Phase 2. Two of these utterances also used -*s* and were noted in Phase 5, but -*s* was not used frequently enough to be considered productive.

If fewer than four coordinated examples were noted, the data were searched for examples of the category that occurred as single words or in phrases that did not include a verb relation. For example, recurrence was not present in coordination with a verb relation, but was found six times in two- or three-word utterances without a verb relation. Thus the category was productive in Phase 2 (see Tables XVI-10 and XVI-11). When the expected content could be determined for a productive form, as "the" or plural -*s*, the percent of expected occurrence was noted in the last column.

Based on the goals for verb relations, Phase 4 or below behaviors that were not productive became goals. More information was needed about behaviors that are listed in early phases and where few examples were found (e.g., rejection). Goals for these categories were written as assessment goals instead of intervention goals:

14. To obtain further information about coding rejection, denial and attribution.

Thus, the remaining goals derived from Table XVI-11 were as follows:

15. To increase the use of plural -*s* (optional goal).
16. To code quantity using "some," "many," and "all."

These goals were also plotted on the schematization of the plan presented in Box XIII-3. To do so, the information from Tables XVI-9 and XVI-11 was directly translated by cross-hatching the productive interactions, double cross-hatching achieved interactions, and circling the interactions for immediate goals (see Box XVI-2). When only partial evidence was available an x was recorded.

TABLE XVI-10
Worksheet for Remaining Analyses[a,b]

CHILD'S NAME *Tommy*

Category	Number of Times Coordinated	Single Words	Noncoordinated Examples[a,b] Syntactic Utterances	Percent of Expected Occurrence
Nonexistence	don't (2)	131 all gone	130 no money (2)[b]; 147 all gone juice;	
Rejection				
Denial		110 no (2)		
Recurrence			160 more money; 166 more toys 162 some more; 171 some more track; 12 two more toys 176 here go again	
Attribution	1			
Possession	my (5) -s (2) your (1)			
Quantity	-s (2) some (1) any (1) numbers (1)		12 two more toys; 8 one dolly; 152 one dollar; 158 nobody home; 166 more toys; 171 some more track	-s 80

476

Mood		
Dative		the 54
Specifier	this (2) that (1) the (7)	33 this way (2); 32 that way (8); 46 in this way
Causal	117 cause; 165 why	
Coordinate		
Place		

Some Examples of Verb Categories with One Constituent

Existence	9 ə dolly; 45 ə baby; 168 ə tunnel; 169 ə train; 170 ə track
Action	49 kiss 156 bite 92 eat
Notice	9 look
Locative action	94 outside 38 upstairs 103 downstairs	54 in the bed (3); 16 in the room (2); 46 in this way; 80 in the kitchen; 120 in there
State	65 tired

[a] Numbers before the utterances refer to the numbers on the transcript.
[b] Number in parentheses indicates number of tokens, if more than one.

TABLE XVI-11

Results of Nonverb Category Analysis

CHILD'S NAME *Tommy*

Content Categories	Phases of Content/Form Interaction							
	1	2	3	4	5	6	7	8
Nonexistence	_1_ sw	_4_ 2-words			___"not" ___"can't" ___"didn't"			
Rejection	__ sw			(__2-words)	___don't			
Denial	_2_ sw				___"not" ___2-words			
Recurrence	__ sw	_6_ 2 words						
Attribution	(__ sw)	(_1_ 2-words)						
Possession	(sw)	(_8_ 2 words)			_2_'s			
Quantity			$\left(\dfrac{4\text{-}s\ (80\%)}{4\ \text{"one" or "two"}}\right)$		___"all" _1_ "some" ___"many"			

Time

Mood

Dative

Specifier

Causal

Coordinate

Epistemic

Antithesis

_1_ "now"   _1_ "be" aux
              __ "ed"
              __ "when"

__ can   __ "should"
              __ "have to"

__ +prep.   __ 2-words

_7_ "the"   _6_ "this"/
(54%)   "that"

(__ "and")   __ su   __ "because"   _1_ "why"
                        __ "so"

              __ "and"   __ "and
              __ su   then"

(__ "what")

              __ "and"
              (__ "but")

Key

sw	= single-word utterance	aux	= auxilliary
su	= successive utterance	prep	= preposition
( )	= goal optional in this phase	(%)	= percent of expected occurrence

479

BOX XVI-2 INFORMATION FROM TOMMY'S LANGUAGE SAMPLE ANALYSIS PLOTTED ON A PLAN FOR LANGUAGE DEVELOPMENT GOALS: CONTENT/FORM

PHASE	EXISTENCE	NONEXISTENCE	RECURRENCE	REJECTION	DENIAL	ATTRIBUTION	POSSESSION	ACTION	LOCATIVE ACTION	LOCATIVE STATE
1	SW	SW	SW	? SW	? (SW)	? (SW)	(SW)	SW	SW	
2	R + S	R + S S + R	R + S S + R			? (Adj + N)	[N P] + N	2 Const	2 Const V + Prep Prep + N	
3	(+Attri-bution) ?					(+ Exist-ence) ?		3 Const	3 Const	**LOCATIVE STATE** 2–3 Const
4	+Recur-rence +Posses-sion "a"	+Action	+Exist-ence +Action	?(R + S)		+Action ?	+Existence	+Attribution*? +Place +Non-existence* +Recurrence* +Intention –ing	+Intention	+Wh-Q +Prep
5	+Wh-Q +Copula	"can't" "didn't" "not" (+Locative Action)	(+State)	"don't" +Action	R + S "not"	(+State)	–'s +Action +Locative Action	+Irregular past +Possession* +Rejection* +Place and Intention +Possession and Intention	V + Prep* +Possession (+Nonexistence*) Patient +3rd Per –s Mover –ing	
6			(+Locative Action)			+Locative Action	(+State)		+Attribution* (+Recurrence*)	
7								(+Wh-Q)		
8										

KEY

sw	= single word utterance	( )	= optional goal— C/F can be postponed until a later phase
R	= relational word		
S	= substantive word	| |	= either one or other of the bracketed forms
N	= noun		
V	= verb	*	= first productions may be with two instead of three constituents
P	= pronoun	○	= immediate goals
Prep	= preposition	✕	= partial evidence available
Const	= major grammatical constituents (Subject—Verb—Complement)	\\\	= productive interaction
		✕✕	= achieved interaction
+	= coordination of two or more categories	?	= further information needed

	STATE	QUANTITY	NOTICE	TIME	COORDINATE	CAUSALITY	DATIVE	SPECIFIER	EPISTEMIC	MOOD	ANTITHESIS
3	2-3 Const	(-s) (numbers)									
4			2-3 Const	-ing +Action Intention +Action +Locative Action							
5	(+Attribution) (+Recurrence)	"some" "many" "all"		-ing +Locative Action-Mover Irregular Past +Action 3rd Pers -s +Locative Action-Patient	SUCCESSIVE CLAUSES Intraclausal "and" (Interclausal "and")		N + N	"this/that"			
6	(+Possession)			"now"		("and")	+Prep "to" "for"	"the"			
7					"and then"	"because" "so"			("what")	"can"	"and" ("but")
8			Complement "what"	Time Specification "when" Progressive "be" Past -ed 3rd Pers -s		+Wh-Q		Relative Clause "that" "where"		["should" "have to"]	

Comparison of Form Goals with Content/Form Goals

The same language sample has now been analyzed three times, and three sets of goals based on developmental data have been devised; two were based on form and one was based on content/form interactions. In general, the similarities are more striking than the differences (see Table XVI-12). The differences can be characterized in three ways: (1) certain behaviors are not analyzed or listed as goals by one method but are by another (e.g., Lee does not include articles); (2) a goal is sequenced earlier or later in an analysis (e.g., articles are sequenced earlier by Tyack and Gottsleben than in the content/form goals); and (3) one specifies content and form while the other two specify form only. The latter difference, the inclusion of content, is least noticeable with goals involving grammatical morphemes, such as plurals, -ed endings, and the like. With most grammatical morphemes, the content is obvious. The content/form goals do however, list some verb inflections according to the content of the verb relation. The difference between form and content/form analyses is most marked in sentence types and sentence modifications that can involve many content categories and their coordinations. Categorization by sentence types, or by the linear arrangement of words according to parts of speech, does not provide information about *what* the child is talking about; it does not allow for differences that occur within these types. Told to teach "noun + verb + noun + noun" sentences, a clinician or teacher might work on indirect object or dative relationship, such as "I gave *the baby* the ball," which is developmentally later than locative prepositional phrases such as "I put the ball *on the table*." In addition, the goal of "noun + verb + noun" may be considered achieved under goals of form if the child produces a number of such utterances about action, although the child may not use this type of construction to talk about locative action, notice, or state.

The suggested analysis of content/form, then, adds another dimension of language to the goals of intervention. Each of the three sets of goals based on the three different analyses provided hypotheses for intervention. At the present time, it appears that enough information is available about the normal development of content/form interactions so that analyses of these interactions are an important part of the analyses of language samples for determining the goals of intervention.

Categorizing Single-Word Utterances

If most of the utterances a child produces are syntactic and goals for most categories are at Phase 3 or above, as in Tommy's sample, it is not necessary to analyze all single-word utterances. When, however, a child is speaking primarily in single-word utterances, all single words are analyzed. Table XVI-13 illustrates the categorization of utterances obtained in a ½ hour

TABLE XVI-12

Comparison of Content/Form Goals with Form Goals for Tommy

Content/Form Goals	Form Goals	
	Lee	Tyack and Gottsleben
Similarities		
Increase use of subject coding agents of actions and locative actions	S-V-O	Goal of N + V + N *achieved*
Increase use of different verbs that code locative actions with subject and complement	S-V-O	Goal of N + V + N *achieved*
Coordinate place with action utterances	*Not included*	N + V + N + N
Prepositions "in" and "on" to talk of static locations	*Not included*	N + V + N + N
Increase use of utterances coding notice with two or three constituents	S-V-O	Goal of N + V + N *achieved*
"Wanna", or "gonna", to code an intention to act	"wanna" and "gonna"	"want" and "wanna" Mod + V + N
Coordinate nonexistence and action	"no" and "not" + verb	"no" and sentence "no" and "not" after subject
Plural -s (optional)	Plural -s	Plural -s
Code present progressive -ing with action	"is" -ing	-ing
Differences:		
Coordinate recurrence with action and existence	Not included in DSS	An earlier goal, V + Mod + N
Coordinate attribution with action and existence	Analyzed in DST but not clear if or when modifiers are goals	Not listed as later goal, but analyzed under N + V + N
Coordinate possession with action and existence		
Use of "same" and "many"	*A later goal*	Not included
Not included	"me"	"me"
Later goal—Wh- Questions of existence	Wh- questions	"What" as question in subject position
Later goal—to use copula with locative state and existence	Copula	N + is + N/Adj
Later goal—"the" to code specification	Not included, although analyzed on DST	Articles
Later goal —irregular past with action	Irregular past	*Much later goal*
Later goal—-s with patient-locative action; -ed, *much later*	-s-ed inflections	*Much later goal*

Key
S-V-O = subject-verb-object
N   = noun
V   = verb
Mod   = modifier

TABLE XVI-13

Analyses of Content/Form Interactions—Single-Word Utterances, for Jay

Relational Words		Nouns
Content Category		*To label static objects:*
Existence	*none*	soup (2)[a], money, doll (Imit.)[b] chin, Jay, umbrella, Judy
Nonexistence	*none*	
Recurrence	*none*	
Rejection	no (2)	*Objects named as he acted*
Denial	no	*upon or located them:*
Attribution	red	truck, soup, button, shoe,
Possession	*none*	mouth, chin, shirt, watch, box, paper, cup, milk, home, money (2), shoe, box,
Action and locative action	open (5), eat (3) tie (5), take, in, off, go out pour (4)	
Time	now	
Causal	why, cause	*Objects named that were not present:* cake, home, gym (Imit.)

Undetermined
  uh, umbrella
Equivocal
  rip (action, attributive
  state) button (action
  verb or noun)

---

[a] Number in parentheses indicates number of tokens, if more than one.
[b] (Imit.) refers to an imitated utterance.

videotape session with a 5-year-old boy, Jay, a student clinician, Judy, and toys including a doll, a play store, and assorted cars and trucks. During the session, Jay also ate a part of his lunch.

Single-word utterances were first separated into nouns and relational words, and then most of the relational words were categorized according to the content categories previously discussed; for example, Jay handed a box to the clinician and said "open" after he had unsuccessfully tried to open it. This utterance was placed under action. The categories for a few relational words were not clear. For example, "rip" was considered equivocal because when Jay looked at a torn bag and said "rip," he may have been referring to the present state of the bag ("the bag is ripped"), or to a past action ("someone ripped it"), or he may have been naming or describing the tear in the bag. Such words were classed as equivocal. There were other utterances that were undetermined because the context was unclear.

Nouns could not be assigned to a content category because they do not code a relationship by themselves (see Bloom, 1973, for discussion of this point). Nouns were, therefore, categorized according to the context in which they were used. The first category included nouns that simply labeled objects, for example:

(Jay holding a can of soup)
What's in there?   soup

(Jay pointing to a picture of an
umbrella on a salt box)   umbrella

The second category included nouns used to label objects that were being acted on in some way. For example:

(Jay pulls a truck out of a box)   truck
(He pushes the truck back and forth)   truck

(Jay tries to get a can of soup from Judy)   soup

(Judy pours milk in a cup)   milk

The last category included nouns that label objects not present in the context. For example:

What did you have for lunch today?   cake

Where do you want to go?   home

These categories are gross and do not directly lead to the content categories, but they do indicate use of nouns for purposes other than identification and in contexts that can be used for future syntactic coding of content categories. These contexts can be further categorized—if desired—to locating contexts, action contexts, notice contexts, and so on. To do this is not to credit the child with such intent or meaning, but may help in deciding if the child needs to use nouns in more varied contexts. Jay labeled objects in many contexts—as he acted on them, located them, requested them, pointed to them, and in response to questions. There appeared to be no need for goals at the single-word level (Phase 1) in these contexts. Rather, such use of single-word utterances points out the contexts to use for teaching multiword utterances for Phase 2 goals.

In addition to the single-word utterances there were a few longer utterances. These, too, were categorized, for example "take shoe off," "Judy eat," "I play," "I watch" (action); "no have umbrella" (nonexistence). Plotting the analyses of single- and multiword utterances according to the sequence of goals listed in Chapters XIII, XIV, and XV, only three categories reached the criterion of productivity: locative action, existence (if we include labeling static objects), and action. Action was considered productive in Phase 1 if we count the two verbs used in two-word utterances, "eat" and "watch," and the single action verbs. There were many categories of Phase 1 that were not coded: denial, recurrence, and possession, and more information was needed about these categories before goals for the categories could be written. (See Table XVI-13.) If they could not be elicited through further assessment procedures, goals would be:

1. To increase number of action and locative action verbs.
2. To code recurrence with "more" or "again."
3. To code nonexistence with "no" or "all gone."
4. To code rejection with "no."
5. To code existence with "this," "that," or "a" plus a noun.
6. To code action with two constituents.
7. To code locative action with two constituents.

And, placed later because they were optional:

8. To code denial with "no."
9. To code attributes with single-word utterances.
10. To code possession with single-word or two-word utterances.

ANALYSIS OF USE

Having completed the analysis of content/form interactions, Tommy's language sample can be analyzed according to the ways in which the child used language. The goals of use that were sequenced in Chapters XIII, XIV, and XV provide the sequence. Since no other sequences are available (i.e., no other program or language analysis procedures have sequenced factors relating to the use of language) only this sequence will be discussed. The analysis will consider use of content/form interactions in relation to nonlinguistic and linguistic contexts and the functions for which language was used.

Comments about the contexts in which utterances were spoken are noted on the worksheets for verb categories. This information about Tommy's language sample was recorded when the utterances were first placed on these worksheets. (See Tables XVI-3 to XVI-8.) The aspects of the linguistic context that were noted included whether the utterance was: initiated by the child (Ch-I); in response to a question (R-Q); or in response to a statement (R-S). If in response to a question or a statement, a (+) or (−) denotes whether the response added information (+) or was inappropriate (−). There were few instances of imitation, a (−) response. The frequency of (Ch-I) utterances suggests that Tommy initiated speech freely and the many (+) responses suggest Tommy was using language in response to language—an important development related to discourse. The function of each utterance was also noted on the verb category charts. Most utterances were comments as Tommy talked mainly about what he was doing, although some demands and requests were noted. He also used language to obtain information and to pretend—suggesting a broad spectrum of functions. Tommy rarely talked about objects that were not present except in pretend activities instigated by the adult. He did not talk about anyone else's activity unless demanding an action and, therefore, goals of use include:

1. To talk about the activities of others (Phases 4 and 5).
2. To talk of events that occurred in the immediate past (Phases 4 and 5).

In terms of the goals presented in the previous chapters, Tommy's language use was commensurate with or beyond his knowledge of content/form interactions. Therefore, priority, in terms of goals, would be given to the achievement of content/form goals in Phases 1 to 3 before the achievement of use goals listed here (which were Phase 4 and 5 goals) and before the content/form goals that were listed in Phases 4 or 5.

Observation of Tommy's motor behaviors and responses to nonverbal cognitive tasks suggested that in many areas, including content, Tommy is delayed in development. He is an illustration of "delay" in the development of content/form/use interactions.

FURTHER OBSERVATIONS IN OTHER CONTEXTS

Often, following analysis of a language sample, further information is needed about particular language behaviors. One of the goals derived from the analysis of Tommy's sample was an assessment goal—to obtain further information about his coding of attribution, denial, and rejection. This further information may be obtained in a number of ways. *Diagnostic teaching* or diagnostic therapy are terms often applied to intervention that is geared to establishing new goals while also teaching to other goals. While working with a child, handnotes should be kept of language behaviors that are different from those observed in initial observation. In addition to ongoing observations during intervention, there are other opportunities for direct observations available to most assessors. The classroom, playground, cafeteria, clinic hall, and waiting room often provide varying situations that are within the environment of the original assessment. Home visits are an excellent source of information about the child's interactions with parents and siblings. Information from all further low structured observations can be added to the analysis sheets and be used to help determine the frequency and context with which certain language behaviors occur; the child's response to the language behaviors of others; and the functions for which a child uses language.

SUMMARY

This chapter considers the use of information obtained from low structured observations in determining the goals of language learning. A number of issues are discussed, including considerations of context, length of observation, and means of recording the language observed. Although a variety of contexts are recommended, some suggestions are made for designing contexts when only one observation is possible. Means of recording recommended are, in order of preference, videotaping, audiotaping, and hand recording. Finally, a number of techniques for analyzing the obtained language samples are discussed. A means of analyzing the content/form interactions (sequenced in Chapters XIII, XIV, and XV) is presented and compared with analyses of form as presented by Lee (1974), Tyack and Gottsleben (1974), and Muma (1973). Both similarities and differences are pointed out. A means of analyzing use in relation to goals suggested in Chapters XIII, XIV, and XV is also presented. Finally, the use of further direct, low structured observations is recommended as a supplement to the analyses of the language sample.

SUGGESTED READINGS

Methods of Analyzing a Language Sample

Crystal, D., Fletcher, P., and Garman, M., *The grammatical analysis of language disability: A procedure for assessment and remediation*. London: Arnold, 1976.[1]

Lee, L., *Developmental sentence analysis*. Evanston, Ill.: Northwestern University Press, 1974.

Longhurst, T., and Schrandt, T., Linguistic analysis of children's speech: A comparison of four procedures. *Journal of Speech and Hearing Disorders, 38,* 240–249, 1973.

Muma, J., Language assessment: The co-occurring and restricted structure procedure. *Acta Symbolica, 4,* 12–29, 1973.

Tyack, D., and Gottsleben, R., *Language sampling, analysis and training: A handbook for teachers and clinicians.* Palo Alto, Calif.: Consulting Psychological Press, 1974.

---

[1] A more recent procedure for analyzing a language sample that became available too late to be included in this chapter. It is an analysis of *form* sequenced according to developmental information.

Chapter XVII
DETERMINING GOALS OF LANGUAGE LEARNING FROM ELICITED INFORMATION

As noted in the previous chapter, information about what a child does with language is best obtained in contexts that are both representative of the child's everyday life and relatively free of observer-imposed constraints— direct observation in a low structured naturalistic context. However, other information is often needed to supplement the language sample obtained in this relaxed structure, in order to learn about certain content/form/use interactions that did not occur, but were expected to occur given the child's other behaviors. When a child is unintelligible or is relatively quiet during the low structured observation, these additional sources of information may even have to serve as the primary source of information.

There are two further types of information that help in determining what a child knows about language; one is information elicited from others who are familiar with the child, and the second is information directly elicited from the child. The first, the use of reported information, was discussed in Chapter XII and is further discussed below. One type of direct elicitation, standardized tests, was also discussed as a means of identification in Chapter XII; in this chapter their use in determining goals of intervention is discussed. Last, direct elicitations that are not standardized are discussed.

REPORTED OBSERVATIONS

One other source of information about a child's behavior in unstructed contexts is the observations of others who are in continual contact with the child. Such information may be successfully elicited, if questions are specific, by use of a questionnaire or an interview.

In a pilot study,[1] information that was obtained by questionnaire from the parents of three children was compared with information that was obtained from analyzing a tape recorded language sample. Questionnaires were constructed with examples of each of the content/form interaction goals listed in Chapters XIII, XIV, and XV. Questions specified the content and the forms used at each phase, for example, "Does your child talk about actions on objects:

1. By using one word such as "hit", "eat", and the like,
2. By using two words such as "hit ball", "eat cake" or "me hit", "mommy eat"?

Questionnaires, with directions, were mailed to the parents; there were no interview data. The information obtained from the questionnaire was strikingly similar to that obtained from analysis of a direct observation. The parents not only reported the same content/form interactions that were found productive through analysis of the tapes, but generally credited the child with other interactions that had not been observed in the clinic. These questionnaires were long and obviously not all parents would be willing to complete them, but the success with which these parents were able to provide information when asked in such a remote fashion (i.e., without direct interview) suggested that at least some parents can be extremely helpful in providing information relevant to determining the goals of intervention.

For clinical use, parents need only be asked about areas where further information is needed and not about each goal. Thus Tommy's parents might have been asked about attribution, denial, and rejection. This could be done in an interview (following direct observation) or with a similar, but shorter, questionnaire that could be sent home with a parent and returned later. It is a good idea to supplement an interview with a questionnaire that is sent home so parents can observe the child at home and record specific examples. Teachers, custodians, nurses, and others in constant contact with the child can also provide information that will be useful for determining goals. Those in charge of a large number of children, however, may have more difficulty in giving specific examples of a child's speech if the child talks in long utterances.

When this information has been compiled and included in the analysis of the child's language behaviors, there may still be questions about or gaps in the information that is needed in order to determine the goals of intervention. In some cases reported observations are not helpful because no one who has contact with the child is available; those available may not understand

---

[1] Carried out by L. Green and L. Recca at Montclair State College, New Jersey, 1975.

what information is being requested; or possible informants may not be cooperative. When information obtained from direct and reported low structured observations is not sufficient to determine which content/form/use interactions must be established, the next step in assessment involves eliciting responses from the child. Elicitation tasks can vary in the degree of structure. The most highly structured are tasks that are a part of a standardized test. Is this information useful in determining the goals of intervention?

USING STANDARDIZED ELICITATIONS

As noted in Chapter XI, standardized elicitations are generally norm-referenced and most applicable to identifying a problem (i.e., for comparing one child to other children). Items selected for elicitation on most norm-referenced instruments are selected in order to differentiate among individuals within a general domain of behavior and not to measure their competence explicitly with particular aspects of that domain. Thus, the results of elicitation can suggest how a child compares with other children in some domain of language, such as vocabulary, syntax, or phonology, but do not give very much information on the child's mastery of particular skills within that domain. For this reason most standardized elicitations are of little help in determining goals of intervention.

If a standardized test has been administered and the responses to different items have been noted, these responses can be used as partial evidence of the presence or absence of a behavior in a child's language system. The term "partial evidence" is important for a number of reasons. First, most standardized tests sample only a limited number of behaviors and sample each of these only once—the presence or absence of a rule for behavior can hardly be predicted on the basis of one example. It is possible to surmount the difficulty of limited sampling within a structured standardized observation by constructing and standardizing tasks that elicit multiple examples of specific language behaviors (e.g., 5 to 10 tasks designed to elicit examples of each interaction listed in the plan). This would, however, still provide only partial evidence for another reason: elicited responses may not represent what the child can and does do with language outside of the test situation because the test situation is usually not representative of normal language use. In order to test the comprehension of a grammatical structure, for example, sentences are devised without semantic and syntactic redundancy and are presented in contexts that do not cue their meaning. Thus, to test certain verb inflections, nouns that are not inflected are used (as in the sentences designed to test the third person singular verb inflection: "The *deer* run home" versus "The *deer* runs home"). Without redundant coding of semantic-syntactic relations that is common to both adult and child speech, emphasis is placed on the specific syntactic structure or morphological inflection being tested—a situation not representative of the child's natural environment.

The use of highly structured observations to elicit language has reportedly underestimated the establishment of certain content/form interactions in a child's language system. Some studies have suggested that behaviors sampled in structured observations do not predict behaviors observed in relaxed, informal observations. In a recent study by Prutting, Gallagher, and Mulac (1975, in *RLDis*), children's responses to the *Northwestern Syntax Screening Test* (Lee, 1971) were compared with their production of the same forms during spontaneous speech in a more informal setting. The results indicated that 30% of the forms found absent or incorrect in the testing situation were produced correctly by the children 50% of the time in their spontaneous speech. The authors concluded that the test could not be used to describe a child's language behavior but only to compare language behavior with that of the child's peers (i.e., as the screening test for which it was designed). With a group of children classified as mentally retarded, Dever (1972) compared the production of grammatical morphemes when elicited in a structured setting with their production when spontaneously used in a relaxed setting. The elicited responses underestimated the use of morphemes in spontaneous speech, and Dever concluded that the test paradigm, a highly structured observation, may not be an appropriate means of sampling language behaviors for this population.

An additional important limitation of highly structured, standardized observations is the limited information that can be obtained about the *use* of language through such techniques. The observer must observe a child in natural settings to find out how the child can use language as a means of communicating ideas and desires, and to determine the purposes for which the child uses language.

Thus, if item analyses are done, standardized elicitations may have some limited value in describing the language of a child. They currently are not, however, very helpful in planning the goals of intervention, because they do not provide enough examples of each behavior, because they do not give evidence about use, and because responses may not be representative of behaviors in the child's natural environment. Information from item analyses can be used to provide first hypotheses when other means of observation are not possible, but the use of nonstandardized elicitations provide another, perhaps more preferable, alternative.

USING NONSTANDARDIZED ELICITATIONS

The purpose of eliciting language behaviors is to supplement the information about which goals have been reached in order to determine the goals of intervention. Some clinicians use nonstandardized elicitations as a major source of information for determining the goals of intervention. When this is the case, a wide range of content/form/use interactions are sampled.

One currently published language assessment instrument—the *Environmental Language Inventory* (ELI, MacDonald and Blott, 1974; and MacDonald and Nickols, 1974)—seems to fit the classification of nonstandardized elicitations more than most published tests, since the procedures are flexible. The ELI was designed to elicit two-word responses that code the content categories of action, locative action, locative state, recurrence, possession, attribution, negation (rejection and denial), and existence. These interactions are comparable to the content/form interactions presented in Chapters XIII and XIV as Phase 2 goals, with the exception of locative state, which is a Phase 3 goal, and negation, where rejection is a Phase 4 goal, and denial a Phase 5 goal. To elicit these interactions, the child is asked to describe an action the examiner performs (such as throwing a ball), and to imitate the examiner, "*say* throw ball." In all instances the event or object is present in the context. Although specific activities are listed, the authors suggested that other nonlinguistic contexts can be used as well, thus allowing flexibility and the opportunity to take advantage of the child's interests. Additionally, MacDonald and Nickols (1974) suggested recording examples of these same content/form interactions (referred to by MacDonald and his associates as semantic-grammatical rules) while the child interacts in a free play setting—thus combining elicitation with observation in a low structured setting—a procedure that is recommended here. The disadvantages of using elicited responses as the primary source of information are similar to the disadvantages discussed under standardized elicitation. One must elicit many examples in varying contexts; it can be more time consuming than analysis of a language sample. Many clinicians, however, use elicitation as a follow-up of analyses of language samples and reported observations, and focus on behaviors that were not observed in the analysis of the sample, or were considered important for some other reason.

WHAT TO ELICIT

The behaviors elicited are those for which insufficient evidence existed in the low structured observations for describing the behavior as productive, but that might be expected to be productive given the level of other productive behaviors that were observed. In the analysis of language samples, one finds many content/form/use interactions established at a particular phase with no, or few, examples of utterances coding other interactions in phases adjacent to, within, or below this phase. The absence of examples may not mean that the child cannot or does not produce these behaviors but, perhaps, that the situation did not call for such productions. These behaviors, which appear developmentally at about the same time as behaviors that were productive within the sample, are chosen as targets for elicitation. For example, there was no evidence that Tommy (whose sample was analyzed in Chapter XVI) had learned to use the grammatical morpheme -ed to code past tense, yet this would not be considered as a target for elicitation, since its use is not expected until Phase 8 and Tommy's other language behaviors were in Phases 3 and 4. More appropriate behaviors to elicit from Tommy would be his coding of recurrence, nonexistence, denial, and possession with forms expected in the early phases. Recall that the purpose of assessment at this point is to determine the goals of intervention. Following a developmental model, the behaviors to elicit are those in phases near the productive language behaviors that were observed.

TECHNIQUES OF ELICITATION

To elicit responses from a child about a particular content/form/use interaction, the assessor must design situations that the child will be willing to respond to and situations that will require the desired response. In certain tasks that are used the stimulus that the child is to produce is presented; that is, the target interaction is modeled to assure an appropriate response (e.g., imitation tasks). In other tasks the situation is designed to elicit responses without modeling the target behavior. Each is discussed below.

Nonmodeled Elicitations

A variety of situations can be designed to elicit the production of different language behaviors. If the desired response is not spoken by another, as the assessor, just prior to the child's utterance, the child's response is considered a nonmodeled elicitation. A nonmodeled elicitation situation is illustrated in the following interaction between Karen, a 9½-year-old girl, and a clinician who was trying to elicit locative action utterances from Karen. (Note that the situation was designed around a nonpresent event. Such a context can only be used if the child has demonstrated, as Karen had, the ability to talk about events not present.)

Do you know how to make a cake, Karen?	yeah/ I know
Can you tell me the steps, the things you must do to make a cake?	yeah/ first cake in box
Then what?	put in bowl
Then what do you do?	put egg
The whole egg, shell too?	no/ break egg/ put in bowl/ mix up
Mix them up?	yeah/ I mix them up

The situation presented so far has illustrated a planned elicitation of locative action utterances without modeling. Karen's use of subject-verb-complement in the utterance "I mix them up" was in response to the clinician's previous production, which modeled both verb and complement, but locative action utterances were not modeled by the clinician. Generally, questions by the clinician were designed to encourage responses about a topic that might demand coding of locative action without modeling the utterance type itself.

Nonmodeled situations can include puppets, toys, or everyday activities. For example, the assessor can manipulate objects such as toy animals, people, and cars and ask the child to describe what is happening. Such activities can illustrate relations of time, quantity, dative, recurrence, action, locative action, and locative state. For example, a child can be asked to describe situations such as those in Box XVII-1.

Some content categories need rather complex situations to elicit desired content/form interactions (e.g., state, notice, negation, and recurrence). To elicit state, one can try engaging a child in an activity where certain objects are missing and needed in order to complete the activity. For example, in painting a picture, perhaps only one color is available and it is hoped that the child will then ask for another color, perhaps using a state utterance ("I need red") or may code nonexistence of the object ("no red" or "red gone"). For denial it is sometimes successful if an object that is not familiar to the

---

BOX XVII-1 INSTRUCTIONS TO THE CHILD: "I'LL MAKE THE DOG DO SOME THINGS AND YOU TELL ME ABOUT THEM".

SITUATION	QUESTION	POSSIBLE RESPONSES
Time plus action		
A dog running and stopping	"Now, tell me, what?"	"He ran"/"he stopped"
A dog running and continues to run	"Now what?"	"He's running"
Quantity plus action		
A boy pets two dogs	"Tell me what's going on?"	"The boy pets the dogs"
One dog barks and stops	"Tell me what's going on?"	"The dog barked"
Two dogs bark and stop	"And now?"	"Two dogs barked"

Note that the target response, in the first situations (time plus action) and in the second situations (quantity plus action), was not coded by the assessor. The *-ing* form was avoided in the questioning about *time* but was used in the question when *quantity* was the target. Thus, the responses would be considered nonmodeled elicitations.

child is identified with the name of a familiar object. For example, a piece of clock mechanism might be shown to the child and identified as a cookie. Occasionally this will elicit denial utterances such as "no cookie" or "not a cookie." If a familiar item such as a penny is identified as a cookie, the response will most likely be "that's a penny" instead of denial. For recurrence, and perhaps recurrence plus state, one might demonstrate a baby doll finishing a bottle of milk and then crying and reaching out, obviously asking for more milk. The child might be asked what is the matter with the baby, and the elicited response may code either state, recurrence, or both by saying "more milk," "more," "want milk," or "she wants more milk." Rejection might be elicited by doing or proposing something that the child would probably reject. Rejection may also be elicited by setting up a scene with puppets or toy dolls, suggesting that one doll won't do anything Mother says, and asking the child to engage in a dialogue between the doll's mother, acted by the clinician, and the doll, acted by the child.

A combination of creativity and experience on the part of the clinician will make it easier to devise situations that are of interest to a child with topics that are appropriate to the child's age level, and that encourage the production of particular language behaviors. The objects and the contexts can vary according to the age and interest of the child. The purpose is to elicit coding of certain content categories and not particular topics. The technique is to devise a situation where the content category or the coordination of categories one is attempting to elicit are obvious to the child and then to request that the child describe the event demonstrated.

For some children, talking through puppets provides motivation. For others, motiviation is increased if they give instructions to another person, that is, if there is a listener to whom they can convey not already obvious information. This can be arranged by having a third person with duplicate toys (i.e., toys similar to those used by the child and clinician) sit with his or her back to the demonstration of the situation to be coded. The child's task might be to observe the clinician's demonstration and then describe the event to the third person so that the third person can recreate it. With other children, token rewards can be used as a means of motivating responses. With most children, however, social praise of efforts and a relaxed atmosphere are generally all that is needed.

The situations designed for nonmodeled elicitations in initial assessment are also useful for reassessment if the context and situations are different from those used in the teaching situation. Topics that are different from teaching are necessary to be assured that the child has generalized the rule as a means of coding content categories and has not just memorized certain topic related utterances.

Attempts can also be made to elicit verbalizations in varying contexts and for varying functions in an attempt to observe aspects of use that have not occurred in the low structured observation. One could obtain responses about events that are not present by asking the child questions and encouraging the child to talk about familiar events at home or at school, events that have taken place at the clinic on a previous day, or about future events that the child may participate in during the coming weeks.

One can also vary contexts in terms of the linguistic input. The assessor can design situations where the child is given an opportunity to respond to both questions and statements. The child's responses to these verbalizations can be taken as evidence of the ability to respond to another's verbalizations by either adding information, repeating and elaborating on the topic presented, imitating, or questioning. Situations can, therefore, be varied both in terms of the presence or absence of the referent and in terms of the verbalizations of others as a means of supplementing the observations made during the low structured sample.

It is also possible to create situations that would elicit the use of language for different purposes or functions. If a child has not given evidence of commenting, certainly asking the child to describe events that the child or others are doing, or to identify and describe objects and pictures, could elicit comments. The use of novel objects, games, and activities very often tends to encourage questioning activity as the child tries to obtain information about these novel situations. Demand utterances may sometimes be elicited by withholding some object that is necessary to complete an activity (e.g., a piece of the puzzle or the block that is necessary to complete a house). The ability to give information and to inform another can be observed in situations where the child is asked to explain a game or activity to a new child or adult. In all cases elicitations of use can be combined with elicitations of content/form interactions.

When low structured observations and nonmodeled elicitations do not provide enough evidence to determine the child's knowledge of certain interactions, the language behaviors that are expected to develop earlier or at the same time as most of the child's productive language behaviors are listed as goals. If, in fact, the behaviors are established, they will probably emerge readily in the teaching contexts and new goals will be set. To err in the direction of setting goals that are already achieved is better than to err in the direction of setting goals that are way beyond the child's current level of functioning and may be too hard for the child to achieve. Early success, even if only apparent (since the behaviors were already established), sets a better climate for learning than long-term frustration.

Modeled Elicitations

Many clinicians and researchers elicit language behaviors by asking the child to imitate an utterance produced by the assessor. Elicited imitation is usually immediate (e.g., "*Say* the boy put the cake in the pan"). It may take place without context, thus stressing form (Carrow, 1974), or in a context that demonstrates content, thus relating form and content (MacDonald and Blott, 1974). Responses may be scored in terms of presence or absence of the forms presented in the model or in terms of the content/form interactions the child produces as they relate to the context or to the meaning of the adult's utterances. Exact repetition of a form may say something about knowledge of form, but it does not provide much information about the establishment of a content/form interaction in a child's language. (See discussion of elicited imitation in Chapter VIII.) One can imitate utterances that are longer than memory span without knowledge of meaning if one is familiar with the form. The recoding of an utterance, however, so that meaning is essentially the same but the form is different, is evidence of content/form interaction and may be used as evidence. Thus, if the assessor says "Say the car stopped," and the child says "no more go," we can credit the child with a syntactic utterance coding nonexistence. Some evidence suggests that modeled elicitations can overestimate what a child knows about language (Fraser, Bellugi, and Brown, 1963); other evidence suggests it may reflect the child's knowledge of structure (Lackner, 1968; and C. Smith, 1970); still other evidence suggests it may underestimate what the child knows about language (Slobin and Welsh, 1973; Bloom, 1974c; and Prutting and Connolly, 1976; see Chapter VIII, for further discussion). It seems the effectiveness of imitation as a means of determining what the child knows about language is not clear; it may tell something about the child's knowledge of form, less about knowledge of content/form interactions, and even less about use.

Another means of eliciting language that involves modeling is the use of questions that demonstrate the utterance type desired. This is illustrated in a continuation of the earlier interaction with Karen—an interaction designed to elicit locative action utterances.

Do you add anything else? Do you put in more things?	milk
Anything else?	put in pan
Put what in pan?	put cake in pan/ in oven
Put cake in oven?	cake oven/ cook/ eat

In this part of the situation the assessor produced three locative action utterances each in the form of a question. Two of the questions asked for specification of the object (e.g., "Put *what* in the pan?"). One could also ask for specification of place, for example, "Put cake where?" or specification of agent, "*Who* puts the cake in the oven?" Thus, modeled elicitation can involve presenting the utterance type in a question and requesting a replacement of a Wh- word or pronoun.

Last, desired utterance types can be modeled by a third party in a play situation. The model, a third party, can pretend to be a resistant child talking to Mother (the assessor). The child may then take the model's role and pretend to be the resistant child. In this case the modeled utterances are presented in a meaningful, although pretend, context and precede the child's utterance by a number of minutes in time. It would seem that the child's production of utterance types in this context is better evidence of knowledge of language behaviors than in the two previous examples of modeled elicitations.

Modeled elicitations are intuitively pleasing to the new clinician, because they are efficient and easy means of eliciting language behaviors and they focus on particular behaviors. Unfortunately, there is little evidence about their effectiveness in determining goals of intervention as compared with, say, the longer task of language sample analyses or even nonmodeled elicitations. Prutting, Gallagher, and Mulac (1975, in *RLDis*) provided some information on the relationship between information obtained in the two tasks, but further research directly tied to establishing clinical goals is needed. How would goals for a particular child differ if information was obtained from (1) a language sample obtained in a relaxed setting; (2) reported observations; (3) elicited nonmodeled responses; or (4) elicited modeled responses?

SUMMARY

This chapter is concerned with language behavior observed by others (reported observations) and with language behaviors observed in response to particular elicitation tasks. The tasks are categorized as nonmodeled elicitations—responses to tasks where the utterance type is not presented to the child before the response, and modeled elicitations—responses to tasks where the utterance type was presented to the child before the response (as elicited imitations). Some examples of techniques used for elicitation are presented.

It is suggested that nonmodeled elicitations and reported observations can be used to supplement direct, low structured observations, but that responses following modeling give the weakest evidence of knowledge of language content/form/use interactions. It is not clear how language goals would be influenced using these different methods of obtaining evidence.

However, since the sequence of goals suggested in Chapters XIII, XIV, and XV is based on language produced in low structured responses, and since this seems to be the most representative context of a child's life, the use such language samples is suggested as the primary source of information for determining goals of intervention based on this developmental sequence. Other information merely supplements this primary source.

SUGGESTED READINGS

In *Readings in Language Disorders*

Prutting, C. A., Gallagher, T. M., and Mulac, A., The expressive portion of the NSST compared to a spontaneous language sample. *Journal of Speech and Hearing Disorders, 60,* 40–49, 1975.

Other

Dever, R. B., A comparison of the results of a revised version of Berko's Test of Morphology with the free speech of mentally retarded children. *Journal of Speech and Hearing Research, 15,* 169–178, 1972.

Part 5
CORRELATES OF LANGUAGE DISORDERS

There is other information about the child with deviant language development that is important to the eventual understanding of the nature of language disorders and, in some cases, to the facilitation of language learning. Focus on correlates of language disorders has led to other descriptions of the child with a language disorder—descriptions based on different types of evidence and different taxonomies—and these different descriptions have often led to goals and procedures of intervention that are different from those discussed previously in this book. The clinical application to the language-disordered child of the information on correlates is discussed in Part 5 in terms of two orientations: a categorical orientation, which groups children according to similar syndromes of behavior, and a specific abilities orientation, which categorizes behaviors felt to reflect skills or abilities necessary for language learning. Both orientations can be considered etiological in relation to language disorders in the sense that both describe and remediate factors felt to be responsible for poor language skills. Language is thus considered a symptom of some other dysfunction.

Chapter XVIII
A CATEGORICAL ORIENTATION: CLINICAL SYNDROMES ASSOCIATED WITH CHILDHOOD LANGUAGE DISORDERS

When similar clusters of behaviors—behaviors that are not expected given a child's age—are found in a number of children, these aggregate behaviors form a syndrome. A syndrome is simply a group of behaviors that differentiates a number of individuals from other individuals. A number of syndromes that include a language disorder as one of the behaviors have been identified in young children and thus have been associated with language disorders in children. When these syndromes have been applied clinically (either to diagnosis or to planning intervention), they are here referred to as a *categorical orientation* that is, an orientation to childhood language disorders that stresses categorizing children with a language disorder according to a cluster of language and nonlanguage behaviors that differentiate them from normal.

Research that is categorically oriented has been aimed at describing and differentiating among children with similar behaviors and histories in order to define clinical categories for classifying children. The clinical categories that have resulted from differentiation research, and that are commonly referred to for clinical and educational management, follow from factors considered necessary for learning language. In order to learn a first language, it is generally felt that a child must have: (1) an intact peripheral sensory system; (2) an intact central nervous system; (3) adequate mental abilities; (4) emotional stability; and (5) exposure to the language. It follows that a deficit in any of these factors could be responsible for difficulty in learning language. The clinical categories relating to deficiencies in each of these factors are respectively: (1) severe hearing impairment or deafness; (2) aphasia or dysphasia; (3) mental retardation; (4) emotional disturbance (primarily autism and schizophrenia); and (5) environmental deprivation.

The categories within the categorical orientation are *global* in nature; that is, they group individuals according to common patterns of behavior that they share. Each category represents a syndrome of behaviors. Clinicians traditionally have been involved in determining the best categorical labels for children based on certain behavioral manifestations; this task has been called differential diagnosis. A categorical label describes how a child is similar to some other children, but different from normal children.

The category in which a child is placed (the diagnosis) is determined by qualitative and quantitative descriptions of behaviors felt to be associated with dysfunctions of sensory systems, nervous systems, mental abilities, or emotional interactions. Language behaviors are often a part of the syndrome that defines each category. (See Myklebust, 1954, for a more complete description of the behaviors associated with many of these categories.)

When a child does not develop facility with the native language, one is most likely to ask "Why?" Indeed, "Why?" is often the first question asked by both parents and clinicians. Attempts to answer this question, both in general and specific instances, have dominated the literature on language disorders in children for the past few decades and have focussed primarily on the clinical categories of hearing impairment, aphasia, mental retardation, and emotional disturbance.

Although these clinical categories have been considered as representing etiologies of a language disorder, they, in turn, have etiologies themselves; that is, there are other factors that precipitate or otherwise underlie the deafness, mental retardation, and so forth. It is, however, these clinical categories that have dominated the thinking about etiology relative to childhood language disorders; it is these categories that will be discussed in relation to a categorical orientation. First, each category will be described and then the usefulness of these categories for facilitating language learning will be discussed.

CLINICAL CATEGORIES

The clinical categories commonly referred to are discussed below both in terms of the general behavioral syndromes that define them and in terms of the language behaviors that have been associated with them. Unfortunately, most studies of the language of children with a language disorder have been quantitative. Thus, language behavior has been described in terms of superficial measures such as the number of different words used, the length of utterance, and the number of complete sentences. Few studies have described how children actually use language to speak and understand messages about states of affairs in the world. The language behaviors that have been associated with a category will be presented, when possible, within the paradigm used throughout this textbook to describe language—content/form/use interactions.

HEARING IMPAIRMENT

Terms used to describe the hearing-impaired individual vary with the purpose of the description. (See Chapter I for a discussion of this same point relative to definitions of language.) Hearing impairment can be defined according to the degree of impairment, the time of onset, causal factors, site of dysfunction in the auditory system, or social impairment (Myklebust, 1964; and Silverman, 1971a, 1971b).

The degree of hearing impairment is usually described in terms of thresholds of sensitivity to pure tones in the speech frequencies (500 to 2000 Hz) as, for example, in Box XVIII-1. The term "deaf" is usually used to describe degree of impairment and in this sense refers to "those who do not have sufficient residual hearing to enable them to understand speech successfully even with a hearing aid, without special instruction" (Silverman,

---

BOX XVIII-1

A classification developed by Davis et al. for the American Academy of Ophthalmology and Otolaryngology (as presented by Silverman, 1971b) includes six classes of loss according to the degree of difficulty in understanding speech: (1) 25 dB (ISO) or less, not significant; (2) 25 to 40 dB (ISO), a slight handicap—difficulty in understanding faint speech; (3) 40 to 55 dB (ISO), a mild handicap—frequent difficulty with normal speech; (4) 55 to 70 dB (ISO), a marked handicap—frequent difficulty with loud speech; (5) 70 to 90 dB (ISO), severe handicap—understands only shouted or amplified speech; and (6) 90 dB (ISO), extreme handicap—usually cannot understand even amplified speech.

1971a, p. 399). In this same sense the term "hard of hearing" refers to those whose hearing, although defective, is functional with or without amplification.

The terms deaf and hard of hearing are also used, however, to refer to educational potential and to distinguish between those who have acquired language and those who have not (Myklebust, 1964). Such a distinction is often closely related to time of onset of the hearing impairment as well as to degree of impairment. Those born with severe hearing impairment, the congenitally deaf, are more likely to have difficulty acquiring language than those who have acquired a hearing loss after the first few years of life. Certainly the ability to acquire language is based on criteria other than degree of hearing impairment and time of onset (e.g., intelligence, environment, and emotional factors).

In addition, language acquisition may be related to the type of loss. There are types of hearing impairment that are not related simply to loss of sensitivity; for example, there are individuals who have difficulty discriminating the speech signal no matter how loud it is. Davis and Silverman (1970) referred to impairment of hearing other than loss of sensitivity as "dysacusis". A child with a mild handicap in terms of threshold of sensitivity but with difficulty in discrimination will no doubt have as much, if not more, difficulty learning language than a child with a more severe loss involving only sensitivity.

Silverman (1971b) noted that it is impossible to draw a composite picture of the hearing-handicapped child because there is too much variation in factors such as intelligence, personality, emotional stability, social behavior and, we might add, language. Because of the variations in the above factors as well as age of onset and degree and type of impairment, the categorical label of *deaf* or *hard of hearing* does not describe qualitative or quantitative differences in language development.

Deaf individuals usually lack intelligible oral speech, so their language has most often been studied in its written form. In general, it has been concluded that sentence structure and vocabulary are stereotypical and include many grammatical errors. Reading scores are generally low, with little progress noted after the middle elementary grade levels. The total number of words used by deaf children is similar to hearing peers in written composition (Heider and Heider, 1940) and less in spoken language (Brannon, 1968, in *RLDis*). Even when amount of verbalization is taken into account, the diversity of vocabulary is not as great (Simmons, 1962; and Brannon, 1968) and the frequency with which different classes of words are used differs from the hearing child (Brannon, 1968, and MacGinitie, 1964; in *RLDis*). When sentences are elicited, the deaf tend to use a greater proportion of nouns, verbs, and articles in their utterances and fewer adverbs, auxilliaries, pronouns, prepositions, and question forms than the hearing child (MacGinitie, 1964; and Brannon, 1968, in *RLDis*). Brannon found this difference was more pronounced with a severe hearing loss than with a moderate hearing loss. In less structured samples, articles and main verbs (particularly the verb "to be") are also often omitted (Tervoort, 1967 and Taylor, 1969, both as presented by Quigley, Wilbur, Power, Montanelli, and Steinkamp, 1976). The average sentence length is shorter for deaf children than for their hearing peers; fewer compound and complex sentences are used; and stereotype carrier phrases and sentence frames are common (Heider and Heider, 1940; and Simmons, 1962).

In summary, analysis of the *form* of language samples has indicated deficiencies in the language of the deaf as compared with their normal hearing peers. Unfortunately, language samples of hearing children have not been compared with language samples of hearing impaired children at similar levels of language learning. Quigley et al. (1976) have conducted a series of studies that compared syntactic knowledge of deaf children age 10 to 18 years with that of hearing children age 8 to 10 years. Both groups of children had the most difficulty with sentences that deviated from the usual subject-verb-object word order (such as passives or relative clauses) and with verbal auxilliaries, although the younger hearing children surpassed the deaf in most tasks. "Most of the oldest deaf students in the study (between 18 and 19 years of age) did not have syntactic development equal to the 8 year old hearing children" (p. 193). The authors concluded that based on the data available at that time "syntactic structures develop similarly for deaf children as for hearing children, but at a greatly retarded rate" (p. 189). Although there were some different syntactic structures used by the deaf children ". . . none of those structures was common to all subjects and most were used by fewer than 50%" (p. 193). Quigley et al. (1976) stressed the importance of describing what each child knows about syntax in order to plan remedial efforts more appropriately.

Blanton (1968) reviewed a series of studies that had investigated the language of deaf individuals by using the cloze procedure. In this procedure the child is presented with a reading passage in which every fifth word is deleted; the task is to complete the blanks representing the deleted words. He also reviewed some studies of the visual memory of deaf individuals for sequences of words presented to them with and without syntactic cues. On the basis of these studies, Blanton concluded that deaf individuals: (1) have excellent visual memory but do not use syntax, as do the hearing individuals, to aid in visual memory of sentences; and (2) know sentence frames and can determine the form class that should be inserted in a sentence frame, but do not understand the use or meaning of specific functor words. It would appear, from the results reported, that deaf children do learn something of the *form* of language as it is written, but possibly do not learn language as a vehicle for coding *content* or for a particular *use*. This may, however, tell us more about the training methods that have been used to teach language to deaf children than about the effect of the loss of the auditory channel on language learning.

Only recently has the study of the communication used by deaf children and adults been directed to sign language as a system. Many young deaf children of deaf parents are exposed to language with visual signals in much the same atmosphere as the young hearing child is exposed to language with auditory signals. In both instances, the children are not consciously taught a linguistic code. Ultimately, such studies may provide information on the effect of the auditory channel on language learning in general. Early reports (Bellugi and Klima, 1972) have suggested that the deaf child who is learning sign language codes the same semantic notions as the hearing child who is learning to speak; although the form of the communication differs, the content is the same.

Furth's (1966) studies of the cognitive development of deaf individuals suggested that their ideas of the world, from which the content of language derives, develop in the same sequence as for the hearing child, and with only slight delay. Thus, it appears from these observational and qualitative studies (as compared with quantitative studies comparing standardized test scores) that the language disorder accompanying deafness can be described as a dysfunction in the interaction of form with content and use, as illustrated in Box XVIII-2. Deaf children may know what they need to know about objects and events in the world and may know how to interact with others in order to communicate, but they may not know the conventional form used for communication in their community.

To know that a child is deaf does not tell the clinician what the child needs to know about language. To know that a child is deaf does not specify that the language system to be taught, either as an auditory-vocal language or as its signed equivalent, is different. Unquestionably the categorization of deafness does lead to hypotheses about how the child might learn language; it certainly requires that techniques of teaching language modify the auditory signal and perhaps supplement the auditory channel. In all other respcts, however, the category is too global to specify other techniques or the content of a language learning program.

CHILDHOOD APHASIA

The category of childhood aphasia has been particularly prone to shifting definitions. The traditional definition—one that concurs with the use of the term aphasia with adults—specifies that the language disorder is a result of dysfunction in the central nervous system and can be described as receptive (a sensory or auditory aphasia reflected in poor comprehension); expressive (a motor aphasia suggesting a child who understands but cannot talk); and mixed or global aphasia (Barry, 1961).

Aphasia in adults refers to loss of language caused by cerebral pathology. Acquired aphasia or loss of language can also exist in children although, if the cerebral insult occurs early in life and involves only one hemisphere, recovery is often rapid and complete (see Lenneberg, 1967, in *RLDis* for further discussion of this point). Other acquired aphasias are associated with convulsive disorders, many of which are transient or are amenable to indirect treatment (see Watters, 1974).

The terms childhood aphasia, congenital aphasia, or developmental aphasia have been used to differentiate the syndrome of aquired aphasia (representing loss of established language skills) from a developmental disorder (failure to develop normal language skills). The lack of complete agreement with a definition of childhood aphasia is apparent in the following comments made by participants in a conference at the Institute on Childhood Aphasia (West, 1962). Wepman felt the term should be restricted to deficits in central integration and should be distinguished from problems in transmission that occur with sensory processing deficits (agnosia) or the coordination of motor output deficits (apraxia). (See Box XIX-2 for the model that illustrates this classification.) In contrast, Karlin said that the term denoted a cerebral form of language dysfunction that included receptive problems—word deafness and auditory imperceptions. Birch noted that the etiology in aphasia is usually unknown but is presumed to be related to cerebral dysfunction. Birch and Wood stressed that the term aphasia describes a syndrome of behaviors where the primary deficit is specifically a language deficit, because the child demonstrates characteristics that suggest that other cognitive abilities are sufficient for language learning. This view is similar to the "operational" definition given by Monsees (1972), who stated that aphasic children are children whose language deficits are more than would be expected considering their hearing level and intelligence. Masland, in a view similar to that expressed by McGinnis (1963) and Calvert, Ceriotti, and Geile (1966), suggested that aphasia is a pragmatic term—one that suggests the need for, or success with, a particular intervention approach.

Eisenson, at the same conference and elsewhere (1972), insisted that there is a rare syndrome of behaviors that he refers to as childhood aphasia that results from cerebral dysfunction and includes more than language deficits. It also includes behaviors such as perseveration, inconsistent responses, hyperactivity, emotional lability, auditory inefficiency, and perceptual and intellectual inefficiences. Eisenson and Ingram (1972, in *RLDis*) listed the following criteria for including a child within the category of childhood aphasia: perceptual dysfunction, particularly in the auditory channel (as observed by problems in speech, sound discrimination, and phonemic sequencing); intellectual inefficiency (functioning that is easily impaired by fatigue, noise, or other distraction); and retardation in language development. Eisenson and Ingram concluded that such a syndrome does exist apart from other complications, that it can be identified, and that dysfunction in auditory perception is the common factor and the reason for poor language skills. They noted, however, that the aphasic child often behaves as if he or she is mentally retarded, deaf, or autistic, and that it is rare to find such a child without complications of hearing impairment, motor impairment, or mental retardation.

Thus, the term childhood aphasia is clearly used to represent a language deficit—the nature of which is not clear—but where the etiology is most often presumed to be pathology in the central nervous system and where a disorder in language behavior is judged to be the primary problem, not a result of low cognitive abilities, deafness, or emotional problems. It is not clear how the term childhood aphasia, thus used, differs from the use of the term language disorder as an explanatory label—that is, as to refer to a diagnostic entity instead of as a descriptive term (as discussed in Chapter X)—or from the term specific language disability as used by some profession-als. The Institute on Childhood Aphasia concluded that the diagnosis of aphasia (i.e., the assignment of this categorical label to a child) was not as much help in determining therapy as would be a description of the language symptoms of each child.

The language behavior of children labeled as aphasic has been more often described and explained in terms of the processing of auditory stimuli than in terms of the production of language. Aphasic children are described as hearing but not understanding, having a short auditory memory span, and having difficulty with temporal sequencing and the repetition of auditory patterns (de Hirsch, 1967, in *RLDis*; and Stark, Poppen, and May, 1967). Such children have been found to have difficulty in reporting the order of auditory stimuli and discriminating stimuli unless the duration between stimuli are extremely long (Lowe and Campbell, 1965; Rosenthal, 1972; Schnur, 1971; and Tallal and Piercy, 1973a, 1973b, 1974, and 1975, in *RLDis*), and more difficulty in discriminating sounds presented in syllables than in isolation (McReynolds, 1966). From these findings it has been concluded that aphasic children have impaired perceptual abilities for auditory stimuli and are therefore slow in learning language (Eisenson and Ingram, 1972, in *RLDis*).

Morehead and Ingram (1973, in *RLDis*) sampled the language perform-ance of a group of children fitting the diagnosis of childhood aphasia and compared it with that of normal children at a comparable level of linguistic ability (as determined by mean length of utterance). They reported that similar rules of grammar were used by both groups of children. Both normal and aphasic children expressed the same grammatical relations, but it seemed that the aphasic children were slower to learn to coordinate these relations in sentences. The major differences between the two groups were delay in onset and slow rate of acquisition of language. They concluded that the language of aphasic children could be described as the result of delayed instead of qualitatively different language development. The same forms were used but were learned at a slower rate and were used less frequently by the aphasic children.

Unfortunately, little has been reported about the content/form/use interactions in the language of aphasic children. The definitions of aphasia, cited earlier, suggest that ideas of the world are more intact than a system of form for coding these ideas—a dysfunction in the interaction between content and form. A cluster analysis of information on children from different clinical categories (Rosenthal, Eisenson, and Luckau, 1972) supported this definition—aphasic and hearing impaired children were differentiated from retarded and autistic children on the basis of higher nonverbal intelligence scores. More recently, Leonard, Bolders, and Miller (1976, in *RLDis*) examined the semantic relations (content) in language samples from a group of children whose primary problem was a language disorder; they concluded that these relations were similar to those of normal children at the same stage of language development. The interactions of use with content/form are less often described. Clinical experience with children labeled aphasic suggests that these children are able to communicate their ideas somehow—that the development of and interaction between content and use are superior to interactions with and development of form. (See Box XVIII-2.) To

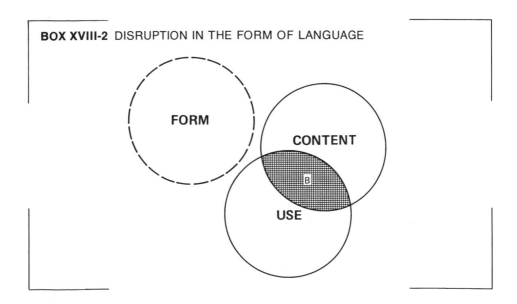

BOX XVIII-2 DISRUPTION IN THE FORM OF LANGUAGE

FORM

CONTENT

USE

know that a particular child has been labeled aphasic does not tell the clinician or teacher what it is that the child needs to learn about language, nor what the child's language development may have consisted of so far.

MENTAL RETARDATION

"Mental retardation refers to significantly subaverage general intellectual functioning existing concurrently with deficits in adaptive behavior, and manifested during the developmental period" (Grossman, 1973, p. 1). Intellectual functioning is generally determined by scores on standardized tests that fall two or more standard deviations from the mean of the test (e.g., an IQ of 70 on the *Wechsler Intelligence Scale for Children*). Adaptive behavior, an important component of the definition, refers to the effectiveness with which an individual meets the levels of personal independence and social responsibility of peers. Children can be categorized by degree of retardation according to IQ level (mild, moderate, severe or trainable-educable), or according to the presumed cause (brain injury, familial, Down's syndrome, etc.).

Many quantitative analyses have been made of the speech of children described as mentally retarded (see, for example, Naremore and Dever, 1975). Descriptions have pointed to impoverished vocabulary, less complex sentence structure, and later development of the use of verbal mediation. In general, an overall relationship has been found between language and IQ, for example, between sentence length and mental age (Goda and Griffith, 1962; Mecham, 1955; and Schlanger, 1954) and between mental age and size of vocabulary (Mein and O'Connor, 1960). Although quantitative studies pointed to differences between the language of the normal child and the retarded child, qualitative analyses have pointed to similarities between the two populations.

A number of studies have described the morphological development of retarded children according to their performance on tests that ask the children to apply morphological inflections (such as plural or possessive -s) either to nonsense words or to familiar lexical items. The results have suggested that such children's spontaneous speech (outside the test situation) yields more advanced levels of performance than test results do, and that test scores do not improve with length of time in school. Morphological inflections were learned in the same sequence by both retarded and normal populations, but the performance of the retarded children was poorer than normals matched for mental age (Dever, 1972; Lovell and Bradbury, 1967; and Newfield and Schlanger, 1968). Two explanations have been offered to account for these results. One explanation is that retarded children may learn inflected words as individual lexical items instead of learning a rule to apply to new situations (e.g., learning the words "hat" and "hats" as two separate words instead of as a single stem word "hat" to which the morpheme -s can be added). This would account for their generally lower performance with nonsense words (which they could not have learned in this same way, having never heard them before). Alternatively, it has been suggested that the testing situation may influence the conclusions that can be drawn from such studies; there may not be a qualitative difference in the performance of retarded and normal children outside of the test context.

Lackner (1968, in *RLDis*) collected samples of speech from retarded and normal children and wrote rules of grammar for the speech of the retarded children. He concluded from his study that the rules used by the retarded children were the same as those found in the adult model and that the grammar became more complex as mental age increased. The structures generated by the grammars were presented to a number of normal children (ages 2, 8 to 5, 9) as imitation and comprehension tasks. The results indicated ". . . an ordering . . . between the complexity of grammars and the mental ages of the retarded children, and the chronological ages of the normal children," suggesting ". . . that the language behaviors of normal and retarded children are not qualitatively different, that both groups follow similar developmental trends . . ." (p. 309).

In a review of research on the language of children with Down's syndrome (mongols), Evans and Hampson (1968) likewise concluded that there is no consistent relationship between Down's syndrome and a unique language pathology. They quoted the findings of Lenneberg, Nichols, and Rosenberger (1964) as evidence that the language development in this population is similar to that of normal children at a younger age.

When retarded and normal children were matched according to average length of utterance (*MLU*), Ryan (1975) found no differences in the proportion of complete (noun phrase plus verb phrase) sentences, incomplete sentences, clichés, or stereotype utterances, and no differences in the range or variety of verb transformations. Errors of both groups were similar. Retarded children matched to normal children on *MLU* had, however, a higher mental age, which Ryan hypothesized may be explained by the emphasis on vocabulary in obtaining mental age. Thus, when children were matched according to average length of utterance, it appeared that their knowledge of syntax was similar to that of normal children learning the form of language, but their knowledge of vocabulary might be greater.

The label of mental retardation is applied to children when their behavior suggests low cognitive abilities. Although late development of language is one of the behaviors used in reaching a diagnosis of retardation, low nonverbal performance is an important factor in determining a child's placement within the category of mental retardation. The language behaviors associated with low nonverbal performance may vary considerably. Learning form, for coding ideas of the world (content), and leaning how to use symbols as a means of representing and communicating these ideas to others are interrelated with and dependent on a child's cognitive abilities in general. For this reason, it is possible that all content/form/use interactions are affected when there is a general defect in cognitive functioning. It is not yet clear whether the accompanying language disorder is best described as a general delay in the normal pattern of development (see Yoder and Miller, 1972, for a discussion of this point), although the data available so far on the development of form suggest that this may be true for learning certain linguistic rules. Data are not yet available concerning either the content that is coded by the language forms learned by these children, or the ways in which they use the language forms that they learn. There is undoubtedly considerable variety within the population in the category of mental retardation (as in the other clinical categories), but it may be that the language disorder accompanying mental retardation is most often a general delay in development.

What is quite clear is that the syndrome of mental retardation does not define a language pathology that is particular to, or unique with, children who are considered to be mentally retarded. The diagnosis of "mental retardation" does not provide any information about what it is that a particular child with that label must learn about language, nor does it provide information on the best procedures to use in teaching language to that child. It does, however, suggest that attention be focussed on teaching the concepts that language codes and on providing the child with redundant and repetitive cues from the context to support the forms of speech being learned. If it is true that inflections on nouns and verbs are not learned as a system of morphological rules, then the diagnosis of mental retardation further suggests the necessity for focussing on inductive techniques in teaching language—techniques that would lead to the induction of rules. Even this may, however, not be unique with mental retardation.

EMOTIONAL DISTURBANCE

Childhood psychosis is a term used to describe children whose relationships with their environments are disturbed. Nine diagnostic signs of child psychosis were agreed on by Creak et al. (1961) and are listed in Box XVIII-3.

Rutter (1968) discussed three subclassifications of psychotic children, according to age of onset, as defined by Eisenberg (1967): psychosis that begins in adolescence and is similar to schizophrenia in adults; psychosis that becomes evident between 3 and 5 years, referred to as childhood schizophrenia; and psychosis that becomes apparent before the age of 3 years, which has been described by Kanner (1943, in *RLDis*) and referred to as autism. According to Rutter (1968), childhood schizophrenia differs from autism in terms of the sex ratio of children affected (a greater male/female ratio for schizophrenia only); social class of parents (higher for autistic

---

BOX XVIII-3 DIAGNOSTIC SIGNS OF CHILDHOOD PSYCHOSIS (from Creak et al., 1961)

1. Gross and sustained impairment of emotional relationship with people (including using people, or parts of people in an impersonal way, or as though they were inanimate objects).

2. Apparent unawareness of personal identity as demonstrated by abnormal behavior toward self, repeated self-directed aggression, and/or, when language is used, a confusion in the person identity of personal pronouns (for example, substituting "you" for "me," etc.).

3. Pathological preoccupation with a few particular objects, to the exclusion of most other objects in general.

4. Continued resistance to change in surroundings, with extreme reaction to any change in daily routine or environment.

5. The occurrence of abnormal perceptual experience with either excessive, diminished, or unpredictable responses to sensory stimuli.

6. Illogical anxiety, possibly precipitated by change in the environment or by certain objects, and yet a lack of fear when presented with real danger.

7. A specific and unaccounted for dysfunction in body movements (hypertension, immobility, bizarre postures, ritualistic mannerisms).

8. Severe and generalized retardation in intellectual functioning, often along with isolated areas of normal intellectual ability.

9. Loss of, lack of, or late development of speech, possibly accompanied by confusions in the use of personal pronouns, echolalia, or other mannerisms of use and diction—as when words and phrases are uttered but convey no sense of a meaningful communication.

---

children); family history of psychosis (in families of schizophrenic children only); intelligence (low with a tendency to scatter for autistic children only); delusions (in schizophrenic children only); and the course of the problem (symptoms of schizophrenia regress with time; autistic symptoms tend to improve). In the same article Rutter described the intelligence scores of the autistic child as stable, predictive of success in adult life, and low on verbal subtests and subtests that demand abstract thought or logic. He commented that the pattern of scores is similar to that found with aphasic children. Wing (1972) reported similar differences and added that the abnormalities of language found in autistic children are different from those found in schizophrenic patients.

A language disorder is an important part of the syndrome of psychosis, particularly autism. In fact, Wing (1972) stated that "unless there are marked problems with both spoken and non-spoken language the diagnosis [of autism] cannot be made" (p. 2). The onset time of language behaviors has been an important prognostic indicator. A history of vocalizations during the first year of life, or the development of any useful speech before the age of 5 years, are considered positive indicators of eventual improvement in social conformity and adaptability (Kanner and Eisenberg, 1956; and Ruttenberg and Wolf, 1967). When speech does occur, it is often described as stereotypical and parrotlike, with much echolalia, being directed at no one, containing many neologisms, confusion over pronouns, immaturity of grammatical structure, and lacking normal prosody patterns (de Hirsch, in *RLIDis*, 1967; Kanner, 1946, in *RLDis;* Wolff and Chess, 1965; Wing, 1972; and Kessler, 1966). Wing further described the language of the autistic child as "aphasic-like" in nonechoed speech with muddled sequencing of sounds and words, confusion of related words, and problems with function words. The autistic child's difficulty in comprehending language without accompanying gestures or context has also been reported (Pronovost, Wakstein, and Wakstein, 1966; and Hingtgen and Coulter, 1967).

There has been considerable variation in language behaviors reported for children in this population. It has been suggested that the cause of the autistic behavior (or a factor that accompanies autistic behavior) in at least some of these children may be quite similar to factors that contribute to the syndrome described in other children as childhood aphasia (Churchill, 1972, in *RLDis;* Cunningham, 1968, in *RLDis*; Rimland, 1962; Ruttenberg and Wolf, 1967; and Rutter and Bartak, 1971). Data from Cunningham (1968, in *RLDis*) suggest that there may be at least two groups of language behaviors within the category of childhood psychosis and that these may not be directly related to the diagnosis of autism versus schizophrenia.

Cunningham (1968, in *RLDis*) compared the language of two groups of retarded children, one diagnosed as psychotic and the other as nonpsychotic. The psychotic children who were all verbal, included children diagnosed as autistic, or schizophrenic, or psychotic but not autistic, and in whom symptoms were evident in early childhood. The retarded and psychotic children were matched according to mental and chronological age and were similar in the mean length of the sentences they produced. The children described as psychotic made significantly more noncommunicative remarks in a free play situation than the nonpsychotic children. Such noncommunicative remarks included delayed and immediate echoing of self and others, remarks classified as thinking aloud, and generally inappropriate or purposeless remarks. In addition, the psychotic children produced more emotionally toned comments related to fears or anxieties. The nonpsychotic children volunteered more information than the psychotic children. There was no difference between the two groups of children in their use of questions or in their use of personal pronouns (only 3 out of the 13 psychotic children reversed pronouns, and they did so inconsistently). The production of questions was related more to the average length of sentences produced than to whether the children were classed as psychotic or retarded; the children using longer sentences tended to ask more questions.

Two clusters of language patterns emerged in the data from the language of the psychotic children. In one cluster were children who used longer sentences, asked questions, and were not excessively echolalic. The structure of their sentences was correct, but the topics of their sentences and the ways certain words were combined with one another were unusual, making their speech appear odd. The second cluster consisted of children who had shorter sentences, poor pronunciation, peculiar intonation patterns, and incorrect or inconsistent sentence structure; these children rarely asked questions or used personal pronouns. Cunningham observed that the language of this second group appeared similar to the language of an aphasic child. This dichotomy did not correlate well with psychiatric diagnosis or age of onset.

Shapiro, Chiarandini, and Fish (1974, in *RLDis*) studied the longitudinal development of the language of 30 severely disturbed children under 7 years of age. Utterances produced in short, naturalistic settings were categorized according to development of form and according to use (communicative versus noncommunicative). Using these categorizations, they defined three groups of children. Group one was made up of children who were severely retarded in the development of form. The remaining children were divided on the basis of their communicativeness. Group two demonstrated echoing and contextually inappropriate utterances so frequently that less than 75% of their utterances were communicative. The children in group three developed communicative speech (greater than 75% of their utterances were communicative) "from very retarded and difficult beginnings" (p. 824). As the children improved in language development (as measured by length of utterance), echoing decreased (at a mean sentence length of approximately 1.9). It was the amount of contextually inappropriate utterances that distinguished group two from group three. There was a general trend to improvement with age (i.e., a move from group one to group three), but each individual child's group placement was highly correlated across the three points in time. From this the authors concluded that the groupings were not simply a measure of development but actually defined a "spectrum of deviant language patterns." Although they believed these children shared language patterns with aphasic children, they felt the terms childhood schizophrenia and autism "segregate a clinical group with rather specific linguistic behaviors in a unique pattern associated with other social behaviors" (p. 284).

It is clear that children who are described as psychotic do not have one unique language pathology. It is not clear how the language of *some* psychotic children is indeed different from the language of the child called aphasic. Among these children, described as emotionally disturbed, there seems to be evidence of a disruption in the interaction of the *form* of their utterances with the *content* or meaning expressed by their utterances. So far there is little evidence to suggest that the syntactic form of such speech is itself qualitatively and consistently different from the syntactic form of the speech of other children. For example, even though personal pronouns may be reversed, the utterance is acceptable in form—it sounds alright—but unacceptable in content/form interaction because the child's self-reference is "him" "her" or "you." Many children, however, have differing suprasegmental form (i.e., unusual prosody patterns). Very little is known about the meanings these children attempt to convey with the forms they do use, or about how the situations in which they use language affects the forms. With other children, there appears to be a disruption in the interaction of *use* with *form* and *content*; the child codes ideas but uses language for strange purposes, and only rarely for interpersonal communication. It seems apparent from what has been observed and reported, that while many emotionally disturbed children produce grammatical utterances, the *form* is often deviant in its relationship to *content* and *use* (distorted interactions of content/form/use). There is a rigidity and lack of creativity or adaptation in their utterances. They show no awareness of semantic-syntactic relations; they do not recombine words; instead, they learn whole units.

The patterns that emerge may be described in terms of the disruptions in content/form/use interactions discussed in Chapter X (see Box XVIII-4): disruptions in form (the children who are in many ways similar to other children diagnosed as aphasic); disruptions in use (the children who code ideas for intrapersonal communication and in contexts unrelated to the ideas); distorted interactions of content/form/use (the children who communicate ideas with unusual forms); and isolation of the three components (the children who utter stereotypic forms for no apparent function). This wide diversity of behaviors that is manifested by children who are labeled emotionally disturbed, or even more specifically as autistic or schizophrenic, negates the usefulness of these diagnoses as descriptions of specific language pathologies or as an explanation of a language disorder. Within the categories of autism and childhood schizophrenia there appear to be qualitative differences in the type of language behaviors that are observed. The categorical labels do not by themselves lead to specific goals or methodology of intervention.

THE COMMONALITIES AND DIFFERENCES AMONG THE CATEGORIES

The typical descriptions of children with a language disorder include reference to a lack of flexibility in their ability to represent information with linguistic forms and limitations in their use of the language they appear to know. An important question continues to be whether some of these children

BOX XVIII-4 DISRUPTIONS IN CONTENT/FORM/USE INTERACTIONS FOUND IN CHILDREN CATEGORIZED AS EMOTIONALLY DISTURBED

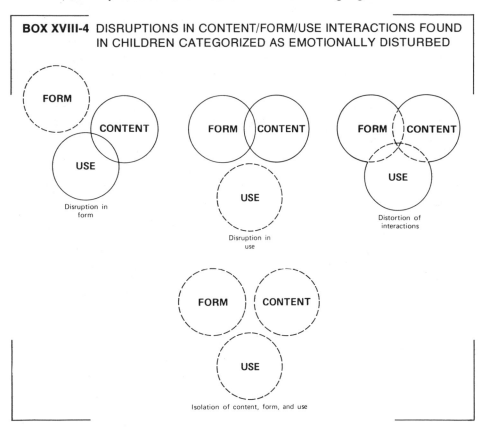

have learned a system of linguistic rules, as has been postulated for the normal child, or whether they have somehow remembered a number of linguistic patterns that they have associated with certain familiar experiences. Unfortunately, there are few descriptions of the language behavior of children who have been described as belonging to one or another of these language-disordered populations, and evidence about their language development is meager. There simply is not enough information available, as yet, to be able to judge whether there might be distinct language pathologies associated with different etiologies. On the contrary, the evidence that has been reported often points out the *commonalities* among children with different etiologies, as well as among the language behaviors that such children actually share with normal children who are first learning language, particularly with form. The qualitative differences reported so far predominate in the use component and are characteristic of *some* children who demonstrate severe impairment in social interactions.

In the area of intelligence, Bortner and Birch (1969) reported that qualitative analysis of patterns of intellectual organization yielded similarities among children with different etiologies that were not revealed when only their gross intelligence scores were compared. When children designated as emotionally disturbed were compared with children designated as brain injured, there was a difference in the total level of intelligence between the groups, but the patterns of intellectual organization, as revealed in their test performances, was markedly similar in both groups. On the basis of this result, Bortner and Birch questioned the *educational* value of the diagnostic categories. Would one reach the same conclusion with a similarly more qualitative analysis—that compares patterns of regularity and consistency in language behavior—of children with a language disorder? It appears that when language analyses include more than word counts or other quantitative measures of utterance length, the similarities of the language of many language-disordered children to normal child language become more evident, e.g., the decrease of echolalic or imitative language as *MLU* increased that was observed in emotionally disturbed children by Shapiro et al. (1974, in *RLDis*), and by Cunningham (1968, in *RLDis*) is similar to that found in normal children by Bloom, Rocissano, and Hood (1976); and Seitz and Stewart (1975).

The paradigm of content/form/use interaction has not yet been used as a framework for describing the speech of children with a language disorder. How do such children differ from normal children in what they talk about, in the form learned to represent their meanings, or in how they use speech? If differences from the normal child exist, to what extent are such differences the result of environmental and teaching situations to which the child has been exposed, or to the developmental pathology that has precipitated and possibly maintained the factors that have interfered with language learning?

As yet the global categories that result from an orientation toward language disorders that is concerned with etiology (to answer the question "Why?"), have not contributed much to understanding the influence of precipitating factors on how language is learned. This lack of progress in understanding language disorders may be attributed partly to the inadeqacy of the tools that have been used for describing language, and partly to the lack of knowledge about normal development. However, it is also true that progress may have been more seriously hampered by the very nature of the categories as predictors of language behavior—the fact that they lack homogeneity and specificity.

THE UNIQUENESS OF CLINICAL CATEGORIES

Some clinical categories include more quantitative definitions than others. For example, deafness can be defined by thresholds of auditory sensitivity, and mental retardation can be partially defined by scores on developmental scales or intelligence tests. Such quantitative definitions lead to more reliable categorizations than information based on inferences from behavior. However, such quantitative definitions are generally dependent on the extent of cooperation from the individual in a formal testing situation. If there is no response or there are incorrect responses, it is often difficult to interpret the results of testing, and reliability becomes a problem within even these apparently well-defined categories.

Unquestionably there are children who fit the common descriptions of behavior patterns associated with each catgory, but it is rare to find many who fit into only one category. Thus, while it is possible for autism, schizophrenia, mental retardation, and aphasia to exist in pure form, in practice they are similar and overlapping conditions. It is not easy to agree on a diagnosis for many children. "The same child may receive four or five different diagnoses, as successive clinics diagnose the case in terms of their special area of interest and experience" (Kessler, 1966, p. 260).

Why should this be so? For one reason, the etiological factors themselves are not mutually exclusive; they can and do easily coexist with one another. Just as a child may be both blind and deaf, a child may also have both a peripheral hearing loss and a central nervous system dysfunction. Multihandicapped children certainly account for some of those children who are not easy to place within an etiological category.

Another reason why the same children may be diagnosed with more than one etiological label is that the manifestation of a dysfunction can be influenced by the way in which the environment interacts with a developing organism. A child who is nonverbal, for whatever reason, may well show signs of emotional disturbance and mental retardation by virtue of the reactions that are or are not received from other individuals. It is often not possible to separate cause and effect relationships when a child is seen for diagnosis. Such children, then, fit the syndromes associated with more than one category and are prone to different diagnoses by different persons.

A final reason why the same child can be diagnosed differently is that it is difficult to associate certain behaviors with only one kind of dysfunction. A child who is neurologically limited in the amount of information that can be processed from the environment may well attempt to control the amount of surrounding stimulation by "turning off" or "tuning out". Thus, what can be described as *autistic* behavior (reducing contact with the environment) may be a useful coping mechanism that was motivated by difficulties in dealing with information from the environment for one child. However, for another child and for other reasons, the same behavior may be motivated by a desire to withdraw from and avoid interaction with other persons. "The more one investigates child behavior, the more one realizes that identical behavior can be the result of radically different causes" (Kessler, 1966, p. 287). For various reasons, then, it is difficult if not impossible to agree on a diagnosis (i.e., a categorical label) for many children.

Are etiological categories in fact unique or independent of each other? Rosenthal, Eisenson, and Luckau (1972) attempted to verify empirically the independence of diagnostic categories used with language-disordered children. All the children they described came from the same diagnostic center, so that there was presumably some agreement in the definitions of the categories that were used. Only 82 out of 200 children seen in the clinic could be placed within a category—highlighting the difficulty there is in such placement. These 82 children had been assigned to diagnostic categories with "high reliability" and formed the population for the study. The categories included: mentally retarded, severe hearing impairment, neurologically handicapped/aphasic, oral apraxic, dysarthric, maturational lag (organic), and autistic. The diagnostic information from medical, psychological, and language evaluations was classified into 32 variables. Cluster analysis of these variables, to determine commonalities among them in terms of the ways the variables coexisted in describing different children, yielded only two clusters. One cluster included the children diagnosed as mentally retarded and autistic, and the second cluster included the children diagnosed as hearing impaired, aphasic, and maturational lag. Discriminant analysis was used to sort out the variables that were different between the two clusters (i.e., the ways in which the children defined by the two clusters were different from each other). Examination of these variables indicated they were primarily measures of nonverbal intelligence; the medical, language, and other psychological measures did not differentiate between the groups; instead, they were differentiated on the basis of nonverbal, problem-solving behaviors. Children diagnosed as hearing impaired, aphasic, and maturational lag did better on nonverbal problem solving than the group diagnosed as mentally retarded or autistic. Thus, in this study using the same data that were used to assign children to diagnostic categories in the first place, the analyses did not support the integrity of such categories. The authors concluded that the categories were "neither unique nor homogeneous with respect to measurements routinely collected in the course of clinical evaluation" (p. 135). There is, therefore, not only a problem in placing a child within only one category, but analyses of the data used to make diagnoses do not support the uniqueness of the categories.

It is certainly important to search for whatever factors interfere with language learning, but attempting to isolate these factors may not be important. Statistical analyses of the data used to make diagnoses has not supported the idea that categories of etiology are unique and distinct from one another. Diagnosticians have difficulty fitting many children into global categories that represent discrete etiological factors. Different diagnosticians do not always agree on the best fit for a child in one or another category. Even when a fit is readily agreed on and the categorical placement does describe a child in comparison with other children, it is necessary to consider whether the category *explains* the child's language disorder.

THE EXPLANATORY VALUE OF CLINICAL CATEGORIES

The category in which a child is placed (i.e., the diagnosis) is determined by qualitative and quantitative descriptions of behaviors felt to be associated with dysfunctions of sensory systems, nervous systems, mental abilities, or emotional interactions. The implication is that each category represents a precipitating factor, but the representation of the precipitating factor is generally inferred from behavior. The factor itself is not tangible or directly observable. For example, it is not possible to observe the inner ear or the central nervous system directly in a diagnostic session, so their dysfunction is generally inferred from the individual's behavioral responses to certain tasks. Verification of an etiology by other than the behavioral manifestations that were used to define the category in the first place is rarely possible— with the exception of hearing impairment where impedance audiometry has become an objective measure of certain types of hearing loss (Jerger, Burney, Mauldin and Crump, 1974) or postmortem examination of brain tissue (Landau, Goldstein, and Kleffner, 1960, in *RLDis*).

In the future, more sophisticated procedures and methods of analyses may assist in validation of all categories that are attributed to organic dysfunctions. At present, however, most statements about organic dysfunction, particularly statements about the central nervous system as a cause of language disorder, are highly inferential. For example, EEG tracings have not clearly differentiated among categories where the precipitating factor was felt to be some central nervous system dysfunction (Goldstein, Landau, and Kleffner, 1958; and Kessler, 1966). Thus, a diagnostic label, such as childhood aphasia or brain damage, represents and is a shorthand description of behavioral patterns—patterns that include a language disorder. The assignment of different labels to different children does not mean that the cause or precipitating factor of any of the observed behaviors, including the language behaviors, has been isolated and identified.

The difficulties in using clinical categories based on behavioral syndromes as an explanation of any of the behaviors within the syndrome is particularly evident when the categories represent nonorganic dysfunctions. In particular, the often referred to categories of mental retardation and emotional disturbance represent hypothetical constructs. One cannot, of course, see or touch the mind, personality, or intelligence of an individual. Inadequate language skills are an important part, if not the major part, of the syndromes that define autism, schizophrenia, mental retardation, and aphasia. It is intuitively unreasonable and unsatisfactory to say that a child is autistic because of certain behaviors and then state that the reason the child behaves in those ways is because he or she is autistic. This circularity of reasoning results when certain behaviors lead to a diagnostic label, and then the diagnosis is used to explain the behaviors.

We are left then with global categories that give us a broad indication of certain patterns of behavior. Even when a fit is readily agreed on, the categorical placement does not explain the language disorder—one does not know the reason for a language disorder when one knows the categorical label assigned to a child. Why are they used? Are they perhaps useful in the educational management of the child?

THE USEFULNESS OF CATEGORIES FOR EDUCATIONAL MANAGEMENT

Because many schools and school systems have programs designed for neurologically impaired, aphasic, deaf, or mentally retarded children, placement within a treatment program is often dependent on such categorical classification. A categorical label must be assigned to each child before admitting the child to any program—and the label determines which program the child is admitted to. Is each of these programs unique and actually different from one another in terms of what they provide for the supposedly different children who are assigned to them? Usually the distinctions among such programs exist more in title than in content, which is not surprising, considering that what an aphasic child needs to learn is the same as what the mentally retarded, deaf, or emotionally disturbed child needs to learn. In fact, what the child with a language problem needs to learn is precisely what the normal child needs to learn at some point in development. The model language is the same for all. At present, there is no reason to suspect that the sequence in which that model is achieved does, or should, differ for different groups of children.

One can only conclude that the clinical categories formed when attention is given almost exclusively to etiological questions may or may not indicate *why* there is a language disorder, but they do not specify a language intervention program (i.e., *what* should be taught). The orientation does, however, stress observing behaviors that may provide information about *how* language intervention should be presented. The information that is sought to determine a diagnosis (i.e., a categorical label) *can* be important to planning a language intervention program *if* such information is viewed in terms of *how* to teach language. Unfortunately, the categorical label itself abstracts the information and too often decreases the understanding of the child.

An additional danger in the use of categorical labels to define children and their problems for educational management is the function it may serve as a self-fulfilling prophecy. Children are often treated in certain ways because of the label applied to them. Some educational and clinical programs are closed to children because of one or another diagnostic label, not because of the child's success or failure within the program. Parents and teachers expect certain behaviors of children who are retarded, emotionally disturbed, or neurologically impaired. Expectancy is an important element in learning. Thus, while many children do manifest common behavioral patterns, seeking to categorize children according to etiological syndromes is rarely useful to educators or clinicians interested in developing language skills. Careful description of the child's behaviors is more important in determining what and how the child will learn.

SUMMARY

The use of the categorical orientation considers the primary cause of the language disorder to be the leading question, with the resulting clinical categories of deafness, mental retardation, aphasia, and emotional disturbance. The categories that have been formed represent dysfunction of one or another of the factors thought to be necessary for the development of language (i.e., an intact sensory system, adequate cognitive function, an intact central nervous system, and appropriate psychosocial development). This orientation to precipitating factors has been a major influence on diagnosis, which is often geared to determining the primary cause or the etiological category that best fits the child's syndrome of behaviors, as well as placement in a treatment program and research having to do with the nature of language disorders. Students of speech pathology and special education in general have been taught to think of each category as distinct and different — if not by direct teaching in differential diagnosis, then by implication in the constant reference to children as being aphasic, mentally retarded, emotionally disturbed, and so forth. As a result, some educators and clinicians feel that the cause of the disorder and not the symptoms should be treated — that by treating the cause, the symptoms will somehow take care of themselves. This view suggests that the content of language intervention programs has less to do with language than with other factors that may or may not be specified by clinical categories.

Unfortunately, the reasons for a lack of language or a severe delay in the development of language are not generally reversible without programs directed to the symptoms. There is no general *cure* for mental retardation, deafness, or aphasia; one can succeed in changing the child's language disorder only by attempting to change the child's language behavior. For example, the child with a severe hearing impairment may benefit from medical treatment or amplification, but will usually still need help in learning language. Such a child may also need as much help with emotional adjustment as the child who is labeled emotionally disturbed. If the primary cause continues to be a maintaining factor and is manipulable, it should be treated. But in all instances the presenting conditions also need to be remedied and dealt with directly. The behaviors of each individual, viewed in terms of some ultimate goal, determine the content of a program. If the goal is language development, behaviors relative to the content/form/use of language must be considered. Certain other factors (e.g., emotional and physical factors) must be considered in all learning whether they were the factors precipitating difficulty in learning or not. Whatever the precipitating factors or whatever categorical label is applied to the child, the child's communication and interactional behaviors determine the goals of an intervention program.

SUGGESTED READINGS

In *Readings in Language Disorders*

Hearing impairment

Brannon, J., Linguistic word classes in the spoken language of normal, hard-of-hearing, and deaf children. *Journal of Speech and Hearing Research, 11*, 279-287, 1968.

Jarvella, R. J., and Lubinsky, J., Deaf and hearing children's use of language describing temporal order among events. *Journal of Speech and Hearing Research, 18*, 58-73, 1975.

Aphasia in children

Eisenson, J., and Ingram, D., Childhood aphasia—an updated concept based on recent research. *Acta Symbolica, 3*, 108-116, 1972.

Landau, W. M., Goldstein, R., and Kleffner, F. R., Congenital aphasia: A clinico-pathologic study. *Neurology, 10*,)15-921, 1960.

Leonard, L., Bolders, J., and Miller, J., An examination of the semantic relations reflected in the language usage of normal and language-disordered children. *Journal of Speech and Hearing Research, 19*, 371-392, 1976.

Lenneberg, E., *Biological foundations of language*. New York: John Wiley & Sons, pp. 145-157, 309-312, 1967.

Morehead, D. M., and Ingram, D., The development of base syntax in normal and linguistically deviant children. *Journal of Speech and Hearing Research, 16*, 330-352, 1973.

Mental retardation

Lackner, J. R., A developmental study of language behavior in retarded children. *Neuropsychologia, 6*, 301-320, 1968.

Emotional disturbance

Churchill, D., The relation of infantile autism and early childhood schizophrenia to developmental language disorders of childhood. *Journal of Autism and Childhood Schizophrenia, 2*, 182-197, 1972.

Cunningham, M. A., A comparison of the language of psychotic and nonpsychotic children who are mentally retarded. *Journal of Child Psychology and Psychiatry 9*, 229-244, 1968.

de Hirsch, Katrina, Differential diagnosis between aphasic and schizophrenic language in children. *Journal of Speech and Hearing Disorders, 32*, 3-11, 1967.

Kanner, L., Autistic disturbances of affective contact: Discussion section. *The Nervous Child, 2*, 1943.

Shapiro, T., Chiarandini, I., and Fish, B., Thirty severely disturbed children: Evaluation of their language development for classification and prognosis. *Archives of General Psychiatry, 30*, 819-825, 1974.

Other

Fromkin, V., Krashen, S., Curtiss, S., Rigler, D., and Rigler, M., The development of language in Genie: A case of language acquisition beyond the "critical period." *Brain and Language, 1*, 81-107, 1974.

Relevant Readings in Other Sources

Dever, R., A comparison of the results of a revised version of Berko's test of morphology with the free speech of mentally retarded children. *Journal of Speech and Hearing Research, 15,* 169–178, 1972.

Swisher, L. P., and Pinsker, E. J., The language characteristics of hyperverbal hydrocephalic children. *Developmental Medicine and Child Neurology 13,* 746–755, 1971.

Another major approach to language disorders in children has emphasized the specific abilities that have been considered necessary for the development and use of language. The specific abilities orientation represented a shift away from categorizing *children* according to common behavioral syndromes, and toward categorizing the *behaviors* of children. In this sense, the taxonomies formed within this orientation were molecular in that they grouped behaviors of people instead of grouping people. Clinically, the shift was away from interest in the precipitating factors of a language disorder and toward diagnosis of the child's present strengths and weaknesses in those abilities and skills that were presumed necessary for the adequate development of linguistic behavior. Children were described in terms of profiles of behavioral categories and not by labels that stressed their similarities or differences in relation to groups of other children. In this chapter the specific abilities will be discussed along with some of the research in information processing for language that has related specific abilities to language disorders. Finally, the usefulness of this approach to educational management will be discussed.

SPECIFIC ABILITIES RELATED TO LANGUAGE

The specific abilities approach has been based on the assumptions that, first, there are certain abilities that are required for language and, second, these abilities can be identified, measured, and remediated. Various models have been proposed to represent the cognitive abilities involved in language processing; each attempts to get inside the human mind to explain what happens between an observable stimulus and an observable response.

Most of the models of language processes that have been proposed include at least three major components: a perceptual component that involves the initial processing of the input signal; a conceptual or representational component that involves meaning and symbolic thinking; and an output component that has to do with planning and command of motor responses. In addition, some models include a feedback component. The perceptual component generally includes signal recognition, discrimination, retention, and intersensory integration. Some of the research related to the perceptual component has been concerned with the perception of verbal stimuli; other research has dealt with nonverbal stimuli. The conceptual component includes the association of meaning with the input or output signal, and the use, or manipulation, of symbols to carry out various tasks. Problem-solving tasks such as analogies and similarities have often been used to evaluate or measure the function of this component. The output component includes a plan for the production of the motor response, for example, the speech signal. Most models also stress the independence of modalities (e.g., visual and auditory). The arrangement and ordering of the different components or elements varies from one model to another, but many schemes suggest some degree of linear processing (e.g., Osgood's 1957 model of language). (See Boxes XiX-1 and XIX-2 for examples of two models.)

The levels and components of language processing are often

BOX XIX-1 A CLINICAL MODEL OF COMMUNICATION PROCESSES

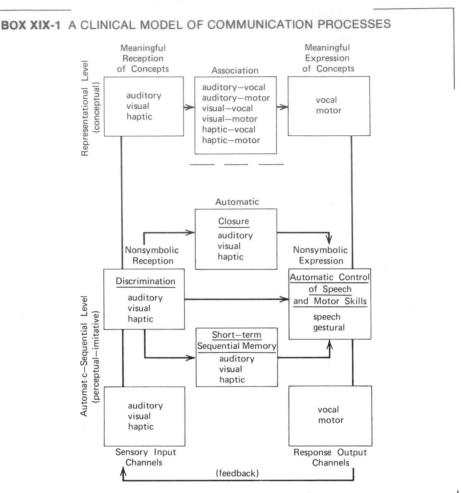

This adaptation of Osgood's model (Kirk and Kirk, 1971) illustrates linear processing from perceptual to conceptual and an independence of the perceptual level from the conceptual level. As do many models, this model suggests that the conceptual level can be bypassed—note the automatic loop (the perceptual-imitative level).

discussed and schematized as though they were discrete and separate from each other, but it would seem that they are actually and necessarily interdependent. Such interdependence among the components is a large factor in the interpretation of much of the research having to do with specific abilities and with the attempts that have been made to apply such information to clinical situations.

SPECIFIC ABILITIES RELATED TO LANGUAGE DISORDERS

Hardy (1965), in an article emphasizing the importance of considering specific abilities in relation to language disorders, pointed out the importance of knowing the modalities of input that are intact when planning remediation for children with language disorders. Considerable research within the specific abilities orientation has focussed on the perceptual processing of auditory stimuli. The interest in the processing of auditory signals spurred the development of a number of tests of auditory perception

BOX XIX-2 AN OPERATIONAL DIAGRAM OF THE LEVELS OF FUNCTION IN THE CENTRAL NERVOUS SYSTEM

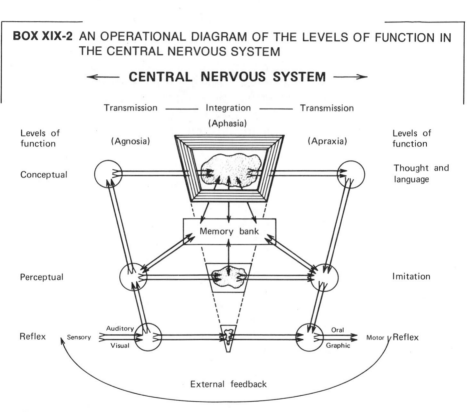

In contrast to the model by Kirk and Kirk (1971, in Box XIX-1) the model by Wepman, Jones, Bock, and Van Pelt (1960) presented here suggests some degree of interdependence between conceptual and perceptual levels through a memory bank. Although the discussion of the model by Wepman et al. focussed mainly on the traces imitation can leave in the memory bank, the arrows suggest recognition of the fact that the memory bank, which is also influenced by the conceptual level, can also influence processing on the perceptual level.

and the viewing of etiology of language problems in terms of a child's inability to process information in the environment—particularly the inability to process verbal stimuli. Much of the research has considered specific abilities in relation to various clinical syndromes. That is, deficits in auditory processing, or the search for other specific ability dysfunctions, has been related to the clinical categories that were discussed in the preceding section. Categories of particular interest in this research have been the populations of children with language disorders who may be labeled brain damaged, aphasic, or emotionally disturbed.

Sabatino (1969) developed a test of auditory perception that measured the discrimination of words and speech sounds, the recall of digit sequences and sentences, the ability to tap auditory patterns, and comprehension of a story. He reported that each subtest discriminated children "with known minimal brain damage" from children without known cerebral pathology, when presented in noise, and that all but the digit and tapping subtests, when presented in quiet, differentiated between the two groups. Because all of the subtests that discriminated between the groups in quiet involved meaningful language (only digit recall and tapping did not discriminate between the two groups in quiet), he concluded "that meaningful language is necessary to discriminate between the auditory perceptual function of normal and neurologically impaired children" (p. 736). Since no description of the subjects' language skills was included in this report, it is difficult to know if the tasks that measured perceptual function were actually a test of the children's knowledge of language. This difficulty with the separation of auditory perception from knowledge of what is being perceived (in most cases language stimuli), has been described by Rees (1973b). Whenever units of language are used as the stimuli to be perceived, the question arises as to whether perceptual dysfunction, identified by response to such stimuli, is a cause or a reflection of a language disorder. (Recall the earlier discussion about the interdependence of levels of processing.)

AUDITORY SEQUENTIAL MEMORY

Reports of research as well as clinical studies have indicated a correlation between many aspects of perceptual dysfunction and language disorder. For example, many language-disordered children present poor auditory recall of sequential information (Masland and Case, 1968; Menyuk, 1964b; and Stark, Poppen, and May, 1967). In a study of the relationship between auditory memory span and language skill in a retarded population, Graham (1968) reported that the ability to imitate and comprehend sentences varied directly with the length of digit span recall. Unquestionably, the ability of the normal child to imitate and comprehend sentences also increases as recall of digits increases, but the high correlation does not specify the direction of the relationship between the two, nor how the one is related to the other.

There seems to be little question that learning and using language involves the processing of sequences of auditory information. It is easy to assume that a deficiency in the reproduction of sequences of auditory stimuli reflects the cause of a language disorder—or that such a deficiency interferes with learning language. The sequence of words within a sentence is a major cue for speech processing by children (Bever, 1970; Lahey, 1974; Sinclair and Bronckart, 1972), but the sequence of words within a sentence is motivated by the semantic relationships among the words. Three-year-old children who can only repeat a list of two or three unrelated words are able to produce and comprehend some rather long sentences because of the semantic relationships that are cued by the words in sequence with one another. Such children also know how to use information about word order to express meaning relationships in their own speech. It is not clear how many unrelated words one must be able to repeat in order to learn language—perhaps only one or two, or perhaps none. The correlation between memory span for sequential auditory information and language development in children may be related to some third factor influencing both, and improvement in one skill may not influence the other. It is also possible that memory span for unrelated information may develop as experience with the use of order relationships in language increases.

According to Olson (1973), auditory memory span may reflect a child's ability to handle verbal information and may not itself be a measure of processing capacity. It may be that the recall of auditory sequential information is a sensitive index of an individual's familiarity with a linguistic code and not a processing ability on which language learning is dependent. Meaningful words are recalled better than nonsense words, concrete words are recalled better than abstract words (Brenner, 1940), and numbers and words are recalled better when presented in the subject's native language than when presented in a second language (Connelly, 1974). It is easier to identify what is well known than to identify newly learned material; thus, memory span may reflect one's knowledge of the signal. (Recall the Wepman et al., 1960, model in Box XIX-2; the imitative perceptual level is connected to the memory bank.) Huttenlocher and Burke (1976) have suggested that the developmental increase in the span of recall is associated with the speed with which subjects can identify incoming items, not with an increase in storage capacity.

To assume that the memory problem causes the language disorder is to assume a linear, unidirectional language model as discussed previously and schematized by Kirk and Kirk's model of communication (1971, Box XIX-1). On the other hand, if one assumes that language processing involves *inter*dependence of processing levels, as schematized by Wepman et al. (1960, Box XIX-2), the finding of poor auditory memory span in language-disordered children may itself be *explained* by the language disorder.

Although increased memory span is related to advanced language skills, no doubt because both are related to some more general, underlying language ability, age-appropriate memory span can coexist with a language disorder. There are language-disordered children, categorized as autistic or schizophrenic, who have average or better than average spans of recall for strings of unrelated words. These same children, however, do not use grammatical structure to aid recall as well as retarded or normal children matched on digit span and vocabulary test scores (Hermelin and O'Connor, 1967; Aurnhammer-Frith, 1969; and Hermelin and Frith, 1971, in *RLDis*). No description of the language of these autistic children was presented in these reports; possibly the autistic children were familiar with the form of language, but did not know much about the content/form/use interactions while the normal and retarded children with similar digit spans were still developing knowledge of each component and of content/form/use interactions.

TEMPORAL CUES

The effect of temporal factors in auditory processing has been investigated in a number of studies. Lowe and Campbell (1965), and Schnur (1971) found that aphasic children needed considerably more time than normal listeners between the presentation of two successive pure tones in order to identify which tone came first—a replication of Efron's (1963) findings with adult aphasics. Rosenthal (1972) has reported that aphasic children, in contrast to normal children, had more difficulty discriminating speech sounds that are different because of temporal cues, such as /ʃ/ and /tʃ/, than between those that are different because of frequency cues, as /s/ and /ʃ/.

More recently Tallal and Piercy (1973a; 1973b; 1974; 1975, in *RLDis*) and Tallal (1976) have reported a series of experiments demonstrating gross deficits in rapid auditory processing by aphasic children. When the intervals between stimuli were decreased and the number of stimuli were increased, aphasic children were adversely affected in their ability to discriminate synthetic speech sounds, but normal children of the same age were not. The same result was not obtained with visual stimuli. They found that less than half of their aphasic population were able to discriminate between different synthetic stop consonants, with their normal rapidly changing formant transitions, but all could discriminate between steady-state vowels. When the rate of formant transition for consonants was artificially extended to twice its original duration, all the aphasic children successfully discriminated the syllables. The authors concluded from these experiments that a constraint on the speed of perception affects the processing of certain speech sounds and underlies the difficulty with learning language.

Thus, even when the experimental task does not demand knowledge of the linguistic code, by using nonverbal stimuli or by using nonsense syllables in experiments, certain language-disordered children have difficulties in the rate at which they can process auditory stimuli. Such difficulties would conceivably interfere with learning the form of spoken language, which is necessarily constrained by temporal factors. There are, however, differences among children and, at present, the language of such children, with demonstrated difficulty in temporal processing, has not been described in any of these research reports. The question remains how the language of those aphasic children who had difficulty with consonant perception differed from the language of those aphasic children who did not experience such difficulty. Is their comprehension of spoken language different? Would children with a different diagnosis (i.e., a different categorical label) or would normal children at a similar language level respond the same way? Such information is still needed before direct connections between auditory processing capacities and a language disorder can be made.

PROCESSING MULTISENSORY INPUT

Another aspect of perception that is logically related to language learning is attention to and integration of separate sensory stimuli from different modalities. It would seem that visual and tactile features of input from the context must be attended to and integrated with auditory impressions, if the interactions between content/form/use are to develop. That is, children need to experience the objects and events referred to by the speech that they hear in order to learn the coding relation between meaning and sound.

Walker and Birch (1970) compared the auditory-visual integration skills of schizophrenic children with those of normal children and found that the schizophrenic children's responses to the integrative task were significantly inferior to the responses by the normal population. Walker and Birch concluded "that the schizophrenic children manifest a clear inability to organize and integrate information coming to them from the environment through the separate organs of sense and that this inability probably reflects a primary peculiarity in the organization of their central nervous systems" (p. 111), which contributes to childhood psychosis. The schizophrenic group was not homogeneous; some of the schizophrenic children performed as well on the integration task as the normal population. Again, there was no description of the children's language presented, so that it is impossible to relate such integrative skill to language behaviors.

If these experimental tasks are representative of the integration of auditory and visual stimuli in real-life situations, then the difficulties exhibited by the child who does not integrate multisensory stimuli might account for difficulties in the interaction between content/form in language development. The child might conceivably learn a lot about the system of linguistic signals through the auditory channel and be able to utter long, complex sentences. But the child might be unable to learn the semantic-syntactic relations in sentences and also their relation to social situations—the connection of form with content/use—because of an inability to integrate knowledge of the world obtained through vision and tactile senses with the vocal linguistic signals. The language of many psychotic children presents such a pattern—referred to as distorted interactions or separation of content/form/use in Chapters X and XVIII. Since the integrative task presented in the Walker and Birch experiment was nonverbal, and since no description was given of the language of the nonintegrating children, such conjecture is only of heuristic interest at the present time.

Instead of an inability to integrate information from different sensory modalities, it may be that some children obtain information from only one modality because they attend to only one type of stimulus during multisensory stimulation; thus they have an attentional deficit, not an integrational problem. Such a possibility was demonstrated by Lovaas, Schreibman, Koegel, and Rehm (1971, in *RLDis*). Three groups of children (normal, retarded, and autistic children of similar age) were reinforced for responding to multisensory stimuli and then tested to see which of the stimuli were responded to when presented separately. They found that the autistic children responded primarily to only one cue, the retardates responded primarily to two cues, and the normal children uniformly responded to all three cues. No one modality was preferred for any group, and the first modality preference of a particular child could be changed suggesting, according to the authors, a problem of "stimulus overselectivity." The results cannot, however, be used to account for differences in verbal behavior, since the language behaviors were not specified; the autistic children were described as severely impaired, with all but one "mute," but the language of the retarded children was not described.

Certainly, such an attentional deficit could also inhibit language learning, since language learning involves processing the simultaneous or near contiguous presentation of both linguistic and nonlinguistic stimuli. An attentional deficit may account for lack of auditory-vocal language (if the auditory modality is continually ignored) or for auditory-vocal behaviors that may be described as a distorted interaction or separation of content/form/ use. On the other hand, selective attention to only one modality may reflect the inability to learn language for some other reason—such as the inability to integrate information from different sensory modalities. The inability to attach meaning to sound may cause a child to "tune out"—either to complex input or to a particular type of input. It is not clear, therefore, that attentional deficits are, in fact, distinct from integrational deficits, nor is it clear whether either is a cause or a reflection of a language disorder.

To determine the cause-effect relationship between poor performance on tasks designed to measure perceptual skills and a language disorder, more information about the language behaviors that differentiate between children who do well and children who do not do well on such tasks is needed (thus, an integration of a specific abilities orientation with a linguistic orientation), as well as developmental information on these skills in both normal and language-disordered children. Meanwhile, does the specific abilities orientation have other than heuristic interest—can it be useful for the educational management of children with language disorders? Are the molecular categories—the elements of processing evolved from models of cognitive functioning—useful to the educator or clinician responsible for developing language skills? Can we measure such functions and, if so, what do they tell us about goals or techniques of intervention related to language learning?

THE USEFULNESS OF THE SPECIFIC ABILITIES ORIENTATION FOR EDUCATIONAL MANAGEMENT

Much of the impetus behind the specific abilities orientation to language disorders came originally from educators who were interested in those schoolchildren who had problems in learning academic skills despite normal overall intelligence and no evidence of severe emotional problems. The concept of weakness in certain specific abilities underlying language and learning in general was appealing, both as an explanation of learning disabilities and as a model for remediation.

There have been two approaches within the specific abilities orientation: one has focussed on delineating weaknesses in cognitive abilities and directly teaching to these weaknesses with the goal of improving such skills—a *specific disabilities* approach; the second has attempted to change brain functioning more generally (and thus remediate deficits in cognitive, particularly perceptual, skills) through indirect means as sensory-motor training—a *motor* approach. Each approach is discussed in the following section, the first more fully than the second because it has had greater impact on planning language intervention.

A SPECIFIC DISABILITIES APPROACH

The most influential and the most elaborate attempt to diagnose specific disabilities has been the *Illinois Test of Psycholinguistic Abilities* (ITPA), published first in an experimental form (Kirk and McCarthy, 1961) and later revised (Kirk, McCarthy, and Kirk, 1968). The objective of the ITPA is to "delineate specific abilities and disabilities in children in order that remediation may be undertaken when needed" (Kirk et al., 1968, p. 5). The purpose of diagnosis is to identify specific areas of defective functioning, and the purpose of intervention is to provide appropriate remediation in the areas so identified.

The ITPA was based on a three-stage mediational model of language (Osgood, 1957) that included: the processes of reception, association, and expression; the modalities of input and output; and levels of processing. (See Box XIX-1 for an adaptation of this model.) The authors of the ITPA modified Osgood's model somewhat to apply it to a clinical population and to the practicality of a testing situation. The test purports to tap both auditory and visual channels of sensory input and motor and vocal channels of output. Each of these channels is considered for the processes of reception, association, and expression at two levels of processing. One level of processing is called the automatic level where information is integrated and organized but does not involve any mediation of meaning. It includes rote learning, automatic production of a sequence of items, and utilization of the redundant codings in heard speech, such as *two* shoes. The second level is called the representational level and involves the processing of meaning and the use of symbols. Twelve subtests are included in the test to observe specific processes through each channel at each level. Each subtest was designed to represent a specific ability, and normative data were presented so that each ability could be compared with a general population of normal children and with each child's other abilities. Remedial programs, based on this approach to specific abilities, are designed with the goal of strengthening each ability. The following section discusses the relevance of this approach to language learning and its application to children who are having difficulty learning a first language (i.e., to language-disordered children).

These are several assumptions that are implied in any orientation to language disorders that attempts to delineate and remediate specific abilities: (1) that the abilities for language are distinct from each other in the learning and use of language; (2) that each ability is a necessary prerequisite for the development and use of language, and weak abilities therefore interfere with the learning or use of language; and (3) that weak abilities can be strengthened by training, and that strengthening specific abilities through remediation training will transfer somehow to general improvement in the knowledge and use of language. These three assumptions are examined below, using the ITPA as a model of such an approach.[1] (See Mann, 1971, and Hammil and Larsen, 1974, in *RLDis* for further discussion of many of these same points.)

Can Abilities be Isolated From One Another?

First, are the abilities that have been defined in the model of language, on which the ITPA was based, actually distinct from each other in language learning and use?

One of the major assumptions underlying the use of the ITPA in this fashion [as a diagnostic instrument to plan remediation of weak abilities] is that the test

---

[1] The ITPA has been selected for discussion because it represents the best organized and most researched attempt to apply this approach. It should be noted that the critique applies only to first language learning and not to the application of this approach or this instrument to later academic learning, such as learning to read.

actually assesses "single abilities" which are mutually exclusive. Factor analysis provides one method of testing the accuracy of this assumption. (Rykman and Wiegerink, 1969)

In a study investigating the construct validity of the test, or the degree to which each subtest measured independent abilities as represented in the Osgood model, different single abilities were substantiated in a fourth-grade population of normal children (Newcomer, Hare, Hammil, and McGettigan, 1973). The investigators included in their factor analyses a set of "criteria tests designed to parallel the functions measured by the ITPA subtests" (p. 3), and found support for Osgood's postulation of levels of organization and input, and of output and organizational processes but no support for different modality channels. They concluded that "all subtests except Visual Reception, Auditory Reception and Visual Sequential Memory can be regarded as measuring separate psycholinguistic abilities . . . that test users would be correct in regarding the subtests as valid representatives of the level and process of psycholinguistic constructs . . ." (p. 17). Such evidence appears to give an affirmative answer to the question of distinct abilities, but the results must be interpreted with caution. As Newcomer et al. warn, different factors, representing different abilities, might emerge with a different population of children. Previous factor analytic studies have supported this warning; they have not isolated 12 distinct abilities, but have found that the number of abilities varied with age (Rykman and Wiegerink, 1969). Fewer factors emerged for younger children, at about the age of 3 years, than for older children, at about the age of 8 years. Thus, for younger children the assumption of single abilities was not supported. In contrast to the findings by Newcomer et al., the aspect of the model that received the greatest support in the review by Rykman and Wiegerink was modality channel. Level and process were not distinctive at the younger preschool age levels, but became better differentiated as the children approached 8 years of age. The lack of support for 12 independent abilities in the studies reported by Rykman and Wiegerink may be caused by the lack of criteria tests included in the data—"a treatment which maximized their intercorrelations" (Newcomer et al., 1973, p. 3)—or may be related to age. The conclusion by Rykman and Wiegerink that the assumption of separate abilities is not supported for young children so that clinical use of the ITPA in this age range should proceed with caution, coupled with the warning by Newcomer et al., that their own findings cannot be generalized to other populations, suggests that the answer to the initial question (Can abilities be isolated from one another?) may be negative for the normal child learning language in the preschool years, at least as measured in this way. For a child with early language skills, the value of the subtests on the ITPA as a measure of distinct abilities underlying the child's knowledge of language is highly questionable.

Are the Specific Abilities Necessary for Language Development?

Is each ability essential for the development and use of language, and do weaknesses within each ability interfere with learning and use of language? Abilities that are specified at the automatic level of the ITPA are not always clearly related to the development and use of oral language.

One subtest, sound blending, taps the ability to synthesize separate phonemes. In fact, research in speech perception (A. Liberman, Cooper, Shankweiler, and Studdert-Kennedy, 1967) and coarticulation studies of speech production (Amerman, Daniloff, and Moll, 1970) have indicated that individuals neither perceive nor produce words by connecting one separate phoneme with another. The acoustic signal of speech cannot be segmented to individual phonemes. For example, the acoustic signals that are perceived as plosive sounds (/p/, /b/, /d/, /g/, /t/, /k/) vary in frequency, and the direction of frequency changes depending on the vowels that precede or follow them. If a perceived plosive phoneme such as /p/ is separated, by tape cutting, from the word in which it is embedded and attached to another syllable, on tape, the resulting phoneme will sound different—for example, like /k/, not /p/ (A. Liberman, Delattre, and Cooper, 1952; Schatz, 1954). Thus, the acoustic signal of our language is not segmentable and there is not a one-to-one correspondence between individual phonemes and the acoustic signal; see, for example Boxes XIX-3 and XIX-4. It is not clear what the unit of perception is, but it is clear the unit is not a phoneme.

A skill in phoneme synthesizing, thus, is certainly not a prerequisite for learning to talk or understand language. It is in fact, even difficult to teach such skills to normal preschool children (I. Liberman, Shankweiler, Fischer, and Carter, 1974).[2] The development of the ability to synthesize speech sounds appears to be more necessary to the use of written language than oral language, and perhaps is best reserved for such academic or remedial training in reading and writing where sounds are necessarily represented by separate letters of the alphabet. Certainly the language pathologist should question teaching sound synthesizing or blending to a child with a language disorder whose language skills are comparable to a 2- or 3-year-old child who, research has shown, is not capable of performance with sound blending tasks. Nevertheless, in many clinics and schools, children who are speaking with syntactic constructions of two and three words that are typical

---

[2] Although the norms on the sound blending subtest of the ITPA go as low as 2½ years of age, thus indicating early acquisition of such a skill, sound blending ability is not really tapped in the early items of the test. On the first eight items of the test, children are asked to choose a picture in response to a phoneme-by-phoneme presentation of the name of an object (e.g., b-a-t). A correct response can very conceivably be made on the basis of the recognition of a part of the word, and actually blending the sounds is really not essential to such recognition. In fact, a psycholinguistic age of 5 years can be reached on the test items without the necessity of phoneme synthesis, and 5-year-old children already have considerable facility with their native language.

BOX XIX-3 THE INFLUENCE OF THE VOWEL CONTEXT ON A PLOSIVE CONSONANT (from A. Liberman, Cooper, Shankweiler, and Studdert-Kennedy, 1967)

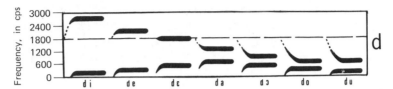

Note that the initial part of the acoustic signal in the figure above is different in each syllable although both syllables are perceived as beginning with /d/.

of early language development have been given training on such skills. The ability to separate and integrate the separate sounds of a word or phrase is a metalinguistic task that has to be taught, and it is not usually taught to children until they demonstrate their readiness at about age 6 or 7 years. Such a metalinguistic task has less to do with language learning than has

BOX XIX-4 THE INTERDEPENDENCE OF PHONEMES (from A. Liberman, 1970)

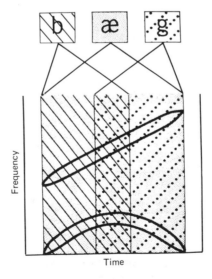

This figure illustrates the interdependence of phonemes; both consonants are influenced by the vowel and the vowel is, in turn, influenced by both consonants.

the ability to understand the use and meaning of words and the semantic-syntactic relations that hold among words.

Another ability tapped on the automatic level of the ITPA and often found deficient in children with a language disorder is auditory memory for sequential information with unrelated words or digits. This problem has already been discussed at length, with the conclusion that the skill in recall of auditory sequences may be a reflection of knowledge of language instead of a separate process that operates independently to interfere with language learning. There are, as yet, no data that support the idea that increasing skills in auditory recall leads to improvement in language skills. On the contrary, whatever evidence that is available does not support the notion that deficiencies in auditory sequential recall are responsible for deficiencies in vocabulary or syntactic skills.

On the grammatical closure subtest of the ITPA, the child is asked to complete sentences with a correct morphological inflection such as a plural or possessive -s. Both the placement of the subtest at the automatic processing level, and the remedial programs designed to train children in this ability, suggest that learning the use of morphological inflections has to do only with form alone—that it is automatic and without relation to meaning. Remediation, for example, is often based on building closure skills with cues from redundancies in the linguistic signal, for example "Here is a boat. Now there are two of them. There are two *boats*." Little time is spent on teaching each morphological inflection as a code for a particular meaning (as adding -s to words indicates possession in one instance, or signals the difference between one and more than one object in another instance). Such procedures strongly imply that coding can be learned as an automatic closure skill.

Since the ITPA taps the child's knowledge of some aspects of certain syntactic skills, such as whether the child can add a plural or possessive -s when required by the syntactic context, it is, to some extent, a test of language knowledge. If a child does poorly on items of the test, one can say that the child does not know the interaction between content/form that is tested, but it is not clear that the child does not know the interaction because of a failure at the automatic level of speech processing unless we simply accept the model at face value, without measures of external validity. From the considerable research that has been done in the development of morphology in the last 15 years, it is quite clear that learning grammatical morphemes is not automatic, but has to do, instead, with important inductions about correspondences between sound and meaning and thus is a part of the representational level of language. The subtest does not measure an ability that is a prerequisite for language learning; it measures an aspect of language knowledge itself (i.e., the knowledge of grammatical morphemes). If children are to learn morphological inflections, they need to induce the rules that underlie the use of morphological inflections through experiencing the morphological forms paired with meaningful contexts. Sentence completion exercises or repetition and memorization of grammatical sentences out of context are not meaningful.

Auditory discrimination is described as a perceptual ability not mediated by meaning and, although not tested on the ITPA, Kirk and Kirk (1971, Box XIX-1) placed auditory discrimination on the automatic level of processing. Training in auditory discrimination often consists of drills for recognizing differences between two sounds presented in isolation and out of context. Although research with young, normal infants has indicated that infants are able to make discriminations among different sounds, toddlers have difficulty discriminating among these same sounds when they are used in meaningful words. (See Chapter III.) Children need to learn or, perhaps, relearn differences between speech sounds when they become aware that aspects of the signal are used to code meaningful differences.

As discussed earlier, certain researchers have found deficits in discriminating temporal aspects of the auditory speech signal among language-disordered children, that is, difficulty in discriminating speech sounds that are differentiated by temporal cues, and in determining order of sounds rapidly presented. Unfortunately, we do not know how these skills develop in normal children—would the differences exist if normal and language-disordered children were matched according to some criterion of phonological or syntactic development? It may very well be that temporal discrimination is yet another process that correlates with and perhaps reflects language knowledge, but is not a specific deficit accounting for a language disorder.

The important point is that many of the tasks used to test the automatic level of processing (i.e., perceptual skills) are difficult to separate from knowledge of language. Thus it is difficult to conclude that low scores on the tests that have been designed to tap these processes are evidence that such processes are weak rather than that language in some more general sense is not well learned. (See Rees, 1973b for further discussion on this point.) The problem is similar on the representational level, where the auditory tests are tests of vocabulary and the manipulation of words. Such tests demonstrate weak language skills; they cannot then be seen to represent the abilities that are necessary for learning language, nor can low scores be said to represent weaknesses in abilities that interfere with language learning or use.

Can the Specific Abilities be Remediated and do Remedial Programs Lead to Improvement in Language Skills?

Kirk and Kirk (1971) have presented treatment case histories as evidence that subtest scores of the ITPA can be improved with remedial training. Whether the increase in subtest scores actually indicates some improvement in a basic ability itself, and not improvement in the ability to perform a specific task, is not clear. Intervention and educational activities often duplicate the type of item that was used to test the ability instead of using different kinds of activities, which also require the ability. It is not surprising that training in an activity might improve some children's ability to perform that activity—and most remedial activities are designed around tasks used for testing the ability. Thus, activities for strengthening auditory sequential memory give the child considerable practice with recall of ordered information—either with unrelated items, poems, or sentence repetition out of context; activities for grammatical closure stress repetition of grammatical sentences and completeness of sentences; activities for sound blending involve analysis and synthesis of phonemes in words; and activities for auditory discrimination often involve identifying differences and similarities between paired sounds or words. Remedial activities such as these are related to language testing, but are far removed from early language learning and use in the young, normal child. It appears that there can be some success in remediating specific abilities with some individual children; that is, their test scores can be raised. When such scores are raised, the more basic question is: Does the improved score represent improved skills within the entire domain of the ability supposedly measured by the test or only in the specific type of skill used to measure the domain of that ability?

In contrast to the individual case histories demonstrating improved test scores after remediation, many studies have reported minimal improvement. Hammill and Larsen (1974, in *RLDis*) reviewed the results of 38 studies that measured the effectiveness of training specific abilities and concluded "it is apparent that for the most part, researchers have been unsuccessful in developing those skills which would enable their subjects to do well on the ITPA" (p. 10). More studies reported improvement in verbal expression than in other subtests; few studies reported improvement with grammatical closure, auditory reception, visual closure, or visual reception. According to Hammill and Larsen, the collective results of the studies they reviewed do not validate the idea that psycholinguistic constructs, as measured by the ITPA, can be trained by existing techniques. They suggested that either the test may not be an appropriate measure of the abilities, the abilities may be untrainable, or the intervention programs reported in the literature may be inadequate. We would add that it may also be that the abilities themselves are inseparable, either from one another, or from some larger, more general language facility.

Children learn language to represent the information that they know about events in the world—not as an empty signal to be discriminated, recalled in sequence, or pulled apart and put together again. A certain metalinguistic sophistication or level of development may be necessary before such operations on the linguistic signal come easily to children, because the use of linguistic signals is closely tied with meaning from the beginning of development. Karpova (1966) found that nursery school children had difficulty identifying individual words within a sentence, but identified groups of words that represented meaning units. Huttenlocher (1964) found that $4\frac{1}{2}$ to 5-year-olds had difficulty separating and repeating backwards words that are normally spoken together but had no difficulty repeating backwards an unrelated list of words. Doing things with words and strings of words without regard for the meaning they represent appears to be possible only after one has had considerable practice with the meaningful use of language. Deficiencies on the automatic or perceptual level of linguistic processing, as measured by tasks such as those that have been discussed, may reflect this lack of experience instead of reflecting the cause of poor language skills. Thus, it appears that remediation should be directed to teaching children linguistic form in relation to the meaning it codes, before teaching children to perform operations on the linguistic signal that do not involve meaning.

The remediation of abilities on the representational level does not involve the same problems as remediation on the automatic level of processing. The representational level involves obtaining meaning from symbols, producing meaning through symbols, drawing relationships from symbols, and manipulating symbolic material. Such abilities are, of course, the essence of the use of language. On this level, remediation is geared to meaning—and language skills are taught directly.

Training on analogies and categorization are a part of the remedial procedures generally suggested for training auditory association. A potential problem with these procedures lies in the selection of priorities or sequence of goals that are implemented in teaching. Activities used to remediate the abilities on the representational level, while teaching language skills, are generally based on the behaviors expected of the normal child with the linguistic ability of at least a 4- or 5-year-old child. For example, younger children of 2 or 3 years, developing language normally, do not readily use or understand analogies, and yet analogies are used as a common remedial exercise for language-disordered children with deficits in auditory association, who have language skills similar to those of a 2 or 3-year-old child.[3]

Another common remedial activity aimed at improving skills at the representational level is training in the ability to categorize objects according to hierarchies. It is not uncommon for children with a language disorder to be given exercises in categorizing common objects (foods, furniture, vehicles, etc.) after a basic vocabulary of nouns has been learned and

---

[3] Even though the auditory association subtest tests analogies and provides norms that extend as low as $2\frac{1}{2}$ years of age, it is nevertheless possible to reach a psycholinguistic age of $4\frac{1}{2}$ on the test without dealing with analogies. Most of the first 14 items on the test can be responded to correctly by understanding only the second of the first and second ideas in the analogy.

before the child expresses ideas in simple sentences. In this way, such superordinate concepts as furniture, fruit, clothing, or size, color, and shape similarities may be presented to children to learn before the coding of the relationships of actor-action-object is presented.

The existing information about early normal language and cognitive development indicates, however, that children know much about coding action and state relationships before they label superordinate categories based on the functional and perceptual similarities among different objects. The early categories that children form in the first 2 years are categories of the same object—that different sizes and shapes of chairs are all *chair*, that different colors and sizes of books are all *book*, and so forth. Subsequent categories that are formed have to do with what the child can do with an object. The linguistic forms that encode the functional or perceptual abstractions that relate different objects to one another are not represented until later in child language.

With this in mind, one might question the use of activities geared to learning opposites, superordinate categorizing, and verbal analogies with a child whose language skills are comparable to those of a 2- or 3-year-old child. In the normal development of language, a child's facility in talking about activities and states precedes talking about relationships between verbal constructs, problem solving with symbols and, in general, the manipulation of symbols without reference in the child's experience. Thus, although the abilities with language that are tapped by the association tasks on the ITPA and by the many tests that measure intelligence are important, eventual goals for all speakers, such skills may entail necessary prerequisites that must be considered first in planning a sequence of goals for any language program.

Certain representational abilities might well be taught before or in conjunction with early language learning if these abilities are precursors to normal language learning. Thus the concept of object permanence, which is achieved in the first 2 years of life, would be a reasonable goal for the prelinguistic child—a behavior both logically and developmentally related to early language learning (content)—but even this goal should be carried out in a setting that incorporates realistic and simple linguistic input.

Abilities such as the ones that have been discussed might best be thought of in conjunction with their use in language contexts. The abilities on the automatic level were questioned in that they isolate the linguistic signal from the meaning it codes, and it was suggested that deficiencies on this level of test performance may be a reflection of the language disorder instead of representing interfering factors in themselves. Remediation of the language skills that are tapped on the representational level may best be considered in terms of the sequence in which these same skills appear in the language development of normal children.

A most important question remains: Is there evidence that remediation of specific abilities leads to or transfers to a general improvement in the knowledge or use of language? Bortner (1971) stated that no body of evidence exists to support the current practice of remediation of specific abilities. We are not aware of any studies that have found improvement in general language development after the remediation of specific abilities— perhaps because few have looked for such transfer of improvement in language use. Without such evidence, however, and without evidence that such abilities are necessary for the development and use of oral language, it is questionable that the remediation of specific abilities should dominate a remedial program for children who are learning language slowly and with difficulty.

One problem with focussing goals of intervention on these abilities that are only associated with language instead of focussing on language itself is the resulting tendency to teach these abilities alone. Such teaching often isolates these abilities from the other language skills the child exhibits and from the sequence in which these abilities are manifested by children who are learning language without difficulty.

Conclusions

The specific disabilities approach represented a shift away from the search for precipitating factors, to a concentration on present abilities. It also represented a shift from global to molecular categorization. Each child was viewed in terms of strengths and weaknesses; remediation was based on assessment. This orientation represented a major thrust forward in diagnostics in that it stressed assessment of present functioning with the purpose of determining the goals and procedures of a remedial program. However, when the specific disabilities approach is used as a search for weak cognitive skills that need remediation before language can be learned, this orientation is also etiological, as was the categorical orientation, but simply on another level.

The information on perceptual processing would appear to be most applicable to determining the procedures or context of intervention, not the goals of intervention; for example, children high on visual skills and low on auditory skills might learn better through the visual than the auditory channel. [As yet, however, even this hypothesis has not been substantiated (Newcomer and Goodman, ms.; and C. M., Smith, 1971) with schoolchildren, although it may be relevant at preschool ages.] Information from the specific disabilities approach may lead to hypotheses about the procedures of teaching, which can be tested through diagnostic teaching. Certainly research within this approach will increase our understanding of children with a language disorder and, as more information is gained, may lead to important information on procedures of language intervention.

It would seem that the dominant theme and goals of a remedial program for children with a language disorder should be the meaningful use of language. Any instrument geared to measuring specific abilities does not give the clinician or teacher information on what the child knows about language or what it is the child needs to know, nor by itself does it tell what uses the child can make of language for problem solving or communication. Such instruments cannot be considered an evaluation or assessment of *language*—they were not so designed and should not be used as such. Language programs should be based on what a child knows about language and what the child is best ready to learn next. It seems a theoretical model of language processes is not the best source of this information.

A MOTOR APPROACH

Like the specific disabilities approach, the motor approach has to do with improving cognitive skills; unlike the specific disabilities approach (which stresses direct remediation of weak cognitive abilities), the motor approach stresses motor development as a means of improving cognitive abilities (e.g., Ayres, 1975; Barsch, 1967; Delacato, 1963; Freidus, 1964; and Kephart, 1960). The motor approach directly remediates motor and perceptual-motor skills. There is considerable variation in the rationale given and the techniques used by proponents of this approach, but the assumptions are the same. When these assumptions are applied to the child with a language disorder, they include: (1) that motor development is a necessary prerequisite to language development; and (2) that training in motor skills will lead to improvement in language. There is certainly a strong correlation between motor development and language development (see Lenneberg, 1967, in *RLDis*), but there is also evidence that degree of motor disability is not directly correlated with language skills. According to Myers and Hammill (1969), "Irwin and Hammill (1964, 1965) have consistently failed to find differences in perception, language, or intelligence between mild, moderate, and severe cerebral palsied youngsters" (p. 130). There is no evidence that supports the assumption that motor training alone improves language expression or comprehension. Thus, if improved language skills are the ultimate goal, this cannot be the primary approach.

Certainly no one would deny the importance of improving the motor skills of any child. Not only is it possible that such improvement will enhance a child's ability to orient in relation to the environment, but it will probably enhance social relationships as well, and, thus, improve self-concept. (as the child is better able to participate in play). However, the assumption that training motor skills should precede or supercede direct help in language learning with a language-disordered child would appear to be misguided. In fact, there is no need for such priority; motor activities make excellent contexts for language stimulation. If a language-disordered child is under any remedial program, it is the task of the speech and language pathologist to insure that language is also an important part of the program and to incorporate language, whenever possible, with other activities.

Most of the motor approaches have had more impact on intervention for the learning-disabled child than for the language-disordered child. However, it becomes more and more obvious that learning disabilities and language disorders are integrally related—that the learning-disabled child often has a language disorder, and vice versa; that the preschool language-disordered child may well be called learning disabled when entering school; and that the move for early identification of learning disabilities will bring the preschool language-disordered child in contact with special educators interested in learning disabilities. Thus the speech and language pathologist and the special educator must be aware of various approaches that exist so they can integrate their approaches for the benefit of the child.

Information and techniques from both approaches within the specific abilities orientation should not provide the goals of language intervention but may well be incorporated into planning the techniques or context for facilitating language learning.

SUMMARY

In this chapter the cognitive abilities and, in particular, the perceptual skills of the language-disordered child are discussed. Many deficits in these abilities are reportedly correlated with language disorders—most often noted are auditory sequential memory, processing of rapid auditory information, and processing of multisensory input. These correlates are usually viewed as causative factors, but each of these correlates may in fact be a reflection instead of a cause of a language disorder. The question raised is the usefulness of this information in planning intervention.

Within this orientation there are two approaches to remediation of language disorders. One, referred to here as the specific disabilities approach, focusses on delineating and remediating weakness in cognitive skills. The assumptions implied in using this approach as the focus of an educational or clinical program for a language-disordered child are discussed using the ITPA as a model of the approach. The conclusion reached is that specific abilities, as currently measured, may not be distinct from one another in language learning; do not appear to be prerequisites for language learning; and may not be improved in most children by current remedial programs. Most important, there is no evidence that the remedial programs designed to remediate these abilities improve general language functioning. Similar problems exist with the second approach within this orientation, the motor approach. The major contribution of the information and techniques that have evolved from this orientation seem currently most applicable to procedures instead of goals of language intervention.

SUGGESTED READINGS

In *Readings in Language Disorders*

Hammill, D., and Larsen, S. C., The effectiveness of psycholinguistic training. *Exceptional Children, 40,* 5–13, 1974.

Hermelin, B., and Frith, U., Psychological studies of childhood autism: Can autistic children make sense of what they see and hear? *Journal of Special Education, 5,* 107–116, 1971.

Lovaas, O. I., Schreibman, L., Koegel, R., and Rehm, R., Selective responding by autistic children to multiple sensory input. *Journal of Abnormal Psychology, 77,* 211–222, 1971.

Tallal, P., and Piercy, M., Developmental aphasia: The perception of brief vowels and extended stop consonants. *Neuropsychologia, 13,* 69–74, 1975.

Other Readings

Myers, P., and Hammill, D., *Methods for learning disorders*. New York: John Wiley and Sons, 1969.

Rees, N., Auditory processing factors in language disorders: The view from Procrustes' bed. *Journal of Speech and Hearing Disorders, 38,* 304–315, 1973.

Part 6
FACILITATING LANGUAGE LEARNING

The final chapters are concerned with language intervention—with how to facilitate language learning in the language-disordered child. The information presented is based on the information in the previous chapters—information about language in general (Part 1), and normal language learning in particular (Part 2), descriptions of deviant language (Part 3), the sequential goals of language learning (Part 4), and correlates of language disorders (Part 5). This information, when applied to an individual child, can be used to assist in planning intervention. Considerations in planning intervention, which are not directly related to the language goals of intervention but to facilitating learning in general, are discussed in Chapter XX. Chapter XXI is concerned more specifically with the facilitation of the interactions of content/form/use.

Chapter XX
GENERAL CONSIDERATIONS OF LANGUAGE INTERVENTION

Language intervention involves modifying a child's environment in a manner that will enhance the ability to induce the interactions among language content/form/use. Certain of these modifications are specific to the contexts in which the goals of language for a particular child will be facilitated; other modifications are more general in that they may apply to many contexts or need to be considered prior to or concurrent with planning specific contextual modifications. Such considerations include (1) reducing the influence of any factors that may be maintaining difficulty with language learning; (2) the context in which language will be facilitated; (3) the child's response behaviors—the techniques of eliciting and maintaining these behaviors, the sense modality to be used, and relative emphasis on comprehension versus production.

REDUCING MAINTAINING FACTORS

A maintaining factor is an aspect of the child or of the child's environment that inhibits language learning and thus acts to maintain the language disorder. A *maintaining* factor may or may not have been a *precipitating* factor (an original reason why language was not learned). For example, profound hearing loss from birth can be considered both a precipitating factor (a reason why auditory vocal language was not learned originally), and a maintaining factor (a factor that is presently inhibiting future language learning); adverse parental reactions to a child who is not talking by the age of 3 years may not have been a precipitating factor but may inhibit future language learning and thus be a maintaining factor; and severe illness in the second year of life may have been a precipitating factor but not a maintaining factor for a 5-year-old who is not learning language.

Maintaining factors that are amenable to change are most important in planning intervention. For example, auditory sensitivity should be routinely checked in all children with a language disorder, because hearing loss certainly is a factor that can interfere with language learning and is a factor that is often amenable to improvement. Children are first referred to the audiologist, who may then make recommendations about further testing, medical referrals, or the use of amplification. Additionally, poor health can affect any learning, including language learning, and should be considered as a possible maintaining factor. Most schools demand periodic medical checkups, and clinics often have such checkups as a routine part of any assessment. When this is not the case, medical referrals should be made if poor health or poor nutrition is suspected.

A number of researchers have reported that interactions between mothers and their language-disordered children are different from the interactions between mothers and children who are learning language normally (Buium, Rynders, and Turnure, 1974; Goldfarb, Goldfarb, and Scholl, 1966; Goldfarb, Levy, and Meyers, 1972; Goss, 1970; and Wulbert, Inglis, Kriegsman, and Mills, 1975, in *RLDis*). Buium et al. noted differences in the grammatical complexity of input to Down's Syndrome children; Goldfarb and his associates reported that mothers of schizophrenic children had inferior speech and language patterns and communicated less clearly with their children; Wulbert et al. noted that mothers of language-delayed children interacted less *with* their children, talked less positively *about* their children, and used shouting, spanking, or threats more often as a means of restricting or punishing the children. These studies matched children according to chronological age, not language skills, so that it is possible that some of the differences found were actually characteristic of normal parent-child interaction at an earlier point in development. This seems particularly possible with the differences in linguistic input described by Buium et al. (See Chapter IX for a discussion of how normal caregiver-child interactions change with linguistic level of the child.) Other patterns, such as those reported by Wulbert et al. and by Goldfarb and his associates, may be a reflection of the parents' frustrations with a child who is not developing as expected—or they may be cues to possible precipitating factors.

Although a cause-effect relationship cannot be assumed, these findings suggest careful attention to caregiver-child interactions in planning intervention. The interactional patterns should include not just the linguistic input, but the general pattern of communication. Nonverbal aspects may be equally, if not more, important for language learning. Whether caregiver' interactional patterns are a cause or result of the child's behaviors, certain of these behaviors could interfere with the child's future language learning. Aberrant speech or language behaviors, lack of clarity in communicating, and lack of responsiveness to the child's attempts to communicate are certainly not factors that can be considered conducive to language learning and are patterns that may be amenable to change through counseling and instruction.

Any factors that may be interfering with language learning (maintaining the language disorder) and are possibly amenable to change are important considerations in planning language intervention. These factors should not replace or preempt the importance of focussing on the language behaviors *per se*, but should be incorporated in intervention plans as a means of facilitating the behaviors.

THE SETTING

Intervention can take place in a variety of surroundings that vary from the child's own playground or classroom to the clinic room, teaching booth, or specially designed classroom. Important aspects of the setting include the degree of structure to be imposed, the persons who will make the immediate environmental manipulation, and the number and type of intervention goals that can be set most reasonably.

DEGREE OF STRUCTURE

It has long been felt that certain children learn best when the amount of stimuli presented to them is somehow constrained (e.g., see Cruickshank, Bentsen, Retzburg, and Tannhauser, 1961; Strauss and Lehtinen, 1947; and Hewett, 1965). These children are often described as having poor attention span, being hyperactive, and being easily distracted. Teaching booths or small classrooms with plain walls, sound treatment, and restraining furniture have been used to reduce background stimuli; the task presented has been highlighted by exaggeration of color, size, and texture. Depressing all sensory input other than that related to the demonstration of the task decreases the child's need to sort out relevant stimuli in both linguistic and nonlinguistic context. Such highlighting of relevant stimuli may increase the ease with which a child can induce content/form interactions.

The most serious drawback of highly structured settings is the limited variety of contextual situations that can occur. The demonstration of many semantic relations may be impossible or very stilted. In addition, the situations in which language can be used (i.e., the functions for which it can be used and the contexts in which it is used) are also constrained. When these problems can be surmounted either within the setting or by supplementing the setting with more natural contexts, the highly structured teaching situation may be a feasible recommendation for particular children— children who appear to learn best when the amount and variety of input stimuli are limited.

The best criterion for determining the appropriate degree of structure for intervention is the child's attention to tasks. The categorical classification of a child (i.e., neurologically impaired, mentally retarded, emotionally disturbed, hearing impaired, or aphasic) cannot be automatically used to recommend high or low structure in a setting for language learning. If a child will focus on a preferred activity when other stimuli (people or sounds) are present, isolation from stimuli may not be necessary or advisable. Hyperactivity and short attention span are behaviors that are influenced by the tasks at hand; the child who is hyperactive or distracted in one setting may well be lethargic or perseverative in another. Settings in which the child is hyperactive may focus on tasks that are too difficult for the child; considerable reduction in hyperactive behavior may occur when the child is involved with tasks that are within motor, cognitive, social, and linguistic capacities. If hyperactivity is influenced in this way, planning language facilitation around activities that a child selects and enjoys will reduce or eliminate the need for severe reduction of stimuli. Gradual modification of these tasks in the direction of new and different activities may then help the child to increase the ability to attend in a variety of situations.

Language intervention in a highly structured setting that is isolated from real life experience is not recommended unless it is impossible to get a child to attend to relevant stimuli without such isolation. Such a decision would be based on observations, both direct and reported, that the child could not focus on any stimuli without the reduction of all competing stimuli and, in addition, that such reduction did in fact aid both in focussing attention and in facilitating inductions of content/form interactions. Even if isolation is necessary, intervention must eventually include situations that are representative of a child's life, so that *use* of language can also be learned.

In contrast to the highly structured setting, a low structured setting generally revolves around a child's everyday activities and may take place in group play situations, perhaps in a nursery school or in a classroom, or they may take place in a one-to-one situation, when the child plays, eats, dresses, or is engaged in other daily activities. In such settings the child's interest or daily routine determines the topics and activities; the facilitator provides the relevant linguistic input that codes these ongoing activities and related states and may at times encourage or demand similar relevant verbalizations from the child. Situations demonstrating various uses as well as content categories of language readily occur in these contexts and do not have to be artificially created. A major advantage of low structured settings is the incorporation of language into the child's daily life, so there is not a problem of *carryover* of skills from artificial contexts.

To facilitate language learning in low structured contexts that are a part of the child's everyday life may mean changing the traditional role of the speech pathologist in many institutions by moving the clinician from the clinic or office to the child's environment. In a school setting it may mean that the speech pathologist will spend a good part of a day on the playground, lunchroom, or classroom in order to facilitate language learning directly and also to make suggestions about how the teacher or parent can facilitate language learning during the rest of the day. Even when highly structured contexts are recommended, they must be followed by language learning in other, more natural, environments. Thus, the current role of the speech pathologist, as viewed by many administrators and speech pathologists themselves, needs to be changed in order to adapt to current ideas about the teaching of early language skills. One cannot be isolated in a room apart from the child's life, see children 1 or 2 hours a week, and expect them to learn early language skills.

FACILITATORS

The speech pathologist will be responsible for planning ongoing assessment and for general advisement, but other persons will, hopefully, be assisting in the language learning process. Whenever possible, persons who live with the child or who spend considerable time with the child are recruited and trained to help. MacDonald, Blott, Gordon, Spiegel, and Hartmann (1974, in *RLDis*) reported on a parent-assisted treatment program where parents were given a 7-week training program in designing nonlinguistic contexts, in modeling linguistic input, and in providing feedback to the child concerning the appropriateness of his or her responses. Pre- and post-testing of three children involved in this program for 4 to 5 months indicated considerable language growth (as measured by *MLU*) when compared with children used as controls. If most children seen in clinics and schools today could be provided with home programs designed to facilitate particular content/form/use interactions, the chances of success in language learning would probably increase substantially. Using parents in this role would not only increase the chances that a child would learn content/form/use interactions (by providing appropriate input, contingencies, etc., during everyday activities), but it would also enable the speech pathologist to see and help more children.

Other potential facilitators include teachers, teachers' aids, houseparents in institutions, and nurses or nurses' aides, all of whom can be given general training through in-service programs. In addition, the speech pathologist can spend time in the classroom, ward, or housing unit, demonstrating how activities such as mealtime, dressing, exercise, gym, playground, and the like, can be used in facilitating language learning.

NUMBER OF GOALS

It is possible to work on only one particular language goal at a time (e.g., the goal of coding action relations with two constituents as comments on self actions); or work on a number of goals for different content categories (e.g., to code possession, recurrence, action, and existence with two constituents as comments on objects and activities that are present in the environment); or to include all goals within a phase level (as all content/form/use interactions for Phase 2). The settings in which facilitation will take place and the choice of persons who will be facilitating language learning influence both the number of goals and the specificity of the goals set. In an informal setting, it is easy to include a number of goals, because the child's day will involve many opportunities for coding the various content categories (action, state, recurrence, possession, time, etc.). In a more formal setting, where context must be created to demonstrate semantic relations, it is often easier to focus on only one or two particular content categories (as action or possession). Thus facilitation in a more structured setting may lead to a focus on one or two goals at a time; facilitation in a less structured setting may lead to the inclusion of a greater number of goals across many content categories. This relationship of number of goals to structure of setting usually coincides with a child's learning styles, since the choice of setting should be partially determined by the child's ability to handle a variety of input. The child who learns best with reduced sensory stimuli will most probably also learn best when the focus of a session is one content/form interaction for one use.

THE CHILD'S LANGUAGE BEHAVIORS

Although it is possible to learn something about language without demonstrating that learning, it is only through observing children's behaviors that the clinician has evidence of learning and is able to plan future modifications. The production of language behaviors also enables children to test hypotheses about their inductions of content/form/use, and thus become more active in the learning process. But what kind of behaviors are most appropriate and how can they be encouraged or elicited? Some questions to be considered in planning the language behaviors that are expected from the child are: "How can behaviors be elicited and maintained?" "What sense modality should be used?" "Should comprehension or production of the code be the major focus?"

TECHNIQUES FOR ELICITING AND MAINTAINING LANGUAGE BEHAVIORS

If the clinician has decided to elicit a language behavior, how is this best done? Most commonly the child is asked to imitate the utterances or actions of the clinician and, when the imitations are appropriate, the child is reinforced. Such procedures are outlined in detail by Lovaas, Berberich, Perloff, and Schaeffer (1966, in *RLDis*), who stressed the production of linguistic forms alone, and by Risley and Wolf (1967), who stressed the production of forms in relation to limited contexts. In essence, the procedure is to teach an imitative set, gradually shape production to approximate the word, and then bring the production under the control of contexts other than the clinician's model utterance. This latter step is done by introducing the object or event that the utterance codes (such as ball) during imitation tasks and then gradually fading the model's utterances. The same techniques can be used to obtain comprehension responses—motor behaviors such as pointing or jumping can be modeled and, when imitated, can be connected to a linguistic stimulus such as "Show me___" or "Jump." Eliciting language through imitation has been central to the studies of language learning that apply behaviorist principles—the child must produce the behavior in order to be reinforced. These studies have clearly demonstrated the effectiveness of this technique (imitation and reinforcement) in establishing behaviors that were not in the child's repertoire before training. The extent of establishment beyond the original training situation is not clear, because it has rarely been studied. It appears in many cases, however, that the child has learned the task at hand but has not induced a rule about the relationship of form to content and use, since the experimenters are often able to reverse the "learning" with short periods of reinforcement for the wrong response. It may be, as discussed by Levine and Fasnacht (1974), that the child has learned more about earning rewards than about language.

A modification of this technique (imitation and reinforcement) has been suggested by Bandura and Harris (1966). They used a *third person* to model the language behavior that the child was to learn. The *model* was rewarded for appropriate language behaviors, but not for errors; errors were occasionally included to increase discriminability of behavior that was to be learned. The *child* was then asked to try the same task and was reinforced for appropriate responses, but not for errors. Thus, there is a component of imitation, but it is delayed and may not be exact imitation, since the child's task may involve topics that differ from those of the model. Using such a procedure, Bandura and Harris (1966) successfully modified the syntactic style of a group of normal second-grade children to include passive sentence construction in response to pictures. Odom, Liebert, and Fernandez (1969) increased the use of prepositional phrases in a group of retarded children using a similar procedure and found that the increase was still retained 3 weeks after initial training but, again, the follow-up was in the experimental setting. Certainly the modeling technique approaches the normal conditions of language learning more closely than the elicited imitation procedure and thus has more intuitive appeal. The use of a model seems to demand more active problem solving or rule induction on the part of the child than does immediate imitation and reinforcement.

Two studies have compared the effects of modeling in contrast to imitation. Whitehurst and Novak (1973) found that imitation plus reinforcement was more effective for increasing the use of different phrase types than modeling—modeling was effective for only some children and some phrase types. In contrast, Courtright and Courtright (1976, in *RLDis*) found modeling to be more effective than imitation, but they did not use reinforcement. None of the modeling studies have looked at teaching early language skills or at the use of this technique with children who are in the early phases of learning content/form/use interactions. The relative effectiveness of either technique may well vary with the level of language skill being learned, with the knowledge the child has about content/form/use interactions and with the learning styles of the child. Certainly it is not clear at this time that one or the other should be used exclusively.

Many clinicians do not follow a formal procedure of imitation or modeling but, instead, elicit behaviors through commands such as "Do this" or questions such as "What is this?" coupled with gestures and, occasionally, the direction to "Say__." Others rarely elicit responses, finding that children respond spontaneously if the language behaviors being stressed are at the child's level. Thus they *model* the behavior but do not formally request or demand similar behavior from the child. If the child will respond without formal elicitation, it seems to be the preferable course of action, since it is more similar to normal language learning than either the modeling procedure presented above or elicited imitation.

When behaviors are obtained, the clinician is concerned with increasing the appropriate behaviors and perhaps decreasing any inappropriate behaviors. This can be accomplished by providing feedback to the child. The term feedback as used here refers to a means of letting the child know how closely a response approximates the response desired or expected by the language facilitator. Feedback can be provided in a number of ways. For one, the facilitator can follow each response of the child with a statement such as, "Yes, you said x right," or "No, listen, x not y, but x" (where x is the desired response and y is an inappropriate response). In this manner the child is promptly informed about the correctness of the response and is given a correct model. Although this type of feedback is used by many clinicians and teachers, Muma (1971) suggested that it is ineffective in language learning if it focusses on errors of form.

Feedback in some language training programs has often been supplemented or replaced by a formal schedule of extrinsic reinforcement. In using reinforcement, a correct response by the child is followed by some consequence designed to increase the frequency of that response (a positive reinforcer); undesired or incorrect responses from the child are either ignored or followed by consequences designed to decrease their frequency (negative reinforcers). What is negative for one child may well be positive for another child; for example, spinning in a chair may be a positive reinforcer for one child but frightening and so a negative reinforcer for another child. Thus those using reinforcement must determine what consequences can be used as positive or negative reinforcers.

There is a variety of consequences that can be considered when looking for positive reinforcers. These include successful communication, social interaction, participation in favorite activities, obtaining desired objects, or food. Perhaps the most natural reinforcers of language are those that approximate the desired effect of language in most environments—successful communication and social interaction. That is, if the child is attempting to manipulate the environment through language and is successful, the success will most likely reinforce this behavior in similar situations. If a child says "want cookie" or "want ball" and obtains the cookie or ball in these contexts, the child is probably more likely to say these same utterances again when these objects are desired than if the child says "want cookie" or "want ball" and someone offers a different object or ignores the vocalizations. In addition, one would expect a relevant response to a comment might be more positively reinforcing than an irrelevant response or no response. For example, if a child says, while riding a bike, "I ride bike," one might expect that the response "And that's a big bike" would be more likely to increase the frequency of meaningful language than the response "Where's Daddy?" or "Let's read a book." Unfortunately, little research has been done on the reinforcing effect of related versus unrelated responses to children's utterances. For many children, appropriate response to their attempts at language may be the only reinforcement needed. For other children, supporting social interaction (praise, smiles, or hugs) may also be needed.

There are children for whom social reinforcers are not at first effective but for whom manipulation of some object as a consequence of an appropriate response is enough to increase that response. For others, preferred activities (watching cartoons, being twirled in the air, sliding down a slide) act as positive reinforcement. Since participation in such activities can be disruptive unless tied directly to the teaching of a content/form/use interaction, many clinicians distribute chips or tokens after a correct response and allow the child to *buy* particular objects with these tokens at specified times. The tokens can be cashed in for some object or event the child desires and thus take on reinforcing properties and act to increase the frequency of the correct responses. A last alternative for children who respond to none of the above types of consequences as a positive reinforcer is the use of food. Most children who have not eaten for a period of time will find food positively reinforcing. Small quantities of well-liked, easily consumed food (e.g., ice cream, Fruit Loops, peanuts, or M&Ms) are given or fed to the child following desired responses. These, too, can interrupt verbalizing and eventually lose reinforcing value if the child becomes satiated; they are, indeed, a last resort.

The use of reinforcements as a means of feedback and a means of increasing or decreasing a response has been extensively written about in a number of sources and will not be discussed further here. Instead, refer to works by Keller (1965); Lovaas, Berberich, Perlof, and Schaeffer (1966, in *RLDis*); Risley and Wolf (1967); and Sloan and McCauley (1968). These readings present both the theory behind reinforcement in learning as well as specific procedures in using reinforcement to aid in language learning. However, reinforcement should be used with caution. A number of studies have shown a decrease in the desired behavior as a result of extrinsic reinforcement when these behaviors had some intrinsic satisfaction prior to the issuing of reinforcers (Levine and Fasnacht, 1974). Although the desired behavior remained at a high level during the use of reinforcement, it dropped below prereinforcement levels when the reinforcements were withdrawn without complicated schedules designed to eliminate extinction. Unless one is willing to follow such extinction procedures, reinforcements that are not a part of the child's natural environment should probably not be used.

SENSE MODALITY OF LINGUISTIC BEHAVIORS

Goals of intervention include a description of the behaviors expected from the child. In Chapters XIII, XIV, and XV goals were presented for the production of linguistic units. The forms described are the forms used in the auditory-vocal language, but they can also occur in a visual-motor language. Speech is the preferred linguistic response because it is the most common means of communication, but alternative systems must be considered for some children—children for whom intelligible speech appears virtually impossible, at least in the immediate future (e.g., children with paralysis of the articulatory tract musculature). Possible alternatives to speech as a linguistic response are sign language, typewriters, and communication boards. Unfortunately, children who have severe difficulty with speech because of poor muscle control often have poor control of other musculature as well, so that the use of sign language and typewriters are not viable alternatives. When this is so, the least preferred response, the communication board, can become the mode of linguistic response for the child. (See Vanderheiden and Harris-Vanderheiden, 1976, for a discussion of techniques for these "nonvocal" children.)

A communication board usually consists of a lap board that is set across the arms of a wheelchair or attached to a bed or a desk and has affixed to it a means of representing objects, actions, and states that are important to the communicator. These representations are most commonly pictures (e.g., a toilet, a glass of water, a bed, mother, and someone eating) and written words—particularly common are the words "yes" and "no." A few boards have been designed with more abstract symbolic representation, using geometric configurations paired with a written word. The use of these abstract configurations instead of pictures increases the possibilities for combinations of symbols and thus broadens the applicability of the communication board. Any communication board is, however, more limiting than an auditory-vocal system, not only in the number of combinations that are ultimately possible, but also in the speed with which communication can take place.

A pilot implementation of an abstract system has been reported by Vanderheiden, Brown, MacKenzie, Reinen, and Scheibel (1975). They used the Bliss symbols (*Bliss Semantography*, Australia: Semantography Publications, as referenced by Vanderheider, et al., 1975) instead of pictures because they felt that pictures limited the generalization of a concept and tied it to a specific object or action; for example, the concept "eat" might be tied to the particular food pictured in the eating process (see Box XX-1 for

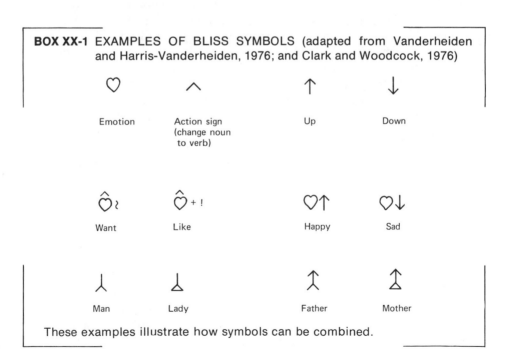

BOX XX-1 EXAMPLES OF BLISS SYMBOLS (adapted from Vanderheiden and Harris-Vanderheiden, 1976; and Clark and Woodcock, 1976)

♡	∧	↑	↓
Emotion	Action sign (change noun to verb)	Up	Down
♡̂⸮	♡̂ + !	♡↑	♡↓
Want	Like	Happy	Sad
⅄	⅄̱	⅄̂	⅄̲̂
Man	Lady	Father	Mother

These examples illustrate how symbols can be combined.

examples of these symbols). Vanderheider et al. used the Bliss symbols instead of words because they felt the symbols were less complex than actual words. However, they printed the words under each symbol on the communication board so that persons communicating with the child would not have to learn the geometric symbols. Spoken language was used by the teacher and was presented with the symbolic representation on the board. Thus objects and people in the environment were labeled with the appropriate spoken words, printed words, and Bliss symbols, and the child's response was to point to the symbols on the board. Theoretically then, the child understood speech but produced language through visual symbols.

More efficient communication boards are needed; information about normal language development may be applicable in both the choice of concepts represented and in the organization of the symbols on the board. For example, relational words, which are used frequently in the single-word utterance period (Bloom, 1973; Chapter IV), can be used to refer to many objects and events, and the verbs used most frequently in early sentences are verbs such as "do," "get," "make," and "go," that can be used in more different events than other verbs such as "catch," "brush," and "fill." Symbols to represent these words may be more efficient than symbols that represent more specific objects or event relations and may be included on first boards and given prominance in other boards. Finally, the categories of content that have evolved from the study of child language (action, time, etc.) may provide a means of organizing symbols that has more relevance to the child first learning language than, for example, traditional parts of speech such as noun and verb. Unquestionably, further refinements in communication boards—refinements in their operation (computer or other electronic controls), in their makeup (the forms and the content coded), and in the organization of the symbols—will make them more efficient.

Alternative modalities for communication have been attempted recently for a number of children with a language disorder—not so much because the child is unable to produce the speech signal but, instead, because the child seems unable to learn content/form/use interactions when the form is the speech signal. These difficulties seem to be more related to processing the linguistic input than to producing the linguistic signal and are discussed in the next chapter.

COMPREHENSION VERSUS PRODUCTION

One question asked by those responsible for facilitating language learning is "What should be the relative importance and sequence of training in comprehension versus production of language?" The question probably arises because so many studies and tests have been directed to either one or the other as evidence of language knowledge. Many studies and language programs have stressed the imitative production of linguistic forms as a first step in language learning for the nonverbal child (Buddenhagen, 1971; Guess, Rutherford, and Twichell, 1969; Hewett, 1965; Lovaas, Berberich, Perloff, and Schaeffer, 1966, in *RLDis*; Sherman, 1965; and McGinnis, Kleffner, and Goldstein, n.d.). Based on the concepts that children learn to speak by imitating and that a behavior needs to be produced in order to be reinforced, it was felt that imitative responses would be the "most beneficial and practical starting point for building speech" (Lovaas et al., 1966, p. 706). When an imitative repertoire was established, contexts (such as objects), which were to eventually elicit these responses, were associated with the response and the model utterance was dropped—thus an aspect of meaning was established (Brawley, Harris, Allen, Fleming, and Peterson, 1969; Hewett, 1965; Risley and Wolf, 1967; and Stark, Giddan, and Meisel, 1968).

Most studies measured the learning of content/form interactions by the degree of generalization of the new behavior to new contexts (such as the production of plurals when shown objects known to the child but not used in training the morpheme). Garcia (1974) trained two profoundly retarded adolescents, speaking in single-word utterances, to "converse" through imitation. They were trained to ask "What is that?" when shown a picture, to label the picture when asked, and to respond "Yes, I do," when asked if they wanted the picture. She noted poor generalization of the same tasks when a different experimenter was used. Most studies have measured generalization within the same setting and with the same person who did the training; few studies have searched for generalizations in the child's natural environment. In one exception, Gray and Ryan (1973) reported that forms taught in formal instruction were used in the classroom "show and tell" discussions with about the same accuracy as in the training program. Furthermore, children were using the same form plus new forms not taught in the program in the home environment. From these observations they concluded:

> Apparently, it is not necessary to build an extensive receptive language repertoire using a non-verbal response (pointing, for example) before teaching expressive language. A child may successfully be asked to emit a verbal response early in the teaching sequence. It is possible that the development of an expressive repertoire may actually enhance the learning of a receptive repertoire [as pointed out by Guess (1969)]. Gray and Ryan (1973, p. 171)

An opposite view is held by Johnson and Myklebust (1967) and by Winitz (1973, 1976) who recommended extensive training in comprehension before training or even encouraging productions of forms. "Our task should be to functionalize the environment so that language and thought can be paired . . . not . . . that of forcing production in order to achieve syntactically correct sentences" (Winitz, 1976, p. 404). Winitz suggested problem-solving situations in which the child would induce rules by listening to forms spoken by the clinician and would be rewarded for selecting the picture appropriate to the meaning of the form. He cited one anecdote where the child spontaneously produced a form that was trained in comprehension only. Winitz based his suggestions on experiences with second language learning (German) by college students. Although Johnson and Myklebust (1967) stressed training in comprehension before production (and also noted spontaneous verbal expression with improved comprehension), they also pointed out that using newly learned words can strengthen comprehension.

Fewer studies have reported training of comprehension only. In one, Striefel and Wetherby (1973) taught an 11-year-old nonlinguistic boy to follow two- to four-word commands that involved actions on objects, occasionally with an instrument ("push car," "rub cheek with washcloth"), but they found no generalization to untrained combinations of actions and objects. Thus, although the child was trained to respond correctly to "point to ear," "point to nose," and "brush hair," he did not correctly respond to "point to hair" but, instead, responded to the action usually associated with the object (i.e. brushing). In contrast, Baer and Guess (1971), Guess (1969), and Guess and Baer (1973) reported generalization of responses to morphological inflections (the child pointed to two objects in response to the name of the object plus the plural morpheme -s when presented with words and objects not used in training). The more difficult task of measuring generalization of this comprehension in natural environments has not been carried out.

The interdependence of comprehension and production has been studied by Guess (1969) and by Guess and Baer (1973). Focussing on the plural morpheme, both studies supported a view of independence between the tasks in at least some children. Guess and Baer (1973) found no generalization across tasks in one subject, only slight generalization in two subjects, and strong generalization in one subject. Thus training in comprehension did not always lead to correct production and training in production did not always lead to correct comprehension. A similar result was reported by Ruder, Smith, and Hermann (1974), who looked at the effect of imitation and comprehension training on the production of nouns. They concluded that neither comprehension training alone nor imitation training alone can be used to achieve production of lexical items but, instead, "the data argue in favor of a training program for lexical items that contains both imitation and comprehension training . . ." (p. 27).

Courtright and Courtright (1976, in RLDis) did not compare comprehension and production directly, but they did compare training procedures that varied in the amount of production required. The procedure that demanded immediate imitation was less successful than the procedure that demanded listening to the correct production of 20 utterances before responding. They concluded "that an abstract rule (for example, a language rule) is best learned by passive observation" (p. 661); quoting Zimmerman and Bell's

(1972) "interference hypothesis," they suggested that verbalization interferes with rule learning, and they questioned the use of imitation approaches.

A number of questions remain unanswered. For example, does the influence of one type of training (comprehension or production) vary with content/form interaction? More important, is it possible that there would be greater interdependence between training in comprehension and training in production if the content/form interaction that was taught was developmentally close to the child's present language skills? For example, if the children taught the plural morpheme had language skills comparable to the normal child who is first productive with this morpheme, would they have learned the rule in both comprehension and production tasks? Is it possible that differences in language skills could account for the differences in generalization that did occur among the children in the study by Guess and Baer (1973)?

Certainly the lack of generalization to commands within the comprehension task reported by Striefel and Wetherby (1973) might well be explained by the level of task compared with the level of language skill brought to the task. The children were reportedly nonverbal, but could produce a few names of objects and could imitate. The generalization task demanded knowledge of verb-object to code action-object relations, and some demanded further knowledge of instrument relations as coded by prepositional phrases. It is not surprising then that on generalization probes, the children responded to only one word in the sentence and produced the action that had previously been associated with that object. Similarly, the lack of generalization to another experimenter reported by Garcia (1974) may be related to the unrealistic level of task—the use of discourse—expected from children who know only a few words.

Gray and Ryan (1973) taught content/form interactions through imitation of forms in relation to pictures (a production approach), and reported generalization to the classroom and home. However, they may have been teaching forms that the children were ready to learn (and perhaps forms they already comprehended to some extent). Ruder, Smith, and Hermann (1974) reported a lack of generalization from training in imitation to comprehension of content/form interactions, which is not surprising, since the content was never presented when children were asked to imitate forms. They also reported lack of generalization from training in comprehension to production, which is less easy to account for, since the children were presented with pictures. The children were certainly developmentally ready for the simple nouns taught, since their language level was reportedly 3.5 years. However, in order to control for prior experience, Spanish words were used for objects that the children probably already had English names for, and this may have accounted for the lack of generalizations.

Thus, it may be, as Winitz (1976) and Johnson and Myklebust (1967) have suggested, that there is no need to force production if the child is exposed to forms in the context of objects and events that code their meaning and use. Production may well follow *naturally but* this may be true *only* if the input is at a level that the child is ready to accept—a level that allows the child to build on present knowledge of language to learn new interactions. The evidence does not support the view that comprehension tasks (identifying, acting out, etc.) need to precede such production tasks as imitation or vice-versa.

In view of this inconclusive evidence, the teacher or clinician has two avenues open. One is to elicit both types of responses—to teach each goal with both elicited responses that evidence comprehension and elicited responses of production. Such an approach is counter to the developmental interaction between comprehension and production discussed in Chapter VIII and there is little evidence to support its value for generalization to spontaneous speech. Alternatively, the clinician or teacher can expose the child to contexts that illustrate content/form/use interactions commensurate with the child's level of development (as determined by methods suggested in Chapters XVI and XVII). If production does not follow after repeated presentation, production can be elicited in the same contexts. Thus, neither comprehension nor production are taught apart from *use* or apart from each other.

SUMMARY

Before planning the specific techniques that can lead to induction of content/ form/use interactions, a number of more general factors must be considered. First, there are factors that may be maintaining the child's difficulty with language learning—factors that are amenable to change—such as hearing loss, poor health, or parent-child interactional patterns. Second, there are some considerations that relate to the setting of intervention. Children may differ in the amount of structure they need in facilitation contexts for inducing content/form/use interactions but, in all cases, the context of learning should resemble the natural environment, and parents or caregivers should be included as facilitators as much as possible. Observation of the child's attentional patterns in different contexts is the best means of deciding the degree of structure needed.

The last general consideration discussed concerns the behaviors that the child is expected to produce. A variety of techniques are available for eliciting and maintaining behavioral responses (e.g., modeling, imitation, reinforcement); there is no one technique that has been demonstrated to be more successful than others for all children. For children who are unable to produce the speech signal, an alternative modality of response is necessary and must be planned for. The nature of this alternative modality will influence techniques used to facilitate language goals. Finally, the relative emphasis on comprehension versus production is discussed. Neither comprehension nor production should be taught apart from each other—both should be included in intervention techniques.

SUGGESTED READINGS

In *Readings in Language Disorders*

Courtright, J. A., and Courtright, I. C., Imitative modeling as a theoretical base for instructing language-disordered children. *Journal of Speech and Hearing Research, 19,* 655–663, 1976.

Lovaas, O. I., Berberich, J. P., Perloff, B. F., and Schaeffer, B., Acquisition of imitative speech by schizophrenic children. *Science, 151,* 705–707, 1966.

MacDonald, J. D., Blott, J. P., Gordon, K., Spiegel, B., and Hartmann, M., An experimental parent-assisted treatment program for preschool language-delayed children. *Journal of Speech and Hearing Disorders, 39,* 395–415, 1974.

Wulbert, M., Inglis, S., Kriegsman, E., and Mills, B., Language delay and associated mother-child interaction. *Developmental Psychology, 11,* 61–70, 1975.

Other Readings

Bandura, A., and Harris, M. A., Modification of syntactic style. *Journal of Experimental Child Psychology, 4,* 341–352, 1966.

Risley, T. R., and Wolf, M. M., Establishing functional speech in echolalic children. *Behavior Research and Therapy, 5,* 73–88, 1967.

Levine, F., and Fasnacht, G., Token rewards may lead to token learning. *American Psychologist, 29,* 816–820, 1974.

Vanderheiden, G., and Harris-Vanderheiden, D., Communication techniques and aids for the non-vocal severely handicapped. In L. Lloyd (Ed.), *Communication assessment and intervention strategies*. Baltimore: University Park Press, pp. 607–652, 1976.

Chapter XXI
FACILITATING THE INDUCTION OF CONTENT/FORM/ USE INTERACTIONS

Learning language is a process of inducing relationships among regularities the child has perceived in: the nonlinguistic world (the concepts that are the content of language); the linguistic signal (the arbitrary units that are the conventional forms of a language); and social interactions (the contexts that affect the use of language as a means of communication). These inductions are necessary for learning language, regardless of age. They are the inductions the normal 2-year-old child is forming spontaneously, but they are also the inductions the 5- or 10-year-old child with a language disorder must make.

If language learning is an induction, how can it be taught? One cannot, in fact, teach a child early language skills, if teaching means imparting information or knowledge. The rules of language cannot be written out, described, or otherwise given to the language learner. One cannot use language to talk about language to a child who is only just learning language. The rules of language must be induced by the learner from tangible experiences with objects and events, lingistic forms, and interpersonal interactions.

The person who intervenes in a child's life to aid in the language learning process is not, then, a teacher in the traditional sense (i.e., one who gives information or trains in skills) but, instead, one who manipulates these tangible aspects of a child's environment in a way that facilitates the formation of these inductions. To stress this important difference, the term "facilitator" will be used to refer to the person directly responsible for intervention procedures (Taenzer, Bass, and Kise, 1974). The role of the facilitator is to arrange external events in the child's life in a manner that will make it easier for the child to induce the relationships among content/form/use.

Language intervention can be viewed in terms of the tangible external events available to the facilitator. The figure in Box XXI-1 illustrates the factors that are external and, thus, available for manipulation, and the inductions that are the internal desired results of intervention. The linguistic forms that are presented to the child are both external and manipulable. The facilitator may choose from among different lexical items and linguistic structures and, in order to increase their salience, may vary the manner and frequency of their presentation. The nonlinguistic context is also manipulable; the facilitator may present certain objects and manipulate these objects in relationship to each other and to the child in order to demonstrate the many concepts that language codes. Finally, the facilitator can vary the social context in order to model, reinforce, or create the need for interpersonal communication. These three manipulable factors are represented as external to the child. The induction of the regularities within each of these factors and the relationship among them are internal.

The term *intervention* is used here to refer to changes that are made in a child's environment for the purpose of facilitating the learning of language.

The environmental manipulations are determined by the goals of intervention (what is to be learned), the learning styles of the child (how he or she learns best), and the contexts in which these modifications occur. Goals of language learning determine the linguistic and the nonlinguistic contexts. Learning styles influence the manner and frequency of stimuli presentation— manipulations geared to increase the salience of the stimuli and their associations with each other, and the manner in which responses are elicited and reinforced. The context determines whether natural situations are restructured, or whether situations need to be created, and who will be responsible for carrying out the change.

BOX XXI-1 A MODEL OF LANGUAGE INTERVENTION

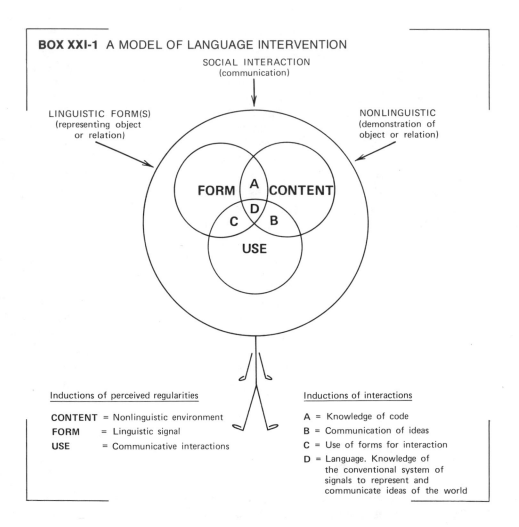

SOCIAL INTERACTION
(communication)

LINGUISTIC FORM(S)
(representing object
or relation)

NONLINGUISTIC
(demonstration of
object or relation)

FORM   A   CONTENT

D

C   B

USE

Inductions of perceived regularities

CONTENT = Nonlinguistic environment
FORM   = Linguistic signal
USE   = Communicative interactions

Inductions of interactions

A = Knowledge of code
B = Communication of ideas
C = Use of forms for interaction
D = Language. Knowledge of
   the conventional system of
   signals to represent and
   communicate ideas of the world

Chapter XX considered modifications based on the child's abilities and styles and discussed the context, or setting, of intervention. This chapter considers the modifications that can be made in a child's environment when facilitating language learning—changes in the linguistic input, the nonlinguistic demonstration of relations, and the social interactions—changes that relate to the goals of content/form/use presented in Chapters XIII, XIV, and XV.

INDUCTION OF CONTENT/FORM INTERACTIONS

Language facilitation involves repeated presentations of tangible events, linguistic events, and nonlinguistic events that will lead to inductions about the interaction of content/form/use in language. In this section the factors that are important in manipulating the tangible input of content and form will be presented and discussed. The important factors to consider are timing and repetition of presented events, the presentation of the linguistic signal, the selection of content/form interactions to be presented, and the presentation of the nonlinguistic input. (Some of these same factors have been discussed by Johnson and Myklebust, 1967.)

TIMING

To induce the relationship between linguistic form and perceived regularities in the nonlinguistic context, the child must hear or see the linguistic forms that represent a concept at the same time that the relationship that is represented in that concept is experienced. To facilitate content/form interaction, then, is to arrange for the child to experience objects and events in the environment at the same time as the linguistic forms that represent such objects and events. It is not yet clear whether the presentation of form should precede, occur with, or follow a nonlinguistic demonstration. The exact timing may vary with the concept being coded, with the extent of the child's participation in the demonstration, and with the child. For example, (1) the mental representation of some actions may best be coded as the child is about to act (as when the child is perched on top of a slide ready to go down) or while the child is acting (as when hammering a nail); (2) the actions of others (sliding or hammering) may best be coded at the same time the action occurs; and (3) the mental representation of an internal state may best be coded simultaneously with the child's experience of that state (as when the child is tired). Considerable research is needed to determine whether these are differences that make a difference and, if so, if they vary with differences among children. In any case, both linguistic form and nonlinguistic demonstration of a concept must occur within the same speech event. The facilitator's task is to provide experiences that clearly demonstrate certain concepts while providing the linguistic forms that code these concepts at a time when the child is attentive to both. Both the concepts and the forms chosen will be based on a careful study of what the child already knows and hypotheses about what the child is ready to learn. See Chapters XVI and XVII.) In some cases this may mean intervening in the nonlinguistic environment by planning particular activities; in other cases it may mean simply talking to the child, using particular forms, about what the child is about to do, is doing, has just done, and about what another person is doing or has just done

REPETITION

In everyday life a child may wait for days to experience clear examples of linguistic forms used concurrently with a nonlinguistic event demonstrating a particular conceptual relation. When facilitating language learning, such experiences must occur many, many times within each session or day. The child is, in essence, bombarded with such coordinated presentations in order to facilitate inductions about content/form interactions. Thus, if the interaction to be established is coding disappearance with the form "all gone," the facilitator would say "all gone" each time objects or events cease to exist in the child's view, and would create situations (such as hiding objects) to increase the frequency with which this relationship could be coded. Facilitating language learning, then, involves increasing the frequency of exposure to certain linguistic forms in the context of the meanings (content) they code.

Often children with language disorders need more repetitions than the normal child in order to learn. McReynolds (1966), for example, found that aphasic children could learn to make some of the same discriminations in auditory stimuli that normal children could make but that it took them many more trials to learn these discriminations. The key to many children is repetition; form with content over and over again may eventually lead to inductions that have not been learned incidentally.

CONSIDERATIONS IN THE PRESENTATION OF THE LINGUISTIC SIGNAL

The linguistic signal can be varied in many ways to increase its salience and to aid a child in processing and categorizing form. The specific variations and degree of variation will differ from child to child and can best be determined by direct observation of the child in response to differences in the presentation of form. Variations of intensity, frequency, and time of the linguistic signal (prosodic patterns) can be decreased or increased (from dull monotone to exaggerated sing-song) and the linguistic signal can be increased or decreased in overall intensity and rate (as compared with normal conversation). For some children the more common, and thus preferred, auditory-vocal modality of form may need to be changed to a visual-motor modality. Finally, the unit of form used as input may vary from meaningful units, such as a word, phrase, or sentence, to nonmeaningful units, such as a phoneme or nonsense syllable. The question is, what, if any, are the variations that will be best for a particular child?

Prosody

Prosody includes variations in stress, intonation, pause, and duration of the linguistic signal. Variable stress is a possible means of increasing the salience of particular forms in contrast to other forms. For example, if a child already uses the single word "more" to code recurrence and the goal is to produce two-word utterances to code the same category of recurrence, the linguistic input might be "more x" (x standing for recurring objects or events that would be named), with x receiving greater stress in relation to the word "more." In fact, the actual lexical items and structures presented to a child may not vary much between one or another of the phases in the acquisition of content/form, although the goals for the child's production may be different and, thus, different forms may be stressed. For example, when talking about an action, such as the child eating a cracker, the input might be "Jim is eating the cracker" at a number of phases of development, but in Phase 1 (single-word utterances) the word "Jim," "eat," or "cracker" might be stressed: "Jim is eating the *CRACKER*." In Phase 5, when one is trying to facilitate inductions about *-ing* to code ongoing actions, the stress could change to "Jim is *EATING* the cracker." And in Phase 8, when the auxilliary verb is the content/form interaction goal, the stress would be changed again: "Jim *IS* eating the cracker." Research supports the use of stress as a means of increasing the probability of imitation (Blasdell and Jensen, 1970), but little is known about its effectiveness in enhancing the learning of content/form interactions.

In addition to stress, some clinicians find that variations in intonation are effective with certain children at certain stages of learning. Teachers of normal preschool children often report that the normal child will attend to story time better if intonational patterns are variable and even exaggerated in contrast to a more flat monotone reading. Lewis (1951) reported that children's first inductions about content/form interactions are based on intonation, not on phonemic elements of the signal. According to Berry (1969), variation in intonation is important for language learning and is an important therapeutic tool.

The effectiveness of variations in prosody as an aid to language learning may, however, vary with the inductions the child is learning. Friedlander (1970), for example, reported that children's early preferences for considerable variation in prosody changed in time to a preference for less variation and more monotonous speech. Furthermore, Lahey (1974) reported that prosodic patterns did not aid 4- and 5-year-olds in comprehending certain complex sentences. On the other hand, LaBelle (1973) found that increasing pause length at the end of clauses aided the comprehension of 3- and 4-

year-olds; input studies (Snow, 1974) report that mothers characteristically increase pause time at sentence and phrase boundaries. Unfortunately, no evidence is available on the influence of prosodic variation on language learning for the child with a language disorder. It may be that certain inductions are best made with variations in prosody, while others are best learned without such variation.

Children learning single-word utterances may find variations in prosody more helpful than children learning word order as a means of coding relations between objects. Thus, while "all gone" spoken with higher pitch on "all" and lowered pitch on "gone" may make the form more salient, exaggerated intonational patterns superimposed on "Jim is eating the cracker" may not aid but, instead, may even hinder the learning of word order to code agent-action relations. It may also be that certain types of variation (intonation, pause, stress) are more effective for the learning of particular behaviors; or that the effectiveness of variations in prosody is different for different children independent of what inductions are being made; or that there may be some interaction among child, type of variation, and the structure being learned. Although considerable research is needed to answer these questions, the role of prosodic variation cannot be ignored by the practicing clinician. Careful experimentation should be carried out with each child for each goal before varying the *normal* prosodic patterns of input words and sentences.

Rate

A second type of form variation involves the rate at which the linguistic signal is presented. Considerable research has suggested that at least some children with language problems have extreme difficulty processing rapid auditory signals (Aten and Davis, 1968; Tallal, 1976; and Tallal and Piercy, 1973a, 1973b, 1974, 1975 in *RLDis*). Although it is not clear that slow speech aids comprehension with these same children, other research suggests that slower speech does improve the comprehension of some children (Nelson, 1976) and that parents speak more slowly to younger children than to older children (Broen, 1972; and Snow, 1974). When first learning a language, increasing the time between words and phrases may help one to segment the sound stream and may provide more time for the processing of each word. Thus the research available coupled with information on normal language learning suggest that a slow rate should be used with children in the early stages of language learning. The ideal rate for a particular child is determined, however, only by observing the results of varying rates with that child.

Modality

Another consideration in planning ways of enhancing the processing and categorization of form relates to the modality of the linguistic signal. The auditory speech signal is the usual modality of linguistic form in first language learning, but it need not be the only modality considered. Recently, a number of professionals have reported using visual input (and some have been using a nonvocal motor output) as a means of facilitating language learning. Baron and Isensee (n.d.), Bonvillian and Nelson (1976 in *RLDis*), and Miller and Miller (1973, in *RLDis*) reported on the use of sign language with autistic children; D. Bricker (1972, in *RLDis*) used motor signals that were later paired with speech and objects as a means of teaching nouns to mentally retarded children; and Carrier (1974a, 1974b) as well as McLean and McLean (1974, in *RLDis*) used chips (plastic or wooden forms) as symbols to teach language to mentally retarded children. Both Bricker and the Millers speak of using this nonverbal linguistic stimuli as a means of facilitating auditory-vocal language learning. (This would seem most likely to occur if both visual and auditory linguistic signals are presented simultaneously.) The results of all these studies suggest alternative modalities for linguistic form may be a viable way of improving the communication skills of some children who have been unsuccessful learning auditory-vocal language although they have received considerable help. The children who will benefit most from the use of alternative modalities may be those, discussed in Chapter XIX, who have difficulty attending to more than one sense modality with multisensory input or difficulty integrating information from different sense modalities.

The combination of another modality with the auditory modality, or the teaching of symbols through the visual modality and then transferring the visual symbol to an auditory symbol may help some children. The *substitution* of the visual modality for the auditory modality is, however, a last resort that should be used only when, despite repeated efforts, auditory forms cannot be associated with the child's conceptions of objects and events in the world. Before switching the modality of form input, it should be clearly established that the problem does not lie in content alone (i.e., in forming concepts of the world) or in the use of language (i.e., demonstrating knowledge of content/form interactions). The modality of the linguistic input should be changed *only* if there is a problem processing auditory stimuli that is so severe that word concepts cannot be learned, or if there is a problem integrating concepts learned through the auditory modality with concepts learned through the visual and tactile modalities.

If a nonauditory linguistic system is to be presented, there are a number of decisions to be made and, unfortunately, little empirical evidence as yet to support such decisions. First, one must decide whether to use geometric forms (Box XXI-2) or hand configurations as symbols (Boxes XXI-3 to XXI-5) and then decide which system, based on these symbols, to use. (See Carrier, 1974a, 1974b; and McClean and McClean, 1974, in *RLDis* for information on chips, and Bornstein, 1973, 1974; Kent, 1974; and Wilbur,

BOX XXI-2 GEOMETRIC FORMS USED AS SYMBOLS (from Carrier 1974b, p. 513)

Boy	Dog		
Girl	Cat		
Man	Bird		
Lady	Horse		
Baby	Cow		

These geometric forms were cut from three-inch squares of masonite. Children were trained to match forms with black line drawings. All symbols were abstract and had no resemblance to the objects pictured.

This is certainly not an efficient means of communication. The placement of forms is a slow process; the child must choose from an array of forms, which takes time, and the number of forms that can be used is limited.

BOX XXI-3 SIGN LANGUAGE (from *A Basic Course in Manual Communication*, 1970, pp. 17–18)

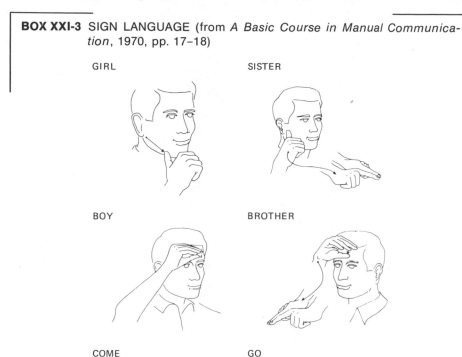

GIRL   SISTER

BOY   BROTHER

COME   GO

Signs make use of hand configurations, direction of movement, and places where hand moves to and from. Also, signs build on semantically related signs. For example, "sister" and "brother" build from "boy" and "girl," and the same motion is used with each to code the sibling relation. Some relationships are represented in a more abstract form than others (e.g., "come" is less abstract than "brother").

1976 for information on signs.) As Mayberry (1976) pointed out, there are a number of systems of sign language with considerable variation among them in their approximation to oral English and in the speed with which they can be used to convey a message. Factors influencing a clinician's decision will include the manual dexterity of the child and the ease with which others in the child's environment (including the clinician) can learn the alternative linguistic system. But even then, the decision making is not completed. The clinician must also decide whether to include the auditory signal with the

BOX XXI-4 SIGN MARKERS (from Bornstein, 1974, p. 334)

Past regular verbs:
walk*ed*, talk*ed*,
want*ed*, kiss*ed*,
learn*ed*

Third person singular:
walk*s*, talk*s*, lead*s*,
eat*s*, sing*s*

Past irregular verbs:
*saw, heard, blew,
forgot, came*

Possessive:
cat'*s*, dog'*s*, pig'*s*,
bear'*s*, grandmother'*s*

ing Verb form:
speak*ing*, sing*ing*,
play*ing*, rain*ing*,
danc*ing*, talk*ing*

Comparatives:
bett*er*, larg*er*,
slow*er*, fast*er*,
small*er*

Adverbs: *ly*
quick*ly*, neat*ly*,
angri*ly*, strong*ly*,
deep*ly*

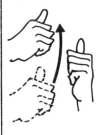

Superlative:
b*est*, larg*est*, slow*est*,
fast*est*, small*est*

Adjectives: *y*
sleep*y*, sunn*y*,
cloud*y*, rain, dream*y*

Regular plural nouns:
bear*s*, chair*s*, house*s*,
table*s*, book*s*

Plural irregular nouns:
(repeat the sign word
twice)
child*ren*, fee*t*,
sheep, mice, geese

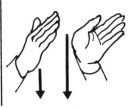

Agent (person
or thing):
tea*ch*er, act*or*,
dent*ist*, sail*or*,
mix*er*, mow*er*

    Some systems of sign language parallel spoken English. One of these, "Signed English," has been developed for preschool deaf children and includes sign markers that stand for the morphological inflections of spoken English. These markers are used in combination with signs that represent words.

BOX XXI-5 THE AMERICAN MANUAL ALPHABET (from Bornstein, 1974, p. 336)

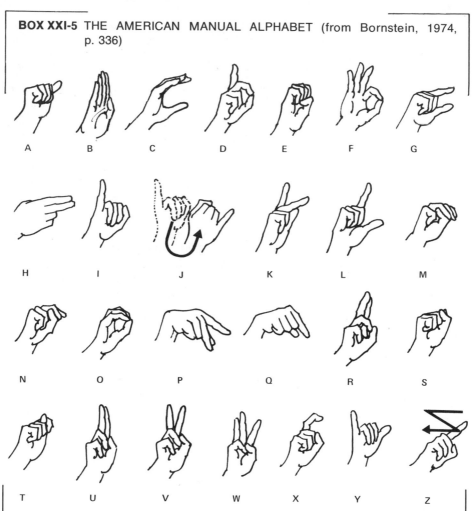

Spelling out words with the manual alphabet is an extremely slow means of communication and is usually used only for uncommon words for which there is no available sign or is used for person and place names.

visual signal, teach only the visual, or teach the visual first and then the auditory. Again, without evidence from research, the decision must be made based on experimental teaching with each child.

Unit of Form

The general assumption in most language programs is that the smallest unit of form presented to a child as linguistic input is the word—a content/

form interaction. Alternatively, the smallest unit of input could be a phoneme or syllable, a unit of form that does not by itself represent any object, event, or relationship (e.g., the phoneme /p/ or the syllable /po/). In a method referred to as the "Association Method" (McGinnis, Kleffner, and Goldstein, n.d.; and Monsees, 1972), the phoneme is the first unit of form presented. Children are presented with both visual (facial movements) and auditory cues to the phoneme concurrent with a visual representation (the letter) of the sound. Sequences of unconnected phonemes (/m/ /æ/ /t/ or /k/ /æ/ /t/) are both heard, produced, and memorized before being "blended" to form words such as "mat" and "cat." This approach is contrary to normal development and to existing knowledge of speech perception. A. Liberman, Cooper, Shankweiler, and Studdert-Kennedy (1967), pointed out, for example, that stop consonants such as /k/ are not invariable independent acoustic segments but transitions that lead into the following vowel. (See discussion in Chapter XIX.) Despite these theoretical arguments against the approach, it has been used, with apparent success, particularly with aphasic children, at the Central Institute for the Deaf (McGinnis et al., n.d.). It is perhaps one of the more extreme distortion of form recommended by any approach and, as with alternative modalities, should be considered only as a last resort.

CONSIDERATIONS IN THE SELECTION OF CONTENT/FORM INTERACTIONS AS INPUT

Planning the content/form interactions to be used as linguistic input is, of course, influenced by the goals for a particular child. The goals do not, however, specify the topic, the specific lexical items, or the larger linguistic context in which you embed the syntactic structures that you wish the child to learn. This choice is sometimes made on the spot and is always dependent on the activities and objects involved. There are, however, a number of ways in which one can talk about particular activities and the relations between objects. On what bases are lexical items and the larger linguistic context chosen as input?

Selection of Lexical Items

One aspect to be considered in the selection of lexical items is the configurations of the signal that will make up the symbols to be presented. Which configurations will be easiest to learn? Again, there is no definitive answer to this question; undoubtedly, there will be variation among children. Certainly one should consider the sounds a child is able to produce when selecting forms to be taught, since this may be the best hypothesis for judging ease of pronounceability. One might also hypothesize that short words of one or two syllables will probably be easier to segment and retain than longer polysyllabic words and most likely will be easier for the child to reproduce. The first words of normal children tend to be monosyllabic, such as "no," or a repetition of one syllable, such as "dada." In addition, as pointed out by Brown (1958), shorter words are the words most frequently used by adults (Zipf, 1965), and so may be the words most often heard by the child. Finally, one might want to select words that are acoustically distinct from each other in order to reduce confusion among the forms presented—thus "car" and "star" would not be presented in the same lesson.

A second consideration in making choices is the efficiency of a lexical item. Certain words, such as "no" or "more," have broader application to objects and events than other words, such as "cookie" or "car," and thus may be heard more often and will serve the child more frequently in his or her efforts to communicate. The more frequently a word is heard by a child, the greater is the chance that the child will make inductions about a content/form interaction; the more often the child is able to use a word in daily life the more opportunity the child will have for practice and reinforcement.

As noted in Chapter IV, words used by young children can be dichotomized as substantive words or as relational words. Substantive words refer to particular objects (e.g., person and place names), or refer to categories of objects (e.g., chair and dog). The choice of particular substantive words as input will depend on the child's environment and should include objects that will be frequently encountered. The child's interest directs the choice of objects to be named, but many objects can be referred to by a number of different words (e.g., "nickel," "five cents," or "money"; "chickadee," "bird," or "animal"; "apple," "fruit," or "food") and the clinician must choose which is appropriate. Brown (1958) noted that children's vocabulary does not simply build from concrete to abstract; for example, the word "fish" is more abstract than the name of a particular fish and less abstract than the term "vertebrate." Many concrete words are not learned until one takes science courses or is interested in different makes of cars. According to Brown, adults appear to use two criteria in making decisions about what a "thing" will be called in their speech to children: the object's most common name, and the word that categorizes the object according to its utilization in the child's life. Thus, coins might first be referred to as money and only later as dimes, nickels, and the like, since the young child is not likely to need the differentiation in daily life; fruits will be specifically identified as apple, pear, and so on, since the differentiation is important to daily meals and snacks. It appears that these criteria of selection have relevance to the language facilitator selecting lexical input for the language-disordered child. The words chosen should be commonly used in the child's environment as labels for objects, and the words should categorize the world in ways that relate to the child's cognitive structure and needs.

Relational words are words that refer to a relationship between objects and include parts of speech such as verbs, adjectives, and prepositions. Relational words are less specific than substantive words and may often be used to refer to many or all objects. For example, "no" can be used to reject, deny, or note the disappearance of any object and event. Certain verbs are less object or event specific than others. Verbs such as "give," "get," "make," and "fall" can refer to more objects than verbs such as "eat" and "throw," and "eat" and "throw" are less specific than verbs such as "drink" or "tear." The adjectives "big" and "dirty" can refer to more objects than can the adjectives "orange" or "round." Thus, in selecting relational words to teach, one might consider first those relational words that are least object specific and that therefore are more likely to be heard, and have the most potential for communication in many different situations because they involve many contexts.

Certain relational words are listed in Table XXI-1 according to the content category they code. These particular words have been singled out for two reasons: (1) they are less specific than many other relational words, and (2)

TABLE XXI-1
Selection of Lexical Items on the Basis of Content and Form: Relational Words[a]

Content	Form	
Content Category	Relational Words that are not object specific	Relational Words that are more specific to objects but still relate to many objects
Rejection	no	
Nonexistence or disappearance	no, all gone, away	
Cessation of action	stop, no	
Prohibition of action	no, don't	
Recurrence of objects and actions on objects	more, again, another	
Noting the existence of or identifying objects	this, there, that	
Actions on objects		give, do, make, get, throw, eat, wash, kiss, broke, close, open, fix, push, take, play, find, hold
Actions involved in locating objects or self		put, go, up, down, sit, fall, out, come, away, stand, climb, fit
Attributes or descriptions of objects		big, hot, dirty, heavy
Notice		see, look at

[a] Adapted from Lahey and Bloom, 1977.

they are frequently found in the lexicons of children learning language normally. These provide hypotheses for which relational words a child may find easiest to learn first.

The selection of lexical items continues to be important in the later stages of language learning. In normal development, Bloom, Miller, and Hood (1975, in *RLDev*) reported more frequent use of three constituents (subject-verb-complement) when familiar lexical items were used and, correspondingly, a reduction in the number of constituents when new lexical items were used. Even as late as elementary school, familiarity with lexical items and their referents enhances linguistic processing of such complex syntactic constructions as the passive. (See Bransford and Nitsch, 1977, for a discussion of some of these studies.) These findings suggest using familiar lexical items when first facilitating inductions about complex syntactic structures.

Complexity of Linguistic Input

The complexity of the sentence in which forms to be learned are embedded is another factor that can influence the salience of the linguistic input. New lexical items might best be spoken in isolation or embedded in very simple and familiar constructions. Thus, new substantive words might best be introduced as single-word utterances or in two- and three-word constructions, as "that's an x" or "more y."

New structures, combinations of words, or grammatical morphemes might also be presented in isolation or in short, linguistic contexts such as "more x," or embedded in short, simple constructions, such as "There is more x," "See more x," "Do you want more x?" In each example, differential stress can be used to accent the words that code recurrence and to deemphasize other words. It may be, however, that any additional words mask the salience of "more x" and that the two words alone would be most effective for some children.

What is to be avoided for all children in the early phases of language learning is the embedding of key words in long and complex utterances (e.g., "If you eat your cereal then you can have more x," or "I thought I saw more x but now I can't find any at all."). These utterances may be appropriate at a later stage of development but, if the child is first learning to code recurrence with two words, the two important words, "more x," are lost in the excessively complicated linguistic context. What needs to be modeled over and over is the form to be taught, in appropriate contexts. In the early stages of language learning, the syntactic level of linguistic input should be just above the level of the child's language. Many beginning clinicians err on the side of too complex and too cluttered input, making it difficult for the child to perceive the important forms in order to induce content/form interactions.

The Child's Actions and Utterances

One basis for the selection of particular topics is to talk about the activities in which the child is engaged or about which the child talks. If the child is continually performing certain actions (sliding, banging, pushing etc.) it may well be that the forms that code these activities will be more easily learned than forms that code activities that are not a part of the usual behavioral repertoire.

Another means of determining the semantic-syntactic input to a child is to base the linguistic input on the child's prior utterance. Muma (1971) discussed a number of techniques for facilitating language learning that are based on the child's utterance: correction, expansion, expatiation, and alternative. The correction technique may be used to correct form (the child says "two book" and the clinician says "not two book, two books") or content (the child looks at an elephant and says "see doggie", and the clinician says "That's an elephant, not a doggie."). Although this is a familiar teaching technique, Muma pointed out that it may be destructive to language *use* when applied to the correction of form, but may be effective for learning content/form interactions when used to point out meaning errors (note the discussion in Chapter IX of mother-child interactions; mothers rarely correct form but often correct content.) Alternatively, one might respond to a child's *utterance* by syntactically expanding the child's prior utterance. Thus, if the child says "there two book," the clinician might respond "Yes, there *are* two books," providing the omitted forms to make a complete adult sentence. Expansions that relate to content—where the clinician adds information— were referred to by Muma as expatiations. In this case the clinician adds information to the child's utterance. When the child says "there two book," the clinician might reply "Yes, there are two big books. The books are heavy. See, pick them up. They are very heavy." Finally, the clinician can respond with an alternative to a child's utterance in a way that points out the logic of the utterance or the situation it codes. For example, about to wash a wall with a dripping sponge, a child says "lots a water;" the clinician might respond "Do you need that much water?" This use of alternatives is outlined and discussed by Blank (1973). Research with the language-disordered child has not yet supported the superiority of one method over another.

CONSIDERATIONS IN THE PRESENTATION OF NONLINGUISTIC INPUT

It is the task of the language facilitator to arrange external stimuli so the concept to be coded by linguistic form will be illustrated in a way that is clear and salient. Considerations in planning nonlinguistic input involve the type of stimuli to be used, the child's involvement in the demonstration, the variety of different contexts demonstrated, and the actual objects and activities used.

Type of Stimuli

Unfortunately, for those who wish to facilitate language in a formal teaching situation, pictures rarely serve as adequate demonstration of a concept during early stages of language learning. Many concepts involve more than the perceptual features of objects (see Chapter III) available from a picture; they involve functional features that come from acting on the objects as well as perceptual features that can only be extracted from three-dimensional objects. Thus, to learn that the word "ball" refers to a category of objects, the child needs to experience the roundness, bouncing, rolling, differences in softness, size, and color in order to learn eventually that all of these are part of the concept and that "ball" is not just a red circle on a card. This is true not only when learning vocabulary (single words to refer to a concept) but also when learning to code the relationships among words. If a child is to learn that the person acting is named before the action is named in order to talk about the agent of an action, the child should experience actual demonstrations of persons acting at the same time as the forms that code the demonstration.

Leonard found that children acquired the subject-verb construction more easily when exposed to ongoing events than when exposed to pictures (1975c) or to only form and referents (1975a, in *RLDis*). Children trained with simultaneous presentation of subject-verb forms with ongoing events could respond to pictures on posttest. However, children exposed to subject-verb forms and pictures did not respond well to *either* ongoing events *or* pictures on posttest. Likewise, children exposed to referents coded by forms but not exposed to a *demonstration* of the referent relationship did not produce subject-verb constructions as often as children exposed to actual events. Leonard concluded that ongoing events demonstrating the relationship coded should be used when facilitating the induction of word order as a means of expressing agent-action relations. It is possible that pictures could be used after an induction has been made to reinforce and practice production or comprehension of the interaction, since the children trained with actual demonstration of events did generalize to pictures in the study by Leonard. In the initial stages of facilitation, however, real objects and people demonstrating relationships should be used for nonlinguistic input.

The types of objects used may also affect the ease with which a content/form interaction is induced. Sailor and Taman (1972) reported that the locative prepositions "in" and "on" were learned faster by autistic children when each preposition was first trained with an unambiguous object (*containers* for "in" and *supports* for "on") instead of contrasting the two prepositions using an ambiguous object (such as a hat and a can, which were containers in one position but supports in another). This finding is contrary to the intuitions of many clinicians who felt an ambiguous object was necessary to demonstrate the *difference* between the two prepositions; it is, however, consistent with the nonlinguistic strategies Clark (1973, in *RLDev*) described for the normal child's comprehension of locative relations.

It should not be surprising that nonlinguistic context influences language learning; there is considerable research demonstrating the effect of nonlinguistic context on the language comprehension and production of normal speakers. Osgood (1971) demonstrated that the nonlinguistic context influenced both the form and content of adults' utterances. By manipulating the sequence of events that were to be described, he influenced the probability that adjectives, articles, negatives, and pronouns would be used. Adjectives were, for example, used more frequently when first describing an object or when similar objects were in the same array. Furthermore, the effect of context on the comprehension of linguistic structure has been consistently demonstrated (Bransford and Johnson, 1972; Bransford and Nitsch, 1977; Huttenlocher, Eisenberg, and Strauss, 1968; Huttenlocher and Strauss, 1968; and Huttenlocher and Weiner, 1971). The effect of similar differences in context has not been described in connection with language learning by the language-disordered child, but it seems possible that they may influence the ease with which a child will learn certain aspects of language. Certainly more research, similar to that by Leonard and by Sailor and Taman, is needed. In the meantime the evidence from their studies and from normal processing suggests that close attention needs to be given to the nonlinguistic demonstration of objects and relations.

Child Participation and Interest

If you watch a 2- or 3-year-old using language it will be clear that children first learning language talk most about what they are doing, are about to do, or want others to do. They talk less about states that they are not involved in or about the actions of others that do not involve them. There is no information about the effect of participation in events versus the observation of events on eventual language learning. In the Leonard (1975a, 1975c) studies mentioned above, the children observed a demonstration; the differences he reported did not relate to observation compared with participation but, instead, to difference in what was observed by the children.

Observations of normal children and clinical experience suggest child participation in the nonlinguistic events that demonstrate the relation being coded may be important in learning early content/form interactions. The importance of the child's participation, however, may vary with the concept being coded. The salience of certain relations may be increased by participation because the sensorimotor experience is an important part of certain concepts. On the other hand, certain actions may so totally involve the child that the linguistic forms are not be attended to. The importance of participation may also vary among children according to conceptual development and attention span. Although future research may help to clarify the role of some of these variables, the clinician must make decisions about how extensively child participation will be intermixed with child observation—decisions based on each child's response.

Certainly planning demonstrations that are of interest to the child is a key to increasing the salience of those demonstrations, whether or not the child is an active participant in the demonstration. Parent interviews as well as unstructured observations are a way of obtaining information about particular interests. For example, if a child likes to bang objects, "bang" may be one of the easiest words for the child to learn.

Variety of Nonlinguistic Demonstrations

Nonlinguistic demonstrations must include more than one example in order for generalization to occur. Even when the lexical items presented refer to specific objects or places (e.g., proper names), the nonlinguistic presentation must involve many contexts that include that specific object (e.g., Mommy or a pet). Thus Mommy is labeled as she enters the room, hugs the child, is pointed to, leaves the room, or throws the ball, to assure that the induction of content/form is not context specific (i.e. that the word "Mommy" refers to only a picture or that person entering the room, etc.)

Similarly, for the child to understand that certain forms (such as most nouns) refer to not just one object, place, or event, but to a *category*, multiple examples of the concept must be experienced with the forms that represent the concept. Thus, if the child is to learn that "ball" refers to many different objects, the child must experience contact with a number of different balls as the child hears the word as well as contact with balls in different situations. Likewise, to learn that the morphological inflection -s can be used to represent plurality, the child must experience demonstrations of *one versus more than one* with many objects (a block and blocks, a truck and trucks, a cat and cats, etc.); to learn subject-verb-object, to express agent-action-object relations, the child must hear the forms at the same time as experiencing a number of different actions as well as the same action with different agents and objects (Mommy eat cake, Doggy eat meat, Mommy wash face, Mommy wash dish, etc.). Thus, all nonlinguistic demonstrations must include a variety of exemplars, because most forms refer to more than one object in one context.

Activities

The activities that best serve to demonstrate the concepts that make up the content of language come from the child's everyday experiences. The situations that consistently arise in life offer opportunities to illustrate concepts that language codes. Which aspect of these activities will be the focus depends on the content the child is learning to code. Keeping in mind the importance of actual demonstration and considering the possibility of the child as participant, some typical home and school activities are listed below according to several of the content categories discussed previously.

The basic idea is to select activities with which the child is familiar, enjoys, and in which he or she can become involved. Most activities can involve the demonstration of many relations; the relations focussed on (by repetition, exaggeration, gesture, etc.) will depend on the content categories the child is learning to code. When goals of intervention include the coordination of categories, two or three relations found within events are focussed on (e.g., describing the object acted on, or located, to coordinate action plus attribution, or locative action plus attribution as in "I'm pouring the hot water" or "I'm putting the big car here.")

1. *Activities for Existence.* After initially pointing out that an object exists, utterances in the category are identification statements.
   a. Identifying objects taken from a bag.
   b. Pointing out interesting objects at the zoo, fire station, store, and so on.

2. *Activities for Disappearance.* After identifying an object, it can be hidden from view or, as the child finishes food or drink, one can comment on its nonexistence or disappearance.

3. *Activities for Recurrence.* Nonlinguistic demonstrations of recurrence should involve both the reappearance or multiple instances of objects as well as events. Again, in a child's normal environment, such situations occur all the time; eating is a continual process of repeated actions ("another cookie," "drink again," etc.). Other situations that lend themselves to the coding of recurrence are:
   a. Playground—slides, seesaws, swings (up and down again).
   b. Shop—bang again, another nail.
   c. Art—another crayon, color more, cut another one.
   d. Blocks and puzzles—another piece or block.
   e. Gym—jump, throw, tumble again.
   f. Looking at a book—another x in the picture, turn another page, turn again.
   g. Sand table—make another one, pour more sand in.

4. *Activities for Possession.* To teach possessor-possessed relationships (Mommy's coat, my hat) the demonstration of the concept should include objects the child associates with particular people. Brown (1973) reported that objects that could conceivably belong to a number of people (alienable objects) were talked about in terms of possessive relationship before body parts (inalienable objects). It is possible that noting the possessor of a bike or cookie is more important (i.e., less obvious), to code than the owner of a nose or an eye. Thus clothing, art work, personal toys, lunches, and assigned storage spaces, chairs, or desks provide opportunities for nonlinguistic illustration; they are alienable and they have associations more permanent than the teaching context. To illustrate possessive relationships, it is impor-

tant that the possessor and possessed object are, in fact, related and not just temporarily assigned for the duration of the lesson.

5. *Activities for Action*. Action is a major portion of a child's life, so there should be little problem finding actions in the child's natural environment. Creating them in a clinic room becomes more of a problem. The following are activities that the child can both participate in and observe. The form to be presented can vary from single words to coordinate and subordinate complex sentences, depending on the content/form interaction of interest. For example, in an activity centered around cooking, "pour," "open," "mix," "stir," and so on, could be presented as single-word utterances or complex causal sentences with "because" for example, "We can't pour the pudding because the box is closed," "Don't touch the pan because it's hot." Thus, particular activities can form the core for learning many content/form interactions. Consider, then, in planning nonlinguistic input for action relations, some of the following inputs and actions.
   a. Playground—slide, run, hop, jump, swing, throw.
   b. Sandtable—build, pour, pat, mix, stir, push, spill, make.
   c. Water play—wash, pour, spill, splash, dry.
   d. Cook—mix, bake, stir, pour, cut, make.
   e. Art—cut, draw, color, paint, paste, tear, fold, make.
   f. Shop—hammer, saw, bang, build, turn.
   g. Snack—eat, drink, open, pour, cut, wash, clean, wipe.

6. *Activities for Locative Action*. Children are often locating objects in their environments. Many opportunities to code such actions occur in the normal classroom and home.
   a. Cleanup time—*putting* many objects in many different places.
   b. Play with trains or trucks and doll houses also involves much locating activity.
   c. Dressing or undressing—*putting* clothes on and off.
   d. Form board and puzzles—*putting* pieces in board.
   e. Telling another or self *where* to hide objects: "dog goes there" (an example of patient-locative action), "you put it there" (an example of agent-locative action), or "You sit there" (an example of mover-locative action)

7. *Activities for Locative State*. Situations referring to the static location of objects are easy to design and certainly are numerous and varied in the child's life. To demonstrate this relationship, it is important to select objects and places that are familiar to the child. One would not choose to use a situation as a microphone on a tape recorder to code locative state if the child has not yet learned about microphones or tape recorders. Static spatial relations follow learning about locative action. Searching activities can incorporate locative state, nonexistence, and wh- questions about locative state.

8. *Activities for Internal State*. It is more difficult to vary external stimuli so that the child will experience an internal state. Ideally, the facilitator will have enough contact with the child to be with him or her when the child

experiences and manifests (nonlinguistically) many states that can be coded, such as "tired," "scared," "sad," "mad," "hungry," "thirsty," or "happy." When these situations occur, the linguistic forms can be supplied.

Wanting is perhaps the easiest state to create and, in fact, the earliest state normal children learn to code. Desired objects can be made almost available and if the child reaches for the object, the form can be provided: "You want x." With enough variety of objects and repetition, it is likely the child will induce that the regularity that the form codes has to do with feelings and desires—that is, the child's internal state relative to the object.

9. *Activities for Time*. Arranging nonlinguistic events to demonstrate temporal relations involves particular attention to the simultaneous presentation of linguistic form with nonlinguistic demonstration. The events may be the same as coded under action, locative action, and state. Ongoing activities need to be coded as they are happening (jumping, drawing, walking, making, stirring, etc.). Intention should be coded as the *child* is about to do something ("I'm gonna jump; now I'm jumping"). Reference to past time should begin with events that have just finished ("I jumped"), that is, events in the immediate past and events the child has just experienced. Temporal relations between events can first refer to chained sequential actions, "you put the milk in the bowl, *and then* you stir—you're pouring the milk/ *and now* you're stirring/ and it's all mixed." Simultaneous time events can also be coded, "I pour *and* I stir" or "I pour *while* I stir" (at the same time).

DISORDERS OF CONTENT/FORM INTERACTION

Children manifesting disorders of content/form interaction may have difficulty with conceptualizing the regularities in the linguistic environment (forming word concepts or linguistic categories); the regularities in their nonlinguistic environment (forming object and relational concepts that are the content of language or nonlinguistic categories); or inducing contact between linguistic and nonlinguistic categories (regularities perceived in the nonlinguistic environment associated with regularities perceived in the linguistic environment). Although each may be a separate problem, the contexts of intervention may not, in fact, differ drastically.

In all cases the goal is an induction of content/form interaction, which involves *contact* between linguistic and nonlinguistic categories. At first it may appear that a child cannot form inductions about content/form *interaction* until being able to form both linguistic and nonlinguistic categories, and, therefore, each should be worked on separately. However, the presentation of forms concurrent with varied demonstrations of concepts may facilitate the formation of categories of both form and content. The child who has difficulty perceiving regularities or discriminating differences in the acoustic signal (speech) may be aided in that perception by the consistent presentation of that signal (made salient as discussed previously) concurrent with regularly occurring and eventually predictable nonlinguistic events.

In this way the child can use his or her concepts of content to aid in building word concepts—strengths the child already has in content can help in learning about form. Furthermore, the ability to see regularities in form may aid in leading a child to discover the regularities in the nonlinguistic environment (Brown, 1956, in *RLDev*). Likewise, the child who has difficulty integrating information from different modalities needs extra repetitions of concurrent linguistic and nonlinguistic presentation. Even when, as a last resort, the visual modality is used to supplement the auditory modality for linguistic forms, both content and form need to be presented concurrently—within the speech event. (See Chapter IX for discussion of contact between linguistic and nonlinguistic categories in development.)

INDUCTIONS ABOUT USE

Inductions about content/form interaction are an important part of language learning, but knowing a code is relevant only if the child can *use* that code in varying contexts and for different functions. Inductions about use are learned concurrent with inductions about content/form interaction. Aspects of use may, in fact, facilitate learning content/form interactions, just as learning about content/form interaction may facilitate learning use.

LEARNING TO COMMUNICATE WITH OTHERS THROUGH LANGUAGE

Certainly a primary function of language is interpersonal communication. Interpersonal functions for which children use language include: establishing contact with others; manipulating another's actions; obtaining desired objects; and getting information. These have been respectively referred to as: interactional; regulatory; instrumental; and heuristic functions by Halliday (1974, in *RLDev*). These communicative functions of language are important considerations in language intervention; they provide the third element of input schematized in Box XXI-1: the social context of language intervention.

The language learner should be placed in many situations where interpersonal interactions are important—situations where making contact with another, requesting an object, manipulating another's actions, and obtaining information are important and rewarding. The alert language facilitator then must tune in carefully to the communicative needs of the child and fully utilize each instance of such needs by presenting the child with the appropriate (in relation to context and level of development) content/form interaction. Attempts by the child to use such content/form interactions are then promptly rewarded by successful communication—for example, if the child requests help, help is given. Taking advantage of communicative desires often supplies considerable motivation for learning content/form interaction. In addition, it provides the child with a natural reinforcer for language.

To make the code useful in this manner means careful observation of the child and a sensitivity that enables one to see a situation from the child's view. (See Box XXI-0). It means a constant awareness of the function and content that will be most useful to the child. The forms presented to help encode the child's communicative intent are selected according to level of

---

BOX XXI-6 FACILITATING LANGUAGE USE (from Itard, 1962, pp. 31 and 32)

On the fourth day of this next experiment I succeeded to my heart's content, and I heard Victor pronounce distinctly, though rather uncouthly it is true, the word lait, *and he repeated it almost immediately. It was the first time that an articulate sound left his mouth and I did not hear it without the most intense satisfaction.*

Nevertheless I made a reflection which in my eyes much diminished the advantage of this first success. It was not until the moment when, despairing of success, I came to pour the milk into the cup which he gave me, that the word lait *escaped him with great demonstrations of pleasure; and it was only after I had poured it again as a reward that he pronounced it a second time. It can be seen why this result was far from fulfilling my intentions. The word pronounced instead of being the sign of his need was, relative to the time when it had been articulated, merely an exclamation of pleasure. If this word had been uttered before the thing which he desired had been granted, success was ours, the real use of speech was grasped by Victor, a point of communication established between him and me, and the most rapid progress would spring from this first triumph. Instead of all this, I had just obtained a mere expression, insignificant to him and useless to us, of the pleasure which he felt. Strictly speaking, it was certainly a vocal sign, the sign of possession. But this sign, I repeat, did not establish any relation between us. It had soon to be neglected because it was useless to the needs of the individual and was swamped by a multitude of irrelevancies, like the ephemeral and variable sentiment for which it had become the sign. The subsequent results of this misuse of the word have been such as I feared.*

It was generally only during the enjoyment of the beverage that the word lait *was heard. Sometimes he happened to pronounce it before and at other times a little after but always without purpose.*

This description by Itard of the facilitation of language with Victor, "the wild boy of Averyon," dramatically pictures Itard's sensitivity to the importance of the pragmatic context of language, but an inflexibility that came from his narrow definition of language use. He was particularly insensitive to the intensity of Victor's recognition and pleasure in this more mathetic use of his *first word*. Children's early use of language is often intrapersonal in just this way.

development and prior decisions about lexical items. For examples, to facilitate interactional and instrumental functions, note the following:

Interactional: A child has completed a block tower, looks and smiles at the adult, looks back at the tower. The adult might say: "Look! Look! Look at that tower" (while looking at it).

Instrumental: A child strains and reaches for a train out of reach, whimpers, and looks at the adult. The adult might say: "Train/ Train/ You want the train— want train" (and then give the child the train).

After considerable input in similar contexts that call for a particular function of language, a response by the child, if not spontaneously given, can be encouraged as a prerequisite for satisfying of the child's intent. Early in development the response may be any vocalization; later it might be one word or a syntactic utterance that codes the intent.

Situations can be devised that increase the need for communication. Important, necessary, or favorite objects can be temporarily misplaced, encouraging the child to ask for information ("Where x?") or to request an object. Novel or unusual objects can be brought in and placed just out of reach, encouraging similar functions. In addition, objects that are hard to operate, open, or fix may encourage requests for help.

For some children, modeling of successful communication by a third party (as discussed by Bandura and Harris, 1966) may help in the induction of language use. Another child, or an adult who is engaged in similar activities as the child, can produce the content/form interaction appropriate to both their needs. The utterance by the model would be quickly rewarded and perhaps repeated by the facilitator. The modeled situation would need to be timed to coincide with the child's attention to the model and the child's communicative need. Repeated examples may help some children induce the content/form/use interactions.

LEARNING TO USE LANGUAGE FOR INTRAPERSONAL FUNCTIONS

Children and adults use language at times when no interpersonal communicative intent is obvious. The child says "up" while climbing up, "down" while climbing down, "stop" while stopping the truck, and "doll fall" after the doll has fallen. In each case, there does not seem to be an attempt to direct the utterance to anyone, nor does there seem to be any observable benefit derived from speaking. Bloom (1970a) referred to such utterances as "comments" and Halliday (1975) suggested that such comments may serve a mathetic function; that is, they may serve to direct the child's activities or aid in concept formation (Rees, 1973a). Although it may never be clear what the exact function of such comments is for the child, they are abundant in the speech of the normal child first learning language.

Clinical observation suggests that comments are less frequent with language-disordered children at the same level of linguistic development. The reasons for this could be many, including age, but the implications are clear. Children who talk about what they see and do certainly have considerable opportunity to practice content/form interaction and to obtain feedback from the environment as to how appropriate or accurate some form is in relation to content. It may also be that these comments help the child to stabilize the concepts, and they may eventually lead to the use of language as a means of self-regulation. For all of these reasons, language-disordered children should be encouraged to talk about their own actions and states. In order to facilitate content/form interaction, the clinician will be talking about what the child is doing. If, *after* much such input, the child does not spontaneously begin to talk about these actions or imitate the utterances of the facilitator, imitation of utterances that code the actions and states might be encouraged.

In the later stages of language learning (e.g., in Phase 8, when the child's *MLU* has been over 3.0 for awhile), the child might be helped to use language as a means of pretending. Using language to pretend about events necessarily follows language used to talk of events that are present in the context. Language can first be used to code pretend play as it happens. For example, while standing at a play sink with dishes but no water, the child may pretend to wash the dishes, and this activity can be coded. More fantasy can later be introduced, as with role-playing: "You be the mommy and I'll be the baby." One would not encourage fantasy until the child could carry out the more literal pretend.

A last intrapersonal use of language that can be facilitated in later stages of development is the expression of emotions—later stages because to learn content/form interactions about emotional states is not easy. A child must hear the forms while experiencing the state (or observe another's experience of the state and relate that to the child's own experiences of that state). The child must understand that the forms refer to the internal emotions instead of to the physical manifestations of emotions, such as crying (sad), hitting (anger), or smiling (happiness).

Intrapersonal functions of language, then, include commenting about ongoing events (particularly one's own actions and states or intended actions); pretend or fantasy; and expression of emotion. Certainly there are many other functions that have not been covered. As more is learned about how normal children use language, the implications of these uses for the language-disordered child can be hypothesized and eventually tested—at least on a child-by-child basis. Certainly if the child appears to use language for additional functions—such as humor—they too should be encouraged.

LEARNING TO USE LANGUAGE IN VARIOUS CONTEXTS

Learning to use language requires making inferences about differences in context and about other persons in relation to context. As has been emphasized in the first part of this chapter, to learn language the child must hear the forms of language in the context of objects that are present and events that are ongoing or intended by the child.

If, however, the language-disordered child has not begun to talk about objects and events that are *not* present in the here and now context by the time content/form interactions are comparable to Phases 6 to 8, this should become a goal of use. To help a child reach this goal, one might begin by talking about objects that are present and are related to similar objects or events in the immediate past or in another place (e.g., the doll in school that is similar to the doll at home). One might also talk about objects and events that are immediately distant from the here and now (e.g., the food that has just been eaten). In all cases, content/form interactions that are well established would be used. This type of input can be combined with activities relating to inducing content/form interactions about temporal relations (discussed earlier).

Finally, the language-disordered child must learn to use language in varying linguistic contexts. The child must learn to initiate conversation and respond to utterances of others. These skills, too, depend on well-learned content/form interactions and are not expected until the child is well along in this development. First, attempts to facilitate discourse would use not only well-established content/form interactions, but the perceptual support of context; that is, the content would be about the here and now. Discourse should include responses to the questions of others, beginning with responses to "what" and "where" questions, and only later including "why" and "when" questions. In addition, the facilitator will want to encourage semantically appropriate responses to statements by others—responses that add information to another utterance. Again, modeling may be used to demonstrate this use to the child. For example, the facilitator says, "Let's build a house" and the model responds "need a block"—a contextually related response; in later stages the model might respond "a big house"— both a contextually and a linguistically related response. (See Chapter VII for a description of the development of discourse.)

DISORDERS OF USE

Some disorders of use seen in the language-disordered child may well be a result of prior techniques that were used by others in an attempt to teach content/form interaction—techniques that focussed on labeling pictures instead of talking about objects and events in the child's natural environment. Some children taught in this way produce routine responses but rarely use language for communication. Some rarely produce the forms outside of the structured learning environment. These disorders of use may even reflect the learning of forms only as a response to certain pictures.

Other children who rarely use language to communicate are children whose interpersonal interactions are limited in every sense. The child withdraws from social contact, touching, and looking at others. The limited use of language appears to be a reflection of general withdrawal from interpersonal contact. With some of these children, content/form interactions are well developed and the language goals focus on increasing the use of the code for interpersonal functions. Work with such children should be closely coordinated with a clinical psychologist or a psychiatrist who is responsible for improving overall interpersonal relations. Other children, however, with limited interpersonal contact may be withdrawing from contact because of difficulty in learning language.

With any child where use is not well developed, it is essential that all attempts by the child to communicate with or without linguistic forms be promptly reinforced. When no forms are used or when the forms used are not appropriate, the facilitator provides the appropriate form at the same time. Thus, facilitating the use of language in many contexts and for many functions involves being sensitive to the communication needs of the child and supplying the content/form interactions that will best serve the child's needs. To learn to use language, the child must experience pleasant interpersonal interactions where language is modeled as a means of communication. Use is probably learned best when one attends to the child and responds meaningfully to the child's linguistic and nonlinguistic interactions in a warm, accepting atmosphere.

SUMMARY

For a child to learn how linguistic forms can be used to represent ideas of the world, the child must repeatedly experience consistent forms along with demonstrations of the concepts these forms represent in the language community. The task of the facilitator is to arrange stimuli in the child's environment so these experiences will be frequent and salient. Considerations in planning the linguistic input include: varying intensity, prosody, and rate to increase the salience of the linguistic signal; selecting lexical items that are short, nonhomophonous, frequently used, efficient and useful to the child; and supplementing the auditory linguistic input with visual nonlinguistic input. Considerations in planning the nonlinguistic input include: actual demonstration instead of picture representations; consideration of the child as a participant; inclusion of different exemplars of a concept; and using the child's life experiences as core activities to illustrate concepts. Whether the child exhibits problems in categorizing the linguistic input (form), the nonlinguistic environment (content), or in integrating form with content, concurrent presentation of content and form is the key to making inductions about the relations between linguistic and nonlinguistic categories.

With some children the task in not so much to aid inductions of form and content but, instead, to facilitate the use of the code they know. Learning to use language includes learning to communicate with others; using language to comment and for other intrapersonal functions; and learning to use alternative forms of language according to the requirements of different contexts.

SUGGESTED READINGS

In *Readings in Language Disorders*

Bonvillian, J. and Nelson, K., Sign language acquisition in a mute autistic boy. *Journal of Speech and Hearing Disorders, 41,* 339-347, 1976.

Bricker, D. D., Imitative sign training as a facilitator of word-object association with low functioning children. *American Journal of Mental Deficiency, 76,* 509–516, 1972.

Itard, J., *The wild boy of Aveyron.* New York: Appleton-Century-Crofts, pp. 67–86, 1962.

Leonard, L., Relational meaning and the facilitation of slow-learning children's language. *American Journal of Mental Deficiency, 80,* 180–185, 1975a.

McLean, L., and McLean, J., A language training program for non-verbal autistic children. *Journal of Speech and Hearing Disorders, 39,* 186–193, 1974.

Miller, A., and Miller, E., Cognitive-developmental training and elevated boards and sign language. *Journal of Autism and Childhood Schizophrenia, 3,* 65–85, 1973.

Other Readings

Sailor, W., and Taman, T., Stimulus factors in the training of prepositional usage in three autistic children. *Journal of Applied Behavior Analysis, 5,* 183–190, 1972.

Wilbur, R., The linguistics of manual language and manual systems. In L. Lloyd (Ed.) *Communication assessment and intervention strategies.* Baltimore: University Park Press, pp. 423–500, 1976.

Appendix A.1
CONVENTIONS FOR TRANSCRIPTION OF CHILD LANGUAGE RECORDINGS[1]

1. All speech by the child and all speech to the child or within the child's hearing is fully transcribed on paper divided by a vertical line. Utterances by the child appear on the right side. Utterances by other speakers appear on the left. The person is identified by an initial (M for Mommy, L for Lois, D for Daddy, etc.). Information about the situational context also appears on the left and is enclosed in parentheses.

    (M takes cookie from bag;
    offering it to A)
    M: Look what I have/
    (A taking cookie)   cookie/

2. An action or event that occurs simultaneously with the child utterance appears on the same line with that utterance.

    (E banging blocks together)   crash/

3. When an utterance precedes or follows an action or event, the utterance appears on the preceding or succeeding line.

    (E throws block)
                                                            no block/
    (E picks up another block)
                                                            more/

4. Note the differential use of verb tenses in describing the situations: progressive for simultaneous action; simple present for actions or events that precede or follow an utterance.

5. For situational information accompanying utterances by someone other than the child, use the same verb tense conventions, but utterances and description can, of course, succeed one another on different lines since there is rarely enough space to put both on the same line.

---

[1] Prepared in collaboration with Lois Hood, and Patsy Lightbown.

(L reaching in bag)
L: Do you know what I have?
(L pulls out truck)
L: I think I'll make the truck go under
    the bridge/

6. Utterances that succeed each other immediately—WITH NO CHANGE IN SITUA-
TION—follow each other on the same line.

(G reaching for box of cookies)   more/ more/ cookie/
If there is any change in situation, the utterances appear on different lines.

(G reaching for box of cookies;   more/
taking box off counter;   more/
reaches in;
pulling out cookie)   cookie/
When in doubt about the situational context, use separate lines.

Punctuation

7. For utterances of child and other speakers, the usual sign of utterance boundary
is a slash (/). The boundary is determined by length of pause before the next
utterance and by its apparent terminal contour. The judgment is sometimes very
difficult to make. With older children and adults, the slash may be considered
equivalent to a period, but it is important to make each judgment carefully and as
objectively as possible.

8. Utterances by adult or child may be followed by an exclamation mark. When a
child utterance is exclamatory, it should be followed by *both* an exclamation
mark and the usual slash.

(Peter takes tire off car)
                           there!/ finish/

9. Adult questions are indicated by question marks. For the child utterance,
however, there are two different ways of indicating that an utterance has question
form. For Wh questions, a question mark may be used.

(P looking in toy bag)   where's ə car?/

When a child utterance seems to be a question because it has rising intonation,
it should be followed by a rising arrow (↑) instead of a question mark.

(P shaking empty box)   no more in there ↑ /

Even for a "well-formed" yes/no question (i.e., one with subject-verb inversion),
the arrow to indicate rising intonation is more informative than a simple question
mark.

(K meeting L at door)   did you bring the toys today ↑ /

In either case, a slash should also be used to mark the utterance boundary clearly.

10. A pause within an utterance is indicated by a dot (·).

   (E trying to fit peg in hole)   put·this one in/

11. A long pause between utterances within the same general situation is indicated by horizontal dots across the center line.

   (P tries to get wheel on car)   wheel goes in there/

      ...

   (P succeeds)

            there!/

12. A long pause between utterances where there is a change in the general situation is marked by three vertical dots on the center line.

   (G trying to stack blocks)   Gia make ə house/
                 ⋮
   (G running to kitchen)   juice!/Gia drink juice/

13. A colon is used to indicate that an utterance or word is drawn out.

   (E trying to fit large block   no:/
   inside small one)

14. A curving arrow is used when there is some kind of utterance boundary, but the utterance sounds unfinished, such as when the child is counting or "listing".

                 one⌒/
                 two⌒/
                 three⌒/

15. Stress marks indicate strongly emphasized words.

   L: Do you want this one? (L giving
      G a blue disc)   no!/
   (G reaching for red one L is
      holding)   thát one/

Capitalization

16. Names are capitalized. Initial letter of child utterance is not. Initial letter of adult utterance may be.

Other "Punctuation"

17. An utterance may be followed by falling arrow (↓) when it is important to emphasize the fact that the utterance had falling terminal contour.

   (P looking in toy bag;   wheel↑/
      pulls out tire for car)
                    wheel↓/

18. When a child or other speaker suddenly interrupts their own utterance—apparently leaving the utterance unfinished—a line (_____) indicates the abrupt stop.

    L: Do you want some _____/
    (E picks up cup and spills juice)

19. When a child or other speaker interrupts their own utterance apparently to change or correct it, a "self-correct" symbol (s/c) is used.

    L: Those are your $_s/_c$ my toys/

    don't $_s/_c$ ə want toys/

20. An unintelligible utterance or portion of an utterance is indicated by three dashes (– – –). If possible, a phonetic transcription is used instead.

    (E pushing over house of blocks,
    making loud crash)   no more/– – –/ house/

Abbreviations

21. When a child or other speaker repeats their own utterance completely and exactly, an X is used to show the repetition. Any change in the utterance must be indicated, including clear changes in intonation.

    L: Be careful/ X/
    (P touching tape recorder)   open/ X/ X /
                                        X!/

22. When an adult repeats a child's utterance, an equal sign (=) is used to show the repetition. When a child repeats an adult utterance, however, the child's utterance is written in full, even if the repetition is exact. An equal sign can never represent a child utterance, although an equal sign may be placed next to the utterance to indicate that it is a repetition of an adult utterance.

                                two cookies/
    M: =/ I only see one in there/

                                one in there/=

23. The symbol # may be used to indicate that there is material on the tape that is not transcribed. It can only appear on the left side and usually represents conversations between adults. The symbol is only used when it is reasonable to assume that the child is not attending to or, in fact, does not hear the conversation.

24. (lf)   = laugh
    (wh)   = whisper
    (cr)   = cry   These abbreviations may be useful for behavior that
    (wm)   = whimper   occurs fairly frequently. The abbreviation should
    (wn)   = whine   appear on the left side of the line.
    (y)   = yell
    (gr)   = grunt

Labeling

25. Pages should be numbered front and back, with numbers in upper right corner.

26. In order to make it easier to locate material on the tape, a number should be placed in the right margin every time the counter on the tape recorder registers a multiple of 50.

27. Every time a new tape or a new side of a tape is started, the tape number, side number (1 or 2) and the date and time of the recording session (if different from the previous tape or side) should be indicated.

Appendix A.2
ADDENDUM TO CONVENTIONS FOR TRANSCRIPTION OF CHILD LANGUAGE RECORDINGS: PROCEDURES FOR TRANSCRIBING VIDEO RECORDED DATA[1]

The aim is to transcribe all speech by the child (column 3) and to the child or within his or her hearing (column 2), to describe the accompanying nonverbal behaviors of the child (column 4) and of other speakers (column 1), and to record information about the context in which the verbal and nonverbal behaviors occur (column 1). The format is illustrated below. Persons other than the child are identified by an initial (e.g., D for Debbie, J for Jerry). Descriptions of nonverbal behaviors and context are enclosed in parentheses.

Column 1	Column 2	Colume 3	Colume 4
Context and behaviors of other speakers	Utterances of other speakers	Child utterances	Child behaviors
(D giving block to S)	D: here's the block/	block//	(S accepting block)

Recording Nonverbal Behavior[2]

1. Nonverbal behaviors consist primarily of actions and gestures. The abbreviation [gs] is used for gestures followed by a description of the type of gesture, for example,

   ([gs] arms straight up over head)

Facial expressions may be included, but are optional.

---

[1] Prepared by Peggy Miller, Lorraine Rocissano, Karin Lifter, and Ellen Tanouye.
[2] The following includes frequently used descriptive terms.
(1) Inspect—to explore visually.
(2) Examine—to explore visually and manually.
(3) Extend—to hold out arm at shoulder level, with or without an object; often an object is extended toward someone in a "display" or "showing" gesture.
(4) Give—to transfer an object from the giver's hand to a recipient; "give" is distinguished from "extend" as follows: (a) an object is always involved; (b) the action is "completed;" that is, another person received the object.

2. The temporal ordering of utterances and behaviors is represented in the following ways.

    a. Utterances or behaviors occurring simultaneously appear on the same line; two or more simultaneous behaviors performed by the same person appear on the same line, separated by commas.

    b. Utterances or behaviors occurring successively appear on successive lines.

1	2	3	4
(M entering room)	M: Where's your truck?/		
		on table/	(putting block aside) (approaches table, smiles)

3. Direction of the child's gaze is noted whenever possible, using the following set of symbols.

    a. Gaze directed toward an object: doll .
    b. Gaze directed toward a person: D , where D is the persons's initial.
    c. Gaze directed toward camera: · .
    d. Shifting gaze: ~ .
    e. Cannot be determined: ? .

Each utterance is followed immediately by one of the above symbols, indicating the direction of gaze that accompanies the utterance. "Accompanies" is defined as "roughly simultaneous" with the utterance. Finer temporal discriminations (e.g., shift of gaze immediately prior to onset of utterance versus during utterance) are not made.

1	2	3	4
			(stringing beads)
		want cookie/ M	(turning toward M)
(M sitting at table)	M: you want a cookie?/		

4. *Optional.* Record direction of gaze of other speakers, using procedures in number 3 above.

5. Direction of child's gaze following (in response to) another speaker's utterance is noted whenever possible, immediately following the speaker's utterance using the following set of symbols.

    a. Gaze directed toward an object: doll .
    b. Gaze directed toward a person: D , where D is the person's initial.
    c. Gaze directed toward camera: ⊙ .
    d. Shifting gaze: ~ .
    e. Cannot be determined: ? .

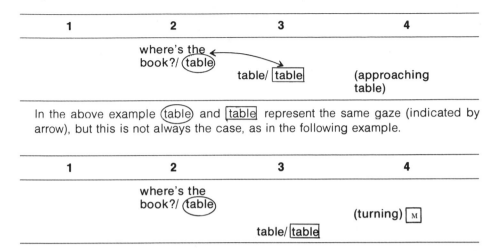

In the above example (table) and |table| represent the same gaze (indicated by arrow), but this is not always the case, as in the following example.

1	2	3	4
	where's the book?/ (table)		
			(turning) M
		table/|table|	

6. Pointing gestures made by the child are represented as follows, with the direction of the gesture enclosed in parentheses.

   a. Pointing toward an object: $\xrightarrow{\text{(cup)}}$.

   b. Pointing toward a person: $\xrightarrow{\text{(K)}}$ where K is the person's initial.

   c. Pointing toward camera: $\xrightarrow{\text{(·)}}$

   d. Cannot be determined: $\xrightarrow{?}$.

   If a pointing gesture accompanies a child utterance, the appropriate symbol is written above the utterance in column 3. "Accompanies" is defined as "roughly simultaneous" with the utterance. Finer temporal discriminations (e.g., pointing immediately prior to onset of utterance versus during utterance) are not made.

1	2	3	4
		$\xrightarrow{\text{(ball)}}$ ball/	(walking toward ball)

   If a pointing gesture does not accompany a child utterance, the appropriate symbol is written in column 4, along with other nonverbal behaviors.

1	2	3	4
		baby eat/	(putting cookie to doll's mouth) (turning toward juice $\xrightarrow{\text{(juice)}}$)

Note here that the action (turning) and the pointing gesture (→) are simultaneous.

1	2	3	4
		baby eat/	(putting cookie to doll's mouth) (turning toward juice (juice) ⟶)

Note here that the action and pointing gesture are successive.

7. *Optional.* Record pointing gestures made by other speakers, using procedures in number 6 above.

Recording Utterances

1. An idiosyncratic pronunciation of a word is indicated with an asterisk as in the following example where "truck" is pronounced "kuk".

1	2	3	4
		truck/*	

2. An adult's misinterpretation of a child's utterance is indicated with a check.

1	2	3	4
	want mine ↑ /√	wait a minute/	

3. Guesses about the form of unintelligible utterances are followed by a question mark and are enclosed in parentheses above the utterance.

1	2	3	4
		(read book?) – – –/	

Miscellaneous

1. An arrow is drawn from one line to the next when an utterance is too long for the space provided.

1	2	3	4
	do you want⤵ ↳to go to the⤵ ↳zoo?/		

2. The exact repetition of a nonverbal behavior is indicated by an "X" enclosed in parentheses. If the actor is someone other than the child, the actor's initial is also given.

1	2	3	4
		bear/	(shakes bear) (X)
(M shakes head negatively) (M X)	poor bear!/		

3. A small diagram of the room and of the subjects' positions relative to one another is drawn at the top of each page, as in the following example.

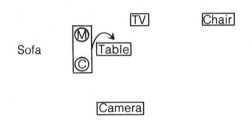

Appendix B
DEFINITIONS OF CONTENT CATEGORIES

Existence. An object exists in the environment and the child either looks at it, points to it, touches it, or picks it up while naming or pointing out its existence with single words such as the word "dish," the word "there" or, even, perhaps, the stereotype question: "What's dis?" The names of objects like "cookie" or "dog" eventually evolve into identification sentences such as: "This cookie" and then, eventually, "This is a cookie." This class of utterances has been called "ostension" by Braine (1971) and Schlesinger (1971) and "nomination" by Brown (1970). *Existence* may be signaled by /ə/ (as an apparent article) or variants of the demonstrative forms "that," "this," and may eventually include some form of the copula verb "to be."

Nonexistence-Disappearance. Utterances are placed in this category if they make reference to the *disappearance* of an object or the *nonexistence* of an object or action in a context in which its *existence* might somehow be expected. Children use terms such as "no," "all gone," "no more," and "away."

Recurrence. Utterances are placed in this category if they make reference to the reappearance of an object, or another instance of an object or event with or without the original instance of the object still present.

Rejection. If the child opposes an action or refuses an object that is in the context or imminent within the situation and uses forms of negation, the utterances are referred to as *rejection*.

Denial. Utterances are categorized as *denial* if the child negates the identity, state, or event expressed in another's utterance or in his or her own previous utterance.

Attribution. Utterances that make reference to properties of objects with respect to (1) an inherent *state* of the object (e.g., "broke" and "sharp"), or (2) *specification* of an object that distinguishes it from others in its class (e.g., "red," "big," and "bread" in "bread book" are categorized as attributions). Another form of coding *attribution* is to refer to an attribute as a condition of the object with a copula sentence such as "the car is big." This *form* of coding *attribution* is placed under *state*.

Possession. Utterances placed in this category make reference to objects within the domains of different persons. A class of words (such as "Mommy," "Daddy," "Baby") can mean the same thing (Possessor) in relation to a class of different words (such as "sweater," "coat," "record") that mean something else (Object Possessed); or, alternatively, Object Possessed can be specified in relation to a constant pro-form such as "my." As with *attribution*, there is an alternative form for coding *possession*; one can specify the possessive state of the object with the copula sentence such as "The car is mine." This form of coding *possession* is placed under *state*.

Action. Utterances placed in this category refer to two kinds of movement when the goal of the movement is not a change in the location or an object or person (see Locative Action). Some utterances refer to *action* that affects an object other than to change its location. Other *action* utterances refer to movements by actors (persons or things) in events where the movement does not affect another person or object.

Locative Action. Utterances in this category refer to movement where the goal of the movement is a change in location of a person or object. The movement that caused this change in location occurs within the speech event. Most *locative actions* entail an agent, an affected object, and a place or the goal of the movement. Where the agent and affected object or person are the same, the single constituent is designated as mover. When utterances in this category specify a movement by an agent that caused another object (patient) to change place, the preverbal constituent, whether or not expressed, is referred to as patient.

Locative State. Utterances in this category refer to the relationship between a person or object and its location, where no movement established the locative relation within the context of the speech event, that is, immediately before, during, or after the child's utterance. *Locative states* entail a person or object located and a place.

State. Utterances in this category make reference to states of affairs usually involving persons or other animate beings.
1. An *internal state,* usually with a verb form such as "like," "need," or "want."
2. An *external state of affairs* as darkness or cold.
3. A *temporary state of ownership or possession.*
4. An *attributive state.*

Quantity. Utterances are placed within this category if they designate the number of objects or persons either by use of a number word, plural -*s* inflection, or adjectives such as "some" or "many."

Notice. Utterances in this category refer to attention to a person, object, or event and necessarily include a verb of notice (such as "see" or "hear"), since such events as seeing or hearing could not be identified by aspects of context and behavior. Eventually, utterances in this category involve two clauses, one of which contains a notice verb focussing on the object of attention, which is the complement of the second clause.

Time. Utterances placed within this category make some reference to time (i.e., ongoing, imminent future, or past), either by use of grammatical morphemes as -*ing,* -*ed,* or irregular past tense of verbs; by adverbs of time such as "now"; or by modals and auxiliary verbs such as "will," "was," or "gonna." Included in this category is the third person singular -*s.* Imminent future was first coded by modal verbs such as "wanna," "gonna," or "have to," and is referred to as *intention.* In addition, utterances are considered under *time* if the relationship between two events and/or states is temporal and this temporal relationship is a dependency relationship. Note that temporal relationships that are not dependent relationships (e.g., a sequential relationship between two independent events and/or states) are placed under the category *coordinate*.

Coordinate. This category includes utterances that refer to two events and/or states that are independent of each other (i.e., the joining of the two does not create a new meaning) but are somehow bound together in space and/or time. The two clauses may include the same or different verbs and may relate to sequential, simultaneous, or static events and/or states. This category is also used here to refer to two objects conjoined intraclausally that are independent of each other but are bound together in space and/or time.

Causality. Utterances included in this category are those that have an implicit or explicit cause and effect relationship between two verb relations, that is, one expressed event or state is dependent on the other for its occurrence. Most often, this relationship is intentional and/or motivational, with one clause referring to an intended or ongoing action or state, and the other clause giving a reason or result of it. This relationship may or may not be expressed by the conjunctions "because" or "so."

Dative. Utterances are included in this category if they designate the recipient of an object or action with or without a preposition.

Specifier. Utterances are included in this category if they specify a particular person, object, or event by contrastive use of the demonstrative pronouns "this" versus "that" or by contrastive use of the articles "the" versus "a." Eventually, specification involves the joining of two clauses, one of which specifies or describes an object or person by function, place, or activity.

Epistemic. When the relationship between two states or an event and a state refers to certainty or uncertainty about an event or state, the relationship is classified as *epistemic*.

Mood. Utterances are included in this category if they express the attitude of the speaker about an event by the use of modal verbs such as "can," "should," or "must."

Antithesis. Utterances are placed within this category when a dependency between two events and/or states exists and the dependency is a contrast between them. Most often the relationship between the clauses is one of opposition, where one clause negates or opposes the other, or exception, where one clause qualifies or limits the other.

Appendix C
INSTRUMENTS THAT ASSESS LANGUAGE
AND LANGUAGE-RELATED BEHAVIORS

Adaptive Behavior Scale (ABS). Washington, D.C.: American Association on Mental Deficiency, 1970.

Agent-Action Test. Ann Arbor, Mich.: University of Michigan Speech Clinic.

Albert Einstein Scales of Sensorimotor Development, by S. K. Escalona and H. C. Corman. New York, Albert Einstein Hospital.

The Arthur Adaptation of the Leiter International Performance Scale, Washington, D.C.: Psychological Service Center Press, 1952.

Assessment of Children's Language Comprehension by R. Foster, J. Giddan, and J. Stark. Palo Alto, Calif.: Consulting Psychologist, 1969, 1973.

Auditory Discrimination Test by J. Wepman. Chicago: Language Research Associates, 1958.

The Basic Concept Inventory: Pupil's Test and Scoring Booklet (Field Research Edition) by S. Engelmann. Chicago: Follett Educational Corporation, 1967.

Berry-Talbott Exploratory Test of Grammar by Mildred Berry. Rockford, Ill.: 1966.

Boehm Test of Basic Concepts by A. Boehm. New York: Psychological Corporation, 1969.

Carrow Elicited Language Inventory by E. Carrow. Austin, Tex.: Learning Concepts. 1974.

Children's Auditory Discrimination Inventory (CADI) by C. Stein. Los Angeles: University of California.

Children's Drawings as a Measure of Intellectual Maturity: A Revision and Extension of the Goodenough Draw-a-Man Tests by D. B. Harris. New York: Harcourt, Brace & World, 1963.

Coloured Progressive Matrices. New York: Psychological Corporation, 1962.

Communicative Evaluation Chart from Infancy to Five Years by R. Anderson, M. Miles and P. Matheny. Cambridge, Mass.: Educators Publishing Service, Inc., 1963.

Denver Developmental Screening Test by W. Frankenburg and J. B. Dodds. Denver, Colo.: LADOCA Project & Publishing Foundation, 1969.

Developmental Articulation Test by R. Hejna. Ann Arbor, Mich.: Speech Materials, 1959.

Detroit Tests of Learning Aptitude by H. Baker and B. Leland. Indianapolis: Bobbs-Merrill Company, 1959.

Fisher-Logeman Test of Articulation Competence by A. Fisher and J. Logeman. Geneva, Ill.: Houghton-Mifflin, 1971.

Full Range Picture Vocabulary Test by R. Ammons and H. Ammons. Missoula, Mont.: Psychological Test Specialists, 1948.

The Goldman-Fristoe Test of Articulation by R. Goldman and M. Fristoe. Circle Pines, Minn.: American Guidance Service, Inc., 1969, 1972.

The Goldman-Fristoe-Woodcock Test of Auditory Discrimination by R. Goldman, M. Fristoe, and R. Woodcock. Circle Pines, Minn.: American Guidance Service, Inc., 1970.

The Houston Test of Language Development by M. Crabtree. Houston: The Houston Test Co., 1958.

The Illinois Test of Psycholinguistic Abilities (Revised Edition) by S. A. Kirk, J. J. McCarthy, and W. D. Kirk. Urbana, Ill.: University of Illinois Press, 1968.

McCarthy Scales of Children's Abilities by D. McCarthy. New York: Psychological Corporation, 1974.

McDonald Deep Test of Articulation by E. McDonald. Pittsburgh: Stanwix House, 1968.

Michigan Picture Language Inventory by L. Lerea. Ann Arbor, Mich.: Speech Clinic, University of Michigan, 1958.

The Miller-Yoder Test of Grammatical Comprehension (M.Y.) by J. Miller and D. Yoder. Madison, Wis.: Communication Development Group, 1972.

Minnesota Preschool Scale by F. Goodenough, K. Maurer, and M. Van Wagenen. Circle Pines, Minn.: American Guidance Service, Inc., 1938, 1940.

Northwestern Syntax Screening Test (NSST) by L. Lee. Evanston, Ill.: The Northwestern University Press, 1971.

Peabody Picture Vocabulary Test (PPVT) by L. Dunn. Circle Pines, Minn.: American Guidance Service, 1959, 1965.

Picture Story Language Test in H. MyKlebust, *Development and Disorders of Written Language, Vol. 1, Picture Story Language Test.* New York: Grune & Stratton, 1965.

Porch Index of Communicative Ability in Children by B. Porch. Palo Alto, Calif.: Consulting Psychologist Press, 1974.

Preschool Attainment Record (PAR) by E. Doll. Circle Pines, Minn.: American Guidance Service, 1966.

Preschool Language Scale by I. L. Zimmerman, V. G. Steiner, and R. Evatt. Columbus, Ohio: Charles Merrill, 1969.

The Pupil Rating Scale: Screening for Learning Disabilities (PRS) by H. Myklebust. New York: Grune & Stratton, 1971.

The Receptive Expressive Emergent Language Scale (REEL) by K. Bzoch, and R. League. Gainesville, Fla.: Language Education Division, Computer Management Corporation, 1971.

Screening Speech Articulation Test by M. Mecham, J. Jex, and J. Jones. Salt Lake City, Utah: Communication Research Associates, 1970.

Sequential Inventory of Communication Development by D. Hedrich and E. Prather. Seattle, Washington: University of Washington Press, 1975.

Slosson Intelligence Test for Children and Adults by R. Slosson. East Aurora, N.Y.: Slosson Educational Publications, Inc., 1963.

Stanford-Binet Intelligence Scale by L. Terman and M. Merrill. Boston: Houghton Mifflin, 1960.

Templin-Darley Tests of Articulation (Second Edition) by M. Templin and F. Darley. Iowa City, Iowa: Bureau of Education Research and Services, University of Iowa, 1969.

Test for Auditory Comprehension of Language by E. Carrow. Austin, Tex.: Learning Concepts, 1973.

TMR Performance Profile for the Severely and Moderately Retarded by A. J. Didula, B. Kaminski, and A. Sternfield. Ridgefield, N.J.: Reporting Service for Children, 1968.

Utah Test of Language Development by M. Mecham, J. L. Joy, and J. D. Jones. Salt Lake City, Utah: Communication Research Associates, 1967.

Verbal Language Development Scale by M. Mecham. Circle Pines, Minn.: American Guidance Service, 1958, 1971.

Washington Speech-Sound Discrimination Test by E. Prather, A. Miner, and L. Sunderland. Danville, Ill.: Interstate Press, 1971.

Wechsler Intelligence Scale for Children (WISC). New York: Psychological Corporation, 1949.

Wechsler Preschool and Primary Scale of Intelligence (WIPSI). New York: Psychological Corporation, 1967.

YEMR: Performance Profile for the Young Moderately and Mildly Retarded by A. Didula, B. Kaminsky, and A. Sternfield. Ridgefield, N.J.: Reporting Service for Children, 1967.

BIBLIOGRAPHY

Abrahams, R. Black talking on the streets. In R. Bauman and J. Sherzer (Eds.), *Explorations in the ethnography of speaking*. London: Cambridge University Press, 1974.

Alajouanine, The., and Lhermitte, F. Acquired aphasia in children. *Brain, 88,* 654-662, 1965.

Allen, D. The development of predication in child language. Unpublished doctoral dissertation, Teachers College, Columbia University, New York, 1973.

Amerman, J., Danilof, R., and Moll, K. Lip and jaw coarticulation for the phoneme /æ/. *Journal of Speech and Hearing Research, 13,* 147-161, 1970.

Amidon, A., and Carey, P. Why five-year-olds cannot understand *before* and *after. Journal of Verbal Learning and Verbal Behavior, 11,* 417-423, 1972.

Ammons, R., and Ammons, H. *Full Range Picture Vocabulary Test*. Missoula, Mont.: Psychological Test Specialists, 1948.

Anderson, R., Miles, M., and Matheny, P. *Communicative evaluation chart from infancy to five years*. Cambridge, Mass.: Educators' Publishing Service, Inc., 1963.

Anglin, J. The extensions of the child's first terms of reference. Paper presented at the Society for Research in Child Development, 1975.

Antinucci, F., and Parisi, D. Early language acquisition: A model and some data. In C. A. Ferguson and D. I. Slobin (Eds.), *Studies of child language development*. New York: Holt, Rinehart & Winston, 1973.

Arthur, G. *The Arthur adaptation of the Leiter International Performance Scale*. Washington, D. C.: Psychological Service Center Press, 1952.

Asch, S. E., and Nerlove, H. The development of double function terms in children. In B. Kaplan and S. Wapner (Eds.), *Perspectives in psychological theory*. New York: International University Press, 1960.

Aten, J., and Davis, J. Disturbances in the perception of auditory sequence in children with minimal cerebral dysfunction. *Journal of Speech and Hearing Research, 11,* 236-246, 1968.

Attneave, F. Transfer of experience with a class-schema to identification-learning of patterns and shapes. *Journal of Experimental Psychology, 54,* 81-88, 1957.

Aurnhammer-Frith, N. Emphasis and meaning in recall in normal and autistic children. *Language and Speech, 12,* 29-38, 1969.

Austin, J. *How to do things with words*. London: Oxford University Press, 1962.

Ayres, A. J. Sensorimotor foundation of academic ability. In W. Cruickshank and D.

Hallahan (Eds.), *Perceptual and learning disabilities in children*. Syracuse: Syracuse University Press, 361–393, 1975.

Baer, D. M., and Guess, D. Teaching productive noun suffixes to severely retarded children. *American Journal of Mental Deficiency, 77*, 498–505, 1973.

Bailey, C. J. Variation resulting from different rule orderings in English phonology. Unpublished manuscript, Georgetown University, 1973.

Baird, R. On the role of change in imitation, comprehension and production. Test results. *Journal of Verbal Learning and Verbal Behavior, 11*, 474–477, 1972.

Bandura, A., and Harris, M. A. Modification of syntactic style, *Journal of Experimental Child Psychology, 4*, 341–352, 1966.

Baratz, J. A bidialectal task for determining language proficiency in economically disadvantaged Negro children. *Child Development, 40*, 889–901, 1969.

Baron, N. The evolution of English periphrastic causatives: Contributions to a general theory of linguistic variation and change. Unpublished Ph.D. dissertation, Stanford University, 1972.

Baron, N., and Isensee, L. M. Effectiveness of manual versus spoken language with an autistic child. Providence, R.I.: Brown University. Unpublished paper. Undated.

Barry, H. *The young aphasic child: Evaluation and training*. Washington, D. C.: Alexander Graham Bell Association for the Deaf, 1961.

Barsch, R. *Achieving perceptual-motor efficiency: A space-oriented approach to learning*. Seattle: Special Child Publications, 1967.

A basic course in manual communication. Silver Spring, Md.: National Association of the Deaf, 1970.

Bates, E. The development of conversational skill in 2, 3, and 4 year olds. Unpublished masters thesis, University of Chicago, 1971.

Bates, E. Pragmatics and sociolinguistics in child language. In D. Morehead and A. Morehead (Eds.), *Normal and deficient child language*. Baltimore: University Park Press, 1976.(a)

Bates, E. *Language in context*. New York: Academic Press, 1976.(b)

Bates, E., Camaioni, L., and Volterra, V. The acquisition of performatives prior to speech. C.N.R. Laboratory Technical Report #129. Rome. Revised version in *Merrill-Palmer Quarterly, 21*, 1975.

Bateson, M. C. Mother-infant exchanges: The epigenesis of conversational interaction. In D. Aronson and R. Rieber (Eds.), *Developmental psycholinguistics and communication disorders. Annals of the New York Academy of Sciences, 263*, 101–113, 1975.

Bauman, R., and Sherzer, J. *Explorations in the ethnography of speaking*. London: Cambridge University Press, 1974.

Beer, C. A view of birds. In A. Pick (Ed.), *The 1972 Minnesota Symposia on Child Psychology*. Minneapolis: University of Minnesota Press, 1973.

Beilin, H. *Studies in the cognitive basis of language development*. New York: Academic Press, 1975.

Belkin, A. Investigation of the functions and forms of children's negative utterances. Unpublished doctoral dissertation, Teachers College, Columbia University, 1975.

Bellugi, U. The acquisition of negation. Unpublished doctoral dissertation, Harvard University, 1967.

Bellugi, U., and Brown, R. (Eds.). The acquisition of language. *Monographs of the Society for Research in Child Development, 29,* (Serial No. 92) 1964.

Bellugi, U., and Klima, E. Roots of language in the sign talk of the deaf. *Psychology Today, 6,* 61–64, 1972.

Bellugi, U., and Klima, E. Two faces of sign: Iconic and abstract. In S. Harnad, H. Steklis, and J. Lancaster (Eds.), *Origins and evolution of language and speech. Annals of the New York Academy of Sciences, 280,* 514–538, 1976.

Bereiter, C., and Engelmann, S. *Teaching disadvantaged children in preschool*. Englewood Cliffs, N. J.: Prentice-Hall, 1966.

Berko, J. The child's learning of English morphology. *Word, 14,* 150–177, 1958.

Berko-Gleason, J. Code switching in children's language. In T. E. Moore (Ed.), *Cognitive development and the acquisition of language*. New York: Academic Press, 1973.

Bernstein, B. Aspects of language and learning in the genesis of the social process. In D. Hymes (Ed.), *Language in culture and society*. New York: Harper & Row, 1964.(a)

Bernstein, B. Elaborated and restricted codes: Their social origins and some consequences. In J. Gumperz and D. Hymes (Eds.), The ethnography of communication. *American Anthropologist, 66,* (16) Part 2, 1964.(b)

Bernstein, B. A sociolinguistic approach to socialization with some reference to educability. In J. Gumperz and D. Hymes (Eds.), *Directions in sociolinguistics: The ethnography of communication*. New York: Holt, Rinehart & Winston, Inc., 1972.

Berry, M. *Berry-Talbott exploratory test of grammar*. Rockford, Ill.: 1966.

Berry, M. *Language disorders of children: The bases and diagnoses*. New York: Appleton-Century-Crofts, 1969.

Bersoff, D. Current functioning myth: An overlooked fallacy in psychological assessment. *Journal of Consulting and Clinical Psychology, 37,* 319–393, 1971.

Bever, T. G. The cognitive basis for linguistic structures. In J. Hayes (Ed.), *Cognition and the development of language*. New York: John Wiley & Sons, 1970.

Bierwisch, M. Semantics. In J. Lyons (Ed.), *New horizons in linguistics*. Harmondsworth, Middlesex, England: Penguin Books, 1970.

Blank, M. *Teaching learning in the preschool: A dialogue approach*. Columbus, Ohio: C. Merrill, 1973.

Blank, M. Mastering the intangible through language. In D. Aaronson and R. Rieber (Eds.), *Developmental psycholinguistics and communication disorders. Annals of the New York Academy of Sciences, 263,* 44–58, 1975.

Blanton, R. Language learning and performance in the deaf. In S. Rosenberg and J. Koplin (Eds.), *Developments in applied psycholinguistics research*. New York: MacMillan, 1968.

Blasdell, R., and Jensen, P. Stress and word position determinants of imitation in first language learners. *Journal of Speech and Hearing Research, 13*, 193–202, 1970.

Bliss, C. *Semantography*. Sydney, Australia: Semantography Publications.

Bloch, O. Les premiers stades du language de l'enfant. *Journal de Psychologie, 18*, 693–712, 1921.

Bloom, B., Hastings, J., and Madaus, G. *Handbook on formative and summative evaluation of student learning*. New York: McGraw-Hill, 1971.

Bloom, L. A comment on Lee's "Developmental sentence types: A method for comparing normal and deviant syntactic development." *Journal of Speech and Hearing Disorders, 32*, 294–296, 1967.

Bloom, L. *Language development: Form and function in emerging grammars*. Cambridge, Mass.: The M.I.T. Press, 1970.(a)

Bloom, L. Child language, adult model. Review of Paula Menyuk, *Sentences children use. Contemporary Psychology, 15*, 182–184, 1970.(b)

Bloom, L. Why not pivot grammar? *Journal of Speech and Hearing Disorders, 36*, 40–50, 1971.

Bloom, L. *One word at a time: The use of single-word utterances before syntax*. The Hague: Mouton, 1973.

Bloom, L. The accountability of evidence in studies of child language. Comment on Everyday preschool interpersonal speech usage: Methodological, developmental, and sociolinguistic studies. In F. Schacter, K. Kirshner, B. Klips, M. Friedricks, and K. Sanders, *Monographs of the Society for Research in Child Development, 39*, (Serial No. 156) 1974.(a)

Bloom, L. Review of J. Hayes (Ed.), *Cognition and the development of language. Language, 50*, 398–412, 1974.(b)

Bloom, L. Talking, understanding and thinking: Developmental relationship between receptive and expressive language. In R. L. Schiefelbusch and L. Lloyd (Eds.), *Language perspectives—Acquisition, retardation, and intervention*. Baltimore: University Park Press, 285–312, 1974.(c)

Bloom, L. Language development. In F. Horowitz (Ed.), *Review of child development research*. Vol. 4. *Society for Research in Child Development*. Chicago: University of Chicago Press, 1975.

Bloom, L. An interactive perspective on language development. Keynote address, Eigth Annual Forum on Child Language Research, Stanford University. In *Papers and reports on child language development*, Department of Linguistics, Stanford University, 1976.

Bloom, L., and Hood, L. Functions of questions in children's spontaneous speech. In preparation.

Bloom, L., Hood, L., and Lightbown, P. Imitation in language development: If, when and why. *Cognitive Psychology, 6*, 380–420, 1974.

Bloom, L., and Lahey, M. A proposed program for the treatment of language disordered children. Teachers College, Columbia University. Unpublished manuscript, 1972.

Bloom, L., Lightbown, P., and Hood, L. Structure and variation in child language. *Monographs of the Society for Research in Child Development, 40* (Serial No. 160), 1975.

Bloom, L., Miller, P., and Hood, L. Variation and reduction as aspects of competence in language development. In A. Pick (Ed.), *Minnesota Symposia on Child Psychology, Volume 9*. Minneapolis, University of Minnesota Press, 1975.

Bloom, L., Rocissano, L., and Hood, L. Adult-child discourse: Developmental interaction between information processing and linguistic knowledge. *Cognitive Psychology, 8*, 521–552, 1976.

Bloomfield, L. *Language*. New York: Holt, Rinehart & Winston, 1933.

Blurton-Jones, N. Introduction: Characteristics of ethological studies of human behavior. In N. Blurton-Jones, (Ed.). *Ethological studies of child behavior*. London: Cambridge University Press, 1972.

Boehm, A. *Boehm test of basic concepts*. New York: Psychological Corporation, 1969.

Bohn, W. First steps in verbal expression. *Pedagogical Seminary, 21*, 578–595, 1914.

Bonvillian, J. D., and Nelson, K. E. Sign language acquisition in a mute autistic boy. *Journal of Speech and Hearing Disorders, 41*, 339–347, 1976.

Bornstein, H. A description of some current sign systems designed to represent English. *American Annals of the Deaf, 118*, 454–463, 1973.

Bornstein, H. Signed English. A manual approach to English language. *Journal of Speech and Hearing Disorders, 39*, 330–343, 1974.

Bortner, M. Phrenology, localization, and learning disabilities. *Journal of Special Education, 5*, 23–29, 1971.

Bortner, M., and Birch, H. G. Patterns of intellectual ability in emotionally disturbed and brain-damaged children. *Journal of Special Education, 3*, 351–369, 1969.

Bower, T. G. R. *Development in infancy*. San Francisco: W. H. Freeman & Co., 1974.

Bowerman, M. *Early syntactic development: A cross-linguistic study with special reference to Finnish*. London: Cambridge University Press, 1973.(a)

Bowerman, M. Structural relationships in children's utterances: Syntactic or semantic? In T. Moore (Ed.), *Cognitive development and the acquisition of language*. New York: Academic Press, 1973.(b)

Bowerman, M. Learning the structure of causative verbs: A study in the relationship of cognitive, semantic, and syntactic development. *Papers and reports on child language*, Department of Linguistics, Stanford University June 1974.(a)

Bowerman, M. Comment on Structure and variation in child language. In L. Bloom, P. Lightbown, and L. Hood, *Monographs of the Society for Research in Child Development, 40*, (Serial No. 160), 1975.

Bradbury, B., and Lunzer, E. A. The learning of grammatical inflections in normal and subnormal children. *Journal of Child Psychology and Psychiatry, 13,* 239-248, 1972.

Braine, M. The ontogeny of English phrase structure: The first phase. *Language, 39,* 1-13, 1963.(a)

Braine, M. On learning the grammatical order of words. *Psychological Review, 70,* 323-348, 1963(b). Reprinted in L. Jakobovits and M. Miron (Eds.), *Readings in the psychology of language.* Englewood Cliffs, N. J.: Prentice Hall, 1967.

Braine, M. On the basis of phrase structure: A reply to Bever, Fodor, and Weksel. *Psychological Review, 72,* 483-492, 1965. Reprinted in L. Jakobovits and M. Miron (Eds.), *Readings in the psychology of language.* Englewood Cliffs, N. J.: Prentice Hall, 1967.

Braine, M. On two types of models of the internalization of grammars. In D. Slobin (Ed.), *The ontogenesis of grammar.* New York: Academic Press, 1971.

Braine, M. Length constraints, reduction rules, and holophrastic processes in children's word combinations. *Journal of Verbal Learning and Verbal Behavior, 13,* 448-456, 1974.(a)

Braine, M., On what might constitute a learnable phonology. *Language, 50,* 270-300, 1974.(b)

Braine, M. Children's first word combinations. *Monographs of the Society for Research in Child Development. 41,* (Serial No. 164), 1976.

Branigan, G. Organizational constraints during the one word period. Paper presented at the First Annual Boston University Conference on Language Development, Boston, October 1976.

Brannon, J. Linguistic word classes in the spoken language of normal, hard-of-hearing and deaf children. *Journal of Speech and Hearing Research, 11,* 279-287, 1968.

Bransford, J., and Franks, J. The abstraction of linguistic ideas. *Cognitive Psychology, 2,* 331-350, 1971.

Bransford, J., and Johnson, M. Contextual prerequisites for understanding: Some investigations of comprehension and recall. *Journal of Verbal Learning and Verbal Behavior, 11,* 717-726, 1972.

Bransford, J., and Nitsch, K. How can we come to understand things that we did not previously understand? In J. Kavanagh and P. Strange (Eds.), *Language and speech in the laboratory, school and clinic.* Cambridge, Mass.: M.I.T. Press, 1977.

Brawley, E. R., Harris, F. R., Allen, K. E., Fleming, R. S., and Peterson, R. F. Behavior modification of an autistic child. *Behavioral Science, 14,* 87-97, 1969.

Brenner, R. An experimental investigation of memory span. *Journal of Experimental Psychology, 26,* 467-482, 1940.

Bricker, D. D. Imitative sign training as a facilitator of word-object association with low-fuctioning children. *American Journal of Mental Deficiency, 76,* 509-516, 1972.

Bricker, W. A. A systematic approach to language training. In R. L. Schiefelbusch, (Ed.), *Language of the mentally retarded.* Baltimore: University Park Press, 75-92, 1972.

Bricker, W. A., and Bricker, D. D. An early language training strategy. In R. Schiefelbusch and L. Lloyd (Eds.), *Language perspectives—Acquisition, retardation, and intervention*. Baltimore: University Park Press, 429–468, 1974.

Bricker, W. A., and Bricker, D. D. A program of language training for the severely language handicapped child. *Exceptional Children, 37,* 101–113, 1970.

Broen, P. The verbal environment of the language learning child. *ASHA Monographs,* Number 17. Washington, D. C.: American Speech and Hearing Association, 1972.

Brown, R. Language and categories. Appendix to Bruner, J. S., Goodnow, J. J., and Austin, G. A. *A study of thinking*. New York: John Wiley & Sons, Inc., 1956.

Brown, R. How shall a thing be called? *Psychological Review, 65,* 14–21, 1958.

Brown, R. *Social psychology*. New York: The Free Press, 1965.

Brown, R. The development of Wh questions in child speech. *Journal of Verbal Learning and Verbal Behavior, 7,* 279–290, 1968.

Brown, R. *A first language, the early stages*. Cambridge, Mass.: Harvard University Press, 1973.

Brown, R., and Bellugi, U. Three processes in the child's acquisition of syntax. *Harvard Educational Review, 34,* 133–151, 1964.

Brown, R., Cazden, C., and Bellugi, U. The child's grammar from I to III. In J. P. Hill (Ed.), *Minnesota Symposia on Child Psychology,* Vol. 2. Minneapolis: University of Minnesota Press, 1969.

Brown, R., and Ford, M. Address in American English. In D. Hymes (Ed.), *Language in culture and society*. New York: Harper & Row, 1964.

Brown, R., and Fraser, C. The acquisition of syntax. In C. N. Cofer and B. Musgrave (Eds.), *Verbal behavior and verbal learning: Problems and processes*. New York: McGraw Hill, 158–197, 1963. Also in Bellugi, U., and Brown, R. The acquisition of language. *Monographs of the Society for Research in Child Development*, (Serial No. 92.), 1964.

Brown, R., and Hanlon, C. Derivational complexity and order of acquisition in child speech. In J. Hayes (Ed.), *Cognition and the development of language*. New York: John Wiley & Sons, 1970.

Bruner, J. The ontogenesis of speech acts. *Journal of Child Language, 2,* 1–19, 1975.

Buddenhagen, R. *Establishing vocalizations in mute mongoloid children*. Champaign, Ill.: Research Press, 1971.

Buium, N., Rynders, J., and Turnure, J. Early maternal linguistic environment of normal and Down's syndrome language-learning children. *American Journal of Mental Deficiency, 79,* 52–58, 1974.

Buros, O. K. (Ed.). *The mental measurements yearbook,* Vol. 7. Highland Park, N. J.: Gryphan Press, 1972.

Butterfield, E. C., and Cairns, G. F., Discussion summary—Infant reception research. In R. L. Schiefelbusch and L. Lloyd (Eds.), *Language perspectives—Acquisition, retardation, and intervention*. Baltimore: University Park Press, 1974.

Bzoch, K., and League, R. *The Receptive Expressive Emergent Language Scale*

(REEL). Gainesville, Fla.: Language Education Division, Computer Management Corporation, 1971.

Calvert, D., Ceriotti, M., and Geile, S. A program for aphasic children. *Volta Review, 68*, 144–149, 1966.

Cameron, T., Livson, M. & Bayley. N. Infant vocalizations and their relation to mature intelligence. *Science,* 1967, *157,* 331–333.

Carrier, J. Application of functional analysis and a non-speech response mode to teaching language. In L. McReynolds (Ed.), *Developing systematic procedures for training children's language. ASHA Monographs*, Number 18, 47–95, 1974.(a)

Carrier, J. Nonspeech noun usage training with severely and profoundly retarded children. *Journal of Speech and Hearing Research, 17,* 510–518, 1974.(b)

Carrow, M. A. The development of auditory comprehension of language structure in children. *Journal of Speech and Hearing Disorders, 33,* 99–111, 1968.

Carrow, E. Assessment of speech and language in children. In J. E. McLean, D. E. Yoder, and R. L. Schiefelbusch, (Eds.) *Language intervention with the retarded.* Baltimore: University Park Press, 1972.

Carrow, E. *Test for Auditory Comprehension of Language.* Austin, Tex: Learning Concepts, 1973.

Carrow, E. A test using elicited imitations in assessing grammatical structure in children. *Journal of Speech and Hearing Disorders, 39,* 437–444, 1974.

Cazden, C. Environmental assistance to the child's acquisition of grammar. Unpublished doctoral dissertation, Harvard University, 1965.

Cazden, C. Subcultural differences in child language: An inter-disciplinary review. *Merrill-Palmer Quarterly, 12,* 185–219, 1966.

Cazden, C. The acquisition of noun and verb inflections. *Child Development, 39,* 433–438, 1968.

Cazden, C. The neglected situation in child language research and education. In F. Williams (Ed.), *Language and poverty, perspectives on a theme.* Chicago: Markham, 1970.

Cazden, C. *Child language and education.* New York: Holt, Rinehart & Winston, 1972.

Cazden, C., John, V., and Hymes, D. (Eds.). *Functions of language in the classroom.* New York: Teachers College Press, 1972.

Cedergren, H., and Sankoff, D. Variable rules: Performance as a statistical reflection of competence. *Language, 50,* 333–355, 1974.

Chafe, W. *Meaning and the structure of language.* Chicago: University of Chicago Press, 1971.

Chambaz, M., Leroy, C., and Messeant, G. Les "petits mots" de coordination: Etude diachronique de leur apparition chez quatre enfants entre 3 et 4 ans. *Langue Francaise*, Apparition de la syntaxe chez l'enfant, *27,* 38–54, 1975.

Chapman, R. Discussion summary—Developmental relationship between receptive and expressive language. In R. L. Schiefelbusch and L. L. Lloyd (Eds.), *Language perspectives—Acquisition, retardation and intervention.* Baltimore: University Park Press, 1974.

Chapman, R. Comprehension strategies in children. In J. Kavanagh and P. Strange (Eds.), *Language and speech in the laboratory, school and clinic.* Cambridge, Mass.: The M.I.T. Press, 1977.

Chapman, R., and Miller, J. Word order in early two and three word sentences. *Journal of Speech and Hearing Research, 18,* 355–371, 1975.

Cherry, C. *On human communication; A review, a survey, and a criticism.* Cambridge, Mass.: The M.I.T. Press, 1957.

Chipman, H., and deDardel, C. Developmental study of comprehension and production of the pronoun *IT. Journal of Psycholinguistic Research, 3,* 91–99, 1974.

Chomsky, N. *Syntactic structures.* The Hague: Mouton, 1957.

Chomsky, N. Review of "Verbal Behavior," by B. F. Skinner. *Language, 35,* 26–58, 1959.

Chomsky, N. *Aspects of the theory of syntax.* Cambridge, Mass.: The M.I.T. Press, 1965.

Chomsky, N. *Cartesian linguistics: A chapter in the history of rationalist thought.* New York: Harper & Row, 1966.

Chomsky, N. Language and the mind. In A. Bar-Adon and W. Leopold (Eds.), *Child language.* Englewood Cliffs, N. J.: Prentice Hall, 1971.

Chomsky, N. *Language and mind.* New York: Harcourt Brace Jovanovich, 1972.(a)

Chomsky, N. *Studies on semantics in generative grammar.* The Hague: Mouton, 1972.(b)

Chomsky, N. and Halle, M., *The sound pattern of English.* New York: Harper and Row, 1968.

Church, J. *Language and the discovery of reality.* New York: Vintage Books, 1961.

Churchill, D. The relation of infantile autism and early childhood schizophrenia to developmental language disorders of childhood. *Journal of Autism and Childhood Schizophrenia, 2,* 182–197, 1972.

Cicciarelli, A., Broen, P., and Siegel, G. Language assessment procedures. In L. L. Lloyd (Ed.), *Communication assessment and intervention strategies.* Baltimore: University Park Press, 777–800, 1976.

Clancy, P. The acquisition of conjunction in Italian. Unpublished manuscript, Berkeley, 1974.

Clancy, P., Jacobsen, T., and Silva, M. The acquisition of conjunction: A cross-linguistic study. Paper presented at the Eighth Annual Forum on Child Language Research, Stanford University. In *Papers and reports on child language development.,* Department of Linguistics, Stanford University, 1976.

Clark, C. R., and Woodcock, R. W. Graphic systems of communication. In L. Lloyd (Ed.), *Communication assessment and intervention strategies.* Baltimore: University Park Press, 1976.

Clark, E. How young children describe events in time. In G. B. Flores d'Arcais and W. J. M. Levelt (Eds.), *Advances in psycholinguistics*. New York: American Elsevier, 1970.

Clark, E. On the acquisition on the meaning of *before* and *after. Journal of Verbal Learning and Verbal Behavior, 10*, 266–275, 1971.

Clark, E. What's in a word? On the child's acquisition of semantics in his first language. In T. Moore, (Ed.), *Cognitive development and the acquisition of language*. New York: Academic Press, 1973.(a)

Clark, E. Non-linguistic strategies and the acquisition of word meanings. *Cognition, 2*, 161–182, 1973.(b)

Clark, E. How children describe time and order. In C. A. Ferguson and D. I. Slobin (Eds.), *Studies of child language development*. New York: Holt, Rinehart & Winston, 1973.(c)

Clark, E. Some aspects of the conceptual basis for first language acquisition. In R. Schiefelbusch and L. Lloyd (Eds.), *Language perspectives—Acquisition, retardation, and intervention*. Baltimore: University Park Press, 1974.

Clark, E., and Garnica, O. Is he coming or going? On the acquisition of deictic verbs. *Journal of Verbal Learning and Verbal Behavior, 13*, 559–572, 1974.

Clark, R. Performing without competence. *Journal of Child Language, 1*, 1–10, 1974.

Clark, R., Hutcheson, S., and van Buren, P. Comprehension and production in language acquisition. *Journal of Linguistics, 10*, 39–54, 1974.

Cohen, L., and Salapatek, P. (Eds.). *Infant perception: From sensation to cognition*, Vols. I and II. New York: Academic Press, 1975.

Cole, P., and Morgan, J. L. (Eds.), *Syntax and semantics. Vol. 3, Speech Acts*. New York: Academic Press, 1975.

Collins, A., and Quillian, M. How to make a language user. In E. Tulving and W. Donaldson (Eds.), *Organization in memory*. New York: Academic Press, 1972.

Condon, W., and Sander, L. Neonate movement is synchronized with adult speech: Interactional participation and language acquisition. *Science, 183* (4120), 99–101, 1974.

Connelly, R. The effect of knowledge of linguistic codes on auditory sequential memory. Unpublished manuscript, Montclair State College, New Jersey, 1974.

Corman, H., and Escalona, S. Stages of sensorimotor development: A replication study. *Merrill-Palmer Quarterly, 15*, 351–61, 1969.

Corrigan, R. Patterns of individual communication and cognitive development. Unpublished doctoral dissertation, University of Denver, 1976.

Corsaro, W. A. Sociolinguistic patterns in adult-child interaction. Unpublished manuscript, Indiana University, n.d.

Courtright, J. A., and Courtright, I. C. Imitative modeling as a theoretical base for instructing language-disordered children. *Journal of Speech and Hearing Research, 19*, 655–663, 1976.

Crabtree, N. *The Houston Test of Language Development*. Houston: The Houston Test Co., 1958.

Creak, M., and committee. Schizophrenic syndrome in childhood. *Cerebral Palsy Bulletin, 3,* 501–504, 1961.

Cromer, R. The development of temporal reference during the acquisition of language. Unpublished doctoral dissertation, Harvard University, 1968.

Cromer, R. The development of the ability to decenter in time. *British Journal of Psychology, 62,* 353–365, 1971.

Cromer, R. The development of language and cognition. The cognition hypothesis. In B. Foss (Ed.), *New perspectives in child development*. New York: Penguin Education, 1974.

Cronbach, L. *Essentials of psychological testing*. New York: Harper & Row, 1970.

Cruickshank, W. M., Bentsen, F. A., Retzburg, F. H., and Tannhauser, M. T. *A teaching method for brain injured and hyperactive children*. Syracuse, N. Y.: Syracuse University Press, 1961.

Crystal, D. *Prosodic systems and intonation in English*. London: Cambridge University Press, 1969.

Crystal, D., Fletcher, P., and Garman, M. *The grammatical analysis of language disability: A procedure for assessment and remediation*. London: Edward Arnold, 1976.

Cunningham, M. A comparison of the language of psychotic and non-psychotic children who are mentally retarded. *Journal of Child Psychology and Psychiatry, 9,* 229–244, 1968.

Cunningham, R. Developing question asking skills. In J. Weigard (Ed.), *Developing teacher competencies*. Englewood Cliffs, N. J.: Prentice-Hall, 1971, 81–131.

Darley, F. L., and Moll, K. Reliability of language measures and size of language sample. *Journal of Speech and Hearing Research, 3,* 166–173, 1960.

Davis, H., and Silverman, S. R. *Hearing and deafness*. New York: Holt, Rinehart & Winston, 1970.

de Boysson-Bardies, B. L'étude de la négation: Aspects syntaxiques et lexicaux. Unpublished doctoral dissertation, L'Université de Paris, Paris, 1972.

de Hirsch, K. Differential diagnosis between aphasic and schizophrenic language in children. *Journal of Speech and Hearing Disorders, 32,* 3–10, 1967.

Delacato, C. H. *The diagnosis and treatment of speech and reading problems*. Springfield, Ill.: Charles Thomas, 1963.

Delack, J. B. Aspects of infant speech development in the first year of life. *Canadian Journal of Linguistics, 21,* 17–37, 1976.

deLaguna, G. *Speech: Its function and development*. Bloomington, Ind.: Indiana University Press, 1963. (First edition, 1927).

Dever, R. A comparison of the results of a revised version of Berko's test of morphology with the free speech of mentally retarded children. *Journal of Speech and Hearing Research, 15,* 169–178, 1972.

Dever, R., and Bauman, P. Scale of children's clausal development. In T. Longhurst (Ed.), *Linguistic analysis of children's speech*. New York: M.S.S. Information Corporation, 1974.

de Villiers, J., and de Villiers, P. A cross-sectional study of the acquisition of grammatical morphemes. *Journal of Psycholinguistic Research, 2,* 267–278, 1973.

de Villiers, J., and de Villiers, P. Competence and performance in child language: Are children really competent to judge? *Journal of Child Language, 1,* 11–22, 1974.

Dittman, A. T. Developmental factors in conversational behavior. *The Journal of Communication, 22,* 404–423, 1972.

Dixon, T., and Horton, D. *Verbal behavior and general behavior theory.* Englewood Cliffs, N. J.: Prentice-Hall, 1968.

Doll, E. A. *Vineland Social Maturity Scale.* Minneapolis: American Guidance Service, 1965.

Donaldson, M., and Wales, R. On the acquisition of some relational terms. In J. Hayes (Ed.), *Cognition and the development of language.* New York: John Wiley & Sons, 1970.

Dore, J. The development of speech acts. Unpublished doctoral dissertation, City University of New York, 1973.

Dore, J. Holophrases, speech acts, and language universals. *Journal of Child Language, 2,* 21–40, 1975.

Dore, J. Children's illocutionary acts. In R. O. Freedle (Ed.), *Discourse processes: Advances in research and theory. Vol. I: Discourse production and comprehension.* Norwood, N.J.: Ablex Publishing Co., 1977.

Dore, J., Franklin, M., Miller, R., and Ramer, A. Transitional phenomena in early language acquisition. *Journal of Child Language, 3,* 13–28, 1976.

Duchan, J. F., and Erickson, J. G. Normal and retarded children's understanding of semantic relations in different verbal contexts. *Journal of Speech and Hearing Research, 19,* 767–776, 1976.

Duncan, S., Jr. Some signals and rules for taking speaking turns in conversations. *Journal of Personality and Social Psychology, 23,* 283–292, 1972.

Dunn, L. *Peabody Picture Vocabulary Test* (PPVT). Circle Pines, Minn.: American Guidance Service, 1959.

Dunn, L. *Expanded Manual: Peabody Picture Vocabulary Test.* Circle Pines, Minn.: American Guidance Service, 1965.

Efron, R. Temporal perception, aphasia, and déjà vu. *Brain, 86,* 403–424, 1963.

Eimas, P. Linguistic processing of speech by young infants. In R. L. Schiefelbusch and L. Lloyd (Eds.), *Language perspectives—Acquisition, retardation, and intervention.* Baltimore: University Park Press, 1974.

Eimas, P. Speech perception in early infancy. In L. Cohen and P. Salapatek, (Eds.), *Infant perception: From sensation to cognition, Vol. II. Perception of space, speech and sound.* New York: Academic Press, 1975.

Eimas, P., and Corbit, J. Selective adaptation of linguistic feature detectors. *Cognitive Psychology, 4,* 99-109, 1973.

Eimas, P., Siqueland, E., Jusczyk, P., and Vigorito, J. Speech perception in infants. *Scence, 171,* 303-306, 1971.

Eisenberg, L. Psychotic disorders in childhood. In L. D. Eron (Ed.), *The classification of behavior disorders.* Chicago: Aldine, 1967.

Eisenson, J. *Aphasia in children.* New York: Harper & Row, 1972.

Eisenson, J., and Ingram, D. Childhood aphasia—an updated concept based on recent research. *Acta Symbolica, 3,* 108-116, 1972.

Emerick, L., and Hatten, J. *Diagnosis and evaluation in speech pathology.* Englewood Cliffs, N. J.: Prentice Hall, 1974.

Engelmann, S. How to construct effective language programs for the poverty child. In F. Williams (Ed.), *Language and poverty.* Chicago: Markham Publishing Co., 1970.

Engler, L., Hannah, E., and Longhurst, T. Linguistic analysis of speech samples: A practical guide for clinicians. *Journal of Speech and Hearing Disorders, 38,* 192-204, 1973.

Ervin-Tripp, S. An analysis of the interaction of language, topic, and listener. In J. Gumperz and D. Hymes (Eds.), The ethnography of communication. *American Anthropologist, 66,* (16) Part 2, 86-102, 1964.(a)

Ervin-Tripp, S. Imitation and structural change in children's language. In E. Lenneberg (Ed.), *New directions in the study of language.* Cambridge, Mass.: M.I.T. Press, 1964.(b)

Ervin-Tripp, S. Discourse agreement: How children answer questions. In J. R. Hayes, (Ed.), *Cognition and the development of language.* New York: John Wiley & Sons, 1970.

Ervin-Tripp, S. On sociolinguistic rules: Alternation and cooccurrence. In J. J. Gumperz and D. Hymes (Eds.), *Directions in sociolinguistics: The ethnography of communication.* New York: Holt, Rinehart and Winston, 1972.

Ervin-Tripp, S. Wait for me roller skate. In S. Ervin-Tripp and C. Mitchell-Kernan, (Eds), *Child discourse.* New York: Academic Press, 1977.

Escalona, S. K., and Corman, H. C. Albert Einstein Scales of Sensorimotor Development: Object Permanence. n.d.

Evans, D., and Hampson, M. The language of mongols. *British Journal of Disorders of Communication, 3,* 171-181, 1968.

Ferguson, C. A., and Farwell, C. B. Words and sounds in early language acquisition. *Language, 51,* 419-439, 1975.

Ferguson, C., Peizer, D., and Weeks, T., Model-and-replica phonological grammar of a child's first words. *Lingua, 31,* 35-39, 1973.

Fernald, C. Control of grammar in imitation, comprehension and production: Problems of replication. *Journal of Verbal Learning and Verbal Behavior,. 11,* 606-613, 1972.

Fillmore, C. The case for case. In E. Bach and R. T. Harms (Eds.), *Universals in linguistic theory*. New York: Holt, Rinehart and Winston, pp. 1-90, 1968.

Fillmore, C., Deixis, I. Unpublished lectures, delivered at the University of California, Santa Cruz, 1973.

Fillmore, C. A proposal for characterizing linguistic abilities. *In* S. Harnad, H. Steklis and J. Lancaster (Eds.), *Origins and evolution of language and speech*. Annals of the New York Academy of Sciences, 280, 1976.

Fodor, J. How to learn to talk, some simple ways. In F. Smith and G. Miller, (Eds.), *The Genesis of language*. Cambridge, Mass.: The M.I.T. Press, 1966.

Fodor, J., Bever, T. G., and Garrett, M. F. *The psychology of language*. New York: McGraw Hill, 1974.

Foster, R., Giddan, J., and Stark, J. *Assessment of Children's Language Comprehension*. Austin, Tex: Learning Concepts, 1973.

Francescato, G., On the role of the word in first language acquisition, *Lingua, 21,* 144-153.

Fraser, C., Bellugi, U., and Brown, R. Control of grammar in imitation, comprehension, and production. *Journal of Verbal Learning and Verbal Behavior, 2,* 121-135, 1963.

Freedle, R., Lewis, M., and Weiner, S. Language acquisition and situational context. Paper presented at the meeting of the Eastern Psychological Association, 1974.

Freedman, P. P., and Carpenter, R. L. Semantic relations used by normal and language impaired children at stage 1. *Journal of Speech and Hearing Research, 19,* 784-795, 1976.

Freidus, E. Methodology for the classroom teacher. In J. Hellmuth (Ed.), *The special child in century 21*. Seattle, Wash.: Special Child Publications of the Seguin School, pp. 303-321, 1964.

Friedlander, B. Z. Receptive language development in infancy. *Merrill-Palmer Quarterly, 16,* 7-51, 1970.

Frishberg, N. Arbitrariness and iconicity: Historical change in American Sign Language. *Language, 51,* 696-719, 1975.

Fromkin, V., Krashen, S., Curtiss, S., Rigler, D., and Rigler, M. The development of language in Genie: A case of language acquisition beyond the "critical period". *Brain and Language, 1,* 81-107, 1974.

Furth, H. *Thinking without language: Psychological implications of deafness*. New York: The Free Press, 1966.

Garcia, E. The training and generalization of a conversational speech form in nonverbal retardates. *Journal of Applied Behavior Analysis, 7,* 137-149, 1974.

Garfinkel, H. *Studies in ethnomethodology*. Englewood Cliffs, N. J.: Prentice-Hall, 1967.

Garnica, O. K. The development of phonemic speech perception. In T. E. Moore (Ed.), *Cognitive development and the acquisition of language*. New York: Academic Press, 1973.

Garvey, C. Requests and responses in children's speech. *Journal of Child Language, 2,* 41–63, 1975.(a)

Garvey, C. Contingent queries. Unpublished manuscript, 1975.(b)

Garvey, C., and Hogan, R. Social speech and social interaction: Egocentrism revisited. *Child Development, 44,* 562–568, 1973.

Gentner, D. Validation of a related-component model of verb meaning. *Papers and reports on Child Language Development.* No. 10, September 1975, Stanford University, Stanford, Calif.

Gibson, E. *Principles of perceptual learning and development.* New York: Appleton-Century-Crofts, 1969.

Gibson, J. J. *The senses considered as perceptual systems.* Boston: Houghton Mifflin, 1966.

Glaser, R., and Nitko, A. Measurement in learning and instruction. In R. Thorndike (Ed.), *Educational measurement.* Washington, D. C.: American Council on Education, 625–670, 1971.

Gleason, H. *Workbook in descriptive linguistics.* New York: Holt, Rinehart and Winston, Inc., 1955.

Gleason, H. Jr. *An introduction to descriptive linguistics.* New York: Holt, Rinehart & Winston, 1961.

Glucksberg, S., Krauss, R., and Higgins, E. T. The development of referential communication skills. In F. Horowitz (Ed.), *Review of child development research,* Vol. 4. Chicago: University of Chicago Press, 1975.

Goda, S., and Griffith, B. C. The spoken language of adolescent retardates and its relation to intelligence, age, and anxiety. *Child Development, 33,* 489–498, 1962.

Goffman, E. *Strategic interaction.* Philadelphia: University of Pennsylvania Press, 1969.

Goldfarb, W., Goldfarb, N., and Scholl, H. The speech of mothers of schizophrenic children. *American Journal of Psychiatry, 122,* 1220–1227, 1966.

Goldfarb, W., Levy, D., and Meyers, D. The mother speaks to her schizophrenic child: Language in childhood schizophrenia. *Psychiatry, 35,* 217–226, 1972.

Goldin-Meadow, S., Seligman, M., and Gelman, R. Language in the two-year old: Receptive and productive stages. *Cognition, 4,* 189–202, 1976.

Goldman, R., Fristoe, M., and Woodcock, R. W. *The Goldman-Fristoe-Woodcock Test of Auditory Discrimination.* Circle-Pines, Minn.: American Guidance Service, Inc., 1969, 1972.

Goldstein, R., Landau, W., and Kleffner, F. Neurologic assessment of some deaf and aphasic children. *Annals of Otology, Rhinology and Laryngology, 67,* 468–479, 1958.

Gordon, D., and Lakoff, G. Conversational postulates. In P. Cole and J. Morgan (Eds.), *Syntax and semantics. Vol. 3, Speech acts.* New York: Academic Press, 1975.

Gorth, W., and Hambleton, R. Measurement considerations for criterion-referenced testing and special education. *Journal of Special Education, 6,* 303–314, 1972.

Goss, R. Language used by mothers of deaf children and mothers of hearing children. *American Annals of the Deaf*, 93–95, March 1970.

Graham, L. W., and House, A. S. Phonological oppositions in children: A perceptual study. *Journal of the Acoustical Society of America, 49*, 559–569, 1971.

Graham, N. C. Short-term memory and syntactic structure in educationally subnormal children. *Language and Speech, 11*, 209–219, 1968.

Gratch, G. Recent studies based on Piaget's view of object concept development. In L. Cohen and P. Salapatek (Eds.), *Infant perception: From sensation to cognition, Vol. II. Perception of space, speech and sound.* New York: Academic Press, 1975.

Gratch, G., Appel, K., Evans, W., LeCompte, G., and Wright, N. Piaget's stage IV object concept error: Evidence of forgetting or object conception? *Child Development, 45*, 71–77, 1974.

Gray, B. B., and Ryan, B. *A language training program for the non-language child.* Champaign, Ill.: Research Press, 1973.

Greenfield, P. Who is "Dada"? Some aspects of the semantic and phonological development of a child's first words. *Language and Speech, 16*, 34–43, 1973.

Greenfield, P., Nelson, K., and Saltzman, E. The development of rulebound strategies for manipulating seriated cups: A parallel between action and grammar. *Cognitive Psychology, 3*, 291–310, 1972.

Greenfield, P., Smith, J., and Laufer, B. *Communication and the beginnings of language.* Unpublished manuscript, 1972.

Grice, H. P. Logic and conversation. In P. Cole and J. L. Morgan (Eds.), *Syntax and semantics. Vol. 3, Speech acts.* New York: Academic Press, 1975.

Grimshaw, A. D. Data and data use in an analysis of communicative events. In R. Bauman and J. Sherzer (Eds.), *Explorations in the ethnography of speaking.* London: Cambridge University Press, 1974.

Grossman, H. J. *Manual on terminology and classification in mental retardation.* Washington, D. C.: Special Publication Series #2, American Association for Mental Deficiency, 1973.

Gruber, J. Topicalization in child language. *Foundations of Language, 3*, 37–65, 1967.

Gruber, J. Correlations between the syntactic constructions of the child and the adult. In C. A. Ferguson and D. I. Slobin (Eds.), *Studies of child language development.* New York: Holt, Rinehart & Winston, 1973.

Guess, D. A functional analysis of receptive language and productive speech: Acquisition of the plural morpheme. *Journal of Applied Behavior Analysis, 2*, 55–64, 1969.

Guess, D., and Baer, D. M. An analysis of individual differences in generalization between receptive and productive language in retarded children. *Journal of Applied Behavior Analysis, 6*, 311–329, 1973.

Guess, D., Rutherford, G., and Twichell, A. Speech acquisition in a mute, visually impaired adolescent. *New Outlook for the Blind, 63*, 8–13, 1969.

Guillaume, P. Les debuts de la phrase dans le language de l'enfant. *Journal de Psychologie, 24,* 1–25, 1927.

Guillaume, P. *Imitation in children.* Chicago: University of Chicago Press, 1968. (Original in French, 1926.)

Guillaume, P., First stages of sentence formation in children's speech. Translated by E. Clark, In C. A. Ferguson and D. I. Slobin (Eds.), *Studies of child language development.* New York: Holt, Rinehart and Winston, 240–251, 1973. Originally in *Journal de Psychologie,* 1–25, 1927.

Gumperz, J. J. Introduction. In J. J. Gumperz and D. Hymes (Eds.), *Directions in sociolinguistics: The ethnography of communication.* New York: Holt, Rinehart & Winston, 1972.

Halliday, M. A. K. Language structure and language function. In J. Lyons (Ed.), *New horizons in linguistics.* Baltimore: Penguin, 1970.

Halliday, M. A. K. *Explorations in the functions of language.* London: Edward Arnold, 1973.

Halliday, M. A. K. A sociosemiotic perspective on language development. *Bulletin of the School of Oriental and African Studies,* University of London. Vol. XXXVII, Part 1, 1974.

Halliday, M. A. K. *Learning how to mean—Explorations in the development of language.* London: Edward Arnold, 1975.

Halliday, M. A. K., and Hasan, R. *Cohesion in English.* London: Longman (English Language Series), 1975.

Hammill, D., and Larsen, S. The effectiveness of psycholinguistic training. *Exceptional Children, 40,* 5–13, 1974.

Hampshire, S. *Thought and action.* New York: Viking, 1967.

Hardy, W. G. On language disorders in young children: A reorganization of thinking. *Journal of Speech and Hearing Disorders, 30,* 3–16, 1965.

Harner, L. Yesterday and tomorrow: Development of early understanding of the terms. *Developmental Psychology, 11,* 864–865, 1975.

Harner, L. Children's understanding of linguistic reference to past and future. *Journal of Psycholinguistic Research, 5,* 65–84, 1976.

Harris, D. B. *Children's drawings as a measure of intellectual maturity. A revision and extension of the Goodenough Draw-A-Man tests.* New York: Harcourt, Brace and World, 1963.

Harris, M. *The nature of cultural things.* New York: Random House, 1964.

Harris, L., and Taenzer, L. Language within a cognitive frame. In *Observational guidelines for the SEEC miniwheel and maxiwheel of developmental milestones.* Schaumburg, Ill.: Community Consolidated School District, 1976.

Harris, P. Development of search and object permanence during infancy. *Psychological Bulletin, 82,* 332–344, 1975.

Harris, Z. Cooccurrence and transformations in linguistic structure. *Language, 33,* 283–340, 1957.

Harris, Z. Discourse analysis. In J. Fodor and J. Katz (Eds.), *The structure of language*. Englewood Cliffs, N. J.: Prentice-Hall, 355–383, 1964.

Hass, W., and Wepman, J. Constructional variety in the spoken language of school children. *Journal of Genetic Psychology, 122,* 297–308, 1973.

Haviland, S. E., and Clark, H. H. What's new? Acquiring new information as a process of comprehension. *Journal of Verbal Learning and Verbal Behavior, 13,* 512–521, 1974.

Heider, F. K., and Heider, G. M. A Comparison of sentence structure of deaf and hearing children. *Psychological Monographs, 52,* 42–103, 1940.

Hejna, R. *Developmental Articulation Test.* Ann Arbor, Mich.: Speech Materials, 1959.

Henderson, K. B. Uses of subject matter. In B. O. Smith and R. H. Ennis (Eds.), *Language and concepts in education.* Chicago: Rand McNally, 43–58, 1961.

Hermelin, B., and Frith, U. Psychological studies of childhood autism: Can autistic children make sense of what they see and hear? *Journal of Special Education, 5,* 107–116, 1971.

Hermelin, B., and O'Connor, N. Remembering of words by psychotic and normal children. *British Journal of Psychology, 58,* 213–218, 1967.

Hewett, F. M. Teaching speech to an autistic child through operant conditioning. *American Journal of Orthopsychiatry, 35,* 927–936, 1965.

Hingtgen, J. N., and Coulter, S. K. Auditory control of operant behavior in mute autistic children. *Perceptual and Motor Skills, 25,* 561–565, 1967.

Hively, W. Domain referenced testing: Symposium. *Educational Technology, 14,* 5–64, 974.

Hockett, C. *A course in modern linguistics.* New York: Macmillan, 1958.

Holzman, M. The use of interrogative forms in the verbal interactions of three mothers and their children. *Journal of Psycholinguistic Research, 1,* 311–336, 1972.

Hood, L. A longitudinal study of the development of the expression of causal relations in complex sentences. Unpublished doctoral dissertation, Columbia University, 1977.

Hood, L., Lahey, M., Lifter, K., and Bloom, L. Observational descriptive methodology in studying child language: Preliminary results on the development of complex sentences. In G. P. Sackett (Ed.). *Observing behavior. Vol. I: Theory and applications in mental retardation.* Baltimore: University Park Press, 239–263, 1978.

Huttenlocher, J. Children's language: Word-phrase relationship. *Science, 143,* 264–265, 1964.

Huttenlocher, J. The origins of language comprehension. In R. L. Solso (Ed.), *Theories in cognitive psychology.* New York: Halsted, 1974.

Huttenlocher, J., and Burke, D. Why does memory span increase with age? *Cognitive Psychology, 8,* 1–31, 1976.

Huttenlocher, J., Eisenberg, K., and Strauss, S. Comprehension: Relation between perceived actor and logical subject. *Journal of Verbal Learning and Verbal Behavior, 7,* 527–530, 1968.

Huttenlocher, J., and Higgins, E. T. On reasoning, congruence and other matters. *Psychological Review, 79,* 420–427, 1972.

Huttenlocher, J., and Strauss, S. Comprehension and a statement's relation to the situation it describes. *Journal of Verbal Learning and Verbal Behavior, 7,* 300–304, 1968.

Huttenlocher, J., and Weiner, S. Comprehension of instructions in varying contexts. *Cognitive Psychology, 2,* 369–385, 1971.

Huxley, R. Discussion. In J. Lyons and R. Wales (Eds.), *Psycholinguistic papers.* Edinburgh: Edinburgh University Press, 1966.

Huxley, R. The development of the correct use of subject personal pronouns in two children. In G. B. Flores d'Arcais and W. J. M. Levelt (Eds.), *Advances in psycholinguistics.* New York: American Elsevier, 1970.

Hymes, D. (Ed.), *Language in culture and society.* New York: Harper & Row, 1964.

Ingram, D. Transitivity in child language. *Language, 47,* 888–910, 1971.

Ingram, D. Phonological rules in young children. *Journal of Child Language, 1,* 97–106, 1974.

Ingram, D., and Eisenson, J. Therapeutic approaches in congenitally aphasic children. In J. Eisenson (Ed.), *Aphasia in children.* New York: Harper & Row, 1972.

Irwin, J., and Marge, M. *Principles of childhood language disabilities.* New York: Appleton-Century-Crofts, 1972.

Irwin, J., Moore, J. M., and Rampp, D. L. Nonmedical diagnosis and evaluation. In J. Irwin and M. Marge (Eds.), *Principles of childhood language disabilities.* New York: Appleton-Century-Crofts, 1972.

Irwin, O. C. Development of speech during infancy: Curve of phonemic frequencies. *Journal of Experimental Psychology, 37,* 187–193, 1947.

Irwin, O. C., and Chen, H. P. Infant speech: Vowel and consonant frequency. *Journal of Speech Disorders, 11,* 123–125, 1946.

Irwin, O. C., and Hammill, D. D. Some results with an abstraction test with cerebral palsied children. *Cerebral Palsy Review, 25,* 10–11, 1964.

Irwin, O. C., and Hammill, D. D. Effect of type, extent and degree of cerebral palsy on three measures of language. *Cerebral Palsy Journal, 26,* 7–9, 1965.

Itard, J. *The wild boy of Aveyron.* New York: Appleton-Century-Crofts, 1962.

Jacobsen, T. On the order of emergence of conjunctions and notions of conjunctions in English-speaking children. Unpublished manuscript, Berkeley, 1974.

Jaffe, J., Stern, D., and Peery, J. "Conversational" coupling of gaze behavior in prelinguistic human development." *Journal of Psycholinguistic Research, 2,* 321–329, 1973.

Jakobovits, L., and Miron, M. (Eds.). *Readings in the psychology of language.* Englewood Cliffs, N. J.: Prentice Hall, 1967.

Jakobson, R. Shifters, verbal categories and the Russian verb. Cambridge, Mass.:

Harvard University Department of Slavic Languages and Literatures. Russian Language Project, 1957.

Jakobson, R. Concluding statement: Linguistics and poetics. In T. A. Sebeok (Ed.), *Style in language*. New York: John Wiley & Sons, 1960.

Jakobson, R. *Child language, aphasia and phonological universals*. The Hague: Mouton, 1968 (originally in German, 1941).

Jakobson, R., and Halle, M., *Fundamentals of language*. (Janua Linguarum, 1.) The Hague: Mouton, 1956.

Jarvella, R. J., and Lubinsky, J. Deaf and hearing children's use of language describing temporal order among events. *Journal of Speech and Hearing Research, 18,* 58-73, 1975.

Jenkins, J., and Palermo, D. Mediation processes and the acquisition of linguistic structure. In U. Bellugi and R. Brown (Eds.), The acquisition of language. *Monographs of the Society for Research in Child Development, 29,* (Serial No. 92), 1964.

Jerger, J., Burney, P., Mauldin, L., and Crump, B. Predicting hearing loss from the acoustic reflex. *Journal of Speech and Hearing Disorders, 39,* 11-22, 1974.

Jespersen, O. *Language: Its nature, development, and origin.* London: Allen & Unwin, 1922 and New York: W. W. Norton, 1964.

Johansson, B. S., and Sjolin, B. Preschool children's understanding of the coordinations "and" and "or." *Journal of Experimental Child Psychology, 19,* 233-240, 1975.

Johnson, D., and Myklebust, H. *Learning disabilities: Educational principles and practices.* New York: Grune and Stratton, 1967.

Johnson, M., Bransford, J., and Solomon, S. Memory for tacit implications of sentences. *Journal of Experimental Child Psychology, 98,* 203-205, 1973.

Johnson, W., Darley, F. L., and Spriesterbach, D. C. *Diagnostic method in speech pathology.* New York: Harper & Row, 1963.

Johnston, J. R., and Schery, T. K. The use of grammatical morphemes by children with communication disorders. In D. M. Morehead and A. E. Morehead (Eds.), *Normal and deficient child language.* Baltimore: University Park Press, 1976.

Josephs, J. Children's comprehension of same and different in varying contexts. Unpublished doctoral dissertation, Columbia University, 1975.

Kanner, L. Autistic disturbances of affective contact. *The Nervous Child, 2,* 217-223, 1943.

Kanner, L. Irrelevant and metaphorical language in early infantile autism. *American Journal of Psychiatry, 103,* 242-266, 1946.

Kanner, L. *Childhood psychosis: Initial studies and new insights.* New York: John Wiley & Sons, 1973.

Kanner, L., and Eisenberg, L. Early infantile autism. *American Journal of Orthopsychiatry, 26,* 556-564, 1956.

Kaplan, E. Intonation and language acquisition. *Papers and reports on child language development.* Stanford: Committee on Linguistics, Stanford University, 1970.

Kaplan, E., and Kaplan, G. The prelinguistic child. In J. Eliot (Ed.), *Human development and cognitive processes*. New York: Holt, Rinehart & Winston, 1971.

Karmel, B., and Maisel, E. A neuronal activity model for infant visual attention. In L. Cohen and P. Salapatek (Eds.), *Infant perception: From sensation to cognition*. Vol. I, *Basic visual processes*. New York: Academic Press, 1975.

Karpova, S. N. Osonznanie slovesnogo sostava rechi rebenkom doshkol' nogo vozrasta. *Voprosy Psikhol, 4,* 43-55, 1955. Abstracted by D. Slobin, Abstracts of Soviet studies of child language. In F. Smith and G. Miller (Eds.), *The genesis of language: A psycholinguistic approach*. Cambridge, Mass.: The M.I.T. Press, 370-371, 1966.

Kates, C. A descriptive approach to linguistic meaning. Unpublished manuscript, Cornell University, 1974.

Keenan, E. Conversational competence in children. *Journal of Child Language, 1,* 163-183, 1974.

Keenan, E., and Schieffelin, B. Topic as a discourse notion: A study of topic in the conversations of children and adults. In C. Li (Ed.), *Subject and topic*. New York: Academic Press, 1976.

Keeney, T., and Wolfe, J. The acquisition of agreement in English. *Journal of Verbal Learning and Verbal Behavior, 11,* 698-705, 1972.

Keller, F. S. *Learning: Reinforcement theory*. New York: Random House, 1965.

Keller-Cohen, D., Repetition in the non-native acquisition of discourse: Its relation to text unification and conversation. In R. O. Freedle (Ed.), *Discourse processes: Advances in research and theory, Vol II. Discourse processes: Multidisciplinary perspectives*. Norwood, N. J.: Ablex Publishing Co., in press.

Kent, L. *Language acquisition program for the retarded or multiply impaired*. Champaign, Ill.: Research Press, 1974.

Kephart, N. C. *The slow learner in the classroom*. Columbus, Ohio: Charles Merrill, 1960.

Kernan, K. Semantic relationships and the child's acquisition of language. *Anthropological Linguistics, 12,* 171-187, 1970.

Kessler, J. *Psychopathology of childhood*. Englewood Cliffs, N. J.: Prentice-Hall, 1966.

Kintsch, W. *The representation of meaning in memory*. Hillsdale, N. J.: Lawrence Earlbaum Associates, 1974.

Kirk, S., and Kirk, W. *Psycholinguistic learning disabilities*. Urbana, Ill.: University of Illinois Press, 1971.

Kirk, S., and McCarthy, J. *The Illinois Test of Psycholinguistic Abilities*—An approach to differential diagnosis. *American Journal of Mental Deficiency, 66,* 399-412, 1961.

Kirk, S., McCarthy, J., and Kirk, W. *The Illinois Test of Psycholinguistic Abilities,* (Revised Edition). Urbana, Ill.: University of Illinois Press, 1968.

Kirkpatrick, E. A. *Genetic psychology*. New York: Macmillan, 1909.

Kleffner, F. *Language disorders in children*. New York: The Bobbs-Merrill Company, Inc., 1973.

Klein, H., The relationship between perceptual strategies and productive strategies in learning the phonology of early lexical items. Unpublished doctoral dissertation, Columbia University, 1978.

Klima, E. Negation in English. In J. Fodor and J. Katz (Eds.), *The structure of language*. Englewood Cliffs, N. J.: Prentice-Hall, 1964.

Klima, E., and Bellugi, U. Syntactic regularities in the speech of children. In J. Lyons and R. Wales (Eds.), *Psycholinguistic Papers*. Proceedings of the Edinburgh Conference, Edinburgh: Edinburgh University Press, 1966.

Kuczaj, S. On the acquisition of a semantic system. *Journal of Verbal Learning and Verbal Behavior, 14*, 340–358, 1975.

LaBelle, J. L. Sentence comprehension in two age groups of children as related to pause position or the absence of pauses. *Journal of Speech and Hearing Research, 6*, 231–237, 1973.

Labov, W. Contraction, deletion, and inherent variability of the English copula. *Language, 45,* 715–762, 1969.

Labov, W. The logic of nonstandard English. In F. Williams (Ed.), *Language and poverty: Perspectives on a theme*. Chicago: Markham Publishing Co., 1970.

Labov, W., Cohen, P., Robins, C., and Lewis, J. A study of the non-standard English of Negro and Puerto Rican speakers in New York City. Cooperative Research Report No. 3288, Vol. I. New York: Columbia University (ERIC ED 028 423), 1968.

Labov, W., and Labov, T. Learning the syntax of questions. To appear in the Proceedings of the Conference on Psychology of Language, Stirling, Scotland, June 1976.

Lackner, J. R. A developmental study of language behavior in retarded children. *Neuropsychologia, 6,* 301–320, 1968. Reprinted in D. Morehead and A. E. Morehead (Eds.), *Normal and deficient child language*. Baltimore: University Park Press, pp. 181–208, 1976.

Lahey, M. The role of prosody and syntactic markers in children's comprehension of spoken sentences. Unpublished doctoral dissertation, Teachers College, Columbia University, 1972.

Lahey, M. Use of prosody and syntactic markers in children's comprehension of spoken sentences. *Journal of Speech and Hearing Research, 17,* 656–668, 1974.

Lahey, M. Disruptions in the development and integration of form, content and use in language development. In J. Kavanagh and W.Strange (Eds.), *Language and speech in the laboratory, school, and clinic*. Cambridge, Mass.: The M.I.T. Press, 1978.

Lahey, M., and Bloom, L. Planning a first lexicon: Which words to teach first. *Journal of Speech and Hearing Disorders, 42,* 340–350, 1977.

Lakoff, G. On generative semantics. In D. Steinberg and L. Jakobovits (Eds.), *Semantics: An interdisciplinary reader in philosophy, linguistics and psychology*. London: Cambridge University Press, 1971.

Lakoff, R. Questionable answers and answerable questions. In B. Kachru, et al. (Eds.), *Papers in linguistics in honor of Henry and Renee Kahane.* Urbana, Ill.: University of Illinois Press, pp. 453-468, 1973.

Landau, W. M., Goldstein, R., and Kleffner, F. R. Congenital aphasia: A clinico-pathologic study. *Neurology, 10,* 915-921, 1960.

Langacker, R. W. *Language and its structure: Some fundamental linguistic concepts.* New York: Harcourt, Brace & World, Inc., 1968.

Lee, L. Developmental sentence types: A method for comparing normal and deviant syntactic development. *Journal of Speech and Hearing Disorders, 31,* 311-330, 1966.

Lee, L. A screening test for syntax development. *Journal of Speech and Hearing Disorders, 35,* 103-112, 1970.

Lee, L. *Northwestern Syntax Screening Test* (NSST). Evanston, Ill.: The Northwestern University Press, 1971.

Lee, L. *Developmental sentence analysis.* Evanston, Ill.: Northwestern University Press, 1974.

Lee, L., and Canter, S. Developmental sentence scoring: A clinical procedure for estimating syntactic development in children's spontaneous speech. *Journal of Speech and Hearing Disorders, 36,* 315-341, 1971.

Leech, G. *Towards a semantic description of English.* Bloomington, Ind.: Indiana University Press, 1970.

Lenneberg, E. *Biological foundations of language.* New York: John Wiley & Sons, 1967.

Lenneberg, E., Nichols, I., and Rosenberger, E. Primitive stages of language development in mongolism. In D. McK. Rioch and E. A. Weinstein (Eds.), *Disorders of communication* (Research Publications of the Association for Research in Nervous & Mental Disease). Baltimore: The Williams and Wilkins Co., *42,* 119-137, 1964

Leonard, L. What is deviant language? *Journal of Speech and Hearing Disorders, 37,* 427-447, 1972.

Leonard, L. Teaching by the rules. *Journal of Speech and Hearing Disorders, 38,* 174-183, 1973.

Leonard, L. From reflex to remark. *Acta symbolica, 5,* 67-99, 1974.

Leonard, L. Relational meaning and the facilitation of slow-learning children's language. *American Journal of Mental Deficiency, 80,* 180-185, 1975.(a)

Leonard, L. Developmental consideration in the management of language disabled children. *Journal of Learning Disabilities, 8,* 232-237, 1975.(b)

Leonard, L. The role of nonlinguistic stimuli and semantic relations in children's acquisition of grammatical utterances. *Journal of Experimental Child Psychology, 19,* 346-357, 1975.(c)

Leonard, L., Bolders, J., and Miller, J. An examination of the semantic relations reflected in the language usage of normal and language-disordered children. *Journal of Speech and Hearing Research, 19,* 371-392, 1976.

Leopold, W. *Speech development of a bilingual child* (4 vols.). Evanston, Ill.: Northwestern University Press, 1939.

Levi-Strauss, C. *Structural anthropology*. Translated by C. Jacobson and B. Schoept. New York: Basic Books, 1963.

Levine, F., and Fasnacht, G. Token rewards may lead to token learning. *American Psychologist, 29*, 816–820, 1974.

Lewis, M. M. The beginning and early functions of questions in a child's speech. *British Journal of Educational Psychology, 8*, 150–171, 1938.

Lewis, M. M. *Infant speech, a study of the beginnings of language*. New York: Humanities Press, 1951.

Lewis, M. M. *How children learn to speak*. New York: Basic Books, 1959.

Lewis, M. M. *Language, thought and personality in infancy and childhood*. New York: Basic Books, 1963.

Lewis, M., and Freedle, R. Mother-infant dyad: The cradle of meaning. In P. Pliner (Ed.), *Communication and affect*. New York: Academic Press, 1973.

Liberman, A. The grammars of speech and language. *Cognitive Psychology, 1*, 301–323, 1970.

Liberman, A., Cooper, F., Shankweiler, D., and Studdert-Kennedy, M. Perception of the speech code. *Psychological Review, 74*, 431–461, 1967.

Liberman, A., Delattre, P., and Cooper, F. The role of selected stimulus variables in the perception of the unvoiced stop consonants. *American Journal of Psychology, 65*, 497–516, 1952.

Liberman, I., Shankweiler, D., Fischer, F., and Carter, B. Explicit syllable and phoneme segmentation in the young child. *Journal of Experimental Child Psychology, 18*, 201–212, 1974.

Lieberman, P. *Intonation, perception, and language*. Cambridge, Mass.: The M.I.T. Press, 1967.

Lightbown, P. Nominal and pronominal forms in the speech of three French-speaking children: A pilot study. Unpublished doctoral dissertation proposal, Teachers College, Columbia University, 1973.

Limber, J. The genesis of complex sentences. In T. Moore (Ed.), *Cognitive development and the acquisition of language*. New York: Academic Press, 1973.

Ling, D. and Ling, A. H. Communication development in the first three years of life. *Journal of Speech and Hearing Research, 17*, 146–159, 1974

Loban, W. *The language of elementary school children*. Champaign, Ill.: National Council of Teachers of English, Research Report No. 1, 1963.

Longhurst, T., and File, J. A comparison of developmental sentence scores from head start children collected in four conditions. Unpublished, undated manuscript, Kansas State University, Manhattan, Kansas.

Longhurst, T., and Grubb, S. A comparison of language samples collected in four situations. *Language, Speech and Hearing Service in the Schools, 5*, 71–78, 1974.

Longhurst, T., and Schrandt, T. Linguistic analysis of children's speech: A comparison of four procedures. *Journal of Speech and Hearing Disorders, 38*, 240–249, 1973.

Lovaas, O. I. Some studies on the treatment of childhood schizophrenia. *Research in Psychotherapy, 3*, 103–121, 1968.

Lovaas, O. I., Berberich, J. P., Perloff, B. F., and Schaeffer, B. Acquisition of imitative speech by schizophrenic children. *Science, 151*, 705–707, 1966.

Lovaas, O. I., Schreibman, L., Koegel, R., and Rehm, R. Selective responding by autistic children to multiple sensory input. *Journal of Abnormal Psychology, 77*, 211–222, 1971.

Lovell, K., and Bradbury, B. The learning of English morphology in educationally subnormal special school children. *American Journal of Mental Deficiency, 71*, 609–615, 1967.

Lovell, K., and Dixon, E. M. The growth of the control of grammar in imitation, comprehension, and production. *Journal of Child Psychology and Psychiatry, 8*, 31–39, 1967.

Lovell, K., Hoyle, H. W., and Siddall, M. Q. A study of some aspects of the play and language of young children with delayed speech. *Journal of Child Psychology and Psychiatry, 9*, 41–50, 1968.

Lowe, A., and Campbell, R. Temporal discrimination in aphasoid and normal children. *Journal of Speech and Hearing Research, 8*, 313–315, 1965.

Lyons, J. *Introduction to theoretical linguistics*. London: Cambridge University Press, 1968.

Lyons, J., and Wales, R. *Psycholinguistic papers*. Edinburgh: Edinburgh University Press, 1966.

Maccoby, E., and Bee, H. Some speculations concerning the lag between perceiving and performing. *Child Development, 36*, 367–377, 1965.

MacDonald, J., and Blott, J. Environmental language intervention: The rationale for a diagnostic and training strategy through rules, context, and generalization. *Journal of Speech and Hearing Disorders, 39*, 244–257, 1974.

MacDonald, J. D., Blott, J. P., Gordon, K., Spiegel, B., and Hartmann, M. An experimental parent-assisted treatment program for preschool language-delayed children. *Journal of Speech and Hearing Disorders, 39*, 395–415, 1974.

MacDonald, J. D., and Nickols, M. *The environmental language inventory*. Columbus, Ohio: Nisonger Center, Ohio State University, 1974.

MacGinitie, W. Ability of deaf children to use different word classes. *Journal of Speech and Hearing Research, 7*, 141–150, 1964.

MacNamara, J. Cognitive bases of language learning in infants. *Psychological Review, 79*, 1–13, 1972.

McCarthy, D. The language development of the preschool child. *Institute of Child Welfare Monograph Series No. 4*. Minneapolis: University of Minnesota Press, 1930.

McCarthy, D. Language development in children. In P, Mussen (Ed.), *Carmichael's manual of child psychology*. New York: John Wiley and Sons, 1954.(a)

McCarthy, D. Language disorders and parent-child relationships. *Journal of Speech and Hearing Disorders, 19*, 514, 1954.(b)

McCarthy, D. *McCarthy scales of children's abilities*. New York: Psychological Corporation, 1974.

McCawley, J. The role of semantics in a grammar. In E. Bach and R. Harms (Eds.), *Universals in linguistic theory*. New York: Holt, Rinehart & Winston, 1968.

McGinnis, M. *Aphasic children*. Washington, D. C.: Alexander Graham Bell Association, 1963.

McGinnis, M., Kleffner, F., and Goldstein, R. Teaching aphasic children. Reprint No. 677. Washington D. C.: The Volta Bureau.

McLean, L. P., and McLean, J. E. A language training program for non-verbal autistic children. *Journal of Speech and Hearing Disorders, 39*, 186–193, 1974.

McNeill, D. Developmental psycholinguistics. In F. Smith and G. Miller (Eds.), *The genesis of language: A psycholinguistic approach*. Cambridge, Mass.: The M.I.T. Press, 1966.

McNeill, D. *The acquisition of language: The study of developmental psycholinguistics*. New York: Harper and Row, 1970.

McNeill, D., and McNeill, N. B. What does a child mean when he says "no"? In E. Zale (Ed.), *Proceedings of the conference on language and language behavior*. New York: Appleton-Century-Crofts, 1968.

McReynolds, L. Verbal sequence discrimination training for language-impaired children. *Journal of Speech and Hearing Disorders, 32* 249–256, 1967.

McReynolds, L. Operant conditioning for investigating speech sound discrimination in aphasic children. *Journal of Speech and Hearing Research, 9*, 519–528, 1966.

Mandler, G. Verbal learning. In T. Newcomb (Ed.), *New directions in psychology, Vol. 3*. New York: Holt, Rinehart & Winston, 1967.

Mann, L. Psychometric phrenology and the new faculty psychology: The case against ability assessment and training. *Journal of Special Education, 5*, 3–14, 1971.

Mann, R., and Baer, D. The effects of receptive language training on articulation. *Journal of Applied Behavior Analysis, 4*, 291–298, 1971.

Maratsos, M. Nonegocentric communication abilities in preschool children. *Child Development, 44*, 697–700, 1973.

Maratsos, M. Preschool children's use of definite and indefinite articles. *Child Development, 45*, 446–455, 1974.

Marler, P. An ethological theory of the origin of vocal learning. In S. R. Harnad, H. D. Steklis, and J. Lancaster (Eds.), *Origins and evolution of language and speech*. Annals of the New York Academy of Sciences, 280, 386–395, 1976.

Masland, M., and Case, L. Limitation of auditory memory as a factor in delayed language development. *British Journal of Disorders in Communication, 3*, 139–142, 1968.

Mayberry, R. If a chimp can learn language, surely my nonverbal client can too. *Asha, 18*, 223–228, 1976.

Mecham, M. The development and application of procedures for measuring speech improvement in mentally defective children. *American Journal of Mental Deficiency, 60,* 301–306, 1955.

Mecham, M. *Verbal Language Development Scale.* Circle Pines, Minn.: American Guidance Service, 1958, 1971.

Mecham, M., Joy, J. L., and Jones, J. D. *Utah Test of Language Development.* Salt Lake City, Utah: Communication Research Associates, 1967.

Mein, R. A study of the oral vocabularies of severely sub-normal patients II: Grammatical analysis of speech samples. *Journal of Mental Deficiency Research, 5,* 52–59, 1961.

Mein, R., and O'Connor, N. A study of the oral vocabularies of severely sub-normal patients. *Journal of Mental Deficiency Research, 4,* 130–143, 1960.

Menig-Peterson, C. The modification of communicative behavior in preschool-aged children as a function of the listener's perspective. *Child Development, 46,* 1015–1018, 1975.

Menn, L., Phonotactic rules in beginning speech. *Lingua,* 26, 225–251, 1971.

Menyuk, P. A preliminary evaluation of grammatical capacity in children. *Journal of Verbal Learning and Verbal Behavior, 2,* 429–439, 1963.

Menyuk, P. Alternation of rules in children's grammar. *Journal of Verbal Learning and Verbal Behavior, 3,* 480–488, 1964.(a)

Menyuk, P. Comparison of grammar of children with functionally deviant and normal speech. *Journal of Speech and Hearing Research, 7,* 109–121, 1964.(b)

Menyuk, P., The role of distinctive features in children's acquisition of phonology. *Journal of Speech and Hearing Research, 11,* 138–146, 1968.

Menyuk, P. *The acquisition and development of language.* Englewood Cliffs, N. J.: Prentice-Hall, 1971.

Menyuk, P., *The development of speech.* New York: Bobbs–Merrill Company, Inc., 1972.

Meumann, E. *Die sprache des kindes.* Zurich, 1903.

Miller, A., and Miller, E. E. Cognitive-developmental training with elevated boards and sign language. *Journal of Autism and Childhood Schizophrenia, 3,* 65–85, 1973.

Miller, G. A. *Psychology: The science of mental life.* New York: Harper & Row, 1962.

Miller, G. A. English verbs of motion: A case study in semantic and lexical memory. In A. Melton and E. Martin (Eds.), *Coding processes in human memory.* New York: John Wiley & Sons, 1972.

Miller, G., A. Galanter, E., and Pribram, K. *Plans and the structure of behavior.* New York: Holt-Dryden, 1960.

Miller, J., and Yoder, D. On developing the content for a language teaching program. *Mental Retardation, 10,* 9–11, 1972.(a)

Miller, J., and Yoder, D. A syntax teaching program. In J. E. McLean, D. E. Yoder, and

R. L. Schiefelbusch (Eds.), *Language intervention with the retarded: Developing strategies*. Baltimore: University Park Press, 1972.(b)

Miller, J., and Yoder, D. *The Miller-Yoder Test of Grammatical Comprehension* (M.Y.). Madison, Wisc.: Communication Development Group, 1972.(c)

Miller, J., and Yoder, D. An ontogenetic language teaching strategy for retarded children. In R. Schiefelbusch and L. Lloyd (Eds.), *Language Perspectives—Acquisition, retardation and intervention*. Baltimore: University Park Press, 1974.

Miller, W., and Ervin, S. The development of grammar in child language. In U. Bellugi and R. Brown (Eds.), The acquisition of language. *Monographs of the Society for Research in Child Development, 29,* (Serial No. 92), 1964.

Minskoff, E., Wiseman, D. E., and Minskoff, J. G. The M. W. M. program for developing language abilities. Ridgefield, N. J.: Educational Performance Associates, 1973.

Mishler, E. Studies in dialogue and discourse: II. Types of discourse initiated by and sustained through questioning. *Journal of Psycholinguistic Research, 4,* 99–121, 1975.

Moerk, E. L. Verbal interactions between children and their mothers during the preschool years. *Developmental Psychology, 11,* 788–794, 1975.

Moffit, A. Consonant cue perception by twenty- to twenty-four-week old infants. *Child Development, 42,* 717–731, 1971.

Monsees, E. K. *Structured language for children with special language learning problems*. Washington, D. C.: Children's Hospital of District of Columbia, 1972.

Morehead, D. The study of linguistically deficient children. In S. Singh (Ed.), *Measurement in hearing, speech and language*. Baltimore: University Park Press, 1975.

Morehead, D., and Ingram, D. The development of base syntax in normal and linguistically deviant children. *Journal of Speech and Hearing Research, 16,* 330–352, 1973.

Morse, P. A. The discrimination of speech and nonspeech stimuli in early infancy. *Journal of Experimental Child Psychology, 14,* 477–492, 1972.

Morse, P. A. Infant speech perception: A preliminary model and review of the literature. In. R. L. Schiefelbusch and L. Lloyd (Eds.), *Language perspectives—Acquisition, retardation, and intervention*. Baltimore: University Park Press, 1974.

Mowrer, O. H. *Learning theory and the symbolic process*. New York: John Wiley & Sons, 1960.

Muma, J. Language intervention: Ten Techniques. *Language, Speech and Hearing Services in the Schools,* No. 5 *American Speech and Hearing Association,* 7–17, 1971.

Muma, J. Language assessment: The co-occurring and restricted structure procedure. *Acta Symbolica, 4,* 12–29, 1973.

Myers, P., and Hammill, D. *Methods for learning disorders*. New York: John Wiley & Sons, 1969.

Myklebust, H. *Auditory disorders in children.* New York: Grune & Stratton, 1954.

Mykelbust, H. *The psychology of deafness: Sensory deprivation, learning and adjustment.* New York: Grune & Stratton, 1964.

Naremore, R., and Dever, R. Language performance of educable mentally retarded and normal children at five age levels. *Journal of Speech and Hearing Research, 18,* 82–95, 1975.

Neisser, U. *Cognitive psychology.* New York: Appleton-Century-Crofts, 1967.

Nelson, K. Structure and strategy in learning to talk. *Monographs of the Society for Research in Child Development, 38* (Serial No. 149), 1973.

Nelson, K. Concept, word and sentence: Interrelations in acquisition and development. *Psychological Review, 81,* 267–285, 1974.

Nelson, K. The nominal shift in semantic-syntactic development. *Cognitive Psychology, 7,*461–479, 1975.

Nelson, N. Comprehension of spoken language by normal children as a function of speaking rate, sentence difficulty, and listener age and sex. *Child Development, 47,* 299–303, 1976.

Newcomer, P., and Goodman, L. Effect of modality of instruction on the learning of meaningful and nonmeaningful material by auditory and visual learners. Unpublished manuscript, undated.

Newcomer, P., Hare, B., Hammill, D., and McGettigan, J. *Construct validity of the Illinois Test of Psycholinguistic Abilities.* Tucson, Ariz.: University of Arizona, LTI-LD Report, Department of Special Education, 1973.

Newfield, M., and Schlanger, B. The acquisition of English morphology by normal and educable mentally retarded children. *Journal of Speech and Hearing Research, 11,* 693–706, 1968.

Newport, E. Motherese: The speech of mothers to young children. In N. J. Castellan, D. B. Pisoni, and G. R. Potts (Eds.), *Cognitive Theory, Vol. 2.* Hillsdale, N. J.: Lawrence Earlbaum Associates, 1976.

Odom, R. D., Liebert, R. M., and Fernandez, L. Effects of symbolic modeling on the syntactical productions of retardates. *Psychonomic Science, 17,* 104–105, 1969.

Oller, D. K., Wieman, L. A., Doyle, W. J., and Ross, C. Infant babbling and speech. *Journal of Child Language, 3,* 1–11, 1976.

Olson, D., and Pagliuso, S. (Eds.). From perceiving to performing: An aspect of cognitive growth. *Ontario Journal of Educational Research, 10,* 1968.

Olson, G. M. Developmental changes in memory and the acquisition of language. In T. Moore (Ed.), *Cognitive development and the acquisition of language.* New York: Academic Press, 1973.

Osgood, C. E. Motivational dynamics of language behavior. *Nebraska symposium on motivation.* Lincoln, Neb.: University of Nebraska Press, 1957.

Osgood, C. E. Where do sentences come from? In D. D. Steinberg and L. H. Jakobovits (Eds.), *Semantics.* London: Cambridge University Press, pp. 497–529, 1971.

Palermo, D. More about less: A study of language comprehension. *Journal of Verbal Learning and Verbal Behavior, 13,* 211–221, 1973.

Parisi, D. What is behind child utterances? *Journal of Child Language, 1,* 97–105, 1974.

Parisi, D., and Antinucci, F. Lexical competence. In G. B. Flores d'Arcais and W. J. M. Levelt (Eds.), *Advances in psycholinguistics.* New York: American Elsevier, 1970.

Park, T. Z. The acquisition of German syntax. Working paper, University of Munster, West Germany, 1970.

Park, T. Z. A study of German language development. Unpublished manuscript, Psychological Institute, Berne, Switzerland, 1974.

Peters, A. M. Language learning strategies: Does the whole equal the sum of the parts? In *Papers and reports on child language development,* Department of Linguistics, Stanford University, 1976.

Phillips, J. Syntax and vocabulary of mothers' speech to young children: Age and sex comparisons. *Child Development, 44,* 182–185, 1973.

Piaget, J. *Judgment and reasoning in the child.* New York: Harcourt, Brace & Co., 1928.

Piaget, J. *The construction of reality in the child.* New York: Basic Books, 1954.

Piaget, J. *The language and thought of the child.* Cleveland, Ohio: The World Publishing Company, 1955 (originally 1924).

Piaget, J. *The psychology of intelligence.* Paterson, N. J.: Littlefield, Adams, 1960.

Piaget, J. *Play, dreams and imitation in childhood.* New York: W. W. Norton, 1951, 1962.

Piaget, J. *Genetic epistemology.* New York: Columbia University Press, 1970.

Piaget, J., and Inhelder, B. *Mental imagery in the child.* New York: Basic Books, 1971.

Pike, K. *Language in relation to a unified theory of the structure of human behavior.* The Hague: Mouton & Co., 1967.

Poole, I. Genetic development of articulation of consonant sounds in speech. *Elementary English Review, 11,* 159–161, 1934.

Popham, W., and Husek, T. Implications of criterion-referenced measurement. *Journal of Educational Measurement, 6,* 1–9, 1969.

Posner, M. Perception. In *Yearbook of Science and Technology.* New York: McGraw-Hill, 1971.

Postal, P. Underlying and superficial linguistic structure. *Harvard Educational Review, 34,* 246–266, 1964.

Powers, M., Functional disorders of articulation symptomatology and etiology. In L. E. Travis (Ed.), *Handbook of speech pathology.* New York: Appleton-Century-Crofts, 1957.

Pronovost, W., Wakstein, M. P., and Wakstein, D. J. A linguistical study of speech behavior and language comprehension of fourteen children diagnosed atypical or autistic. *Exceptional Children, 33,* 19–26, 1966.

Prutting, C., and Connolly, J. Imitation: A closer look. *Journal of Speech and Hearing Disorders, 41*, 412-422, 1976.

Prutting, C., Gallagher, T., and Mulac, A. The expressive portion of the N.S.S.T. compared to a spontaneous language sample. *Journal of Speech and Hearing Disorders, 40*, 40-49, 1975.

Quigley, S. P., Smith, N. L., and Wilbur, R. B. Comprehension of relativized sentences by deaf students. *Journal of Speech and Hearing Research, 17*, 325-342, 1974.

Quigley, S. P., Wilbur, R. B., Power, D. J., Montanelli, D. S., and Steinkamp, M. W. *Syntactic structures in the language of deaf children.* Urbana, Ill.: University of Illinois, Urbana-Champaign, 1976. Final Report Project No. 232175, U. S. Department of Health, Education and Welfare, National Institute of Education.

Ramer, A. Syntactic styles in emerging language. *Journal of Child Language, 3*, 49-62, 1976.

Reed, C. (Ed.). *Language learning.* Champaign, Ill.: National Council of Teachers of English, 1971.

Rees, N. The role of babbling in the child's acquisition of language. *British Journal of Disorders of Communication, 4*, 17-23, 1972(a).

Rees, N. Bases of decision in language training. *Journal of Speech and Hearing Disorders, 37*, 283-305, 1972(b).

Rees, N. Noncommunicative functions of language in children. *Journal of Speech and Hearing Disorders, 38*, 98-110, 1973(a).

Rees, N. Auditory processing factors in language disorders: The view from procrustes' bed. *Journal of Speech and Hearing Disorders, 38*, 304-315, 1973(b).

Rheingold, H., Gewitz, J. and Ross, H. Social conditioning of vocalizations in the infant. *Journal of Comparative Physiological Psychology, 52*, 68-73, 1959.

Richards, M., Come and go reconsidered: Children's use of deictic verbs in contrived situations. *Journal of Verbal Learning and Verbal Behavior, 15*, 655-665, 1976.

Rimland, B. *Infantile autism.* New York: Appleton-Century-Crofts, 1962.

Risley, T. R., and Wolfe, M. M. Establishing functional speech in echolalic children. *Behavior Research and Therapy, 5*, 73-88, 1967.

Rocissano, L. Cognitive factors in language and play. Unpublished paper. Teachers College, Columbia University, 1975.

Rodd L., and Braine, M. D. S. Children's imitations of syntactic constructions as a measure of linguistic competence. *Journal of Verbal Learning and Verbal Behavior, 10*, 430-433, 1971.

Rosch, E. Cognitive reference points. *Cognitive Psychology, 7*, 532-547, 1975.

Rosch, E., Mervis, C. B., Gray, W., Johnson, D., and Boyes-Braem, P. Basic objects in natural categories. *Cognitive Psychology, 8*, 382-439, 1976.

Rosenthal, W. Auditory and linguistic interaction in developmental aphasia: Evidence from two studies of auditory processing. *Papers and Reports in Child Language Development.* Palo Alto, California: Stanford University Press, *4*, 19-35, 1972.

Rosenthal, W., Eisenson, J., and Luckau, J. A statistical test of the validity of diagnostic categories used in childhood language disorders: Implications for assessment procedures. *Papers and Reports in Child Language Development.* Palo Alto, California: Stanford University Press, *4,* 121–143, 1972.

Ruder, K., and Smith, M. Issues in language training. In R. Schiefelbusch and L. L. Lloyd (Eds.), *Language perspectives—Acquisition, retardation and intervention.* Baltimore, Maryland: University Park Press, 1974.

Ruder, K., Smith, M., and Hermann, P. Effect of verbal imitation and comprehension on verbal production of lexical items. In L. McReynolds (Ed.), Developing systematized procedures for training children's language. *American Speech and Hearing Association Monographs,* No. 18, 1974.

Ruttenberg, B., and Wolf, E. Evaluating the communication of the autistic child. *Journal of Speech and Hearing Disorders, 32,* 314–325, 1967.

Rutter, M. Behavioral and cognitive characteristics. In J. K. Wing (Ed.), *Early childhood autism: Clinical, educational and social aspects.* Oxford, N. Y.: Pergamon Press, 1966.

Rutter, M. Concepts of autism: A review of research. *Journal of Child Psychology and Psychiatry, 9,* 1–25, 1968.

Rutter, M., and Bartak, L. Causes of infantile autism: Some considerations from recent research. *Journal of Autism and Childhood Schizophrenia, 1,* 20–32, 1971.

Ryan, J. Early language development: Towards a communicational analysis. In M. P. M. Richards (Ed.), *The integration of the child into the social world.* London: Cambridge University Press, 1974.

Ryan, J. Mental subnormality and language development. In E. Lenneberg and E. Lenneberg (Eds.), *Foundations of language development.* New York: Academic Press, 269–278, 1975.

Ryckman, D., and Wiegerink, R. The factors of the Illinois Test of Psycholinguistic Abilities: A comparison of 18 factor analyses. *Exceptional Children, 36,* 107–115, 1969.

Sabatino, D. The construction and assessment of an experimental test of auditory perception. *Exceptional Children, 35,* 729–739, 1969.

Sachs, J., Brown, R., and Salerno, R. Adult speech to children. Paper given at the International Symposium on First Language Acquisition, Florence, Italy, 1972.

Sacks, H. Unpublished lecture notes. University of California at Irvine, Calif, 1972.

Sailor, W., and Taman, T. Stimulus factors in the training of prepositional usage in three autistic children. *Journal of Applied Behavior Analysis, 5,* 183–190, 1972.

Salapatek, P. Pattern perception in early infancy. In L. Cohen and P. Salapatek (Eds.), *Infant perception: From sensation to cognition. Vol. I, Basic Visual Processes.* New York: Academic Press, 1975.

Sankoff, G. A quantitative paradigm for the study of communicative competence. In R. Bauman and J. Sherzer (Eds.), *Explorations in the ethnography of speaking.* London: Cambridge University Press, 1974.

Sankoff, G., and Cedergren, H. Some results of a sociolinguistic study of Montreal French. In R. Darnell (Ed.), *Linguistic diversity in Canadian society.* Edmonton: Linguistic Research, 1971.

Sankoff, G., and Laberge, S. On the acquisition of native speakers by a language. Paper presented at the Northeastern Linguistic Society Annual Meeting, 1971.

Sapir, E. *Language.* New York: Harcourt, Brace & World, 1921.

Schaerlaekens, A. A generative transformational model for child language acquisition: A discussion of L. Bloom, *Language development: Form and function in emerging grammars. Cognition, 2,* 371-376, 1973.

Schatz, C. The role of context in the perception of stops. *Language, 30,* 47-56, 1954.

Schegloff, E. A. Notes on a conversational practice: Formulating place. In P. Giglioli (Ed.), *Language and social context.* Middlesex: Penguin Education, 1972.

Schiefelbusch, R. L. (Ed.). *Language of the mentally retarded.* Baltimore: University Park Press, 1972.

Schiff, N. The development of form and meaning in the language of hearing children of deaf parents. Unpublished doctoral dissertation, Columbia University, 1976.

Schlanger, B. B. Environmental influences on the verbal output of mentally retarded children. *Journal of Speech and Hearing Disorders, 19,* 339-343, 1954.

Schlesinger, I. Production of utterances and language acquisition. In D. Slobin (Ed.), *The ontogenesis of grammar.* New York: Academic Press, 1971.

Schlesinger, I. Relational concepts underlying language. In R. L. Schiefelbusch & L. Lloyd (Eds.), *Language perspectives—Acquisition, retardation and intervention.* Baltimore: University Park Press, 1974.

Schnelle, H. Language communication with children, toward a theory of language use. In. J. Bar-Hillel (Ed.), *Pragmatics in natural languages.* Dordrecht, 1971.

Schnur, M. Auditory discrimination and temporal ordering by children with normal language and children with language impairments. Unpublished doctoral dissertation, Teachers College, Columbia University, 1971.

Schwartz, E. Characteristics of speech and language development in the child with myelomingocele and hydrocephalus. *Journal of Speech and Hearing Disorders, 39,* 465-468, 1974.

Searle, J. *Speech acts: An essay in the philosophy of language.* London: Cambridge University Press, 1969.

Seitz, S., and Stewart, C. Imitations and expansions: Some developmental aspects of mother-child communications. *Developmental Psychology, 11,* 763-768, 1975.

Shapiro, T., Chiarandini, I., and Fish, B. Thirty severely disturbed children: Evaluation of their language development for classification and prognosis. *Archives of General Psychiatry, 30,* 819-825, 1974.

Shapiro, T., Roberts, A., and Fish, B. Imitation and echoing in young schizophrenic children. *Journal of the American Academy of Child Psychiatry, 9,* 421-439, 1970.

Sharpless, E. Children's acquisition of person pronouns. Unpublished doctoral dissertation, Columbia University, 1974.

Shatz, M. The comprehension of indirect directives: Can two year olds shut the door? Paper presented at the summer meeting, Linguistic Society of America, Amherst, Mass., 1974

Shatz, M. On the development of communicative understandings: An early strategy for interpreting and responding to messages. In. J. Glick and A. Clark-Stewart (Eds.), *Studies in social and cognitive development*. New York: Gardner Press, 1977.

Shatz, M., and Gelman, R. The development of communication skills: Modifications in the speech of young children as a function of listener. *Monographs of the Society for Research in Child Development, 38,* (Serial No. 152), 1973.

Sherman, J. A. Use of reinforcement and imitation to reinstate verbal behavior in mute psychotics. *Journal of Abnormal Psychology, 70,* 155–164, 1965.

Sherman, J. A. Imitation and language development. In H. W. Reese (Ed.), *Advances in child development and behavior Vol. 6*. New York: Academic Press, 1971.

Shipley, E., Smith, C., and Gleitman, L. A study in the acquisition of language: Free responses to commands. *Language, 45,* 322–342, 1969.

Shvachkin, N. The development of phonemic speech perception in early childhood. In C. A. Ferguson and D. I. Slobin (Eds.), *Studies of child language development*. New York: Holt, Rinehart & Winston, Inc., 1973.

Silverman, S. R. The education of deaf children. In L. E. Travis (Ed.), *Handbook of speech pathology and audiology*. New York: Appleton-Century-Crofts, 1971.

Silverman, S. R. Hard-of-hearing children. In L. E. Travis (Ed.), *Handbook of speech pathology and audiology*. New York. Appleton-Century-Crofts, 1971.(b)

Simmons, A. A. A comparison of the type-token ratio of spoken and written language of deaf and hearing children. *Volta Review, 64,* 417–421, 1962.

Sinclair, H. The transition from sensory-motor behavior to symbolic activity. *Interchange, 1,* 119–126, 1970.

Sinclair, H. Sensorimotor action patterns as a condition for the acquisition of syntax. In R. Huxley and E. Ingram (Eds.), *Language acquisition: Models and methods*. New York: Academic Press, 1971.

Sinclair, H. Language acquisition and cognitive development. In T. Moore (Ed.), *Cognitive development and the acquisition of language*. New York: Academic Press, 1973.

Sinclair, H., and Bronckart, J. P. S.V.O. A linguistic universal? A study in developmental psycholinguistics. *Journal of Experimental Child Psychology, 14,* 329–348, 1972.

Skinner, B. F. *Verbal behavior*. New York: Appleton-Century-Crofts, 1957.

Sloane, H. N., and McCauley, B. D. (Eds.). *Operant procedures in remedial speech and language training*. Boston: Houghton Mifflin, 1968.

Slobin, D. I. Imitation and grammatical development in children. In N. Endler, L. Boulter, and H. Osser (Eds.); *Contemporary issues in developmental psychology*. New York: Holt, Rinehart & Winston, 1968.

Slobin, D. I. (Ed.). *The ontogenesis of grammar: Some facts and several theories.* New York: Academic Press, 1971.

Slobin, D. I. Cognitive prerequisities for the development of grammar. In C. A. Ferguson and D. I. Slobin (Eds.), *Studies of child language development.* New York: Holt, Rinehart & Winston, 1973.

Slobin, D. I. *Psycholinguistics.* Glenview, Ill.: Scott, Foresman & Co., 1974.

Slobin, D. I., and Welsh, C. A. Elicited imitation as a research tool in developmental psycholinguistics. In C. A. Ferguson and D. I. Slobin (Eds.), *Studies of child language development.* New York: Holt, Rinehart & Winston, 1973.

Slosson, R. *Slosson Intelligence Test for Children and Adults.* East Aurora, N.Y.: Slosson Educational Publications Inc., 1963.

Smith, C. An experimental approach to children's linguistic competence. In J. R. Hayes (Ed.), *Cognition and the development of language.* John Wiley & Sons, 1970.

Smith, C. Review of T. Moore (Ed.), Cognitive development and the acquisition of language. *Journal of Child Language, 2,* 303–335, 1975.

Smith, C. M. The relationship of reading method and reading achievement to I.T.P.A. sensory modalities. *Journal of Special Education, 5,* 143–149, 1971.

Smith, F., and Miller, G. (Eds.). *The genesis of language.* Cambridge, Mass.: The M.I.T. Press, 1966.

Smith, J. The development and structure of holophrases. Unpublished honors thesis. Harvard University, 1970.

Smith, M. An investigation of the development of the sentence and the extent of vocabulary in young children. In B. Baldwin (Fd.), *University of Iowa studies in child welfare.* Iowa City, Iowa: University of Iowa Press, 1926.

Smith, M. Grammatical errors in the speech of preschool children. *Child Development, 4,* 183–190, 1933.(a)

Smith, M. The influence of age, sex, and situation on the frequency, form and function of questions asked by preschool children. *Child Development, 4,* 201–213, 1933.(b)

Smith N. *The acquisition of phonology.* Cambridge: Cambridge University Press, 1973.

Snow, C. Mothers' speech to children learning language. *Child Development, 43,* 549–565, 1972.

Snow, C. Mothers' speech research: An overview. Paper presented at the Conference on Language Input and Acquisition, Boston, September, 1974.

Snow, C., and Ferguson, C. (Eds.) Talking to children: Language input and acquisition. London: Cambridge University Press, 1977.

Soderbergh, R. The fruitful dialogue, the child's acquisition of his first language: Implications for education at all stages. Project Child Language Syntax, Reprint No. 2, Stockholm University, Institutionen for Nordiska Språk, 1974.

Spitz, R. *No and yes.* New York: International Universities Press, 1957.

Staats, A. Linguistic-mentalistic theory versus an explanatory S-R learning theory of language development. In D. Slobin (Ed.), *The ontogenesis of grammar.* New York: Academic Press, 1971.

Stampe, D. The acquisition of phonetic representation. *Papers from the fifth regional meeting,* Chicago Linguistic Society, 433–434, 1969.

Stampe, D. A dissertation on natural phonology. Unpublished doctoral dissertation, University of Chicago, 1972.

Stark, J., Giddan, J., and Meisel, J. Increasing verbal behavior in an autistic child. *Journal of Speech and Hearing Disorders, 33,* 42–48, 1968.

Stark, J., Poppen, R., and May, M. Effects of alterations of prosodic features on the sequencing performance of aphasic children. *Journal of Speech and Hearing Research, 10,* 849–855, 1967.

Stern, C., and Stern, W. *Die Kindersprache.* Leipzig: Barth, 1907.

Stern, D. A micro-analysis of mother-infant interaction. *Journal of the American Academy of Child Psychiatry, 10,* 501–517, 1971.

Stern, D., Jaffe, J., Beebe, B., and Bennett, S. Vocalizing in unison and in alternation: Two modes of communication within the mother-infant dyad. In D. Aronson and R. Rieber (Eds.), *Developmental psycholinguistics and communication disorders. Annals of the New York Academy of Sciences, 263,* 89–100, 1975.

Strauss, A. A., and Lehtinen, L. E. *Psychology and education of the brain injured child.* New York: Grune & Stratton, 1947.

Stremel, K. Language training: A program for retarded children. *Mental Retardation, 10,* 47–49, 1972.

Stremel, K., and Waryas, C. A behavioral psycholinguistic approach to language training. In L. McReynolds (Ed.), Developing systematic procedures for training children's language. *ASHA Monographs,* Number 18, 1974.

Streng, A. *Syntax, speech and hearing.* New York: Grune & Stratton, Inc., 1972.

Striefel, S., and Wetherby, B. Instruction-following behavior of a retarded child and its controlling stimuli. *Journal of Applied Behavior Analysis, 6,* 663–670, 1973.

Strohner, H., and Nelson, K. The young child's development of sentence comprehension: Influence of event probability, nonverbal context, syntactic form, and strategies. *Child Development, 45,* 567–576, 1974.

Swisher, L. P., and Pinsker, E. J. The language characteristics of hyperverbal hydrocephalic children. *Developmental Medical Child Neurology, 13,* 746–755, 1971.

Taenzer, S., Bass, M., and Kise, L. The young child—A language explorer: A Piagetian-based approach to language therapy. Paper presented at the American Speech and Hearing Association, Las Vegas, Nev., 1974.

Taenzer, S., Harris, L., and Bass, M. Assessment in a natural context. Paper presented at the American Speech and Hearing Association National Convention, Washington, D.C., 1975.

Tallal, P. Rapid auditory processing in normal and disordered language development. *Journal of Speech and Hearing Research, 19,* 561–571, 1976.

Tallal, P., and Piercy, M. Defects of non-verbal auditory perception in children with developmental aphasia. *Nature, 241,* 468–469, 1973. (a)

Tallal, P., and Piercy, M. Developmental dysphasia: Impaired rate of nonverbal processing as a function of sensory modality. *Neuropsychologia, 11,* 389–398, 1973. (b)

Tallal, P., and Piercy, M. Developmental aphasia: Rate of auditory processing and selective impairment of consonant perception. *Neuropsychologia, 12,* 83–93, 1974.

Tallal, P., and Piercy, M. Developmental aphasia: The perception of brief vowels and extended stop consonants. *Neuropsychologia, 13,* 69–74, 1975.

Tanz, C. Learning how *it* works. In *Papers and reports on child language development,* Department of Linguistics, Stanford University, 1976.

Taylor, L. A language analysis of the writing of deaf children. Unpublished doctoral dissertation, State University of Florida, 1969.

Templin, M. *Certain language skills in children.* Minneapolis, Minn.: University of Minnesota Press, 1957.

Templin, M., and Darley, F. *Templin-Darley Tests of Articulation.* 2nd Ed. Bureau of Education Research and Services. Iowa City: University of Iowa, 1969.

Terman, L., and Merrill, M. *Stanford-Binet Intelligence Scale.* Boston: Houghton Mifflin, 1960.

Tervoort, B. T. *Analysis of communicative structure patterns in deaf children.* (Final Report, Project No. R.D.-467-64-65), Washington, D. C. U.S.O. H.E.W., Vocational Rehabilitation Administration, 1967.

Thomson, J., and Chapman, R. Who is "Daddy" revisited: The status of two-year olds' overextended words in use and comprehension. To appear in *Journal of Child Language,* 1977.

Thorndike, E. L. *The original nature of man.* New York: Teachers College, Columbia University, 1913.

Thorndike, E. L. Studies in the psychology of language. *Archives of Psychology, 231,* 1938.

Trager, G., and Smith, H. An outline of English structure. *Studies in linguistics: Occasional papers.* Washington, D. C.: American Council of Learned Societies. 1957.

Traugott, E. Explorations in linguistic elaboration: Language change, language acquisition, and the genesis of spatio-temporal terms. In J. Anderson and C. Jones (Eds.), *Proceedings of the First Historical Conference on Historical Linguistics,* Edinburgh, September 2–7, 1973.

Tronick, E. Stimulus control and the growth of the infant's effective visual field. *Perception and Psychophysics, 11,* 373–376, 1972.

Tulving, E. Episodic and semantic memory. In E. Tulving and W. Donaldson (Eds.), *Organization in memory.* New York: Academic Press, 1972.

Tyack, D., and Gottsleben, R. *Language sampling, analysis and training: A handbook for teachers and clinicians.* Palo Alto, Calif.: Consulting Psychological Press, 1974.

Uzgiris, I. C., and Hunt, J. Mc. V. *Assessment in infancy.* Urbana, Ill.: University of Illinois Press, 1975.

Vanderheiden, D., Brown, W., MacKenzie, P., Reinen, S., and Scheibel, C. Symbol communication for the mentally handicapped. *Mental Retardation, 13,* 34–37, 1975.

Vanderheiden, G., and Harris-Vanderheiden, D. Communication techniques and aids for the nonvocal severely handicapped. In L. Lloyd (Ed.) *Communication assessment and intervention strategies.* Baltimore: University Park Press, 1976.

Volterra, V., Il "no". Prime fasi di sviluppo della negazione nel linguaggio infantile. Unpublished paper, 1971.

Vosniadou, S. Strategies in the acquisition of Greek. Unpublished M.A. Thesis, Teachers College, Columbia University, 1974.

Vygotsky, L. S. *Thought and language.* Cambridge, Mass.: The M.I.T. Press, 1962.

Walker, H., and Birch, H. Neurointegrative deficiency in schizophrenic children. *Journal of Nervous and Mental Disease, 151,* 104–113, 1970.

Warden, D. The influence of context on children's use of identifying expressions and references. *British Journal of Psychology, 67,* 101–112, 1976.

Wasz-Hockert, O., Lind, J., Vuorenkoski, V., Partanen, T., and Valanne, E. The infant cry: A spectographic and auditory analysis. Clinics in Developmental Medicine. No. 29. Spastics International Medical Publication in Association with William Heinemann Medical Books, Ltd., 1969.

Waterson, N. Child phonology: A prosodic view. *Journal of Linguistics, 7,* 179–211, 1971.

Watt, W. On two hypotheses concerning developmental psycholinguistics. In J. Hayes (Ed.), *Cognition and the development of language.* New York: John Wiley & Sons, 1970.

Watters, G. The syndrome of acquired aphasia and convulsive disorder in children. *Canadian Medical Association Journal, 110,* 611–612, 1974.

Wechsler, D. *Wechsler Intelligence Scale for Children* (WISC). New York: Psychological Corporation, 1949.

Wechsler, D. *Wechsler Preschool and Primary Scale of Intelligence* (WIPSI). New York: Psychological Corporation, 1967.

Weiner, S. On the development of more and less. *Journal of Experimental Child Psychology, 17,* 271–287, 1974.

Weir, R. *Language in the crib.* The Hague: Mouton, 1964.

Weisberg, P. Social and nonsocial conditioning of infant vocalization. *Child Development, 34,* 377–388, 1963.

Wepman, J. *Auditory Discrimination Test.* Chicago: Language Research Associates, 1958.

Wepman, J., Jones, L. V., Bock, R. D., and Van Pelt, D. Studies in aphasia: Background and theoretical formulations. *Journal of Speech and Hearing Disorders, 25,* 323–332, 1960.

Werner, H. *Comparative psychology of mental development.* New York: Science Editions, Inc., 1948.

Werner, H., and Kaplan, B. *Symbol formation.* New York: John Wiley & Sons, 1963.

Werner, H., and Kaplan, E. The acquisition of word meanings: A developmental study. *Monographs of the Society for Research in Child Development, 15*(1), 1952.

West, R. (Ed.). *Childhood aphasia.* (Proceedings at the Institute on Childhood Aphasia Conference, 1960). San Francisco: California Society for Crippled Children and Adults, 1962.

Wetstone, H., and Friedlander, B. The effect of word order on young children's responses to simple questions and commands. *Child Development, 44,* 734–740, 1973.

Whitehurst, G. J., and Novak, G. Modeling, imitation training, and the acquisition of sentence phrases. *Journal of Experimental Child Psychology, 16,* 332–345, 1973.

Wilbur, R. The linguistics of manual languages and manual systems. In L. Lloyd (Ed.), *Communication assessment and intervention strategies.* Baltimore: University Park Press, 1976.

Wilbur, R., Quigley, S., and Montanelli, D. Conjoined structures in the language of deaf students. *Journal of Speech and Hearing Research, 18,* 319–335, 1975.

Wing, L. What is an autistic child? *Communication, 6,* 5–10, 1972.

Winitz, H. *Articulatory acquisition and behavior.* New York: Appleton-Century-Crofts, 1969.

Winitz, H. Problem solving and the delaying of speech as strategies in the teaching of language. *Asha, 15,* 583–586, 1973.

Winitz, H. Full time experience. *Asha, 18,* 404, 1976.

Winitz, H., and Preisler, L. Discrimination pretraining and sound learning. *Perceptual Motor Skills, 20,* 905–916, 1965.

Wolff, P. H. The natural history of crying and other vocalizations in early infancy. In B. M. Foss (Ed.), *Determinants of infant behavior, Vol. IV.* London: Metheun, 1966.

Wolff, S., and Chess, S. An analysis of the language of fourteen schizophrenic children. *Journal of Child Psychology, 6,* 29–41, 1965.

Wulbert, M., Inglis, S., Kriegsman, E., and Mills, B. Language delay and associated mother-child interactions. *Developmental Psychology, 11,* 61–70, 1975.

Yoder, D., and Miller, J. What we may know and what we can do: Input toward a system. In J. McLean, D. Yoder, and R. Schiefelbusch (Eds.), *Language intervention with the retarded: Developing strategies.* Baltimore: University Park Press, 1972.

Zimmerman, B. J., and Bell, J. A. Observer verbalization and abstraction in vicarious rule learning, generalization, and retention. *Developmental Psychology, 7,* 227–231, 1972.

Zimmerman, I. L., Steiner, V. G., and Evatt, R. *Preschool Language Scale.* Columbus, Ohio: Charles Merrill, 1969.

Zipf, G. K. *The psycho-biology of language: An introduction to dynamic philology.* Cambridge, Mass.: The M.I.T. Press, 1965.

AUTHOR INDEX

Abrahams, R., 202
Allen, D., 171
Allen, K., 565
Amerman, J., 540
Amidon, A., 180
Ammons, H., 355, 614
Ammons, R., 355, 614
Anderson, R., 354, 613
Anglin, J., 116, 117
Antinucci, F., 164, 211
Appel, K., 84, 97
Arbor, A., 613, 614
Aronson, D., 97
Arthur, G., 356
Aten, J., 576
Attneave, F., 81
Aurnhammer-Frith, F., 534
Austin, J., 130, 202, 210, 212, 235
Ayers, A., 548

Baer, D., 248, 249, 566
Bailey, C. J., 60
Baird, R., 244
Baker, H., 613
Bandura, A., 559, 567, 569, 595
Baratz, J., 250
Bar-Hillel, Y., 236
Baron, N., 105, 577
Barry, H., 509
Barsch, R., 548
Bartak, L., 516
Bass, M., 444, 571
Bates, E., 81, 93, 97, 202, 204, 205, 210, 211, 216, 219, 235
Bateson, M., 93, 208
Bauman, R., 9, 65, 216, 317
Bee, H., 252
Beebe, B., 93, 94, 97, 208
Beer, C., 3, 33, 34, 52, 65

Beilin, H., 194
Belkin, A., 188, 189, 190, 239, 444
Bell, J., 566
Bellugi, U., 99, 166, 177, 184, 191, 192, 244, 245, 248, 253, 262, 267, 271, 277, 280, 285, 498, 508
Bennett, S., 93, 94, 97, 208
Bentsen, F., 555
Berberich, J., 559, 562, 565, 569
Bereiter, C., 393
Berko, J., 27, 64, 336, 500
Berko-Gleason, J., 218, 280
Bernstein, B., 212, 213
Berry, M., 314, 355, 575
Bersoff, D., 440
Bever, T., 9, 51, 180, 262, 267, 271, 284, 533
Bierwisch, M., 58
Birch, H., 509, 520, 535, 536
Blank, M., 586
Blanton, R., 507
Blasdell, R., 575
Bliss, C., 563, 564
Bloch, O., 272
Bloom, B., 327
Bloom, L., 30, 31, 32, 35, 40, 42, 46, 47, 48, 50, 52, 56, 57, 61, 81, 82, 83, 91, 105, 106, 107, 108, 110, 111, 112, 114, 116, 117, 129, 130, 134, 136, 138, 140, 141, 144, 146, 147, 150, 152, 153, 157, 158, 160, 164, 166, 167, 168, 169, 170, 171, 172, 173, 175, 176, 177, 179, 184, 188, 189, 190, 191, 192, 194, 199, 200, 212, 215, 219, 221, 225, 226, 227, 228, 229, 232, 235, 239, 240, 243, 248, 250, 253, 256, 259, 262, 263, 267, 269, 273, 276, 277, 278, 283, 284, 285, 313, 322, 323, 327, 328, 336, 380, 392, 445, 485,

SUBJECT INDEX

Note: Italicized pages refer to material in boxes in the text.

ACKNOWLEDGEMENTS

We are grateful to the following for granting permission to reprint previously published materials:

Academic Press, New York, N.Y., for permission to include: Figure 3, p. 400 from "Imitation in language development: If, when and why," by Lois Bloom, Lois Hood and Patsy Lightbown, *Cognitive Psychology,* Vol. 6, 1974; excerpts from p. 281–282 from "The development of Wh questions in child speech," by Roger Brown, *Journal of Verbal Learning and Verbal Behavior,* Vol. 7, 1968; and Figure 5, p. 309 from "The grammars of speech and language," by Alvin Liberman, *Cognitive Psychology,* Vol. 1, 1970.

American Psychological Association, Washington, D.C., for permission to include Figure 2, p. 46, from "Perception of the speech code," by Alvin Liberman, Franklin Cooper, Donald Shankweiler and Michael Studdert-Kennedy, *Psychological Review,* Vol. 74, 1967.

American Speech and Hearing Association, Washington, D.C., for permission to include Figure 1, p. 334 and Figure 2, p. 336 from "Signed English: A manual approach to English language development," by Harry Bornstein, *Journal of Speech and Hearing Disorders,* Vol. 39, 1974; Figure 1, p. 513 from "Nonspeech noun usage training with severely and profoundly retarded children," by Joseph Carrier, Jr., *Journal of Speech and Hearing Research,* Vol. 17, 1974; Table 1, p. 433 from "What is deviant language?," by Laurence Leonard, *Journal of Speech and Hearing Disorders,* Vol. 37, 1972; Figure 2, p. 326, from "Studies in aphasia: Background and theoretical formulations," by Joseph Wepman, Lyle Jones, R. Darrell Bock, and Doris Van Pelt, *Journal of Speech and Hearing Disorders,* Vol. 25, 1960.

Cambridge University Press, New York, N.Y., for permission to include excerpts from p. 103, from "The influence of context on children's use of identifying expressions and references," by David Warden, *British Journal of Psychology,* Vol. 67, 1976.

Edicom N.V. on behalf of Mouton and Co., Laren (N-H), Holland, for permission to include excerpts from pages 48, 51–53, 155–156, 192, 193, 195 and Table 4, page 68 and Table 7, page 104 from *One Word at a Time,* by Lois Bloom, copyright 1973.

Sibylle K. Escalona and Harvey H. Corman, for permission to include excerpts from Albert Einstein Scales of Sensorimotor Development, unpublished manual, Albert Einstein College of Medicine, New York, N.Y.

Harcourt, Brace Jovanovich, New York, N.Y., for permission to include excerpts from pages 11–13, from *Language,* by Edward Sapir, copyright 1921, by Harcourt, Brace Jovanovich, Inc.; renewed, 1949, by Jean V. Sapir. Reprinted by permission of the publishers.

University Park Press, Baltimore, Md., for permission to include Table 1, page 112, from "Some aspects of the conceptual basis for first language acquisition," by Eve Clark, in *Language Perspectives–Acquisition, Retardation, and Intervention,* edited by Richard Schiefelbusch and Lyle Lloyd, copyright 1974, University Park Press; and Table 1, page 244 and Table 5, page 249, from "The use of grammatical morphemes by children with communication disorders," by Judith Johnston and Terris Schery, in *Normal and Deficient Child Language,* edited by Donald Morehead and Ann Morehead, copyright 1976, University Park Press.

In addition, Chapter VIII was published originally as a chapter, "Talking, understanding and thinking," by Lois Bloom, in Richard Schiefelbusch and Lyle Lloyd (Eds.), *Language Perspectives–Acquisition, Retardation and Intervention,* University Park Press, copyright 1974. We thank the University Park Press for permission to include it here in its present revised and expanded form. The first few pages of Chapter IX were published originally as part of a chapter, "Language development," by Lois Bloom, in Frances Horowitz (Ed.), *Review of Research in Child Development,* Vol. 4, The University of Chicago Press, copyright 1975. Portions of Chapter II appeared in a somewhat different form, as the comment "Accountability of evidence in studies of child language," from "Everyday preschool interpersonal speech usage: Methodological, developmental, and sociolinguistic studies," in Frances Fuchs Schachter, Kathryn Kirshner, Bonnie Klips, Martha Friedricks and Karin Sanders, *Monographs of the Society for Research in Child Development,* Vol. 39, 1974.